America's Armed Forces

AMERICA'S ARMED FORCES

A Handbook of Current and Future Capabilities

Edited by Sam C. Sarkesian
and Robert E. Connor, Jr.

Greenwood Press
Westport, Connecticut • London

Library of Congress Cataloging-in-Publication Data

America's armed forces : a handbook of current and future capabilities / edited by Sam C. Sarkesian and Robert E. Connor, Jr.
p. cm.
Includes bibliographical references and index.
ISBN 0–313–29012–1 (alk. paper)
1. United States—Defenses. 2. National security—United States. 3. World politics—1989– I. Sarkesian, Sam Charles. II. Connor, Robert E.
UA23A66323 1996
355'.033073—dc20 95–6704

British Library Cataloguing in Publication Data is available.

Library of Congress Catalog Card Number: 95–6704
ISBN: 0–313–29012–1

First published in 1996

Greenwood Press, 88 Post Road West, Westport, CT 06881
An imprint of Greenwood Publishing Group, Inc.

Printed in the United States of America

The paper used in this book complies with the Permanent Paper Standard issued by the National Information Standards Organization (Z39.48–1984).

10 9 8 7 6 5 4 3 2 1

Copyright Acknowledgments

The editor and publisher gratefully acknowledge permission to reprint material from the following copyrighted sources:

Excerpts reprinted with the permission of The Free Press, a Division of Simon & Schuster, Inc. from *For the Common Defense: A Military History of the United States of America* by Allan R. Millett and Peter Maslowski. Copyright © 1984 by The Free Press.

Table 8.1 reprinted from William W. Kaufmann, *Glasnost, Perestroika and U.S. Defense Spending*. Washington, DC: Brookings Institution, 1990, Tables 1 and 3.

Excerpts and Table 8.5 reprinted from John Allen Williams and Charles Moskos, ''Civil-Military Relations after the Cold War,'' paper delivered at the American Political Science Association, Annual Meeting, September 2–5, 1993; Table pp. 5a and 5b. Reprinted with permission.

CONTENTS

Part II. Wars, Military Conflicts, and Noncombat Contingencies

FIGURES AND TABLES

FIGURES

TABLES

PREFACE

Studying the American armed forces in this period of transition and uncertain external environment is a difficult task. It would be a more certain undertaking to wait until the fog of peace clears and the military is fixed in its restructuring and strategic orientation. But important issues affecting the U.S. armed forces, strategy, and defense policy do not wait for the surfacing of clear directions and ordered domestic and international environments. Indeed, the most critical time to undertake such an analysis is during the difficult transition period, even if directions and end results are uncertain. It is at such times that clarification of strategic and policy directions is most needed. This is the purpose of this volume.

The contributing authors are authorities in their fields. Each is aware of the difficulties in studying the military in this period of transition. Yet they also recognize the importance of undertaking such a study.

The volume is divided into two parts. In addition, there is an introductory and a concluding chapter. The Introduction provides a broad overview of the strategic landscape, the American political scene, and the concept of national security. The focus is to set the international and domestic political context for the study of the U.S. military. The concluding chapter summarizes several major themes in the book and focuses on two particularly troubling issues facing the American military: the conflict environment and civil-military relations. In this respect, the chapter concludes by assessing future problems for the military.

Part I consists of six chapters. Each of the first four addresses one of the services, one focuses on the reserve forces, and the last provides a summary and conclusions. This part is a straightforward study of the Army, the Navy, the Air Force, the Marine Corps, and the Federal Reserve and National Guard, with attention to command structure, force organization, doctrine, weaponry, and projections into the future. This part of the book covers the forces under the Department of Defense, within the military chain of command. The authors also address the problems faced by each of the services in responding to the changed landscape.

Part II contains six chapters focusing on the various conflicts and contingencies from the Gulf War (conventional conflict) to operations other than war, including unconventional conflicts (insurgency and counterinsurgency). Beginning with the American way of war, the topics include the Gulf War and regional conflicts, peacetime engagements, drug wars and revolutionary groups, noncombat operations, and unconventional conflicts. Also addressed in each chapter are the capability of the U.S. military in responding to each contingency and the problems posed in maintaining capability in the primary military mission.

There is a degree of overlap between most of the chapters. Given the nature of this study and the interconnections between each subject, this is not only to be expected but is important in providing a realistic view of the military and the contingencies to which it is expected to respond. Each chapter also contains a selected bibliography, and again there is a degree of overlap and repetition of some sources for the reasons already noted.

Aside from broad editorial guidelines, we have avoided directing the authors to fit their chapters into a rigid format. We particularly want to avoid an operating-manual format that may be aimed at a particular audience. While we may not agree with the assessments of individual authors, we believe that the study of the American armed forces is better served by each individual author's own analysis and insights.

Not all of the answers to problems faced by the U.S. military in this transitional period or for the future are here, and we recognize that analysis is complicated by the changed power base in Congress with the control of both houses of Congress now in the hands of the Republican Party as a result of the 1994 midterm elections. It seems clear that domestic, foreign, and national security policies will change and that the changes will affect U.S. military posture and force structures, adding to the uncertainties of the transition. Nonetheless, we believe that the authors have not only provided essential information and acute analyses, but also have set out directions and posed questions important in developing perceptive insights into the U.S. military. The final responsibility for identifying the various topics, for material included and omitted, and for strategic judgments expressed in chapters 1 and 14 rests with the editors.

Sam C. Sarkesian
Robert E. Connor, Jr.

America's Armed Forces

Chapter 1

INTRODUCTION

Sam C. Sarkesian

The dissolution of the Soviet Empire and the unification of Germany signalled the end of the Cold War. Thus began a period of transition from the relative predictability of international politics to the uncertainties of the new world order—or disorder. The major strategic change for the United States was the end of the superpower era with its clear threats to the United States—the disappearance of the "Evil Empire"—and the beginning of a host of lower-level challenges and threats that have vague significances for U.S. national interests. Yet it is also true that any number of problems that were submerged under the East-West dichotomy but had their roots in the Cold War period have surfaced. Thus, while there is a clear demarcation between the Cold War and the post–Cold War periods, the fact is that there are also lingering continuities. At the same time, there are a number of relatively unique characteristics of the new world order that are shaping the strategic landscape.[1]

This has raised serious questions not only about the meaning of American national interests and strategy, but also about the utility of military force and the applicability of prevailing military strategy and doctrine. Although the strategic landscape is ill defined and the notion of a new world order remains elusive, the American armed forces need to establish strategic concepts that provide directions and guidelines for developing doctrine, force structures, and weaponry.

This is complicated by the fact that in the first part of the 1990s questions remain regarding the objectives of American foreign and national security policy. Critics have argued that the United States has lacked both a clear concept of national interests and a strategic vision. For example, from 1991 into 1995

U.S. policy on Bosnia-Herzegovina reflected hesitation, bluffs, and on-again, off-again air strikes. This led to serious questions regarding U.S. involvement in the North Atlantic Treaty Organization (NATO) and the U.S. relationship with the United Nations.

The U.S. military does not have the luxury of waiting until this tangled web of policy and strategy is untangled. It must be prepared to respond to a variety of conflicts across the conflict spectrum in the present as well as future landscapes. Its uncertain position is exacerbated by a variety of peacekeeping and noncombat missions under the rubric of operations other than war. The complexity and problems associated with many of the issues raised here, particularly those dealing with the U.S. military, strategic plans, and defense planning, are well summed up by Lynn-Jones and Miller:

> The passing of the Cold War has swept away many of the familiar and convenient frameworks of analysis and categories of thought about international politics. Scholars and policy makers alike are unanchored from previous intellectual moorings, and the certainties of the past have given way to the ambiguities of the present.[2]

Compounding these problems is that a revolution in military affairs is occurring—some call it war in the information age, others call it the third-wave warfare.[3] Regardless of the label, there is little question that the American military is faced with the prospect of preparing for ill-defined and uncertain strategic environments, innovations in weaponry and communications, and the electronic/microchip age. In the process it confronts a fundamental dilemma. The "revolution" is aimed at a military preparing for its primary purpose: success in battle. At the same time, however, the challenges facing the military include operations other than war—or what have in the past been labelled operations short of war—encompassing everything from peacekeeping and humanitarian missions to unconventional warfare. The dilemma is rooted in the fact that sophisticated electronics and weaponry may have minimum impact on operations other than war, particularly unconventional conflicts.

To analyze what all of these uncertainties may mean and the challenges they present to the American armed forces, this introductory chapter provides an overview of the new world order and strategic landscape, clearly recognizing that such an overview is fraught with uncertainty reflecting the characteristics of the international world. Nonetheless, such an overview can serve as a reference point and map for analyzing directions, characteristics, and potentials that may evolve in the new world order. Equally important, the U.S. military and its capabilities in the current and future strategic landscape cannot be analyzed realistically without placing these matters within the context of the domestic and international political environments.

The analytical framework to address these various issues and how they may affect the U.S. military consists of the following: (1) national security as a concept; (2) the interests/power/strategy equation; (3) the international dimension and its security setting; (4) the American political system; (5) continuities and changes; and (6) the U.S. military: overview. While these categories are listed separately, they are not intended to suggest clear distinctions. Rather, all overlap and are linked. Establishing categories is an effort to provide an orderly analytical path and a critical focus within each category without isolating one from the other. This is important because, as will be shown, there is a degree of synergism in the aggregate that compounds the problems facing the U.S. military.

NATIONAL SECURITY AS A CONCEPT

The new international security landscape has clouded the concept of national security. Moreover, the interpretation of American values and national interests into meaningful national security policy has become a difficult process. This problem has been well summed up by one expert:

> No formal definition of national security as a field has been generally accepted; none may be possible. In general, it is the study of the security *problems* faced by nations, of the *policies and programs* by which these problems are addressed, and also of the governmental *processes* through which the policies and programs are decided upon and carried out.[4]

National security must be seen in the context of foreign policy. Foreign policy is that policy of a nation that encompasses all official relations with other countries. The instruments of foreign policy are primarily diplomatic and secondarily economic and psychological. National security differs from foreign policy in at least two respects: (1) national security purposes are more narrow and focused on security and safety of the nation; (2) national security is primarily concerned with actual and potential adversaries and their use of force, which means that there is a military emphasis that is not usually the case in matters of foreign policy. However, national security policy overlaps with foreign policy; indeed, sometimes they are almost indistinguishable.

While it is difficult enough to design effective national security policy to further national interests, this is compounded by the difficulties in determining with clarity U.S. national interests, and establishing national security priorities is complicated by the link between national security and domestic policy. The domestic economic impact of certain national security policies (such as economic sanctions, an embargo on agriculture exports to adversaries or potential adversaries, illegal immigration and refugees, diminished foreign oil sources, and the export of technologically advanced industrial products) connects American domestic interests and policies to the international security arena.

The point is that many national security issues cannot be isolated from domestic policy. In brief, in addition to the relationship and linkage between foreign and national security policy, there is also a domestic policy linkage that is an important factor in establishing priorities and interests. Indeed, this issue is viewed by some scholars as ''intermestic'' politics and policies.[5]

For many policymakers and nationally elected leaders, however, national security has become more than the capacity to conduct wars in the international arena. Accordingly, challenges to U.S. national security may take on any number of nontraditional forms ranging from economics to refugee assistance and immigration control. Yet it is also true that the capacity to wage nuclear war and conventional conflicts remains essential for the conduct of national security policy even in the security era of the 1990s.

Moreover, some scholars argue that

> the concept of ''security'' must include protection against all major threats to human survival and well-being, not just military threats. . . . Given the multiplicity of pressing world hazards, the concept of ''national security'' must be integrated with that of ''world security.'' . . . In today's interdependent world . . . the quest for security is rapidly becoming a *positive sum* process, whereby national well-being is achieved jointly by all countries—or not at all.[6]

How one incorporates national security into world security in a realistic fashion has yet to be determined. Moreover, the tendency in such perspectives is to view virtually everything as a national security issue.

It is the view here, however, that national interests and national security policy must be carefully crafted and applied according to priorities that distinguish survival (vital) interests from others. Too often national security is used synonymously with any interest, raising the specter that all interests are survival priorities. If national security policy and strategy followed such a pattern, the United States would be placed in a position of having to defend everything with the end result of being unable to defend anything—a repeat of Sun Tzu's admonition. Resources and forces would be scattered throughout the world and rarely would be in a position to bring sufficient force to bear on a particular issue that might well be a survival matter.

Nonetheless, national security rests primarily on the notion that there is a high propensity for the use of military force in a combat environment. To take a page from Sun Tzu, if almost everything is a matter of national security, then the concept of national security becomes virtually meaningless.[7] Distinctions must be made between domestic policy and national security as well as between foreign policy and national security. The primary distinction rests in the propensity for the use of military force and the fact that the military is the primary instrument in the implementation of national security policy. While many other matters are important in the overall concept of national interests, they are best incorporated into foreign policy and the overlap between foreign policy and national security.[8]

These observations are the basis for defining national security policy. National security policy is that part of government policy primarily concerned with formulating and implementing national strategy to create a favorable military en-

Figure 1.1
Organization for National Security

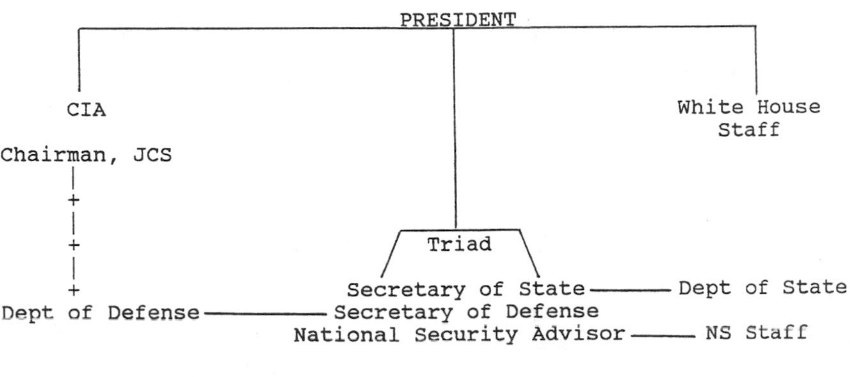

Source: Adapted from Sam C. Sarkesian, *U.S. National Security: Policymakers, Processes, and Politics*, 2nd ed. (Boulder, CO: Lynne Rienner Publishers, 1995), p. 12.

vironment for U.S. national interests. An integral part of this is to prevent the effective use of military force by the nation's adversaries or potential adversaries in obstructing or denying U.S. ability to pursue its national interests.

Short of clear threats to the territory of the United States, Americans may disagree, and do, over priorities. Even when there is agreement on priorities, there is disagreement regarding resource commitment and strategy. Nonetheless, a system of priorities provides a way of identifying levels of threats and helps in designing strategies. But all of this must be guided by the meaning of national security and its conceptual dimensions.

While the national security system is organized around the President as the focal point, there are any number of structures within that system that have an impact on the concept and implementation of national security. Figure 1.1 shows the organization for national security.[9]

There are two overriding priorities in national security interests: first, the protection of the American homeland and the survival of its political system; second, the maintenance, nurturing, and expansion of "open systems." This generally means democratic systems. (The concept of "open systems" is used here with the idea that there are various forms of democracy, and, indeed, there may be socialist systems that have established the basis of openness and are nonthreatening to neighbors and to world peace.) These priorities need to be examined in the context of the international security setting and the strategic landscape.

THE INTERESTS/POWER/STRATEGY EQUATION

National Interests

American national interests are expressions of American values projected into the international arena. The purpose of these interests includes the creation and perpetuation of an international environment that is not inimical or antagonistic to the peaceful pursuit of these values. It follows that such interests are those that nurture and expand democracy and open systems. Conversely, these interests are those that prevent the expansion of closed systems by the use of force or indirect aggressive means.

At the core of American national interests is the survival of the homeland and the American political order. But survival cannot be limited to the "final" defense of the homeland. In light of today's weapons technology and ideological imperatives, among other things, the concept of survival of the homeland means more than retreating to the borders of the United States and threatening total destruction of any who attack.

If national interest is invoked only in those cases where the homeland is directly threatened and its survival is at stake, then the concept is of little use. Indeed, it may be too late if Americans wait until survival is at stake. If the concept of national security is to have any meaning in terms of policy and strategy, then it must mean something more than survival of the American homeland. It is the interpretation and application of this broader view that sparks a great deal of debate and disagreement between the executive and legislative branches of government and between a variety of groups in the American political arena. The media also become involved in these matters, more often than not, with their own agenda.

However, the national security establishment, policymakers, and the U.S. military rarely have the luxury of endless debate. Nor do they have unlimited time or all of the necessary facts in any given situation. Yet policy must be made and strategy options examined and implemented regardless of these conditions and while debates and disagreements remain intense.

The fact is that at some point in time policy must be decided upon and implemented. Before that is done, the American national interest for that particular situation must be identified and articulated. At the same time, national interests over the long range must be considered. Custom, usage, and constitutional powers have usually given the President the basis for articulating the meaning of American national interests. Although in the contemporary period some Americans may challenge this notion, initiatives in foreign and national security policy usually rest with the President.

Congress has an important role in these matters, but the President must take the lead and is the only legal representative of the United States with respect to relations with foreign countries. For better or for worse, therefore, it is the President who articulates the national interests and Congress that responds. The same holds true with respect to the President and the variety of interest groups in the public arena, as well as the government bureaucracy.

In summary, four points need to be restated. First, American values as they apply to the external world are at the core of national interests. Second, national interests do not mean that U.S. strategy is limited to the immediate homeland of the United States. These interests may require power projection into various parts of the world. Third, the President is the focal point in defining and articulating American national interests. To do this effectively, the President must demonstrate leadership and understanding of the domestic and international setting. Fourth, the U.S. military must function within the context of the first three points.

National Power

The ability to successfully carry out national security policy is a direct result of the power the nation possesses and its ability to use that power effectively. But here again we are faced with problems of definition. National power can be seen from two dimensions. It can be defined in universal terms and also with respect to power in any given situation. In the first instance, national power can be measured by a variety of indicators, ranging from the total number in the armed forces, the ability of a nation to mobilize for war, to the nation's economic capacity. In these terms, only relatively large states favored by large populations and resources can become powerful. But in any given situation, large states may not have usable and effective power. In such cases, smaller states may have power based on other considerations. For example, in the case of Vietnam, many argued that the United States did not have usable power to bring the Vietnam War to a successful conclusion. The minor state of North Vietnam had more effective power in that particular case and was able to prevail. It may very well be that the Soviet Union faced a similar power relationship with respect to the Afghanistan War in 1987.

In brief, national power is a complex and often an ambiguous concept. Nonetheless, there are a number of important elements of national power that a nation must possess if it is to pursue its national interests on a global scale.

According to one authority,

> National power . . . is a mix of strategic, military, economic, and political strengths and weaknesses. It is determined in part by the military forces and the military establishment of a country but even more by the size and location of territory, the nature of frontiers, the population, the raw-material resources, the economic structure, the technological development, the financial strength, the ethnic mix, the social cohesiveness, the stability of political processes and decision-making, and, finally, the intangible quantity usually described as national spirit.[10]

It is from this concept of national power that we design a more abbreviated one that may be useful for a road map of the national security landscape. National power is based on four major elements: military power, geostrategic importance, national character, and psychological sustenance.

Military power is a measure of the total (aggregate) physical attributes of the armed forces of a country. This includes such indicators as the quality and quantity of equipment, mobility, and combat effectiveness (skills, leadership, and will to fight).

Geostrategic importance refers to the location of the country in terms of the international economy, international security, and the national security of other states. For example, the Strait of Hormuz in the Persian Gulf area is of geostrategic importance, given its international character as a waterway to oil resources, among other things. Further, geostrategic importance includes the availability of important resources within the country and its climate and terrain.

National character is another important consideration. Because of its highly subjective nature, some discount its relevancy to national power. Nonetheless, it is important in providing insights into the nation's political processes and cohesiveness. National character is measured by such things as the homogeneity of the population, including its size and growth, population education and skills, economic system and capability, the degree of commitment to the political system, and the legitimacy and efficiency of the governing structures.

Finally, psychological sustenance is an inextricable part of national power. This is an obviously subjective dimension and, as expected, the most difficult to measure. The fact is that all of the elements of national power may be useless if the people of a nation are unwilling to use them in the pursuit of national interest. Moreover, if other states perceive that the nation with power is hesitant to use it and that its people are divided over the proper courses of military action, then those states will ultimately perceive the powerful nation as a "paper tiger" whose power is based solely on rhetoric. Similarly, even when a nation has all of the other elements of power, its own people may perceive such power as useless and, for all practical purposes, diminish the nation's real power.

Thus military power and the other elements of power are real only if they are buttressed by national will, political resolve, and staying power to develop an effective strategy to pursue national interests. At the same time, there must be a commitment to persist over the long run—staying power to see the matter through, once committed. It is with national will and staying power that the United States as an open system has the most difficult problems. This is particularly true when national interests and national security must deal with issues outside the homeland (some second-order and all third-order interests).

Measuring national power is even more complex than each of these elements individually suggests. The problem becomes acute in trying to link these elements, determine their relationships, and identify their total impact on other states. Yet attention to national power does provide a sense of the relative power of the country. It also focuses attention on the need to translate national power into usable power and link it through the national security establishment and the policy process to the pursuit of national interests. Much of this has to do with strategy.

National Strategy

There is a great deal of confusion in the use of the terms *policy* and *strategy.* Many use these terms synonymously. The fact is that there is an important difference, particularly when these terms are used in the study of national security. Policy refers to the major objectives of the state, whether in foreign policy or national security. Strategy, however, refers to the methods and means used to achieve these purposes.

> The term ''strategy,'' derived from the ancient Greek, originally pertained to the art of generalship or high command. In modern times, ''grand strategy'' has come into use to describe the overall defense plans of a nation or coalition of nations. Since the mid-twentieth century, ''national strategy'' has attained wide usage, meaning the coordinated employment of the total resources of a nation to achieve its national objectives.[11]

The term *strategy* as used here refers primarily to national strategy. From time to time references will be made to what some call national military strategy, focusing on ''the generation of military power and its employment in state to state relationships.''[12]

At the highest level, grand strategy is the usual label given to the way a state intends to pursue its national security goals. From this a number of other strategies are designed that are focused on specific regions or issues. Thus there are military strategy, economic strategy, political strategy, and psychological strategy. Also, there is a U.S. strategy for the Middle East and other parts of the world. No wonder there is confusion in using terms such as *strategy, policy,* and *doctrine.* Writing in the eighteenth century, Carl von Clausewitz concluded, ''Strategy is the use of the engagement for the purpose of the war. The strategist must therefore define an aim for the entire operational side of the war that will be in accordance with its purpose. . . . Everything in strategy is very simple, but that does not mean that everything is very easy.''[13]

There is, of course, more to these terms than this brief explanation. But the differences are clear: policy refers to goals; strategy is the means to reach these goals. It follows that strategy or strategies cannot be realistically designed and implemented if policy is unclear or vacillating. In this study of national security, the terms *policy* and *strategy* are used as defined here. Additionally, *doctrine* is taken to mean a body of beliefs and teachings about national security and its implementation.

THE INTERNATIONAL DIMENSION AND ITS SECURITY SETTING

The international dimension and its security setting affect the U.S. national security policy process in a number of ways. First, the international dimension is characterized by contradictory forces creating complexities and difficulties that are often intractable in terms of U.S. national security. Thus there are limits to what the United States can do in any given national security issue. The complexities have become even greater in the security landscape of the 1990s, where real threats to American core security interests have diminished and the notion of national interests has become vague. The difficulty now is to determine what and who are threats to American national interests.

Second, the international security setting is not a neat and clearly delineated order, nor is it necessarily driven by a set of rational forces. On the one hand, there are a number of commonalities; on the other hand, there are distinct characteristics associated with each security issue and challenge. Thus each U.S. national security issue may require a unique set of responses. The international security setting also may require a broad policy that is implemented by a variety of strategies, at times appearing to be contradictory. Further, the traditional concepts of military force may have limited utility in such a setting.

Third, international security issues may quickly develop into crisis situations demanding rapid and flexible response. In such cases, it may be difficult for U.S. policy processes to be effective because of the character of the U.S. political system. Additionally, the American establishment tends to be cumbersome in trying to react quickly and legitimately in crisis situations.

Fourth, U.S. national security policy may require secrecy or covert operations. Given the nature of the U.S. system, trying to undertake effective covert operations promises to be difficult at best and ineffective at worst. This makes it difficult for the United States to develop a coherent policy and strategy to respond to the most likely conflicts—unconventional ones, which may require "indirect" approaches and secrecy. Further, the resurgence of Congress into the national security policy area (some call this congressional micromanagement) and the continuing debate and disagreement over the defense budget add to the problem. This is particularly true when such policies and strategies stray from mainstream American views and ways of war.

Fifth, the problem of strategic cultures poses a relatively new issue for U.S. national security. Strategic cultures evolving out of non-Western traditions govern the political and security orientation of many states in the Southern Hemisphere as well as China and India. The character of conflicts and the meaning of victory or defeat may differ in foreign strategic cultures in contrast to U.S. strategic principles.[14] Yet the United States cannot compromise its strategic culture without eroding its legitimacy and capacity as a major world power. Maintaining and nurturing its culture in both domestic and international arenas is an essential part of its identity.

Sixth, the focus of U.S. intelligence services is changing from the superpower-era confrontations to a variety of lesser challenges. While such intelligence was also part of the intelligence-gathering system during the Cold War, these challenges have become more prominent and have been given greater importance in the new world order. Equally important, the intelligence community in the

United States is being shaped to become involved in economic intelligence—industrial intelligence, given the complexity of the international security setting and the expanded notion of national security.

The major conclusion is that the international dimension and its security setting are characterized by uncertainties and ill-defined threats and challenges and are in the process of evolving. This leads to a great deal of disagreement and debate within America regarding U.S. national security and the use of military force (always aside from real threats to the homeland). Disagreements are likely to occur within the national security establishment, between the establishment and other branches and agencies of government, and between all of these and the public in general. The intensity of the disagreement increases in direct proportion to the size of the gap between policies and strategies, on the one hand, and well-established American perspectives, expectations, and political-military posture, on the other. When we add to this the differing views of allies and adversaries and their national security efforts, it is not difficult to conclude that simply examining the U.S. military and defense planning does not do justice to the complexities and complications inherent in U.S. national security and the use of military force. This is best summed up by the following:

> The defense planning process . . . is beset with multiple dilemmas. Assessing the threat and acquiring the force structure to meet that threat require an efficient crystal ball—not only in the sense of defining the future in the here and now in terms of events and dangers. The process also requires accurately estimating the national mood years before the critical event.[15]

THE AMERICAN POLITICAL SYSTEM

American Values and Culture

American values and culture are the bases for interpreting and projecting national interests into the international security environment, and they shape national security policy. Moreover, values and culture are the psychological and moral sustenance of the military and create boundaries and limitations for the role and function of the military. In addition, these factors have a major impact on the role of the U.S. military and the principles of military professionalism.

The term *American values* refers to what is esteemed and absolutely essential as the philosophical, legal, and moral basis for the continuation of the American system—in other words, those principles from which the American political system and social order derive their innate character and give substance to American culture. Many of these values evolve from the Judeo-Christian heritage, the Reformation, the Renaissance, the philosophies of John Locke and Jean-Jacques Rousseau, and the principles rooted in the American Revolution, the Declaration of Independence, and the Constitution. While all of these sources cover a wide range and a variety of historical reference points, we can identify at least six fundamental values that are particularly relevant to American national interests and their role in the international world.[16]

First is the right of self-determination, which is the presumption that each nation-state has the right to determine its own policy and to govern itself as it sees fit. An important corollary is that the people within that nation-state also have the right of self-determination. From the point of view of the United States, this means that through a mechanism of free and fair elections, people within each nation-state have a right to determine by whom and how they will be ruled, with the option of replacing their rulers as they see fit. This process is to operate within a system of laws and peaceful change.

Second, it follows that there is an inherent worth to any one individual in his or her relationship to others, to the political system, and to the social order. What does this mean? In the simplest terms, every person is intrinsically a moral, legal, and political entity to which the system must respond. Each individual has the right to achieve all that he or she can without encumbrances, other than those that protect other individuals and those required for the protection and survival of the homeland. Individual worth must, therefore, be reflected in economic, political, and legal systems.

Third, "governors" and those who have been selected to rule owe their power and accountability to the people. The people are the final authority regarding who should rule. Further, there is a continuing responsibility by the governors, as well as those appointed to positions in the system, to rule and function according to the moral and legal principles embodied in the concept of "power to the people." The right of the people to change governors is absolute. In this respect, there must not be any one consuming power dominating government or establishing its own rationale for rule. The furthering of individual worth necessitates limited government with no absolute and permanent focal point of power. To insure this, rule and governance must be open. In the main, this means decisions and policies openly arrived at with input from a variety of formal and informal groups. The system of rule must be accessible to the people and their representatives. This is the essence of "open systems."

Fourth, policies and changes in the international environment must be based on the first three values. Thus peaceful change brought about by rational discourse between nation-states is a fundamental value. Resort to war can only be acceptable if it is clearly based on protection and survival of the homeland, and then only if all other means have failed. In this respect, diplomacy and state-to-state relationships must be based on mutually acceptable "rules of the game."

Fifth, for the United States, it is a fundamental proposition that systems professing these values and seriously attempting to function according to them must be protected and nurtured. Further, nation-states whose values are compatible with those of the United States are thought to be best served by an international order based on the same values.

Finally, there is a moral underpinning to American values that owes its inception to the Judeo-Christian heritage. For many Americans, therefore, this instills a sense of "humanity," a sensitivity to the plight and status of individuals, and a search for divine guidance. This moral underpinning adds a dimension to what is seen to be proper and just in the minds of many Americans, and it is considered by many to be beyond the legal definition of government.

It is not suggested that these values are perfectly embodied in the American system. There are many historical examples of value distortions and their use to disguise other purposes. But the fact is that in the American system, no matter how imperfect, these values are esteemed in their own right and are embodied in the political-social system. Further, the system of rule and the character of the political system have institutionalized and "operationalized" these values, no matter how imperfectly. The expectations of Americans and their assessment of other states are, in no small measure, an application of these values.

American Values: Into the Twentieth Century

The collapse of the old order in Europe following World War I set the stage for the evolution of democratic systems in Europe, on the one hand, and tyrannical and Marxist-Leninist systems on the other. Until that time, "Pax Britannica" had provided a sense of stability and order to European affairs as well as to the United States and its relationships with Europe. But for many Americans, involvement in the "Great War" to save Europe seemed a mistake. The United States withdrew into a splendid isolationism that only ended with the start of World War II.

Even in the aftermath of World War I, Americans had been accustomed to a world dominated by a European order compatible, more or less, with the general nature of American values and national interests. While this was an imperfect order, it was not threatening to what Americans felt was the proper order of things and their own value system. At the beginning of the twentieth century, American values seemed to be best expressed by the progressive period of Theodore Roosevelt's presidency and Franklin Roosevelt's New Deal, both focusing on individual Americans and the government's responsibility to them.

There was little need to translate these values for use in the external world. America's interest only rarely extended beyond its own shores. Yet it was also in the beginning of the twentieth century that the United States became a "world" power with its acquisition of territory resulting from the Spanish-American War. A decade later, involvement in World War I was seen as a way of making the world safe for democracy and subduing a tyrannical Old World power. In the aftermath, most Americans were glad to see their government distance itself from the Old World again and focus on internal domestic matters. "It's their problem, not ours," was a common American attitude with respect to Europe and the outside world. American isolationism during the 1920s and 1930s is a well-recognized historical fact. World War II changed all of that, even though most Americans wanted no part of the European War (beginning in 1939) right up to the bombing of Pearl Harbor in 1941.

In between the two Great Wars, Americans presumed that American interests were also world interests; American values were morally unassailable and therefore were those to be sought by the rest of the world. In this context national security was primarily a narrow view focused on the protection of the American homeland, which required only minimum armed forces and limited strategies. Further, there was little need to struggle with issues of American values and how to protect them in the external world, except occasionally in terms of international economics.

Regardless of America's desire to return to its splendid isolation in the aftermath of World War II, the United States was in the world to stay. It became clear that American responsibilities now extended beyond the nation's borders. It was also becoming clear that democracy and American values could not be nurtured and expanded by simply "staying at home." Democracy made political and moral demands that required its nurturing in all parts of the world. Beyond protection of the American homeland, what did America stand for? And how did it intend to achieve these goals, whatever they were?

These questions were less difficult to answer in the negative—that is, America was against Marxist-Leninist systems as well as other types of authoritarian systems. Containment became the major U.S. policy to prevent the expansion of the Soviet Union. Positive responses to such questions were seen in the U.S. role in rebuilding Europe—the Marshall Plan. These responses placed the United States in a leadership role of the West, a reflection of the earlier Puritan view of the "chosen people."[17] This provided the moral basis for involvement in the Korean and Vietnam wars.

But the end of the Cold War and the emergence of a new security landscape made many Americans feel that it was time to focus on domestic issues at home. There was a turning inward, reinforced by the conviction that the fear of major wars had diminished considerably and the United States had won the Cold War. But this new landscape was muddled and lost in the "fog of peace." Indeed, some even argued that America would miss the Cold War.[18]

Moreover, turning inward, Americans became concerned with issues of multiculturalism. Some critics argued that while the United States may never have been a "melting pot," it did benefit from the waves of immigrants who brought with them a rich cultural heritage. But this heritage, according to critics, is being promoted at the expense of "Americanism." That is, the notion of American cultural heritage and Western tradition, in which the roots of democracy lie, are being eroded by the increasing prominence of other cultures and loyalties. The greatest charge is that such a development can lead to the "balkanization" of the United States. Regardless of the pros and cons, it is clear that demographics and cultural issues can have an impact on the national security policy, strategy, and the U.S. military. U.S. involvement in Africa, for example, must surely be sensitive to the views of African-Americans. The same is true with respect to Latin America.

The Domestic Setting

The characteristics of the American political system complicate the difficulties of coming to grips with national security and the role of the military in the new world order. Changing domestic political-social issues and the diffusion and decentralization of power within the American political system, not only within and between the various branches of government, are some of the factors within the domestic setting affecting the security environment. These are likely to be highlighted by the change brought about by the 1994 midterm elections, with the Republican Party controlling both houses of Congress for the first time in four decades.

In the 1990s the American domestic setting was changing. The rise of multiculturalism and political correctness caused some to fear the erosion of traditional views of Americanism and others to fear the ''balkanization'' of America. In such an environment it may become increasingly difficult to develop and maintain a domestic consensus about the strategic landscape, except in clear cases of aggression against the United States. The issue of multiculturalism spilled over into the military ranks.

Participatory politics and single-issue politics, the erosion of political-party cohesion, changing domestic demographics, the policy role of the media, and internal power problems within the government have made it almost impossible for the President to undertake any foreign policy or national security initiatives that are perceived as outside the mainstream or that appear to challenge U.S. constitutional principles. To successfully induce changes and to place his own stamp on national security policy, the President and his domestic allies must build a political base within the government and the general public, as well as convince the media of the appropriateness of new policies and strategies. This usually means that the matter (1) must be seen as a major national security issue, with the U.S. position clearly proper and morally correct, and (2) must involve minimum risk and a high expectation of success.

The American fear of concentration of power ingrained in the constitutional principles of separation of powers and checks and balances has provided clear limitations to the exercise of power of any one branch of government. Yet these restraints can also prevent effective response to challenges that require a concentration of power. The legal niceties of U.S. constitutional practice may have little influence in the international security setting, where power and politics are often inextricable. It is in this context that the U.S. national security establishment and the process by which security policy is formulated and implemented and military force is used meet their greatest test.

An important part of how the United States responds to and perceives the international security setting is the view of its own historical experience, including ideology, culture, and character of the political system. A great deal has changed since the end of the Cold War. This was also the case at the end of World War II. Each generation has witnessed enormous changes in relations between nation-states, in the nature of conflicts, and in the nature and character of adversaries. Indeed, change has become so commonplace that it is a truism that the only permanent thing in the world is change.

From the U.S. perspective, there are two continuities from the Cold War period that spill over into the 1990s and beyond: nuclear weapons and weapons proliferation, and the Vietnam War. In addition, there are four characteristics of the post–Cold War period that, when they are combined with continuities from the Cold War, create a complex strategic landscape. These are the shape of the new world order, the conflict environment, interdependence, and communications technology. There are, of course, other important points ranging from the shape and character of Russia to international terrorism. These are specific national security issues and are not the major focus of this chapter. The continuities and reference points, however, are springboards for shaping mind-sets and world views of those in the national security establishment who fashion national security posture.

CONTINUITIES AND CHANGES

Cold War Continuities

Nuclear Weapons and Weapons Proliferation

In the post–Cold War era, the proliferation of nuclear technology, as well as biological and chemical weapons, has become an increasing danger. Fears of nuclear war persist, even if at a lower level for major powers. Nuclear proliferation has also become intertwined with weapons proliferation in general, and there is a fear that such proliferation is expanding throughout many parts of the world that heretofore were relatively isolated from it.

Russia and three of its former republics, the Ukraine, Belarus, and Kazakhstan, along with the United States, have a large share of the world's nuclear weapons. Agreements are in place or planned to dismantle strategic nuclear weapons and to monitor the reduction of these weapons. However, China, India, and a dozen other states have nuclear weapons. Iran and China, for example, have bought modern weapons from Russia. Also, in 1995 fears persisted that North Korea and Iraq were acquiring (or had) nuclear weapons. A number of other states have the capability to develop them or are in the process of doing so, including Iran. In addition, many states have chemical and biological weapons and capabilities.

At the same time, conventional weapons, many of them of the sophisticated variety, have developed into a major economic market. In the post–Cold War period, the United States has become the most prominent arms-sales state. It has been estimated that the United States sold over $22 billion worth of arms in 1993. In the 1994 Paris weapons show, for example, the United States displayed for sale everything from helicopters and night-vision devices to Patriot missiles and armored vehicles. The proliferation of weapons has triggered an arms race in East Asia. More recently, there was evidence that the new leader of North Korea, Kim Jong-Il, was in the process of expanding North Korea's conventional arms sales to areas in the Middle East and Africa in order to acquire hard currency.[19]

With its roots in the Cold War, the black market in plutonium and high-tech weapons has become a major problem for the United States and Western powers. The fear is that the illegal transfer of plutonium to any number of countries could result in the accumulation of enough material to develop nuclear weapons. In addition, there is a growing fear that terrorists could acquire such material and eventually develop a nuclear device with which to threaten the United States, among others.

Complicating the weapons-proliferation problem is the fact that a number of Russian scientists have been hired by some Middle East states to develop their own nuclear capacity and technology. These intellectual mercenaries may be the most serious challenge in the long run. Transferring knowledge about nuclear weaponry and delivery systems to states with access to vast amounts of money through oil resources allows such states to develop their own nuclear industries that not only pose a formidable long-range threat to control and limitation of nuclear weapons, but also establish the bases for regional hegemony and regional conflicts.

In the long term, such developments may prompt states such as Japan to change their views on nuclear development and as a matter of national security to move into nuclear technology and development. Given the fact that China has already progressed a considerable distance in this regard, Japan may well be rethinking its present posture, if not in the general public as yet, at least among some in the Self-Defense Force. Also, the historical animosity between India and China bodes ill for limiting weapons proliferation.

In sum, the "arms bazaar" continues with increasing efforts at acquiring sophisticated weapons and nuclear technology. Not only does this complicate U.S. national security issues, but it adds difficulties in defense planning and the contingencies faced by the U.S. military.

The Vietnam War

Even though many Americans have tried to put "Vietnam behind us," the fact is that it is deeply embedded in the American landscape. The impact of Vietnam on the U.S. military remains real and lasting. To a lesser extent this is also true for the American public. Constant reminders of the Vietnam War appear in the literature, but the most visible reminder is the Vietnam War Memorial in Washington. The issues of prisoners of war and missing in action (POW/MIA) from the Vietnam War and the large number of Vietnam veterans in society are likely to make the Vietnam War a visible part of society for the foreseeable future. But, some argue, the Vietnam generation is in the process of passing into history. This is true in the U.S. military as well as for those who have been elected to national office. Indeed, the Gulf War generation is emerging as the driving force in the U.S. military. Nonetheless, the constant reminders of Vietnam, the sacrifices in the war, and its disputed outcome remain part of American history and the military experience.

This is reinforced by the volumes written about the Vietnam War ranging from "I was there" books and military performance assessments to analyses of policy and the role of national and military leaders. This does not include the studies and books written by Vietnamese who were involved in the war or by Frenchmen who were involved in the First Indochina War. Without trying to address the various themes from such a diverse range of literature, it is important to point out that the U.S. involvement spanned three presidencies, and as the war progressed, it created much divisiveness in the U.S. public and later within the military. The emotions that the war spawned in the United States added to the divisiveness and the heated political debates. To many Americans, particularly those in the military, the war became a very visible issue again when it was revealed that President Bill Clinton had avoided military service during the Vietnam War and his past comments about loathing the military were brought to light. This, among other things, resulted in a gap between the military and the Commander-in-Chief that in 1995 has yet to be reconciled.[20]

Vietnam has become a criterion for assessing post-Vietnam conflicts into the post–Cold War period. For the U.S. military the Vietnam War has become a measure against which other conflicts and contingencies are assessed. Even during the 1991 Gulf War, Vietnam surfaced. It became important to point out that the Gulf War was not like Vietnam: General Norman Schwarzkopf, the commander of the allied coalition in the war, was allowed to run the war from the battle area. Equally important, the military objectives were clear, the adversary was clear, the battle was short and pointed, and modern weaponry and sophisticated operational techniques were brought to bear to defeat Iraq, all in direct contrast to Vietnam. In the public realm, civilian leaders are wary of any conflict that hints even slightly of "another Vietnam."

In sum, Vietnam has become a part of the American psyche. Whether one believes that it was a "noble cause" or a major blunder, the fact is that Vietnam is an important psychological component as well as policy consideration in the new strategic landscape. A serious study of U.S. national security and the U.S. military in the post–Cold War era cannot dispense with the long-term impact of Vietnam on the psyche of the American people or on strategic plans and the use of military force. This does not mean that everything regarding military involvement or strategic plans should be totally rooted in Vietnam experience. But the lessons drawn from that war remain a part of the total strategic package for the future. These lessons include the impact of the U.S. withdrawal, its operational doctrines, the link between conflicts and the American people and political leadership, and, of course, what the Vietnam War did to the American military.

The Post–Cold War Era: Changes

The New World Order

It is common knowledge that the post–Cold War era—the new world order—ended the superpower era with the breakup of the Soviet Empire and the emergence of Russia and independent republics of the former Soviet Union. With this emerged a world order that some have called disorder. The relative predictability of the superpower era differs considerably from the new world order.[21] Indeed, for some the new world order reflects the disorder of the 1930s. What seems clear in the new world order is that there is a degree of disorder caused by shifting and evolving forces and ideologies that make it extremely difficult to come to grips with an international "system." Indeed, the notion of "ordered chaos" may be an optimistic view of the new world order.

While the final shape of the new world order remains elusive, there are some signs of what may be evolving. These have an important bearing on U.S. foreign policy, strategy, and military force.

First, the dissolution of the Soviet Union also meant the disappearance of the "Evil Empire." Combined with the collapse of the superpower era, this has led to a new strategic landscape characterized by a number of ethnic, religious, ideological, and nationalistic conflicts—or a combination of some or all of these. At the same time these conflicts have been compounded by the reshaping of some state systems, for example, Yugoslavia, and the potential of the breakdown of some existing states, such as Rwanda. In this strategic landscape Russia remains a major player on the world scene, particularly with its existing strategic nuclear stockpiles, its resources and population, and its influence with the independent republics. However, Russia is still struggling to reform its economic system and trying to resolve its internal political problems.

One of the most far-reaching attempts to explain such changes was presented by Samuel Huntington.[22] He argued that future conflicts would be a clash of civilizations:

> Groups or states belonging to one civilization that become involved in war with people from a different civilization naturally try to rally support from other members of their own civilization. As the post–Cold War world evolves, civilization commonality . . . is replacing political ideology and traditional balance of power considerations as the principal basis for cooperation and coalitions.[23]

To be sure, there are those who criticize Huntington's view.[24] But the fact is that there are some signs that religious loyalties and foreign strategic cultures may be developing transnational groupings and superimposing them over traditional state structures.

Second, regional hegemons are in the process of forming. That is, major states within various regions are attempting to dominate the specific regions in which they are located. Thus Iran and Syria may be embroiled in an implicit struggle over control of events in the Arab Middle East. That is, one or the other may well be attempting to be the leader of Islam. The fundamentalistic Islamic movement plays a major role in such matters, as do the evolving Israeli-Palestinian peace efforts.

Third, any number of states are facing internal struggles over control and response to destabilizing forces. In 1995 Bosnia-Herzegovina, Somalia, Rwanda, and Haiti were cases in point. But other states in sub-Saharan Africa, for example, were facing similar problems. At the same time former Soviet republics were still in the process of trying to create effective political and economic systems, and some were struggling over borders, as in the conflict between Christian Armenia and Moslem Azerbaijan.

Fourth, international economics have created what some call a global village. The European Community (EC), the North American Free Trade Agreement (NAFTA), the evolving Association of Southeast Asian Nations (ASEAN), and the Asian Pacific Economic Organization were attempts to bind regions together in trade pacts. At the same time, trade efforts reached global proportions as it became clear that economic growth did not lie solely in the homeland. The 1994 international efforts in signing the General Agreement on Tariffs and Trade (GATT) reflected a global economic vision.

Fifth, old alliances and treaties are becoming irrelevant. At the same time, former enemies may become friends, and former friends may become adversaries in the economic realm and power position of the United States. Also, new adversaries are evolving who perhaps do not pose the same threat as the former Soviet Union, but rather regional threats. Nevertheless, they may challenge U.S. national interests.

Sixth, there is a widening economic and military gap between developed industrial democracies and most of the Third World. (The concept of Third World is simply intended to denote a distinction in types of political systems and strategic cultures that are different from Western systems and cultures. It is not intended to denote a monolithic world nor one that is characterized by common economic and political systems.) This gap could be the basis for continuing conflicts within the Third World and between certain Third World systems and the United States and the West.

These matters raise a number of questions from the U.S. perspective. What role should (can) the United States play in shaping the international environment? What remains of the old alliances? Who are friends and who are adversaries? What is the concept of national power in the new world order? How can such power be utilized to achieve national security objectives? Perhaps the most complex and difficult issue is what U.S. national interests and national security mean in this new world order. In 1995 these questions remain unanswered and troubling.

The Conflict Environment

The changes in the international environment and the security landscape have changed the conflict environment. There is a popular view in the United

States that the possibility of major wars has considerably diminished. This also seems to be the growing conviction among leaders of major powers. Yet it is also true that there are any number of lesser conflicts and unconventional conflicts in the world ranging from the former Yugoslavia to the Caucasus, areas in Southeast and Southwest Asia, sub-Saharan Africa, and parts of Latin America. Also, the potential for conflicts remains high in the Middle East and Korea.

Many of these conflicts may not necessarily follow the patterns of conventional conflict such as those in the 1991 Gulf War. Many are likely to be unconventional conflicts encompassing everything from revolution and counterrevolution to terrorism and counterterrorism operations. Even though the 1994–1995 conflicts in Bosnia-Herzegovina seemed, on the surface, to follow conventional lines, the fear was that these not only could expand, but eventually could include unconventional conflict. Moreover, the U.N. command and control system for such conflicts came under criticism, not only for the hesitancy with which decisions were made, but also because of the very limited response to overt Serbian military efforts.

A pressing problem for the United States is the drug-cartel/revolutionary-group coalitions, such as those in Colombia and Peru. Not only do such coalitions pose a serious threat to the indigenous systems involved, they are a threat to American domestic tranquility and counterdrug operations. This intermix of domestic and international dimensions makes effective U.S. response extremely difficult. The visible use of mainstream military forces, for the most part, is limited to the external environment and normally is in support of other agencies. Moreover, effective response to such coalitions does not necessarily rest with conventional forces and doctrine.

In 1992 another dimension surfaced in the United States. This was labelled "wars of conscience." Such conflicts do not necessarily challenge or threaten U.S. national interests, but involvement is moved by humanitarian concerns. In 1994 U.S. involvements in Somalia and Rwanda were prime examples. Some even suggested that such U.S. involvement was being video driven. That is, the constant showing of suffering in Somalia and Rwanda, particularly that of children, played on the American conscience and created the environment for committing the United States. In 1994 refugees from Haiti and later from Cuba raised questions regarding the goal of U.S. policy in both cases even with U.S. military involvement. This occurred in Haiti in 1994 only after some complicated missteps by the United States. Yet the character of conflicts in this decade and the form of possible U.S. involvement may not follow European or Gulf War scenarios. This raised a number of questions about the utility of military force, military operational doctrines, and long-term support of the American people. But the more critical issue is how well prepared the American military is to engage in what are now called operations other than war (OOTW), including unconventional conflicts that are shaped by foreign strategic cultures. Equally important, will the American people support such involvement, and if so, for how long? Can the United States design an effective strategy or strategies that take into account foreign strategic cultures and a variety of nonconventional considerations?

Global Interdependence

The new world order has focused attention on a variety of issues that cross national boundaries. These include environmental considerations, humanitarian impulses, the drug trade, and perhaps most important, economic power as an instrument of national policy. Many of these issues have been placed in the context of national security. Environmental issues, for example, are seen as threats to the survival of the state and to the well-being of people. Similarly, it is argued that unless all peoples have some level of quality of life and are not hounded by hunger and poverty, a serious security environment is created that threatens the security and well-being of states and people who are relatively well off. But the most visible dimension of interdependence is economic. Historically, economic strength has been part of national security, but it was overshadowed by the focus on military power. However, in the new era where many accept the notion of the decreasing utility of military power, economic power has gained a particular prominence as a major component of national security. For some, the use of the economic instrument can now achieve national security objectives unattainable by the use of military power.

Economic power rests primarily on domestic economic strength—productivity and competitive capability in the external world. This forges a close link between national security and domestic economic and political issues. It is also argued that the ability to bring economic power to bear against other states, both explicitly and implicitly, shapes security and foreign policies. But it is also true that small states with important resources such as oil can have a major impact on larger states whose need for oil is critical. Thus smaller states in the Middle East, for example, are important players in the national security field by virtue of their oil resources.

The economic dimension is also part of the notion of "global village" and interdependence. The clear implication is that no state can exist in an economic vacuum; domestic economics are closely linked to the international economic arena. This linkage forges close ties between the domestic economic issues of major states and international economic issues and is reinforced by the increasing economic gap between developed industrial states and a number of underdeveloped states in the Southern Hemisphere. This is viewed in terms of economic power or its lack.

From another perspective, economic development is crucial to the well-being of any state. The continuation of those in power is in no small measure contingent upon the ability to implement specific policies to further the economic well-being of its people. Indeed, the 1992 presidential elections in the United States turned on such an issue.

In the final analysis, those in the national security establishment must incorporate a number of considerations that tend to create an interdependent international community or global village. The most prominent of these is economic power. This needs to be incorporated into the national security equation to a greater extent than has been envisioned in the past. The more difficult problem is to design appropriate strategies for responding to interdependent issues and the use of economic power to achieve national security objectives. Complicating the matter is that economic power cannot be viewed in isolation. It must be systematically incorporated with other national security instruments and in strategic planning. In brief, for many policymakers in the United States, strategic thinking must go beyond the use of military power, incorporate a variety of instruments, consider a variety of options including economic strategies, and perhaps even demand the creation of new instruments.

Communications Technology

A revolution in communications technology has not only added to the notions of global interdependence, it has dramatically exposed the workings of government and the political instability characterizing much of the international environment. Moreover, it has made information available almost instantaneously throughout the globe. This has been called the information age. The technological revolution in communications promises to continue unabated. What does this mean in terms of national security?

The ability of government to communicate across national boundaries almost at will not only reinforces the notions of interdependence, but also reshapes diplomacy and can provide a wealth of information on any particular state or groups of people. Equally important, the ability to use satellite communications makes it increasingly difficult to control the media and to censor news reports.

Also, such technology has had an impact on the ability to conduct wars. The highly sophisticated communications networks established by the coalition against Iraq in the Gulf War were an extremely important factor in controlling forces and in conducting a successful military operation in Kuwait. This was particularly true in the use of air power, air-to-ground missiles, and surface missiles. Also, the ability of news personnel to use satellite communications provided instantaneous reports on battlefield operations throughout the globe. Further, command centers in Washington had a better grasp of military operations through the use of the communications network than even commanders in the field in Saudi Arabia. These developments have driven the notion of a revolution in military affairs.

At another level, the dramatic increase in personal computers, fax machines, and camcorders, among other devices, in possession of individuals throughout the world increases people power and offers direct person-to-person communications across national boundaries. The total government control of such communications is a difficult if not impossible task.

The implications seem clear. Access to information and the ability to transmit information quickly and relatively cheaply link not only states more closely, but also people. Moreover, authoritarian systems that had a monopoly on communications now find it harder to maintain such a monopoly. Also, the ability of governments to shape the news and give it a particular spin is more limited, given direct access to a variety of news sources made available by the communications explosion.

Those in the national security establishment must account for the communications technology not only in designing national security strategy, but also in implementing security policies, collecting and evaluating intelligence information, and assessing the political-psychological dimension of national security issues. It is also the case that in the use of military force, care must be taken regarding the role of the media and access to information that ultimately comes with military operations. National security has become, on the one hand, a more complex arena with the communications technology. On the other hand, it has become a more visible arena as access to information by more governments and individuals increases. It is becoming increasingly difficult to find a place to hide.

Summary

The continuities from the Cold War era and the major characteristics of the post–Cold War period shape the new world order. More specifically, they fashion the security landscape that is emerging in the new world order. Thus the nuclear age and the Vietnam War from the earlier period, combined with the changing conflict environment, interdependence, and communications technology, underpin the shape of the new world order. All of these developments create dilemmas for the United States because they contain contradictory forces and pose difficult and serious challenges. For our purpose, how these developments are perceived and interpreted, and how U.S. policy and strategy are designed to respond, are part of the broad patterns of the politics of policymaking, affect the mind-sets of those in the national security establishment, and shape the role and capabilities of the U.S. military.

THE U.S. MILITARY: OVERVIEW

The U.S. military, as noted earlier, does not have the luxury of waiting until the new world order is stabilized and clear strategic issues emerge. It must design military strategies, doctrines, and force posture and weaponry to respond to contemporary as well as long-range contingencies. This design is based not only on perceptions of the new strategic landscape but on the so-called revolution in military affairs. In brief, American strategic posture is evolving with roots in the dissolution of the Soviet Union, the Gulf War, and peacekeeping contingencies. The response by the Bush administration was based on peacetime engagements and the beginning of military redeployment and reductions in force. The Clinton administration has put into place plans to reduce the size of the military even more and to create a strategic posture that appears to be driven by budget considerations rather than serious strategic insights. Also, considerable attention is now being placed on operations other than war (peacekeeping and humanitarian missions). At the same time, the second two years of the Clinton administration are likely to be dominated by Republican Party agendas, with emphasis on the congressional role in shaping the military and defense policy.

Another potentially serious problem that has emerged is the renewing of interservice rivalries.[25] While such rivalries historically have been part of the military system, with the reduction in defense budgets and planned reductions in military manpower, these disputes take on special significance. Battles over missions, turfs, and shares of the defense budget (which is getting smaller) are emerging in full array. These were signalled by the publication of various manuscripts designed to rationalize the importance of each service in future conflicts. *Land Warfare in the 21st Century* emphasized the technical military revolution and the impact this will have on land warfare; combined with *Army Focus 94: Force XXI: America's Army in the 21st Century,* it showed the importance of ground forces now and well into the next century.[26] The Air Force monograph *Global Reach—Global Power* and the Navy's *. . . From the Sea* are similar efforts for each of those services.[27]

Peacetime Engagements

At the beginning of this decade, the concept of ''peacetime engagements'' was articulated by the Bush administration in response to the changing strategic environment.[28] Subsequently, then Secretary of Defense Dick Cheney provided a detailed statement of peacetime engagements describing Strategic Deterrence and Defense, Forward Presence, Crisis Response, and Reconstitution.[29] The Regional Defense Strategy rests on four essential elements:

Strategic Deterrence and Defense—a credible strategic nuclear deterrence capability, and strategic defense against limited strikes.

Forward Presence—forward deployed or stationed forces (albeit at reduced levels) to strengthen alliances, show our resolve, and dissuade challengers in regions critical to us.

Crisis Response—forces and mobility to respond quickly and decisively with a range of options to regional crises of concern to us.

Reconstitution—the capability to create additional new forces to hedge against any renewed global threat.

Strategic deterrence and defense were based on the need to continue to ''maintain a diverse mix of survivable and highly capable offensive nuclear forces . . . and a defensive system for global protection against limited ballistic missile strikes—whatever their source.'' Forward presence reaffirmed the need to redeploy most U.S. armed forces to the United States, but acknowledged that ''some U.S. forces must remain deployed overseas in areas of U.S. interests.''

Crisis response stated that ''U.S. conventional forces must be able to respond rapidly to short-notice regional crises and contingencies that threaten U.S. interests.'' Finally, force reconstitution was based on the view that the United States ''must maintain the ability to reconstitute a larger force structure if a resurgent threat of massive conflict returns.'' This also assumed that collective security was a central focus of U.S. strategy. Cheney further stated that peacetime engagement was ''a coordinated combination of political, economic, and military actions, aimed primarily at counteracting local violence and promoting nation-building.''

The military began to restructure in order to respond to the requirements of peacetime engagements. These efforts continued into the Clinton administration. However, the *Bottom-Up Review* and operations other than war (OOTW) added to the increasingly difficult contingencies placed on the military.

The Bottom-Up Review

The Clinton administration embarked on its own version of military posture in 1993. Although much of the peacetime engagement concept remained guiding principles, new names and labels were put into place. This began with then Secretary of Defense Les Aspin's *Bottom-Up Review*.[30] This envisioned restructuring and reduction of the U.S. military while still making it effective in responding to two major regional conflicts (MRCs) simultaneously. Much of this was based on the experience of the Gulf War, the diminution of the fear of major wars, and the changed strategic environment. But it was also clear that much of the peacetime engagement perspectives remained part of this review.

By 1999 the *Bottom-Up Review* planned for an Active Army of 10 divisions (down from 14); the Marine Corps reduced from 182,000 to 174,000 personnel; 13 Air Force fighter wings, reduced from 16; and 11 Navy aircraft carriers, down from 13. A number of other reductions were also planned in nuclear forces. A greater reliance on reserve forces was also part of the review.

A number of critics of Aspin's plan argued that the plan was budget driven, devoid of serious strategic guidance, lacking in strategic reality, or all of these. According to some authorities,

> Aspin's Bottom-Up Review reveals serious discrepancies between what it says the Pentagon ought to have and what it is likely to get. . . . According to the analysis Aspin undertook last year as Chairman of the House Armed Services Committee, the Clinton Administration's defense budget doesn't provide nearly enough funds to buy a win-hold-win force structure.[31]

Les Aspin resigned as Secretary of Defense in 1994 among much talk that his effort to increase defense spending or at least stop the erosion of defense spending had led to major disagreements within the Clinton circle. Indeed, some even argued that for all practical purposes Les Aspin was fired.

As noted earlier, the Republican Party sweep of the 1994 midterm elections, resulting in the capture of the House and Senate for the first time in more than four decades, had an impact on defense policy and national security issues in general. The Republican Party blocked further erosion of the defense budget and provided more financial resources to the U.S. military. Also, there is likely to be a more concerted effort by Congress in its oversight role regarding the commitment of U.S. forces. How all of this will play in the 1996 presidential elections will, in no small way, determine whether the Republican Party will maintain control of Congress.

All of the efforts at establishing a different military posture must be considered in combination with coalition strategies, joint operations, the revolution in military affairs, operations other than war, and a changing military society relationship. It seems clear that the U.S. military is in a state of transition, groping for clear strategic guidelines and operational doctrines for a new set of threats and challenges.

CONCLUSIONS

The U.S. military cannot operate in a vacuum; nor can it successfully engage in contingencies that are contrary to the national will; nor can it divorce itself completely from society. Its force composition, structure, organization, weaponry, and operational doctrines are shaped by the strategic landscape, the American political system and its values, and the ability to transfer national power into usable power. In addition, it must be guided by national interests, the strategic vision of the national leadership, and, in the long term, by the national will and the political resolve and staying power of that leadership and the American people. The study of the U.S. military and the national security establishment, therefore, cannot be seriously undertaken without some attention first to such matters. Moreover, in addition to a reduction in force and increasingly limited resources, the U.S. military is going through a revolution in military affairs, at least in terms of its weaponry and command and control system. Thus to say that there are serious challenges facing the U.S. military may well be an understatement.

The seriousness of these matters was well stated by General Gordon R. Sullivan and Lieutenant Colonel James M. Dubik (General Sullivan was the Chief of Staff of the U.S. Army) with regard to the U.S. Army. Their remarks apply as well to all of the services.

> American political leaders are requiring the military to *contract* in both size and budget, *contribute* to domestic recovery, *participate* in global stability operations, and *retain* its capability to produce decisive victory in whatever circumstances they are employed—all at the same time. . . . Simply put, international and domestic realities have resulted in the paradox of declining military resources and increasing military missions, a paradox that is stressing our armed forces. The stress is significant. It requires fundamental changes in the way the nation conducts its defense affairs.[32]

The chapters that follow examine the specifics of each of the services and how they respond to the environment and challenges described by Sullivan and Dubik, including some discussion of the command and control system of the American armed forces, the organization and capabilities of the various services, and what steps have been and are being taken to prepare the armed forces for the new strategic landscape. Subsequent chapters examine contingencies and conflicts that are likely in the new world order, identifying their characteristics and challenges to the U.S. military. In addition, the chapters give some attention to operations other than war (OOTW); the reduction and restructuring of the armed forces; society and the military; and the revolution in military affairs. As stated previously, all of these issues with respect to the U.S. military must be placed in the broader context of the changing environments in which the military must operate. It is only through such a contextual perspective that the seriousness of the challenges posed to the U.S. military can be realistically examined.

NOTES

1. A number of themes in this chapter are from Sam C. Sarkesian, *U.S. National Security: Policymakers, Processes, and Politics,* 2nd ed. (Boulder, CO: Lynne Rienner Publishers, 1995).

2. Sean M. Lynn-Jones and Steven E. Miller, *The Cold War and After: Prospects for Peace,* expanded ed. (Cambridge, MA: MIT Press, 1993), p. xxi.

3. See, for example, Steven Metz and James Kievit, *The Revolution in Military Affairs and Conflict Short of War* (Carlisle Barracks, PA: Strategic Studies Institute, U.S. Army War College, 25 July 1994).

4. Richard Smoke, *National Security and the Nuclear Dilemma,* 2nd ed. (New York: Random House, 1987), p. 301.

5. See, for example, John Spanier and Eric M. Uslaner, *American Foreign Policy Making and the Democratic Dilemmas,* 4th ed. (New York: Holt, Rinehart and Winston, 1985), pp. 17–22.

6. Michael T. Klare and Daniel C. Thomas, eds., *World Security: Challenges for a New Century* (New York: St. Martin's Press, 1991), p. 3.

7. Sun Tzu, *The Art of War,* translated and with an introduction by Samuel B. Griffith (New York: Oxford University Press, 1971).

8. Carnes Lord, "Strategy and Organization at the National Level," in *Grand Strategy and the Decisionmaking Process,* ed. James C. Gaston (Washington, DC: National Defense University Press, 1992), pp. 141–159.

9. Headquarters, Department of the Army, *FM 100-25: Doctrine for Army Special Operations Forces* (Washington, DC: U.S. Government Printing Office, 12 December 1991), p. 4-2.

10. Ray S. Cline, *World Power Assessment: A Calculus of Strategic Drift* (Washington, DC: Center for Strategic and International Studies, 1975), p. 11.

11. Bruce Palmer, Jr., "Strategic Guidelines for the United States in the 1980s," in *Grand Strategy for the 1980s,* ed. Bruce Palmer, Jr. (Washington, DC: American Enterprise Institute for Public Policy Research, 1978), p. 73.

12. Klaus Knorr, "National Security Studies: Scope and Structure of the Field," in

National Security and American Society: Theory, Process, and Policy, ed. Frank N. Trager and Philip S. Kronenberg (Lawrence: University Press of Kansas, 1973), p. 6.

13. Carl von Clausewitz, *On War,* ed. and trans. by Michael Howard and Peter Paret (Princeton, NJ: Princeton University Press, 1976), pp. 177 and 178.

14. See Adda B. Bozeman, *Strategic Intelligence and Statecraft: Selected Essays* (Washington, DC: Brassey's [US], 1992).

15. Frederick H. Hartmann and Robert L. Wendzel, *Defending America's Security* (Washington, DC: Pergamon-Brassey's, 1988), p. 146.

16. For a useful study, see Eugene R. Wittkopf, ed., *The Domestic Sources of American Foreign Policy: Insights and Evidence,* 2nd ed. (New York: St. Martin's Press, 1994).

17. See, for example, Kenneth D. Wald, *Religion and Politics in the United States,* 2nd ed. (Washington, DC: CQ Press, 1992).

18. See, for example, John Mearsheimer, "Why We Will Soon Miss the Cold War," *Atlantic,* August 1990, pp. 35–50.

19. Terrence Kiernan and Barbara Opall, "North Korea's Kim Likely to Expand Arms Sales," *Army Times,* 1 August 1994, p. 31.

20. David Silverberg, "Clinton and the Military: Can the Gap Be Bridged?" *Armed Forces Journal International,* October 1993, pp. 53–54. See also Richard Kohn, "Out of Control: The Crisis in Civil-Military Relations," *National Interest,* Spring 1994, pp. 3–17.

21. Mearsheimer, "Why We Will Soon Miss the Cold War."

22. Samuel P. Huntington, "The Clash of Civilizations," *Foreign Affairs* 72, no. 3 (Summer 1993): 22–49.

23. Ibid., p. 35.

24. See replies by a number of authors in "Comments: Responses to Samuel P. Huntington's 'The Clash of Civilizations?' " *Foreign Affairs* 72, no. 4 (September/October 1993): 1–26.

25. See Tom Donnelly, "Services Outline Their Futures in High-Stakes Era," *Army Times,* 26 April 1993, p. 25. See also Molly Moore, "War Exposed Rivalries, Weaknesses in Military," *Washington Post,* 10 June 1991, pp. A-1, A-17.

26. General Gordon R. Sullivan and Lieutenant Colonel James M. Dubik, *Land Warfare in the 21st Century* (Carlisle Barracks, PA: U.S. Army War College, Strategic Studies Institute, February 1993); *Army Focus 94: Force XXI: America's Army in the 21st Century* (Washington, DC: Headquarters, Department of the Army, September 1994). See also Gordon R. Sullivan, *America's Army: Into the Twenty-First Century* (Cambridge, MA: Institute for Foreign Policy Analysis, 1993).

27. Secretary of the Air Force, *Global Reach—Global Power* (Washington, DC: Pentagon, n.d.); Department of the Air Force, *Reaching Globally, Reaching Powerfully: The United States Air Force in the Gulf War: A Report,* September 1991. See also Department of the Navy, Office of the Chief of Naval Operations, *The United States Navy in "Desert Shield," "Desert Storm,"* Washington, DC, 15 May 1991.

28. President George Bush, "Reshaping Our Forces," speech delivered at the Aspen Institute, Aspen, Colorado, 2 August 1990, *Vital Speeches of the Day,* 1990, p. 677.

29. Dick Cheney, Secretary of Defense, *Defense Strategy for the 1990s: The Regional Defense Strategy* (Washington, DC: Department of Defense, January 1993), p. 11.

30. Les Aspin, *The Bottom-Up Review: Forces for a New Era* (Washington, DC: Department of Defense, 1 September 1993).

31. Kim R. Holmes and Baker Spring, ''Aspin's Defense Review: Top-Down, Not Bottom-Up,'' *Armed Forces Journal International,* August 1993, pp. 39 and 40.
32. Sullivan and Dubik, *Land Warfare in the 21st Century,* p. 8.

SELECTED BIBLIOGRAPHY

Bozeman, Adda B. *Strategic Intelligence and Statecraft: Selected Essays.* Washington, DC: Brassey's (US), 1992.

Eitelberg, Mark J., and Stephen L. Mehay, eds. *Marching toward the 21st Century: Military Manpower and Recruiting.* Westport, CT: Greenwood Press, 1994.

Gaston, James C., ed. *Grand Strategy and the Decisionmaking Process.* Washington, DC: National Defense University Press, 1992.

Jordan, Amos A., William J. Taylor, Jr., and Lawrence Korb. *American National Security: Policy and Process.* 4th ed. Baltimore, MD: Johns Hopkins University Press, 1993.

Murray, Douglas J., and Paul R. Viotti, eds. *The Defense Policies of Nations: A Comparative Study.* 3rd ed. Baltimore, MD: Johns Hopkins University Press, 1994.

Sarkesian, Sam C. *U.S. National Security: Policymakers, Processes, and Politics.* 2nd ed. Boulder, CO: Lynne Rienner Publishers, 1995.

Sarkesian, Sam C., and John Mead Flanagin, eds. *U.S. Domestic and National Security Agendas: Into the Twenty-First Century.* Westport, CT: Greenwood Press, 1994.

Shultz, Richard, Roy Godson, and Ted Greenwood, eds. *Security Studies for the 1990s.* Washington, DC: Brassey's (US), 1993.

Snow, Donald M. *National Security: Defense Policy for a New International Order.* 3rd ed. New York: St. Martin's Press, 1995.

Sullivan, General Gordon R., and Lieutenant Colonel James M. Dubik. *Land Warfare in the 21st Century.* Carlisle Barracks, PA: U.S. Army War College, Strategic Studies Institute, February 1993.

Sun Tzu. *The Art of War.* Translated and with an introduction by Samuel B. Griffith. New York: Oxford University Press, 1971.

von Clausewitz, Carl. *On War.* ed. and trans. by Michael Howard and Peter Paret. Princeton, NJ: Princeton University Press, 1976.

Weigley, Russell F. *The American Way of War: A History of United States Military Strategy and Policy.* Bloomington: Indiana University Press, 1977.

Wittkopf, Eugene R., ed. *The Domestic Sources of American Foreign Policy: Insights and Evidence.* 2nd ed. New York: St. Martin's Press, 1994.

PART I

THE ARMED FORCES

Chapter 2

THE ARMY

Daniel J. Kaufman

The end of the Cold War reduced dramatically the risk of strategic nuclear confrontation while, paradoxically, heightening the need to be able to respond to a wide range of conventional contingencies. In the years since Operation Desert Storm provided a glimpse of what information-age warfare will be, the pace of change for the U.S. Army has been enormous. In many ways, the turn-of-the-twenty-first-century Army will be as different from the Army of Desert Storm as George Marshall's Army of World War II was different from Ulysses Grant's Army of the Potomac. New challenges, new missions, new ways to accomplish those missions, and new technologies have combined to produce a transformation that is fundamentally changing every aspect of the Army.

The disintegration of the Soviet Union removed the paramount security concern of four and a half decades, but left other significant dangers undiminished. Indeed, the demise of the Soviet Union unleashed new and destabilizing trends. The rise of new centers of influence, radical ethnic or religious groups, and new regional powers will enhance competition for power, resources, and territory.

The breakup of nation-states and the rupture of civil society, such as we have witnessed in the former Yugoslavia, have had a significant impact on regional peace and stability. Traditional national and ethnic enmities will sustain the demand for high-technology weaponry, retarding economic development while raising the costs of conflict. Ethnic divisions that were suppressed by the Cold War now erupt with suddenness and ferocity, as the tragedy in Bosnia-Herzegovina demonstrated all too graphically.

Uneven economic development will prolong poverty throughout many parts of the globe, promoting terrorism and malignant drug-based economies. The gap between rich and poor societies has expanded dramatically, separating nations and continents into fundamentally different worlds. The collapse of Communist regimes threatens millions with deprivation, insecurity, and conflict. As events clearly have demonstrated, the peaceful transition of these nations into democratic regimes cannot be taken for granted.

The United States has addressed these challenges with a national security strategy designed to enlarge the community of democracies and free-market economies. U.S. national military strategy focuses on dealing with four dangers: the spread of nuclear, biological, and chemical weapons; aggression by major regional powers or ethnic and religious conflict; the potential failure of democratic reform in the republics of the former Soviet Union and elsewhere; and the potential disruption of the stable international environment necessary for free trade to flourish.[1]

MISSIONS OF THE ARMY

The Army is reshaping itself in order to be responsive to the requirements of the national military strategy and to meet the challenges of the post–Cold War era. What are these challenges? The Army must maintain forces capable of power projection and forcible entry, forces that would then conduct land combat operations ranging from large-scale armored combat to smaller-scale, primarily infantry operations. The Army also must retain the capability to carry out what are now styled ''operations other than war,'' including foreign assistance, humanitarian aid, and peacekeeping or peace-enforcement operations. Specifically, the national military strategy requires that U.S. armed forces must be capable of conducting two nearly simultaneous major regional contingencies, as well as a variety of smaller operations such as peacekeeping.[2]

In order to accomplish its new missions, the Army has changed from a forward-deployed heavy force designed to deter and defeat large armored formations on the plains of Central Europe to a power-projection force—a strategically and operationally flexible force capable of deploying from the continental United States to protect and defend American interests anywhere in the world. The Army is designed to project decisive force across the broad spectrum of operations—from humanitarian assistance to high-intensity war, in any climate or terrain.

ORGANIZATIONAL SIZE AND STRUCTURE

Size

The Army is comprised of three ''components'': soldiers serving in the active force; soldiers serving in the Reserve Components (Army National Guard and Army Reserve); and civilian employees. After the drawdown in size following the end of the Vietnam War, the Active Army stabilized at a strength of about 780,000 soldiers. As the table below indicates, that was the size of the Active Army when the Berlin Wall came down in late 1989. Since that time, every component of the Army has been reduced in size significantly.

Army Endstrength (Thousands)

	1989	1992	1993	1994	1995
Active	780	610	572	540	510
Reserve	776	727	686	670	642
Civilian	403	334	294	293	281

By the end of the decade, the Active Army will be about 500,000 soldiers, while the Reserve Component will be slightly larger at 575,000. The reduction in the size of the Army since 1989 is reflected in the lower number of combat divisions retained in the force. In 1989 there were eighteen divisions in the active force. By 1994 that number had been reduced to twelve. By 1999 there will be ten divisions in the Active Army.

Structure

The structure of the Army reflects the variety of functions that it is required to accomplish. These major functions are the following:

1. To organize, train, and equip forces for the conduct of prompt and sustained operations on land, to defeat enemy land forces, and to seize, occupy, and defend land areas
2. To provide forces for appropriate air and missile defense and space control operations
3. To develop airborne doctrine, procedures, and equipment that are common to the Army and the Marine Corps
4. To provide Army forces for joint amphibious, airborne, and space operations
5. To provide forces for special operations
6. To provide forces for humanitarian assistance and disaster relief at home and abroad

Army forces are organized as combined-arms teams. Combined-arms forces consist of combat (armor and infantry), combat support (artillery, aviation, engineers, signal, intelligence, and air defense), and combat service support (logistics, maintenance, transportation, medical, and the like) units. These arms and services are integrated at each command level, from battalion through corps.

Tactical Army units stationed in the United States and abroad provide the direct means by which the Army accomplishes its functions. However, there is an extensive institutional support structure necessary to recruit, train, and equip soldiers before they are assigned to operational units.

The Secretary of the Army and the Chief of Staff of the Army are responsible for recruiting, training, and equipping soldiers as well as providing supervision of the organizational structures needed to carry out these functions. The Chief of Staff also oversees the support functions of the Army Staff (personnel, operations, logistics, and resources) in Washington, D.C.

All soldiers are assigned to one of the twenty-one branches of the Army. The branches of the Army are grouped by whether their primary mission is to engage in combat, to support the combat elements directly, or to provide combat service support or administration to the Army as a whole. The branches of the Army are as follows:

Combat and Combat Support

Infantry	Armor	Field Artillery	Air Defense
Engineer	Signal	Special Forces	Aviation
Military Intelligence	Civil Affairs	Military Police	Chemical

Combat Service Support

Ordnance	Quartermaster	Transportation
Finance	Chaplain	Adjutant General
Medical	Inspector General	Judge Advocate General

The Army's Training and Doctrine Command supports a network of training centers and schools that train soldiers in their specialties (for example, armor, infantry, or artillery) upon entry into the Army and at regular intervals during every soldier's career. The Command and General Staff College at Fort Leavenworth, Kansas, trains midcareer officers in the operational level of war. Senior officers study strategy at the Army War College in Carlisle, Pennsylvania. The Training and Doctrine Command also is responsible for the development of the doctrine that is the common frame of reference on operational matters for all Army units. Each branch school contributes to the development of the relevant aspects of Army doctrine.

The Army Materiel Command is responsible for an extensive community of laboratories and arsenals that develop and procure everything from main battle tanks and helicopters to combat boots and Army socks. Subordinate organizations such as the Tank-Automotive Command and Missile Command conduct research and development in specific areas, as well as supervise the production of materiel procured by the Army.

The Active Army's operational units consist of four corps (a corps consists of two or more divisions), twelve divisions, two armored cavalry regiments, five Special Operations Groups, and a number of separate brigades comprised of specialized forces such as aviation, field artillery, air defense artillery, engineer, signal, military police, and military intelligence units. The composition and deployment of Army units is discussed in detail in the following sections.

Force Composition

The Army's force structure and weaponry reflect its commitment to the concept of combined-arms operations. The Army's principal maneuver unit is the division. There are six different types of divisions in the U.S. Army: mechanized infantry, armored, light infantry, airborne, air assault, and infantry. Regardless of type, each division has a "base" that includes a command and control headquarters and essential functional units, to include a cavalry squadron, an aviation brigade, an artillery brigade, a support brigade, a signal battalion, an air defense battalion, and an engineer battalion. A division normally is composed of three maneuver brigades, each of which is made up of three combat battalions. The organic artillery brigade consists of three artillery battalions. The size of each unit depends on the type of division. The composition of Army combat units is depicted at figure 2.1.

Mechanized infantry and armored divisions have about 17,000 soldiers assigned. As their names suggest, these types of divisions contain significant numbers of tanks and infantry fighting vehicles. A mechanized infantry division has five mechanized infantry battalions, each consisting of about 850 soldiers, and five armored battalions of 550 soldiers each. An armored division has six tank battalions and four mechanized infantry battalions. Each armored division contains 348 tanks and 216 infantry fighting vehicles; a mechanized division has 290 tanks and 280 fighting vehicles. There are four mechanized infantry divisions and three armored divisions in the Army. Light infantry divisions, containing about 10,000 soldiers, are designed to be strategically mobile. They have no tanks or fighting vehicles assigned. A light infantry battalion has about 600 soldiers assigned. There are two light infantry divisions in the Army's force structure.

The one airborne division contains about 16,000 soldiers and is the only unit capable of forced entry via parachute assault. The one air assault division also has about 16,000 soldiers; its organic helicopter assets give it the ability to conduct extensive air mobile operations. The sole infantry division has only two tank battalions among its maneuver battalions; its infantry battalions are not heavily mechanized.

Every division has additional combat power in the form of artillery and attack helicopters. Additionally, there are artillery, aviation, air defense, signal, intelligence, and engineer units assigned to the corps commander that augment divisional capabilities.

Combat service support units are a vital part of a modern army. These forces include maintenance, transportation, ammunition storage and handling, logistical, and medical units. Every division has an integral division support command that provides these functions. Corps and theater commanders also have combat service support assets to sustain their deployed combat and combat support units.

In addition to the heavy and light divisions, the Army also maintains a significant number of Special Operations Forces. These forces include five active

Figure 2.1
Army Combat Organization

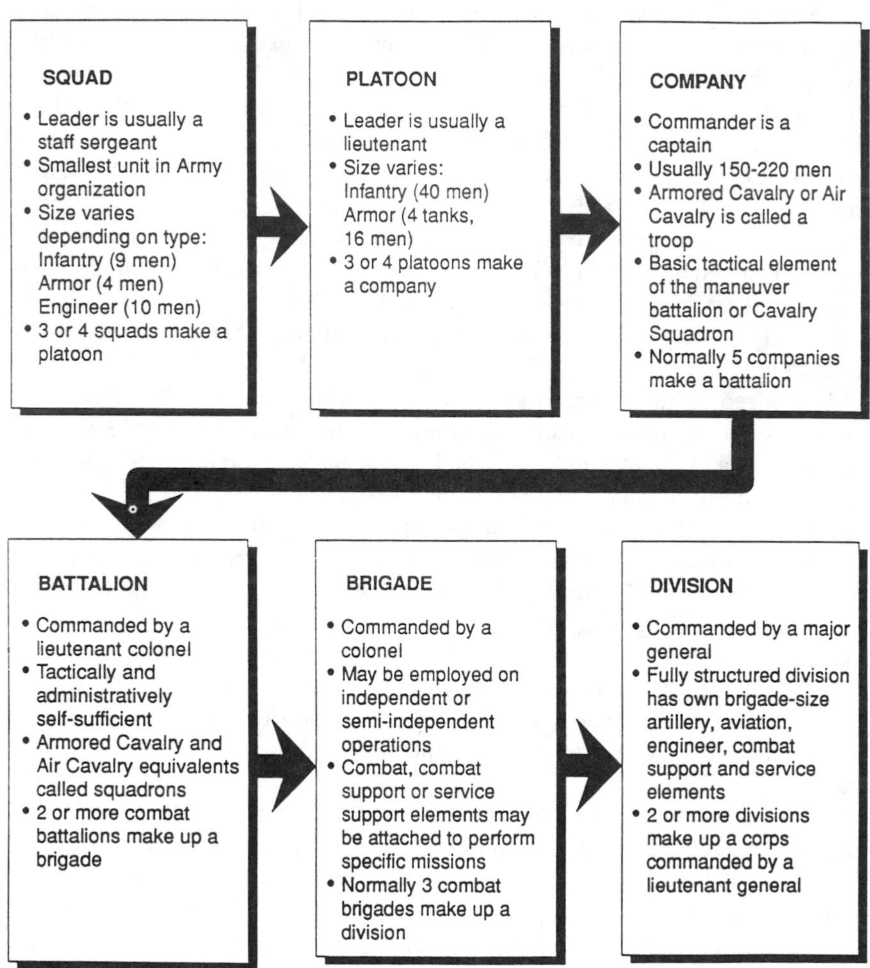

and four reserve Special Forces Groups, a ranger regiment, a Special Operations Aviation regiment, and a Civil Affairs and Psychological Operations Command. Special Operations Forces conduct a variety of functions, including unconventional warfare, foreign internal defense, special reconnaissance, counterterrorism, civil affairs, and psychological operations.

Force Mix

Active forces alone cannot fulfill the requirements of the national military strategy. Reserve Component forces (National Guard and Army Reserve) are a key aspect of a power-projection force the size of the post–Cold War Army. Indeed, Reserve Component forces will provide fully 60 percent of the combat support and combat service support for early deploying contingency forces, as was the case during Operation Desert Storm. Critical early deploying reserve combat support and combat service support units must be ready within thirty days of mobilization or sooner.

Reserve Component combat units pose a somewhat different problem. Lessons learned from the Persian Gulf War and the inherent difficulty of maintaining combat proficiency in the limited amount of training time available to Reserve Component units indicate that even the most ready Reserve Component combat brigade will require a minimum of ninety days of postmobilization training prior to deployment. Consequently, the Army will sustain fifteen National Guard Enhanced Readiness Brigades to round out Active Army divisions. These brigades will be maintained at readiness levels such that ninety days of postmobilization training will be sufficient prior to deployment. Another twenty-five brigades will be organized in five to eight National Guard divisions that will be maintained at lower levels of readiness. They will serve as reinforcing forces, providing the capability to mobilize, train, and deploy forces in the event of a large-scale protracted war.

Deployment and Stationing

The deployment of Army forces reflects the major changes that have taken place in the aftermath of the Cold War. The Army has changed from a forward-deployed force focused on conflict in Central Europe to a power-projection force primarily stationed in the United States focused on regional conflict. In 1989 there were 285,000 soldiers stationed in Europe; by 1995 that number will have been reduced to 65,000.

Major overseas deployments of Army forces consist of elements of two divisions (1st Armored and 3rd Mechanized Infantry) and a corps headquarters (V Corps) in Europe; an infantry division (2d Infantry) and associated support troops in Korea (totaling about 30,000 soldiers); one light infantry division (25th Infantry) in Hawaii; and a separate infantry brigade in Panama and Alaska.

The three remaining corps and eight divisions are stationed in the continental United States. The deployment of Army forces is portrayed in figure 2.2. This deployment pattern supports the scheme by which the Army would deploy forces abroad in the event of conflict. The XVIII Airborne Corps, located at Fort Bragg, North Carolina, is the rapid-reaction contingency corps. Depending on the situation, elements of the corps from the 82d Airborne Division at Fort Bragg, the 10th Mountain Division at Fort Drum, New York, the 24th Mechanized Infantry Division at Fort Stewart, Georgia, or the 101st Air Assault Division at Fort Campbell, Kentucky, could be deployed within eighteen hours of notification.

Reinforcing forces under the command of III Corps at Fort Hood, Texas, where the 1st Cavalry Division and the 2d Armored Division are located, or I

Figure 2.2
Active Army Division Locations

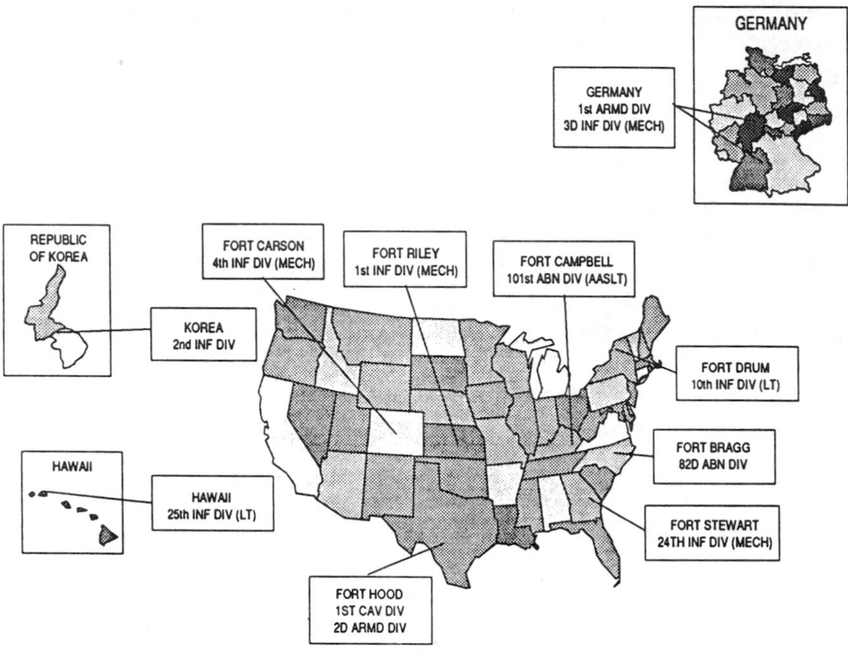

OTHER MAJOR COMBAT UNITS OF THE U.S. ARMY

UNIT	LOCATION
XVIII Airborne Corps	Fort Bragg, NC
Army Special Operations Command	Fort Bragg, NC
III Corps	Fort Hood, TX
I Corps	Fort Lewis, WA
V Corps	Heidelberg, Germany
2d Armored Cavalry Regiment (Light)	Fort Polk, LA
3d Armored Cavalry Regiment	Fort Bliss, TX

Corps at Fort Lewis, Washington, would support initially deployed contingency forces. Other available forces for reinforcement include the 1st Mechanized Infantry Division at Fort Riley, Kansas, and the 4th Mechanized Infantry Division at Fort Carson, Colorado. As discussed in detail later, the Army's goal is to be able to deploy three divisions anywhere in the world in thirty days, and a five-division corps with necessary support anywhere in the world in seventy-five days.

In addition to the 125,000 soldiers permanently stationed abroad in Europe,

Korea, and Panama, the Army has on average 20,000 more soldiers forward deployed carrying out a variety of missions in over sixty other countries. These missions range from peacekeeping operations in the Sinai Desert and Macedonia to military-to-military programs that educate soldiers in newly emerging democracies on the appropriate role of the military establishment in a democratic society.

Maneuver Battle Systems

The primary purpose of Army forces is to dominate the ground war and overwhelm enemy forces. Land forces are the instrument of decision; they provide the means by which the nation can achieve decisive victory, that is, the rapid termination of conflict on terms favorable to the United States with a minimum of casualties on both sides. In order to accomplish its mission, the Army must maintain an overmatching capability in maneuver forces. A number of weapons systems in the Army inventory contribute to the ability of the Army to dominate the ground battle.

Weaponry

M1A1 Abrams Tank

The Abrams tank is the Army's primary ground combat weapon system for closing with and destroying enemy forces. The tank relies on a combination of firepower, mobility, and shock effect to overwhelm enemy defenses. The special armor used on the Abrams makes it the most survivable tank in the world. It mounts a 120-millimeter main gun that fires a high-speed (more than 4,500 feet per second) round capable of penetrating the armor of any other tank at ranges of up to 2,500 meters. The Abrams also contains a nuclear-biological-chemical protection system that provides additional survivability in a contaminated environment. The tank weighs 67 tons, is powered by a 1,500-horsepower gas turbine engine, and contains an advanced thermal imaging sight system that enables it to operate under all light and climate conditions. It can travel at speeds up to 42 miles per hour on roads and 30 miles per hour across country. There are 14 Abrams tanks in every tank company and 58 in each armored battalion. The Army has a total of about 7,000 Abrams tanks in its inventory; both active and reserve units are equipped with the Abrams.

M2/M3 Bradley Fighting Vehicle System

The Bradley provides the mechanized infantry with a full-track, lightly armored fighting vehicle, and scout and armored cavalry units a vehicle for their screening, reconnaissance, and security missions. Both the infantry fighting vehicle (IFV) and the cavalry fighting vehicle (CFV) have a two-man turret that mounts a 25-millimeter automatic stabilized cannon, its primary armament with a range of 2,700 meters, and the tube-launched, optical-tracked, wire-guided missile (TOW) system, which is capable of destroying armored targets at ranges of up to 3,750 meters. The Bradley weighs 30 tons, is powered by a 600-horsepower diesel engine, and can swim inland waterways. The overall mobility of the Bradley is comparable to that of the Abrams tank, a critical capability that enables the mechanized infantry to keep up with tanks in high-speed cross-country operations. The IFV carries a three-man crew and six infantrymen; the infantry squad dismounts when necessary to conduct operations that require soldiers on the ground. The CFV carries a three-man crew and two scouts.

Each mechanized infantry company is equipped with 13 IFVs; every mechanized infantry battalion has 54 IFVs. Scout platoons in armored and mechanized infantry units have 6 CFVs; each division cavalry squadron (a battalion-sized reconnaissance unit) has 40 CFVs. The Army will purchase a total of about 6,725 Bradleys for use in both active and reserve mechanized infantry and cavalry units.

Apache Attack Helicopter

The AH-64 Apache attack helicopter is designed to be an airborne antitank weapon. The Apache is armed with the Hellfire antitank missile, as well as with a 30-millimeter cannon and rocket pods that carry 2.75-inch rockets. The Hellfire can destroy tanks or other armored vehicles at ranges in excess of 7,000 meters. The Apache is equipped with a target-acquisition and night-vision system that enables it to operate at night and in adverse weather conditions. The Apache carries a crew of two and can reach speeds of 150 miles per hour. The aviation brigade of every heavy division has 36 Apaches; light divisions have 21; the airborne division has 18. Corps-level aviation brigades and the air assault division have 54 AH-64s.

Additional antitank and antivehicle capabilities are provided by other systems such as the improved TOW vehicle, which is an armored personnel carrier modified to carry the antitank missile rather than infantrymen. The Dragon antitank missile, which can be carried by the individual soldier or mounted on a vehicle, is a wire-guided missile that has a range of about 1,000 meters.

Artillery

Indirect fire support is provided primarily by artillery. Armored and mechanized infantry divisions are equipped with the M109 self-propelled howitzer, which fires a 155-millimeter projectile. The latest version of this howitzer can fire a rocket-assisted projectile to a maximum range of 30 kilometers. Regular rounds have a maximum range of 24 kilometers. There are a number of types of artillery rounds available for employment. In addition to the regular high-explosive fragmentation round, there are smoke, illumination, and white phosphorus (for spotting) rounds. Modern munitions can deliver scatterable mines to disable tanks and other vehicles or conventional submunitions to attack more than one target. The laser-guided precision round, named Copperhead, can be used to destroy individual hard targets, such as tanks.

Each heavy division has 72 howitzers in its artillery brigade, with each of the three artillery battalions having 24; an artillery battalion normally supports each of the three maneuver brigades in the division. These weapons also are found in corps artillery brigades. Light, airborne, and air assault divisions have a smaller, lighter, towed 105-millimeter howitzer. The reduced size makes the howitzer more easily transportable, an essential consideration for these rapid-deployment forces.

Multiple-Launch Rocket System

The latest addition to the Army's indirect fire capabilities is the Multiple-Launch Rocket System (MLRS). MLRS consists of a 12-round launcher mounted on a highly mobile track vehicle; the system fires a free-flight artillery rocket one at a time or in rapid ripples to ranges of about 30 kilometers. The MLRS rocket is 13 feet long and 9 inches in diameter. The MLRS can deliver conventional as well as smart munitions. MLRS greatly improves the indirect-fire capability of the Army. For volley fire, each MLRS launcher can cover the same area as a battalion of 155-millimeter howitzers. There is a battery of 9 MLRS launchers in each heavy division. Corps artillery MLRS battalions have 24 launchers.

Army Tactical Missile System

Modern reconnaissance, surveillance, and target-acquisition systems make it possible for ground commanders to engage targets beyond the range of currently deployed artillery and MLRS projectiles. Deep fires are provided by the Army Tactical Missile System (ATACMS). The ATACMS is a ground-launched, conventional, surface-to-surface, inertially guided missile with an antipersonnel and antimateriel warhead. The ATACMS is fired from a modified MLRS launcher using the same targeting, engagement, and command and control systems as the basic MLRS. ATACMS is designed to be used against high-value targets deep in the enemy's rear such as missile sites, bridges, ammunition and logistics sites, and long-range rocket launcher or artillery batteries. ATACMS is capable of engaging point targets at ranges beyond 100 kilometers.

Black Hawk Utility Helicopter (UH-60)

The Black Hawk is used in air assault, air cavalry, and aeromedical evacuation missions. The Black Hawk can carry a squad of 11 combat-equipped soldiers or a payload of over 2,600 pounds. It can reposition a 105-millimeter howitzer, its crew of 6, and 30 rounds of ammunition in a single lift. The Black Hawk cruises at a speed of 145 knots, with a maximum cruising range of 330 nautical miles. There are 117 UH-60s in a corps aviation brigade. The aviation brigade of the air assault division has 99 Black Hawks; there are 33 in the airborne division, and 21 in each heavy division. Additionally, the air reconnaissance squadron of each type of division also is equipped with the UH-60, as is the combat aviation squadron of the armored cavalry regiment.

Combat Support Systems

In addition to the weapons systems designed to dominate the maneuver war, there are other important systems that contribute to the Army's ability to conduct sustained land combat operations. Surveillance, target-acquisition, and command, control, and communications systems are vital components of any modern military force, as are systems designed to protect ground forces from aerial attack by aircraft or missiles.

Joint Surveillance Target Attack Radar System (JSTARS)

JSTARS is an aerial-mounted wide-area surveillance and target-acquisition radar system. JSTARS detects and classifies ground targets with sufficient accuracy to allow them to be attacked by precision weapons from extended ranges. JSTARS is a joint Army and Air Force program. The Air Force is responsible for the airborne platform and the associated radar and communications systems. The airborne components of JSTARS are mounted on a militarized version of the Boeing 707. The Army is responsible for the ground-station components of the system. Orbiting a safe distance behind friendly lines, JSTARS radar surveys a wide area at great depth behind enemy lines. Targeting and intelligence data are transmitted to the ground stations, where they are distributed to tactical operations centers at army, corps, or division level.

Stinger

Stinger is a shoulder-fired, infrared homing antiaircraft missile system that provides air defense coverage to combat units. The missile homes on the heat emitted by the aircraft or helicopter engine; it employs a navigational system that allows it to fly an intercept course to the target. The missile weighs thirty-five pounds and has an effective range of over four kilometers. The missile is stored in a sealed tube that requires no maintenance. Once the gunner visually acquires the target and electronically interrogates it to determine if it is friend or foe, the missile notifies the gunner when it has a lock on the target. When fired, the missile travels a safe distance from the gunner before its main engine ignites and propels it toward the target.

Patriot

The Patriot air defense missile is designed to provide theater air defense capabilities against aerial attack. The system is composed of a radar set, an engagement control station, a power plant, and eight remotely located launchers. Each launcher contains four ready-to-fire missiles. The single radar provides for surveillance, target acquisition and track, and support of missile guidance. The missile has an effective range of 120 kilometers, enabling targets to be engaged at extended distances.

Special Units

Special operations are actions conducted by specially organized, trained, and equipped military and paramilitary forces to achieve military, diplomatic, economic, or psychological objectives by unconventional means. The five principal missions of special operations are unconventional warfare, direct actions, special reconnaissance, foreign internal defense, and counterterrorism. Special Operations Forces also may participate in other activities such as humanitarian assistance, antiterrorism, counterdrug operations, and personnel recovery. Typical special operations missions include interdicting enemy lines of communications and destroying military and industrial facilities. Collateral missions are intelligence collection, target acquisition, terminal guidance for strike aircraft and missile systems, and location of weapons of mass destruction. Special Operations Forces conduct psychological operations to demoralize the enemy, as well as train, equip, and advise resistance forces in guerrilla warfare.

Army Special Operations Forces consist of five types of units: Special Forces, rangers, Army Special Operations Aviation, psychological operations forces, and civil affairs forces. The U.S. Army Special Operations Command at Fort Bragg, North Carolina, is responsible for all Special Operations Forces in the United States. The John F. Kennedy Special Warfare Center and School at Fort Bragg is responsible for training and doctrine for Special Operations Forces.

Special forces units are organized, trained, and equipped to conduct all principal and collateral special operations missions. There are five active, two reserve, and two National Guard Special Forces Groups in the Army. Each group has a specific geographic area of responsibility. For example, the 1st Special Forces Group stationed at Fort Lewis, Washington, is responsible for special operations in Asia and the Pacific. Each Special Forces Group consists of three battalions; each battalion contains three line companies composed of six twelve-man Special Forces "A Teams," a support company, and a headquarters detachment.

Ranger units are rapidly deployable, airborne capable, and trained to conduct joint strike operations with special operations units of all services. Rangers also can conduct strike missions in support of conventional operations and can operate as conventional light infantry. The 75th Ranger Regiment, stationed at Fort Benning, Georgia, has three ranger battalions under its command. Each ranger battalion has about 550 soldiers assigned.

Army Special Operations Aviation units provide a mix of short-, medium-, and long-range lift and limited attack capabilities. In addition to supporting all principal and collateral missions, they also can conduct autonomous reconnaissance and direct-action missions. Special Operations Aviation assets include fixed-wing and rotary-wing aircraft. Army Special Operations Aviation units are assigned to the 160th Special Operations Aviation Regiment at Fort Campbell, Kentucky.

Psychological operations forces are employed to influence favorably the attitudes and behavior of specific foreign audiences and to reduce the will of hostile forces to wage war or oppose U.S. interests. Psychological operations forces are equipped with audiovisual, print, loudspeaker, radio, and television broadcasting capabilities. The 4th Psychological Operations Group is stationed at Fort Bragg, North Carolina.

Civil affairs forces are employed to enhance relationships between military forces and civilian authorities and populations in the area of operations. Civil affairs units are used to reduce civilian interference with military operations and to foster public understanding of and support for required military measures. The U.S. Army Civil Affairs and Psychological Operations Command is headquartered at Fort Bragg. There is one active-duty civil affairs battalion in the Army; there are three civil affairs commands, nine civil affairs brigades, and twenty-four civil affairs battalions in the Army Reserve.

OPERATIONAL DOCTRINE

The Purpose of Doctrine

Doctrine is the statement of how an army intends to conduct its operations. As an authoritative statement of intent, it must be definitive enough to guide specific operations, yet adaptable enough to address diverse and varied situations. Doctrine is a condensed statement of how army commanders should conduct campaigns, major operations, battles, and engagements. Doctrine essentially is a guide for action and a common way of thinking.

Doctrine is, or ought to be, the institutional glue that binds the disparate elements of a military organization together. Doctrine guides training, weapon and equipment development, tactics, communications, and organizational design. The development of doctrine is influenced by many factors: technological advances, changes in the nature of threats, national security policies, rivalries between branches of a service, rivalries between services, available resources, and the personal views of senior military and government leaders.

The Evolution of Army Doctrine

U.S. Army doctrine has evolved continuously for the past half century, reflecting many of the influences just noted. In the 1930s the Army lacked practical experience and effective doctrine for the employment of large combat units. Although corps and armies had been employed during the Civil War, the Army had not conducted large-scale maneuvers since 1865. In order to test operational concepts and evaluate its leaders, force structures, and equipment, in 1941 the Army conducted large-scale maneuvers between two armies consisting of over

400,000 soldiers operating in an area of over 30,000 square miles. The exercise was called Louisiana Maneuvers, and the lessons learned about integrating combined arms, coordinating air and ground operations, and the importance of logistical support helped guide the Army through World War II.

In the years immediately following World War II, the Army continued to rely on the doctrine that had proven to be so successful during the war. Doctrine was dominated by the offense and was primarily designed to conduct battles of annihilation by overwhelming an enemy with masses of combat power. The Army would rely on the ability of the U.S. economy to mobilize and to outproduce any enemy in the weapons and equipment of war. With the end of the U.S. nuclear monopoly came substantial revisions in doctrine. The mobile defense replaced the offense as the key to operational planning. Tactical nuclear weapons would be used to compensate for the lack of adequate numbers of forces to defend against a Warsaw Pact thrust into Western Europe.

As the nuclear arsenals of both sides in the Cold War grew, the Army adopted the concept of flexible response. The use of nuclear weapons would not be assumed; the Army would have to conduct sustained conventional operations. Consequently, mechanized infantry was introduced into the force structure to operate with armored formations, and improvements in mobility and command and control reflected the requirement to conduct nonnuclear defensive operations against the Warsaw Pact.

The pace and destructiveness of the 1973 Mideast War demonstrated that the United States could no longer depend on mobilization as the basis of its approach to conflict. U.S. forces would have to be prepared to fight outnumbered and win from the very first battle. The concept of the active defense was designed to force the enemy to mass most of his forces forward, where they would be more vulnerable to destruction by the precision-guided weapons that were beginning to be deployed in significant numbers. The goal of the active defense was to provide an operational concept that would cope with the massive numbers of Warsaw Pact armored forces facing NATO in the central region of Europe.

As the lethality and range of battlefield weapons increased and as the ability to see deeper into an enemy's rear improved, Army doctrine moved to a more offensive orientation with a concept of nonlinear warfare called ''AirLand Battle.'' Army studies clearly indicated that in order to defeat a Warsaw Pact attack in Central Europe the Army required a doctrine that enabled U.S. forces to attrite enemy combat power without becoming engaged in a war of attrition. The doctrinal solution was to employ the capabilities of modern sensing systems and precision weapons by attacking deep into the enemy rear area with missiles, helicopters, and Air Force tactical air power. In so doing, the Army would reduce the number and effectiveness of enemy forces that reached the forward edge of the battle area. AirLand Battle doctrine moved away from the traditional focus on linear battles of annihilation by balancing attrition with maneuver and by emphasizing the coordination of modern communications, surveillance, target-acquisition, and weapons systems.

Current Army Doctrine

In the aftermath of the Persian Gulf War, the Army refined its operational doctrine to incorporate the lessons learned from that conflict, to reflect the continuing and broadening impact of modern information-gathering and communications systems as well as increasingly lethal precision weapons, and to codify the Army's participation in what it styles "operations other than war."[3] Indeed, the major innovation in the latest doctrinal revision is the emphasis accorded the conduct of noncombat operations.

Army doctrine retains its focus on combined-arms operations. Combined-arms warfare is designed to overwhelm an enemy's ability to react by synchronizing direct and indirect fires from ground- and air-based platforms; assaulting with armor, mechanized, air assault, and dismounted units; jamming the enemy's communications; and attacking from several directions at once.

Simultaneous operations are designed to overwhelm the enemy's ability to react or to coordinate his response. Simultaneous attacks are launched against multiple objectives, day and night. Linear battles of attrition have been replaced with combined-arms operations throughout the depth of the battle area.

Tenets of Army Operations

Successfully orchestrating the components of modern military units in simultaneous, nonlinear operations is a complex undertaking. In order to prepare commanders at all levels to think systematically about the application of the assets they have available, Army doctrine posits five operational tenets it believes are essential for victory.

Initiative

Initiative sets the terms of battle, normally through offensive action. The intent is to deprive the enemy of freedom of action through surprise, speed and vigor of execution, and anticipation of response.

Agility

Agility is the ability to react faster than the enemy. Forces concentrate rapidly against enemy vulnerabilities, disrupting the enemy's plans and leading to late, uncoordinated, or piecemeal responses. Successive concentration against locally weaker or unprepared enemy forces enables smaller forces to disorient, fragment, and eventually defeat much larger opposing formations.

Depth

Depth is the extension of operations in time and space. Commanders take advantage of all available resources, attacking enemy forces and capabilities simultaneously throughout the battlefield. Using joint assets, commanders observe enemy movements and activities, then attack both committed and uncommitted forces. These deep attack operations degrade the enemy's freedom of action, attrite his combat, command and control, and logistics capabilities, and reduce the combat power he can bring to bear against friendly forces.

Synchronization

Synchronization is orchestrating available assets to mass at the decisive place and time. Integrating intelligence, fire-support, and logistics activities with the plan of maneuver results in synchronized operations. Synchronization also entails the effective sequencing of required activities. For example, jamming enemy communications, suppressing air defenses, and emplacing barriers and obstacles occur before the decisive maneuver battle begins. Effective synchronization produces the maximum use of available resources.

Versatility

Versatility is the ability of units to meet diverse mission requirements. Forces must be capable of moving rapidly from one geographical region to another and from one type of warfare to another. Versatility implies the capacity to operate across the full range of military operations and to perform at the tactical, operational, and strategic levels of war. The same is true for operations other than war. Using their inherent capabilities and command and control structures, Army units can assist effectively in nation-building, disaster relief, civil-disturbance, or peacekeeping operations.

Operations Other Than War (OOTW)

Army forces have participated in what are now styled ''operations other than war'' throughout their history. The Army protected citizens on the frontiers of an expanding America, built roads, bridges, railroads, and canals, and assisted other nations' internal development. The post–Cold War environment presents a complex and diffuse international system in which Army forces could be used to support a variety of sensitive and difficult operations. In recognition of the fact that ''nontraditional missions'' may well become commonplace, Army doctrine has incorporated the consideration of such operations in a formal way.

Specific operations other than war that have been included in the latest version of Army doctrine are as follows:

1. Support to domestic civil authorities
2. Humanitarian assistance and disaster relief
3. Security assistance
4. Noncombatant evacuation operations
5. Arms-control monitoring and verification
6. Nation assistance
7. Support to counterdrug operations

8. Combatting terrorism
9. Peacekeeping operations
10. Peace-enforcement operations
11. Show of force
12. Support for insurgencies and counterinsurgencies
13. Attacks and raids[4]

Operational Army units now include these subjects in their formal training schedules and field exercises.

INTO THE FUTURE

The Power-Projection Army

As a result of the changes in U.S. national military strategy that attended the end of the Cold War, the Army began to transform itself from a forward-deployed army focused on deterring and, if necessary, defeating a global Soviet threat into a smaller, primarily U.S.-based force prepared to project power into regions where U.S. interests are threatened and, if necessary, wage and win a major regional conflict. Inherent in this change of strategic orientation are a number of significant doctrinal and institutional changes.

First, the European focus that dominated Army planning for over four decades has been replaced by the requirement to respond to regional crisis and to conduct a regional conflict, even though the exact region cannot be known in advance. Consequently, Army forces cannot be structured for combat in a specific theater, but rather must train for a more generic set of battle tasks and must be tailored at the appropriate time for the requirements of the particular region in which they are to be employed.

Second, a power-projection army must be deployable. The Army must be able to project combat power rapidly from the continental United States to the region where U.S. interests are threatened. Consequently, strategic mobility is a cornerstone of the nation's post–Cold War military strategy. The congressionally mandated Mobility Requirements Study defined the strategic-lift requirements needed to carry out the national military strategy and recommended a number of specific programs to redress the strategic-lift shortfalls.

The study recommended that the Air Force continue to buy the C-17A strategic-lift aircraft. A significant improvement over the aging C-5A and C-141B fleets, the C-17A will allow access to an additional 3,000 airfields worldwide that cannot be used by current strategic-lift aircraft. The study also recommended that the Navy should build or convert twenty large, medium-speed, roll-on/roll-off ships (LMSRs). Nine of these ships would be used to preposition afloat an Army combat maneuver brigade equipment set and the associated support supplies and equipment needed to sustain the brigade for thirty days. The other eleven LMSRs would be used to deploy Army heavy divisions from the United States to reinforce units already deployed to the region.

In addition to the procurement of new air and sea lift capabilities, the Ready Reserve Fleet (RRF) would increase the number of roll-on/roll-off (RO/RO) ships from seventeen to thirty-six. Finally, infrastructure improvements in the United States would include upgrading railroads, prepositioning rail cars, and making improvements in highways and port-handling equipment to enhance the "fort-to-port" infrastructure and facilitate the rapid movement of forces and materiel.

The recommendations of the Mobility Requirements Study are being implemented. The Air Force has taken delivery of the first operational C-17s. The Army has completed loading the equipment of a heavy combat brigade and its supporting units. The brigade set is deployed afloat, available for use in either Southwest or Northeast Asia. The Navy has awarded contracts to convert five container ships to LMSRs and to build the first two new LMSRs. The Department of Defense will purchase or build nineteen LMSRs by 2001. The RRF had twenty-nine of the recommended thirty-six RO/RO ships at the beginning of 1994; the remainder will be purchased by the end of 1995. The Army spent nearly $500 million in 1993 and 1994 on infrastructure improvements ranging from the purchase of one hundred new heavy-duty railroad flatcars to improvements in the outload infrastructure at Fort Hood, Texas, and Fort Stewart, Georgia.

Prepositioning of equipment in critical regions also will enhance the Army's power-projection capabilities. In addition to the heavy brigade set of equipment prepositioned afloat, eight additional brigade sets of modern equipment will be located around the world in places such as Korea, Italy, Germany, and Kuwait. In times of crisis, soldiers will fly to forward staging areas and link up with this equipment. As a result of the improvements in strategic-lift capabilities, the Army will be able to attain the following power-projection goals:

1. A light brigade anywhere in the world within four days
2. A light division anywhere in the world in twelve days
3. A heavy brigade (prepositioned afloat) anywhere in the world within fifteen days
4. Two heavy divisions from the continental United States anywhere in the world within thirty days
5. A five-division corps with support (more than 150,000 soldiers) anywhere in the world within seventy-five days

The transformation from a forward-deployed force to a power-projection force also mandates changes in the institutional support structure. Consequently, the sustaining base needed to support deployed forces has been reconfigured. War reserve stockpiles have been consolidated in the United States, where the materiel is more readily available to support regional contingency operations. The number of war reserve stockpiles has been reduced from nineteen to five. An automated materiel management system called Total Asset Visibility keeps track of 600 weapons systems and more than 210,000 separate items, including repair parts and ammunition, that support these systems.

The Revolution in Military Affairs

Technological innovations, many of which were previewed in the Persian Gulf War, are giving rise to what is being called a "revolution in military affairs." As history makes clear, however, technological change by itself is insufficient to bring about such a revolution. A revolution in military affairs occurs when the application of new technologies into military systems combines with innovative operational concepts and organizational adaptation to alter fundamentally the character and conduct of military operations. Five dominant trends in the conduct of land warfare suggest that such a revolution in military affairs is indeed taking place: lethality and dispersion, volume and precision of fire, integrative technology, mass effects, and invisibility and detectability.[5]

Lethality and Dispersion

As weapons have become more lethal over time, units and individuals have become more dispersed. Rifling, introduced in the mid-nineteenth century, extended the range of artillery pieces and individual weapons. As rifles and artillery became more effective over much greater distances, units could no longer deploy in the dense, shoulder-to-shoulder formations that marked the age of the musket.

The lethality of weapons continued to improve throughout the twentieth century. Consequently, tactics, organizations, doctrine, equipment, force mixes, and methods of command and control all changed in response to increasing lethality and the corresponding requirement for dispersion. The Persian Gulf War demonstrated the ability of modern weapons to deliver increasingly lethal fire over ever-extended distances. Systems such as the Abrams tank, the Bradley fighting vehicle, the Apache helicopter, and the Multiple-Launch Rocket System (MLRS) all confirm the trend toward greater lethality at greater ranges and the increased dispersion of units and individuals.

Volume and Precision of Fire

The second trend concerns the volume (ordnance delivered within a given time) and precision of fire. Muzzle-loading rifles and cannons meant low rates of fire. The volume of fire began to increase significantly with the introduction of breech-loading rifles, smokeless powder, magazines, belts, and other automatic loading devices. Along with the ability to deliver an increased volume of fire came increases in the precision of weapons systems. Precision-guided weapons such as antitank missiles, laser designators that guide artillery rounds as well as bombs dropped from aircraft, modern fire-control systems such as those found on the Abrams and the Bradley, longer-range precision weapons like the Apache, ATACMS, and MLRS, and the "brilliant" systems (the next generation of precision-guided munitions) now in development ensure that increased precision will accompany increases in the volume of fire.

The introduction of new high-energy weapons, electromagnetic rail gun technology, superconductivity, and other yet-to-be-discovered technological improvements will continue the trend of major increases in the volume and precision of fire. Greatly dispersed land force units will be able to deliver increasing volumes of increasingly accurate fire. Integrative technology will enhance the ability of dispersed ground forces to coordinate their schemes for fire and maneuver.

Integrative Technology

Modern integrative technology began with the telegraph and railroad. The telegraph enabled information to be moved around the battlefield quickly. Near-"real-time" information assisted in the command and control of forces and increased the potential for coordinated effort throughout the theater of operations. The railroad provided the means to realize the potential that the telegraph offered. Rail made it possible to move large numbers of troops, equipment, supplies, and weapons quickly.

Advanced technologies provide the opportunity for the integration of reconnaissance and intelligence gathering systems with command and control, fire-control, and maneuver elements, as well as with logistical support centers. While the realities of the battlefield preclude the attainment of "perfect information," the degree of situational awareness that integrative technology will provide to ground forces will increase the commander's understanding of the battlefield enormously.

The incorporation of digital technology into battlefield systems will enable information now transmitted by radio and synchronized on acetate overlays and paper charts to be synchronized automatically, computer to computer. Modern command and control systems will create a common perception of the battlefield. Commanders will be able to transmit their operational concepts to subordinate commanders instantly; leaders at every level will "see" the same battlefield, thereby facilitating the effective allocation of reconnaissance, maneuver, fire-support, and logistical assets.

Mass Effects

The effects of the first three trends combine to reinforce a fourth: the ability of smaller units to achieve decisive effects. The advent of modern weaponry allowed fewer soldiers and smaller units to concentrate the effects of more firepower. Improvements in mechanization, aviation, and communications meant that ground forces not only had at their disposal more lethal weapons, but also could employ these weapons systems from physically remote locations. Furthermore, ground forces could move across, or over, the battlefield much faster than could their predecessors.

The second source of the increased ability of smaller units to achieve decisive effects stems from an organizational response to technological advances: the adoption of combined-arms formations at every level from company to corps. Units comprised of infantry, armor, artillery, and aviation assets are standard; consequently, commanders have at their disposal the full range of combat and combat support capabilities.

Maneuver is the third source of the increased effects of smaller units. Modern tanks, infantry fighting vehicles, self-propelled artillery, and logistics vehicles have improved significantly the ability of ground units to maneuver cross-country at ever-greater speeds. Aviation systems such as troop-carrying helicopters and attack helicopters capable of destroying tanks and armored vehicles contribute to the commander's ability to maneuver combat forces quickly, concentrating the effects of fire and maneuver at the decisive point.

Integrative technology reinforces the effects of improved maneuverability. Internally, integration includes the ability of all members of a combined-arms unit to talk and coordinate among the combat, combat support, and combat service support elements of the unit. Externally, integration enhances the ability to synchronize the contributions of land, air, and naval forces. Fully integrated joint forces can be tailored to fit the specific geographical, political, and military conditions of a particular situation.

Invisibility and Detectability

Improvements in long-range intelligence and target-acquisition systems, as well as in precision-guided weapons, work in both directions. Consequently, U.S. ground forces must adopt practices that reduce their visibility to an enemy while enhancing the ability of friendly forces to detect and engage enemy forces at extended distances. Invisibility—the ability to hide from the enemy—in its most basic form involves movement at night and the use of vegetation and terrain to conceal the deployment of troops, equipment, and supplies. Detectability—learning the location and disposition of enemy forces—historically was limited to what one could see with scouts, spies, and cavalry. Airplanes extended the ability to ascertain the nature of the enemy forces arrayed in a particular area of operations.

Electronic intelligence-gathering measures provide the capability to detect an enemy well beyond the horizon. Electronic countermeasures can mask the location of friendly forces, increasing their invisibility to enemy detection efforts. Deception operations using electronic transmissions to create a false image of the battlefield also contribute to invisibility.

Holography, virtual reality, televideo, and other modern signal and image-producing capabilities promise to increase invisibility even more. Low-observable (stealth) technology applied to ground combat vehicles will make detection of these systems more difficult. Conversely, advanced land-, air-, and

Figure 2.3
Information-Age Warfare

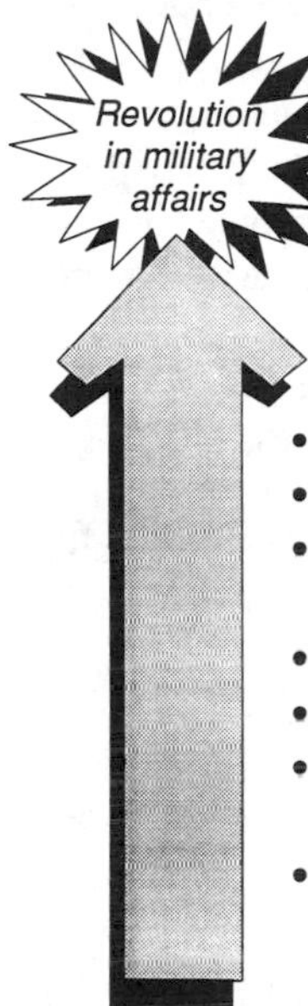

- High-tech weapons
- Information warfare
- Precision strike and decisive maneuver
- High-tempo, dispersed battle
- Smaller forces, greater effects
- Joint, multinational, interagency operations
- Coexistence of high and low-tech warfare

space-based information-gathering systems such as JSTARS and unmanned aerial vehicles will continue to expand the range at which the ground commander can detect enemy forces, improve the quality of the information gathered, and disseminate the information more rapidly over digitally integrated communications networks.

Information-Age Warfare

The five trends discussed here portend the nature of ground combat in the information age. The familiar form and structure of military campaigns as a chain of sequential operations will be transformed by the revolution in military affairs. Modern military forces will have the capability to achieve multiple operational objectives nearly simultaneously throughout the theater of operations. This simultaneity, coupled with the influence of near-real-time military and public communications, may well blur the traditional distinctions between the strategic, operational, and tactical levels of war.

Modern ground forces will be smaller and more expensive to equip, train, and maintain. As noted in figure 2.3, mid- to high-intensity military operations conducted by these armies will involve the use of high-technology equipment, smart weapons platforms and precision weapons, joint or multinational forces, and enhanced situational awareness. Such operations will be conducted under the threat of air and ballistic missile attack with conventional, chemical, biological, or nuclear warheads.

Future mid- to high-intensity wars will tend to be shorter when one side dominates the other in modern military power. However, more evenly matched foes could quickly reach a stalemate as both soldiers and inventories of modern munitions are exhausted. Warfare characterized by sharp, highly lethal, and intense periods of combat, followed by lulls during which both sides try to reconstitute their military power, may become the norm for conflicts between modern armies.

Information-age armies will conduct operations designed to result in the near-simultaneous paralysis and destruction of enemy forces, enemy war-making capability and potential, and enemy information networks throughout the theater of operations. Modern armies will develop a shared situational awareness based on common, real-time, near-complete information on both friendly and enemy forces distributed to every element of the task force.

The U.S. Army will be able to locate enemy forces quickly and precisely, whether that enemy is an information-age peer, an industrial-age army, or an agrarian warlord. The Army will know where its own forces are much more accurately than in previous conflicts, and it will be able to deny that knowledge to the enemy to a much greater extent. Information about friendly and enemy forces will be distributed to every element of the committed force—land, sea, and air—to create a common perception of the battlefield.

This shared situational awareness, coupled with the ability to conduct continuous operations, will enable the Army to observe, decide, and act faster than its adversaries. Every element of the force—armor, infantry, artillery, aviation, and command and control assets—will be linked digitally to facilitate the coordination and application of combat power against enemy formations. Domination will be achieved through simultaneous, around-the-clock, all-weather, air and ground operations directed against enemy formations and command centers throughout the width and depth of the battle area. Fire support will be directed against enemy forces with remarkable accuracy from platforms that may be hundreds of miles away. Speed and precision will be the dominant requirements for war in the information age.

Modernization

As the Army becomes smaller, it will have to rely more heavily on technologically advanced systems to preserve its ability to ensure land force dominance. To retain this land force dominance, the Army's modernization strategy focuses on five areas where the Army must retain its decisive edge over potential adversaries:

1. Project and sustain the force
2. Protect the force

3. Win the battlefield information war
4. Conduct precision strikes throughout the extended battlefield
5. Dominate the maneuver battle

Taken together, these attributes comprise the characteristics that will be required for the Army to achieve decisive victory in future conflicts.[6]

Project and Sustain the Force

In order to support the national military strategy, the Army must be capable of projecting and sustaining substantial combat power. Strategically, of course, the pace of deployment will be determined by airlift and sealift assets. For the Army, two specific implications follow from this requirement: contingency forces must have adequate combat power to contain the situation until heavy follow-on forces arrive; and adequate support capabilities must be integrated with the combat forces to provide efficient distribution of critical materiel and supplies while minimizing airlift and sealift requirements.

Two systems currently under development are designed specifically to enhance the lethality of early arriving contingency forces. The Armored Gun System (AGS) is a light tank that will provide antitank direct-fire capability to light forces when early deployment of Abrams tanks and Bradley fighting vehicles is not feasible. Javelin is a soldier-portable antitank system that features fire-and-forget technology and twice the target-acquisition and engagement range at two-thirds the weight of the Dragon antitank missile it will replace.

Combat service support programs focus on improving tactical transportation and distribution capability through the development of modern tactical support vehicles. New vehicles include the heavy, high-mobility, multipurpose wheeled vehicle and the family of medium tactical vehicles. The palletized load system will improve significantly ammunition-distribution and resupply capabilities.

Protect the Force

As the use of Scud missiles by Iraq during the Persian Gulf War demonstrated, relatively low-cost ballistic and cruise missiles can carry conventional or nonconventional warheads deep behind the front lines. Consequently, defense against theater ballistic missiles, cruise missiles, and unmanned aerial vehicles will be required in any foreseeable contingency to protect critical bases, ports, maneuver forces, and population centers. An effective counterfire capability also is needed to destroy enemy ballistic missile launchers as well as to counter enemy artillery.

As engagement ranges increase and sustained operations are conducted at night and in adverse weather, combat identification through passive and non-passive means will be essential to identify friend from foe in all conditions and at distances commensurate with weapons engagement ranges. Finally, the Army will have to protect its forces from weapons of mass destruction while maintaining the capability to operate in a chemical or biological warfare environment.

The Patriot advanced capability-3 (PAC-3) missile reflects the continued evolution of theater ballistic missile defense systems. PAC-3 will provide the lower level of defense against theater ballistic missiles, while the upper layer will be provided by the theater high-altitude area defense (THAAD). THAAD and the projected corps surface-to-air missile (corps SAM) are in early development.

Improvements in force-protection capabilities also will result from the integration of sensors and detection systems such as JSTARS with modern long-range precision weapons such as ATACMS and MLRS. Protection against air strikes will be provided by the Air Force as well as by ground-based systems such as Stinger.

Win the Battlefield Information War

To win the battlefield information war, the Army must have the capability to gather information, process it, and transmit it around the battlefield quickly while denying any enemy the capability to do the same. Digital integration will provide a shared view of the battlefield and yield significant improvements in real-time command and control.

Essential elements for conducting war in the information age include air-, ground-, and space-based sensors that can locate and identify targets; intelligence-fusion systems that process and collate information quickly and accurately; command and control systems that disseminate information to appropriate users; fire-control systems that translate information into targeting data; and smart munitions that can attack high-value targets accurately.

One method of developing these capabilities is to improve dramatically the capabilities of equipment already in the field. Horizontal technology insertion, the process of applying new technologies across a number of weapons systems, will improve the capability, performance, and overall combat power of systems already deployed. For example, the integration of the Inter-Vehicular Information System on the Abrams tank and Bradley fighting vehicle dramatically improved maneuver-unit performance in field tests by producing a common picture of the battlefield for leaders at every level. Similarly, incorporation of second-generation forward-looking infrared (FLIR) devices will enhance the performance of every combat platform equipped with a night sight.

The Comanche helicopter currently under development will not only improve the range and firepower of the Army's fleet of attack helicopters, it also will be an information-gathering platform with the ability to share its view of the battlefield with maneuver forces on the ground. The synchronization of maneuver forces, artillery fire, and aviation assets will depend, in large measure, on the ability to gather, process, and disseminate information quickly and accurately.

Conduct Precision Strikes throughout the Extended Battlefield

To strike and destroy enemy forces throughout the extended battlefield—laterally, in close proximity, and well forward of friendly forces—the Army must have modern artillery, attack helicopters, and missile systems with the requisite range, munitions, and communications linkages with target-acquisition and fire-control systems. The munitions suite must include systems that defeat armored vehicles as well as munitions to destroy high-priority, short-dwell targets such as tactical ballistic missile launchers, command and control centers, and enemy air defenses. Long-range sensors such as unmanned aerial vehicles and JSTARS are critical components of the reconnaissance and target-acquisition system.

In order to conduct precision strikes, a variety of weapons systems—artillery, rockets, missiles, and attack helicopters, all with appropriate ranges and sophisticated munitions—will be required. The Paladin upgraded howitzer overcomes many of the operational limitations of the outdated M109 howitzer, providing longer-range fires, substantially improved rates of fire, and increased mobility. Complementing the Paladin is the sense and destroy armor (SADARM) munition, launched from the howitzer or from an MLRS launcher. The principal targets for SADARM are enemy armored vehicles and self-propelled artillery pieces. The Army Tactical Missile System (ATACMS) and the triservice standoff attack missile (TSSAM) will provide medium- to long-range fires. The brilliant antiarmor submunitions (BAT) precision submunition currently under development will provide long-range precision attacks against multiple moving targets.

For the long term, the Advanced Field Artillery System (AFAS) and its armored resupply vehicle remain a high-priority development project. The AFAS, with a regenerative liquid propellant gun and a new armored chassis, will provide order-of-magnitude improvements in range, rate of fire, and mobility, as well as reductions in personnel and logistical support requirements. The AFAS also will serve as the testbed for advanced armored vehicles and associated integrated systems for use in follow-on tactical vehicles.

The Longbow fire-control radar and radar-seeking fire-and-forget missile are being developed for integration into the already-deployed Apache attack helicopter and later into the Comanche reconnaissance and attack helicopter when it is produced and deployed. The Longbow targeting radar and missile can be used day or night, in adverse weather, and in conditions where battlefield obscurants such as smoke have been employed. Longbow can be used as an aerial sensor to provide reconnaissance information to ground commanders and targeting data to other weapons systems, and as an advanced weapons platform to engage targets with its missiles when required.

Dominate the Maneuver Battle

Decisive operations entail the destruction of the enemy's land combat capability. Therefore, the Army must maintain an overmatch in close combat capabilities. Overmatch is the product of a number of characteristics. Real-time intelligence and combat information must be available to commanders in order to synchronize the assets available to them. Shared situational awareness and common perceptions of the battlefield facilitate maneuver and the distribution of fires.

Direct-fire systems must dominate the maneuver battle with mobility, shock action, and overwhelming firepower at the decisive point. Funding constraints preclude the deployment of new close combat systems for the foreseeable future. Therefore, existing maneuver systems—the Abrams tank, the Bradley fighting vehicle, and the Apache attack helicopter—will remain the mainstays of Army combat units. Consequently, improvements in close combat capabilities will come from upgrades to these systems rather than from the introduction of new platforms.

Upgrades to the Abrams tank include position navigation equipment and a digital communications architecture that allows electronic distribution of target and friendly position data to other similarly configured tanks, upgraded Bradleys, Longbow Apaches, and fire-support networks for artillery, rocket, and missile systems. The Bradley upgrade program will modernize existing vehicles by increasing their survivability, enhancing their lethality, and providing them with a digital communications capability compatible with the upgraded Abrams and Longbow Apache.

MANAGING CHANGE

Since the end of the Cold War, the pace of change has been enormous for the Army. New size, new deployment patterns, new doctrine, new operational planning focus, new missions—how can they all be accommodated in a severely constrained resource environment while maintaining a force trained and ready to carry out two nearly simultaneous major regional contingencies as well as being engaged every day in a considerable number of ''operations other than war''? The answer, of course, is that not everything can be accommodated. The overall Army budget declined from $93 billion in 1989 to $61 billion in 1995.[7] The budget for research, development, and acquisition declined 45 percent from 1989 to 1995. The modest Army modernization program reflects these fiscal realities.

Despite the institutional instability of the post–Cold War era, the Army has established a number of organizational initiatives designed to facilitate the development and integration of new doctrine, force structure, and equipment. The Louisiana Maneuvers program (the name for which was taken from the major series of exercises directed by General George Marshall in 1941 to prepare the Army for World War II) uses a combination of simulations, command-post exercises, and actual maneuvers to test new organizational and operational concepts.

Another institutional innovation is the establishment of six ''battle labs'' to conduct appraisals of critical capability requirements needed to meet the changing nature of warfare. Battle labs use simulation technology such as virtual reality and virtual prototyping to experiment with new technologies to ascertain their effects on the dynamics of the ground battle.

There are six battle labs; each addresses a specific aspect of battlefield dynamics, which are the categories of military activity where there appears to be the greatest potential for change. Battle labs have been established for the following categories: early entry lethality and survivability; mounted battle space; dismounted battle space; depth and simultaneous attack; battle command; and combat service support. Each battle lab can conduct its own experiments independently; all of the laboratories are linked electronically so that major tests involving every category can be executed. Examples of battle lab inquiries include horizontal technology integration, technology insertion, materiel acquisition, and operational testing and evaluation.

The Army's Force XXI initiative will study the organization and design of battalions, brigades, divisions, and corps to determine how they ought to evolve to a size and composition that will provide the versatility needed to succeed in the variety of operational environments in which the Army is likely to find itself. The aim of the Force XXI initiative is to develop the right mix of soldiers, leaders, skills, functions, weapons, and equipment needed to employ information-age technologies decisively in ground combat.

The Combat Training Centers at Fort Irwin, California, Fort Polk, Louisiana, and Hohenfels, Germany, remain the premier training facilities in the world. These fully instrumented training areas enable battalion- and brigade-size units to meet realistic opposing forces in an operational environment where the performance of every vehicle can be measured and every engagement can be assessed by sophisticated monitoring devices. The Joint Readiness Training Center at Fort Polk emphasizes low-intensity and peacekeeping operations. Representatives from international organizations such as the International Red Cross and World Vision, as well as journalists and other media representatives, participate in the training exercises.

PREDICTIONS ARE RISKY

Americans tend to forget their Army between wars. For all of the doctrinal, operational, organizational, and technological changes that have marked the post–Cold War Army, ultimately the key to whether or not the Army will retain its effectiveness derives from the support it receives from the American public. As the nation's declared status as the world's only superpower collides with the realities of an unstable and unpredictable international environment, it remains very much to be seen if the American people will sustain the Army to the degree necessary for it to carry out the multitude of missions that fall to those who profess the status of global leader.

NOTES

1. Les Aspin, *Report on the Bottom-Up Review* (Washington, DC: Department of Defense, October 1993), pp. 1–2.

2. Ibid., p. 7.

3. Headquarters, Department of the Army, *FM 100-5: Operations* (Washington, DC: U.S. Government Printing Office, June 1993). The discussion of the tenets of Army doctrine is drawn from chapter 2.

4. Ibid., chap. 13.

5. For a more complete discussion of the impact of technological changes on land warfare, see General Gordon R. Sullivan and Lieutenant Colonel James M. Dubik, *Land Warfare in the 21st Century* (Carlisle Barracks, PA: Strategic Studies Institute, February 1993), pp. 12–25.

6. U.S. Department of the Army, *The Army Modernization Vision* (Washington, DC: U.S. Government Printing Office, November 1993). See also General Gordon R. Sullivan, ''Statement before the U.S. House of Representatives Armed Services Committee on the Fiscal Year 1995 Budget Proposals,'' March 1994.

7. Richard Cheney, Secretary of Defense, *Annual Report to the President and the Congress* (Washington, DC: U.S. Government Printing Office, January 1994), p. B-2.

SELECTED BIBLIOGRAPHY

Brown, Frederic J. *The U.S. Army in Transition II.* Washington, DC: Brassey's, 1993.

Keegan, John. *A History of Warfare.* New York: Alfred A. Knopf, 1993.

Luttwak, Edward N. *Strategy: The Logic of War and Peace.* Cambridge, MA: Belknap Press of Harvard University Press, 1987.

Odom, William E. *America's Military Revolution: Strategy and Structure after the Cold War.* Washington, DC: American University Press, 1993.

Pfaltzgraff, Robert L., Jr., and Richard H. Shultz, Jr., eds. *The United States Army: Challenges and Missions for the 1990s.* Lexington, MA: Lexington Books, 1991.

Rosen, Stephen P. *Winning the Next War: Innovation and the Modern Military.* Ithaca, NY: Cornell University Press, 1991.

Toffler, Alvin, and Heidi Toffler. *War and Anti-War.* Boston: Little, Brown, 1993.

U.S. Department of the Army. *Field Manual 100-5: Operations.* Washington, DC: U.S. Government Printing Office, June 1993.

van Creveld, Martin. *Command in War.* Cambridge, MA: Harvard University Press, 1985.

———. *Technology and War.* New York: Free Press, 1989.

Chapter 3

THE NAVY

John Allen Williams

The U.S. Navy has come a long way from its Reagan administration goal of a 600-ship Navy centered around fifteen deployable aircraft carriers. This level was not quite achieved, and with the end of the Cold War and the subsequent military retrenchment the plans have now been completely revised. At the same time, thorny personnel issues continue.

Issues of strategy, forces, missions, and personnel are intertwined in such a way that it is difficult to discuss one without understanding the others. In view of its central position, however, it is best to begin with Navy strategy and describe how it has evolved in response to changing international conditions.[1]

STRATEGIC ISSUES

The U.S. Navy moved quickly to fill the theoretical void left when the breakup of the Soviet Union changed the dangers against which it needed to prepare. No longer was the primary threat from a major maritime power with a large submarine force that would attempt to interdict supplies moving across the Atlantic to reinforce U.S. and allied land forces in Europe. There was a growing awareness, emphasized by Operation Desert Storm in 1991, that new dangers were emerging from regional powers, and that Navy strategy needed to evolve to deal with them.

The Maritime Strategy

For the last several decades the primary military question was how to fight and win a global conventional war with the Soviet Union.[2] U.S. Army and Air

Force attention was focused on Central Europe and the problem of stopping several echelons of Soviet and Warsaw Pact shock troops before they reached the Atlantic. AirLand Battle 2000 was the Army's campaign plan to fight such a war, combining mobility and firepower to keep the attacker off balance and prevent him from reaching his objectives. The threat of escalation to tactical nuclear weapons was explicit, as the doctrine of "extended deterrence" envisioned the first use of battlefield nuclear weapons by allied forces if this became necessary to stop an attack.

The U.S. Navy was presented with a dilemma: its primary contribution to this high-priority scenario was to keep the Atlantic "sea bridge" to Europe open so that supplies could flow to the troops in the field, yet it had worldwide responsibilities to protect U.S. interests that required far more forces than would be needed for sea control in the Atlantic. The problem was particularly acute during the Carter administration, which tried unsuccessfully to reduce military spending early in its term by cutting forces not directly related to the central mission of repulsing an attack on the central front of Europe.

The Navy's solution to this strategic and budgetary dilemma was to develop a strategy that arguably could make a difference on the ground in Europe, and in so doing justify forces needed elsewhere, such as in the vast areas of the Pacific, where enduring U.S. interests also lay. The result became known as the Forward Maritime Strategy and received its most explicit public description in a 1986 supplement to the semiofficial *Proceedings* of the U.S. Naval Institute, a technically private organization headquartered at the U.S. Naval Academy in Annapolis.[3]

The key feature of the Maritime Strategy was its expansive notion of sea control.[4] Defensive, local-area sea control would not be sufficient to stop the powerful naval and air forces that were expected to attack the slow and vulnerable merchant ships bringing supplies to Europe. Offensive sea control was thought needed to deal with the threat of nuclear-powered Soviet attack submarines (SSNs) and increasingly sophisticated bombers of Soviet Naval Aviation making large-scale, coordinated missile attacks on convoys and the naval forces protecting them. In an attempt to deal with the "archer" rather than the "arrows," attacks were planned on the bases from which these forces would emanate, primarily in the Crimea (requiring attacks from the Mediterranean Sea) and the northern Kola Peninsula (requiring attacks from the Norwegian Sea). In a leap of logic left implicit, U.S. Navy forces, rather than other U.S. or allied forces, were thought necessary by the Navy to attack these threats to their forces, and campaign plans were developed to do so.

In brief overview, U.S. Navy forces would move forward on the northern and southern flanks of the North Atlantic Treaty Organization (NATO) into position in the Norwegian and Mediterranean seas, and also in the Western Pacific to freeze land-based Soviet forces there. U.S. naval forces would be in a position to attack Soviet ballistic-missile-firing submarines (SSBNs) in their bastions under the Arctic ice and in the Sea of Okhotsk, and also to carry out attacks on

Soviet bases threatening U.S. Navy forces and resupply shipping. The idea was to pin Soviet forces down as far as possible from the sea lanes and simultaneously reduce the numbers of strategic missiles targeted at the United States. The escalatory possibilities from such a strategy were a prime source of criticism, of course.

Such an expansive notion of sea control, combined with power projection involving attacks on the Soviet homeland, required large numbers of the most sophisticated ships and weapons systems to accomplish.[5] This served the Navy's purpose of participating directly in the highest-priority U.S. military mission and also justified the kind and level of forces needed for operations elsewhere. It also posed a severe threat of nuclear escalation, as the Soviets would not look kindly at the close approach of a nuclear-weapon-capable U.S. aircraft carrier battle group (CVBG) to their shores and could reasonably be expected to destroy it however they could.[6]

It would be a mistake to assume, as many in the Army and Air Force did, that the Maritime Strategy was simply a ''Potomac strategy,'' designed only as a force builder for the Navy. Whatever may have been the motivation of then Secretary of the Navy John Lehman, the strategy was crafted inside the Pentagon by the staff of the Chief of Naval Operations and at the Naval War College in Newport, Rhode Island, as a legitimate military response to a genuine military problem.[7] The suspicions of the other services notwithstanding, the Maritime Strategy was seen by its creators as a genuine war-fighting strategy to guide the development of campaign plans.

Forward... From the Sea

With the demise of the Soviet Union, and therefore of the threat of attack on Western Europe, the naval forces formerly arrayed against the West were no longer a particular problem. Not only were their numbers, state of readiness, and deployment patterns reduced, there was no plausible scenario that envisioned a conflict with them in the foreseeable future. The new threat was underlined by the 1990 attack on Kuwait by Iraq: aggressive regional powers posing a threat to the interests of the United States and its allies. The resulting Gulf War, or Operation Desert Shield and Operation Desert Storm, was seen by many as the prototype of the new military challenges to be faced, although never again is there likely to be such a highly developed host-nation support system in place for the use of the U.S. Army and Air Force.

Due in large part to weapons transfers from the major powers (especially the United States, the Soviet Union, Britain, and France, but also lower-tier powers such as Brazil), minor powers in the Third World developed sophisticated arsenals that posed a significant threat to forces approaching their shores.[8] Thus the level of sophistication of naval forces required to operate against them increased, although not to the level required to defeat Soviet forces. Combined with the need to reduce U.S. casualties, caution dictated that naval forces would continue to be the best available to ensure success at the lowest possible human cost to the United States.

The nature of the military problem had changed for the Navy, however. No longer was the primary threat from a global power able to project military forces at great distances and to threaten a resupply effort in midocean. It was still necessary to plan to bring material reinforcements in the event of a land conflict, but the open-ocean (''blue-water'') antisubmarine warfare (ASW) problem was replaced by the need to operate in littoral regions near a potential adversary (that is, in relatively shallow ''brown water''). In Soviet Admiral Sergey Grigoriyevich Gorshkov's famous phrase, the focus shifted to ''the battle against the shore.'' Such a battle requires naval forces, if they are to be relevant, to operate close to shore in support of the land campaign being waged by other U.S. forces, possibly including those of U.S. allies.

The question of how to make Navy strategy relevant to the emerging strategic situation assumed the highest priority in the staffs of the Secretary of the Navy and the Chief of Naval Operations. Over several months in 1993 a panel of Navy and Marine Corps flag and general officers (that is, Navy admirals and Marine Corps generals) developed a series of concepts based on the new strategic considerations that resulted in a new basic strategic document called . . . *From the Sea* (and, in a 1994 revision, *Forward . . . From the Sea*). These concepts envision that the U.S. Navy will operate far forward in a future engagement in support of land forces engaged against the enemy. They call for naval expeditionary forces to be shaped for joint operations, operating forward from the sea and tailored for national needs. Certain operational capabilities are required, including command, control, and surveillance; battlespace dominance; power projection; and force sustainment.[9] . . . *From the Sea* marked a significant departure from the strategic presuppositions of an entire generation of naval officers. If it were taken seriously, it would also shift the relative importance of the various communities of which the U.S. Navy is comprised. Submarine officers, who had come to dominate the upper reaches of the Navy, found their specialty in less demand as the importance of open-ocean ASW decreased. There was less need for nuclear-powered attack submarines (SSNs), and the rationale for an entire new generation of SSN-21 Seawolfs designed to counter the Soviet threat was undermined. Amphibious warfare and mine warfare officers found the importance of their specialties greatly increased as the focus of the Navy shifted to assisting the U.S. Marine Corps in mounting amphibious assaults from the sea and ensuring that the attacks were not undone by enemy minefields. Indeed, one of the severe problems uncovered in Operation Desert Storm was the degree to which enemy minelaying operations, even of unsophisticated mines, could derail both amphibious operations and naval gunfire support.[10]

Despite the major change in strategy, carrier-based aviation became, if anything, even more central to Navy plans. Carrier battle groups were needed to control the battlespace and to protect forces both ashore and afloat. With proximity to hostile forces comes vulnerability to land-based as well as sea-based weapons systems, and warning time is likely to be short. Aircraft are essential for protection in such a situation, and the Navy may need to operate where no land-based aircraft are available. The continuing relevance of carrier aviation to Navy planning will be apparent later, when force levels are discussed.

ORGANIZATIONAL ISSUES

Like the other U.S. military services, the Navy has both an administrative and an operational organization, or "chain of command." The administrative chain of command is concerned with building and maintaining forces and providing trained personnel to operate them. Activities such as deployments and combat are conducted under the operational chain of command, although the administrative chain continues to be involved in providing the forces and personnel. The head of each chain is the President of the United States, the constitutional commander-in-chief of the armed forces. From him authority flows to the Secretary of Defense, and from there the path differs depending on the chain of command in question.

Navy Administrative Organization

Department of the Navy

The Navy administrative organization is the Department of the Navy, headed by a civilian Secretary of the Navy who reports to the Secretary of Defense. The Secretary of the Navy currently has an Under Secretary and four Assistant Secretaries of the Navy. The titles of the Assistant Secretaries give an indication of the range of responsibilities of the administrative chain of command: Manpower and Reserve Affairs; Research, Development, and Acquisition; Installations and Environment; and Fiscal Management. In addition, the military chiefs of the Navy and Marine Corps (the Chief of Naval Operations [CNO] and the Commandant of the Marine Corps [CMC], respectively) work directly for the Secretary of the Navy. The principle of civilian control is clear in this organization (figure 3.1).[11]

The CNO's Pentagon Staff: OPNAV

The staff of the Chief of Naval Operations is called the Office of Naval Operations, or OPNAV. In a major 1992 reorganization the staff was changed to reduce the autonomy of the "platform advocates" responsible for air, surface, and undersea warfare. These positions were downgraded from three-star (Vice Admiral) to two-star (Rear Admiral) rank, and they no longer report directly to the CNO. Instead, they are responsible to a new three-star position, the Deputy Chief of Naval Operations for Resources, Warfare Requirements, and Assessments (N8, in the new OPNAV parlance). This is not just a paper reorganization, because it makes it easier to balance the requirements to execute strategy with

Figure 3.1
U.S. Navy Organization

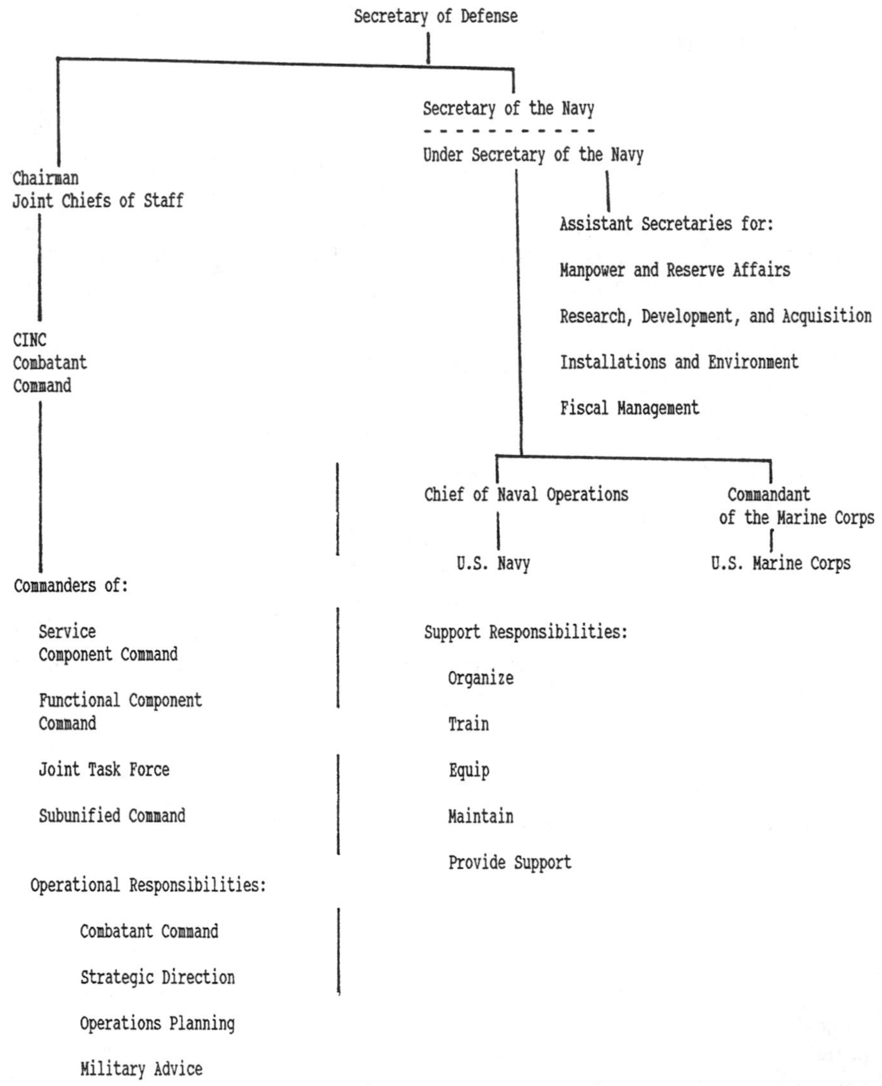

Source: Adapted from Headquarters, Department of the Army, *FM 100-25: Doctrine for Army Special Operations Forces* (Washington, DC: U.S. Government Printing Office, 1991), p. 4-2.

the needs of the particular community, whether it be air, surface, or subsurface, and trade-offs can now be made more easily.

Planning and Budgeting

Perhaps the greatest result of this reorganization is in the way in which the budget is developed. Instead of allocating a fixed percentage to each of the platform types (air, surface, and subsurface), a careful review process has been instituted to ensure that budgetary proposals allocate funds more rationally among the branches of the Navy. The Navy budget is now assessed not by platform, but by Joint Mission Area (JMA): joint strike, joint littoral warfare, joint surveillance, joint space and electronic warfare/intelligence, forward presence, strategic deterrence, and strategic sealift/protection. As a result, programs are now tied more directly with specific missions to be accomplished, and justifications must be linked to those areas. The Vice Admiral who is J8 chairs a special forum of flag officers called the Investment Balance Review (IBR), which discusses the tradeoffs among various programs and reduces the parochialism apparent under the old system.[12]

Outside the Pentagon

Under the Chief of Naval Operations for administrative purposes are the Commander-in-Chief, Atlantic Fleet (CINCLANTFLT), and the Commander-in-Chief, Pacific Fleet (CINCPACFLT). Each of these, in turn, has five subordinate "type commanders" responsible for air, surface, subsurface, training, and construction. Also directly subordinate to the CNO is the Commander, Naval Reserve Force, who operates through the commanders of the Naval Air Reserve and the Naval Surface Reserve Forces.[13] The importance of the Naval Reserve should be emphasized, since it provides all of the Navy's heavy logistics aircraft, embarked advisors, and mobile inshore undersea warfare (harbor defense) capability, and over 80 percent of its naval control of shipping, cargo handling, and military sealift forces. It has maintained this level of support despite dropping from over 142,000 personnel in fiscal year 1992 to some 113,000 in fiscal year 1994, with no end to the reductions in sight.[14]

Navy Operational Organization

The chain of command for operations, including war fighting, is a joint one; that is, it contains elements of more than one service. The trend toward "jointness" is the most important element driving defense origination and operations since the Goldwater-Nichols Defense Reorganization Act was passed in 1986, after the inadequacies of interservice cooperation were revealed in the 1981 invasion of Grenada.

Navy Operational Chain of Command

As with the administrative structure, the operational chain of command begins with the President and includes the Secretary of Defense. At that point, it moves to the military officers who are the Unified Commanders-in-Chief. It bypasses the civilian service secretaries such as the Secretary of the Navy. As noted later, operational orders do not pass through the Joint Chiefs of Staff as a collectivity, although they are transmitted through JCS communication links.

Unified Commanders-in-Chief

There are currently nine Combatant Commands, also called Unified Commands because they include elements from each service. Five of these commands are defined geographically and four functionally. The geographic commands are Central Command (the Persian Gulf area), European Command, Pacific Command, USA Command (formerly Atlantic Command and frequently still referred to in that way), and Southern Command. Each of these has a naval component commander. The functional commands are Special Operations (low-intensity warfare), Strategic (nuclear delivery), Space, and Transportation.[15] All operations are carried out through one or another of these joint commanders.

The operating forces of the Navy are divided into four fleets: Second (headquartered in Norfolk, Virginia), Fifth (Pearl Harbor, Hawaii), Sixth (Gaeta, Italy), and Seventh (Yokosuka, Japan). Depending on the operation, the fleets will be working for one or another of the Unified Commanders.[16]

The Joint Chiefs of Staff

The members of the Joint Chiefs of Staff are not technically in either chain of command, although orders from the Secretary of Defense pass through JCS channels en route to the Unified Commanders-in-Chief. The JCS include the military chiefs of the Army, Navy, Air Force, and Marine Corps and are headed by a Chairman and Vice Chairman. Like the other military chiefs, the Chief of Naval Operations is ''double hatted'' with both joint and service-specific responsibilities.[17] This can pose a problem if a joint initiative is not in the bureaucratic interest of a particular service.

DEPLOYMENT AND STATIONING

The U.S. Navy is a force of global reach, able to project power at great distances from home ports and able to remain on station for extended periods of time. If an area is sufficiently important, it is possible to maintain a continuous naval presence there indefinitely. Although this exacts a heavy toll on personnel and equipment, it can be done. Given finite resources, however, it is not possible to maintain a presence everywhere.

Forward Presence

"Surge" Forces versus Forward Presence

With their ability to operate indefinitely from international waters, naval forces are uniquely suited to promote U.S. interests abroad. The Navy has a strong preference for forward presence, with as many forces as possible stationed so as to provide timely support for U.S. interests should they become threatened. Forward presence is seen as a way to show U.S. commitment to an area or an ally and to contain crises before they get out of hand. The forward-presence mission may require more forces than actually would be used in a foreseeable conflict, due to the need to rotate units to provide proper upkeep and crew morale.

The alternative is to base the bulk of naval forces in the continental United States (CONUS). These forces could be at a high level of readiness and could be sent wherever needed on short notice. But given the relatively slow speed of ship transits, they would not arrive quickly. As a result, there is a danger of forces arriving too late to control a crisis or to assist an ally. The Center for Naval Analyses has estimated that there were some 207 U.S. responses to international incidents between the World War II and 1990 in which U.S. naval forces were involved in a major way.[18] It is doubtful that such forces would be as effective if they needed to come from locations in the United States. While it is true that Army and Air Force units can participate in the forward presence mission, neither is able to do so with the flexibility of naval forces (which include the U.S. Marine Corps).

Locations

Given their high degree of mobility, naval forces can operate from international seas worldwide. As Navy spokespersons are fond of saying, 80 percent of the world's population is within 500 miles of the shore.[19] This means that the Navy can put the vital assets of most nations at risk without the assistance of the other services, although a ''go it alone'' strategy is generally not contemplated for any major crisis. The capability for independent operations has accounted for much Navy foot-dragging on joint organizations in the past, including the establishment of the Department of Defense in 1947. For numerous reasons, including costs and political pressures, the Navy is now very supportive of ''jointness'' in its operations and planning. With a new generation of Navy officers who are experienced in joint operations now reaching senior ranks, this support appears to be genuine.[20]

The U.S. Navy has maintained a sustained presence in the Mediterranean Sea and the Western Pacific areas, and since the fall of the Shah of Iran in 1980 and the Persian Gulf War has devoted increasing resources to the Indian Ocean and Southwest Asia. These extended deployments would tax the Navy even more than they do if the United States did not have a carrier homeported in Yokosuka, Japan. This greatly reduces the transit times to critical areas, and the carrier is considered "on station" even when it is in drydock.[21]

Forces Required

Types of Forces

The forces needed in a particular situation will vary according to the specific circumstances that require their presence. It is important to remember that military force deployments are an implicit threat to perform particular missions and thereby influence the actions of one's opponents. In order for such actions to be effective and not merely a hollow bluff, the forces must be capable of performing the mission implicitly threatened, and there must be a perception that there is the political will on the part of the United States to use them.

Perceptions of political will are developed over a period of time as prospective opponents take the measure of the United States and its leaders. Military capability is easier to assess. It would be best to send the most versatile and capable platforms, the carrier battle groups, whenever they are needed, but that is not always possible. Carrier force levels are drawing down to a total of twelve, one of which is technically a "reserve" carrier.[22] Therefore, the traditional carrier battle group deployments can be augmented by deployments of Air Force ground-based aircraft and/or Army units. Other Navy ship combinations are also possible, including "maritime action groups" of surface ships and submarines and "surface action groups" of surface ships centered around a sophisticated cruiser. Many ships used for amphibious landings have the capacity to operate vertical takeoff and landing aircraft, and these make an excellent carrier substitute in some lower-threat situations.

Force Ratios

It was indicated earlier that several ships are needed to maintain one on station. The old rule of thumb was that a three-for-one ratio was required; that is, two ships were required back in the United States undergoing repairs and conducting training for each ship deployed forward. Actually, as Ronald F. O'Rourke of the Congressional Research Service has pointed out, the figure can be much higher than that, depending on the home port and the destination. For example, counting transit times and the need for training and periodic overhauls, it takes 8.6 San Diego–homeported nuclear-powered aircraft carriers (CVNs) to maintain one CVN on duty continuously in the Indian Ocean. It would take 6.6 of them if they were homeported in Norfolk, but this assumes the availability of the Suez Canal.[23] As discussed earlier, the need for forward presence can be more taxing on fleet resources than an actual conflict. In a conflict or an emergency, routine maintenance could be postponed and the need for crew rest ignored, but this tempo of operations (OPTEMPO) cannot be sustained indefinitely.

A particularly important factor is the effect of successive lengthy deployments on Navy personnel. The Navy decided on three limits on what is called PERSTEMPO, or the tempo of operations for personnel: deployments should not exceed six months, two days should be spent in operations near home for each day deployed, and sailors should expect to spend at least 50 percent of their time in home port over a five-year period.[24] This limits flexibility in ship scheduling, increasing the number of ships required to maintain a presence overseas at a given level.

NAVAL FORCES

We turn now to an overview of the kinds of forces that make up the U.S. Navy and the major weapons systems employed. It is important to understand that the Navy is in a period of severe retrenchment as it scales back from its earlier plans for a 600-ship force. The Navy is now at some 424 ships, on its way down to some 330 ships by 1999.[25] By the time these words are read, the Navy is likely to be below 400 ships for the first time in a generation.

Space does not permit a discussion of all forces and weapons, but a review of the major platforms will give an indication of the current Navy force posture and some Navy plans for the future. Although a particular platform may have several possible uses, it is useful to distinguish among those that are primarily strategic in nature, as opposed to general-purpose and special-warfare forces.

Strategic Forces

The prime mission of strategic forces is to deter an attack on one's own forces or homeland by holding those of an opponent hostage to one's own nuclear weapons. The most obvious form of deterrence is nuclear deterrence, in which the threat of destruction of his homeland deters an aggressor from attacking a nuclear-armed opponent. The doctrine of "extended deterrence" contemplates the first use of nuclear weapons, if necessary, to deter or counter chemical, biological, or even large-scale conventional attacks. This was official NATO policy and meant that member countries could not sign a pledge of "no first use" of nuclear weapons. The Navy plays a large and increasing role in nuclear deterrence.

Ballistic-Missile-Firing Submarines

The primary Navy strategic weapon is the ballistic-missile-firing submarines (SSBNs) and their associated missiles. There are currently fourteen of the new *Ohio*-class SSBNs, eight of which carry the older Trident I (C-4) missile and six of which carry the newer Trident II (D-5) missile, a larger missile with greater payload, accuracy, and range. Congress is unlikely to permit the Navy to backfit the older *Ohio*-class ships with the D-5 missile, but will probably permit the Navy to reach a total of eighteen SSBNs. In order to keep within the limits of the START II treaty, it may be necessary to reduce the number of missiles per ship, the number of ships, or the number of warheads per missile. The advantage of fewer ships is cost, but at the expense of putting a greater proportion of the retaliatory force in each particular ship.[26]

Land Attack Cruise Missiles

Although they are no longer deployed at sea in their nuclear configuration, Tomahawk cruise missiles (that is, air-breathing missiles that fly like miniature airplanes) have a nuclear variant that could attack targets at a distance of some 1,350 nautical miles. These could be launched from surface or subsurface vessels.[27]

Aircraft Carriers

Although they have not been a primary strategic strike weapon since the Kennedy administration, and although the Navy no longer carries nuclear weapons at sea, aircraft carriers (CVs or CVNs, depending on whether they are nuclear powered or not) are still capable of handling, transporting, and delivering nuclear weapons. It is this capability that made them so worrisome to the Soviets, especially when they were the centerpiece of the Maritime Strategy that called for them to sail well within range of major Soviet assets and attack them. Like most conservative military analysts, the Soviets measured the degree of threat they faced by enemy capabilities, not intentions or strategy, and never discounted the strategic value of the aircraft carrier.

General-Purpose Forces

With the end of the Cold War, the importance of flexible conventional warfighting forces is more evident as the U.S. military plans for a range of contingencies at varying levels of conflict and radically diverging situations.

Aviation Forces

In the new strategic environment the aircraft carrier is proving to be even more relevant than in the Cold War scenario. A typical *Nimitz*-class aircraft carrier may have nine air squadrons, with 85 to 90 aircraft on board. These may include the following, although the numbers carried will vary[28]:

F/A-18 Hornet (20–24 on board), capable of air-to-air combat and air-to-ground attack. A major upgrade is under consideration.[29]

F-14 Tomcat (20–24), used to defend the carrier battle group against air attack. As is the case with the F/A-18 Hornet, a major upgrade is being considered to provide land-attack as well as antiair capability.[30]

A-6 E Intruder (14), a venerable all-weather attack bomber that is being phased out with no clear replacement in sight. This is the Navy's longest-range bomber, and its loss without replacement will cause the Navy to lose its manned-bomber deep-strike mission.

EA-6 B Prowler (5), based on the Intruder but used for electronic warfare.

S-3 A Viking (8), used to detect and attack enemy submarines.

SH-60 Sea Hawk helicopter (4), used for ASW and for search and rescue. These frequently fly "plane guard" during takeoffs and landings to rescue downed pilots.

Other aircraft may also be deployed, such as carrier onboard delivery ("COD") aircraft used to ferry vital personnel and materiel, or the AV-8 B Harrier vertical takeoff and landing (VTOL) aircraft used by the Marines. Army helicopters have been embarked for special missions, a trend that is likely to continue as the services become more accustomed to working together and the need for a Navy steaming in littoral waters to combat land-based forces becomes more evident. The transport of large Army helicopters on the attack carrier *Dwight D. Eisenhower* in advance of the 1994 Haiti operation rendered the carrier inoperational and was a most unusual (and, in the opinion of the author, ill-advised) use of such a naval weapons platform.

During the Reagan administration the Navy pressed for a 600-ship force based on fifteen deployable carriers. Since one carrier would be in long-term overhaul undergoing a service life extension program (SLEP), this meant that there needed to be sixteen carriers. With the advent of the Clinton administration, there was great trepidation that the Navy would be left with ten or fewer carriers. Given the realities of the force-level-to-forward-deployment ratio, this would cut the heart out of a posture requiring forward deployments.

Soon after assuming office, Secretary of Defense Les Aspin undertook what he called a "bottom-up review" to assess defense needs in the light of the new strategic realities and the need to fight two nearly simultaneous major regional conflicts (MRCs). To the surprise of many, the report accepted the Navy's argument that a total of twelve carriers was necessary, one of which would be nominally a reserve training carrier. This twelfth carrier will actually be both highly capable and fully deployable and will be manned predominantly with active-duty personnel.[31]

In addition to its carrier-based aircraft, the Navy operates a fleet of transport aircraft and P-3 Orion maritime patrol aircraft. There are currently twenty-four active-duty and nine reserve P-3 squadrons, with the active-duty squadrons scheduled to be reduced to thirteen. P-3 missions have been primarily antisubmarine warfare, but the emphasis on surface surveillance and antisurface ship missions will be increased.[32]

Surface Forces

With the limited number of aircraft carriers likely to be available, the forward-presence mission will need to be performed in part by surface forces. Several ship types need to be discussed in order to get an idea of the range of vessels available.

Under the Reagan administration the four World War II–vintage *Iowa*-class battleships (BBs) were brought out of mothballs, upgraded with modern weapons systems in addition to their powerful 16-inch guns, and put back into commission. Although *New Jersey* saw some action in Vietnam, *Iowa, Missouri,* and *Wisconsin* had been laid up since the 1950s. Personnel, fuel, and upkeep costs drove the battleships back out of service, but they are an example of the long life of naval platforms and the ability to upgrade them with modern systems. They were very useful for naval gunfire support and were effective and highly visible centerpieces for surface action groups.

Cruisers and destroyers (CGs, CGNs, and DDGs) may be thought of as smaller and newer battleships. The newest of them are equipped with the Aegis combat system, a highly sophisticated suite of sensors and weapons to defend against air and missile attacks. They also serve as the primary ships for surface action groups. The main issue is how many of the DDG-51 *Arleigh Burke*–class guided missile destroyers to build. At $820–$900 million apiece, they are one of the largest parts of the defense budget. To date twenty-nine of these modern ships have been funded, and the administration would like to build fifteen more.[33]

With the increasing importance of littoral warfare and projecting power from the sea, amphibious ships are an important part of the Navy's plans. These include the LHD-1 *Wasp*-class amphibious assault ship, which is essentially a small aircraft carrier, and the "LX" amphibious assault ship, to be delivered after the turn of the century. The same considerations increase the importance of mine countermeasures, and a total of fourteen MCM-1 *Avenger*-class mine-countermeasures ships are currently contracted. Also, three of a total of twelve planned MHC-51 *Osprey*-class coastal mine-hunter ships will be delivered by the end of fiscal year 1994.[34]

Submarine Forces

The U.S. Navy was building to a fleet of more than ninety nuclear-powered attack submarines (SSNs) during the Reagan administration. With the demise of the Soviet Union, and therefore of the "blue-water" submarine threat, the primary rationale for SSNs was eroded. A major consideration when planning nuclear-powered ship construction is to maintain the highly complex industrial base required. If there is a gap during which such ships are not built, the capability to build them will erode, and it will become extremely expensive to rebuild it.[35] Perhaps with the desire to preserve force structure in mind, the Navy's submarine division put out a glossy pamphlet highlighting the roles submarines have played in addition to ASW, including precision strikes, surveillance, and inserting small numbers of troops clandestinely.[36] A more recent pronouncement from the same office emphasizes the continuing relevance of

ASW, but also discusses alternative missions.[37] SSNs can carry torpedoes, mines, cruise missiles, and even special operations personnel.

Three attack submarine programs are now under way.[38] The SSN-688 *Los Angeles*–class submarines are the oldest, and greatly improved models are still coming into the inventory. A total of sixty-two will have been built when the program terminates in 1996.

The SSN-21 Seawolf program was justified as a counter to new generations of Soviet submarines, their primary opponent. With a displacement half again as great as the 688 class, they cost $1.9 billion each, compared to the $800 million of the 688 class. Their biggest advantage was to be quiet operation at higher speeds, and thus less vulnerability to detection. Although the Navy would like to purchase more, the program will likely terminate with three.

Given the need to replace a large number of 688-class submarines when they reach the end of their service lives later this decade, plus the high cost of the SSN-21, the Navy is developing a New SSN (NSSN) in what was originally called the Centurion program. Despite the projected lower cost, the top Navy submarine officer reported that "it will be a better submarine, in terms of all the requirements, than the SEAWOLF-class or LOS ANGELES-class submarines."[39] If that is so, of course, one wonders about earlier pronouncements about the indispensability of the Seawolfs.

Navy Special Forces

U.S. special forces, which include Army, Navy, and Air Force units, are assigned to the Special Operations Command. The Navy special forces are the SEALs (for sea, air, and land) and are divided into ten 16-man platoons. (Women are not yet permitted to serve as SEALs.) Support elements include special boat squadrons, special boat units, and command and control elements.[40] Service in Naval Special Warfare (NSW) is not an obvious route to becoming Chief of Naval Operations, since these units are seen as a narrow specialization.

PERSONNEL ISSUES

Although there is a continuing need for quality personnel accessions, the reduced Navy force structure means that fewer personnel are needed overall. The Chief of Naval Operations has reported that 20,000 fewer officers and 170,000 fewer enlisted personnel will be needed in 1999 than were on active duty in 1989. The question is how to achieve such a large reduction while maintaining quality and minimizing costs to career personnel. The Navy's goal was to prevent forced separations of people in midcareer, before they became eligible for retirement benefits. Although many are still being forced to leave the service before they had intended to, the new fifteen-year retirement (at reduced benefits) has eased the transition for many.[41]

"People programs" are designed to improve the quality of life for Navy personnel and their families. This is genuinely seen as the right thing to do and has the additional benefit of increasing loyalty to the Navy as an organization. A sailor on deployment worrying about his family is operating at greatly reduced efficiency and may even pose a safety hazard to himself and others. Part of this emphasis is the importance of maintaining a reasonable PERSTEMPO so that ships are in home port as much as possible. A most important initiative from an effectiveness as well as personnel perspective is the widespread adaptation of Total Quality Leadership (TQL) to Navy needs and its implementation throughout the service.

Homosexuals in the Navy

As part of the Department of Defense (DOD), the Navy falls under Defense Department regulations concerning the service of homosexuals in the armed forces. The DOD policy on homosexuality is consistent with Title 10, United States Code, which was amended in 1983 to emphasize that homosexual activity is prohibited among military members, on or off duty.[42] The close living quarters on Navy ships are thought to pose special problems for morale if open homosexuals are integrated into the crew. Because of the sensitivity of this issue and the strong feelings it engenders, it is difficult to have a dispassionate discussion on the merits of this assumption or the degree to which civil rights and military effectiveness should be balanced. As a result, the Navy, together with the other services, may find itself unprepared for such an integration if it is forced upon it, most likely by the courts.

The Role of Women

One of the most embarrassing chapters in recent memory for the Navy was the mistreatment of women at the 1991 Las Vegas convention of the Tailhook Association, an organization of naval aviators.[43] ''Tailhook'' has become a code word for unacceptable behavior toward women, and the failure of the Navy to find and punish individuals responsible for sexual harassment and assault at that convention badly tarnished the image of the service. As a partial response, the Navy has gone out of its way to open career fields to women, including pressure to end the combat ban on women's service. Women are now being assigned to combat vessels, including aircraft carriers, destroyers, and amphibious ships. By the end of 1993 there were over 8,000 women assigned to ships.[44]

CONCLUSIONS: INTO THE FUTURE

Barring unforeseen circumstances, one may expect the trends now visible in the Navy to continue through the turn of the century. Like the other armed services, the Navy faces the problem of translating military power into political results. The situations in Somalia, Bosnia, and Haiti in 1994 showed the difficulty of accomplishing this. The Navy will continue to plan for Third World contingencies, which will severely strain the resources of a shrinking force. A revival of a hostile global power would change the priorities of the Navy, particularly if that power had a strong navy capable of interdicting U.S. merchant ships on the high seas. But naval forces require long lead times to design and procure, so too great a reduction in force levels would be very risky. For now, the path of . . . *From the Sea* seems likely to continue.

The Navy will continue to tailor its organization to fit in with joint operations and structures. A smaller Navy will require a more streamlined organizational structure to provide a reasonable "tooth-to-tail" ratio. More reliance will probably be placed on the Naval Reserve as personnel levels of the active force decline.

Forward operations will continue to the extent that the ships and personnel are available to do them. The Navy is a strong supporter of a forward presence, and it is inconceivable that it would willingly move to a "surge" strategy.

Trends toward a smaller but more capable force will continue, but there is a limit below which one cannot prudently reduce. The world is not shrinking geographically, and even the most capable ship cannot be in two places at once. With a small force level, the response time also increases as naval forces try to contain crises or act in other ways to support U.S. national interests.

The group of people to be led is growing more diverse in terms of race, religion, gender, language, and possibly sexual orientation. The challenge for Navy leadership will be to ensure that each member of the naval service is able to make a contribution to the best of his or her ability.[45] This will be the severest test for Total Quality Leadership, and the result will determine the effectiveness of the U.S. Navy for the next generation.

NOTES

1. For an overview of theoretical Navy forces and missions and an earlier U.S. Navy perspective on them, see John Allen Williams, "U.S. Navy Missions and Force Structure: A Critical Reappraisal," *Armed Forces and Society* 7, no. 4 (Summer 1991): 499–528.

2. The course of a war in the event of nuclear escalation was too difficult to predict effectively. Consequently, it was not dealt with deeply in most war games, apart from some "what if" excursions.

3. Admiral James D. Watkins, USN, "The Maritime Strategy," *U.S. Naval Institute Proceedings,* January 1986, pp. 2–17.

4. For an extended discussion of the Maritime Strategy, see John Allen Williams, "The Maritime Strategy in a New Security Era," in *The U.S. Army in a New Security Era,* ed. Sam C. Sarkesian and John Allen Williams (Boulder, CO: Lynne Rienner Publishers, 1990), pp. 217–235.

5. John J. Mearsheimer, "A Strategic Misstep: The Maritime Strategy and Deterrence in Europe," *International Security* 11, no. 2 (Fall 1986): 3–57, and Linton F. Brooks, "Naval Power and National Security: The Case for the Maritime Strategy," *International Security* 11, no. 2 (Fall 1986): 58–88.

6. Barry R. Posen, ''Inadvertent Nuclear War? Escalation and NATO's Northern Flank,'' *International Security* 7, no. 2 (Fall 1982): 28–54.

7. The development of the Maritime Strategy occurred primarily in the Strategic Concepts Branch, OP-603 (now N513 after the recent reorganization to bring the ''OP codes'' into line with the other services' structures). Several versions of a briefing were developed, at varying levels of classification, and presented to Navy and non-Navy audiences for their information and feedback.

8. This point was underlined to the British during the 1982 Falklands War when they lost a naval destroyer to an Argentine Exocet missile acquired from France.

9. John H. Dalton, J. M. Boorda, and Carl E. Mundy, Jr., *Forward . . . From the Sea: Preparing the Naval Service for the 21st Century* (Washington, DC: Department of the Navy, 1994), pp. 5–12.

10. See *Conduct of the Persian Gulf War: Final Report to Congress* (Washington, DC: Department of Defense, April 1992), pp. 286–287.

11. Richard Cheney, Secretary of Defense, *Report of the Secretary of Defense to the President and the Congress* (Washington, DC: U.S. Government Printing Office, January 1994), p. A-5. We will not be concerned with Marine Corps organization in this chapter.

12. Department of the Navy, *Force 2001: A Program Guide to the U.S. Navy* (Washington, DC: Department of the Navy, July 1993), pp. 22–23, 27–28. The forward-presence JMA was added with the publication of the 1994 edition of this document. See also Vice Admiral William A. Owens, USN, ''Building the New Navy,'' in *Forward Presence and the National Military Strategy,* ed. Robert L. Pfaltzgraff, Jr., and Richard H. Shultz, Jr. (Annapolis, MD: U.S. Naval Institute Press, 1993), pp. 221–226.

13. Department of the Navy, *Force 2001: A Program Guide to the U.S. Navy* (1994 edition) (Washington, DC: Department of the Navy, 1994), pp. 121–123.

14. ''Major Naval Reserve Mission Areas,'' *All Hands,* no. 921 (January 1994): 32.

15. Richard Cheney, Secretary of Defense, *Annual Report* (January 1994), p. A-4.

16. Department of the Navy, *Force 2001* (1994 edition), pp. 122–123.

17. The title Chief of Naval Operations is a misnomer. He or, eventually, she does not command the operating forces of the U.S. Navy.

18. Adam B. Siegel, *The Use of Naval Forces in the Post-War Era: U.S. Navy and U.S. Marine Corps Crisis Response Activity, 1946–1990* (Alexandria, VA: Center for Naval Analyses, May 1991), p. 1.

19. Department of the Navy, *Force 2001* (1994 edition), p. i.

20. Technically, the Defense Department was called the National Military Establishment until 1949.

21. Ronald F. O'Rourke, ''Aircraft Carrier Homeporting,'' *CRS Report for Congress* (Washington, DC: Congressional Research Service, 2 October 1992), p. 3.

22. The degree to which this carrier, the *John F. Kennedy,* is actually a ''reserve'' carrier is problematic. It will be fully capable of deployment and will be crewed almost exclusively by active-duty personnel. Many observers believe that it was declared a ''reserve'' carrier to get it past congressional scrutiny.

23. Ronald F. O'Rourke, ''Naval Forward Deployments and the Size of the Navy,'' *CRS Report for Congress* (Washington, DC: Congressional Research Service, 13 November 1992), p. 14.

24. O'Rourke, ''Aircraft Carrier Homeporting,'' pp. 3–4.

25. Richard Cheney, Secretary of Defense, *Annual Report* (January 1994), pp. 27, 270.

26. "U.S. Navy Submarines," *All Hands,* no. 921 (January 1994): 46; *National Defense Authorization Act for Fiscal Year 1994: Report of the Committee on Armed Services, House of Representatives, on H.R. 2401* (Washington, DC: U.S. Government Printing Office, 30 July 1993), p. 50 (henceforth cited as *HASC Report on H.R. 2401*).

27. *All Hands,* no. 921 (January 1994): 47.

28. *All Hands,* no. 921 (January 1994): 34–35. See Richard Cheney, Secretary of Defense, *Annual Report* (January 1994), p. 182, for a discussion of the evolution of carrier air wings in the 1990s. One possibility is to reduce the number of combat aircraft carried and augment the numbers in a crisis by planes based in CONUS. Another possibility is the development of a short takeoff and vertical landing (STOVL) aircraft.

29. *Department of Defense Appropriations Bill, 1994: Report of the Committee on Appropriations, House of Representatives* (Washington, DC: U.S. Government Printing Office, 22 September 1993), p. 231.

30. *HASC Report on H.R. 2401,* pp. 132–133.

31. Les Aspin, *Report on the Bottom-Up Review* (Washington, DC: Department of Defense, October 1993), pp. 26–27, 47–55.

32. Richard Cheney, Secretary of Defense, *Annual Report* (January 1994), pp. 174–175.

33. Congressional Budget Office, *Reducing the Deficit: Spending and Revenue Options* (Washington, DC: U.S. Government Printing Office, March 1994), p. 39.

34. Department of the Navy, *Force 2001* (1994 edition), pp. 65–68.

35. The U.S. Navy has no interest in procuring diesel-powered submarines, despite the fact that they are superior to nuclear-powered submarines for some missions. Diesel submarines running on their batteries are quieter than nuclear submarines. This factor, the proximity to land, and difficult sound-propagation characteristics make shallow-water ASW a problem that the Navy is addressing urgently.

36. Assistant Chief of Naval Operations for Undersea Warfare, *Submarine Roles in the 1990's and Beyond* (Washington, DC: Department of the Navy, 18 January 1992). With this document the "silent service" went public in a big way.

37. Edward L. Walsh, "Ryan Reaffirms Primacy of ASW for SSNs," *Sea Power* 37, no. 7 (July 1994): 17–18.

38. This section is based on Ronald F. O'Rourke, "Navy Seawolf and Centurion Attack Submarine Programs: Issues for Congress," *CRS Issue Brief* (Washington, DC: Congressional Research Service, 4 January 1994), pp. 2–6.

39. Walsh, "Ryan Reaffirms Primacy of ASW for SSNs," p. 18.

40. Richard Cheney, Secretary of Defense, *Annual Report* (January 1994), p. 217.

41. Department of the Navy, *Force 2001* (1994 edition), pp. 37–39.

42. *National Defense Authorization Act for Fiscal Year 1994: Conference Report to Accompany H.R. 2401* (Washington, DC: U.S. Government Printing Office, 10 November 1993), pp. 128–131.

43. The association is named for the hook on the tail of carrier-based aircraft that is used to catch one of the four wires of the arresting gear on an aircraft carrier and thereby stop the airplane when it lands on the deck.

44. *Status and Plans for Women in the Navy: Surface Warfare* (Washington, DC: Navy Bureau of Personnel, 1 December 1993).

45. For a discussion of this issue and how it relates to leadership, see John Allen Williams, "Interpersonal Influence and the Bases of Military Leadership," *Military Review* 62, no. 12 (December 1982): 56–65.

SELECTED BIBLIOGRAPHY

Brooks, Linton F. *Peacetime Influence through Forward Naval Presence.* Alexandria, VA: Center for Naval Analyses, 1994.

Dalton, John H., J. M. Boorda, and Carl E. Mundy, Jr. *Forward . . . From the Sea.* Washington, DC: Department of the Navy, 1994.

Department of the Navy. *Force 2001: A Program Guide to the U.S. Navy* (1994 edition). Washington, DC: Department of the Navy, 1994.

Department of the Navy. *Naval Doctrine Publication 1: Naval Warfare.* Washington, DC: Department of the Navy, 1994.

George, James L. *The U.S. Navy in the 1990s: Alternatives for Action.* Annapolis, MD: U.S. Naval Institute Press, 1992.

Gray, Colin, and Roger Barnett. *Seapower and Strategy.* Annapolis, MD: U.S. Naval Institute Press, 1989.

Joint Chiefs of Staff. *Joint Warfare of the U.S. Armed Forces.* Washington, DC: National Defense University Press, 1991.

Kaufmann, William W. *A Thoroughly Efficient Navy.* Washington, DC: Brookings Institution, 1987.

Chapter 4
THE AIR FORCE

James A. Mowbray

The U.S. Air Force has a relatively short history. As a result of the personal interest of President Theodore Roosevelt, Brigadier General James Allen, the Army's chief signal officer, established the Aeronautical Division of the Signal Corps, effective 1 August 1907. The aviation arm of the Army retained this title until it was redesignated the Army Air Service by executive order on 21 May 1918. This was made law by the Army Reorganization Act of July 1920.

In 1926 the Air Corps Act was signed into law, creating the Army Air Corps, with effect 2 July 1926. Although the Air Corps continued to be the aviation branch of the U.S. Army, the operational forces of the Air Corps were reorganized immediately prior to World War II. The Army Air Forces, one of the three components of the U.S. Army, along with the Army Ground Forces and the Army Service Forces, was created by executive order on 20 June 1941.[1] The AAF, as it came to be known, coexisted with the Air Corps, which remained the branch to which personnel were assigned.

Following the close of World War II, Congress passed the National Security Act of 1947, creating three military service departments under a new Department of Defense. On 18 September 1947 the U.S. Air Force "stood up," in the vernacular of the service, as a separate and independent branch of the armed forces of the United States.[2]

The National Security Act, as amended, provides that the Air Force will be organized, trained, and equipped for prompt and sustained air offensive and defensive operations. These air operations include everything above the surface of the globe in air and space, and the term *aerospace* encompasses the two together as a single operational medium. That medium, the aerospace environment, knows no absolute boundary between the atmosphere and space. Nations recognize political boundaries in the atmosphere, but by convention there are no boundaries in space.[3]

AIR FORCE BASIC AND OPERATIONAL DOCTRINE

The doctrinal history of the U.S. Air Force has been short but troubled.[4] The Air Force first tried to write doctrine in the aftermath of World War I while still an organic part of the U.S. Army. It confronted numerous problems then, just as it has ever since that time. One problem, reflected in the way that the Air Force still develops its doctrine, as opposed to the manner in which the other services develop their doctrine, is the levels of concern that confront theater air commanders, which in turn are reflected in the terminology that the service uses.

Because of the service's early history of doctrine development and thinking, and because of the nature of air power, the Air Force Component Commander must think, make decisions, and execute simultaneously at all three levels of war: strategic, operational, and tactical. It is rare for component commanders below the level of a theater commander-in-chief (CINC) to be faced with this prospect. For the Air Commander it is central to his way of war. Air forces are able to attack target arrays, target systems, target sets, and individual targets concurrently, if required. Surface forces, by their very nature, must attack things in sequence because they cannot reach targets in the depth available to airmen. This, in turn, requires the airman to think and act in terms of what will most contribute to winning the war, then the campaign, and finally the battle at hand. Most ground commanders and commanders of naval forces at sea have a campaign or battle objective, knowing that these have theoretically already been fitted into a war-winning strategy. Because CINCs are almost always nonairmen, the airman as advisor to the CINC must be able to function at all three levels concurrently.

As a result, air doctrine has often been written first and foremost at the "basic doctrine" level. This is a level that other services can virtually disregard in their doctrine. The Air Force, on the other hand, has had difficulty in writing doctrine at the operational level of war in contrast to the Army and Marines, and to a lesser extent the Navy. This disconnection has created most of the problems of jointness on the battlefield for the Army and Air Force. What each service does is uniquely suited to its own responsibilities, but each service has difficulty in relating to what the other services do well in terms of doctrine development—they live in different worlds focusing on different operational doctrine.

The term *basic doctrine* appeared in 1940, when it was applied by the Army Air Forces to *FM 1-5: Employment of the Aviation of the Army,* according to the leading Air Force doctrine historian, Frank Futrell.[5] Basic doctrine establishes fundamental principles that describe and guide the proper use of aerospace forces in war. This is the foundation of all aerospace doctrine. It provides broad, enduring guidance that should be used when deciding how Air Force forces should be organized, trained, equipped, employed, and sustained. Basic doctrine is the cornerstone and provides the framework from which the Air Force develops operational and tactical doctrine.[6]

Operational doctrine as a term appears later than basic doctrine. In the 1930s, when airmen were trying to write air doctrine, they had no definition of the term *operational* in the modern sense of that expression. One of the earliest uses of the term *operational* was postwar and meant that "the activity is in operation," that is, ongoing.[7] Operational doctrine was first conceived at Air University about 1947 as one of three categories of air doctrine.[8] In the modern sense, operational doctrine establishes principles that guide the use of aerospace forces in campaigns and major operations. It examines relationships among objectives, forces, environments, and actions to ensure that aerospace operations contribute to achieving assigned objectives.[9]

CURRENT AIR FORCE BASIC DOCTRINE

In March 1992 the Air Force Chief of Staff, General Merrill A. McPeak, signed out a brand-new Air Force basic doctrine manual, *Air Force Manual 1-1: Basic Aerospace Doctrine of the United States Air Force.*[10] This manual is unique in the annals of Air Force basic doctrine in several respects.

First is the fact that it is in two volumes, the design of which is a first volume of just twenty-seven pages containing the doctrine itself: what the Air Force believes about the best way to employ aerospace power in war. The second volume contains a set of essays, which are referenced in the first volume at the point where each is appropriate. These essays are discussions about why the Air Force believes in the doctrinal statements to which it subscribes.

The second way in which the manual is unique is in the thorough manner in which space is integrated with air. The Air Force has subscribed to this view since the publication of the first *AFM 1-1* in 1965 during General Curtis E. LeMay's tenure as Chief of Staff of the Air Force. However, it has consistently had a problem with getting the concept down on paper in a completely coherent fashion understandable to its officer corps. This effort, even if some have been critical of it, is nonetheless the best to date, and it comes at an opportune time, since the Air Force is charged with leadership of the unified U.S. Space Command.

The third unique feature lies in the fact that general officers experienced in air warfare actually put their hands to the task and wrote, or rewrote, substantial portions of the draft manual. They deserve great credit for this step, for while it may open them to criticism, it ensures that the manual is more properly aligned on war fighting. This has not been the case with any previous edition since *FM 100-20: Command and Employment of Air Power,* which was published in the wake of the North African campaign.[11] That manual was written in part by General Laurence Kuter, of Air Corps Tactical School and World War II fame.

He had been the deputy commander of the Northwest African Tactical Air Force in the defeat of Panzer Armee-Afrika in 1943.

The current doctrine establishes the Principles of War, the same nine used by the Army since the 1920s, as part of Air Force doctrine. This has been the case with most previous doctrine manuals. It discusses the nature of war and the nature of aerospace power and spells out the four basic roles of aerospace forces: aerospace control, force application, force enhancement, and force support.

The first of these, aerospace control, is the establishment of control of the combat environment, that is, the traditional role of air superiority, now to include space superiority. The second is force application, the application of combat power, such as strategic attack, interdiction, or close air support of ground or maritime forces. The third is force enhancement, actions that multiply combat power, to include air and space lift, air refueling, electronic combat, special operations, and reconnaissance or surveillance. The fourth is force support, actions to sustain forces in war or peace. These include logistics, combat support, on-orbit support, base defense, and ensuring base operability.

A fourth unique feature is the establishment, for the first time, of guidelines identified as Tenets of Aerospace Power. These tenets are seven in number and are considerations second only to the Principles of War themselves as guidelines for commanders for the conduct of combat operations.

Centralized Command/Decentralized Execution: Airmen believe, based on vast experience, that aerospace assets must not be squandered, nor their potential wasted, by parceling them out across the battlefront to many commanders. Execution of assigned missions, however, gains efficiency when led at the lowest level of effective command.

Flexibility/Versatility: Aerospace power is both flexible and versatile, and these features should not be compromised by limiting the capability of air forces to concentrate their fighting power at the decisive points.

Priority: Airmen believe that the priority order for missions are their essentiality to the war, then the campaign, and finally the battle at hand.

Synergy: Airmen believe that aerospace power working each of its parts (the roles) coherently can achieve a much greater impact than if they are worked separately; the same thing is true if aerospace and ground or aerospace and maritime forces work together in coordinated plans and actions.

Balance: It is believed that combat opportunity, necessity, effectiveness, and efficiency must be balanced against the inherent risk to high-value aerospace assets. This is central to success.

Concentration is nearly a repetition of the principle of mass, but in this case speaks to "focus of effort" to all intents and purposes.

Persistence: If there is one thing that a student of strategy learns early and often, it is the essentiality of persistence in war, balanced by knowing when to change in order not to plunge into disaster.

The balance of the manual discusses employing aerospace forces, the concept of operational art, orchestrating roles and missions, "airmindedness," and preparing the Air Force for war. This, then, is current Air Force Basic Aerospace Doctrine today.

It is important to note that the Air Force is now earnestly interested in producing "operational doctrine" across the scope of Air Force interests and activities. Currently, there is very little up-to-date operational doctrine in the Air Force, albeit the tactical-level manuals, the 3-series doctrine manuals, are sometimes heavy in operational matters, and they are very up-to-date and quite good. The new Air Force doctrine-writing shop at Langley Air Force Base, Virginia, has an immense task in front of it for the foreseeable future since it is charged with the development of this new body of operational-level doctrine.

It is important to recognize that basic and operational doctrine properly determines for the service what technology and equipment it should select.[12] As "Hap" Arnold said at the end of World War II, "[A]ny Air Force which does not keep its doctrines ahead of its equipment, and its vision far into the future, can only delude the nation into a false sense of security."[13]

COMMAND STRUCTURE AND ORGANIZATION

The Air Force is structured around four fundamental elements: (1) Headquarters, Department of the Air Force, which includes Headquarters, United States Air Force, (2) the Major Commands, (3) the Field Operating Agencies, and (4) the Direct Reporting Units. Figure 4.1 is a simplified version of the Air Force Headquarters command and staff system.

The following two sections cover the first two components in detail. While the Field Operating Agencies and the Direct Reporting Units are important components of the Air Force Command Structure and Organization, they refer primarily to logistical and administrative components and the reserve and National Guard system. In brief, a Field Operating Agency (FAO) is an element of the U.S. Air Force responsible for specialized activities under a senior Air Force headquarters. These agencies have special functions and responsibilities which are similar to those of major commands, but require fewer personnel, facilities, and assets. Such agencies include activities ranging from the Air Force Audit Agency, Air Force Center for Environmental Excellence to Air Force Real Estate Agency, the Air Force Reserve, Air National Guard, and Center for Air Force History.

Direct Reporting Units (DRUs) are large, highly specialized commands which report to the Office of the Chief of Staff of the Air Force. These include the Air Force District of Washington, Air Force Operational Test and Evaluation Center, and the United States Air Force Academy.

Command Structure

The Department of the Air Force is administered by the civilian Secretary of the Air Force, who conducts the fiscal, production, procurement, and legal plans

Figure 4.1
U.S. Headquarters Command and Staff System

```
                    Secretary of the Air Force
                    - - - - - - - - - - - - - -
                 Under Secretary of the Air Force


Deputy Under Secretary of the Air Force
     (International Affairs)


Assistant Secretaries of Air Force:

     Financial Management & Comptroller

     Space

     Acquisition

     Manpower, Reserve Affairs, Installations, and Environment


                         Air Force Chief of Staff
                           Vice Chief of Staff

                                               Special Assistant for
                                                 Theater Air Defense

Deputy Chiefs of Staff for                Assistant Chief of Staff,
                                                Intelligence
     Personnel

     Plans and Operations

     Logistics

     Command, Control, Communciations
     and Computers


Chief of Air Force Reserve


National Guard Bureau
```

and programs of the service. The Secretary is not involved with operations. The Office of the Secretary includes the Under Secretary of the Air Force, a Deputy Under Secretary for International Affairs, a Small and Disadvantaged Business Utilization Office, and four Assistant Secretaries of the Air Force: (1) Financial Management and Comptroller; (2) Space; (3) Acquisition; and (4) Manpower, Reserve Affairs, Installations, and Environment. The staff of the Office of the Secretary is rounded out by the General Counsel, an Administrative Assistant, the Director of Legislative Liaison, the Director of Public Affairs, the Auditor

General, and the Inspector General. These are advisors to the Secretary for the functions assigned to them. Three of the assistant secretariats and three of the staff functions (public affairs, auditor, and inspector) have field operating agencies under their direct control. These are dealt with under that section of this chapter. The Assistant Secretaries are empowered to act in their areas of responsibility for the Secretary.

The professional head of the service is the Chief of Staff, United States Air Force (CSAF). The Chief of Staff of the Air Force is the military head of the Air Force and is directly responsible to the Secretary for the efficiency and operational readiness of the service. The CSAF is a member of the Joint Chiefs of Staff (JCS). The Vice Chief of Staff (VCS) conducts most of the day-to-day business under the direction of the Chief of Staff. The VCS is assisted by the Air Staff.

The Air Staff is a headquarters functional organization under the Chief that serves the Chief and the Office of the Secretary in carrying out management functions that cannot be delegated or decentralized elsewhere. The Air Staff operates under the Office of the Chief of Staff, which consists of the Chief of Staff (CSAF), the Vice Chief of Staff (VCS), the Assistant Vice Chief of Staff, the Chief of Staff of the Air Force's Operations Group (headed by a full colonel), and the Chief Master Sergeant of the Air Force. In addition, a Special Assistant for Theater Air Defense (a major general) reports directly to the Office of the CSAF.

The Air Staff itself consists of a large number of specialized functional offices, including four Deputy Chiefs of Staff, one each for (1) Personnel, (2) Plans and Operations, (3) Logistics, and (4) Command, Control, Communications, and Computers, each of whom is a lieutenant general. There is one Assistant Chief of Staff, Intelligence, who is a major general in rank. The balance of the Air Staff is composed of military or civilian officials who function essentially as directors of specialized staff areas.

These specialized staff areas are Civil Engineer (major general), Chief of Safety (brigadier general), Chief of Security Police (brigadier general), Air Force Historian (Ph.D. in history), Chief Scientist (Ph.D. in a scientific discipline), Chief of Air Force Reserve (a reserve major general), and the National Guard Bureau (headed by a Chairman and with a Director at the rank of major general). In addition, the USAF Scientific Advisory Board (headed by a civilian Ph.D.), the Judge Advocate General (the chief lawyer of the Air Force), a Director of Tests and Evaluation (a civilian), a Director of Programs and Evaluation (a major general), the Surgeon General of the Air Force (a lieutenant general), a Chief of Chaplains (a major general), and a Director of Services (a brigadier general) are part of the Air Staff. The Director of Services has under him, in addition to a civilian deputy, a Chief of Resources Management, a Chief of Programs, a Chief of Strategic Plans and Evaluation, and a Chief of Plans and Force Management (civilians, lieutenant colonels, or full colonels).

Major Commands

Air Combat Command (ACC)

The Air Combat Command was established 1 June 1992 with headquarters at Langley Air Force Base (AFB), Virginia. This was a result of the merger of Tactical Air Command and Strategic Air Command. The command has a number of missions. It operates U.S.-based USAF combat-coded attack aircraft, bombers, and fighters and provides nuclear-capable forces for the U.S. Strategic Command as directed. It also organizes, trains, equips, and maintains combat-ready air forces in the United States. The ACC also tests new combat equipment. In addition, it is involved in the monitoring and interception of illegal narcotics traffic.

Other responsibilities include supplying aircraft to the five geographical unified commands: USA (formerly Atlantic), European, Pacific, Southern, and Central Commands. It provides air defense forces to the North American Aerospace Defense Command (NORAD). The command also operates certain air mobility forces in support of the U.S. Transportation Command.

The force structure includes the following major units:

First Air Force with headquarters at Tyndall AFB, Florida

Eighth Air Force with headquarters at Barksdale AFB, Louisiana

Ninth Air Force with headquarters at Shaw AFB, South Carolina

Twelfth Air Force with headquarters at Davis-Monthan AFB, Arizona

Air Reserve Component (ARC) units gained by Air Combat Command on mobilization

The ARC units gained by ACC include United States Air Force Reserve Wings, headquartered at the Tenth Air Force at Bergstrom AFB, Texas, and Air National Guard Wings/Groups. A number of Air National Guard Fighter and Reconnaissance Wings/Groups pass to ACC on mobilization.[14] Air National Guard Fighter Interceptor Wings and Groups are the nation's frontline air defense forces against attack by air-breathing threats, including aircraft, cruise missiles, and airborne narcotraffic. The fighter squadrons in this category fall under the command of one of the First Air Force air defense sectors for operational purposes. Air National Guard Airlift Wings/Groups are essentially "tactical" airlift assets, although they are no longer so designated.

Air Combat Command now controls through its numbered air forces and two direct reporting units 4 Bomb Wings, 7.8 Fighter Wing equivalents in the active duty Air Force, 6.8 Fighter Wing equivalents in the Air National Guard, and 1.9 Fighter Wing equivalents in the Air Force Reserve. As budget cuts continue, these numbers will sink to a total of about 13 Fighter Wing equivalents over the next couple of years.

Air Education and Training Command (AETC)

The AETC was established (by merging the Air Training Command and Air University) on 1 July 1993 at Randolph Air Force Base, Texas. It has the following missions: It recruits, accesses, commissions, and trains USAF enlisted and officer personnel. This includes providing basic military training, initial and advanced training, officer training, and flying training for USAF personnel. The command also provides, through Air University, professional military education (PME) at the graduate, undergraduate, technical, and continuing-education levels. As corollary missions, AETC conducts joint training (for all of the services) in intelligence, law enforcement, air navigation, fire fighting, and other areas. It provides medical service, readiness, and security assistance training.

Other responsibilities include the recall of Individual Ready Reservists and mobility and contingency tasking support to combatant commands. The force structure includes the following major units:

Second Air Force with headquarters at Keesler AFB, Mississippi, has the responsibility for supervising all technical training in the Air Force.

Nineteenth Air Force with headquarters at Randolph AFB, Texas, has responsibility for all flying training in the Air Force.

Other Flying Training Units include a variety of Active and Air National Guard units.

The Air University, with headquarters at Maxwell AFB, Alabama, has primary responsibility for all Air Force professional military education (PME) and technical education.[15] It includes the following units:

The Air War College (AWC) conducts PME for lieutenant colonels and colonels in strategy, national security studies, war fighting, and leadership/management (10-month course).

The Air Command and Staff College (ACSC) conducts PME for senior captains and majors in command and staff responsibilities, air operations, and campaign planning (10-month course).

The School of Advanced Air Power Studies (SAAS), a part of ACSC, conducts a second-year program of historical studies for selected graduates of the one-year course of study at ACSC.

The Squadron Officer School (SOS) conducts PME for company-grade officers in administrative and personnel matters and other areas of special interest to maturing staff personnel.

The Air Force Institute of Technology (AFIT) at Wright-Patterson AFB, Ohio, offers scientific graduate degrees to specially selected officers and enlisted personnel.

Ira C. Eaker College for Professional Development (CPD), located at Maxwell AFB, offers selected personnel highly specialized courses, including courses for incoming judge advocate (legal) personnel, management courses, and instruction for officers selected as base and wing commanders, along with similar educational programs.

The College of Aerospace Doctrine, Research, and Education (CADRE), located at Maxwell AFB, serves to educate selected officer personnel in research and professional-level writing skills in subject areas of vital interest to the service.

The College for Enlisted Professional Military Education was formerly the Senior NCO Academy and is located at Gunter Annex to Maxwell AFB. It is responsible for educating senior noncommissioned officers in the duties, skills, and requirements of the positions associated with senior and chief master sergeants.

The Community College of the Air Force (CCAF), located at Maxwell AFB, coordinates the educational activities for Air Force personnel enrolled in two-year college degree programs immediately related to their assignments in the Air Force.

The Air Force Quality Institute (AFQI) is at Maxwell AFB and directs and educates the Air Force community in the implementation of the Quality Air Force (QAF) management programs worldwide.

The Air Force Reserve Officer Training Corps (ROTC) is headquartered at Maxwell AFB and directs the junior and college-level reserve officer training corps programs nationwide.

The Officer Training School (OTS) at Maxwell AFB educates college graduates seeking commissions in the Air Force to be officers.

The Extension Course Institute at Gunter Annex to Maxwell AFB provides continuing education to officers, noncommissioned officers, enlisted personnel, and civilians worldwide through distance educational programs (correspondence).

Headquarters Civil Air Patrol—United States Air Force at Maxwell AFB coordinates the programs and activities of the United States Air Force Auxiliary worldwide. Civil Air Patrol is a civilian auxiliary of the USAF, founded in 1941 to provide aviation support to the national defense effort from the private aviation community not eligible for military service. It also includes a preinduction training program for teenagers, now the Cadet Program, engaged in aerospace education in the United States and on military bases overseas. The aviation assets are committed to disaster relief, air search for lost aircraft, and counter-narcotics efforts with Customs and the Drug Enforcement Administration (DEA).

The Air University Library, located at Maxwell AFB, is probably the finest aviation library in the world, and one of the better general military libraries also. It is open to the public.

Other components of AETC include the following: Headquarters Air Force Recruiting Service at Randolph AFB, Texas; Air Force Security Assistance Training Squadron at Randolph AFB, Texas; and the 59th Medical Wing (Wilford Hall Medical Center) at Lackland AFB, Texas.

Air Force Materiel Command (AFMC)

The AFMC was established on 1 July 1992 by merging Air Logistics Command and Air Force Systems Command. Its headquarters is located at Wright-Patterson AFB, Ohio. The missions include the following: management of the integrated research, development, testing, acquisition, and sustainment of USAF weapons systems and the production and acquisition of advanced systems; operation of major product centers, logistics centers, testing centers, and specialized laboratories (called "superlabs" in the vernacular); and operation of the USAF School of Aerospace Medicine and the USAF Test Pilot School. The force structure includes four major product centers; four "super" laboratories; three test centers; five air logistics centers; and four specialized centers (organized under four separate categories of activity in order to rationalize a large organization with diverse responsibilities).

Air Force Space Command (AFSPC)

The AFSPC was established on 1 September 1982 with headquarters at Peterson AFB, Colorado. The Commander AFSPC is also CINC NORAD and CINC U.S. Space Command. The missions are to operate the USAF ICBM forces for U.S. Strategic Command and the ground-based missile warning radars, sensors, and satellites for NORAD. It also operates the national space launch facilities and operational boosters and the worldwide space surveillance radars and optical systems. Further, the command provides command and control for DOD satellites, and ballistic missile warning to NORAD and U.S. Space Command. In addition, there is a corollary mission to develop and integrate space support for U.S. military personnel involved in combat and manage the USAF helicopter resources. Other responsibilities include providing communications, computer, and base support to NORAD and supplying range and launch facilities for military, civilian, and commercial space launches.

The main force structure is as follows:

Fourteenth Air Force with headquarters at Vandenberg AFB, California, has responsibility for all Air Force space operations.

Twentieth Air Force with headquarters at Francis E. Warren AFB, Wyoming, has responsibility for all Air Force Intercontinental Ballistic Missile (ICBM) Operations under U.S. Strategic Command direction.

Air Force Special Operations Command (AFSOC)

Located at Hurlburt Field, Florida, the AFSOC was established on 22 May 1990. Its mission includes the following: It serves as the air component of U.S. Special Operations Command, a unified command, deploying specialized air power for a worldwide presence with a unique set of capabilities in peace or war. Primary missions are unconventional warfare, direct action, special reconnaissance, counterterrorism, and foreign internal defense in support of the unified commands. Corollary missions of the command include providing humanitarian assistance and personnel recovery (''combat rescue''), psychological operations (''psyops''), and counternarcotics operations as directed.

The force structure includes a number of Special Operations Groups, Wings, and Squadrons located in the United States and overseas installations. In addition, the command operates the USAF Special Operations School at Hurlburt Field, Florida. A number of Air Reserve Component (ARC) units are gained by AFSOC.

Air Mobility Command (AMC)

The AMC was established on 1 June 1992 with headquarters at Scott AFB, Illinois, by reorganization of Military Airlift Command and elements of Strategic Air Command. Its missions include the following: to provide rapid, global airlift and aerial refueling for U.S. armed forces, to serve as the USAF component of the U.S. Transportation Command, and to support wartime taskings by providing forces to theater commands. Corollary missions include providing operational support aircraft, stateside aeromedical evacuation missions, and visual documentation support.

The force structure is as follows:

Fifteenth Air Force with headquarters at Travis AFB, California.

Twenty-First Air Force with headquarters at McGuire AFB, New Jersey.

Air Reserve Component (ARC) units subordinate to Air Mobility Command are United States Air Force Reserve Wings that pass to AMC on mobilization. Fourth Air Force with headquarters at McClellan AFB, California, is the headquarters for these units. It passes to Air Mobility Command on mobilization.

Twenty-Second Air Force with headquarters at Dobbins AFB, Georgia, is the headquarters for a number of units that pass to Air Mobility Command on mobilization. This includes Air National Guard Wings/Groups.

Air Mobility Command now controls through its numbered air forces 2 air mobility wings, 5 airlift wings, and 6 air refueling wings in the active-duty Air Force. There are 13 airlift wings, of which 5 are associate wings (no aircraft, crews only), and 2 air refueling wings in the Air Force Reserve. In addition, there is 1 associate airlift group in the Reserve. The Air National Guard contains 3 airlift groups and 7 air refueling wings.

Pacific Air Forces (PACAF)

The Pacific Air Forces was established on 1 July 1957 with headquarters at Hickam AFB, Hawaii. The missions include the planning, conduct, and coordination of offensive and defensive air operations in the Pacific and Asian theaters. PACAF is responsible for maintaining resources to conduct air operations.

The force structure includes the following major units:

Fifth Air Force with headquarters at Yokota Air Base (AB), Japan

Seventh Air Force with headquarters at Osan AB, Korea

Eleventh Air Force with headquarters at Elmendorf AFB, Alaska

Thirteenth Air Force with headquarters at Andersen AFB, Guam

Air National Guard Squadrons available to Pacific Air Forces

United States Air Forces Europe (USAFE)

USAFE was established on 15 August 1947 with headquarters at Ramstein AB, Germany. The major missions of USAFE include the following: to plan, conduct, control, coordinate, and support air and space operations to achieve U.S. national and NATO objectives based on taskings assigned by the Commander-in-Chief, U.S. European Command. Corollary missions are to support U.S. military plans and operations in parts of Europe, the Mediterranean, the Middle East, and Africa.

The major units in the force structure are as follows:

Third Air Force with headquarters at RAF Mildenhall, United Kingdom

Sixteenth Air Force with headquarters at Aviano AB, Italy

Seventeenth Air Force with headquarters at Sembach AB, Germany

AIR FORCE WEAPONRY

The purpose of this section is to familiarize the reader with the functions of aircraft surveillance devices and various munitions in the Air Force inventory. For details of aircraft, refer to any standard aircraft reference work.

Attack Aircraft

The A-10A and OA-10A Wart Hog attack aircraft come in two virtually identical versions, the OA-10A being a standard A-10A converted for forward air control work, that is, the direction of strike aircraft against ground targets, in which role it may carry marking rockets rather than the standard A-10A ordnance load. The Wart Hog is employed for close air support missions against targets nominated by ground forces. The aircraft carries a 30-millimeter GAU-8 Gatling gun with armor-penetration capabilities and up to 16,000 pounds of munitions. These munitions are usually antiarmor and ground-attack munitions, but AIM-9 air intercept infrared missiles may also be carried.

The AC-130A/H/U Spectre gunship is a Hercules C-130 airframe modified by mounting a variety of guns and electro-optical sensor systems that are computer controlled and are used for attack of ground targets, day, night, or in foul weather. The guns, depending upon the model of aircraft, range from a 105-

millimeter howitzer through 40-millimeter and 20-millimeter automatic cannons down to 7.62-millimeter Gatling machine guns. All models carry multiple guns.

Bomber Aircraft

The B-52H Stratofortress long-range heavy bomber is the last Boeing bomber in the Air Force inventory. Although now very old, the B-52H is capable of delivering up to 20 air-launched cruise missiles (ALCMs) with nuclear or conventional warheads and a conventional bomb load of 25,500 pounds. Other loads are possible, with an absolute weight limit of 77,000 pounds of munitions. (The B-52Gs are all now retired.)

The B-1B Lancer long-range heavy bomber is the Air Force's third-generation nuclear bomber. It will remain the backbone of the ACC bomber fleet for the future and operates primarily in the nuclear delivery mode. In due course it will be modified to deliver a wide range of conventional munitions, including ''smart'' munitions (guided) or ''dumb'' bombs (gravity weapons). Its bomb load remains classified.

The B-2A Spirit long-range nuclear bomber was designed as a stealthy nuclear weapons delivery system for very long-range strategic attack, but it will also be modified for delivery of conventional munitions. It is the first of the fourth-generation nuclear bombers. Since it is built around stealth technology, it is primarily, if not exclusively, a night-only weapons delivery system. As with the B-1B, the bomb load of the B-2A is classified.

Fighter Aircraft

The F-4G Wild Weasel electronic combat aircraft containing the APR-47 antiradar (radar homing and warning receiver) system is designed to detect, classify, prioritize, lock onto, and destroy surface-to-air radar systems programmed into it. The aircraft is armed with a mission-specific munitions load of AGM-88 high-speed antiradiation missiles (HARMs), AGM-78 standard antiradiation missiles (SARMs), AGM-45 Shrike supersonic antiradiation missiles, or AGM-65 Maverick guided air-to-surface missiles and often carries an ALQ-119 jamming pod. (All of these munitions come in a series of variants with different capabilities and seeker heads.) As of October 1994 there were only three F-4G squadrons in the Air Force, the 189th Fighter Flight and 190th Fighter Squadron, Air National Guard, at Boise International Airport, Idaho, and the 561st Fighter Squadron in the 57th Fighter Weapons Wing at Nellis AFB, Nevada. By 1995 only the 561st will still be active.

The RF-4C Phantom II tactical reconnaissance fighter is the only tactical reconnaissance platform that can make images of ground targets and return them to commanders who require the information for mission planning. The aircraft was scheduled to be phased out by 1994. However, since the F-16 tactical reconnaissance pod is on budgetary hold, the RF-4C squadron still in the Air

National Guard, the 192nd Fighter Squadron at Reno Municipal Airport, Nevada, will very probably remain an RF-4C unit for the indefinite and unforeseeable future.

The F-15 Eagle air superiority fighter is the Air Force's standard air-to-air fighter. It comes in four air-to-air variants, the F-15A and F-15C single-seat air superiority aircraft and the F-15B and F-15D two-seat conversion and familiarization variants. The A and B versions go together with identical systems, as do the later C and D models. The APG-63 radar in the A and B models is being upgraded to the later APG-70 lightweight and long-range version in the C and D models. This radar is capable of tracking very small targets down to treetop level at long range. It is an X-band pulse-Doppler radar. The F-15Cs and Ds achieved 36 of the Air Force's 39 air-to-air kills in the recent Gulf War. The F-15s use a 20-millimeter Gatling gun close-in and the AIM-7, AIM-9, and AIM-120 (AMRAAM) air-to-air missiles at longer ranges. In addition, they are equipped with the ALR-56C radar warning receiver and ALQ-135 electronic countermeasures set for use in their missions.

The F-15E Strike Eagle two-seat strike fighter is a two-seat dual-role totally integrated fighter for all-weather air-to-air and deep interdiction (ground-attack) missions. The F-15E is capable of carrying 24,500 pounds of ordnance. The APG-70 radar and a LANTIRN (Low-Altitude Navigation and Targeting InfraRed for Night) pod, along with a wide-field forward looking infrared (FLIR) system, give the airplane enormous night and foul-weather capabilities. It is intended to be the replacement for the F-111F aircraft.

The F-16 Fighting Falcon single-seat multirole fighter is the Air Force's standard multirole single-seat fighter and was the first fly-by-wire computer-stabilized aircraft to enter operational service anywhere in the world. Currently the F-16A single-seat and F-16B two-seat aircraft have been essentially replaced throughout the active and air reserve component fighter squadrons. Some As and Bs have been upgraded with APG-66 radar and AMRAAM capabilities as F-16 ADFs (air defense fighters) to equip the Air National Guard continental air defense squadrons. The F-16C single-seat and F-16D two-seat fighters are now the standard F-16 equipment in all squadrons of the Air Force. These aircraft have APG-68 multimode radars, 20-millimeter Gatling guns for close-in fighting, AIM-9 IR missiles, and seven hard points (load-bearing attachment points) for fuel and munitions. With significant avionics and electronic-combat capabilities, the Cs and Ds are significantly more capable aircraft than their predecessors. The F-16 is still one of the most maneuverable combat aircraft in the world, being at least 20 percent more maneuverable than the MiG-29. The two-seat version is essentially a conversion aircraft for new pilots, but it is fully combat capable.

The F-22 Lightning II or Rapier single-seat advanced-technology multirole fighter is the Air Force's newest fighter aircraft, employing the most advanced technology available. The F-22A will be a single-seat highly maneuverable air-to-air fighter with a secondary-strike fighter role. In the strike role it can be expected to carry munitions still in development, including the Triservice Standoff Attack Missile, a guided munition with a range of more than 300 miles, and the Joint Direct Attack Munition, a short-range precision-guided munition. It will carry an internal Gatling gun, AIM-9 Sidewinder IR missiles, the AIM-120 AMRAAM air intercept missiles, sophisticated sensor systems, and electronic countermeasures equipment, now standard on U.S. fighters, and will cruise above Mach 1 at high altitude (about 30,000 feet) without afterburners. The F-22 is a highly stealthy aircraft and is in fact the first of the second-generation stealth aircraft to be fielded by the U.S. Air Force. The F-22B will presumably be the usual two-seat conversion and training companion to the single-seat fighter, as in the F-15 and F-16 programs.

The F-111F Aardvark variable-geometry strike aircraft and the EF-111A Raven or Electric Fox Electronic Combat Aircraft are the family of aircraft, after a nightmare development cycle, that have proved to be one of the world's premier strike aircraft developments. Many are concerned today that even the redoubtable Strike Eagle will not be as capable as the F-111F strike aircraft. The F-111F is simply faster than any likely adversary aircraft and is easily concealed in the terrain-following radar (TFR) mode of operation. It carries a 20,000-pound ordnance load, including some of the heaviest precision-guided munitions in the world, capable of killing most hard targets. The F-111F is very similar to the EF-111A, but lacks the prominent electronic sensor on the top of the vertical stabilizer.

The EF-111A is a strike-aircraft conversion to a radar- and communications-jamming aircraft of capability and power unparalleled anywhere in the world. It is an essential element to any successful air strike against a heavily defended target or an integrated air defense system.

The F-117A Black Jet single-seat strike fighter is the first stealth aircraft to enter service with any nation's air forces. It carries an ordnance load of over 5,000 pounds, chiefly precision-guided munitions. It has sophisticated avionics and electronic-combat capabilities. The aircraft has an Inertial Navigation System (INS), a recently installed Global Positioning System (GPS) receiver, and forward-looking infrared (FLIR) and downward-looking infrared (DLIR) systems, as well as a boresighted laser designator and an automatic laser tracking system in a maneuverable turret underneath the aircraft to ensure ultra-accurate munitions delivery. Like all stealthy aircraft, it is a night-only aircraft. New avionics and cockpit instrumentation have been added, and upgrades are continuous. It is air refuelable and can deploy worldwide on short notice with tanker support.

Helicopters

The HH-1H and UH-1N Iroquois utility helicopters are early 1960s helicopters still in use in the Air Force for a variety of purposes, including missile site support and cargo movement. The single-engine HH will lift about 2,400 pounds of cargo, and the twin-engine UH will lift 4,000 pounds.

The CH-3E and HH-3E Jolly Green Giant cargo and rescue helicopters and the later MH-53J Super Jolly Green Giant special operations helicopter are derivatives of the Navy's SH-3A Sea King helicopter. The original Jolly Greens were first used in Vietnam. The CH version is present in small numbers for cargo and utility transport operations. The HH rescue version is being rapidly replaced by the newer Black Hawk. The later and larger H-53 or Super Jolly Green Giant was the final version and has now been modified in Air Force service as the MH-53J special operations helicopter for night and foul-weather operations employing the Pave Low III Enhanced System. This system is built around the AN/APQ-158 terrain-following and terrain-avoidance navigation radar, with forward-looking infrared (FLIR) and an integrated digital avionics suite. The electronic combat and electronic countermeasures suite includes an AN/ALQ-162 continuous-wave radar missile jammer, ALQ-153 infrared missile jammer, ALE-40 flare/chaff dispenser, and an ALR-69 missile warning receiver. Upgrades now going into the aircraft include ALQ-136 radar missile jammers, the AAR-47 missile plume detector, and an Integrated Defense Avionics System to automate all of these defensive systems.

The MH/HH-60G Pave Hawk special operations and rescue helicopter is now the standard Air Force air-search-and-rescue helicopter worldwide. It is equipped with multiple navigation systems, including Global Positioning System (GPS), Inertial Navigation System (INS), and Doppler radar, completely integrated. The MH-60G is the special operations aircraft and includes a KG-10 map reader and FLIR equipment along with its integrated navigation suite. Both types are armed with 7.62-millimeter miniguns, and the MH can carry the .50-caliber heavy machine gun.

Reconnaissance and Electronic-Combat Aircraft

The U-2R/RT strategic reconnaissance aircraft has been around a long time. With new engines, similar to those being used in the B-2A, the aircraft has a range of 3,000 miles unrefueled and can operate at or above 90,000 feet. With a variety of pods it can undertake a wide range of reconnaissance activities.

The EC-130E Commando aircraft is a psychological warfare aircraft operated exclusively by the 193rd Special Operations Squadron of the 193rd Special Operations Group, Pennsylvania ANG. The EC-130H Compass Call aircraft is a communications-jamming aircraft operated by the 41st and 43rd Electronic Combat Squadrons, 355th Wing, 12th Air Force.

The EC/RC-135 Stratolifter Aircraft is the original Boeing cargo model 717 airframe that has provided a variety of military aircraft, just as it gave rise to the civilian passenger variant, the famous model 707. The EC-135C/E/J/P/Y are airborne command and control aircraft in use in ACC, PACAF, and USAFE. EC-135K aircraft are used by ACC for overseas deployment of fighters. Four

EC-135A/E aircraft are range instrumentation birds flown by the 452nd Flight Test Squadron at Edwards AFB, California. The RC-135S/U/V/W/X are electronic/signals intelligence-gathering aircraft with differing capabilities. These are all flown worldwide by the 55th Wing out of Offutt AFB, Nebraska. The same wing operates several other specialized aircraft: the OC-135B to monitor the Open Skies Treaty of 1992, an NKC-135 as a special data collector for certification of C-135 radomes, and an NC-135E, which is an optical data collector for space and other specialized activities.

The E-3B/C Sentry Airborne Warning and Control System (AWACS) aircraft, notable for its saucer radome mounted above the aircraft, is built on the Boeing 707-320B airframe. It serves as the command and control platform for fighter and other airborne operations and is able to sort out friendly from enemy aircraft while simultaneously handling multiple intercepts and a high volume of traffic. Endurance is six hours.

The E-4B NEACP airborne command post aircraft was originally intended as the national emergency airborne command post for the National Command Authority (NCA) in time of alert or war. These four aircraft are now used for a variety of purposes at the direction of the NCA. They are highly sophisticated communications systems.

The E-8A Joint STARS Joint Surveillance and Target Attack Radar System aircraft is a system that can see behind enemy lines from friendly airspace, determine the nature, volume, speed, and direction of enemy ground movements, and direct attacking forces onto the identified targets. Although pictures have been released from the Gulf War showing all of this, the exact capabilities of the system are not yet released, and since the aircraft and the system itself are in prototype stage, it is difficult to know what their limitations might be.

The E-9A electronic surveillance aircraft remains in the Air Force inventory, but only two are left, and they are operated by the Gulf Test Range units at Tyndall AFB, Florida. They are used for sea surveillance to keep civil craft off of the range when live munitions are in use, and to help measure the range activities. Tyndall AFB is one of the air-to-air training ranges used by Air Combat Command for training and upgrade of fighter pilots. These aircraft are DHC-8 Dash 8M-100 airframes built by Boeing of Canada (de Haviland of Canada).

The EC-18B/D ARIA aircraft are "advanced range instrumentation aircraft" with modified Boeing 707-320 airframes used to monitor and control missile range operations and collect data on missile impacts and related range information.

The WC-130E/H Hercules aircraft are the only flying weather forecasters left in the Air Force and are operated by the 53rd Weather Reconnaissance Squadron of the Air Force Reserve (AFRES) from the 403rd Wing under the 22nd Air Force.

Transports and Tankers

The C-5A/B Galaxy heavy logistics transport is a long-range transport that will move 261,000 pounds of cargo, or 374 troops, for 3,434 miles unrefueled (maximum payload), or it will fly 6,469 miles with maximum fuel load and a reduced cargo. There are seventy-seven C-5A aircraft and fifty C-5B aircraft in the Air Force inventory.

The C-9A/C Nightingale aeromedical airlift transport is a long-range flying ambulance that will move 40 passengers with a medical team of 5 persons on board more than 2,000 miles unrefueled. This is the DC-9 of commercial service.

The C-12C/D/F Huron personnel/cargo transport is the Beech Super King Air 200 and is used for multiengine pilot training and proficiency and the time-sensitive movement of personnel and small cargoes. Forty-one of these aircraft are in use in the Air Force.

The C-17A Globemaster III heavy airlifters—the first C-17A heavy lifters—have been assigned to the 437th Airlift Wing at Charleston AFB, South Carolina. Each such squadron will have twelve aircraft, up to a total of three squadrons under the present procurement planning. Given the age of the C-141B fleet, more C-17A aircraft will be required to maintain America's "Global Reach." Each C-17A will lift 160,000 pounds with a range of 2,765 miles unrefueled, at a cruising speed of 518 miles per hour.

The C-20A/B/H Gulfstream III/IV personnel transport aircraft is purchased from Grumman/Gulfstream "off-the-shelf" for VIP transportation duties. The three C-20As are assigned to USAFE at Ramstein AB, Germany, and the seven C-20Bs belong to the 89th Airlift Wing at Andrews AFB, Maryland. The newer Hs are being delivered to the 89th also.

The C-21A Learjet personnel/aeromedical evacuation aircraft, like the Hurons and Gulfstreams, are used for personnel movement, including aeromedical evacuation operations. They are generally used for time-sensitive missions. They operate in PACAF, USAFE, and CONUS.

The C-22B personnel transports are four Boeing 727 transports all operated by the Air National Guard in support of personnel-movement requirements of Air Mobility Command.

The C-23A Sherpa light transports are three Short Brothers Model 330 cargo haulers originally acquired for intratheater airlift in Europe because their 6-foot-6-inch-square, 29-foot-long cargo hold could be opened at both ends and handle a fully assembled F100-series jet engine. A Sherpa can carry 5,000 pounds 770 miles at 218 miles per hour. They are now operated by Air Force Materiel Command for similar purposes.

The VC-25A personnel transports are two new Boeing 747-200B aircraft operated by the 89th Airlift Wing as presidential aircraft in support of the White House. They have an unrefueled range of 7,140 miles at Mach 0.84 with a crew of 23 and passengers up to 70 in number.

The C-26A/B Metro III personnel/cargo transport aircraft are being procured by the ANG and Guard Bureau. When procurement is completed, there will be as many as sixty-four of these Fairchild Metro III commuter transports in service nationwide. With a quick-change interior, they can be used for medical evacuation, personnel, cargo, or a variety of more specialized tasks. They operate in what is referred to as "the mission support role."

The C-27A Spartan airlifter is the commercially available Alenia G222 medium airlifter in the basic Spartan airframe, and ten have been purchased for use in Southern Command, headquartered in Panama, as short takeoff and landing (STOL) aircraft. As many as eight more may be added in the future. The aircraft will lift 14,850 pounds of cargo or 34 troops and has a ferry range of 1,727 miles with a maximum fuel load.

The C-130E/H Hercules Transport Aircraft has been the standard tactical airlifter since its introduction in the mid-1950s. With four engines it has an unrefueled range, with maximum payload, of 2,356 miles. It is air refuelable and can lift a maximum load of 42,673 pounds, or 92 troops, 64 paratroops, 74 litter patients, or 5 463L standard freight pallets. This airframe has numerous other adaptations: MC-130E/H Combat Talon II/III special operations aircraft are equipped with AN/APQ-170 precision terrain-following radar and other specialized night and foul-weather equipment, which allow operations under very difficult conditions, as befits AFSOC forces. HC-130N/P Combat Shadow/Tanker aircraft equip both Special Operations and Combat Rescue units at home and abroad. They double as helicopter refuelers and have extensive night and foul-weather operational capabilities, as befits their primary duties. JC-130H aircraft are specially modified for recovery of space vehicles reentering the atmosphere. DC-130H aircraft are modified for control of airborne target drones over operational ranges, such as those at Tyndall AFB, Florida, and Nellis AFB, Nevada.

The KC-135A/E/Q/R/T Stratotanker aircraft are the primary aerial refueling aircraft of the Air Force. The Es and Rs are the backbone of the fleet, with specialized birds like the Q, which refueled the SR-71 aircraft when they were still in service, being in the fleet in small numbers.

The C-135B Stratolifter aircraft are still operated by the Air Force in very small numbers, including a couple of TC-135S/W variants in the 55th Wing at Offutt AFB, Nebraska, for training purposes. These aircraft are used for cargo hauling in support of ACC operational requirements and the operational requirements of the overseas Air Forces, the "combat air forces."

The VC-137B/C Stratolifter aircraft are Boeing Model 707 transports modified for VIP duties. They have a 5,150-mile range unrefueled and are operated by the 89th Airlift Wing at Andrews AFB, Maryland, in support of the NCA. The C-135B and VC-137B/C have the same basic airframe but with sufficient variations to require a new designation under USAF rules.

The C-141B StarLifter heavy airlift aircraft is the standard strategic airlifter of the Air Force. It can carry 68,725 pounds normally and 89,000 pounds war emergency load, or 13 standard 463L pallets, 200 troops, 155 paratroops, or 103 litters with attendant medical crew. Unrefueled the range is 2,170 miles with maximum load, but the aircraft is capable of air refueling. First entering service in April of 1965, the C-141 fleet now may be expected to have a limited useful life, and the C-17A will gradually replace the StarLifter before they must be rebuilt or retired. About 270 aircraft were originally acquired.

The KC-10A Extender tanker/cargo aircraft is designed to double as a cargo aircraft and as a tanker aircraft. These DC-10 Series 30CF Douglas-built machines number 59 in the Air Force inventory. The maximum cargo load is 169,409 pounds of fuel/cargo, with seating for up to 75 persons or 27 pallets as alternate loads. Its range, with maximum cargo, is 4,370 miles unrefueled at a cruising speed of Mach 0.825.

Training Aircraft

The T-1A Jayhawk trainer is a twin-jet trainer for conversion of pilots to heavy airlift equipment; AETC is the chief operator of these aircraft.

The T-3A Firefly trainer is a single-engine low-wing monoplane that is the Air Force's principal undergraduate pilot training (UPT) aircraft.

The T-37B Tweet trainer is the AETC's primary jet trainer.

The T-38A and AT-38B Talon trainers are the Air Force's standard advanced twin-jet trainers and are capable of supersonic speeds.

The T-43A and CT-43 navigation trainers are based on the Boeing 737-200 airframe and are the standard navigator training aircraft. A couple have been converted to personnel transport duties, and one each is assigned to the 58th Airlift Squadron at Ramstein AB, Germany, and the 310th Airlift Squadron at Howard AB, Panama.

Strategic Missiles

The LGM-30F Minuteman II and LGM-30G Minuteman III are missiles with a three-stage solid-fuel intercontinental ballistic missile lifting a bus containing three independently targeted reentry vehicles (MIRVs) of either the Mk 12 or Mk 12A type.

The LGM-118A Peacekeeper has three solid-fuel stages and a fourth stage fueled with storable liquid fuel. This ICBM lifts 10 Mk 21 independently targeted reentry vehicles.

The AGM-86B/C air-launched cruise missiles (ALCMs) carry a nuclear warhead 1,500 miles at a speed of 500 miles per hour. They are low-altitude vehicles of very small radar cross-section. Heavy bomb wings still have the delivery capability to employ the 86B. The AGM-86C is the conventional-munitions high-explosive-warhead version used with great effectiveness in the recent Gulf War. Its performance is similar to that of the 86B.

The AGM-129A advanced cruise missile (ACM) is a nuclear delivery mechanism that carries a warhead 1,865 miles at high speed with an Inertial Navigation System. It is far easier to program than the ALCM, which preceded it into service (AGM-86B).

Munitions (Selected)

The AIM-7 Sparrow is a radar-guided air-to-air intercept missile that requires the launching aircraft to lock on a target and keep a radar pulse on the target so that the missile will receive the reflected signal and guide on it to the targeted aircraft. The AIM-7F is the standard missile currently in use, but the AIM-7M has a monopulse system to give improved performance in the look-down back-clutter arena. These missiles give very good results against antiship missiles due to improved fusing and electronics, and the AIM-7R deals with sophisticated electric counter measures (ECM) by adding an infrared (IR) seeker mode. Speed is Mach 3.5 over a 25-mile range with an 86-pound warhead.

The AIM-9 Sidewinder is a close-range air-to-air intercept missile with an IR seeker head for use in maneuvering combat. AIM-9L and AIM-9M versions, the most recent, give all-aspect acquisition capability and have improved anti-countermeasures capabilities to reduce jamming. The missile speed is Mach 2.0 or greater over 10 or more miles with a 20.8-pound warhead.

The AIM-120A advanced medium-range air-to-air missile (AMRAAM) is a fire-and-forget missile that has inertial midcourse guidance and terminal radar homing to produce a formidable air-to-air weapons system capable of all-weather, all-environment operations with great effectiveness. Its speed is Mach 4.0 or greater over a range of 30 or more miles with a warhead of unspecified weight.

The AGM-65 Maverick is a launch-and-leave air-to-surface missile with either TV guidance (AGM-65B) or imaging-infrared guidance (AGM-65D) and a shaped-charge warhead or a 298-pound blast-fragmentation warhead for hard targets carried on the AGM-65G model. This is primarily an antiarmor, anti-vehicular weapon that can be employed against any hard target, mobile target, or other appropriate target.

The AGM-84A Harpoon is an airborne, all-weather, antiship missile with sea-skimming radar altimeter monitored cruise capability and active radar terminal homing. The missile has a high subsonic speed over a range that exceeds 57 miles carrying a 488-pound penetrating high-explosive warhead.

The AGM-88C high speed antiradiation missile (HARM) has a 145-pound high-explosive warhead that fires tungsten-alloy cubes as shrapnel when it detonates against a radar-receiving antenna. The missile seeker head has a memory circuit to ensure arrival at the location of the antenna upon which it originally locked. Flying at supersonic speed, it has a range of 10 or more miles and operates effectively between sea level and an altitude of 40,000 feet.

The GBU-15 and AGM-130A: The guided glide bomb unit 15 is an unpowered Mk 84 bomb of 2,000 pounds or a BLU-109 (bomb live unit) of the same class, coupled to a television or imaging-infrared seeker (guidance) unit capable of giving pinpoint accuracy against an identifiable target. The AGM-130A is a rocket-powered version of the same ordnance and seeker-head arrangement.

The GBU-24/27 Paveway III low-level laser-guided bombs are units attached to Mk 82 500-pound bombs or Mk 84 2,000-pound bombs to produce a guided munition that can be released at very low level in a standoff mode of operation. These units are replacements for the GBU 10/12 series expended during the Gulf War.

The GBU-28 Bunker Buster is a guided bomb unit with a GBU-10 tail unit and a GBU-24 guidance kit fitted to a 12-foot section of 16-inch-bore naval rifle that is filled with 660 pounds of Tritonal explosive. It is a powerful penetrating weapon.

The AGM-137 TSSAM (triservice standoff attack missile) is designed to be a subsonic 2,300-pound stealthy missile with an infrared guidance system and submunitions that will be acoustically guided to their targets upon release. The system is intended for use in the B-1B, B-2A, B-52H, F-22A, and F-16 aircraft of the Air Force, plus Navy A-6s and F/A-18s.

The joint direct attack munition (JDAM) will be a highly accurate all-weather inertial guidance system for use with the Mk 83 (1,000-pound bomb), Mk 84 (2,000-pound bomb), or BLU-109 munitions. Initial operational capability (IOC) is expected to be fiscal year 1997.

The joint standoff weapon (JSOW) is a Navy-led interdiction standoff weapon to be used by both Air Force and Navy aircraft.

The AGM-142 Have Nap is the Israeli-built Popeye medium-range standoff weapon that will equip U.S. B-52Hs committed to theater CINCs in the conventional attack role. With a 50-mile range and a 750-pound warhead of the blast-fragmentation type, it will be a formidable system.

INTO THE FUTURE

The United States is and will continue to be the leading aerospace nation, relying on its freedom to use air routes, airspace, space orbits, and access to deep space for commercial, government, and national security purposes. It is clear that even a government committed to a domestic agenda cannot set aside or ignore the role of the U.S. Air Force in preserving the nation's access to world markets and resources and in maintaining long-standing commitments to vital interests around an increasingly violent world. Our old allies and new friends expect us to carry on a responsible if measured role in the maintenance of world order and stability, in spite of fewer sizable threats to our own and their vital interests. More than ever before, aerospace power is the key to quick, timely, and effective intervention to preserve order, restore order, or defend those vital interests. Aerospace power can provide surveillance of the globe as can no other force in order to give government timely warning in most cases of potential disorder. Aerospace power can go where no ship can reach, and it can place the ultimate peacekeeper, the infantryman, on the ground and sustain him there as no other force can.

In the event of one or more major or minor regional conflicts, aerospace forces are the key to timely and effective intervention. Aerospace power can often deter an aggressor and may well be able to slow or hold him until the arrival of air-transported ground forces. It is now recognized that in any war, whatever its nature, it is essential to gain and maintain aerospace superiority in order to fight and win. Aerospace power cannot very often "go it alone." It is also the case that when committed, the Army seeks a friendly aerospace envelope for its missions.

Organization

It is difficult to predict the future of the active Air Force's force structure and manning. In the early twenty-first century it is entirely likely that the Air Force will be reduced to as few as ten fighter wing equivalents and fewer than 500 fighters—barring the United States becoming involved in a war of some significance.

The number of bomb wings may be about 20 percent of that, probably no more than 100 bombers of all types, until the last B-52s are retired. Then the number may go as low as a total of 70. It will be several years before the B-52s can be retired, since the B-1B and B-2A units are not yet trained or equipped to do some of the missions allocated to the redoubtable "Buffs."

The strategic airlift force will decline through airframe attrition, which Congress has no interest in replacing. The number of C-17A aircraft is unlikely to be able to meet the needs of any large-scale crisis in a remote area. So long as crises remain small or response fails to gain the support of the American people and Congress, no large-scale commitment may be expected. Yet there is no guarantee that such crises will not emerge. The airlift force is now down from more than 800 aircraft to a little over 550, and it is continuing to shrink.

The Air Force will continue to reduce in manpower proportionate to the numbers of airframes and units. With such a small force, a problem will come when it again becomes necessary to commit the force to sustained operations. Even with a large Air Force Reserve and National Guard force structure (about half the size of the active Air Force, except in the airlift arena, which may be larger), the Air Force will not be able to sustain any significant amount of attrition in either its aircraft or its pilot force. Air forces, unlike ground forces, are less well able to reconstitute themselves because of their unique nature. Once aircraft factories disappear, their rebuilding takes an interminable length of time. Once the shooting starts in conventional conflicts, it is likely that air forces will be the first to engage the adversary. The ground forces are likely to be in the process of mobilizing and being moved overseas. The pilot force is the center of gravity of any air force, and if one loses that cadre early on, there can be no short-term reconstitution of the force structure lost in an unanticipated war.

The space assets of the U.S. Air Force will be reduced as the ICBMs are removed from service, but presumably the boosters under the warheads will be diverted to space lift. The future of the Air Force is in space, and it must face that vast emptiness, just as early airmen were willing to face the unknown of aviation. *Man-in-space is the essential future of the Air Force.* Unmanned systems will remain vital to national security, the environment, and peacekeeping and peacemaking, just as will men on the ground and in the air overhead. Space is to the Air Force today what aviation was to the Army aviators in the 1920s—the future.

The Special Operations components of the Air Force will grow and be of increasing importance in the future. At present AFSOC is small, but with the most probable forms of conflict in the immediate future likely to be U.N.–related operations, peacekeeping, peacemaking, and changing governments in remote regions of the world, Special Operations forces are likely to be very much in demand. The American military has spent most of its existence in the constabulary role, and that seems a very likely prospect for the immediate future.

Future Weaponry

Stealth technology is a long way from being perfected, and countermeasures are probably far in the future—although one can never be certain of such a speculative proposition. The Air Force will continue to buy stealth technology, if Congress will fund any more of it. There are innumerable ''Black World'' programs under way on new technology, the very nature of which is known to only a few. The Air Force intends to stay in front of technology, as it has always striven to do. What that means, however, is still unclear at this time.

Perhaps the most important new technologies in the Air Force will be those associated with ''information war,'' a new and growing field with implications beyond anyone's ability to predict. Computers, masses of data, and the manipulation of the media are already matters in which many countries are involved. In the Gulf War, for example, Saddam Hussein made major efforts to manipulate the media. In sum, psychological warfare and the use of sophisticated communications are major strategies, ones that are likely to become increasingly important with the communications revolution.

Future Doctrine

In 1994 yet another research effort was under way at Air University to get out in front of technology and policy with Spacecast 2020.[16] The intent is to give as much creative and innovative thought as possible to the future of space and space technology, and, like the first Forecast effort of the early 1960s, to get the Air Force back out in front across the board.[17] However, what is of even greater significance is the recent change in doctrine writing by the Air Force. Recently the Air Force Doctrine Center at Langley Air Force Base was charged with the mandate to produce an entire set of doctrine publications, apart from all other Air Force publications. For the first time since 1946, the Air University is charged with educating the entire Air Force in matters of doctrine. Among other things, operational doctrine is included in the new publications to be produced.

In each of the cases when the Air Force has published operational doctrine, the Air Force Chief of Staff has apparently been instrumental. For example, General Henry H. Arnold ensured the publishing of the Air Corps Tactical School (ACTS) doctrine in 1941 under the guise of Air War Plans Division-Plan 1 (AWPD-1), partly by whom he selected to write it. In the mid-1950s General Hoyt S. Vandenberg ensured the timely publishing of the post–Korean War manuals. In the mid-1960s General Curtis LeMay directed the publication of operational doctrine before he retired. In the next few years, if the Doctrine Center is to have success in publishing operational doctrine, it will require the intervention of a strong and determined Air Force Chief of Staff.

Still vexing is the fact that the doctrine process is not yet institutionalized. It has been moved one more time. The writing of basic doctrine is in its fourth location, and operational doctrine is in its fifth or sixth location. The Air Force is still plagued by a high degree of paranoia about its survival as a service, in spite of its track record of success.[18] Once again the Air Force is writing doctrine with no evidence that it is going to be rooted in a comprehensive, or even a limited, theory of aerospace power. If the new group of doctrine writers is as chary about committing to writing what the Air Force believes it can deliver to other forces on the battlefield, the service will be trapped in the same deadly closed loop that has plagued it for seventy years. Only time will determine how well these problems will be identified and resolved.

There are individuals today who argue about the need for the Air Force to reexamine its theoretical base and to develop new air power theories for the present and future. Unfortunately, air power theory is unlikely to be relevant to the modern Air Force. The Air Force is an aerospace force, and its future is now in space as certainly as in 1926 it was in the air.

The Air Force must work toward a first-generation theory of the integrated employment of aerospace assets for war fighting. Airplanes are not going to disappear in the foreseeable future, but the required aerospace theory must be futuristic, not retrospective. The focus should not be on the current assets, but rather on the future theory. That theory must look far into the future, a future of war fighting in and from space. Nor should the Air Force think in terms other than the need to send military man into space, for we cannot see the future, and the theory must provide for unforeseeable contingencies. Airmen are as essential in space as they are within the atmospheric envelope. The cost will not be small, but in terms of today's world and economy such requirements are no more unreachable than what Giulio Douhet was theorizing about when he saw air power as a war-winning concept in 1922.

What the Air Force needs now, above all else, is creative thinkers to work on a true aerospace theory upon which its future concept of warfare, and therefore its doctrine, can be based. Spacecast 2020, were it pursued continuously hereafter, effectively, systematically, and with proper intellectual integrity, might be a starting point for such a theory of aerospace power. In the interim, however, the Air Force may have to rely on a complete rethink of its theoretical underpinnings until new, visionary theories can be developed. It must, at least temporarily, reground its doctrine in theoretical concepts of war winning through aerospace power.

As we have seen, the Air Force has been unable to institutionalize its doctrine-writing program in the manner of the Army. If the Air Force is able to institutionalize its doctrine-writing process at Langley with its new doctrine center, give the staff support, education, and longevity in the job, and leave it alone for the next half century, instead of moving the function every few years, it may get what it is paying for and desperately needs: sound and realistic operational doctrine to serve into the future of air-breathing air forces. The writers may be creative enough to work the aerospace theory and future doctrine issues as well. But this will require a cerebral atmosphere, one not routinely turned end for end. The Air Force must give up its predilection to develop its doctrine in ad hoc fashion, and it must commit cerebral personnel long-term to the preparation of doctrine, particularly operational doctrine so that it can talk to the Army and Navy at appropriate levels of endeavor. In addition to institutionalizing the process, the Air Force must ensure that whatever doctrine it has is effectively transmitted into, and understood by, the officer corps that must fight with it.

Doctrine should be taught routinely, effectively, thoroughly, and with hands-on, ''get your hands dirty'' exercises to thoroughly familiarize everyone with its application in all possible situations, from the cockpit to the Joint Forces Air Component Commander (JFACC) level, as determined by the officer's rank and experience. Every PME institution should be required to instruct its officer corps in such a manner.

In the immediate future the Air Force must write operational doctrine that is accepted servicewide. The Air Force does not need another Tactical Air Command Manual 2-1 (TACM 2-1) experience in which the service itself cannot agree on how it is to do its mission. The USAF could not make TACM 2-1 an Air Force Manual (AFM) because U.S. Air Force Europe (USAFE) could not agree to the contents. The problem in developing Air Force doctrine is discussed in more detail in the section on Air Force Basic Doctrine. The Air Force, in an increasingly joint world, must commit with clarity and without equivocation to what it can do for the theater commander, the ground-component commander, and the naval-component commander, how effectively it believes that it can do those things to which it does commit, and what factors will limit or impair its ability to live up to those commitments. That is what operational doctrine should be about. The task is not easy, but it is almost certainly necessary at this point in time, and the Air Force can do it, and do it well, even as it works on new theories of aerospace power.

Central to doing these things is the elimination of the paranoia that still plagues the Air Force. No country can win a war, or even stay on the battlefield, without its air power in control of the skies overhead. Paranoia is simply wrong in this day and age, but it is rampant in the officer corps today, and at all levels. This is in part because the Air Force does not do a very effective job, at any PME level, of educating the officer corps about the modern realities of aerospace power. The service must work at putting the paranoia behind it. This paranoia is rooted in history that is no longer relevant. The Air Force must expend its energy on thinking about its theoretical and doctrinal underpinnings and its future as the dominant aerospace force on the battlefield and in space.

NOTES

1. This reorganization was announced in Army Circular 59, dated 2 March 1942.

2. There have been numerous statutory measures over the years that have affected the organization of the Air Force. This is merely an outline history of its various organizational stages.

3. *Air Force Manual 1-1: Basic Aerospace Doctrine of the United States Air Force,* 2 vols. (Washington, DC: Headquarters, U.S. Air Force, March 1992), vol. 1, p. 5.

4. For the sake of simplicity, the modern title is used throughout as a generic term for the Air Service, the Army Air Corps, and the Army Air Forces. The Air Force's titles historically were the Aeronautical Division of the Signal Corps, 1 August 1916 to 21 May 1918; the Air Service, 21 May 1918 to 2 July 1926; the Army Air Corps, 2 July 1926 to 18 September 1947; the Army Air Forces, coexisting with the Air Corps, which was the branch to which personnel were assigned, as a component of the U.S. Army from 20 June 1941 to 18 September 1947. Since that date the service has been the United States Air Force.

5. Robert Frank Futrell, *Ideas, Concepts, Doctrine,* vol. 1, *Basic Thinking in the United States Air Force, 1907–1960* (Maxwell AFB, AL: Air University Press, 1989), p. 95.

6. *Air Force Manual 1-1,* vol. 2, p. 274.

7. *Air Force Pamphlet 5-1-1: Joint Chiefs of Staff Dictionary* (Washington, DC, 1948), p. 62.

8. For which see Futrell, *Ideas, Concepts, Doctrine,* vol. 1, p. 369.

9. *Air Force Manual 1-1,* vol. 2, p. 296.

10. *Air Force Manual 1-1.*

11. *FM 100-20: Command and Employment of Air Power* (Washington, DC: War Department, 21 July 1943).

12. Futrell, *Ideas, Concepts, Doctrine,* vol. 1, p. 180.

13. Futrell, *Ideas, Concepts, Doctrine,* vol. 1, p. 180, quoted Arnold on this relationship of doctrine ahead of equipment. Carl H. Builder, *The Icarus Syndrome: The Role of Air Power Theory in the Evolution and Fate of the U.S. Air Force* (New Brunswick, NJ and London: Transaction Publishers, 1994), pp. 83–87, discussed another example of how doctrine preceded the development of the technology, the classic example of the correct relationship between doctrine and technology.

14. The wing organizations as shown here have been traditional, but since the units

frequently lie in different states, there is no command relationship; moreover, it is the intent of the Air Force at this writing to call up ANG units piecemeal as required, not as complete units; these wing headquarters should not be expected to deploy overseas at any time.

15. The 2nd and 19th Air Forces handle ''training'' for the Air Force, while Air University and its components conduct professional ''education,'' including technical/scientific degree programs at the Air Force Institute of Technology (AFIT), described later.

16. This forecast effort was launched at the express instruction of the Chief of Staff of the Air Force, General Merrill McPeak.

17. It is worth noting that the Air Force has commissioned several ''forecasts'' over the years. I have mentioned only one or two of particular note from a doctrinal point of view; see Futrell, *Ideas, Concepts, Doctrine,* vols. 1 and 2, *Basic Thinking in the United States Air Force, 1961–1984* (Maxwell AFB, AL: Air University Press, 1989), passim.

18. The author has been on the faculty of Air War College for ten years, with ample opportunity to teach and talk with Air Command and Staff College students as well. This paranoia, albeit a fact of life for Air Force officers, is something very few will admit to publicly, but many will freely discuss privately. They admit that it is conveyed from one generation of officers to the next, almost as though it were the sacred legacy of the service.

SELECTED BIBLIOGRAPHY

Air Force Magazine, May 1995: *USAF Almanac 1995* (published by the Air Force Association annually in May of each year).

Burrows, William E. *Deep Black: The Startling Truth behind America's Top-Secret Spy Satellites.* New York: Random House, 1986.

Cochran, Thomas B., William M. Arkin, and Milton M. Hoenig. *Nuclear Weapons Databook.* Vol. 1, *U.S. Nuclear Forces and Capabilities.* Cambridge, MA: Ballinger Publishing Co., 1984.

Donald, David, ed. *U.S. Air Force Air Power Directory: Space, Espionage, and National Security.* London: Aerospace Publishing; Westport, CT: Airtime Publishing, 1992.

Flintham, Victor. *Air Wars and Aircraft: A Detailed Record of Air Combat, 1945 to the Present.* New York: Facts on File, 1990.

Godden, John, ed. *Shield and Storm: Personal Recollections of the Air War in the Gulf.* London: Brassey's, 1995.

Gunston, Bill. *The Illustrated Encyclopedia of Aircraft Armament: A Comprehensive Guide to Modern Airborne Weapons and Sensing Systems, Their Operating Principles, and Tactical Deployment.* New York: Orion Books, 1988.

Jane's All the World's Aircraft, 1993–4.

Korb, Edward L., ed. *The World's Missile Systems.* Pomona, CA: General Dynamics Corporation, 1988.

Miller, Samuel Duncan, ed. *An Aerospace Bibliography.* Washington, DC: Office of Air Force History, 1986.

Chapter 5
THE MARINE CORPS

Allan R. Millett

The dawn of the post–Cold War strategic era may prove a rebirth of sorts for the U.S. Marine Corps and Navy. As Marine and Navy planners struggle with shrinking budgets and manpower levels, the demands of the next twenty years will place an increasing burden on those forces that remain. Even with the collapse of one superpower, the world remains an uncertain and dangerous place for U.S. economic and geostrategic interests and places an even greater strain upon the U.S. military's ability to plan and prepare for future conflicts. What remains clear, however, is that the post–Cold War world places a premium on those forces that are capable of responding rapidly, yet possess the ability to deliver sustained combat power. These same forces will be required to retain an even greater amount of flexibility capable of intervening in a variety of scenarios short of a major war. This mixture of rapid response, sufficient firepower, tactical flexibility, and mobility can be found in the U.S. Marine Corps.

For the U.S. Marine Corps, the role of premier rapid-deployment force began with reorganization and realignment of the functions of the armed services in the National Security Act of 1947. The Marine Corps' status was refined by Congress with the passage of the Douglas-Mansfield Act (PL 416) in 1952. The roles and missions of the post–World War II Marine Corps were, in fact, largely forged by the legislative battle that took place in both the House of Representatives and the Senate even as Marines responded to the North Korean invasion in June 1950. These same missions and roles largely reflected the Corps' tra-

The author thanks Major Larry Alexander, USMC; Staff Sergeant Leo J. Daugherty III, USMCR; and Sergeant Mike Nelson, USMCR, for their assistance in preparing this chapter.

ditional ties to the Navy as well as its newer role as an amphibious force-in-readiness.

Buoyed by its reputation for amphibious assaults during World War II, Marine Corps Commandant (CMC) General Alexander A. Vandegrift fought to retain the wartime Fleet Marine Force as an air-ground force-in-readiness. After a bitter political battle in Washington, the Marine Corps received the primary responsibility for developing amphibious warfare doctrine and equipment. It could expand during a war if it did not threaten the Army as the principal land combat service. The eventual 1947 statement on roles and missions specifically outlined that the Marine Corps, a separate service within the Navy Department, "shall provide fleet marine forces of combined arms, together with supporting air components, for service with the fleet in the seizure and defense of advanced naval bases and for conduct of such land operations as may be essential to the prosecution of a naval campaign."[1]

The Marine Corps' role within the newly established Department of Defense was further refined during the subsequent debate that raged from March 1948 to early 1952 over both its size and wartime role in the nation's defense. Headquarters Marine Corps (HQMC) and influential pro-Corps senators and congressmen halted an Army and Air Force attempt to curtail the size of the Corps through Public Law 416, which authorized the Marine Corps to maintain three divisions and three wings in peacetime and allowed expansion in wartime to a 400,000-man ceiling.[2] The current law governing the Marine Corps' size and mission, Title 10 United States Code 5063, reflects the compromise of 1952, with the only addition being that the Commandant of the Marine Corps is now a full member of the Joint Chiefs of Staff and may serve as chairman (1978).

STRATEGY AND MISSIONS: THE IMMEDIATE POST–VIETNAM PERIOD, 1975–1980

As the Marines withdrew from South Vietnam during 1969–1971, the Corps refocused on the amphibious warfare mission as well as the reinforcing role in NATO. Headquarters Marine Corps watched with great interest the developments in the field of armored and maneuver warfare, highlighted by the 1973 Arab-Israeli War, and the massive Soviet conventional buildup of the mid to late 1970s. Commandant Robert E. Cushman, Jr., and his successor, General Louis H. Wilson, Jr., introduced a series of reforms and policies that reflected the most likely contingencies in which Marines might become involved. They sought improved armored vehicles such as the M60A1 and M60A3 tanks and an improved amphibious assault vehicle. They sought more sealift in order to enhance the Corps' amphibious readiness. These improvements set the stage for General Wilson's emphasis on preparing the Marine Corps for its rapid reinforcing role in NATO, especially on the northern flank, and later participation in the Rapid Deployment Joint Task Force (RDJTF).

The commandancy of General Louis H. Wilson (1976–1980) was marked by the adoption of better artillery (M198 155-millimeter howitzer), as well as by better infantry assault weapons such as the M203 grenade launcher, the shoulder-launched multipurpose assault weapon (SMAW), and the Dragon antitank missile system, all of which greatly enhanced the fighting power of Marine infantry units. Commensurate with the addition of the increase in firepower was the reorganization of the Marine infantry battalion, the basic tactical element of the Marine Corps. Reflecting the shift from manpower to firepower, Marine infantry battalions were reduced in total strength but were provided with the addition of a weapons company. The three (down from four) rifle companies were likewise provided with the crew-served weapons of the deleted company in order to bolster their firepower.[3] This increase in firepower enhanced the combat effectiveness of Marine units, thus strengthening the Corps' claim that it could preserve its war-fighting capability with a relatively modest investment in modernization.

General Wilson's decision to turn Marine Corps Base, Twentynine Palms, California, into the Corps' mobile warfare center encouraged Marine tactical commanders to think in terms of mobile as well as amphibious warfare. The role of Twentynine Palms as "a combined-arms training center" at first met with some skepticism and institutional opposition from purists on both the ground and air sides. The Combined Arms Exercises (CAXs) soon found general approval. These exercises simulated battles against a Soviet-style enemy in the high desert, a good representation of the Middle East. General Wilson and his successor, General Robert H. Barrow, paved the way for the Marine Corps' participation in the Rapid Deployment Joint Task Force, commanded by Lieutenant General (later Commandant) P. X. Kelley. Wilson and Barrow also initiated improvements of the Marine Corps well into the 1980s.[4]

Coinciding with the continued emphasis on mobile warfare and rapid deployment, the Marine Corps benefited from the increased defense spending in the last year of the Carter administration and the first five years of the Reagan administration. The material improvement of the Fleet Marine Force coincided with the movement away from the noninterventionist policies of the late 1970s toward the increased opposition to Soviet/Cuban activity in the Third World. The fall of the Shah of Iran, coupled with the Soviet invasion of Afghanistan in 1979, demonstrated the vulnerability of U.S. geostrategic interests in Southwest Asia, as well as the need for a force that could respond to any crisis within a matter of days. The appointment of General Kelley to head the newly created Rapid Deployment Joint Task Force was recognition that the Marine Corps would be a key element in U.S. power projection in the Middle East and Southwest Asia.

Despite the buildup that began in 1980 and the increased infusion of dollars under the first Reagan administration, both the RDJTF and General Wilson's revamped Marine Corps remained untested. Studies concluded after the Vietnam War, notably Martin Binkin and Jeffrey Record, *Where Does the Marine Corps Go From Here?*, questioned the need for a Marine Corps.[5] Binkin and Record reflected the views of many critics, who argued that the U.S. experience in Vietnam showed the futility of Third World intervention. The events in Iran and Afghanistan, coupled with the fall of Anastasio Somoza in 1979 and the election of a Marxist regime in Grenada, however, kept the issue of power projection alive.

The election of Ronald Reagan in 1980 and the continued Soviet involvement in Afghanistan and Central America signalled not only the rearming of the U.S. armed forces but a return to a maritime strategy. The construction of a 600-ship Navy, advocated by then Secretary of the Navy John Lehman, ended only in 1990. The 50 percent increase in spending permitted the Navy and the Marine Corps to acquire new weapons as well as expand their research programs. For the Marine Corps, this research and development effort concentrated on enhancing its mobile war-fighting capability with the eventual addition of the six-wheeled light armored vehicle (LAV) as well as the upgrading of the infantry battalion's small arms.

The new administration quickly set about dispelling the notion that Vietnam had crippled the U.S. ability to protect U.S. interests. A Marine peacekeeping force went to Lebanon (1982–1984), while a Marine amphibious unit participated in the combined operation that liberated the Caribbean nation of Grenada (October 1983). The operation in Grenada demonstrated shortcomings in joint training, organization, and tactics.

The Marine Corps emerged from Grenada with deficiencies to correct, which included the physical training of its men, inadequate equipment (the lack of a mobile assault vehicle), and the need for another restructuring of the infantry battalion. Operation Urgent Fury revealed that Marines were capable of operating for short periods of time without rest, but needed more physical fitness training. The training issue did not stop there. Combat in Grenada likewise suggested that Marines in noninfantry military occupational specialty (MOSs) had forgotten the basic Marine adage: "Every Marine a rifleman." These problems were addressed by Commandant P. X. Kelley, but more intensely by Commandant Alfred M. Gray. Gray, in fact, again revamped the Marine Corps infantry battalion and ordered that all new Marines would receive thirty days of specialized infantry training.[6]

The eventual acquisition of the light armored vehicle (LAV) and the upgrading and increased firepower of the LVPT7 amphibious assault vehicle (AAV) corrected the deficiencies in fire support for Marine battalions. (The numerous vehicle designations show variations of a basic vehicle such as light armored vehicle [LAV], landing vehicle personnel track [LVPT], landing vehicle track [LVT], amphibious assault vehicle [AAV], and amphibious assault vehicle personnel [AAVP]. For accuracy, the numbers such as LVPT7, LVPT7A1, AAVP7A1 indicate different model numbers of the same vehicle with modifications. For accuracy, the appropriate model numbers are indicated where applicable.) This was dramatically revealed during the subsequent operations in Panama in December 1989, when a joint U.S. force stormed into Panama City in order to install the democratically elected government of Panama, which had been blocked by Panamanian strongman General Manuel Antonio Noriega. Marine light armored infantry teams (LAI) in Operation Just Cause (December 1989) seized all their objectives in minimum time with few casualties.

The United States demonstrated in Grenada and Panama that it could still selectively employ military force whenever it deemed this necessary. The barracks bombing in Beirut, Lebanon (October 1983) as well as the continuing Soviet/Cuban role in Africa and Central America, however, raised serious questions regarding the military's role in civil wars where U.S. interests seemed vague. These same questions renewed the debate over the roles and missions of the various branches of the military, as each service sought to shape its war-fighting doctrine according to the newly ordained emphasis on "low-intensity conflict." When both the Soviet Union and the Warsaw Pact collapsed at the end of the 1980s, the missions of the U.S. military became even more debatable. For the Marine Corps, the answer was simple: it prepared for global expeditionary warfare with a continued emphasis on power projection from the sea.

Despite the collapse of Soviet military power, other countries—notably Iraq, Iran, North Korea, China, and the new Russia—have filled the void of potential threats vacated by the dismembered Soviet Union. The victory over Iraqi forces during Operation Desert Storm in 1991 came about largely due to the absence of Soviet intervention. For the Marine Corps, Desert Storm resulted in one of the quickest, least costly, and most visible victories in its history, though it remains to be seen if a victory of Desert Storm's scale can be repeated. Despite President Clinton's pledge to retain American military strength, the shift from one major adversary to a host of regional threats calls into question traditional planning and force structure.

ORGANIZATION

The Marine Corps by law is authorized to maintain an active-duty three-division and three-aircraft-wing Fleet Marine Force. A Marine Corps no larger than 200,000 has been a constant defense planning factor since the end of the Korean War. Only during the height of U.S. involvement in the Vietnam War did the Marine Corps surpass the Korean War level of 230,488, reaching 314,417 Marines in 1969. The Corps at the end of fiscal year 1994 numbered 174,000 on active duty. Its end strength is planned to stabilize at this level, retaining the ability to form three Marine Expeditionary Forces (MEFs) if augmented by its organized reserve force of 42,000 officers and enlisted Marines and the 70,000 more Marines in the Individual Ready Reserve.[7]

During the "Base Force" planning developed by the Chairman of the Joint Chiefs of Staff in 1991, the Marine Corps received guidance that it should plan for a Fleet Marine Force (FMF) built upon a total strength of 159,000 officers and men. A Commandant's Force Structure Planning Group in 1992 produced a three-division–three-wing FMF to fit such a personnel level (unhappily so), but this force bore scant resemblance to the FMF as it then existed. For example, each division would drop an infantry regiment and fill the void with a combined-arms armored regiment that looked much like an Army mechanized brigade and would have been too expensive to equip and too immobile to deploy on amphibious shipping. Nevertheless, the FMF received official approval when Commandant Carl E. Mundy, Jr., published *Marine Corps 2001,* a ten-year plan for force modernization. Headquarters Marine Corps, however, never embraced the 159,000 ceiling and worked to overturn the CJCS recommendation the following year (1993). General Mundy ordered another study, made by the Structure Review Group, that reported that *Marine Corps 2001* had already been overtaken by events. To meet its likely commitments, the Marine Corps required 177,000 active-duty members to man an adequate (and reduced) Fleet Marine Force, which could be streamlined by eliminating command elements (the brigades) and some combat support and combat service support elements. In the meantime, the continuing shrinkage of the Corps down to 183,000 produced relatively little institutional trauma, for 1993 was not 1973.[8]

Then Secretary of Defense Les Aspin's decision to set Marine Corps end strength at 174,000 reflected a realization, especially in Congress, that regional warfare required the existence of an amphibious ready force capable of rapid crisis response. The "new internationalism" of the Clinton administration emphasized the need for naval expeditionary forces that require little or no additional augmentation to carry out missions short of all-out war. Secretary Aspin's *Bottom-Up Review* (September 1993) established that forward deployment, crisis response, and the capability to fight two major regional conflicts required a Fleet Marine Force of five active brigades, but military planners thought this number too low by half. Such persistent strength-missions disconnects are not new for the Marine Corps, but they are no less troublesome.[9]

The readiness of the Marine Corps is found within the framework of the Marine Air-Ground Task Force (MAGTF). This organization provides a force structure that is tailored for specific missions. The MAGTF provides a fleet commander or theater commander with a highly trained, flexible force that can be task organized for a variety of missions from noncombatant evacuation operations (NEOs) to humanitarian missions to combat. This flexibility was in fact demonstrated during these operations:

Provide Comfort	1991	Iraq
Sea Angel	1991	Bangladesh
Guantanamo	1992	Haiti and Cuba
Provide Promise	1992	Yugoslavia
Provide Relief	1992	Kenya/Somalia
Provide Hope	1992	Somalia

The Marine Air-Ground Task Force (MAGTF)

A Marine Air-Ground Task Force is an integrated, combined-arms force containing ground combat, air, and combat service support elements under a single commander. It is structured and equipped for amphibious operations and the defense of advanced naval bases in support of a naval campaign.[10] The origin of the MAGTF dates back to the winter maneuvers off Culebra, Puerto Rico, in January 1914 with the introduction of the airplane into Marine operations. Despite the limited capabilities of the early aircraft, Marine Corps visionaries, notably Major Alfred A. Cunningham, the "father" of Marine Corps aviation, foresaw the potential of ground-air cooperation. Marines pioneered the use of aircraft in the role of close air support during counterinsurgency operations, first in Haiti (1919) and later in Nicaragua (1927–1931). During the Pacific campaign in World War II (1941–1945) and the Korean War (1950–1953), the air and ground Marine combat units, together and separately, conducted major amphibious landings and extended ground operations. The Marine air-ground expeditionary force, codified by an agreement between the Army and the Navy as early as 1927, was the forerunner of today's MAGTF. This agreement stated that the Marine Corps would provide and maintain forces "for land operations in support of the fleet for the initial seizure and defense of advanced bases and for such limited auxiliary land operations as are essential to the prosecution of the naval campaign."[11] Established in 1933 to execute this mission, the Fleet Marine Force (FMF) proved its value in World War II.

While the Fleet Marine Force remains the administrative and operational headquarters, the MAGTF serves as the actual combat power in the execution of a naval campaign. A MAGTF would, in fact, be the "task-organized" element of an FMF, "an integrated, balanced air-ground combined arms force organized for combat with its own combat service support element (CSSE) . . . [and] . . . employed to apply ground combat power supported by the MAGTF's own aviation combat element and CSSE."[12]

MAGTFs may vary in size, but the organizational structure will always include a single Command Element (CE) with a Ground Combat Element (GCE), Aviation Combat Element (ACE), and a Combat Service Support Element (CSSE). Although there are always four major elements within a MAGTF, other temporary, separate task organizations may be required to perform combat service support (CSS) functions. The commanders of these separate organizations report directly to the MAGTF commander. These organizations may include, but are not limited to, landing support, engineer, force reconnaissance, artillery, and electronic warfare task organizations.[13] The flexibility built into the MAGTF is deliberate since the FMF serves as "the nation's primary hedge against strategic uncertainty, and their operational planning and task organizational concepts have been developed to meet that role on short notice."[14]

The successful defense of Saudi Arabia can be attributed to the rapid deployment of Army and Marine forces after the initial Iraqi invasion of Kuwait. Part of this success can be credited to the fleet of prepositioned logistics shipping in the Indian and Pacific oceans. Another part was the rapid deployment of a Marine expeditionary brigade during the first two weeks of Operation Desert Shield. The Marine-Army response was, in fact, a primary example of how the rapid deployment force might have reacted to a Soviet invasion of Iran in a similar scenario. The ability of the Marine Corps and Army to deploy rapidly during the initial days of Desert Shield demonstrated the intrinsic value of such floating supply depots as an enhancement to expeditionary forces in general and amphibious forces in particular.

There are two basic types of Marine Air-Ground Task Forces that can be utilized to perform any number of missions. They are the Marine Expeditionary Unit (MEU) and the Marine Expeditionary Force (MEF). The MEU is the smallest MAGTF and is thus restricted in the missions it is capable of carrying out. The MEF provides the combat power necessary for any initial lodgement on a hostile shore and sufficient firepower to defend an area until reinforced by U.S. or allied forces. The MEF's war-fighting capability is enhanced by its ability to employ both fixed- and rotary-wing aircraft for complex offensive air operations, all integrated with ground combat units' mobile warfare.

The Marine Expeditionary Unit (MEU)

The MEU is built around a Battalion Landing Team (BLT) and a composite aviation squadron. It is commanded by a colonel and is attached to a naval task force that patrols a major ocean or sea in support of U.S. geostrategic interests. Weaponry of a MEU includes standard infantry battalion weapons, an artillery battery, a company of amphibious assault vehicles, a platoon of light armored reconnaissance vehicles (LAVs), and a platoon or more of tanks. With its command and support elements, it numbers around 2,000 Marines. The MEU provides an immediate reaction capability to crisis situations and is capable of limited combat operations. The operations most associated with a MEU are the following:

Humanitarian and disaster relief assistance

Noncombatant evacuation operations

Tactical recovery of aircraft and personnel

Counterdrug operations

Amphibious raids

Embassy security and protection of U.S. government property

Show-of-force operations

Each MEU that leaves Camp Lejeune, North Carolina, Camp Pendleton, California, or Okinawa is required to be trained and certified as ''special operations capable'' and receives the designation MEU (SOC). This force is capable of performing limited special operations without additional reinforcements. The MEU receives sustainment from the accompanying fleet and is not self-sufficient in combat operations beyond fifteen days.

In the event of major commitments, a MEU will be reinforced with other Marine units and placed under the control of the next higher echelon, the Marine Expeditionary Force. The Marine Expeditionary Force is built around at least a Regimental Landing Team, a composite Marine Aircraft Group, and a combat service support group (strength 5,000–6,000) and is commanded by a general officer. The MEF may be deployed afloat or dispatched to a crisis area by air to join maritime or land prepositioned supplies and equipment. The advance elements of a MEF can be forward deployed for extended periods, receiving their support from a sea base or facilities ashore. The MEF could consist of a fly-in echelon, an amphibious assault echelon, and an assault follow-on echelon. The MEF's organic Combat Service Support Element enables the force to move rapidly into a hostile environment until reinforced or withdrawn. Aviation support for the MEF is either carrier based or shore based at advanced airfields. The MEF will also be capable of participating in joint operations ashore with Army and other allied forces in time of war. A MEF, besides the standard infantry weapons organic to one or more Marine infantry regiments, has artillery battalions, tank companies, light armored reconnaissance companies, and antitank (TOW) companies. In short, the MEF can carry out a wide range of combat operations from low- to mid-intensity levels. These include the following:

1. A follow-on reinforcement for a committed MEU or other forces
2. Amphibious operations, that is, assaults, raids, demonstrations, or withdrawals
3. Operations in support of a maritime campaign, such as the seizure or defense of an advanced naval or air base
4. Low-intensity-conflict operations, such as counterinsurgency, counterterrorism, counterdrug actions, peacekeeping, or peacetime contingency operations
5. Humanitarian assistance/disaster relief
6. Evacuation operations/protection of U.S. government property or individuals

A MEF may be organized with variable task organizations and structure, tailored for any intensity of combat and capable of deploying to any geographic region of the world. Forming a MEF can include combining existing forward-afloat forces, land-based forces, mission-deployed forces, maritime and prepositioned equipment and supplies, additional forces from another MEF, and units of Selected Marine Corps Reserve (SMCR) or the members of the Individual Ready Reserve (IRR).

Special Purpose Marine Air-Ground Task Force (SPMAGTF)

The SPMAGTF is designed for a highly specialized mission of limited duration that requires relatively small numbers (fewer than 1,000 Marines and sailors) and high-skill combat and support specialities. The SPMAGTF concept received its first test in 1988 during a series of raids upon Iranian oil platforms serving as maritime commando bases in the Persian Gulf. One characteristic of the SPMAGTF is that it is capable of operating from ships that are not usually assigned as amphibious assault ships, for example, a Navy attack carrier or a landing ship dock. The SPMAGTF has thus far received mixed reviews since its ''special'' characteristics are of limited capability, and its operating functions are incompatible with those of an attack carrier. SPMAGTF enthusiasts argue that an *Iowa*-class battleship (four are now in storage) could be reconfigured to handle a SPMAGTF that would take its own naval gunfire with it.

Maritime Prepositioning Ships (MPSs)

A major concern for the deployment of the MEF is the shortage of amphibious shipping. Although the Navy enjoyed a decade of unparalleled growth in the 1980s, amphibious ships did not top the list of building priorities. This shortage of sufficient amphibious lift remains a serious constraint on deploying a Marine Expeditionary Force with its entire complement of combat power. To meet the needs of a Marine Air-Ground Task Force, estimated at a minimum of 15,000 Marines, the Navy and Marine Corps developed the concept of Maritime Prepositioning Ships (MPSs), whereby a squadron of combat-loaded cargo and conveyor vessels are prepositioned in the Indian Ocean, Western Pacific, and Eastern Atlantic. Designed to join the forward-deploying elements of a Marine Expeditionary Force, providing replenishment and reinforcement with heavy armor and assault vehicles as well as spare parts, fuel, and other critical logistical needs, MPS squadrons ensure a rapid buildup. The Marine Corps has three MPS squadrons, composed of thirteen ships, assigned to the Fleet Marine Force. Each squadron carries the supplies for a 16,000-man expeditionary force for thirty days. The MPS squadrons, as occurred in the Persian Gulf crisis, will sail upon activation to a point of rendezvous with the ground service support elements. The ability to sustain such a force with a self-contained logistics capability is a key element in amphibious operations as well as a crisis in Southwest or Southeast Asia. Lessons learned from Desert Storm, as well as the Marine Corps' adoption of the M1A1 Abrams tank, revealed the necessity for an increase in lift capability. Plans are under way to put an MPS squadron in the Mediterranean. The Commandant and the Chief of Naval Operations (CNO) agree that the addition of one more MPS to each of the three squadrons will go a long way toward addressing the shortfall in amphibious prepositioning.[15]

Amphibious Ready Group (ARG)

Under current JCS requirements for an Amphibious Ready Group (ARG), one for each of three critical theaters, the Navy plans to maintain eleven amphibious squadrons, but would like twelve. At the center of each ARG is the ''big-deck'' amphibious assault ship in three different classes: the third-generation LHA; the second-generation LHD; and the first-generation LPH. The Navy plans to replace four other current ship classes with the LPD-17 amphibious assault ship, a program it wants to start in fiscal year 1996. The current forty-ship amphibious fleet will remain stable through fiscal year 1998 with seven additions and seven retirements. The long-term plan is to have an amphibious force in 2008 of thirty-six ships: twelve LHA/LHDs, twelve LPD-17s, and twelve LSD-41s, which will replace all other classes of ships designed for assault and logistical functions. This force alone will not provide the number and types of ships the Marine Corps needs.[16]

The Marine Corps Reserve

One of the more important tests of Desert Shield/Desert Storm was the activation and employment of Selected Marine Corps Reserve (SMCR) units and members of the Individual Ready Reserve (IRR). The successful augmentation by Marine reserve forces during the war in the Persian Gulf validated the Total Force concept. A post–Desert Storm analysis of the Marine Corps Reserve's participation highlighted this last point:

> Beginning in August 1990 over 31,000 Marine reservists (24,300 SMCR/IMA; 6,200 IRR; 600 retirees) were activated, and 13,000 deployed to SWA [Southwest Asia]. This mobilization [of the Marine Corps Reserve], the first for the Marine Corps since 1950, was a massive and demanding test of existing policies, structures and procedures.[17]

The successful activation of the Marine Corps Reserve during the Persian Gulf War has, nonetheless, raised the issue of its future. With the drawdown cutting both reserve and active budgets, the entire Marine Corps Reserve may require restructuring in order to meet future crises. Indeed, the SMCR went to war in August 1990 very much like it would have against a Soviet-led invasion of Iran or Norway, incrementally, with the mind-set that the "war would go on for some time or that even later arriving force would still be required." As Lieutenant Colonel Mark Cancian wrote, "Current planning assumption is for regional conflicts that provide for shorter warning times and conflicts." Cancian added that the philosophy of "better late than never" no longer applies, replaced by "better never than late" since forces that cannot deploy rapidly are useless.[18] Despite these and other criticisms, maintenance of a well-structured Marine Corps Reserve force not only is necessary, but will be vital in the post–Cold War era. One reason is the fact that Marine Corps SMCR units as well as the IRR offer a vital "surge" of trained manpower into the existing Fleet Marine Force. The second is the low-cost–high-return value of reserve forces. Congress is less likely to cut reserve forces.

Recognizing the inherent value of potent reserve capability, HQMC has reorganized the reserves into a single command, Marine Reserve Forces (MARESFOR). Activated on 1 July 1992 to streamline the command and control of the 4th Marine Division (4th MarDiv), 4th Marine Aircraft Wing (4th MAW),

4th Force Service Support Group, and the Marine Corps Reserve Support Command (MCRSC), MARESFOR is commanded by a regular major general with a consolidated general staff, headquartered in New Orleans.

The mission of MARESFOR

> is to provide trained units and qualified individuals to augment, reinforce, or reconstitute the Active Component in time of war, national emergency, and at such other times as national security requires; during peacetime the MARESFOR organizes, trains, and prepares Marine Reserve units and individuals for involuntary active duty as directed by a presidential call-up or mobilization order.[19]

Marine Reserve Forces will remain a vital component of the FMF. The Select Marine Corps Reserve is expected to remain at 42,000 officers and enlisted men and the IRR at around 60,000.

DEPLOYMENT AND STATIONING

The post–Cold War environment has brought about significant changes in the deployment and stationing of U.S. forces abroad. For the Marine Corps and the Navy, the loss of Subic Bay in the Philippines imposes some limitation on operations in the Pacific. The reduction in U.S. military personnel will also influence current and future deployment patterns for Marines. Current operational requirements have resulted in 23 percent of all Marines being deployed at any given time. Department of Defense (DOD) figures indicate that Fleet Marine Force units spend an average of 43 percent of their time deployed. Prior to the restoration of a 174,000-man Marine Corps, the DOD-mandated force reductions would have restricted the FMF size to 94,000 Marines (roughly the number of Marines in the Persian Gulf in February 1991) with the same missions of today's 119,000-Marine FMF.[20] This would have resulted in FMF units being deployed an average of 57 percent of the time. Critics of the reductions and the increased deployment time claim that both readiness and quality of personnel would suffer as a result of this high operational tempo. The Marine Corps, under the newly mandated force restructuring, will be able to maintain a FMF at a force level of 115,000 Marines.

Historically, reduced personnel and increased operational deployments have resulted in a degradation of readiness as well as turmoil in personnel assignments. One study compared the unavoidable increase in personnel deployment rates and resulting morale problems to the chaos immediately after the Vietnam War. During that period the Marine Corps faced serious external criticism and internal argument about its mission, force structure, and personnel policies. Despite the stresses that resulted from its war in Vietnam, the Marine Corps quickly refocused its attention on amphibious warfare and several neglected training programs. Force modernization and retraining succumbed to the pressure of reduced budgets and personnel problems that then affected the FMF's ability to support NATO during the early to mid-1970s as well as meet routine contingency deployments.

Former Commandant of the Marine Corps General Alfred M. Gray in his annual report to Congress for 1989 summed up the problem:

> We cannot allow ourselves to regress to an era of budget driven strategy. Rather our strategy must be firmly based upon our enduring national interests and an assessment of the threat to these interests.[21]

Borrowing a line from the nineteenth-century naval theorist Alfred Thayer Mahan, Gray added:

> As a maritime nation, we cannot dismiss our geography and the unique requirements it imposes. We are dependent on the free use of the sea lines of communication and access to the natural resources of the world for our economic and security needs. . . . The changes in the international security environment provide a golden opportunity for us to reassess our position, take advantage of these changes and pursue our goals in a manner consistent with our national character.[22]

. . . From the Sea

In September 1992 the Navy Department published a reshaped concept for naval strategy. The naval strategy of . . . *From the Sea* replaced the ''Maritime Strategy,'' which focused on naval forces designed to secure command of the seas from the Soviet fleet. The new concept stresses naval expeditionary forces capable of projecting U.S. power into the littoral regions of the world. This littoral strategy places a premium on the capability to enter a region by force if necessary, exploiting military organizations that possess the capability to operate from the sea and are able to project land and air combat power beyond the shoreline.[23]

. . . *From the Sea* is a return to the expeditionary role the Marine Corps and the Navy held prior to World War II. The term ''expeditionary implies a mind set, a culture, and a commitment to forces that are designed to operate forward and to respond swiftly.'' According to . . . *From the Sea,* naval expeditionary forces are

> *Swift to Respond, on Short Notice, to Crises in Distant Lands:* Naval Forces, deployed overseas, are poised to respond to national tasking. Recent examples include the initial rapid response to meet the requirements for Desert Shield and provide the assistance to storm-battered Bangladesh and the war-torn Kurds following Desert Storm.
>
> *Structured to Build Power from the Sea When Required by National Demands:* The Navy and Marine Corps ''sea-air-land'' team is capable of a full range of action—from port visits and humanitarian relief to major offensive operations. Even as Desert Shield intensified, tailored naval forces responded to evacuation requirements in both Liberia and Somalia.

Able to Sustain Support for Long-Term Operations: Ships at sea in remote areas of the world have a healthy self-sufficiency. Naval forces can remain on station for extended periods. Amphibious forces remained off Liberia for seven months. The USS *Eisenhower* task force remained in the Indian Ocean at sea for five months during the Iranian Hostage Crisis.

Unrestricted by the Need for Transit or Overflight Approval from Foreign Governments in Order to Enter the Scene of Action: The international respect for freedom of the seas guarantees legal access up to the territorial waters of all coastal countries of the world. This affords naval forces the unique capability to provide a peaceful presence in ambiguous situations before a crisis erupts.

The MAGTF, in short, allows the Amphibious Task Force to project one kind of combat power ashore ''at a time and place of its choosing.'' The Marine Corps hopes to redefine the traditional notion of sequential, phased amphibious assaults with the more flexible concept of Operational Maneuver from the Sea (OMFTS), which treats the shoreline as a ''permissive boundary, not a crude natural defense that limits maneuver.'' The assumption is that faster amphibious ships, landing craft, and aircraft will allow the landing force to avoid obvious landing sites and prepared enemy defenses. The amphibious force can also maneuver with greater freedom to avoid air and missile attacks. The landing force and the amphibious force can maneuver in such ways as to deceive the enemy, take advantage of natural conditions like weather and night, and counter the enemy's electronic warfare efforts. The doctrine of . . . *From the Sea* builds upon the operational concept of over-the-horizon landings to project sufficient combat power ashore within a limited period of time. The Navy's Landing Craft Air Cushion (LCAC) and the ongoing development of the V-22 Osprey will enhance the MAGTF's capability for a wide range of operations with more speed and surprise. Incorporating technological advances of the past decade, the doctrine of . . . *From the Sea* reaffirms the Marine Corps role as an expeditionary force-in-readiness.

Force Composition

. . . *From the Sea* depends upon the ability of the Marine Corps to form a MAGTF of appropriate combat power for each crisis. The Ground Combat Element (GCE) provides ground combat task forces of infantry, armor, and artillery. The GCE also has engineer, reconnaissance, amphibious assault, maintenance, supply, medical, and communications units. The GCE, in most instances, is formed around an infantry battalion landing team (1,000-plus Marines). The regimental landing team is built upon three infantry battalions that have an organic fire-support capability (mortars and antitank weapons as well as light and heavy machine guns) and their own combat service support (CSS) capability. A Marine division has three infantry regiments, an artillery regiment, and tank, amphibious assault, light armored reconnaissance, and combat service support battalions. While Marine infantry regiments are essentially foot mobile, they can be moved by the division's motor transportation assets as well as their own light tactical vehicles.[24]

The Aviation Combat Element (ACE) consists of a Marine aircraft wing, group, or squadron that is task organized to provide tactical air support before or during ground operations. The ACE can establish expeditionary airfields after the execution of an amphibious landing. One of the ACE's main tasks during an amphibious landing and the subsequent push inland is to provide close air support for the MAGTF. The MAGTF commander, in fact, may have at his disposal the V/STOL AV-8B Harrier, F/A-18 Hornet, A-6 Intruder, and the AH-1W Cobra attack helicopter for a wide range of tactical air missions. Some aircraft can support operations from the decks of the various classes of amphibious assault ships as well as from fixed bases and Navy carriers.

The ACE is also tasked with carrying out other support functions that include offensive air support, reconnaissance, antiair warfare, assault support, electronic warfare, and the control of aircraft and missiles. These functions are provided in accordance with the tactical situation and the size of the MAGTF. Each ACE has much the same combat support and combat service support components found in the GCE. There is only one aviation combat element in a MAGTF. It includes those aviation command and air control agencies, combat, combat support, and combat service support units required by the mission. Its helicopter component is tailored to perform a wide range of missions that include the insertion of Marine reconnaissance units, heliborne assaults, and retrieving downed aircraft and pilots as well as assisting in the evacuation of American and foreign nationals.

During both the air and ground phases of Operation Desert Storm, Marine Corps aviation flew close air support and air interdiction missions for Marine and coalition troops in the Kuwait Theater of Operations. While the overall performance of Marine air assets was judged good to excellent, problems did appear that in a protracted conflict could have resulted in reducing the air campaign's overall effectiveness. These problems, while not as severe as during the Vietnam War, suggested that in a future conflict "we cannot fight as we did in the last war." Problems included a degradation in the intelligence, communications, and command and control of air assets as well as the predictable discovery that the F/A-18, while an excellent air-superiority and close-attack fighter, is not a level bomber in the class of the A-6. As one Marine Corps assessment of the air war during Desert Storm stated:

> The War in Southwest Asia did not prove that we could defeat a well motivated, competently led and modern equipped force. Even though the Marine Corps was probably the best prepared for battle in the initial stages of this war, its initial deployment did not prove that the Marine Corps could have successfully defended itself against a disciplined attack.[25]

The single most important current aviation issue is the development of the tiltrotor V-22 Osprey, a twin-engined aircraft that is intended to replace the venerable CH-46 Sea Knight and CH-55D Sea Stallion transport helicopters, which have been in the Corps' inventory since the 1960s. Production problems, in-flight accidents, cost, and skeptical defense officials have put the aircraft's future in doubt. While the V-22's future remains uncertain, its lift capability and troop-carrying capacity make it a prime candidate to replace the CH-46 as the expeditionary aircraft of the next century.

The last major part in the MAGTF is the Combat Service Support Element (CSSE). The CSSE is a task organization that provides combat service support that air and ground organic elements cannot provide. Combat service support units are responsible for any or all of the logistical functions required by a MAGTF: supply, first- and second-echelon maintenance, landing support, engineer, medical/dental, automated data processing, material-handling equipment, personnel administration, military police, and motor transport. A CSSE can be formed to support any size or type of MAGTF.

Marine logisticians during Desert Shield and Desert Storm demonstrated the need for mobile, well-equipped, and well-organized logistics forces. The war in Southwest Asia proved again that efficient logistical support affords a commander more flexibility and allows the attack to continue uninterrupted with as little loss in momentum as possible. The 2nd Force Service Support Group (FSSG) prior to the ground war, for instance, moved 34,000 short tons of ammunition, POL (petroleum, oil, and lubricants), and other supplies ninety miles from Kibrit in eastern Saudi Arabia to a new logistics base in the desert. This new logistics base close to enemy territory provided immediate support to the two Marine divisions that breached the Iraqi lines in Kuwait with such astonishing rapidity. The other logistics success story came from the aviation side of the Marine Corps. Aviation logistical support, one post–Desert Storm analysis concluded, was excellent and matched the operational tempo.[26]

Most postwar analyses of Marine Corps logistics during Desert Shield gave overall Marine performance high marks for the speed of unloading and distribution of the MPS equipment and supplies during the first months of the operation. While these efforts by the 1st and 2nd FSSGs were commendable, logistical limitations might have spelled disaster had the Iraqis attacked the support forces. These problems included the disorganized unloading of supplies from the MPS ships at Al Jubayl. The muddled distribution and transportation of such items as spare parts and JP-4 fuel eroded the effectiveness of the first Marine combat units deployed along the Saudi-Kuwaiti border area. Given the tempo of both the ground and air campaigns during Desert Storm, the logistics system might not have functioned efficiently had the war continued much beyond forty-odd days.

While Marine logistics support in the Gulf was initially capable of handling the massive influx of supplies coming off the MPS shipping during the first weeks of Desert Shield, serious flaws developed in the unloading and distribution of supplies because of the misidentification and disorganization of the numerous containers unloaded at Saudi ports. This latter problem was largely due to the initial lack of trained FSSG personnel (Landing Support Battalion) at the outset of Desert Shield as well as an insufficient number of heavy vehicles capable of moving the supplies forward. Marine logisticians encountered "monumental difficulties created by the geography and environment, the constant shortage of organic assets, the demanding organizational taskings required for maneuver warfare, and the battlefield distance factor." Prior to Desert Shield/ Desert Storm, truck companies were deleted from the division, degrading Marine transportation capabilities.[27]

While overall performance of Marine combat service support operations was rated good, a much broader analysis of the operational performance of CSSE units during the war in the Gulf is necessary before any reduction of CSSE assets is undertaken. Current plans call for the retention of two 8,000-man Force Service Support Groups, stationed at Camp Lejeune and Camp Pendleton, respectively. A third FSSG, numbering approximately 4,000 Marines, would remain in Okinawa, to be reinforced from the United States by both active-duty and reserve Marines in time of war. Marine Corps CSSE capabilities may be a major limitation upon the expeditionary mission.[28]

Current Deployment

Current MAGTF deployments provide the National Command Authority with accessible, combat-ready forces that can be deployed within forty-eight hours of notification and even less time for an afloat MEU, depending on its location. By utilizing the three squadrons of MPS shipping, strategic airlift, and amphibious ships, the Marine Corps can dispatch an expeditionary force to a regional "hot spot" with a mix of ground and air units. These units are capable of establishing a lodgement until relieved or reinforced by more Marines or by U.S. Army or allied forces.

The normal operating areas of the three Marine Expeditionary Forces reflect the geographical regions of potential crises. The I MEF is based at Camp Pendleton, Twentynine Palms, and the El Toro air base, California. I MEF can dispatch forces to the Western Pacific, the Caribbean, and the Mediterranean. I MEF also provides a standby Marine expeditionary force aligned with MPSRON-2 in the Indian Ocean for employment in the United States Central Command (USCENTCOM) area of responsibility in Southwest Asia and the Middle East.

II MEF is stationed at Camp Lejeune and Cherry Point, North Carolina, and has as its main responsibility Europe, the west coast of Africa, and the eastern coastline of South and Central America. II MEF's operations and responsibilities are focused on Southwest Asia, the Middle East, or on the Korean peninsula, but it has historically focused on reinforcing NATO in northern Europe (primarily Norway, Denmark, and northern Germany) or its Mediterranean flank (Italy, Greece, Turkey). If employed in northern Europe, it can use equipment prepositioned in Norway during the Cold War.

III MEF is stationed in the Western Pacific with its headquarters and major forces located at Okinawa and Iwakuni, Japan, and it controls the 1st Marine Brigade located at Kaneohe Bay, Hawaii. III MEF has as its area of responsibility Japan as well as Korea, mainland Asia, and the Western Pacific. III MEF in time of war can reinforce or be reinforced by I MEF, particularly on the Korean peninsula. III MEF also has units continuously deployed aboard ships of the Seventh Fleet. While each MEF has different methods and contingency plans shaped by its regional area of responsibility, they are organized to ensure interoperability.

WEAPONRY

Despite the success enjoyed by the Marine Corps during Desert Shield/Desert Storm, the performance of certain weapons demonstrated the critical need to replace or refine existing systems. While the war proved the viability of the Corps' maneuver warfare doctrine, the return to maritime expeditionary warfare requires innovation in the use of existing weapons systems and the fielding of new materiel. The requirements of amphibious or riverine warfare will demand not only the integration of a new line of amphibious assault vehicles, but also the adoption of either the revolutionary V-22 Osprey or a new medium-lift helicopter. These two critical systems will largely determine the operational flexibility of the MAGTF in the post–Cold War era.

The current amphibious assault vehicle, the LVTP7A1, entered the Fleet Marine Force in 1972 and has undergone several improvements, the latest completed in 1986. These improvements have included rearmament and structural strengthening in order to increase survivability on the modern battlefield. The last series of changes to the LVTP7A1 ended with the addition of the MK19 40-millimeter grenade launcher and plates of ceramic tile in order to absorb the impact of Soviet antitank guided missiles (ATGMs).

Despite these upgrades, however, the current AAV's service life is limited to ten more years. The decision to replace the AAV-7 is almost as old as the current family of waterborne assault vehicles itself. In fact, when the AAV-7 entered the FMF in early 1973, Marines wondered if the speed of the LVT-7 was sufficient to support advanced concepts of amphibious operations. This perception was reinforced by the U.S. Navy's belief that ship vulnerability would require more standoff distance from the shore. The Navy wanted an ''over-the-horizon'' (OTH) capability, which meant that all forms of ship-to-shore transport would require more speed and range.[29] The high-speed system the Navy chose is the Landing Craft Air Cushion (LCAC), which entered the inventory in 1985, but Marines do not regard the LCAC as an AAV substitute. The Marine Corps studied alternatives to the AAV that would provide the Marine Corps with a vehicle that had high water speed, the capability to land Marines from ships twenty-five miles out to sea, and reduced vulnerability.

Despite the Navy's insistence that the Marine Corps acquire one experimental vehicle, Commandant Louis H. Wilson, Jr., cancelled the Marine Corps' participation in the program (1978), citing the vehicle's prohibitive cost and maintenance and operational complexities. Testifying before the House Armed Services Committee, Wilson refuted the Navy's claim that an amphibious force would have to stand twenty-five miles off shore or more from a defended beach. The Commandant believed that "such a standoff distance is not required for the initial assault wave." Despite this Marine Corps action and subsequent block upgrades of the AAV, the Navy insisted upon the "over-the horizon" employment concept. Since a new high-water-speed amphibious assault vehicle might not be necessary for a successful amphibious assault, a 1983 Department of the Navy study hinted at the need for "multimission craft" capable of high-water-speed operations and a heavy-load logistical capability. This study left unanswered the problem of finding a suitable vehicle for the inland phase of an amphibious assault, when the AAV serves as an armored personnel carrier.

The Marine Corps has decided to upgrade again the current AAV-7s despite their slow water and land speeds. The upgrading of the AAV-7A1 has been termed a block upgrade program. According to the Director, Amphibious Vehicle Test Directorate, there are five phases to the upgrade, and testing has started on the Block II (second-phase) upgrade. The Block II upgrades are an improved suspension, improved transmission, and a 500-horsepower engine sometime after fiscal year 1997. The upgrades are linked to the advanced amphibious assault vehicle program and will stop if and when the AAAV program is approved.[30] The service life of the current AAV-7A1 has been extended to the first decade of the next century with the hope that the AAAV or some variant will then enter the Fleet Marine Force.

Marine Corps officers recognize that, despite the upgrades of the AAV-7A1, its battlefield survivability could be limited in any future conflict because of its low water speed; lack of firepower; inadequate armor protection; inadequate nuclear, biological, and chemical (NBC) and electromagnetic protection; low cross-country speed; and inadequate night/all-weather fighting capability. The performance of the AAV during the Gulf War was, nonetheless, creditable enough for its continued use as an infantry carrier until the AAAV enters service. Those AAVs that had upgraded weapons stations provided an even greater capability to deliver suppressive fire. Those AAVs that had appliqué armor were better suited for combat. Unfortunately, appliqué armor, new weapons, and sensors were not in sufficient supply to outfit the entire mechanized force.[31]

The Marine Corps seeks a replacement to the 7A1 series of amphibious assault vehicles. After testing thirteen candidates, the evaluators concluded that a high-water-speed advanced amphibious assault vehicle (AAAV) is "the most operationally effective system of all the options under consideration."[32] The AAAV concept is currently being evaluated by Headquarters and primary contractors that include General Dynamics, AAI Corporation, and FMC, the primary contractor for the current family of Marine AAVs. In response to the Navy's "From the Sea" doctrine, the Marine Corps had established that any new amphibious tractor must be able to "successfully conduct operational maneuver from the sea . . . beyond the range of enemy conventional surface radar and direct fire weapons." Marine planners base their analysis on a decline of the number of Navy amphibious carriers and the expectation that the AAAV will enter service in conjunction with a new medium-lift helicopter or the V-22. With the introduction of the AAAV and the V-22, along with the high-speed LCACs, the Commander Amphibious Task Force (CATF) will have at his disposal a more mobile landing force. Critics of the AAAV concept claim, however, that the introduction of the LCAC has already given the Marine Corps the necessary over-the-horizon capability that combines speed with the ability to bring sufficient tanks and artillery ashore quickly.

Requirements for the AAAV include the ability to travel faster than twenty knots (twenty-three miles per hour) over water rather than the current eight miles per hour in water. While either amphibious assault vehicle can achieve the same land cruising range of twenty-five to thirty miles per hour, the AAAV's 30-millimeter Bushmaster chain gun and a state-of-the-art navigation system make it an improvement over the AAV-7A1. The AAAV's greater armor protection system will enable it to defeat an impact from a 14.5-millimeter armor-piercing projectile at 300 meters. The AAAV has a much better nuclear, chemical, and biological detection and protection system that may be a necessity even for fighting a Third World foe. The disadvantages of the AAAV include its weight, which is approximately ten tons more than the current AAV, which means that it will use more fuel ashore. Maintenance and performance concerns (both on ship and in the field) have placed severe restraints on the research and development of the AAAV. The AAAV is at best a decade away from becoming an operational reality. Current plans call for the fielding of approximately 900–1,000 vehicles of all types. Full funding for the AAAV program may not occur until the beginning of the next century. The Corps will pursue development of the AAAV or a suitable replacement while maintaining the current fleet of AAV-7A1s until at least 2005.[33]

The V-22 Osprey

First tested in 1989, the V-22 Osprey represents another milestone in the Marine Corps' involvement with unique aircraft. The Osprey, currently under development by Bell Helicopter's Textron Division and Boeing Helicopter, is the culmination of tiltrotor development. The V-22 combines the best features of the helicopter and turboprop aircraft. This aircraft will represent a further refinement of the Marine Corps' concept of vertical assault if and when it joins the Fleet Marine Force.

The Osprey, much like the troubled AAAV program, has met with several near-fatal setbacks that threatened to halt further development of the program. Crashes, budgetary restraints, the presence of a less expensive competitor, and a reluctant Secretary of Defense have delayed the full production of the V-22. Development and production of the V-22 will greatly enhance the ability of a Marine Expeditionary Force to strike beyond the Force Beachhead Line (FBHL) during the initial phases of an amphibious landing. The V-22 will also assist Special Purpose Marine Air-Ground Task Forces in carrying out raids, reconnaissance, and intelligence missions more effectively than the current fleet of CH-53s.

The Osprey combines the capabilities of a fixed-wing turboprop aircraft with those of a helicopter. The V-22 can carry payloads farther and faster than conventional helicopters. The Osprey provides the Marine Corps with flexibility far beyond the available helicopters. The speed of the V-22, able to cruise at speeds up to 300 knots, gives the Marines the ability to strike more quickly from as far as 200 miles away. If armed with a cannon and Hellfire antitank missiles as well as an assortment of air-to-air defenses, the V-22 might provide better inflight and air-to-ground fire support for a Marine assault force. Equipped with automatic folding wings, as many as sixteen V-22s can be deployed aboard current Navy amphibious assault ships of the LHA and LHD types. In one wave, 384 combat-loaded Marines (24 per aircraft) can be inserted well beyond the FBHL, thus enabling the ground combat element to widen the battlefield faster than traditional airborne or heliborne operations. The V-22's lifting capability enhances its ability to insert heavy weapons as external loads. The lifting capability will provide Marine infantrymen with more firepower at a much faster rate than with the current fleet of CH-53s and CH-46s.[34]

Production and development problems, however, have set the V-22 program back. Although five V-22 prototypes have been built since 1989, two have crashed, further delaying the decision to proceed with production of this aircraft. Former Secretary of Defense Richard Cheney, the most outspoken critic of the V-22, suggested that further testing of the V-22 be halted in favor of developing a more suitable medium-lift helicopter. Congress ignored Cheney and other critics and authorized continued funding of the tiltrotor aircraft in addition to the research and development of a new medium-lift helicopter. Before leaving office, Cheney proposed that limited funding continue until "such problems as the weight, engine, and flight-test shortcomings" are solved or a new medium-lift helicopter program is introduced. The former Secretary of Defense added that a "final decision of whether the V-22, or a new medium-lift helicopter would be the means to meet the further needs of the armed forces would be left for future years, when the value of each approach has been shown."[35]

Despite the problems that have beset the V-22 program, the tiltrotor enhances the ability of the Marine Corps to conduct deep vertical assault operations. Like all past innovations, including the development of helicopters, the Osprey, when combined with the AAAV and LCAC, would enhance future amphibious capabilities. The Osprey, the LCAC, and the AAAV represent advanced technology applied to the reformulation of Marine Corps war-fighting doctrine.

A New Medium Lift-Helicopter

Whatever the outcome of the debate over the V-22, a replacement for the fleet of CH-46 helicopters will be necessary by the end of the decade. While Congress and Headquarters attempt to keep the development of the V-22 intact, the search has begun for a possible replacement or, given the prohibitive cost of acquiring a one-for-one replacement for the CH-46 with the Osprey, a mix of Ospreys and medium helicopters. Civilian analysts suggested that the Marine Corps adopt the Army's Blackhawk helicopter, but Marines prefer a helicopter with more range, speed, and troop-carrying capability. Despite the attempts to upgrade the current fleet of CH-46 helicopters, the increased emphasis on an over-the-horizon capability places more pressure on the Corps to find a medium-lift helicopter possessing some of the range and cargo-carrying capacity of the V-22. While a Boeing upgrade package has been designed to "ensure that the CH-46 will be mission-capable into the 21st century," the Marine Corps may have to accept another rotary-wing aircraft in the coming decades instead of the Osprey.

One possible solution to the Marine Corps' search for a medium-lift helicopter is the Augusta-Westland EH101, a proposed aircraft to fill the medium-lift role of the Marine rotary-wing community. The EH101 can carry twenty-five fully equipped Marines or a TOW-mounted high mobility multipurpose wheeled vehicle (HMMWV). The EH101 could be armed and equipped with an over-the-horizon autonomous navigation system (long-range capability). The EH101 can reach a maximum speed of 180 knots with a cruising speed of 147 knots and has a maximum range of 493 nautical miles, which makes it compatible with the requirements of Operational Maneuver from the Sea.

Aviation

Other aviation issues require further evaluation by the Marine Corps. One is the performance of the F/A-18 A/C/D aircraft in Southwest Asia. While the Hornet was "uniformly regarded by its aircrew as a superb aircraft," its performance as a close air support weapon was not fully tested. One postwar assessment conducted by Marine officers pointed to several critical concerns expressed by pilots and bombardier/navigators regarding the F/A-18's overall performance as the Corps' premier close air support (CAS) aircraft. These areas include (1) the need for greater fuel capability that will allow for greater on-station time and (2) the capability for greater ordnance payloads. While the F/A-18s were able to deliver precision-guided missiles (PGMs) with good overall results, "the ordnance racks on the present aircraft were judged to be of insufficient capacity and should be replaced with higher capacity racks." When the

F/A-18s were equipped with PGMs, the lack of a laser target designator inhibited the F/A-18s' effectiveness. Similar limitations affected other close air support aircraft such as the A-6 Intruder and the AV-8B Harrier.

The A-6 Intruder and AV-8B Harrier performed well during the air campaign in the Gulf. While Marine Harriers proved vulnerable to enemy hand-held SA-14/16 missiles, this aircraft and the venerable Intruder demonstrated a remarkable ability to fly and fight, the latter at night as well as during periods of bad weather. Doubts remain about the Harrier's effectiveness in CAS strikes because of its complex and vulnerable engines. The A-6, in fact, remained the Marine Corps' night-attack and all-weather aircraft of choice in the Gulf.

While shortages occurred in the availability of PGMs as well as night-vision goggles for pilots and bombardier/navigators, the most serious gap in the Marine air war in the Persian Gulf occurred in the intelligence field. As one postwar analysis illustrated, ''Another factor influencing Marine aviation in the Gulf was the lack of real-time intelligence analysis.'' The intelligence provided to Marine pilots and air crews (not to mention ground commanders) was often dated and of little or no use in planning missions or locating critical targets. Part of this lack of critical real-time intelligence has been blamed on a variety of factors such as the decision prior to the war to retire Marine RF-4B Phantom reconnaissance jets; the failure to implement a much better Marine Air-Ground Imagery System (MAGIS) capability before the war; and lack of HUMINT or human-based intelligence. Marine pilots on follow-up missions relied upon crews returning from missions to pinpoint exact locations and targets rather than wait for the Wing or MEF G-2 staff to produce timely intelligence. The Wing's dependence on satellite intelligence and other interservice imagery led to delays that might have caused greater losses during the Gulf air war if the Iraqi air force had fought back. Intelligence data are only useful when they are being properly analyzed and distributed. In the Gulf a lack of timely, well-analyzed intelligence caused some disruption in the air attack on Iraqi targets.

Although the use of the F/A-18D as a ''FastFAC'' (Fast Forward Air Controller) proved highly successful in providing real-time intelligence to Marine aircraft arriving on station, Marine air assets may have been disproportionately committed to deep air strikes (DAS), not traditional close air support (CAS), a consequence of Air Force tasking. This trend can be largely attributed to the pace of the ground war as well as support missions flown by the Marines for the Allies, notably the British. Marine armed helicopters (AH-1W Cobras) often filled the mission requirements with great effectiveness. Marine aviation, in short, while successfully carrying out its traditional mission of close support during the war, will have to be careful in drawing lessons from a conflict that lasted forty-three days. Shortcomings in aircraft and ordnance delivery systems, intelligence, suppression of enemy air defense assets (SEAD), and traditional close air support doctrine will require some attention to be effective if enemy defenses are more difficult to locate and suppress.[36]

The long-range plans for Marine aviation foresee a continued refinement of the ACE's expeditionary capability. One way to simplify deployment and sustainability is to reduce the number of types of aircraft. Basically, the Marine Corps plans to cut the number of current aircraft types in half with a fixed-wing force built around the A/F-18, an advanced AV-8 Harrier, and further models of the C-130, which provides air refueling and resupply capabilities. The rotary-wing force would fall from five types to three: the V-22 Osprey, a heavy-lift helicopter to replace the CH-53E, and a light helicopter that would perform all the functions now associated with the family of Cobras and UH-1Ns. The Structure Review Group (1993) recommended ten F/A-18 squadrons and eighteen medium-lift helicopters/Osprey squadrons. This force could operate from a new Expeditionary Airfield 2000 (EAF 2000) that would come with a 3,800-foot strip and all the supporting construction and equipment to support a seventy-five-aircraft force. In the short term the Marine Corps will improve its night and poor-weather capability by placing advanced avionics in its existing aircraft.

MARINE GROUND FORCES

Since the Marine Corps plans to fight across the spectrum of regional conflicts, more emphasis should be given to upgrading existing weapons systems, especially the lethality of the Marine infantry battalion, despite the cutbacks in manpower. A strategy to meet regional crises will require a Marine Corps of 174,000 or more active-duty Marines. This will allow the Marine Corps to place its Ground Combat Elements (GCEs) on any battlefield by retaining the high tempo of operations and training for individual Marines that ensures that they can operate in any type of environment.

Despite the emphasis on the acquisition of new weapons systems such as the V-22 Osprey and the AAAV, Marine planners will take a critical look at the arsenal of the Marine infantry battalion, the GCE's main maneuver element. A Marine battalion commander has at his disposal a wide range of direct-fire weapons (for example, rifles and machine guns); indirect-fire weapons (for example, grenade launchers and mortars); assault weapons (for example, rocket launchers and flame weapons); and antiarmor weapons (Dragon, AT-4). The improvement in the Marine infantryman's Vietnam-era M16 assault rifle has increased the firepower a battalion commander can employ on the battlefield. The addition of the M203 40-millimeter grenade launcher has increased the ability of Marine infantrymen to deal with enemy bunkers and unprotected vehicles.

The Marine infantry battalion's firepower has been further enhanced with the addition of a light machine gun, the squad automatic weapon (SAW), and the shoulder-launched multipurpose assault weapon (SMAW), which is a lightweight, man-portable 83-millimeter rocket weapons system. The addition of three SAWs to each Marine rifle squad has greatly increased the fighting potential of Marines by enabling them to deliver a heavy volume of firepower. The SAW is a welcome addition to the Marine infantryman's arsenal, since the Browning automatic rifle (BAR) was phased out of the Marine squad during the early 1960s. It also allows more effective employment of a company's M-60 machine guns. The addition of the SMAW provides Marines with a weapon that is capable of breaching fortified positions and destroying bunkers and lightly armored vehicles. With the addition of the new high-explosive antiarmor (HEAA) round, the SMAW is capable of defeating some main battle tanks up to a maximum range of 500 meters. While the SMAW's performance during military operations in the Kuwait Theater of Operations was judged to be good, "problems with the electrical connectors constantly wearing down" reduced the weapon's overall effectiveness on the battlefield. The SMAW, nevertheless, remains a formidable and lethal assault weapon.

The two weapons that most pleased Gulf War Marines were the MK19 40-millimeter grenade launcher and the M2 .50-caliber machine gun. Both the MK19 and the M2 were employed successfully while mounted on either the AAVP7A1 or the multipurpose HMMWV. Both these weapons continue to provide excellent point-of-fire support when assaulting enemy strongpoints and have successfully demonstrated their value as effective fire-suppression weapons.

As for the Marine battalion's inventory of indirect-fire weapons, the only new addition in recent years has been the 60-millimeter Light Weight Company Mortar System (LWCMS). The LWCM 60-millimeter mortar provides a significant improvement in both range (over two miles) and lethality over the older M19 60-millimeter mortar, phased out of the infantry battalions during the 1980s. The addition of the LAV-25 (light armored vehicle) and its six variants, as well as the HMMWV, has contributed significantly to a reinforced Marine infantry battalion's ability to maneuver and deliver a maximum amount of firepower on the battlefield.

While Desert Storm proved to be a valuable test for the Corps' new weapons systems and maneuver warfare doctrine adopted during the late 1970s and 1980s, the war revealed the hard use experienced by the individual Marine's M16A2 rifle, M-60E3 machine gun, and the Beretta 9-millimeter pistol. Many Marines complained that frontline units received worn equipment that was prone to stoppages and breaking. One Marine stated that "during this war the units that didn't need the stuff [new small arms equipment] had it, and others who needed it most didn't get it." Another Marine, citing problems with the M16A2 service rifle, told one interviewer that the weapon should be "updated . . . [because] it jams too easy . . . [unlike the] AK-47 which proved to be a superior weapon in the desert." The war in the Gulf resurrected the call for a return to a larger-bore, more dependable rifle such as the Israeli Galil for combat in a desert environment. The M16A2 would be used for jungle, urban, or special-purpose missions such as raids. Despite these and other equipment-related problems, there have been important but undramatic improvements in the Marine infantryman's arsenal of small arms since the end of the Vietnam War.[37]

Marine infantrymen performed splendidly during the ground-war phase of Desert Storm. The investments made in training, weapons acquisitions, and personnel made the difference. Despite the victory, the Marine Corps will need to reevaluate existing weapons systems and doctrine in order to meet the expeditionary needs of the next century.

SPECIAL-PURPOSE UNITS: ELITE AMONG THE ELITE

The Marine Corps–Navy team emphasizes readiness *now* for its role as the American ''911 force.'' Marines, for example, went to Liberia during Operation Eastern Exit in September 1990 to rescue American and other foreign nationals and did the same thing in Somalia in January 1991 during Operation Sharp Edge. These operations involved a Marine Expeditionary Unit Special Operations Capable (MEU SOC). The MEU (SOC) is a small air-ground task force that numbers around 2,000 sailors and Marines, normally a reinforced infantry battalion and a composite helicopter squadron. The MEU (SOC) provides an immediate reaction capability for operations of relatively short duration. Because of its limited size, combat power, and sea-based sustainability, a MEU (SOC) would not conduct major amphibious assaults. MEU (SOC) is designed to perform limited, special-purpose missions from a sea-based contingency force.[38]

Separate from the MEU (SOC) are the Marine Corps Security Forces (MCSF). These Marines perform a wide variety of operations that range from protection of key naval installations to embassy security and counterterrorist operations. The MCSF battalion contains a Fleet Antiterrorism Security Team (FAST) company. FAST Marines have the ability to deploy within a limited amount of time to protect high-priority targets, or they can provide additional security to nuclear fueling and loading facilities. The Fleet Antiterrorist Security Teams were effectively employed during Operations Just Cause (Panama), Sharp Edge (Mogadishu, Somalia), and Desert Storm.

THE MARINES AND MANEUVER WARFARE

The Marine Corps' concept of fighting an enemy tank-heavy force as well as conducting its traditional amphibious operations appears to have been validated in the Persian Gulf War. The results of Desert Storm may vindicate those in the Corps who vigorously fought to modernize the force and expand the Marine Corps' roles and missions throughout the decade of the mid-1970s and into the 1980s. It remains to be seen what shape this doctrine will take as force reductions dominate the operational planning for the post–Cold War era. As the Marine Corps prepares to meet the challenges of the twenty-first century, it plans ''to employ a sophisticated, highly-structured version of maneuver warfare as its principal tactical doctrine.''[39]

The Corps' interest in maneuver warfare was an evolutionary process that began in the wake of the October 1973 Arab-Israeli War. After this conflict the Marine Corps and the Army reevaluated their own assumptions about firepower and maneuver and found them dated. The Soviet Army's modernization for a ''blitzkrieg'' war against NATO forces on the central plains of Germany gave the issue urgency. The Marine Corps had focused upon delivering sustained firepower, with little thought given to mobility and maneuver. The Marine Corps, in essence, was thinking more in terms of fighting and defeating an enemy through attrition rather than through disruption and annihilation. Military theorists in and out of uniform, often confusing tactics with operations, resurrected the ideas of the 1920s: the goal of combat was to destroy the organizational cohesion of enemy forces and their leaders' power to command. They emphasized the importance of maneuver rather than firepower.

The strongest advocate of maneuver warfare became former Marine Corps Commandant General Alfred M. Gray. While Commanding General, 2nd Marine Division, General Gray preached maneuver warfare, but the Corps' senior leadership reserved judgment on a doctrine it considered much too close to the Army's AirLand Battle doctrine, which was designed for a European war. When General Gray became Commandant in 1987, maneuver warfare was elevated to official doctrine. Complementing this doctrinal shift away from attrition-style warfare was the publication of *OH-6-1: Ground Combat Operations* (1988), *FMFM 1: Warfighting* (1989), and *FMFM 1-1: Campaigning* (1990). These manuals confirmed the maneuver warfare doctrine advocated by Gray and provided further arguments for over-the-horizon amphibious operations.

Maneuver warfare as defined by *OH-6-1* is ''an approach to war which emphasizes disrupting the cohesion of the enemy's tactical units and the mental process of the enemy commander—his ability to make correct and timely decisions—rather than simply attempting to inflict casualties at a greater rate than they are sustained.''[40] The doctrine places emphasis on what Clausewitz identified as the main aim in war, the destruction of the enemy. Despite the Corps' acceptance of maneuver warfare as its principal operational doctrine, serious questions remain as to the organization, command and control, and the relationship of maneuver warfare to the Marine Corps' principal mission of amphibious warfare. Another issue is the integration of the air element in a war dominated by maneuver and fire. While Marine commanders may think of maneuver warfare in terms of the attacks upon a decisive point of exploitation, serious questions remain about the adaptability of maneuver warfare within the framework of a MEF-size force structure. Much like the Army's AirLand Battle doctrine, maneuver warfare doctrine is still in its infancy as a real match of tactics, operations, techniques, and technology.

With the publication of *FMFM 2-1: MEF Doctrine: Fighting the MEF,* maneuver warfare will move from its embryonic stage to an actual war-fighting doctrine. While confirming maneuver warfare as the Corps' operational doctrine, *FMFM 2-1* recognizes seven primary operational challenges during Desert Shield/Desert Storm. These were command and control, maneuver, engineer operations, aviation, supporting fires, intelligence, and combat service support. Furthermore, the refinement of the Corps' maneuver warfare doctrine should produce a more manageable system that will increase battlefield flexibility and adaptability and will encourage Marine ground commanders to function despite the ''friction'' or ''fog'' of war.[41] The operational concepts of the new doctrine will guide weapons acquisition and force restructuring into the next century. Specifically, the union of doctrine and technology can be seen in the acquisition of the light armored vehicle (LAV) and the organization of three light armored infantry (LAI) battalions, now reorganized as armored reconnaissance battalions. Maneuver warfare has contributed to the Corps' ability to conduct rapid exploitation of a beachhead once the landing force is ashore and ready to push inland beyond the force beachhead line (FBHL). If and when the AAAV and V-22 Osprey join the Corps' arsenal, the CATF and Commander Landing Force (CLF) will have an even more powerful force-projection capability.

Given the emphasis on operational maneuver from the sea and over-the-horizon amphibious capability, maneuver warfare is a doctrine that will enhance the power-projection capability of an amphibious task force. The increased lethality of enemy arsenals—particularly in surface-to-surface missiles, surface-to-air missiles, and ATGMs—will require that the MEF possess the capability to secure an objective quickly. As the Marine Corps heads toward the adoption of an over-the-horizon assault capability, the possession of a mature maneuver warfare doctrine will enhance its battlefield proficiency as an expeditionary force-in-readiness.

CONCLUSIONS: INTO THE FUTURE

The U.S. Marine Corps of the post–World War II era was forged from its World War II experience in the Central Pacific campaigns, which created the integrated Marine Air-Ground Task Force. Refined and modernized through trial and error during the Korean and Vietnam wars, the MAGTF emerged during the 1970s and 1980s as a preeminent assault force-in-readiness that successfully integrates new concepts in doctrine and weapons. Although Marines in Operation Desert Storm conducted only a minor amphibious linkup with I MEF during the third day of the ground war, the presence of an amphibious task force off the coast of Kuwait prevented the Iraqis from reinforcing their inland positions against General Norman Schwarzkopf's main effort.

The MAGTF will have to be trained and tailored to respond rapidly and effectively to any threat from any quarter of the globe that threatens vital U.S. interests. This ''tailoring'' will require the addition of a new medium-lift helicopter and a new generation of amphibious assault vehicles able to meet the Navy's over-the-horizon requirements and retain the Marine Corps' ability to introduce sufficient combat power ashore at the outset of a naval campaign. Marine Colonel Patrick Collins best summed it up when he wrote:

> Helicopter-borne infantry operating from over-the-horizon amphibious shipping, combined in a single command with attack helicopters and vertical short-take-off and landing Harriers, affords a revolutionary maneuver potential to a force projected from the sea.

Such a force could maneuver at three or four times the speed of the fastest mechanized forces ashore.[42]

The Marine Corps' claim as an expeditionary force-in-readiness will be effective only if it can develop an operational war-fighting doctrine that is compatible with its structure for amphibious operations.

While the MAGTF is structured to meet regional contingencies, its overall focus must not shift from its primary mission, which is to project ashore a sufficient level of combat power in the shortest possible amount of time. Given the absence of a major threat comparable with the Soviet Union, the Marine Corps, like the other branches of the U.S. military, will be operating within the framework of reduced budgets and manpower for the foreseeable future. The MAGTF commander will be required to fight, hold, and win with a unit as small as a reinforced infantry battalion in some situations. The Marine infantry battalion landing team, even if provided with superior and overwhelming firepower, is capable of supplying only a limited amount of sustained combat power until relieved or reinforced.

The MAGTF, in short, is capable of providing a force that can be rapidly deployed to a regional crisis within a relatively short time period, that is armed with sufficient firepower to accomplish military missions, and that is able to offer maximum flexibility in the achievement of specific geostrategic goals. Moreover, the MAGTF can float offshore for months, out of sight until it is needed in a crisis. This will become a key advantage in any future post–Cold War crisis like Somalia or Bosnia where it is diplomacy and global politics that count.

Despite the MAGTF's flexibility and expandability, however, the lack of sufficient amphibious lift, reduced manpower, the need to replace the aging CH-46 and AAVP7A1, and declining modernization could degrade the Corps' ability to project sufficient combat power in regional contingencies. While the Marine Corps has based its operational and organizational structure on meeting a number of conventional contingencies since the end of World War II, the post–Cold War era has rendered such planning obsolete. Even with the shift in focus toward peacekeeping and humanitarian and rescue operations, the Marine Corps will require both the equipment and the manpower to carry out the missions implied in the new "From the Sea" doctrine and the "Bottom-Up Review."

The demise of the Soviet Union and the U.S.-led coalition victory against Saddam Hussein have not made all of the world a safer place to live. The world has witnessed the deepening of ethnic and tribal conflicts that were either suppressed or redefined while the Cold War defined foreign policy. These problems have now emerged as the flashpoints that could destroy the stability many believed would follow the end of the Cold War. Moreover, as the nations of sub-Saharan Africa, Asia, Southwest Asia, and South and Central America emerge to take their places in the post–Cold War world, old tensions may become new rivalries, threatening to disrupt the peace and security of all. These new tensions will place even greater demands on the ability of the U.S. armed forces to project military power into areas of the world that would have been unthinkable or technologically unfeasible until the 1990s. Hence the Marine Corps' adoption of the ''From the Sea'' strategy simply redefines an expeditionary-based operational concept within the uncertainty of world events.

NOTES

1. Allan R. Millett, *Semper Fidelis: The History of the United States Marine Corps,* rev. and exp. ed. (New York: Free Press, 1991), pp. 456–474; United States Marine Corps, *Fleet Marine Force Field Manual 1–2: The Role of the Marine Corps in the National Defense* (Quantico, VA: Marine Corps Combat Development Center, June 1991), p. 3-3-3-7. Also see Colonel Gordon W. Keiser, *The U.S. Marine Corps and Defense Unification: The Politics of Survival, 1944–1947* (Washington, DC: National Defense University Press, 1982).

2. Millett, *Semper Fidelis,* p. 506.

3. Marine Corps Combat Development Center, *OH-6-3: Operations of the Reorganized Rifle Battalion* (Quantico, VA: MCCDC, October 1979).

4. Verle E. Ludwig, *U.S. Marines at Twentynine Palms, California* (Washington, DC: Headquarters, U.S. Marine Corps, History and Museums Division, 1989), p. 68.

5. Martin Binkin and Jeffrey Record, *Where Does the Marine Corps Go from Here?* (Washington, DC: Brookings Institution, 1976).

6. Philip Gold, ''The New Marine Is Still Trained the Old Way,'' *Insight,* 25 September 1989, pp. 12–13.

7. Millett, *Semper Fidelis,* pp. 506, 628; ''Sea Power/The Marines,'' *Sea Power,* January 1993, pp. 12–13; ''Marine Corps End Strength Reduction Profile,'' Headquarters Marine Corps, *1992/1993 Top-Level School Reference Papers,* Special Projects Directorate, (Washington, DC: HQMC, 5 June 1992).

8. Review of reports of Force Structure Planning Group and Structure Review Group, as briefed to the author, Marine Corps Combat Development Command, March 1994.

9. Les Aspin, Secretary of Defense, *The Bottom-Up Review: Forces for a New Era,* Washington, DC: Department of Defense, 1 September 1993.

10. United States Marine Corps, *OH-2: The Marine Air-Ground Task Force* (Quantico, VA: Marine Corps Development and Education Command, March 1987), p. 1-1.

11. The Joint Board, *Joint Action of the Army and the Navy 1927* (Washington, DC: Joint Board, 1927), p. 3.

12. U.S. Marines Corps, *OH-2: The Marine Air-Ground Task Force,* p. 2-1; Headquarters Marine Corps, Quantico, VA: *Fleet Marine Force Organization 1992,* FMFRP 1-11 (1992).

13. United States Marine Corps. *IP-1-4: Fleet Marine Force* (Quantico, VA: Marine Corps Combat Development Command, March 1986), pp. 2–5.

14. U.S. Marine Corps, *Role of the Marine Corps in the National Defense,* pp. 4–7.

15. United States Marine Corps, *Concepts and Issues 1994* (Washington, DC: Headquarters Marine Corps, 1994), pp. 1-1 to 1-5; Department of the Navy, *1994 Posture Statement* (Washington, DC: Department of the Navy, 1994).

16. ''Amphib Forces in Transition,'' *Marine Corps Gazette* 77 (December 1993): 4; U.S. Marine Corps, *Concepts and Issues 1994,* pp. 2–6.

17. Lieutenant Colonel Mark F. Cancian, USMCR, *Marine Corps Reserve Forces in Southwest Asia* (Quantico, VA: Marine Corps Combat Development Center, Battle Assessment Team, July 1991), p. 1.

18. Ibid., p. 3.

19. Headquarters Marine Corps, "Establishment of a Marine Reserve Force (MARESFOR)," *Top Level Reference Papers,* 8 July 1992, p. 1.

20. "Sea Power/The Marines," *Sea Power,* p. 201.

21. General A. M. Gray, "The Annual Report of the Marine Corps to Congress," *Marine Corps Gazette* 74 (4 April 1990), p. 62.

22. Ibid.

23. Secretary of the Navy Sean O'Keefe, *"From the Sea:" A New Direction for the Naval Service* (Washington, DC: Department of the Navy, September 1992), p. 3.

24. United States Marine Corps, *FMFM 0-1: Marine Air-Ground Task Force Doctrine* (Washington, DC: Headquarters Marine Corps, August 1979), p. 2-2.

25. M. A. Roberts, *Aviation Operations in Southwest Asia* (Quantico, VA: Marine Corps Combat Development Center, June 1992), p. 39.

26. Ibid.

27. Robert T. Forte, *Combat Service Support Operations in Southwest Asia* (Quantico, VA: Marine Corps Combat Development Center, July 1991), pp. v–vi.

28. "Sea Power/The Marines," *Sea Power,* p. 202.

29. Colonel Ky L. Thompson, "Cost, Complexity May Doom USMC's Advanced Amphibian," *Armed Forces Journal International,* April 1990, p. 66; U.S. Marine Corps, *Concepts and Issues 1994,* pp. 2–10.

30. Letter from Major James R. Davis, Director, Amphibious Vehicle Test Directorate, Marine Corps Base, Camp Pendleton, California, to Leo J. Daugherty III, 5 August 1993.

31. According to a post–Desert Storm analysis, AAVs in the role of armored personnel carriers provided suppressive fire on suspected enemy positions despite the limitations offered by some vehicles outfitted with the older electric drive weapons station (EDWS) and despite the low level of preconflict training. Those AAVs that had the upgraded weapons stations provided an even greater capability to deliver suppressive fire. Those AAVs that had appliqué armor were likewise better suited to be used as an infantry fighting vehicle (IFV). Unfortunately, both appliqué armor and up-gun weapons station (UGWS) were not in sufficient supply to outfit the entire mechanized force, hence limiting the effectiveness of the AAV as an infantry fighting vehicle in the initial assault. See John F. Kelly, Douglas Seal, William B. Harrison, and Robert Esposito, *Armor/AntiArmor Operations in Southwest Asia* (Quantico, VA: Marine Corps Combat Development Center, July 1991), p. 15.

32. "Advanced Amphibious Assault Program in the Spotlight," *Marine Corps Gazette* 77 (August 1993), p. 4.

33. Headquarters Marine Corps, "Advanced Amphibious Assault (AAA) Program," *Top Level Reference Papers,* 9 April 1992, p. 2.

34. Bell Helicopter Corporation, *The V-22 "Osprey" Tiltrotor, V/TOL: A "New Dimension"* (Ft. Worth, TX: Bell Helicopter/Textron Company, 1993), p. 25.

35. "Sea Power/The Marines," *Sea Power,* p. 211.

36. Roberts, *Aviation Operations in Southwest Asia,* pp. 34–35.

37. Captain John Studt, *Individual Weapons/Equipment in Southwest Asia* (Quantico, VA: Marine Corps Combat Development Command, July 1991).

38. U.S. Marine Corps, *Concepts and Issues 1994,* p. A-7.

39. Major Kenneth F. McKenzie, ''On the Verge of a New Era: The Marine Corps and Maneuver Warfare,'' *Marine Corps Gazette* 77 (July 1993), p. 63.

40. United States Marine Corps, *OH-6-1: Ground Combat Operations* (Quantico, VA: Marine Corps Combat Development Command, January 1988), pp. 1–5.

41. McKenzie, ''On the Verge of a New Era,'' p. 67.

42. Colonel Patrick Collins, ''A Doctrinal Concept for the Employment of a Naval-Marine Air Ground Amphibious Task Force in the 1990–2010 Time Frame,'' Marine Corps Combat Development Center, Warfighting Center, October 1988, pp. 3-1, 3-5.

SELECTED BIBLIOGRAPHY

''Advanced Amphibious Assault Program in the Spotlight.'' *Marine Corps Gazette* 77 (August 1993): 4.

''Amphib Forces in Transition.'' *Marine Corps Gazette* 77 (December 1993): 4.

Headquarters Marine Corps. ''Establishment of a Marine Reserve Force (MARESFOR).'' *Top Level Reference Papers,* 8 July 1992.

———. *Fleet Marine Force Organization 1992.* FMFRP 1-11 (1992).

McKenzie, Major Kenneth F. ''On the Verge of a New Era: The Marine Corps and Maneuver Warfare.'' *Marine Corps Gazette* 77 (July 1993): 62–67.

Millett, Allan R. *Semper Fidelis: The History of the United States Marine Corps.* Rev. and exp. ed. New York: Free Press, 1991.

O'Keefe, Sean. *''From the Sea'': A New Direction for the Naval Service.* Washington, DC: Department of the Navy, September 1992.

United States Marine Corps. *Concepts and Issues 1994.* Washington, DC: Headquarters Marine Corps, 1994.

———. *Fleet Marine Force Manual 1-2: The Role of the Marine Corps in the National Defense.* Quantico, VA: Marine Corps Combat Development Command, June 1991.

———. *OH-2: The Marine Air-Ground Task Force.* Quantico, VA: Marine Corps Development and Education Command, March 1987.

Chapter 6
TOTAL FORCE: FEDERAL RESERVES AND STATE NATIONAL GUARDS

Charles E. Heller

The United States has evolved a unique reserve system for its military establishment. It is a system that was originally constructed partly as a result of an eighteenth-century fear of standing armies and strong centralized governments and is embedded in myth and tradition. It is a system that is laced with domestic politics, spiced with states' rights, and contains strong citizen-soldier lobby groups. The reserves today are divided between the state militias or National Guards and Federal Reserves for the Army and Air Force, while the Navy, Marines, and Coast Guard have only the latter. Although U.S. wars are fought and won by citizen armies, the reserve system has rarely met the readiness claims of its citizen-soldiers or the regular, now called Active Component (AC), establishment. Each component, active and reserve, of each military service warily regards the other with skepticism and, at times, hostility. American society has accepted the contentious nature of the relationship between the regular establishment and citizen-soldiers, be they reserves, wartime volunteers, or conscripts. However, in the public's eyes citizen-soldiers are the nation's saviors in wartime. The fact that the regular establishment has traditionally borne the first onslaught of a conflict or that its professionalism has molded the citizen forces

This chapter is a slightly revised version of the report ''Total Force: Federal Reserves and State National Guards'' (Carlisle Barracks, PA: U.S. Army War College, Strategic Studies Institute, 17 October 1994). The views expressed in this chapter are those of the author and do not necessarily reflect the official policy or position of the Department of the Army, the Department of Defense, or the U.S. government.

mobilized to fight the nation's wars is usually lost in the euphoria of the citizen-dominated armed forces' victory over an enemy.

THE TOTAL FORCE POLICY

Today, the armed forces' Reserve Components (RC), to include the U.S. Coast Guard, which, although under the Department of Transportation in peacetime, is part of the Navy during a national emergency or war, play a greater role than ever in national security. The Cold War was partly responsible for this increased reliance because the Soviet threat appeared so overwhelming and the cost of maintaining large active forces was prohibitive. Then too, it is due partly to the failure to mobilize, except for a small number, the RC for the Vietnam War. After this Asian war many defense analysts and military leaders claimed that the eventual lack of public support could be attributed, in part, to President Lyndon Johnson's failure to fully mobilize the reserves, and that this politically motivated decision, in turn, did not fully commit the American public.

As a consequence, when the Vietnam War ended, a new policy was evolved that had significant impact on the nation's reserve forces. On 21 August 1970 the Total Force Policy for the armed forces was introduced by Secretary of Defense Melvin Laird. It was a vehicle to promote a reduced response time for the reserves to back a small active establishment in a national emergency. It was also seen as an economy measure in anticipation of the defense budget's growth to eventually accommodate the increased cost of all-volunteer forces planned for commencement in 1972. In 1979 the policy was spurred on by the beginning of a massive rearmament program initiated by President Jimmy Carter's administration after the Soviets invaded Afghanistan. According to the Department of Defense Reserve Forces Policy Board, the Total Force Policy "implies an increased interdependence of active and reserve forces. It absolutely requires that the availability and readiness of reserve forces must be as certain as the availability of active forces."[1] Thus, once again, the RC, as they were prior to Vietnam, would be the immediate and primary source of additional forces in a national emergency.

The armed forces' responses were varied. Those that are "platform" oriented, that is, depend on large weapons systems such as aircraft and vessels, the Navy, Coast Guard, and Air Force, approached the policy differently than the two services that are manpower intensive, the Army and Marines. Obviously, the loss of a number of ships and aircraft in a major war, given the length of time required by defense industry to replace such high-technology weaponry, would result in excess manpower. In the Air Force, for example, some reserve pilots have greater experience because of prior active duty with the AC and civilian jobs with airlines that equate to more flying hours than their active counterparts. As for the Navy's experience, it is almost impossible to man a vessel with reservists in any considerable number because of the complexity of modern technology. Such is not the case with the Marine Corps and the Army. A conflict of any proportion would result in initial manpower and unit requirements. Also, combat losses would need to be replaced immediately, initially from the reserves. It is also expensive to keep on active duty certain types of units such as graves registration and civil affairs for which there is no immediate requirement upon mobilization.

The 1990–1991 Persian Gulf War saw a return to the use of the RC in a national emergency and was seen by many as the Total Force Policy's vindication. The reserves of all the services mobilized and deployed, sometimes in advance of active forces. Reserve combat and support units representing the Marine Corps, Navy, and Air Force, and Army support units deployed. No combat maneuver elements of the Army's RC reached the Gulf. Thus the policy's only significant failure came with the inability of the Army National Guard (ARNG) combat maneuver "roundout" brigades (units assigned to round out an active division to three brigades) to be certified as deployable prior to the war's end.

The Gulf War can now be seen as a unique event coming at the end of the Cold War. As a consequence, both the AC and the RC were better prepared than in the nation's past major wars. In large measure this traditional unpreparedness of all the armed forces, active, Federal Reserve, and state National Guards, is due to the public's inclination, after a conflict, to return to normalcy as rapidly as possible. This attitude carries over to defense appropriations and strength authorization so that active and reserve peacetime establishments are usually minimum forces. The surprising part of this traditional approach to war is that the ACs of all services have had, in varying degrees, problems successfully integrating their reserves within their establishments in peacetime for reasons that range from the traditional hostility between citizen-soldiers and regulars to competition for scarce dollars. The successes and problems with attempts at integration will become readily apparent as the reserves are examined in this chapter.

THE LEGAL BASIS FOR THE RESERVE FORCES OF THE UNITED STATES

The constitutional basis for state reserve forces resides in Article 1, Section 8, giving Congress the power to call out the militia of the states and to "provide for organizing, arming, and disciplining" citizen-soldiers. However, it became apparent, beginning in President George Washington's first administration, that other citizen forces would be required to support the nation's regular forces during wartime. Thus an unsuccessful attempt was made to create a "Federal Militia." However, the wars that followed the birth of the Republic used federal volunteers and then, for the first time during the Civil War, citizen conscription. All these actions were authorized under the Constitution's Article 1, Section 8, which gave Congress the power to "raise and support Armies."

Today the legislative basis for all U.S. reserve forces is *Title 10, United States Code, Armed Forces* (*10 USC*). This legislation states the Reserve's purpose:

> To provide trained units and qualified persons available for active duty in the armed forces, in time of war or national emergency and at such other times as the national security requires, to fill the needs of the armed forces whenever, during, and after the period needed to procure and train additional units and qualified persons to achieve the planned mobilization, more units and persons are needed than are in the regular components.[2]

Title 10, United States Code lists the reserve components of the armed forces within the Department of Defense (DOD) as the Army National Guard of the United States (ARNG); Army Reserve (USAR); Naval Reserve (USNR); Marine Corps Reserve (USMCR); Air National Guard of the United States (ANG); Air Force Reserve (AFRES); and Coast Guard Reserve (USCGR). As indicated earlier, the latter reports to the Department of Transportation (DOT) in peacetime, and the Coast Guard may become a part of the Navy in war or national emergency. Within these reserve forces there are three categories in which individual reservists are placed regardless of the service—the Ready Reserve, Standby Reserve, and Retired Reserve.

RESERVE CATEGORIES OF SERVICE AND ACTIVE DUTY

Ready Reserve

The Ready Reserve consists of units and individual "reserves" liable for call-up by the President under the authority of section 673b of *10 USC*. There are over 1,800,000 individuals in this category. Within the Ready Reserve are several separate categories.

Selected Reserve

The Selected Reserve is composed of units manned and equipped to serve as required and totals about 1,000,000 individuals.[3] The members of the Selected Reserve are "drilling" reservists who perform regularly scheduled training of forty-eight paid drill or training assemblies that are four-hour periods (IDT—Inactive Duty for Training) and perform Annual Training (AT) of not less than fourteen days per year. At home station in their local communities, reserve units usually conduct Multiple Unit Training Assemblies (MUTAs), which are four twenty-four-hour periods, one weekend per month. These are called MUTA-4.

The Selected Reserve contains full-time support personnel in the Active Guard/Reserve (AGR) program. The term AGR is used by the Army and the Air Force; however, the Navy refers to the program as TARs (Training and Administration of Reserves) and the Marine Corps FTS (Full-Time Support). Within these programs are reserve personnel who have volunteered for active-duty status to perform a variety of duties to include organizing, administering, recruiting, and instructing the reserves. Those individuals in units are assigned authorized mobilization positions.

The Selected Reserve category also includes Individual Mobilization Augmentees (IMAs). This program is available in the Federal Reserves only. Individual reservists augment the staffs of AC units, major commands, and executive branch departments such as DOD and the Federal Emergency Management Agency (FEMA). These reservists are required to perform at least fourteen days of AT. There is also a small subcategory of IMA called Drilling IMA (DIMA). Individuals in this program perform the same number of Inactive Duty for Training (IDT) (paid, but a lesser category than AT) and Annual Training days as units. The Selected Reserve is unique because the President is authorized to order it to active duty other than during a declared war or national emergency (*10 USC 673b*). Section 673b states that not more than 200,000 members of the Selected Reserve may be on active duty at any one time. These reservists are authorized to serve for 270 days. The Congress can extend the time further, as it did for ARNG combat maneuver units in the 1990–1991 Gulf War. This authority is popularly known as the "200K call-up."

Individual Ready Reserve

The Ready Reserve also contains the Individual Ready Reserve (IRR). The IRR is a pretrained manpower pool of individuals who have served in an AC or one of their Selected Reserves and have not completed their mandatory service obligation, which is currently eight years. It has about 776,000 members.[4] It is only applicable for federal reservists. The IRR can be ordered to active duty involuntarily for training, but this is rarely done. Its members have a low priority in terms of training, and unless they volunteer and funds are available, they will not be trained. These individuals are not affected by a presidential 200K call-up. However, the President can call the IRR to active duty involuntarily along with the Selected Reserve if he declares a national emergency (*10 USC 673*). In 1984 Congress mandated that each service screen its IRR annually.

Inactive National Guard (ING)

Distinct and apart from the IRR is a category of National Guard soldier or airman in the Inactive National Guard (ING). These approximately 7,000 guardsmen are inactive individuals attached to an Army or Air National Guard unit, but are not part of the Selected Reserve.[5] They are required to muster once a year, but do not train or receive compensation.

Standby Reserve

The Standby Reserve is composed of individuals, approximately 26,000, who retain their military affiliation, but are not part of the Ready Reserve.[6] They have been designated key civilian employees or have a temporary disability or hardship. They do not train and are not in units. This also is an exclusive Federal Reserve category. Over the years since Vietnam, DOD has made strenuous efforts to reduce this manpower pool. Individuals in this category may be involuntarily called to active duty during a war or national emergency with the approval of the appropriate service Secretary and Secretary of Defense.

Retired Reserve

The Retired Reserve is composed of individuals who have been honorably retired and are receiving retired pay on the basis of having over twenty years of active duty: all reserve soldiers eligible for retired pay at age sixty not serving in the Ready or Standby Reserves. A service Secretary has the authority to order to active duty involuntarily retirees if such a call-up is in the interest of national security. Retirees, by DOD directive, are placed in one of three categories by age. Category I contains those who have been retired not more than five years and are under age sixty. Category II are those individuals retired more than five years, under age sixty, and physically fit. Category III includes all other retirees.

In addition, there are several other categories of active duty in which a reservist can serve. One is Active Duty for Training (ADT). In this category a reservist can obtain additional training to enhance his or her skills, to gain new skills such as airborne qualification, or to learn a new military occupation specialty (MOS). ADT may also include attendance at any level of training or schooling from Initial Entry Training to Senior Service College. It is also used for training on active duty beyond AT. IRR soldiers can volunteer to perform ADT as "fillers" for active and reserve units engaged in major exercises such as Reforger in Europe. Another category is Active Duty Special Work (ADSW). This does not involve training per se, but rather uses the expertise of the individual to perform work to enhance the RC's readiness. Lastly, there is Temporary Tour of Active Duty (TTAD). A reservist who volunteers in this category is selected by virtue of his/her skills not readily available in the Active Components. While serving in each category except TTAD, reservists serving less than 179 days are not counted against the AC strength, which, like the reserve, is established by law.

MANAGEMENT OF RESERVE FORCES: CONGRESS AND THE DEPARTMENT OF DEFENSE

Congress, under the U.S. Constitution, Article 1, Section 8, is the final authority to manage the reserves of the various armed services. Reserve issues are overseen by the House and Senate Armed Services Committees and the Defense Subcommittee of the Appropriations Committee in each house of Congress. Congress enacts laws establishing policies and guidelines from pay and allowances to officer promotions and force structure. Of special interest to reserve forces is annual congressional action establishing strength authorizations, which, in turn, are used to support pay and allowances. Congress can and does insure, from time to time, that moneys appropriated go directly to the respective reserve component for installations and equipment purchase. These funds are, therefore, "fenced" for specific purposes within the reserves.

The Secretary of Defense delegates overall responsibility for reserve forces to the Assistant Secretary of Defense (Reserve Affairs) (ASD/RA). This office works directly with the service Secretaries of the various departments and with the armed forces leadership. Acting through the ASD/RA is the Reserve Forces Policy Board (RFPB). By statute, this board is chaired by a civilian and is composed of general officer representatives from all the armed forces and their Reserve Components. Membership also includes the civilian Assistant Secretaries (Manpower and Reserve Affairs) of each service. The board, the principal advisory group to the Secretary of Defense on reserve matters, is required to submit an annual report on the Reserve Components' status to Congress and the President. The report focuses on reserve readiness and makes recommendations as to how the reserves can be improved.

Unique within the management structures of the Army and Air Force is the National Guard Bureau (NGB). The bureau fulfills the need for the defense establishment to have a centralized agency to work with the fifty-four separate state and territory National Guards. By law, *10 USC Section 3040,* the NGB is both a staff and operating agency whose chief reports to the Secretaries of the Army and Air Force through their respective service chiefs. The NGB is the avenue by which the federal government communicates with the states, that is, the governors and the Adjutant Generals, the latter usually appointed. The NGB then becomes the clearinghouse for dealing with individual states. The bureau controls funding, total strength, force structure, and equipment. It also develops state regulations for the National Guards.

Pay, Benefits, and Entitlements for the Reserves

Pay, benefits, and entitlements eligibility are directly related to the reservist's type of service. As with the AC, basic pay and allowances depend on length of service and rank. Reservists may receive special pay as aviators or medical personnel or hazardous-duty pay for personnel in authorized positions such as airborne duty or deep-sea diving.

Benefits are available depending upon the service member's reserve status. When performing IDT for pay and for exchanging one four-hour drill period for one day of privileges, Ready Reserve members and their families may use a post/base exchange, a department-type store. Ready Reservists and their families also have access to commissaries (food stores) based on the number of training days performed during the previous calendar year, up to twelve days. Ready Reservists may use military clothing stores, recreation facilities, clubs, and other services while on IDT, ADSW, TTAD, AT, and ADT. They are eligible for full-time serviceman's group life insurance and may participate in the Montgomery GI Bill Educational Assistance program. While on active duty they may also receive limited medical care. Since 1986 reservists have been subject to the Uniform Code of Military Justice in an IDT status as they are when on active duty. Reservists can be recalled to answer for crimes committed in any active-duty category.

Full-Time Support of the Reserves

In 1906 a system of providing full-time support (FTS) to reserve units was begun. As technology increased and warfare became more complex, full-time support programs emerged for all the RC. FTS personnel insure continuity and stability, which improve unit readiness. They provide administrative, logistical, operational, and training support to reservists. Currently, there are three FTS categories. The first is Active Guard/Reserve (AGR). This category was described previously in the section ''Reserve Categories of Service and Active Duty.'' Next is FTS Military Technicians and Air Reserve Technicians, which apply only to the Army and Air Force RC. These are Selected Reservists who are federal civilian employees providing FTS in reserve organizations and units. Closely related to this category are those in Civil Service, both federal and state, who also support units and organizations, but are not required to be drilling reservists. Lastly, a small number of AC personnel are assigned or attached to RC organizations and units. These soldiers provide advice, liaison, management, administration, and maintenance support.

GAINING ACCESS TO THE RESERVES

Currently, five mobilization levels can be utilized to gain access to U.S. reserve forces. Also, reservists may and are asked to volunteer their services to enter active duty in peace and war. Legally, under *Title 10, United States Code,* the threat's seriousness to national security governs the mobilization level. The reserves are affected by each level.[7]

Selective Mobilization (*10 USC 3500, 8500; 10 USC 331, 332; 10 USC 673*)

Congress or the President may order the expansion of the AC armed forces by mobilizing reserve units and/or individuals. This level of mobilization would not be used for a contingency operation required to meet an external threat to national security, but rather a domestic threat to the safety and well-being of citizens. The 1992 Los Angles riot is an example of this mobilization level.

Presidential Selected Reserve Call-Up (*10 USC 673b*)

The President, by executive order, may augment the AC to meet operational requirements by calling to active duty up to 200,000 reserve personnel for up to 270 days. As indicated previously, this authority is known as the ''200K call-up.'' The President is required to notify Congress and explain the reasons for his actions. President George Bush exercised this option after the invasion of Kuwait in August 1990.

Partial Mobilization (*10 USC 673, 673b; 10 USC 6485*)

Congress or the President may declare a national emergency and the President may issue an executive order for the augmentation of AC armed forces with up to one million soldiers as individuals or in units from the Ready Reserve for up to twenty-four months. Congress can pass legislation establishing any limit for a partial mobilization. Preparations for offensive Operation Desert Storm required a partial mobilization after a presidential declaration of a national emergency in January 1991 that was issued in order to freeze Iraqi assets in the United States.

Full Mobilization (*10 USC 671a, 672[a]*)

Congress is required to pass legislation, by public law or joint resolution, declaring war or a national emergency. All reserve units and individuals within the force structure would be mobilized, and authority is available for national conscription. An example of this level is the 1940 U.S. mobilization after the German conquest of France in the spring of that year.

Total Mobilization (*10 USC 671a, 672[a]*)

Congressional declaration of war or national emergency, by public law or joint resolution, is required for this mobilization level. Not only are all reserve units and individuals called up, but additional units are created beyond the force structure in existence, by national conscription if necessary. All the nation's resources are mobilized to sustain the expanded armed forces. World Wars I and II are examples of total mobilization.

THE ARMY'S RESERVE COMPONENTS

Background

Because the Army's reserve system is the first, largest, and most complex, its historical development is important in understanding the other armed forces reserve systems. There are two reserve categories for the Army: the state militias and the federal Army Reserve. The former are the nation's first citizen reserve, today's Army National Guard (ARNG). The National Guard traces its origins to the colonial militias formed in each community as a defensive force. Service in these militias was mandatory, and regular drills or musters were conducted.

During the American Revolution both long- and short-term militia units were raised to augment the Continental Army.

The militias were and continue to be dual-mission forces with dual loyalties. Each remains under the governor's control in peacetime, but is available to the federal government in time of war or national emergency. Although guard units that meet AC standards receive federal recognition in peacetime, the parent armed forces, by law (*Titles 10* and *32 USC*), can only advise and coordinate training in peacetime. The Constitution makes it clear that the federal government does not have direct access except upon mobilization or what is known as "federalizing" the guard for war or a national emergency.

The militia's performance in the American Revolution and in the wars that followed was questionable. As a consequence, the federal government, beginning with George Washington's administration, attempted from time to time to create a federal militia in peacetime and call for volunteers in war. Both actions met with opposition from militia supporters. In the Mexican War the federal government began calling for volunteers who, although formed into units by the states, were immediately reorganized and placed in federal service. At the onset of the Civil War President Lincoln called for militia. However, of the over 1,780 regiments raised, only 15 were in existence prior to the war.[8] State-designated regiments were, in reality, federal volunteers. The militias, resurrected after the Civil War for domestic disturbances, were renamed National Guard in honor of the unit the Marquis de Lafayette formed during the French Revolution. They continued, however, to suffer from deficiencies that became apparent on mobilization for the Spanish-American War. Further, legal opinion was that the Constitution forbade militia deployment overseas. In the Spanish-American War guardsmen volunteered as individuals. As a consequence, the 1903 Dick Act became the first legislation in 111 years aimed at reforming the militia. Basically, the act called for enforced federal standards, Regular Army instructors, and inspectors, as well as increased federal expenditures for equipment.

Increasingly concerned over the legal restrictions barring the guard from overseas deployment and lack of enforcement of federal standards in peacetime, the guards' dual missions and loyalties, and the forces' traditional unpreparedness, the Army sought alternative reserve forces. The Army moved modestly and cautiously in 1908 to create a Medical Officer Reserve Corps. The new corps was legislated into existence under the Constitution's Army clause. The National Guards' condition after they were called up in 1916 for border duty during the Mexican Punitive Expedition prompted the Army and Congress to expand the Medical Reserve in the National Defense Act of 1916 to include both officers and enlisted personnel in all branches of the Army. The two new reserve organizations were called, respectively, the Officer Reserve Corps and the Enlisted Reserve Corps. After both proved of value during World War I, the two were merged in the National Defense Act of 1920 as the Organized Reserve Corps (ORC). This Federal Reserve is today's Army Reserve. Under subsequent amendments to the 1916 act, the National Guards would become part of the

Army of the United States when ordered into federal service. Federal financial assistance was increased, and guard units could receive federal recognition in peacetime if they met Army standards.

Based on wartime experience, the Army planned a post–World War I force comprised of twenty-seven ORC and eighteen National Guard divisions. In 1933 legislation was enacted to allow for overseas deployment of guard units.[9] Unfortunately, the small defense appropriations of the interwar period insured that World War II mobilization mirrored past deficiencies of AC, reserve, and guard forces.

At the war's conclusion the armed forces struggled to rebuild in a constrained budgetary environment. The National Defense Act of 1947 created separate service secretaries. Shortly after the new organization was established, the first Secretary of Defense ordered a committee to examine the state of the nation's reserves. The committee issued its report, *Reserve Forces for National Security,* named ''Gray Report'' after its chairman, Assistant Secretary of the Army Gordon Gray. Critical of state forces, it recommended that all Reserve Components be federal. The emphasis on combat arms in modern times has always been difficult to comprehend in light of the guard's dual missions. The Gray Report noted that ''the use of the National Guard with its present powerful armament is not generally suitable for the execution of state missions . . . and not consistent with sound public policy'' and that ''the same forces can no longer be expected to perform both local and national functions and that a modern Federal striking force cannot be prepared adequately under state control.''[10] At the urging of the National Guard, Congress ignored the study.

The Cold War, commencing with Korea, brought further increased reliance on the reserves to fight a global war against the Soviet Union. For the Korean War, individual reservists and reserve units were mobilized. After analyzing the Reserve and National Guard's lack of readiness, Congress passed legislation attempting to improve their readiness and bring the ORC into parity with the state forces in regard to regulations and funding. This legislation changed the name of the ORC to U.S. Army Reserve (USAR).

Problems continued to plague reserve readiness and were apparent during the 1962 Berlin call-up. Intent on streamlining the Army's cumbersome and expensive dual reserve system, Secretary of Defense Robert McNamara attempted to merge the ARNG with the USAR. Failing to accomplish this, he then sought to move all combat arms (infantry, armor, and artillery) into the ARNG, maintaining the USAR as a support force. In this latter attempt he was only partially successful, for the Army, with congressional acquiescence, asked for and received back a number of USAR combat maneuver units. However, this laid the basis for further migration of combat units to the ARNG, leaving the USAR's composition primarily, but not completely, support units.

Breaking with the past, President Lyndon B. Johnson made a political decision not to fully mobilize the reserves for the Vietnam War. As indicated previously, only a small number of reservists and reserve units were called to active duty

Figure 6.1
Total Army Combat and Combat Service Support Structure

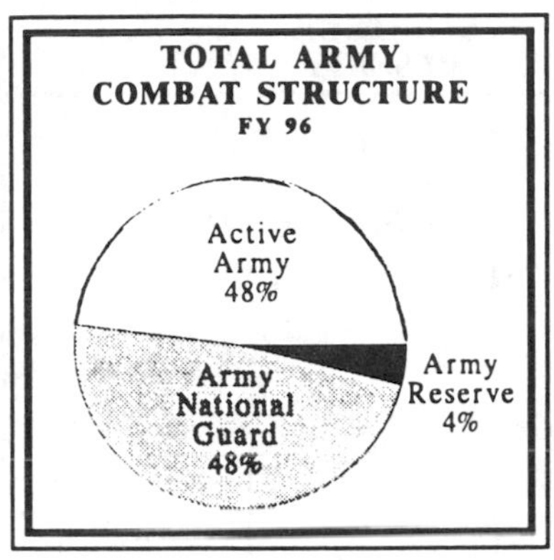

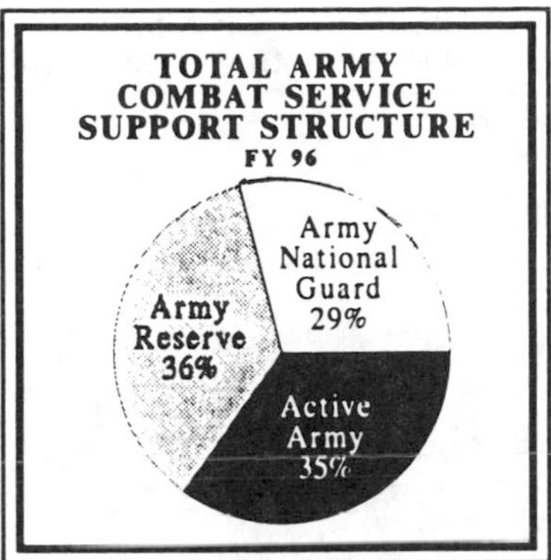

Source: Department of the Army, *Special Report* (Washington, DC: Office Chief Army Reserve, 1993), p. 9.

during this unpopular conflict. The reserves became a haven for young men attempting to avoid conscription. Manpower was obtained by increasing draft calls and expanding the Reserve Officer Training Corps and Officer Candidate School quotas.

The 1990–1991 Gulf War partially broke the tradition of reserve unpreparedness. The USAR and ARNG deployed support forces. In this sense this conflict vindicated the Total Force Policy. It also proved that reserve forces could be successful when used in a complementary role. However, there was a downside: the ''roundout'' brigades, units designed to fill out an Active Army division on mobilization by becoming the third brigade, failed to deploy. These combat maneuver forces did not meet standards, and only one completed postmobilization training and validation for deployment, but just at the war's conclusion.

The Army's Reserve Components Today

At the Cold War's end the total Army is going through massive changes in the number of personnel, structure, equipment, training, and missions. As the AC is drawn down, the RC's importance to the total force has continued to grow. Figure 6.1 shows the nature of this dependency based on projected fiscal year 1996 statistics. Within the total Army, 53 percent of the personnel will be in either the ARNG or USAR while 47 percent will be AC. In terms of combat structure (infantry, armor, artillery, air defense, special forces, combat engineers, combat aviation), in percentages the Active Army has 48, the ARNG 48, and the USAR 4 percent. Combat support (signal, chemical, military police, civil affairs, engineers, aviation, military intelligence, psychological operations) and

Figure 6.2
Army Base Force

FORWARD PRESENCE	CRISIS RESPONSE	EARLY REINFORCE	STRATEGIC RESERVE	TRANSITION
AC Unit Personnel 66K	120K	58K	17K	
ARNG Unit Personnel 15K	15K	51K	134K	43K
		USAR UNIT 7K Personnel		
USAR: Individuals 16K				
AC: CS/CSS 143K Unit Personnel				62K
USAR: CS/CSS 144K Unit Personnel				
ARNG: CS/CSS 124K Unit Personnel				

SUSTAINING BASE

AC: 120K	USAR: 60K	NG: 31K

*Numbers are approximate due to constant changes in appropriations during FY 1993-1994.
Source: Office Chief Army Reserve, Policy and Liaison Division, May 1994.

combat service support (medical, finance, supply and service, quartermaster, transportation, ammunition, judge advocate general, railway, and maintenance) break down into the following percentages: Active, 35; ARNG, 29; and USAR, 36.[11]

In overseas deployment planning for contingency operations, figure 6.2 shows the number of Reserve Component personnel dedicated to what the Army calls "warfighting," which includes units already deployed overseas, "forward presence"; those forces immediately deployed, "crisis response"; and "early reinforcement" units that would be the follow-on forces to support those already deployed. The ARNG combat units are part of a "strategic reserve" and what is called "transition" or expansion. The other-than-wartime-mission forces also are indicated for all three components.[12]

As one can readily observe, the reserve forces' contribution to the total Army is significant. No contingency operation can take place today without mobilizing the Army's two reserves. In order to better understand the two citizen-soldier components, the following is a brief description of today's ARNG and the USAR.

Army National Guard

The ARNG is composed of fifty-four state and territorial forces of varying strength and unit composition. Currently, the ARNG is authorized 410,000 sol-

Figure 6.3
Army National Guard and Air National Guard Command and Control

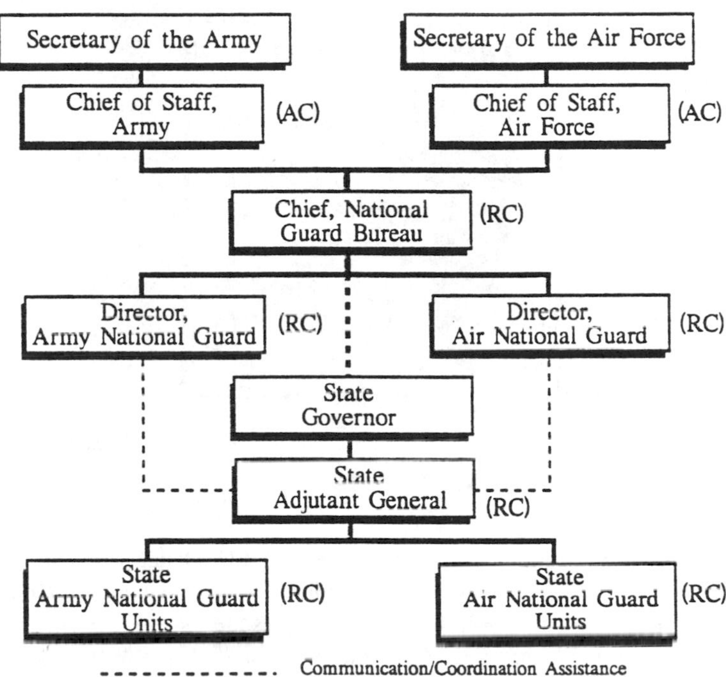

Source: Department of Defense, *Annual Report of the Reserve Forces Policy Board*, Fiscal Year 1993 (Washington, DC: U.S. Government Printing Office, 1994), p. 186.

diers. Each state guard has a dual mission and "performs federal tasks, for national defense and for domestic emergencies, and state tasks, for local emergencies."[13] Within the NGB is the Director, ARNG. The director and his staff allocate available resources to provide units for the ARNG's federal combat mission. His office conducts long-range planning, submits programs and budgets to the Army Staff, and administers resources for personnel, force structure, training, and equipment.

The ARNG maintains the Army National Guard Personnel Center, which operates as an NGB field agency. In peacetime the center manages the Official Military Personnel Files of all ARNG officers and is directly involved with those guardsmen, officers and enlisted men, who are in the AGR program. Enlisted records are maintained by the states and territories. Officer and enlisted personnel data are on one personnel management information system, the Standard Installation/Division Personnel System. The center is also responsible for the dissemination and monitoring of ARNG peacetime personnel policies.

The ARNG management structure (figure 6.3) flows from the chief, NGB, to the Director, ARNG. Because the ARNG is composed of independent state

Figure 6.4
ARNG Composition

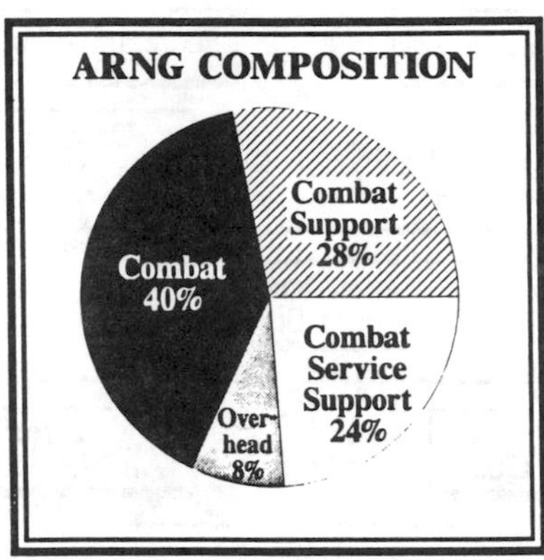

Source: National Guard Bureau, Force Management Briefing, *National Guard Command Plan*, May 1994, Slide 12.

forces, there is no "chain of command" from the Department of Defense. Rather, there is a "channel of communication" to each state and territorial governor and the usually politically appointed state official (South Carolina elects), The Adjutant General (TAG), a major general who may or may not have federal recognition of his rank outside the state. The governor is the commander-in-chief and the TAG his chief of staff who commands all state military forces. The District of Columbia is unique in that the President of the United States is the commander-in-chief both of it and of the armed forces. A State Area Command (STARC) exercises command and control of a state's force in peacetime and assists during premobilization activities.

Historically, from the minutemen at Lexington and Concord, the ARNG has been primarily a combat arms force. Currently, the ARNG has eight divisions and forty-five combat maneuver brigades. Approximately 40 percent of the ARNG's strength is in the combat category. Twenty-eight percent is combat support, while 24 percent is in combat service support. Because each state controls its own forces, it has about 8 percent of its strength in administrative support, and this includes those individuals at Departments of the Army and Defense levels (figure 6.4).[14] As part of the Army's plans for downsizing, the current structure will be modified to allow for fifteen "enhanced brigades" in a high state of readiness and twenty-two others at a lesser level that are considered a "strategic insurance" force.

Units in the Army National Guard vary in size from military history detachments to combat divisions. Some ARNG major units, such as the 35th Division Mechanized, are spread over as many as seven states. Major units by state, for example, range from a sole infantry brigade in Connecticut to the units in California, where the ARNG has a troop command, a mechanized infantry division, an area support group, a medical brigade, and a military police brigade. As with the Active Army, within large combat formations are smaller combat and combat service support units. Since a large percentage of the ARNG is combat arms, the Army's drawdown has allowed the migration of modern weapons systems such as M1A1 main battle tanks and Bradley infantry fighting vehicles to the state forces.

U.S. Army Reserve (USAR)

The U.S. Army Reserve is a federal reserve comprised of regional units and individuals located throughout the United States that is centrally commanded and administered. Currently, it is authorized 230,000 Selected Reserve soldiers. Additionally, about 440,000 soldiers are in the IRR. The USAR's primary mission is to support and augment the AC. It is, in peace and war, "under direct and immediate federal control. . . . As a consequence, the roles and missions of the Army Reserve are assigned directly by the Army and the Congress."[15] It can be utilized like the ARNG for domestic missions, but only upon a declaration of a national emergency or partial mobilization. However, unlike state forces, its units are not restricted by state boundaries because it is a federal force with a direct chain of command from the smallest detachment to the Chief, Army Reserve.

The Chief, Army Reserve, has three primary responsibilities: Chief, Army Reserve; Commander of the U.S. Army Reserve Command; and deputy commanding general of Forces Command. As Chief, Army Reserve, he also serves as the advisor to the Army Chief of Staff on USAR issues.

The Office, Chief Army Reserve (OCAR), is the staff agency that advises and is responsible for the Army Reserve. This office manages planning, training, mobilization, readiness, and maintenance of the USAR. The office is responsible for three appropriations: pay and allowances, operations and maintenance, and construction. OCAR, as an Army Staff component, engages in the formulation of Department of the Army policies regarding the USAR. The office also develops long-range plans for the USAR. Figure 6.5 shows the USAR command and control relationships.

The U.S. Army Reserve Command (USARC) is responsible for the resourcing, personnel, and facilities management of all USAR units located in the continental United States (CONUS), excluding those units under control of Special Operations Command and overseas commands. Under a recent reorganization plan yet to be approved, the Army Reserve will reduce the number of subordinate commands directly reporting to the USARC in Atlanta to thirty-one. Twenty-one of these would be organized to encompass geographic regions. These Army Reserve Commands (ARCOMs) are either administrative entities or wartime-deployable units, and the "divisions" are either exercise or training. The plan also creates a total of ten Regional Support Commands aligned with

Figure 6.5
Army Reserve Command and Control

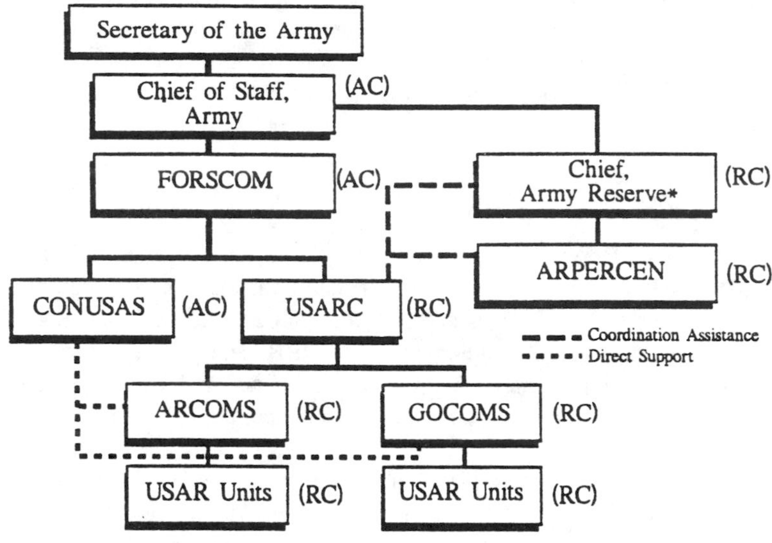

*The Chief Army Reserve also serves as DCG, FORSCOM; CDR, USARC

Source: Department of Defense, *Annual Report of the Reserve Forces Policy Board*, Fiscal Year 1993 (Washington, DC: U.S. Government Printing Office, 1994), p. 187.

the current ten Standard Federal Regions utilized by the FEMA and other governmental agencies.[16]

However, today there are twenty-two regional ARCOMs. These commands provide administrative support to USAR units within their geographic boundaries. Also located within ARCOM areas are forty-three USAR General Officer Commands (GOCOMs). These are primarily in the combat support and service support area and range from medical and civil affairs to maneuver area, signal, and support commands. Additionally, the USAR has twelve training divisions and two separate infantry brigades. The total USAR Troop Program Unit (TPU) composition is divided into four functional areas (figure 6.6): 56 percent combat service support, 18 percent combat support, 6 percent combat, and the balance, 20 percent, "mobility base expansion" (training divisions/brigades, garrisons, U.S. Army Reserve Forces schools, hospitals, depot support, and port operations).[17] As with the ARNG, units range from detachments to large units such as Theater Army Area Commands. As support-type units, they are to a greater extent independent because they provide unique functions.

A Field Operating Agency of OCAR, the Army Reserve Personnel Center (ARPERCEN) commands and controls USAR soldiers not in TPUs. Its mission is similar to the AC's Personnel Support Command. It provides life-cycle man-

Figure 6.6
USAR Troop Unit Composition

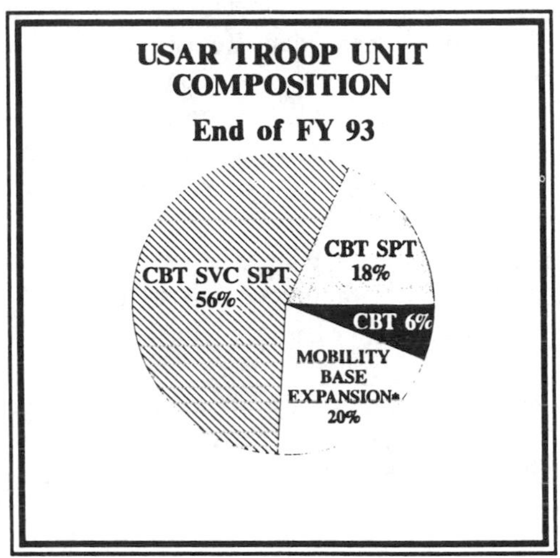

*Training divisions, training brigades, garrisons, schools, hospitals, depot support, port operations
Source: Office Chief Army Reserve, Special Report FY 1993, p. 8.

agement for those soldiers not assigned to USAR units and is assuming similar responsibilities for TPU members. The center is also responsible for the administration and records of the IRR, the IMA program, the Standby Reserve, and retirees of all components to include the Retiree Recall Program. USAR AGRs are managed by the Full-Time Support Manning Center colocated with ARPERCEN but reporting directly to OCAR. Although ARPERCEN's motto is "Management for Mobilization," it has inherited mission responsibilities that have little to do with the reserve such as management of records for World War II Philippine Scout veterans. These missions are holdovers from the old Reserve Components Personnel and Administration Center operated by the Army's Adjutant General.

Equipping USAR units has not been as easy as with the ARNG. Since the USAR does not mirror the AC as does the ARNG, equipment does not migrate in similar quantities. Additionally, the types of major end items of equipment for bakeries and laundries do not appear as glamorous as M-1A1 tanks and Bradley fighting vehicles and therefore do not appear as necessary for war. Therefore, the reserve must rely heavily on programs such as Dedicated Procurement. As a consequence, "the USAR still lags significantly behind all other DOD Reserve Components in the amount of equipment actually on hand when compared to wartime requirements."[18]

Training the Army's Reserve Components

The Total Army Training Study conducted in 1984 developed the Reserve Components Training Development Plan. Revised annually, this document integrates all reserve training initiatives into a comprehensive plan that provides the blueprint for pre- and postmobilization training for individuals and units. The study identified requirements and recommended methods, new and existing, to train the ARNG and USAR to Army standards as individuals, crews, and units.

Individual enlisted soldiers and officers may attend any AC school or course provided there is a need for the training or education, a space is available, and the soldier meets certain admission criteria. Some admissions, especially in the federal USAR, require board approval for such schooling as the Sergeants Major Academy and Command and General Staff College. There are a number of major training programs to enhance the ARNG and USAR's unit readiness. One of the most significant is CAPSTONE, a management tool that aligned the reserves and the AC within a wartime organizational structure. The program formally aligns reserve units with active units so that upon activation/mobilization, the reserve units have detailed familiarity with an active organization and can connect directly to it. The organizational structure was then used as a basis for planning and training USAR and ARNG units, allowing them to make the fullest use of limited training time to focus on wartime missions and build a relationship with the AC units they would operate with in wartime. Other programs such as Affiliation, Partnership, and Counterpart, as the names imply, build closer relationships between the AC and the USAR and ARNG. The Overseas Deployment Training (ODT) program further expands CAPSTONE by allowing reserve units to deploy and train in overseas areas they might be sent to after mobilization in a national emergency.[19]

New programs continue to be introduced. As a result of the inability to deploy the ARNG roundout brigades for the Gulf War, Congress passed the Army National Guard Combat Readiness Reform Act of 1992. Also in 1992, Bold Shift, a program in which AC teams assist in individual, unit, and leader training in the USAR and ARNG, was introduced. The ARNG's Project Standard Bearer and the USAR's Priority Reserve Initiative in Mobilization Enhancement (Project PRIME) focus on training units identified as part of the Contingency Force Pool (CFP), those that would be mobilized and deployed early in a crisis.[20]

THE AIR FORCE'S RESERVE COMPONENTS

Background

As with the Army, the U.S. Air Force has a dual reserve. A National Guard air arm began in 1908 when the New York National Guard volunteered to form the Signal Corps' 1st Aero Company. After the creation of a Regular Air Service in 1907, the first National Guard fixed-wing unit appeared. In 1911 an aero detachment was formed in California, and in 1915 the First Aero Company, New York National Guard, was federally recognized.[21] The 1916 National Defense Act established an Aviation Section in the Signal Corps and created a Federal Reserve of 296 officers and 2,000 enlisted personnel. As a consequence, the first Air Force Reserve Aero Squadron organized in 1917 and deployed to France that same year. The Army Air Corps gained equal status with other Army branches in 1926 when it became the U.S. Army Air Corps.[22] In the interwar period, from 1919 to 1940, the AC ORC and the ARNG's air assets suffered from limited funding. In fact, the Air Corps was so chronically undermanned that it used reservists who were not counted against manpower ceilings on a regular basis. Both were relatively insignificant in terms of providing units during the mobilization for World War II. The ORC provided 1,500 trained pilots for the Army Air Corps during the critical period just after Pearl Harbor.[23]

At the conclusion of World War II the Air Force was reorganized. An Air Defense Command was established for continental U.S. air defense. This command was given the mission to provide for the organization, administration, training, and maintenance of the National Guard and Reserve Air Force elements. The former expressed a desire to ''reconstitute the air capability'' of the state National Guards. The Army Air Force was less than enthusiastic. However, Chief of Staff George C. Marshall overrode objections in an effort to obtain support for postwar universal military training and supported the establishment of the Air National Guard (ANG) in late 1945. However, the Air Force continued to object to the lack of a direct control and reporting chain to state air assets.[24]

The National Security Act of 1947 created a new ''National Military Establishment'' that authorized the Air Force as a separate service. Three military departments, headed by civilian secretaries, Army, Navy, and Air, would report to a Secretary of Defense. The National Guard Bureau would have two separate divisions, one Army and the other Air Force. The bureau itself would remain under the Department of the Army. The Air Force was still concerned about this Army oversight and the lack of direct control of state forces and questioned why a governor required state air elements. The controversy came to a head following the Gray Report. The Secretary of the Air Force convinced the Defense Secretary to request legislation merging the ANG with the AFRES. The National Guard lobby killed the proposed merger. However, the legislation made it clear that the National Guard Bureau would be denied the power to interfere with Air Force and Army operations through the bureau's divisions.[25]

Once the issue was resolved, the Cold War insured emphasis on both the AFRES and ANG. During President Dwight D. Eisenhower's administrations increased attention was paid to the AFRES and ANG, primarily as a result of the successful use of air power during the Korean War and a deliberate attempt by the Chief of Air Force Reserve to influence congressional delegations in favor of his service. In addition to continental U.S. air defense, the ANG absorbed additional missions such as those in the Tactical Air Command, which included fighters, reconnaissance, troop transporters, heavy-equipment lift, and medical evacuation. The AFRES was similarly tasked and duplicated these missions. Unlike the Army, the Air Force, over the following years, used both the ANG and AFRES in real-world missions without the need to mobilize by using individual volunteers. Examples of such mission deployments range from Berlin and the Pueblo Crisis in 1961 and 1968, respectively, to the airlift into Grenada in 1983 and Just Cause in Panama in 1989. Indeed, the Total Force Policy was very much a part of the Air Force philosophy after the Korean War and prior to its introduction in the early 1970s. It was and is much easier for the Air Force AC to validate standards because it was dealing with a more manageable force that applies its skills frequently. Some, but not all, have related civilian experience in aviation. These factors account for the relatively short time to mobilize and deploy air assets. As a platform-oriented service composed of small crews, formations, and individuals, it has been far easier for the active force to integrate the ANG and the AFRES into a total force.

During the 1990–1991 Gulf War the ANG provided early augmentation of the deployment with two Military Airlift Groups on a voluntary basis prior to mobilization. These were quickly followed by reconnaissance and air refueling tanker units. After mobilization other ANG support units followed, including a Mobil Aerial Port Squadron and two F-16 squadrons.[26] The AFRES deployed twelve out of fourteen C-141 and C-130 squadrons, all of its C-5 assets, one A-10 fighter unit, all of its medical elements, and other smaller support assets such as aerial port, security police, and fire protection units.[27]

The Air Force's Reserve Components Today

The Air Force has faced the realities of the Cold War's end. Its performance in the Gulf War, heightened by media attention, has not exempted it from downsizing. Even prior to the current reductions, beginning in 1973, missions had been slowly migrating to the reserves and the guard. The active force's manning level has decreased by one-third since 1986. During that time the RCs have grown slightly to match increasing missions. However, the Air Force continues to be a power-projection force that can be immediately deployed to the scene of a conflict anywhere in the world. Indeed, the Air Force was able to respond first with major deployments of assets to Saudi Arabia in August 1990, and it also transported the 82nd Airborne Division and other Army units to the Gulf from the United States and Europe. In accomplishing this, heavy reliance was placed on ANG and AFRES units and individuals.

Today, the ANG comprises 117,676 (19 percent) and the AFRES 81,539 (13 percent) of the Air Force Total Force of 623,180 (figure 6.7).[28] Also, about 112,000 airmen are in the IRR. The RCs dominate many Air Force missions. For example, the AFRES contributes 100 percent of the aerial spraying capability, 71 percent of the aeromedical evacuation assets, and 50 percent of the

Figure 6.7
Manning the Total Force

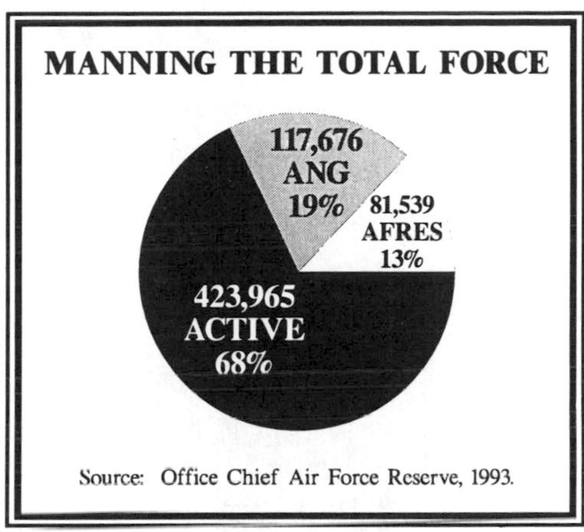

strategic airlift crews. The ANG provides 92 percent of the continental U.S. interceptors, 86 percent of the tactical/weather reconnaissance assets, and 70 percent of the communication units. For a complete breakdown of ANG and AFRES contributions to the Total Force, see figure 6.8.[29]

All reserve units in peace and war are assigned to an AC command. These major commands are Air Mobility, Air Combat, Air Force Special Operations, Pacific Air Forces, Air Force Materiel, Air Force Intelligence, Air Training, and U.S. Forces Europe. These commands set training standards, provide advisors, and evaluate the Reserve Components. Through these commands both the ANG and the AFRES perform worldwide missions.[30] These missions include airlift support to the U.N. force in Somalia, domestic counternarcotics efforts, fighting forest fires, and many other real-world tasks both at home and abroad.

Both the ANG and the AFRES, like their Army counterparts, are separate and distinct components. What follows gives a general overview of these reserve forces.

Air National Guard

At the NGB level there is a Director of the ANG who has equal status with the ARNG director. The constitutional constraints also apply to the ANG, and, therefore, as with the ARNG, there is a "channel of communication" from the Department of Defense (see figure 6.3). The ANGs are state and territorial forces available to the federal government when required. While not all the aircraft and units within the ANG are compatible with state missions, some, such as medical and engineering and security units, are used by governors, as are individual airmen. The fifty-four state and territorial governors are the Command-

Figure 6.8
Air Reserve Component Contributions

ANG Contributions to the Total Air Force

Unit	Percentage of Total Air Force
CONUS Interceptor	92
Tactical/Weather Rec	86
Communications Units	70
Tactical Airlift	38
Air Rescue	36
Civil Engineering	27
Tactical Fighters	26
Support Aircraft	25
Strategic Tankers	22
Weather Units	14
Aerial Port Units	13
Medical Personnel	12
Strategic Airlift	6
Special Operations	6

0 20 40 60 80 100

Percentage of Total Air Force

USAFR Contributions to the Total Air Force

Unit	Percentage of Total Air Force
Aerial Spraying Cap	100
Weather Recon	100
Aeromedical Evac	71
A/C Battle Damage	59
Strategic A/L Crews	50
Aerial Port Units	48
Tanker/Cargo Crews	43
Air Rescue/Recovery	41
Strategic A/L Maint	40
Aeromed A/L Crews	30
Tactical Airlift	26
Civil Engineering	13
Special Operations	12
Strategic Airlift	11
Tactical Fighters	9

0 20 40 60 80 100

Percentage of Total Air Force

Source: Department of Defense, *The Reserve Components of the United States Armed Forces* (Washington, DC: Office, Assistant Secretary of Defense for Reserve Affairs, June 1992), pp. 25–26.

ers-in-Chief of their respective guards, which are immediately available for state missions. The Adjutant General is the Chief of Staff for both the Air and Army National Guards, making state forces joint in nature. The ANG shares responsibilities in the State Area Command (STARC); however, each state and two of the four territories maintain an ANG headquarters. Every state and territory has at least one of the eighty ANG installations in its geographic boundaries.

Also similar to the ARNG, the ANG has a larger percentage of its approximately 400 units in the combat category of continental interceptor and tactical fighter wings than in support areas. As with the ARNG, the 117,000 Air Guardsmen either are unit members or in an inactive status. Other than combat formations, ANG units include tactical control and combat communications, engineering installation, communications and mission support, weather, aircraft control and warning, civil engineering, medical, security police, and range control. Examples of the types of units within a state range from the New York ANG with two airlift groups, a rescue group, a fighter group and wing, and a tactical control group to Delaware with a single airlift group.[31]

Many ANG units fly the same type and model aircraft flown by the AC. At times there is a migration of older aircraft; however, as the Air Force becomes smaller, much of the equipment passed to the ANG is in the current state-of-the-art category. Air combat units utilize F-16, F-15, A-10, F-4G, and RF-4C aircraft. ANG units, which provide personnel and cargo transportation capabilities, are equipped with KC-135, C-5A, C-141, and C-130 aircraft.

Air Force Reserve (AFRES)

The AFRES is a federal reserve. Its chain of command (see figure 6.9) flows directly from the Air Force Chief of Staff to the Chief of Air Force Reserve, who is dual hatted. The latter heads the Office of Air Force Reserve and is the principal advisor to the Chief of Staff. In this capacity the Chief of Air Force Reserve establishes policy and develops plans and programs. In addition to staff functions, the Chief of Air Force Reserve also commands the Air Force Reserve.

Headquarters, AFRES, is located at Robins Air Force Base, Georgia. From there the Chief of Air Force Reserve exercises control over three Air Force Commands. The 4th Air Force at McClellan Air Force Base, California, is responsible for providing airlift, C-9 aeromed evacuation, rescue, and special operations units; the 10th Air Force at Bergstrom Air Force Base, Texas, oversees five fighter wings, an air refueling wing, and one composite wing; and the 22nd Air Force at Dobbins Air Force Reserve Base, Georgia, supports airlift and weather reconnaissance units. These major commands provide for the administration and supervision of the unit programs, provide logistic support, review and manage unit training, and validate combat readiness of units in their respective geographic regions. Most of the AFRES units, upon mobilization, are gained by either the Air Combat Command or Air Mobility Command. A field

Figure 6.9
Air Force Reserve Command and Control

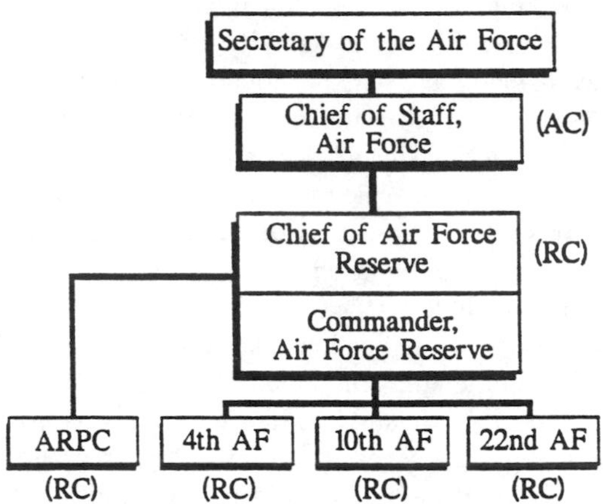

Source: Department of Defense, *Annual Report of the Reserve Forces Policy Board*, Fiscal Year 1993 (Washington, DC: U.S. Government Printing Office, 1994), p. 187.

operating agency, the Air Force Reserve Personnel Center, located in Denver, Colorado, provides personnel services to all AFRES and ANG members.

AFRES units are equipped with cargo C-141, C-130, C-5, and KC-135 aircraft. Combat aircraft in the AFRES include F-16, A-10, and HH/MH-60 (helicopter). As a Federal Reserve, the AFRES has an Associate Aircraft Program that provides trained crews and maintenance personnel for approximately 300 AC aircraft. This program pairs a reserve unit with an AC unit who then share a single aircraft. Aircraft types in the program include C-5, C-17, C-141, C-9, KC-10, and B-52.

Training the Air Force's Reserve Components

Reservists are trained at AC Air Force training and educational facilities, which range from crew and pilot training to Senior Service College. Unit training is conducted by full-time technicians who are civil service employees during the week and reservists on drill weekends. Much of what is considered training is performed as real-world missions such as humanitarian airlifts and support of all AC missions.

THE NAVAL RESERVE (USNR)

Background

President Thomas Jefferson believed that the nation was best served not by standing military forces but by citizen militias. As a consequence, he suggested creation of a national naval militia in 1805. In the same period several seacoast states established naval militias. A number of these units survived to augment the Union Navy during the Civil War. In May 1888 Massachusetts brought back the concept by establishing a naval battalion as part of the state militia. A decade later sixteen states followed suit. In 1898 these militias served in the Spanish-American War. The Navy Department eventually established, in 1914, a Division of Militia Affairs. A year later, in March 1915, Congress legislated into existence a Federal Naval Reserve, the forerunner of the modern Naval Reserve.[32] This federal organization eventually supplanted the state militias.

The federal U.S. Naval Reserve (USNR) has provided personnel in every war since its establishment. Over 300,000 reservists served in World War I, and all draftees, 2,000,000, were classified as reservists in World War II. USNR spearheaded the salvage of the space shuttle *Challenger,* and in 1987 two USNR minesweepers deployed at the height of the war between Iraq and Iran. In the Gulf War USNR personnel deployed to the Gulf. Over half of these reservists were medical specialists. USNR sealift specialists, air naval gunfire liaison officers, harbor masters, cargo handlers, Seabee (construction) battalions, search and rescue detachments, and port security personnel deployed to the Gulf. During the war other reservists augmented Navy commands worldwide.[33]

The Naval Reserve Today

A reserve or AC rear admiral heads the USNR command and control structure (figure 6.10) and is based in Washington, D.C. As the Chief of Naval Reserve, this officer is also the Director of Naval Reserve and Commander, Naval Reserve Forces. The Chief of Naval Reserve is the principal advisor to the Chief of Naval Operations for planning, policies, programming, and budgeting.

The Naval Reserve Force Command is a field command operating in New Orleans. It has primary responsibility for operations, training, administration, and readiness of all Navy reservists. Its responsibilities include the TAR, IRR, and IMA programs. Colocated are two subordinate commands, Naval Surface Reserve Forces and Naval Air Reserve Forces. Both are commanded by reserve flag (general) officers. The senior of the two is the Deputy Commander, Naval Reserve Forces. There is also a third reserve command located in New Orleans, the Naval Reserve Recruiting Command, responsible for the recruitment of manpower to fill Naval Reserve units and individual Selected Reserve positions. The Selected Reserve is authorized a strength of 118,000, which is 12 percent of the Navy. Another approximately 160,000 are in the IRR.[34]

Selected Reservists serve either in "commissioned" or "augmentation" units in over 250 training sites across the nation. Commissioned units, comprising 20 percent of the Selected Reserve, are self-contained organizations possessing their own major end items of equipment. These units are structured to mobilize and be functionally independent or deploy alongside AC units. The types of units in this category include ships, aircraft squadrons, construction battalions, cargo-

Figure 6.10
Naval Reserve Command and Control

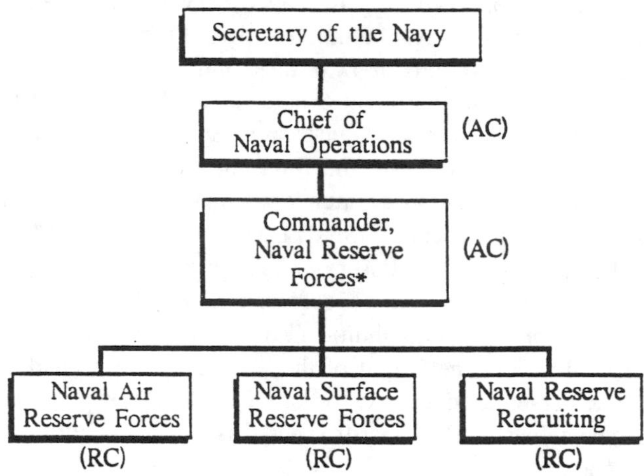

*The Commander, Naval Reserve Forces, also serves as Director, Naval Reserve, and as Chief of Naval Reserve.

Source: Department of Defense, *Annual Report of the Reserve Forces Policy Board*, Fiscal Year 1993 (Washington, DC: U.S. Government Printing Office, 1994), p. 188.

handling battalions, mobile inshore undersea warfare units, and special boat units. Eighty percent, approximately 2,500 units, are in the augmentation category. These units are composed of reservists with professional skills in, for example, medicine, intelligence, and law. These units augment just about every AC organization. Upon mobilization these skilled personnel are immediately available to serve in an individual asset or as unit members.[35]

The USNR's contribution to the Navy's Total Force is significant. The force contributes 100 percent of the Navy's total assets in five areas: heavy airlift, composite aircraft, strike rescue, embarkation assistance, and harbor protection. Over 50 percent of the Navy's total assets are contributed by Reserve units in the areas of shipping control, cargo handling, military sealift, Seabee battalions, and intelligence/security (figure 6.11).[36]

Training the Naval Reserve

USNR personnel attend Navy educational and training institutions as required. Contributory support (reservists using their skills to support ongoing fleet operations) not only enhances readiness training, but also adds needed manpower to support the AC in peacetime. Other training programs are available. One of the newest is the Naval Surface Reserve's Innovative Naval Reserve Concept. It has been applied to the Fast Frigate Program. Eight FF-1052 *Knox*-class frig-

Figure 6.11
Naval Reserve Contributions

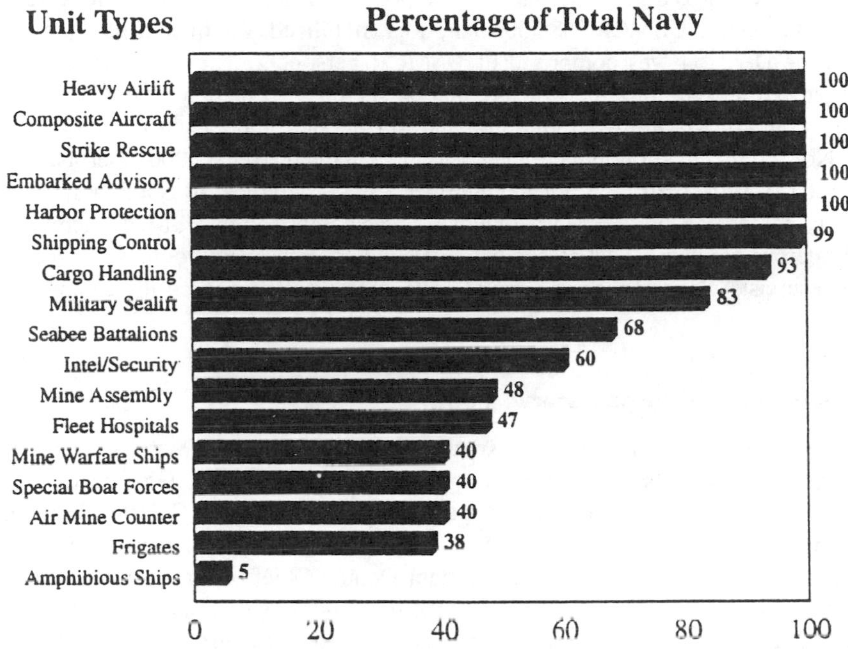

Source: "The Reserve and the Total Force: America's Future National Security," *Officer*, February 1993, p. 178.

ates have been designated training "platforms" and are under the USNR's operational control. Each frigate in the program trains a Selected Reserve crew and four cadre crews. The cadre will then be available as nucleus activation crews for decommissioned ships.

THE U.S. MARINE CORPS RESERVE (USMCR)

Background

The authority for the U.S. Marine Corps Reserve (USMCR) resides in an appropriations act passed by Congress on 29 August 1916. Two days later the Navy Department issued General Order 231 establishing "a U.S. Marine Corps Reserve to be a constituent part of the Marine Corps."[37] When war was declared in April 1917, USMCR strength consisted of 3 officers and 32 enlisted men. By the end of World War I the authorized strength had climbed to almost 80,000. In the interwar period the Congress passed an act to establish a formal organizational structure for the USMCR. The basic unit became Fleet Marine Corps

Reserve company. When World War II broke out, there were twenty-three Marine Reserve battalions and thirteen Reserve air squadrons. Ultimately, 68 percent of the Corps during the war was composed of reservists. During the Korean War the entire USMCR, 88,500 men, was mobilized. At Inchon half the 1st Marine Division was comprised of USMCR personnel. The USMCR was reorganized in 1962 into the structure that exists today. It includes the 4th Marine Division, 4th Marine Aircraft Wing, and 4th Service Support Group.

Not mobilized for Vietnam, the USMCR activated over 31,000 reservists for the 1990–1991 Gulf War. Of this number 13,000 deployed to Southwest Asia. Forty percent of the 2nd Marine Division was comprised of USMCR members. Numerous smaller USMCR combat and support units were composed entirely of reservists. Several reserve combat units successfully engaged the enemy.[38]

The Marine Corps Reserve Today

Because the Marine Corps is a smaller service within the Navy, its reserve is integrated within its own command and control structure. The Commandant of the Marine Corps is responsible for the USMCR. His Deputy Chief of Staff for Manpower and Reserve Affairs, an AC general officer, is the principal staff officer for USMCR matters. The Assistant Deputy Chief of Staff for Manpower and Reserve Affairs is responsible for the day-to-day operations of the Reserve Affairs Division. The USMCR command and control structure is shown in figure 6.12.

An AC general officer commands the Marine Reserve Force (MARESFOR), which is headquartered in New Orleans. In this command are five Fleet Marine Force major subordinate commands and a support command. The headquarters provides a centralized command structure for all USMCR elements, and its staff is comprised of both AC and reserve personnel.

Subordinate to the MARESFOR are a number of USMCR elements. The AC Fleet Marine Forces' USMCR units are organized in a Marine Division (MARDIV), a Marine Aircraft Wing (MAW), a Force Service Support Group (FSSG), and two Marine Expeditionary Brigade (MEB) commands. These organizations are each commanded by reserve general officers and are colocated with MARESFOR. The MARDIV consists of nine infantry battalions, two tank battalions, one armored infantry assault battalion, and one light armored battalion and combat and combat support units. The MAW has 19 squadrons of fixed- and rotary-wing aircraft and an antiaircraft battalion plus support units. The FSSG is composed of seven support battalions. The MEB command elements are organized as command and control nuclei for a Marine Air-Ground Task Force upon mobilization. All in all, the USMCR comprises 25 percent of the total Marine force structure and 33 percent of the manpower, 42,000 Selected Reserve authorized strength with approximately 70,000 IRR.[39] The USMCR contains 100 percent of the Marine Civil Affairs Groups and 50 percent of the force recon-

Figure 6.12
Marine Corps Reserve Command and Control

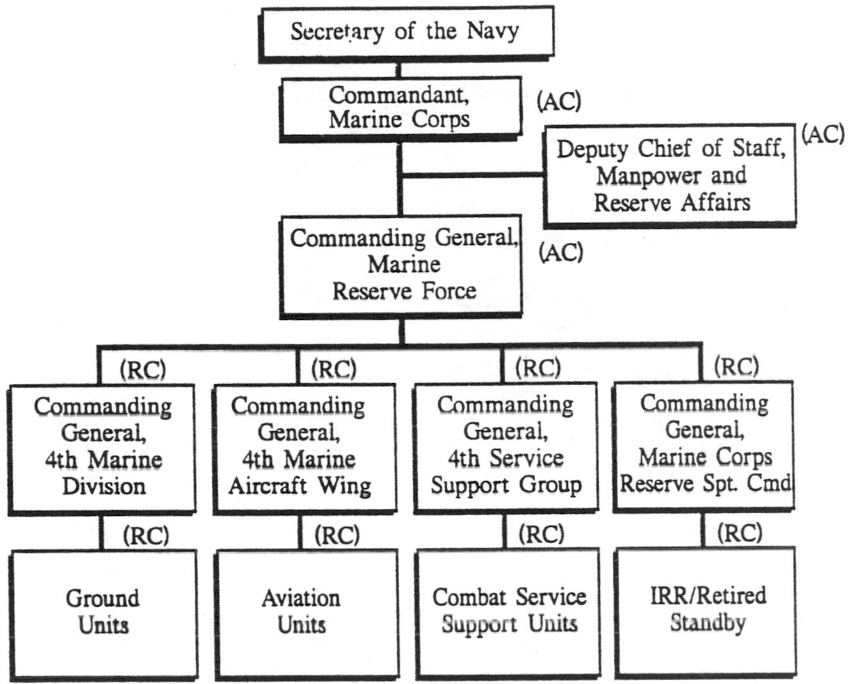

Source: Department of Defense, *Annual Report of the Reserve Forces Policy Board*, Fiscal Year 1993 (Washington, DC: U.S. Government Printing Office, 1994), p. 189.

naissance and air naval gunfire units as well as significant percentages of other types of units (figure 6.13).[40]

Under MARESFOR is the Marine Corps Reserve Support Command headquartered in Overland Park, Kansas. Commanded by a reserve general officer, the center administers the IRR, provides training opportunities to USMCR members during AC exercises, and may activate IRR members on a voluntary basis to support special projects, mobilization screening, and professional education courses.[41]

Training the Marine Reserve

The small Marine Corps strength minimizes segregated training for USMCR personnel. Reservists are educated and trained by the AC across the board. Special two-week courses for the USMCR are available at regular intervals. They are primarily military occupation specialty refresher training or review specific aspects of Marine Corps doctrine. Reservists, like their AC counterparts,

Figure 6.13
U.S. Marine Corps Reserve Contributions

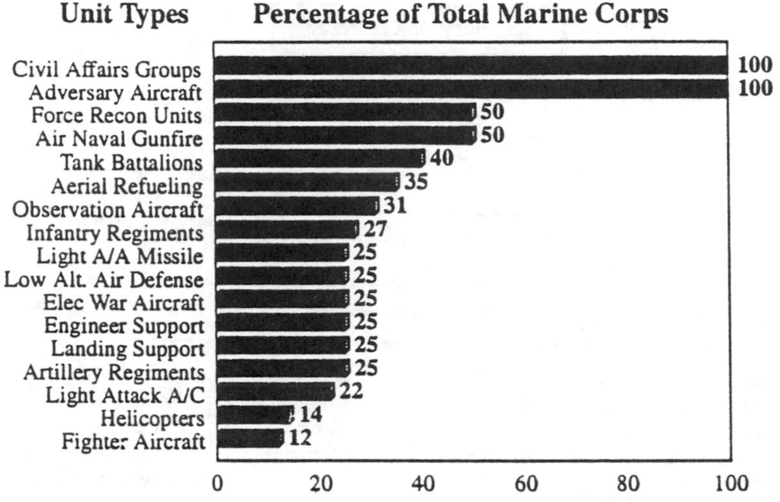

Source: "The Reserve and the Total Force: America's Future National Security," *Officer*, February 1993, p. 179.

may attend a full range of training and education programs provided by the other armed services. Unit members and IMAs train on an annual basis. The USMCR is called upon annually to augment AC exercises. Lastly, there is the Reserve Counterpart Training program. This type of training allows individual reservists to serve alongside their AC counterparts for two to four weeks working in the specialty.[42]

U.S. COAST GUARD RESERVE (USCGR)

Background

The Coast Guard was first established in January 1915 when the Revenue Cutter Service merged with the Life-Saving Service. Although the Coast Guard, since 1967, has operated as part of the Department of Transportation, it is, by law, one of the U.S. armed forces. It operates as part of the Navy in war or national emergency; its personnel and ships are transferred to operational control of Navy commanders.

In 1939 the first Coast Guard Reserve was established. On 19 February 1941 this civilian component became the Coast Guard Auxiliary. The Coast Guard Reserve provided 144,000 personnel for World War II. After the conflict the civilian auxiliary languished until the end of the decade when reserve personnel began to meet informally to train without compensation. Several years later,

Figure 6.14
Coast Guard Reserve Command and Control

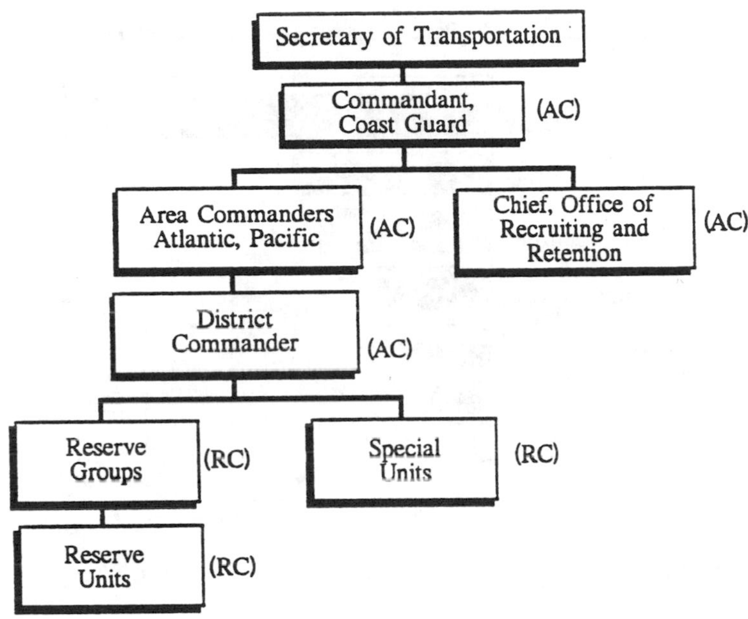

Source: Department of Defense, *Annual Report of the Reserve Forces Policy Board*, Fiscal Year 1993 (Washington, DC: U.S. Government Printing Office, 1994), p. 191.

legislation passed in 1950 drastically increased the Coast Guard's port security mission. With the growing tensions brought about by the Cold War, Congress, as part of an across-the-board strengthening of the armed forces, created a paid drill Coast Guard Reserve. The first unit of this peacetime force was organized in October 1950 in Boston. For the wars that followed there were no reserve activations. However, as in the armed forces reserves, individual members volunteered for the Korean War and Vietnam. During the Gulf War over 1,600 Coast Guard Reservists were called to active duty to perform in-theater port security and port out-loading in the United States.

The U.S. Coast Guard Reserve Today

The USCGR is "directed" by an AC Rear Admiral who serves as Chief, Office of Readiness and Reserve, reporting directly to the Coast Guard's Commandant. The Director does not command the USCGR. The reserve chain of command does not differ from that of the AC. The USCGR is organized into ten Reserve Districts and forty-six "Groups" encompassing units in thirty-nine states, the District of Columbia, Puerto Rico, and Guam. Units are the responsibility of local AC commanders (figure 6.14).[43]

Figure 6.15
USCGR Contributions

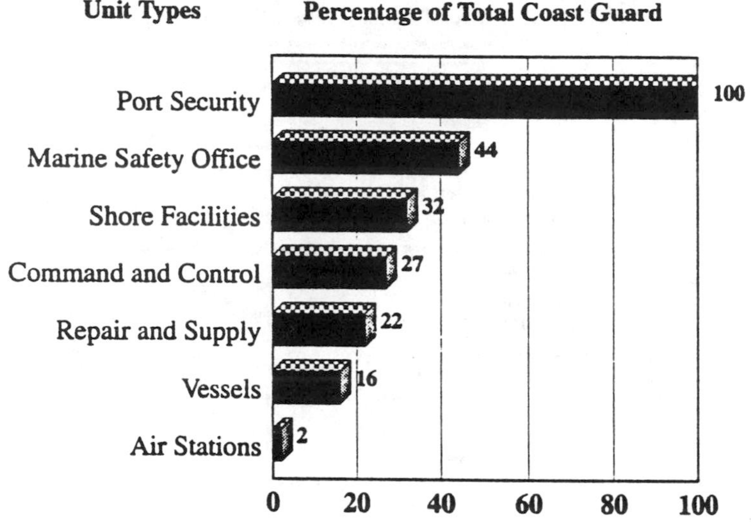

Source: "The Reserve and the Total Force: America's Future National Security," *Officer*, February 1993, p. 180.

Currently, under *Title 14, U.S. Code* and unlike the other four Federal Reserves of the armed services, only the USCGR can be involuntarily called to active duty for not more than thirty days in a four-month period and not more than sixty days in a two-year span to meet the surge demands caused by a man-made or natural disaster without a presidential declaration of a national emergency. Also, this reserve force is not restricted from acting in a law-enforcement capacity, as are the other Federal Reserves.[44]

The USCGR has an authorized Selected Reserve strength of 10,000 serving in units and about 8,000 in the IRR.[45] Most of the units directly augment local AC commands. One hundred percent of the Coast Guard's deployable port security units are in the USCGR. Other types of units include small stations, marine safety offices, operational shore facilities, command and control elements, repair and supply, and air stations. Only 3.5 percent of the Total Force USCGR personnel serve aboard vessels (figure 6.15).

Since USCGR personnel are primarily augmentation forces, they are integrated in a number of Coast Guard missions and have specific responsibilities, for example, port management operations. They perform port security, safety, and environmental inspections at all levels: district, group, and marine safety offices. Additionally, reservists are integrated into the operations of small boat units where they stand watch and perform as crew members, coxswains, and boat engineers. This type of augmentation is especially useful for "surge operations'' such as narcotic interdictions, intercepting illegal immigrants, and combatting natural disasters. Some 200 reservists were called to active duty for Hurricane Andrew, and 500 more served in Midwest flood relief operations in 1993.

Training the Coast Guard Reserve

USCGR members attend formal training and education programs similar to those of their Active Component counterparts. The reserve performs over 53 percent of its training duties in direct support of operational missions.

CONCLUSIONS: RESERVE FORCES OF THE UNITED STATES AND THE FUTURE

Postwar and peacetime environments have never been easy for U.S. armed forces. In the peacetime periods between war, especially in the twentieth century, there has been a struggle between active and reserve components for personnel strength and portions of a decreasing defense budget. Coupled with this fratricidal warfare for scarce dollars are other contentious issues: end strength, force mix, missions, and recruiting, equipping, and training reservists.

In many ways today's post–Cold War demobilization is vastly different than those in the past. There is a difference because of the introduction and institutionalization of two concepts: first, the Total Force Policy, and second, the elimination of conscription and the introduction of the smaller, but costly all-volunteer forces. Both have placed the armed forces reserves into a position to assume greater roles in defense than ever before in the nation's history.

Prior to his resignation, Secretary of Defense Les Aspin conducted what he called *The Bottom-Up Review: Forces for a New Era.* The results were announced on 1 September 1993. The armed forces, the review stated, must be prepared to ''field forces sufficient to fight and win two nearly simultaneous major regional conflicts.''[46] However, only by using the reserves extensively would the armed forces be able to accomplish this requirement. As indicated in the individual reserves' training programs, emphasis is being placed on reserve forces' readiness. *The Bottom-Up Review* has remained the Clinton administration's defense blueprint, thus insuring a prominent role for the reserves well into the future. However, problems exist for the armed forces because of the built-in dependency on their pretrained citizen-soldier forces.

One problem that affects all the services is accessibility to their reserves in conflicts less than major regional contingencies, the type of conflicts that are more likely in the future. In a Department of Defense–contracted study by the Institute for Defense Analyses released during the spring of 1994, there was general agreement that there will be a ''need for RC units and individuals in lesser contingencies and operations other than war (OOTW).''[47] One significant example is the deployment of U.S. forces to Somalia. A postal unit available from the USAR was required. Because access to a Selected Reserve unit could not be gained without the President invoking a 200K call-up under *10 USC 673b* or declaring a national emergency, volunteers were called for and a provisional unit was created that did not function well. Another problem in Somalia was that after combat forces landed, the mission, in the author's opinion, should have been turned over to civil affairs units, which have members who in their civilian lives manage cities and towns from sanitation to government and police forces, exactly what was needed for a country in chaos. This was not done because these units are in the RC. Had these units been deployed, the results for the military, the administration, and Somalia might have been better.

The Defense Department's response to the growing need for reservists and reserve units was to ask for legislation that would allow the Secretary of Defense to call up 25,000 Selected Reserve members for contingencies and operations other than war. In the fall of 1994 Congress refused to act upon the request, but later agreed to reexamine the issue. Not certain that such authority will be forthcoming, DOD is continuing to examine the long-standing policy of seeking reserve volunteers for operations and institutionalizing procedures. A recent study on volunteerism acknowledges that the Air Force "uses volunteers routinely for peacetime operations."[48] The reason is simple: air crews are small and the skill levels of reservists are equal to or better than those of members of the AC. The other services, especially the Army, require greater numbers of individuals in units or vessels that require lengthy postmobilization training and cohesion prior to deployment. In the final analysis, volunteerism is less than a satisfactory option for all but the Air Force. However, the DOD will continue to institutionalize this option as long as it lacks the secretarial 25,000 call-up authority.

The services have long been uncomfortable with large reserve formations and the command of these by senior reserve officers. Volunteerism precludes the need and perceived "problem" created by bringing large reserve forces and reserve senior officers onto active duty.

Another problem that will plague the reserves in the future is the inevitable reduction in training operations tempo (OPTEMPO). *The Bottom-Up Review* requires that maximum effort be made to ready reserve forces for combat. However, in fiscal year 1995, for example, the budget allows the USAR to train only those units in the Contingency Force Pool (preidentified units that would be required early in an emergency).[49] Other than enhanced ARNG combat maneuver brigades, which would be necessary if there were two major regional contingencies, the fiscal year 1995 budget does not contain funds for any other guard brigades.

The absence or reduction of meaningful RC training in the past has led to a decline in reenlistment, which has created a significant annual turnover of personnel and ultimately resulted in lower readiness levels. With the uncertainty about the ultimate size of the reserves, there is also a reluctance to enlist, and once the reserve drawdown is completed in 1999, recruiting for the reserves will become even harder.

The other difficulty facing the reserves is the increasing technological revolution and pace of modern maneuver warfare. As a consequence, it is increasingly unlikely that combat maneuver forces in the ARNG will deploy in a contingency without extensive and lengthy postmobilization training despite *The Bottom-Up Review*'s claims. With a downsized AC, the numbers of personnel used to conduct RC postmobilization training will not be available. Thus, even if funds were appropriated, the one element that funding will never be able to buy is training time. Warfare in the twenty-first century will be deadly and complex, so much so that it is unlikely that ARNG combat brigades will ever be used except as a late-deploying strategic insurance force.

On the other hand, the future of the USAR as a consequence of an ''off-site'' agreement announced in December 1993 by then Secretary Les Aspin appears bright. One result of the agreement was the eventual migration of most of the remaining combat arms structure from the USAR to the ARNG, leaving the former Reserve Component primarily combat service support. It is likely that there will be further moves to define the support role for the USAR and the combat role for the ARNG.[50] As a consequence, the USAR will form the bulk of early mobilized and deployed reserve units. Almost all of the USAR's Troop Program Units will be part of the Contingency Force Pool, and its other units, which support mobilization, will be utilized even before the deployment of AC units in the event of a regional conflict.

The same holds true for the USNR. The complexities of modern naval warfare limit the use of ships that are exclusively manned and commanded by reservists. Those ships ''manned'' by reservists are actually 80 percent Active Component personnel crews. The Navy also has limited need for large numbers of reserve personnel in the future because if ships are lost in combat, there will be more than enough crews available since the industrial-base lead time will preclude launching replacements for a conflict. However, there probably will be an increased dependency on shore-based USNR support units and individual reservists in specialty areas.

The USMCR will change little. Although there will be budget cuts and small force reductions, the Marine Corps' utilization of its reserve will remain basically the same: small combat units easily integrated with the bulk of the reserve in support units, and command positions filled by both AC and reserve officers.

In regard to the Coast Guard, faced with budget cuts, its leadership has decided to make the USCGR the bill payer to maintain the AC's strength. This decision will have more impact on the Coast Guard's domestic missions than on its small, but not insignificant, national security role. The most significant consequence will be on AC personnel, for they will be required to perform more weekend and holiday duty.

The AFRES, and to a lesser extent the ANG, are the most integrated of all the RCs with their ACs. The Air Force war plans show its intent to make full use of its reserve assets early in any contingency operation. This is partially because the Air Force is platform oriented; that is, the mission revolves around aircraft. As the AC downsizes, more and more modern equipment will flow to the reserves. However, in the distant future, should the defense budgets continue to decline, there will emerge a problem of aging aircraft. It is becoming increasingly clear that there is also less need for ANG fighter units. The future will probably see a substantial reduction in these units. It remains to be seen, however, if the existing guard assets are moved into the support arena.

For those armed forces that depend heavily on having available large numbers of pretrained individuals, the Army and the Marine Corps, the Individual Ready Reserve will be increasingly important as fillers and casualty replacements. The downsizing of the AC forces will swell this reserve program, as did the large Cold War forces, and then by the next century its numbers will decline. The Clinton administration firmly opposed abolishing the Selective Service System, which, in the distant future, once the IRR declines in numbers, will become increasingly important as a manpower source.[51]

The other individual manpower pool, the IMA, may eventually be removed from the Selected Reserve and returned to the Mobilization Designee Program, which consisted of volunteers within the IRR. The armed forces will, by necessity, increasingly rely on Selected Reserve units. Further cuts in the Selected Reserve will be unacceptable, and thus the IMA program may transfer to the IRR so that it does not count as part of the Selected Reserve strength.

In the future the RCs will become the "compensating leverage," according to Secretary of Defense William Perry, to reduce the potential risks accrued by accepting smaller AC forces.[52] In addition to providing support in the worse-case scenario, two major regional contingencies, the reserves will also be involved in peacekeeping, peacemaking, peace enforcement, and humanitarian missions both at home and abroad.

To be able to provide that leverage regardless of the roles or missions they assume, the armed forces reserves must meet four "imperatives" noted by the Reserve Forces Policy Board. First is that they must be well organized, provided the most modern equipment, fully trained within the time limits imposed, and fully sustained annually. Second, they must continue to be affordable, that is, not only less costly, but more effective and efficient in what they do. Third, they must be relevant. To be so requires further integration into their ACs and thus being properly molded to meet national security and domestic requirements in the future. Last, there must be immediate access to reserve individuals and units by the Secretary of Defense.[53] If the nation continues to rely on citizen-soldiers, then the mechanism must be in place that allows for accessibility to reserve forces in peace and war. If all these imperatives are met, the nation will continue to be well served by its citizen-soldiers.

NOTES

1. Department of Defense, *Annual Report of the Reserve Forces Policy Board,* FY 1975 (Washington, DC: U.S. Government Printing Office, 1976), p. 2.

2. U.S. Congress, *Title 10, United States Code, Armed Forces* (Washington, DC: U.S. Government Printing Office, 1989), p. 79.

3. Department of Defense, *Annual Report of the Reserve Forces Policy Board,* Fiscal Year 1993 (Washington, DC: U.S. Government Printing Office, 1994), p. 197.

4. Ibid.

5. Ibid.

6. Ibid.

7. Department of the Army, *Mobilization and Deployment: Reference and Theory* (Fort Leavenworth, KS: Command and General Staff College, n.d.), p. 2-1.

8. John K. Mahon, *History of the Militia and the National Guard* (New York: Macmillan, 1983), pp. 97–100.

9. Ibid., p. 175.

10. Department of Defense, *Reserve Forces for National Security: Report to the Secretary of Defense by the Committee on Civilian Components* (Washington, DC: Office of the Secretary of Defense, 30 June 1948), p. 14.

11. Department of the Army, *Special Report* (Washington, DC: Office Chief Army Reserve, 1993), pp. 9–10.

12. Department of the Army, ''The Army Reserve'' (briefing slides), Office Chief Army Reserve, Policy and Liaison Division, May 1994.

13. John R. D'Araujo, Jr., ''National Guard: The Dual-Role Force,'' *Army 1993–94 Green Book* (Arlington, VA: Association of the United States Army, October 1993), p. 120.

14. Army National Guard Public Affairs Office, ''Restructuring the Army National Guard Campaign Plan'' (briefing slide), May 1994.

15. Department of the Army, *Special Report,* p. 3.

16. U.S. Army Reserve Command, ''Memorandum for MUSARC PAOS: Subject: Public Affairs Guidance—USARC Command and Control (C2) Plan,'' 17 July 1994.

17. Department of the Army, *Special Report* (Washington, DC: Office Chief Army Reserve, 1933), p. 8.

18. Ibid., p. 55.

19. Ibid., pp. 44, 50.

20. J. H. Binford Peay III and John R. D'Araujo, ''Building America's Army for the 21st Century,'' *National Guard,* January 1994, pp. 28–29.

21. Mahon, *History of the Militia and the National Guard,* p. 146; Department of Defense, *The Reserve Components of the United States Armed Forces* (Washington, DC: Office, Assistant Secretary of Defense for Reserve Affairs, June 1992), p. 23.

22. Robert Frank Futrell, *Ideas, Concepts, Doctrine: Basic Thinking in the United States Air Force, 1907–1960,* vol. 1, (Maxwell Air Force Base, AL: Air University Press, December 1989), pp. 21–22.

23. Department of Defense, *Reserve Components,* pp. 23, 24.

24. Mahon, *History of the Militia and the National Guard,* p. 203.

25. Ibid.

26. National Guard Association, ''The Army and Air National Guard of the 54 States, Territories and the District of Columbia,'' *National Guard,* January 1991, pp. 23–25.

27. Office Air Force Reserve, *Issues Brief: Desert Storm* (Washington, DC: 1994), briefing slide no. 29.

28. John A. Bradley, ''Air Force Reserve Briefing to the U.S. Army War College,'' 21 March 1994.

29. Department of Defense, *Reserve Components,* pp. 25, 26; ''The Reserve and the Total Force: America's Future National Security,'' *Officer,* February 1993, p. 174.

30. National Guard Bureau, *Air National Guard Update* (Washington, DC: National Guard Bureau, July 1993); ''Reserve and the Total Force,'' p. 177.

31. National Guard Association, *National Guard,* January 1994, pp. 82 and 83.

32. Department of Defense, *Reserve Components,* p. 16.

33. Ibid., p. 17.

34. Department of Defense, *Annual Report of the Reserve Forces Policy Board for Fiscal Year 93,* p. 197.

35. Ibid., pp. 17–18.

36. ''Reserve and the Total Force,'' p. 178.

37. Susan L. Alone, ''The Reserves Turn 75,'' *Marine Corps Gazette,* September 1991, p. 59.

38. Department of the Navy, *Marine Corps Reserve Forces in Southwest Asia* (Quantico, VA: Marine Corps Research Center, July 1991), pp. 1, 5.

39. Department of Defense, *Annual Report of the Reserve Forces Policy Board for Fiscal Year 93,* p. 197.

40. Department of Defense, *Reserve Components,* p. 21; ''Reserve and the Total Force,'' p. 179.

41. Department of Defense, *Reserve Components,* p. 21.

42. Department of the Navy, *Marine Corps Reserve: Information Pamphlet* (Overland Park, KS: Marine Corps Reserve, n.d.), pp. 11–12.

43. Department of Defense, *Annual Report of the Reserve Forces Policy Board,* Fiscal Year 1993, p. 191.

44. ''Reserve and the Total Force,'' p. 179.

45. *Annual Report of the Armed Forces Reserve Policy Board,* p. 197.

46. Les Aspin, *The Bottom-Up Review: Forces for a New Era* (Washington, DC: Department of Defense, 1 September 1993), p. 10.

47. Stan Horowitz, ''Reserve Component Volunteerism,'' briefing prepared by the Institute for Defense Analyses, Washington, DC, 20 May 1994, slide no. 6.

48. Ibid., slide no. 8.

49. Office Chief Army Reserve, ''AGR Senior Advisor Position Validation Meeting,'' Washington, DC, 19 May 1994.

50. ''Peay: Force Overhaul Is 'Success Story' '' (Interview with General James H. Binford Peay III), *Army Times,* 30 May 1994, p. 26.

51. ''Clinton Continues Registration for Draft,'' *Washington Times,* 19 May 1994, p. 4.

52. Department of Defense, *Annual Report of the Reserve Forces Policy Board,* Fiscal Year 1993, p. 3.

53. Ibid., pp. 4–5.

SELECTED BIBLIOGRAPHY

Aspin, Les. *The Bottom-Up Review: Forces for a New Era.* Washington, DC: Department of Defense, 1 September 1993.

Department of Defense. *Annual Report of the Reserve Forces Policy Board,* Fiscal Year 1993. Washington, DC: U.S. Government Printing Office, 1994.

———. *The Reserve Components of the United States Armed Forces.* Washington, DC: Office, Assistant Secretary of Defense for Reserve Affairs, June 1992.

Department of the Army. *Mobilization and Deployment: Reference and Theory.* Fort Leavenworth, KS: Command and General Staff College, n.d.

Mahon, John K. *History of the Militia and National Guard.* New York: Macmillan, 1983.

Peay, J. H. Binford, III, and John R. D'Araujo. ''Building America's Army for the 21st Century.'' *National Guard,* January 1994, p. 146.

U.S. Congress. *Title 10, United States Code, Armed Forces.* Washington, DC: U.S. Government Printing Office, 1989.

Chapter 7

SUMMARY AND CONCLUSIONS

Robert E. Connor, Jr.

The purpose of the preceding chapters is to acquaint the reader with the missions, structures, capabilities, and future uses of the various entities that make up the U.S. armed forces. Though all the services, active and reserve, are linked to a common aim, each is unique. This uniqueness is reflected in each service or entity's mission, configuration, and doctrine. The challenge to national security planners, as it has ever been, is to harmonize the capabilities of these entities in order to satisfy policy. It is the challenge of military leaders to advise in that process, make the harmonization work, and then translate the resulting synergism into victory.

Each of the services is the result of a historical process. Each, with the exception of the more recently created Air Force, has rather more than two centuries of experiences that have shaped (some might say ''hammered'') them into the singular organizations that they are today. This means that to an extent each is a living historical artifact that has responded and still responds, however unwittingly, to its past experiences. Some of these experiences are sensed only dimly, but they, to some degree, made an impression and influence the future. Additionally, the effects of these experiences or history operate asymmetrically on each military entity, making the establishment of any historical common ground a difficult proposition.

History's influence on institutions like any of the services has both beneficial and detrimental effects. It can cause an army to fight an industrial-age war in

The author gratefully acknowledges the assistance of Roger J. Spiller, Ph.D., Richard M. Swain, Ph.D., and Lieutenant Colonel Greg R. Hampton in the preparation of this chapter.

blue coats and red pants, or it can be a primal factor in inspiring heroic behavior, as at Gloucester Hill. For the services as institutions, however, history, or, alternatively, tradition, generates a sort of gravity from which it is exceedingly hard to pull free; it tends to cause those who are entrapped to think in a certain, myopic way. This does not preclude innovation, progress, or achievement; but the innovation and progress will be within the narrow confines of the tradition, and any achievement will only reinforce the tendency. The U.S. armed forces have been conditioned by their past to think a certain way about the waging of war and the accomplishment of their various missions.

The result of this thought pattern on service leaders can be a chronic blindness that denies a service the ability to think clearly and open-mindedly about its future. The Gulf War is an example. This conflict fit squarely into the institutional comfort zones of all the services. It was a conventional conflict fought on terrain that, though naturally hostile to humans, was well suited for the military technology that had been developed for the Cold War. The operations were conventional, the forces used were conventional, the equipment was technologically advanced, and the campaign was successful. The services finally got the war, albeit on a much reduced scale, they had waited such a long time to fight. The services, especially the Air Force, legitimized their organizations, their training programs, and much of their equipment without ever having to leave their institutional comfort zones.

Therefore, breaking free of experience to effect change within the services requires an intellectual effort of no mean magnitude. This is not to say that the services are not progressive, just that they have their own singular pace. Because they are hierarchical and by nature conservative institutions, the progress can at times be painfully slow, often the result of irresistible official pressure or, if speedy, the result of calamity. Since World War II the services, with the possible exception of the Marine Corps, have seduced themselves into believing that advances in technology are the same as progress. This is especially true in the Army. Progress has been measured more by the sophistication of systems than by the sophistication of thought. This is the real Cold War paradigm that entraps our services, and now that the Cold War is over it is time to realize that the old, comfortable belief that technology will win out in the end, regardless of the situation, should change. The challenge facing the services in this new security era is, as it ever has been, an intellectual one.[1]

As each service matured, it strove to accommodate the needs of the Republic that it served. Often this was not an easy task to accomplish. The Republic, faithful to its own set of historical experiences, had and still has its own ideas about the necessity and utility of the armed forces. Thus the authors of the U.S. Constitution, when considering national defense, expressed their deep conviction that standing armies were the traditional tools of despots to oppress citizens and deprive them of their rights. That is why the Constitution gives Congress the authority to ''raise and support armies,'' but only for two years at a time.[2] On the other hand, Congress, by that same document, is directed to ''maintain'' a navy.[3] Navies, after all, are no immediate threat to the citizenry and are necessary for the protection of commerce, the Republic's lifeblood. Finally, the Constitution further and more deeply affected the development and character of the services by clearly subordinating them to civilian control by making the President, the freely elected, civilian head of state, commander-in-chief. In this embryonic stage of our nation's development, therefore, a historical mark that was both basic and lasting was imprinted on the armed forces.

Several times in our nation's past the services (typically but not exclusively the Army) found themselves in the somewhat uncomfortable position of trying to persuade Congress, never wholly convinced that a standing army was either safe or necessary, of its continuing viability while the Navy pushed for expansion and modernization. One such example was engendered by the closing of the West in 1890. Allan Millett and Peter Maslowski ably captured this period:

> With the Indian wars' ending, the Army lost its most active mission. Police duty was an unsatisfactory substitute, and no strategist envisioned sending large expeditionary forces abroad. . . . The Army embraced a new fortifications program, for coastal defense seemed its sole remaining significant function. While reminding the public of the Navy's role in aiding businessmen abroad, naval officers propagandized for the new Navy among select groups . . . shipbuilders, steel firms, and weapons manufacturers who would benefit from naval construction. Navalists also supported an expanded merchant marine, hoping they could convince the business community that more commerce justified more warships.[4]

Though the newest and arguably the most "modern" of the services, the Air Force has its own history that informs its present and will affect its future. Intellectually, the modern Air Force was born when Billy Mitchell took his first flight over the static, deadly, wasting trenches of the western front. Russell Weigley quoted what Mitchell wrote about his experience:

> One flight over the lines gave me a much clearer impression of how the armies were laid out than any amount of traveling around on the ground. A very significant thing to me was that we could cross the lines of these contending armies in a few minutes in our airplane, whereas the armies had been locked in the struggle, immoveable, powerless to advance, for three years. . . . It was as though they were knocking their heads against a stone wall, until their brains were dashed out. They got nowhere, as far as ending the war was concerned.
>
> It looked as though the war would keep up indefinitely until either the airplanes brought an end to the war or the contending nations dropped from sheer exhaustion.[5]

Not a word here is said about strategic bombing, nor is there a hint of the claim that the "bomber will always get through." What is expressed here is the fundamental creed of the U.S. Air Force: in modern war decision cannot be obtained without air power.

David MacIsaac pointed out that in its earliest days military aviation attracted young, impetuous, daredevil enthusiasts rather than the reflective, philosophical fellow. The thoughts and writings of these young zealots were therefore usually enormously sanguine about their arm of service.

> In so far as such people talked or wrote of their experiences, it was usually of the air as a new environment of endeavor, utterly untrammeled or impeded by the usages or customs of the past. Passionately committed to flying and the general advancement of aviation, the writers who emerged from among the aviation pioneers were rarely analytical and never dispassionate. Their vision of the role air power could play in warfare invariably outran the reality of the moment, provoking disappointment among the converted and derision from the unbelievers.[6]

Some may suggest that this historically fundamental intellectual proclivity has clung to the Air Force to this day. Whether it has or not, what is basal to the U.S. Air Force is the intellectual credo that air power can be the decisive factor in warfare, and without it decision on the modern battlefield is chimerical.

In order to maintain itself on the leading edge of aeronautic technology, the Air Force, like the other services, must contend for dwindling resources in what may be viewed as a hostile environment. That the armed forces are a pestiferous drain on the Republic's treasury has been and probably will ever be an article of faith for the U.S. government. This historical circumstance is, therefore, woven into the very fabric of our services. It is the foundation for the most recurrent phenomenon in their history. As Roger Spiller has pointed out, this phenomenon goes by several euphemisms according to the style of the day: "downsizing," "retrenchment," or simply "reduction in force." But when all is said and done, the process inevitably becomes one of demobilization.[7] It is during these periods, which are usually, but not always, associated with the end of a war or threat of war, that the services find themselves in heated competition, not only with other government agencies, but among themselves (and within themselves) for resources. The result of one particularly ferocious and rancorous competition was the "revolt of the admirals" following the demobilization after World War II. The armed forces of the United States are faced with a similar situation today, and how they respond will have as much to do with their past experiences—their history—as with any real or perceived threat or change in the strategic landscape.

As the reader reviews each of these chapters, certain points may become apparent: the similarity, or even redundancy, in some of the services' missions, capabilities, or configurations; the obvious reliance some services have on others, especially in an era of "power projection"; or, perhaps, the difficulty inherent in properly training, stationing, equipping, and configuring modern forces capable of securing victory (whatever that may be in each circumstance) in a menacing and volatile world. These challenges and a plethora of others that attend them do, in fact, face our military leaders and strategic planners.

One fundamental method that military organizations use to clarify what they are about is to construct a clear, concise, achievable mission statement. This is true of organizations as big as the services themselves and as varied as infantry battalions and the Army–Air Force Exchange Service. Once an organization is clear as to what it is about, it can start devising ways of doing its job. In order for all branches of a given service and the various units within a single branch to work synergistically toward a commonly understood goal, the services have adopted doctrines.

As all our authors have pointed out, doctrine has become a focal point in the post–Cold War armed services. We will speak more fully on this topic later in this chapter, but a few words are appropriate here. Each service has found it necessary to make "authoritative statements" about how it will carry out its operations. The services are in broad agreement as to a definition of the word *doctrine.* For the Army doctrine is

> the statement of how America's Army . . . intends to conduct war and operations other than war. It is the condensed expression of the Army's fundamental approach to fighting. . . . As an authoritative statement, doctrine must be definitive enough to guide specific operations, yet remain adaptable enough to address varied situations worldwide.[8]

The Navy, for example, is in general agreement: "Naval Doctrine is the foundation upon which our tactics, techniques and procedures are built. It articulates operational concepts that govern the employment of naval forces at all levels."[9]

The services agree, therefore, that doctrine is a crucial, fundamental element in mission accomplishment. Even so, questions arise about this critical element called doctrine. In a world like the one in which we now live, one might ask, is such a thing as an "authoritative statement" governing all the possible missions that may face our armed forces possible? If so, is that which we now have "it"? Last, in such an uncertain strategic landscape, what must we look for to bind all the disparate parts of the separate services' doctrines together? These questions concern the topics of theory, doctrine, and joint operations or "jointness." This chapter will deal with each of these critical areas, but first let us review what our authors have said about the current and future capabilities of the various armed services and what the future may hold for each.

THE ARMY

Daniel Kaufman presents an authoritative and detailed summary of the current and future capabilities of the United States Army. He correctly focuses his comments on the remarkably altered strategic environment and how this will affect the most senior of the armed forces. Vital to his chapter is his concern about the "new and destabilizing trends" that the demise of the Soviet Union has unleashed upon the world. The bottom line to Kaufman's concerns is, as he quite plainly states, that the eagerly sought rewards of victory, such as the much-touted "peace dividend" attending the end of the Cold War, are a mirage.

Kaufman describes the Army's part in this dramatically changed environment, by linking it to national leadership views on national security strategy. It is from this expression of national strategic concerns that the services draw their missions and create the national military strategy. Changing missions have their effects on the size and shape of the Army as well as on the way it sees itself actually conducting operations. With a set of missions as diverse as those expressed in U.S. national military strategy, the Army finds itself once again reshaping itself to respond to the requirements of the Republic. It is on this reshaping that Kaufman next focuses our attention.

The fundamental change between the Army of today and the Cold War Army of yesterday is, as Kaufman points out, that instead of being ''forward deployed'' in places like Europe, the Army is becoming a ''power-projection'' force. This army will be based in the continental United States and will be deployed to any point on the globe where the National Command Authority (NCA) deems it necessary. As Kaufman asserts, this calls for a redesign of the force.

The Army that for over forty years was trained and poised to do battle with the heavy, massive Soviet ground force was itself heavy. In order to be any sort of viable threat to the Soviet Army, our Army had to organize, train, and equip itself to engage and defeat the armor-heavy Soviets on the plains of Central Europe. Army planners and trainers therefore focused on modernizing tanks, armored personnel carriers (APC), antiarmor weapons, and a myriad of air defense capabilities. This was expensive but intellectually easy. Today the Army is expected to deploy across the globe into any type of climate and terrain to fight or aid any culture, no matter how diverse or alien to that of the United States; do it quickly, cheaply, and successfully while suffering minimum casualties; and do it with fewer people. This is intellectually much more difficult.

Kaufman gives us the present configuration of the Army and what it is designed to do. Of crucial importance is the idea that the Army is configured with different types of fighting formations, each with its own special capabilities and limitations. That is, while the light infantry formation may be more rapidly deployable, it lacks the tactical power of a heavy or mechanized infantry formation or, even more so, an armored formation. Therefore, the most rapidly deployable Army formation, the airborne infantry or Marine amphibious formation, is also its least powerful. This is the dilemma a power-projection force faces: the most rapidly deployable forces are, in terms of sustaining combat, by definition the least potent fighting units when challenged with a heavy enemy ground threat. A rapidly deployable force, no matter how famous, therefore, does not necessarily equate to a decisive or even potent fighting force.

It must be kept in mind that the present variety and mix of the various fighting formations in the Army were dictated by the military predictions of the Cold War world. Though the Army is ''downsizing'' with the post–Cold War world in mind, combat division and lower organization is still very much as it was during that period. The Army is looking very hard at its formations and using a multitude of means to test different combinations and configurations, as Kaufman makes clear. It is too early now to make any guess as to what, if any, great changes might be made, but one can plainly see by Kaufman's lucid account that the Army has a myriad of formations and cutting-edge technologies upon which it can draw to accomplish its mission.

The most important part of Kaufman's chapter is that which deals with the Army's struggle to cast itself as a viable fighting force for the twenty-first century. It is in dealing with this subject that a debate is heating up within the Army. The controversy hinges on a difference of opinion about what type of mission the Army should prepare for.

In any document dealing with the Army and the future, the first thing the author will be likely to say, and quite rightly so, is that the Army recognizes that it will be called upon to react to any one of the full spectrum of possible challenges, from a major regional conflict to disaster relief. This is saying quite a lot. First there is a spectrum of conflict itself. This ranges from low-intensity through mid-intensity to high-intensity warfare. Then there are all the other possibilities that do not necessarily entail conventional combat. These have been lumped together by the Army as operations other than war (OOTW). Though the acronym OOTW is an invention of the Army's "capstone" doctrinal statement, *Field Manual 100-5,* these missions have been the bread and butter of the Army since the Whiskey Rebellion.

Historically, the Army has conducted far more OOTW missions than it has conventional wars, a fact that has been recognized and thoroughly examined by such scholars as Sam C. Sarkesian.[10] The post–Cold War world and the language of the national security strategy will most likely add to this list. What some critics are seeing, and this is at the heart of the controversy, is planners putting the Army's pocketbook and, what is more crucial, its intellectual effort behind large-scale, conventional wars. This is being done, so the critics say, while ignoring those missions that continue to be the Army's bread and butter in favor of an aberration like the Gulf War.

A counterargument to this is that by preparing for "the big one" the Army can best be ready to deal with the entire spectrum of eventualities. This very simple argument actually has much to recommend it. Would it, after all, be possible or desirable to organize, equip, and train an entire army around such disparate missions as disaster relief, security and advisory assistance, arms control, and peacekeeping? If the Army continues to build, at least technologically, and train for major regional conflicts, will it not be in the best possible position to deal with the smaller, more subtle affairs?

On the surface, given the realities of the time, the counterargument seems to be plausible. But there are serious problems with it. There are inherent dangers associated with training, organizing, and equipping for one sort of conflict and conducting another. These dangers range from putting soldiers trained for conventional war in charge of roadblocks where the rules of engagement are perilously restrictive and change daily, if not more often, to completely mistaking the nature of the conflict into which the Army has been committed and thereby inviting disaster. One does not have to travel far back in time to find an example where the fact that the nature of the conflict was misunderstood was at the root of a military disaster for the United States and its Army.

Roger Spiller once described the failure in Vietnam as fundamentally intellectual.[11] Strategic planners failed rather miserably to look beyond their current paradigm of warfare and past the seemingly irresistible superiority of their technology in order to understand the nature of the conflict in which they found themselves. The U.S. Army was not only organized, trained, and equipped for a conventional, European war but was woefully ill prepared to deal intellectually with anything else. Clausewitz considered understanding the nature of a conflict an elemental part of victory: "The first, the supreme, the most far-reaching act of judgment that the statesman and the commander have to make is to establish . . . the kind of war on which they are embarking; neither mistaking it for, or trying to turn it into, something that is alien to its nature."[12]

Vietnam was not the first time since World War II that the U.S. Army was caught mistaking the nature of a conflict. In Korea the Army was not only intellectually unprepared to fight a limited war in the nuclear age, it was woefully ill prepared materially as well. Many nervous critics today look at the shrinking defense budget and the shrinking Army and fear, not without reason, a reprise of the "hollow Army" of 1950 or, for that matter, the late 1970s.

Korea was not the war the Army was prepared to fight. The war, if it came, would take place on the plains of Europe, barring the preemptive use of nuclear weapons, against an invading conventional armor-heavy force. This was the paradigm of the bipolar Cold War world. This was the "worst-case" scenario of the Cold War era, and it provided service planners with a rather neat (if frightening) homogeneous mission upon which to base force structure, systems development, strategy, and doctrine.

Happily, the feared Soviet invasion of Western Europe never took place. The Korean War, though it eventually involved prodigious amounts of personnel and materiel, was unlike that which the armed forces had fought in Europe during the World War II. It was predominately a ground war in which naval fleet action did not take place. The enemy, while numerous, was basically a light infantry force that generally lacked a great deal of combat support and combat service support assets. The enemy's strength lay in his numbers, his tactics, and his resolve. The Communist forces tended to attack at night and were masterful in their ability to infiltrate, cut off, and isolate U.N. troops yet maintain momentum. U.N. forces conventionally stopped Communist offensives by blunting them with overwhelming air and field artillery support. After the Communist forces absorbed this punishment, the offensive would typically fail, having reached its culminating point, due to the inability of the Communists to sustain these massive drives, allowing the U.N. forces to go over to the offense. This is not to denigrate the contribution of the maneuver forces. Their steadfastness, especially after the first year of combat, was remarkable. What was equally remarkable and tragic, however, was the undeniable unpreparedness of the U.S. forces in the early stages of that conflict.

Compounding this unpreparedness on the part of the soldiers was the remarkable inability of the operational commanders to break away from the northern European scenario, which was not applicable to the barren, mountainous, and backward environs of Korea. Motorized American columns found the terrain nearly impossible to traverse, and operational and tactical commanders found the enemy's use of this very terrain difficult to understand or counter.

Finally, there was the example of the supreme commander who could not force his own mind, powerful as it was, from the paradigm of total war. MacArthur could not, or refused to, realize that he was engaged in a war of a different nature. Korea was a limited conflict where the military solution of complete and final victory was no longer valid. Simply put, MacArthur violated Clausewitz's primary rule.

Volumes have been written about the startling lack of U.S. readiness to engage in an armed conflict just five years after bringing the Axis powers to their knees. This lack of preparedness was especially keen in the ground forces that were first committed to the Korean peninsula. The reasons for this were many and involved, but chiefly they stemmed from a war-weary nation's deep desire to hang up the mailed fist and enjoy the fruits of peace, from a misperception of the enemy and his intentions, and a mistaken reliance on technology. Many cannot resist pointing out the obvious parallels with today's situation.

Perhaps sensing this, then Army Chief of Staff, General Gordon R. Sullivan, stated emphatically that there will be no more Task Force Smiths. By this one must assume that General Sullivan meant that not only will the Army never again send just over four hundred poorly trained, underequipped infantrymen and a battery of artillery to stop the better part of a tank brigade and two infantry regiments, but that it will guard against the broader, deeper reasons for the U.S. reversals early in the Korean war.[13] The implied pledge is that the U.S. armed forces will be intellectually as well as physically prepared to face the next challenge whenever and wherever it may occur; that with cries for a ''peace dividend,'' downsizing, and a changing world strategic environment notwithstanding, the armed forces of the United States will be ready.

While we pray this is true, one cannot avoid the uncomfortable feeling that the Army's senior leadership is once again failing to look past a paradigm that in this case is the false paradigm of the Gulf War. It is not easy, one must add, to look beyond the prevailing attitude, but it is absolutely necessary. Even in the eighteenth century at least one military practitioner and thinker expressed his lack of patience with generals who could not see beyond the ordinary:

> I look upon them in the light of persons who are confounded and rendered incapable of discernment; and who don't know how to execute any other business than what they have been accustomed to all their lives. . . . The reaction of this defect is, because very few officers study the grand detail . . . when therefore they arrive at the command of grand armies, they are totally perplexed, and from their ignorance [of] how to do what they ought, are very naturally led to do what they know.[14]

Are not the grand designs for the future Army of which Kaufman speaks merely adjustments within a false paradigm? Army planners, while acknowledging the wide variety of possible missions the Army may be assigned, are not paying any meaningful attention to those missions. Both history and future prognostications indicate that OOTW and low-intensity conflict will form the mainstay of the Army's activities; yet, as Kaufman's chapter so clearly demonstrates, the Army unfortunately lacks any serious intellectual effort in that arena.

In a recently published white paper, General Sullivan expressed his thoughts on the future orientation of the Army, an official view of how the Army should be used in this transformed strategic environment. Though one might think that such a document would better serve at the beginning of a Chief of Staff's tenure rather than at the end, this document spelled out what his thoughts were. In this paper the Chief of Staff declared flatly that the "United States Army is America's force of decision" and that it "has changed to meet the challenges of the world today."[15] Strategically this new Army has four purposes. In the international arena they are to compel, deter, and reassure; on the domestic scene its purpose is to support.

The three international activities are closely linked. They share the common assumption that if a military force is to be of any use, it must be viable and seen as such by friend and foe alike. Such a force in being, Sullivan argued, has the salutary effect of deterring potential adversaries from the use of force. If deterrence fails, the Army must fight or otherwise compel the enemy into acceding to U.S. wishes. Compulsion, of course, lies anywhere on the great spectrum of military involvement from general war calling for the unconditional surrender of the enemy to securing a less extreme policy. Finally, the Army can be used to reassure allies by its very existence either as a rapidly deployable power projection army (for which it is completely dependent on other services), or by being "forward deployed," as in Korea. Regardless of how the Army is used, Sullivan asserted, and irrespective of the fact that it will always act as part of a joint services team, the Army's unique contribution to national security is the fact that it remains the only service that offers the statesman decisiveness—the ability to win a war.

As far as domestic missions are concerned, Sullivan pointed out that the Army has the equipment, manpower, and organization to rapidly succor victims of disaster, such as Hurricane Andrew in 1992. Sullivan curiously, but no doubt diplomatically, also included civil disturbances under the heading of support rather than compulsion. We should not wonder at this; the army of a republic should be reticent about publicizing its role of being the central government's last resort against its own citizens. Sullivan was, after all, merely cataloging the various potential uses of the Army to make a point. The point is that a great deal of thought must be expended to properly organize, equip, and train a force capable of all these missions.

There can be no doubt, as Sullivan suggested, that as long as people live on land, the Army will continue to be the one tool that gives the statesman the possibility of decision if military force is used. This is because only the Army has the assets, the organization, and the expertise to carry out sustained operations on the ground. If it is to be truly useful in this unique role in the new strategic setting, however, the Army as an institution must effect a fundamental reappraisal of the element in which it operates. As mentioned earlier, breaking a paradigm is a herculean task, but now may be the time to effect such a change. This would involve for the Army a reevaluation of war itself, its nature, and its progress. The Army has for too long concerned itself with the battlefield (a battlefield, no matter how realistically reproduced by modern computer technology, is always comfortingly familiar); it is time now for it to reconsider the phenomenon of war itself in this new security era.

The real value of General Sullivan's paper is that it represents a process of thoughtful reflection on the Army's place in the Republic. Such intellectual effort must be highly regarded. General Sullivan's example of thinking thoroughly about the future and having those thoughts published and challenged is worthy of emulation by future military leaders. One problem with the paper, however, is that it has no intellectual foundation. This is a fault shared by the entire U.S. military establishment. Individually and collectively the services lack a pervading theory of war. The need for such a theory will be discussed later in this chapter.

THE NAVY

In his chapter, John Williams offers a keenly perceptive view of the Navy and its future capabilities. A key comment in his chapter is the statement that the Navy "moved quickly to fill the theoretical void left when the breakup of the Soviet Union changed the dangers against which it needed to prepare." It reminds us that political changes that have so affected the world had a profound impact on the U.S. Navy. Williams addresses these changes both perceptively and concisely.

Though Williams does not drag the reader through the long and sometimes convoluted history of naval theory and practice, he relates enough of it to demonstrate to the reader the line of causation that compels the Navy, or any service, to alter its strategy. It is not only, as Williams points out, "the threat," real or perceived, that shapes these strategies but also the political priorities of the current administration. This is why, as mentioned earlier, the services must be looked at as historical entities. They are products of their historical context, and that context may be, and usually is, complex. In the context of the Carter administration, due to certain political imperatives, the Navy attempted to meet the needs of the Republic by formulating the Forward Maritime Strategy.

Williams goes on to explain quite clearly the progress of and the challenges to naval strategy to the present day, while discerningly commenting on and critiquing that progress. His discussion of the operation of the Forward Maritime Strategy is a case in point. While detailing some of the landlocked targets included in the ''expansive notion of sea control'' that was the heart of this strategy, Williams states, ''In a leap of logic left implicit, U.S. Navy forces, rather than other U.S. or allied forces, were thought necessary by the Navy to attack these threats to their forces, and campaign plans were developed to do so.'' He goes on to explain, insightfully, how this strategy was viewed at the time and what its practical ramifications were. One of the planned by-products of this aggressive and ambitious plan was to justify ''the kind and level of forces needed for operations elsewhere.'' Williams goes on to explain, however, that to assume that the Maritime Strategy was entirely a blind to garner more of the budget and not a ''legitimate military response to a genuine military problem'' would be a mistake.

Undoubtedly the greatest benefit to be derived from Williams's chapter is his informed and intelligent discussion of current Navy thought. While recognizing the reality that the new naval doctrine, From the Sea, is a result of the Gulf War, he refuses to endorse, and quite correctly too, the notion that the Gulf War with all its anomalies should serve as a model for future conflict. Indeed, Williams argues that if From the Sea is ''taken seriously,'' it will mark a startling departure from the Cold War scenario. This departure is underscored by its effect on certain platforms. Submarines, the ascendant platform of the Cold War, have lost their premier position to the notion of ground combat support. Minesweepers and amphibious warfare ships are enjoying the limelight in this new naval doctrine.

Of course, the position of the aircraft carrier has, if anything, been enhanced by the lessons of recent experiences (not all the lessons of the Gulf War are invalid). The unique abilities of the aircraft carrier to quickly project potent U.S. military power globally as well as supporting ground operations render its position in the arsenal secure for the foreseeable future.

This, of course, is in keeping with the historical traditions of the Navy. It has demonstrated time after time its ability to accomplish missions in remote parts of the world, away from forward-deployed troops, in places where U.S. or allied air bases are inadequate or do not exist. This unique ability has proven more eloquently than any budgetary briefing ever could the continuing need for a strong sea force. Let us look at just one moderately recent historical example.

After the 1956 Suez crisis, Soviet influence in the Middle East steadily increased while that of France and the United Kingdom declined. In July 1958 Soviet-backed Iraqi military officers toppled the monarchy in a sanguinary coup. Fearing the same end, Lebanese President Camille Chamoun appealed to President Dwight Eisenhower for immediate assistance. Though not completely convinced of the urgent nature of the situation, Eisenhower asked the Chief of Naval Operations to land forces on the coast of Lebanon within thirteen hours of the initial request. A carrier task force of the USS *Essex* was sent to rendezvous with the amphibious force to cover the landings. By noon the following day, 16 July 1958, there were a total of 5,000 Marines ashore. The Marines effected a linkup with Lebanese forces and marched with the U.S. Ambassador and President Chamoun into Beirut.

Floyd Kennedy described the less successful efforts of the Army and Air Force contingents of this operation:

> The Army and Air Force units that were assigned to reenforce the Marine assault were thrust into a single staging area at Incerlik, Turkey. The logistics of the situation were impossible. A "fast reaction" composite air strike force . . . took five days to reach Incerlik. Upon their arrival they discovered the airfield so congested with transport aircraft assigned to lift Army troops from Germany that the airplanes of the composite group could not even taxi to parking spaces. On July 18 there were 150 aircraft, most of which were large transports, cluttering the airfield. . . . The proximity of Incerlik to Soviet air bases would have facilitated a rapid, effective Soviet intervention, but even the total destruction of Incerlik would not have effected the success of the Navy-Marine landings.[16]

There are, of course, many explanations for the immediate availability of those Marine and Navy forces and extenuating circumstances for the unfortunate performance by the Army and Air Force in this instance. But the incontestable fact remains that the Navy was able to offer policymakers a unique and indispensable function that, in this particular instance, could not be matched by the other services. One must be mindful, however, of the parameters of the Lebanese crisis of July 1958 lest dangerous generalities be reached about the viability of the various services.

The unique capabilities of the Navy remain. These special properties form the basis of the Navy's modern doctrine. "The ultimate source of peacetime persuasive power . . . lies in the implied guarantee that both the intent and capability to protect our national interests are present *just over the horizon,* with the fortitude and staying power to sustain operations as long as necessary" (emphasis added).[17] These are the unique capabilities upon which the Navy is relying to secure its place in the new security era, and as an argument for viability, it is a strong one indeed. Constant forward deployment is the idea upon which the Navy's strategy hinges, as is made clear by its doctrinal document *Naval Doctrine Publication (NDP) 1: Naval Warfare.* This publication is to the Navy what *Field Manual 100-5* is to the Army. Some may find it strange that *NDP 1,* dated 28 March 1994, is the Navy's first essay in written, servicewide doctrine. The Navy's lack of a statement of doctrine has been a bone of contention within that service, and for those who have operated with it, for many years.

In 1915 Lieutenant Commander Dudley Knox won the Naval Institute's essay prize for a piece criticizing the Navy for its lack of written doctrine. To Knox the benefits of doctrine were both legion and undeniable. Was it enough, he asked, to have a Navy that could merely steam and shoot? Perhaps he felt that the self-evident need for doctrine was understood by the Navy hierarchy when he wrote:

> The navy is comprehending with greater clearness every day that a fleet is more than just a mere collection of ships; that a "bare ship for ship" superiority over a possible enemy is not a guarantee of victory; that before the ships are ready to go into action, no matter how efficient individually, they must be welded into a body, whose various members can be well controlled from a single source and can act collectively as a unit, free from embarrassing internal friction; and that the problem of the proper utilization of the abilities to steam and shoot—that is, the problem of command is not only less elementary but also much more difficult of a solution than any yet undertaken by us.[18]

Sailors like Knox and the Navy would have to wait nearly eighty years for a published doctrine.

Though Knox would no doubt have applauded the production of naval doctrine, he might have been perplexed at the shape it took. Knox would probably have expected doctrine that described great fleet actions where the prime objective would be to seek out the enemy's main battle fleet, bring it to decisive action, and destroy it. This would have been the doctrine of Alfred Thayer Mahan, the nineteenth-century naval theorist. This is not what one finds in *NDP 1.*

As already discussed, Professor Williams gives us a clear picture of the intellectual process that the Navy went through in its examination of the post–Cold War world and its production of its new doctrine. Without the formidable Soviet fleet as a potential adversary, the U.S. Navy has looked beyond the seductive promises of Mahanian theory to see the realities of the new security era. As Williams says, the new naval doctrine is every inch a "significant departure from the strategic presuppositions of an entire generation of naval officers," which, as we have mentioned, is no mean feat.

Indeed, such a change in orientation runs strongly against the Navy's historical grain, as Williams points out. He refers to the "go it alone" mentality that "accounted for much Navy foot-dragging on joint organizations in the past." As Williams suggests, the capability translated into an attitude, the attitude into an article of faith. It is extremely difficult for any service to subordinate itself even in part to another or to the idea of "jointness." In light of this it is not hard to imagine that any naval officer would chafe at the idea of his or her service being made over as a water-borne taxi service for the Army with additional duty as an offshore, floating battery.

The Navy, as is evident in the language of *NDP 1,* is mindful of its historic mission. "The ability to engage the enemy at sea decisively will always remain paramount to our naval forces."[19] Since the demise of the Soviet Union this priority, as Williams suggests, has diminished. This will only serve to improve the chances of true cooperation with the other services. In the past the overriding need for the Navy to maintain a strong, offensive surface and submarine fleet for the specific purpose of engaging and sinking a like enemy force practically precluded meaningful cooperation. This situation was due to a number of factors, among which are theory and doctrine, which will be discussed in more detail later. As Williams says, barring the resurgence of a world naval power, ''the path of . . . *From the Sea* [*NDP 1*] seems likely to continue.''

THE AIR FORCE

One of the difficulties historians have when dealing with the Air Force or the idea of air power is the fact that this service and this notion have a very limited pedigree. As David MacIsaac pointed out, air power, because it is a relatively new idea (particular to the twentieth century), ''continues to defy our attempts at analysis.''[20] James Mowbray's perceptive and informative chapter underscores MacIsaac's point of view. Perhaps the hardship lies somewhere in the dichotomy between the traditional promise of air power and actual results. Air power, as suggested at the beginning of this chapter, has always held out to military thinkers the seductive prospect of quick, decisive, and relatively bloodless (for the wielder of air power) victory. The results of the use of air power, however, have always been controversial. The most obvious example of this controversy is the still hotly debated effectiveness of the Allied bombing campaign in the European theater in World War II.

Even though air power did not accomplish a quick and decisive victory, Malcolm Smith argued that it is dangerous to assert that because ''airmen did not actually achieve what they set out to achieve and leave it at that . . . is to undervalue the real importance of Allied performance in the air.'' One must not separate the strategic air campaign from the tactical, Smith maintained. To do so would be to ''undervalue the contribution of air power to the war on land and on the sea.''[21] (This idea of the totality of the Air Force mission is emphasized by Mowbray in his section dealing with doctrine.) When one examines the historical context of the idea of strategic air power, Smith asserted, the distance between the promise and the results comes into sharper focus:

> The idea that the bomber would be the decisive weapon in any renewed war rested on a depressed faith in the future of advanced industrial society, with its economic recessions and social divisions. If industrial economies were indeed inherently unstable, how could they withstand a rain of high explosive? It was easily argued that an attack on important sectors of the economy could bring the entire structure crashing down under the cumulative weight of its interdependence. Similarly, how could civilian morale take the strain of bombardment, when societies were barely surviving the divisive effects of mass unemployment?[22]

Air power theorists of the interwar period, therefore, committed a grievous contextual error in their predictions as to the true meaning of air power.

Interwar theorists, Smith went on to say, were also victims of their own unshakable faith in the lasting superiority of swift, high-flying technology: the bomber. There was no real evidence in the years before World War II that the bomber could be stopped. Formations of these mechanical marvels would simply brush past any abortive attempt by pursuit aircraft to stop them, then fly over ground artillery's puny efforts at air defense and on to devastate the enemy. These early theorists were blind to ideas like an enemy with indomitable will or his ability to blunt or even turn back the technological edge with developments of his own, or the impracticability of the notion that any Air Force possessed the ability to deliver a single, knockout blow to German industry.

Even today, the issue of the true decisiveness of air forces is disputed. Some air power enthusiasts assert that the ''Line Backer'' series of air operations in Vietnam are a plain indication of what a well-planned air offensive can achieve quite on its own. Well-publicized accounts of the Air Force's successes in the Gulf War have been used to suggest the superfluousness of ground forces. Of course the time-honored (and as yet not disproven) counterargument to the most strident claims of air power is that there is, in fact, no evidence that air assets alone can force a decision from an enemy. Indeed, the exact opposite might even be true. As T. R. Fehrenbach said:

> Americans in 1950 rediscovered something that since Hiroshima they had forgotten: you may fly over a land forever; you may bomb it, atomize it, pulverize it and wipe it clean of life—but if you desire to defend it, protect it, and keep it for civilization, you must do this on the ground, the way the Roman legions did, by putting your young men into the mud.[23]

Such arguments rage on within the services but produce very little in the way of positive results. It is when the services see their role as vital parts of the whole that productive thought is accomplished. Such a thoughtful and satisfying discussion of present and future Air Force potential is presented by Mowbray, who brushes aside what he sees as parochial polemics and takes for granted the need and the will of that branch to stay on the technological leading edge while focusing our attention on what he sees as the real challenge facing the Air force today—the intellectual challenge.

The U.S. Air Force, as Mowbray sees it, faces the danger of writing doctrine that has no intellectual or theoretical foundation. This would be most seriously felt if the Air Force invested time and effort in formulating an ''up-gunned'' air power theory. According to Mowbray, the intellectual challenge of today's Air Force leadership is to transcend the intellectual paradigm of the day and devise a theory that embraces the ''employment of aerospace assets for war fighting.'' A more detailed discussion of the need and role of theory will be presented at the end of this chapter.

THE MARINE CORPS

The U.S. Marine Corps presents the observer with a paradox. It is undeniably a unique organization; indeed, it invests a great deal of energy in emphasizing its singularity. Its uniform, its focus on tradition, and its internationally notorious initial-entry training methods all serve to stress its exceptionality. On the other hand, it strikes some observers that in appearance, equipment, and general mission the Marines constitute an institutional redundancy with the Army. Why is it, one may ask, that both exist?

Allan Millett addresses that question in his perspicacious and informative chapter on the Corps. Operation Restore Democracy has served to fan the flames of this rather old controversy. In this instance the argument centers around the fact that though Marine expeditionary forces had been steaming around Haiti since October 1993, the mission to occupy Port-au-Prince (initially planned as an invasion) was given to the Army's 82d Infantry Division (Airborne) and 10th Infantry Division (Mountain). The Marine Corps sees this as a clear encroachment onto their turf.[24] As Millett has made clear in his chapter, the Haitian operation is not the first time that the Marine Corps has been involved in disputes with other services over its role in the national security of the United States.[25]

Historically linked to the Navy, the Marine Corps' continued existence relied on that services' good offices. Due to its role as part of the Navy, the Marine Corps remained a small and fragile service until the end of the nineteenth century. Jack Shulimson put it succinctly:

> During the days of sail, Marine sharpshooters, positioned in the fighting tops of men of war, cleared the decks of opposing ships with musket fire. When this mission receded with the coming of steam, Marines continued to assist in manning gun batteries and serving as ship's police. They also formed the nucleus of any landing party. On shore, Marines provided the security forces to protect vital naval installations. Occasionally, when needed, the Marine Corps formed ad hoc battalions to keep the peace or to reinforce the Army.[26]

The Marine Corps of the late nineteenth century, therefore, was in a wasteland where its strength lay at about 2,000, dispersed into small garrisons. Its senior officer was only a colonel, and promotions were excruciatingly slow.[27]

During the last decades of the nineteenth century, the services, led by far-sighted senior officers like Admiral David Porter, General William Sherman, and the Marine Corps' own Commandant, Colonel Charles Haywood, enjoyed a period of professionalization and revitalization that was marked by the establishment of such institutions as the Naval Institute, the Military Service Institute, the Naval War College, the Army's School of Application for Infantry and Cavalry, and the Marine Corps School of Application. For the Marines, who were still, as Shulimson put it, an "organizational anomaly," the Spanish-American War marked a turning point in their history.[28]

Before the outbreak of the war with Spain, the Navy had proposed making the Marines the nucleus of any and all landing forces, but when the United States entered the war, this proposal had not been formally accepted; the Marine Corps still had no mission. Disputes, however, with the Army over securing of advanced bases, coupled with the successful use of the ad hoc Marine battalion formed at the start of the war, finally gave the Corps its place in the national strategy. "In 1900 the Navy General Board's assignment of the advance base mission to the Marine Corps finally gave the Marine officer that clear connection to the Navy that had elluded him over the previous two decades."[29]

World War I found the Marine Corps' main effort focused on its infantry brigade, which formed part of the Army's 2d Infantry Division on the western front in France. Indeed, the Marine brigade's commander, John A. Lejeune, succeeded to the command of that division. It was in the interwar years, though, that the future of the Marine Corps was to take shape. Spearheaded by Major General Lejeune, now Marine Corps Commandant, the Marine Corps' effort to seize its permanent place in the defense establishment centered around the most significant challenge posed by War Plan Orange: the lack of forward bases available to U.S. Navy forces. Lejeune's point man in this was the enigmatic Lieutenant Colonel Earl H. "Pete" Ellis.

> Ellis wrote a study . . . "Advanced Base Force Operations in Micronesia," which Lejeune endorsed in 1921. With a brilliant fusion of faith and realism, Ellis thought that he had identified and solved the fundamental problems of seizing a defended island. Naval gunfire and air strikes would provide the fire superiority that conventional artillery could not provide while waves of landing craft brought infantry, machine guns, light artillery and tanks to the beaches. The concentrated violence of the beach assault would carry the Marines through the beach defenses, provided the Navy could keep the reinforcements and the supplies coming in the ship-to-shore movement. Henceforth the Marines would make the impossible amphibious assault possible, since the Navy could not advance across the central Pacific without the bases the Marine Corps would seize for it.[30]

By the time of World War II the Marines had become the nation's amphibious assault experts, and the stage for . . . *From the Sea* was set.

Millett succinctly relates how this amphibious expertise has easily translated itself into the post–Cold War era. Marine organization, training, and expertise and the Marine Corps' formal connection with the Navy make it admirably suited to the demands of the new security era. Millett very aptly describes the Marine Corps as adapting its venerable "expeditionary-based operational concept within the uncertainty of world events."

THE RESERVES AND STATE NATIONAL GUARDS

Charles Heller's chapter on the reserve forces of the United States does an excellent job of reminding the reader of the fundamental and remarkably lasting reason our reserve components look and behave as they do today. He is quite correct when he points out that the reserve establishment of the United States is an amalgam of eighteenth-century fears, modern politics, and widely held misconceptions about the history of American warfare. The reserve forces, perhaps more than any other segment of the U.S. defense establishment, are a product of their history and their very special relationship with the Republic that they serve. It is, therefore, often astonishing to observers that this relationship rests so heavily, as Heller points out, on misperception and myth.

The image of "the embattled farmer" is etched so deeply in the American ethos that equating victory with the citizen-soldier has become a shibboleth to the American people and, it at times seems, to the defense establishment itself. One of the most influential American military thinkers in our history, however, was not so blinded by myth, politics, and misperception. The erratic and brilliant Major General Emory Upton communicated his discontent with the American idea of militia in the late nineteenth century in his *Military Policy of the United States,* published posthumously in 1904 (Upton committed suicide in 1881 following the revelation that he was suffering from a terminal illness). Let us appeal once again to Millett and Maslowski for a synopsis of Upton's heretical thoughts:

> As Upton perceived it, U.S. policy contained near-fatal weaknesses. Excessive civilian control was a fundamental flaw, since most congressmen, presidents and secretaries of war were inexperienced in military matters. The nation as a whole had an "unfounded jealousy of not a large, but even a small standing army." Thus America relied upon unreliable citizen soldiers. Although volunteers and militiamen could be brave, Upton considered their short enlistments, lack of discipline, dual state and federal control, and untrained officers as crushing liabilities, making them useless as a reserve force. Since these defects prevented adequate preparations, the country's wars usually began with failures, were longer than they should have been, and entailed "enormous and unnecessary loss of life and treasure." "Ultimate success in all our wars," warned Upton, "has steeped the people in the delusion that our military policy is correct and that any departure from it would be no less difficult than dangerous." Nothing, he argued, could be farther from the truth.[31]

At the time, Emory's discontent was widely shared in a service of antiquated organization, slow promotion, and civilian indifference toward their "military saviors."[32]

Upton, whose own military career was nothing short of meteoric, spent two years abroad studying foreign armies and became a great admirer of the Prussian service. He envied its relative freedom from civilian control, its large regular component, its efficient and farseeing general staff, and its reserve establishment. "Germany relied on conscription and assigned its veterans to seven years' service in the reserves, which were under national control."[33] The reforms that Upton pressed were not as radical as one might suspect. He realized that this Republic could not reform its military completely along the lines of the German model, but as Millett and Maslowski argued, his suggestions had a "definite Teutonic ring."[34] His reforms included adoption of the Great German General Staff organization, boosting the powers of the professionals relative to the civilian secretaries, and an enlarged, expansible regular force.

Though Upton no doubt would be unhappy to see how few of his recommendations were adopted even in spirit by the Republic, his overall theme that the very nature of reserve forces should be carefully scrutinized irrespective of past victories bears remembering. This is especially important today when, as Heller has so clearly stated, organizationally the reserve forces are so intimately linked with the Active Component. The same question Upton asked over one hundred years ago is still pertinent, perhaps even more so, today due to the recognition of the types of missions facing U.S. armed forces: Are the reserves as presently constituted a viable fighting force?

Colonel Heller cites recent examples that suggest that in a world where regional crises of low intensity or those incidents that qualify as OOTW are the norm, the reserve forces as they are presently constituted are in fact presently not well prepared to respond to the needs of the services. This, coupled with the increasingly complex technology of modern war, the reality of a downsizing Active Component, and shrinking training budgets, creates an alarming picture of a reserve force unable to properly prepare itself for future conflicts. We see here the dichotomy in which our reserve forces find themselves: in order to save money the reserve forces have taken on more and more of the combat service and combat service support activities vital to sustained operations of the Active Component. Due, however, to other fiscal imperatives those vital functions are now being jeopardized, thus putting the ability of the armed forces as a whole to accomplish the missions that may be assigned them into serious question. When this dichotomy is viewed in light of the four imperatives that, Heller tells us, were formulated by the Reserve Forces Policy Board, one starts to get a sense of the enormity of the challenge being faced by the Reserve Components of all the services.

Colonel Heller argues persuasively that the time has come to take stock of the constitution of the reserve forces. A much tighter and more realistic bond must be forged, particularly in the Army, between the vital reserve forces, with their combat support (CS) and combat service support (CSS) responsibilities, and the Active Component. In this era when OOTW have been recognized as an imperative, the reserves must, Heller warns, be not only trained on the latest technology, but accessible. The reserves as presently constituted have not left the Cold War paradigm. What is needed, therefore, is intellectual movement away from that paradigm toward an establishment that will meet the requirements of the new security era.

JOINTNESS, DOCTRINE, AND THEORY

Though it may not be readily apparent, the topics of jointness, doctrine, and theory are intimately related in the context of the new strategic environment that faces the armed forces. Each of our authors has pointed out, either by quoting official documents or by observing the reality inherent in a force-projection military, that jointness is inescapable. Joint operations are, of course, nothing new, but the emphasis U.S. services have placed on them has increased greatly in the wake of the Goldwater-Nichols Act, which was passed to address the faults discovered in Operation Urgent Fury. As we have seen, the various services have created guides for conducting operations within their purview that are called doctrine. Doctrine has also been written, in a series of documents, to guide joint operations. The impetus that the Goldwater-Nichols Act imparted to the creation of joint doctrine was in no small measure responsible for the Navy creating a body of doctrine for the first time in its history. The capstone document for the conduct of joint operations is *Joint Pub 1: Joint Warfare of the U.S. Armed Forces.*

Joint Pub 1 describes doctrine as ''authoritative but not directive,'' presenting ''fundamental principles that guide the employment of forces.''[35] This definition generally agrees with that preferred by the doctrinal manuals of the individual services. What *Joint Pub 1* also includes that is omitted by the individual services' doctrinal manuals is a clear reference to theory. Just as the need for a joint doctrine is crucial to the smooth functioning of joint operations, so theory is fundamental and critical to the development of doctrine. It is only through the development of a suitable theory of war, or the acceptance of an existing theory, that the defense establishment can, at the end of the day, produce forces trained, organized, and properly equipped to face the myriad of challenges abroad in the new security era.

Doctrine is a very necessary commodity for the services, but one of the drawbacks of this commodity is that it is usually based on the last conflict—the last experience the service had in fighting a war. In a lecture delivered to a British audience in 1973 Michael Howard focused on the difficulties of developing doctrine in the absence of conflict, referring to this challenge as sailing on ''in a fog of peace.''[36] Howard went on to say:

> I am tempted indeed to declare dogmatically that whatever doctrine the Armed Forces are working on now, they have got it wrong. I am also tempted to declare that it does not matter that they have got it wrong. What does matter is their capacity to get it right quickly when the time comes. . . . Still it is the task of military science in an age of peace to prevent the doctrines from being too badly wrong.[37]

What will help keep our military thinkers from getting doctrine ''too badly wrong''?

Every new student at the U.S. Army Command and General Staff School (CGSS) is subjected to rote memorization of the nine Principles of War, the five tenets of Army operations, the seven dynamics of combat power, and a multitude of other laundry lists that were compiled to reduce the amount of time devoted to thought. The staff-college students endure this barrage because it makes sense to them. Such lists and abbreviations of thought, though perhaps tedious to learn, are comforting in their organization, brevity, and the sanctity of official approval. These same students are also subjected to the world of military theory. Their discomfort and confusion during what they obviously consider an ordeal faithfully reflect the Army's attitude toward the subject of theory.

Though each of the services has a "capstone" doctrinal manual, these documents only allude to theory. These documents include the joint doctrinal literature, which, although it has a section dealing with the "nature of war," does so in the most narrow, self-serving sort of way that concludes that the "nature of warfare in the modern era . . . is synonymous with joint warfare."[38] Nowhere do the services either individually or collectively express clearly what they consider to be a theory of war. Instead they offer platitude-like snippets of Clausewitz and then plunge straight into the calmer, more familiar, safer waters of doctrine, principles, and operations. The problem with this approach is that formulating doctrine without first establishing a sound theoretical base constitutes starting in the middle: theory is the element that will keep military thinkers from being, in Howard's words, too badly wrong.

What, then, does theory offer the services? What form should theory take? In this context, theory offers two indispensable services: it organizes thought and it gives a sense of purpose. The organization of thought is fundamental to those who are trying to concert the efforts of institutions whose historical tendency is toward separatism. The services as a collective whole find themselves, therefore, between the opposing forces of tradition and jointness. The force that tradition exerts on the services is essentially centrifugal, forcing the services away from each other, even though history is replete with examples of joint operations, while the forces of jointness are centripetal in nature, forcing the services together. Jointness demands that the services recognize their mutual dependence not only in the theater of operations, but in getting to the theater of operations and, perhaps most important, in resourcing for the new security era.

As to what form theory should take, this is a subject of fiery debate among some staff-college students. Though most Army officers are agnostics when it comes to theory and some are openly hostile to the idea of the need for theory, those who have an opinion tend to prefer Sun Tzu largely because he is clear, concise, and easily read. Conversely, the colossus of the Western tradition, Clausewitz, is considered to be too obscure, too wordy, and too difficult. Additionally, some see Clausewitz as locked in the context of his own time and thus of less and less value as history progresses. As an example of this, some scholars have cast doubt on the continuing relevance of Clausewitz in what they see as a post-Westphalian world.[39] Their argument is that because of his historical context, Clausewitz irrevocably linked policy to the nation-state. With the apparent dissolution of nation-states due to the fall of the Soviet Union, so the argument goes, Clausewitz's primary proposition that "war is merely the continuation of policy by other means"[40] has lost its validity. Obviously Clausewitz had the Western European, Westphalian paradigm in mind when he wrote, but this in no way means that his postulation does not operate in a post-Westphalian world, for the operative word in Clausewitz is *policy.*

Any human grouping, whether it is an industrialized nation-state or a Stone Age tribe, will, in its intercourse with other, similar groupings, develop policy. As long as this remains true (and the argument here is that it does), Clausewitz remains valid, or, as Richard Swain argued, ''Clausewitz' theory . . . is transcendent so long as the central proposition remains valid.''[41] This is the crucial property of any theory: that it transcends its time and place. For a theory to be and remain valid, it must have the ability to be taken from its context, though it may be framed in the language of that context, and successfully applied to a different paradigm.

There are other necessary signatures of a desirable theory:

> A theory that performs its function appropriately does not stand in some fixed relation to knowledge. It organizes and synthesizes new knowledge by providing for dynamic relationships. Clausewitz was able to establish intellectual dominion over the dynamism inherent in war by conceiving a theory designed specifically to expand when it was challenged by the dynamic relationships of war. He did not erect artificial barriers to emerging knowledge; he provided means by which new developments in war could find their place in the theory itself. His theory was meant to be inclusive and expansible, and it was phrased in such a way as to admit new developments from any quarter that gave them birth. This is why, despite pronouncements to the contrary, the way in which Clausewitzian theory is constructed forms the model of military theory and action today.[42]

Therefore, a theory commensurate to the demands of the new security era must be able to accept the disparate elements of this age and unify them through thought. It also must fundamentally organize thoughts on war and bind them by means of a central, unifying idea. The hoped-for result would be an intellectually organized, tightly bound body of knowledge on the nature and practice of war rather than ''a loose collection of worrisome developments, roughly superimposed upon traditional thinking.''[43]

As stated earlier, most military men doubt the utility of theory. They tend to believe that theories hold little value for those engaged in the practical world of war fighting. They, as do others, equate theory with difficult, ethereal concepts written in obscure language by impractical people. What often is lost in the shuffle is that theory is an eminently practical and necessary element that can be, and has been, expressed in the most practical of terms: ''The art of war is simple enough. Find out where your enemy is. Get at him as soon as you can. Strike at him as hard as you can as often as you can, and keep moving on.''[44] Ulysses S. Grant's observation holds the kernel of a theory. This particular quotation has been criticized as the typically anti-intellectual mutterings of a habitually drunk battlefield butcher, but nothing could be further from the truth. The quote in itself is quite profound, but Grant expanded on it to say that if men conducted operations in ''slavish observance'' to rules, their efforts would be attended by failure, and that wars are, by their very character, progressive, as are ''all the instruments and elements of war.''

A theory is not a set of rules, nor is it a collection of platitudes (like Sun Tzu's), no matter how profound or pithy. The purpose of theory in the military context was best summed up by its greatest proponent, Carl von Clausewitz:

Figure 7.1
Military Theory and Its Impact

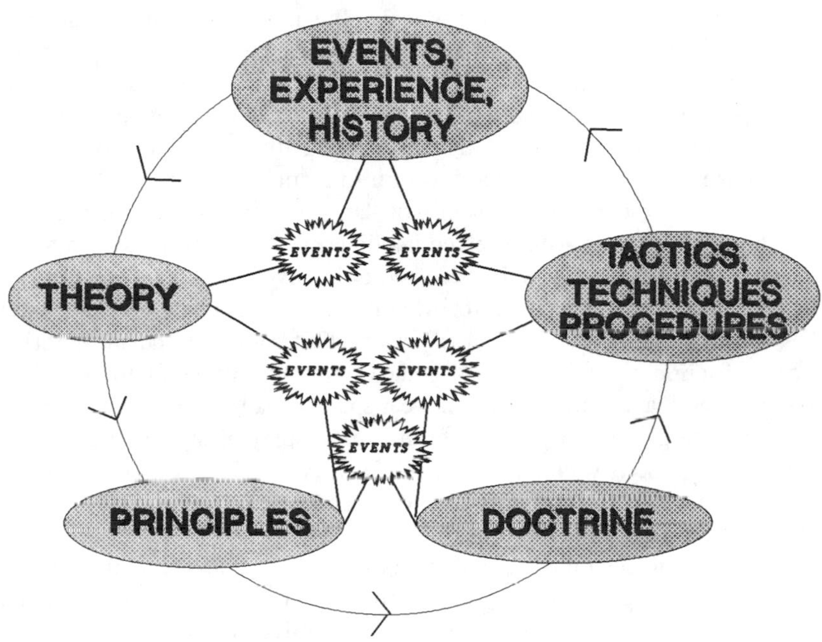

> Theory will have fulfilled its main task when it is used to analyze the constituent elements of war, to distinguish precisely what at first sight seems fused, to explain in full the properties of the means employed and to show their probable effects, to define clearly the nature of the ends in view, and to illuminate all phases of warfare in a thorough critical inquiry. Theory then becomes a guide to anyone who wants to learn about war from books; it will light his way, ease his progress, train his judgement, and help him to avoid pitfalls.[45]

Theory, by its organizing quality, serves to make sense and order out of historical events, principles, doctrine, tactics, techniques, and practices. It can do this because theory is itself a child of history. All these elements ''fire'' in random order, and each, in the military context, affects the other as shown in figure 7.1, which expresses the operation of theory and its relationship to the other elements. Theory therefore is indispensable to well-ordered military thought.

By organizing thought, a sound theory will enable the practitioner to break away from past paradigms that can stifle true progress. It appears that the Navy might be traveling along the road of true progress if, as Williams mentions, it is faithful to its words. The Army, on the other hand, seems mired in its now-institutional mind-set that technology will ensure victory. This can be no better shown than by observing the Army's own preparations for the twenty-first century.

One of the most disturbing by-products of the Army's headlong plunge toward technology is the presumption that the critical need is for the commander to have absolute and superior real-time intelligence every minute during an operation. The Army, which is currently captivated by ''third-wave'' warfare, believes that if the commander is sufficiently informed, he can be virtually indefatigable. The fundamental flaw in this assertion is the assumption that information equals understanding—that by making the commander omniscient, we can create genius. An abundant flow of information will serve, as Clausewitz warned, only to obscure the true nature of the battlefield. If a commander is to do anything constructive with received intelligence, it must be presented to him or her in a useful way; it must be accepted or believed by the commander; and most of all it must be understood for what it really is. As Clausewitz remarked, ''This difficulty of *accurate recognition* constitutes one of the most serious sources of friction in war'' (emphasis in the original).[46] For the future battlefield, it is envisioned that a commander will wear special headgear with a night-vision device that will give him a sort of ''heads-up'' display of the entire battlefield. This technology, derisively termed ''*coup d'oeil* goggles'' by the skeptical, cannot provide understanding. Theory and all the beneficial elements that flow from it do, however, offer understanding.

Of course, even technologically highly advanced and convincing information, if not accepted and acted upon by the commander, will be of no use to anyone, as the abortive Operation Market Garden of 1944 demonstrated. The operation was scheduled to commence 17 September 1944, but by 10 September the chief intelligence officer of the British Airborne Corps, Major Brian Urquhart, had received intelligence through interception and from the Dutch underground that the 9th and 10th SS Panzer Divisions of the 2nd SS Panzer Corps were in and near Arnhem (one of the designated objectives of the operation was the Rhine bridge at Arnhem). The devastating nature of this intelligence was immediately recognized by Urquhart, who later stated, ''Even if these formidable fighting units had been badly mauled in Normandy and were short of armoured vehicles, they were a deadly threat to lightly armed airborne troops landing in their vicinity.''[47] Urquhart went on to record what transpired next:

> When I informed General Browning (overall in charge of the operation) and Colonel Walch, his chief of operations, of this development they seemed little concerned and became quite annoyed when I insisted on the danger. They said, as I remember, that I should not worry unduly, that the reports were probably wrong, and that in any case the German troops were refitting and not up to much fighting.[48]

The outcome of this operation was artfully retold by Cornelius Ryan in *A Bridge Too Far;* it is sufficient to say here that it was not a success. The British Army's 1st Airborne Division suffered almost 8,000 casualties (1,200 dead), and Arnhem was never secured.

William T. Sherman had something to say on the subject of *coup d'oeil,* though he neither used that term nor the word *intelligence.* In speaking to a friend, Sherman expressed his soldierly admiration for his superior, Ulysses S. Grant, and at the same time made a perceptive observation on battlefield information:

> Wilson, I am a damn sight smarter than Grant. I know a great deal more about war, military history, strategy, and grand tactics than he does; I know more about organization, supply, and administration, and about everything else than he does. But I tell you where he beats me, and where he beats the world. He don't care a damn for what the enemy does out of his sight, but it scares me like hell. . . . I am more likely to change my orders, or to countermarch my command than he is. . . . He issues his orders and does his level best to carry them out without much reference to what is going on about him.[49]

This should not be construed as a call for the immediate cessation of technological advancement in the armed forces. The services must stay on the forward edge of new armaments and other developments. One may become concerned, however, that the services are focusing too much of their attention and resources on it and not enough on thought. The American armed forces' faith in technology has, in fact, often been rewarded with success; just as often, however, it has not. When too much faith is placed on technology, one tends to fall into what Brigadier R. G. S. Bidwell termed the fallacy of the magic weapon.[50] When military men commit this fallacy, they often also start to consider future conflict without regard to a resourceful, resolute enemy, which can have disastrous consequences. It is not axiomatic that because the United States has satellite links, laser-guided munitions, and computer-enhanced intelligence systems, all of its potential enemies will be overwhelmed. Our technological edge availed us little in Vietnam. When one notices this mind-set, Hilaire Belloc's sanguine British soldier ironically named Blood comes to mind. Beset on every side by swarms of hostile natives, Blood's faith in the ultimate superiority of modern technology remained unshaken. The soldier exclaimed that the British had ''the Maxim gun, and they have not.''[51] This Maxim-gun mentality is all well and good until the thing jams or runs out of bullets before it runs out of enemy.

For a moment the end of the Cold War gave rise to hopes of world peace. It was not long, however, before reality set in. This reality dictates that the world is by no means a safer place; indeed, it is less stable than it was. In a recent lecture Roger Spiller stated that nothing he knows of military history leads him to conclude that a new age of peace is upon us or that the specter of a dangerous international environment will ''dissuade our policy makers in the least from demobilizing as quickly as we can.''[52] In fact, what the military history of the United States does clearly indicate presents a very bleak picture indeed. It is a legacy that the service chiefs are working very diligently to avoid, but perhaps the struggle should be more intellectual than technological.

This post–Cold War world has presented our armed forces with a variety of seemingly overwhelming and mutually exclusive challenges. The services, as they enter the new security era, and as they face the alarming multitude of challenges attendant to it, would be well served by closely examining their individual and collective intellectual stock, for it is in this realm that the most serious challenges can be successfully met. Chief among the intellectual projects that must be completed by the service heads is the establishment of a theory of war. The practical benefits of this have already been described, but there is yet one more. The exercise itself would unify the service staffs and bind them to a common view of war that, if correctly constructed, will serve as the foundation for all other intellectual efforts undertaken by the services or joint staffs. Therefore, the first and most serious challenge facing the services, individually and collectively, is intellectual.

NOTES

1. See Sam C. Sarkesian and John Allen Williams, eds., *The U.S. Army in a New Security Era* (Boulder, CO: Lynne Rienner Publishers, 1990), and Sam C. Sarkesian, *Unconventional Conflicts in a New Security Era: Lessons from Malaya and Vietnam* (Westport, CT: Greenwood Press, 1993), for a complete discussion of what is meant by the phrase ''new security era.''

2. Constitution of the United States, section 8.

3. Ibid.

4. Allan R. Millett and Peter Maslowski, *For the Common Defense: A Military History of the United States,* (New York: Free Press, 1984), p. 251.

5. Russell Weigley, *The American Way of War: A History of United States Military Strategy and Policy* (Bloomington: University of Indiana Press, 1973), p. 224.

6. David MacIsaac, ''Voices from the Central Blue: The Air Power Theorists,'' in *Makers of Modern Strategy: From Machiavelli to the Nuclear Age,* ed. Peter Paret, (Princeton, NJ: Princeton University Press, 1986), p. 626.

7. Roger J. Spiller, ''The Military Faces a New World'' (Paper delivered at the Northern Great Plains Historical Conference, October 1992), p. 3.

8. Headquarters, Department of the Army, *Field Manual 100-5: Operations* (Washington, DC: U.S. Government Printing Office, June 1993), p. 1-1.

9. Department of the Navy, *Naval Doctrine Publication 1: Naval Warfare* (Washington, DC: Department of the Navy, 1994), p. i.

10. Sam C. Sarkesian, *America's Forgotten Wars: The Counterrevolutionary Past and Lessons for the Future* (Westport, CT: Greenwood Press, 1984).

11. Roger J. Spiller, conversation with the author, 1992.

12. Carl von Clausewitz, *On War,* ed. and trans. Michael Howard and Peter Paret (Princeton, NJ: Princeton University Press, 1976), p. 88.

13. T. R. Fehrenbach, *This Kind of War* (New York: Macmillan, 1963), p. 104.

14. Maurice de Saxe, *Mes Reveries* (Westport, CT: Greenwood Press, 1971), p. 162.

15. Gordon R. Sullivan, ''Decisive Victory, America's Power Projection Army,'' (Washington, DC: The Pentagon, 1994), p. i.

16. Floyd D. Kennedy, Jr., ''The Creation of a Cold War Navy, 1953–1962,'' in *In Peace and War: Interpretations of American Naval History, 1775–1978,* ed. Kenneth J. Hagan (Westport, CT: Greenwood Press, 1978), p. 321.

17. Department of the Navy, *Naval Doctrine Publication 1,* p. iii.

18. Dudley W. Knox, "The Role Of Doctrine in Naval Warfare," *United States Naval Institute Proceedings* 41, no. 2 (March–April 1915): 325–354.

19. Department of the Navy, *Naval Doctrine Publication 1,* p. 29.

20. MacIsaac, "Voices from the Central Blue," p. 625.

21. Malcolm Smith, "The Allied Air Offensive," in *Decisive Campaigns of the Second World War,* ed. John Gooch (London: Frank Cass and Company, 1990), p. 68.

22. Ibid., p. 70.

23. Fehrenbach, *This Kind of War,* p. 427.

24. Bruce B. Auster, "Turf Wars at the Pentagon: Infighting on a Second Front," *U.S. News and World Report,* 26 September 1994, p. 47.

25. See Allan R. Millett, *Semper Fidelis: The History of the United States Marine Corps,* rev. and exp. ed. (New York: Free Press, 1991), or Jack Shulimson, *Marine Corps' Search for a Mission, 1880–1898* (Lawrence: University Press of Kansas, 1994).

26. Shulimson, *The Marine Corps' Search for a Mission,* p. 1.

27. Ibid.

28. Ibid., p. 11.

29. Ibid.

30. Millett and Maslowski, *For the Common Defense,* pp. 375–376.

31. Ibid., p. 257.

32. Weigley, *American Way of War,* p. 168.

33. Millett and Maslowski, *For the Common Defense,* p. 257.

34. Ibid.

35. *Joint Pub 1: Joint Warfare of the U.S. Armed Forces* (Washington, DC: 11 November 1991), p. 5.

36. Michael Howard, "Military Science in an Age of Peace," *Journal of the Royal United Services Institute for Defence Studies* 119 (March 1974), reprinted in U.S. Army Command and General Staff College, *C610 Syllabus/Book of Readings* (Fort Leavenworth, KS: USACGSC, August 1993), p. 229.

37. Ibid., p. 232.

38. *Joint Pub 1,* p. 2.

39. See Martin van Creveld, *The Transformation of War* (New York: Free Press, 1991); John Keegan, *A History of Warfare* (New York: Alfred A. Knopf, 1993); and Alvin Toffler and Heidi Toffler, *War and Anti-War: Survival at the Dawn of the 21st Century* (Boston: Little, Brown, 1993).

40. Clausewitz, *On War,* p. 87.

41. Richard M. Swain, "The Hedgehog and the Fox," *Naval War College Review* 43, no. 4 (Autumn 1990): 107.

42. Roger Spiller, "The Theory and Practice of Post-Industrial Conflict" (Unpublished paper in possession of the author), p. 6.

43. Ibid., p. 26.

44. Peter G. Tsouras, *Warrior's Words* (London: Cassel Arms and Armour Press, 1992), p. 32.

45. Clausewitz, *On War,* p. 141.

46. Ibid., p. 117.

47. Brian Urquhart, "The Last Disaster of the War," *New York Review of Books,* 24 September 1987, pp. 27–30. Reprinted in U.S. Army Command and General Staff Col-

lege, *C610 Syllabus and Book of Readings* (Fort Leavenworth, KS: USACGSC, July 1992), p. 248.

48. Ibid.

49. T. Harry Williams, *McClellan, Sherman, and Grant* (New Brunswick, NJ: Rutgers University Press, 1962), p. 59.

50. Brigadier R. G. S. Bidwell, O.B.E., A.D.C., "The Five Fallacies: Some Thoughts on British Military Thinking," reprinted in U.S. Army Command and General Staff College, *C600 Syllabus/Book of Readings* (Fort Leavenworth, KS: USACGSC, July 1991), p. 240.

51. Hilaire Belloc, "The Modern Traveller," as quoted in John Ellis, *The Social History of the Machine Gun* (Baltimore, MD: Johns Hopkins University Press, 1986), p. 94.

52. Spiller, "Military Faces a New World," p. 17.

SELECTED BIBLIOGRAPHY

Clausewitz, Carl von. *On War.* Edited and translated by Michael Howard and Peter Paret. Princeton, NJ: Princeton University Press, 1976.

Fehrenbach, T. R. *This Kind of War.* New York: Macmillan, 1963.

Keegan, John. *A History of Warfare.* New York: Alfred A. Knopf, 1993.

Millett, Allan R., and Peter Maslowski. *For the Common Defense: A Military History of the United States.* New York: Free Press, 1984.

Paret, Peter, ed. *Makers of Modern Strategy: From Machiavelli to the Nuclear Age.* Princeton, NJ: Princeton University Press, 1986.

Sarkesian, Sam C. *America's Forgotten Wars: The Counterrevolutionary Past and Lessons for the Future.* Westport, CT: Greenwood Press, 1984.

Sarkesian, Sam C., and John Allen Williams, eds. *The U.S. Army in a New Security Era.* Boulder, CO: Lynne Rienner Publishers, 1990.

Toffler, Alvin, and Heidi Toffler. *War and Anti-War: Survival at the Dawn of the 21st Century.* Boston: Little, Brown, 1993.

Tsouras, Peter G. *Warrior's Words.* London: Cassel Arms and Armour Press, 1992.

van Creveld, Martin. *The Transformation of War.* New York: Free Press, 1991.

Weigley, Russell. *The American Way of War: A History of United States Military Strategy and Policy.* Bloomington: Indiana University Press, 1973.

PART II

WARS, MILITARY CONFLICTS, AND NONCOMBAT CONTINGENCIES

Chapter 8
THE AMERICAN WAY OF WAR

Stephen J. Cimbala

There is, broadly speaking, an American way of war. Consistent with U.S. strategic culture, the American way of war emphasizes the taking of moral high ground in political disputes or the appearance of having done so; an emphasis on conventional or mainstream military operations; a preference for overwhelming firepower and campaigns of annihilation in order to minimize U.S. and allied casualties; an imperfect policy consensus on war aims between the executive and legislative branches, and between civilian and military leaderships; and, since World War II, the involvement of military leaders in debates about policy in addition to their more traditional participation in questions of strategy and force structure.

Within a stable constitutional framework for civil-military relations, the U.S. armed forces have evolved from modest beginnings into twentieth-century superpower status. The period from 1945 to 1990 represents a significant departure from previous U.S. history. Prior to the Cold War, peacetime military preparedness was a hit-or-miss affair.[1] The Cold War armed forces of the United States, as a result of the Soviet threat, peacetime alliance commitments, and nuclear weapons, were poised for immediate involvement in large-scale conventional or nuclear war. The expectation of possibly imminent transition from peace to major coalition war caused new departures in civil-military relations,

I am grateful to Professor Sam C. Sarkesian for his encouragement to undertake this chapter. I also appreciate the permission of Professors Charles Moskos and John Allen Williams to cite an unpublished study authored by them. None of these persons shares any responsibility for the contents of this chapter with the author, who is solely responsible.

in force structure, and in military-operational doctrines for the various services.[2] The demands of the Cold War also forced eventual consolidation of service management.

The issue of military legal and political subordination to duly constituted civil political authority has long been a decided issue in American politics.[3] Nevertheless, the Cold War presented to U.S. policymakers and military planners some unexpected and unprecedented challenges.[4] The Cold War U.S. military was qualitatively as well as quantitatively different from its predecessor.[5] The first half of the discussion identifies some of the most important attributes of the Cold War U.S. armed forces and their political setting in terms of their implications for civil-military relations.[6] In the second part of this chapter an attempt will be made to anticipate the future international environment and the potential for U.S. uses of force in the new world order, including those uses of force on behalf of collective security or other peacekeeping missions.

BIPOLARITY AND THE U.S.-SOVIET CONFLICT

The international system of the Cold War was an unexpected outcome of an unexpected war. Between World War I and World War II the United States had sought to disconnect itself from any responsibility for collective security or for preserving the balance of power in Europe. U.S. armed forces were demobilized from their World War I peaks. However, this effort at interwar military self-effacement had already been compromised by several factors. First, the U.S. imperialist experience in the aftermath of the Spanish-American War gave to Americans a heady sense of world engagement, however selective that engagement might be. Second, European security concerns would not go away from American national interests. To the contrary, during the 1930s the two became inextricably linked. The major significance of Franklin Roosevelt's election to the presidency was not apparent at first blush; while he was trumpeted by his partisans as an economic savior, his actual innovation was to brilliantly guide an isolationist Congress and polity toward European engagement.

Given the size and competency of its military establishment during the 1930s, the United States could not extend deterrence on behalf of the status quo in Europe and Asia against rising hegemons in Berlin and Tokyo. The League of Nations proved to be feckless. The power vacuum that resulted when Britain and France only belatedly grasped the ring of antifascist resistance had to be filled from outside of Europe. Russia was a possible source of rescue, but Hitler's initial diplomatic moves had neutralized Stalin as an opponent until Germany was ready to deal with Russia. As France crumbled and Britain scrambled to evacuate Dunkirk, American political leaders were forced to confront their responsibility for global political order. The Japanese attack in December 1941 influenced the timing of U.S. national awakening, but the content of that awakening had already been settled.

Forced to rearm on a scale unprecedented before or since, Americans were divided in their assumptions about the probable shape of the postwar world and of U.S. civil-military relations within that world. Some maintained that wars were caused by renegade states and perverse ideologies. Once these states and ideologies had been defeated and discredited, a return to normalcy in U.S. overseas commitments and in the size of the U.S. military establishment could be expected. Others who saw the causes for World War II as more complicated doubted that the United States could extricate itself from postwar responsibility for world peace. President Roosevelt and his advisors, clearly in sympathy with the internationalist viewpoint of postwar global engagement, expected that the United States and other great powers, including the Soviet Union, could cooperate through the United Nations to deter disruptions of world peace.[7]

This expectation was to be disappointed, and bitterly so. There are various explanations for why events turned out so much against the optimism of U.S. wartime leaders. Most important for the discussion here was the immediate postwar distribution of global military power. The bipolar international system that followed the collapse of Axis military power left the United States and the Soviet Union in a position of uniquely global reach. It became the perception of U.S. and Soviet Cold War leaders that world politics was a constant-sum game in which the winnings of one side would have to take place as a consequence of the other's losses.[8] As suspicion hardened into hostility during crises over Greece and Turkey, Iran, Czechoslovakia, and Berlin, President Truman was persuaded that only diplomatic firmness and military preparedness would deter further Soviet adventurism. The Truman Doctrine and the Marshall Plan declared U.S. universal and regional interests in keeping friendly regimes outside of the Soviet political orbit. But Truman was not prepared to pay the defense costs for these expanded commitments until the outbreak of war in Korea in 1950.

The U.S. postwar military establishment was not returned to a status similar to that awaiting the U.S. armed forces after World War I. Although more than ten million men were demobilized as rapidly as possible, the Truman administration did not foresee the peacetime period ahead as one of pacific deterrence through international organization and U.S. disengagement, as had been the expectation of President Woodrow Wilson following World War I. Instead, the United States committed itself to oversee the postwar reconstruction of Japan and Germany, the former as a political democracy and the latter according to the four-power division of the pie agreed to during wartime conferences. In the event, Germany was permanently divided and rearmed, but not before the United States confronted the need for the rearmament of Europe along with the economic reconstruction of it.

THE EUROPEAN LANDSCAPE

The rearmament of free Europe had to be undertaken with some awareness of U.S. and European sensitivities: U.S. political neuroses about overseas commitments in peacetime, and European sensitivities about being dominated by American guns and capitalism. The solution for incorporating Western Europe within an American strategic protectorate was NATO, a voluntary alliance of unprecedented scope and inclusiveness in peacetime Europe. NATO grew up along with the maturing of the U.S. nuclear arsenal and the hardening of Cold War lines between the Soviet sphere of interest and the Western one. Eventually the Soviet side copied NATO's approach and organized the Warsaw Pact as a belated answer to NATO's European rearmament, although decisions were not taken by democratic consent within the pact as in NATO.

The extension of U.S. peacetime defense commitments to Western Europe, followed by the stationing of permanent American garrisons there, was a politico-military strategy for Cold War competition. But it was also a strategy for freezing the status quo in the center of Europe, thereby reducing the risk of inadvertent war between the United States and the Soviets.[9] NATO was to contain the independent proclivities of the British, French, and Germans to fight with one another as a by-product of its importance for deterring Soviet attack. Although not fully appreciated even now, NATO's political role was as important as its military one. Most U.S. foreign policy influentials did not anticipate an actual shooting war in Europe during the latter 1940s or early 1950s. As George F. Kennan had anticipated, what was more probable was the slow squeeze of Kremlin pressure against American and allied interests both directly, as in the Berlin crisis of 1948, and through surrogates, as in Korea in 1950.

THE KOREAN WAR

Prior to the outbreak of the Korean War, the Truman administration had a hard sell for military buildup, including a rapid expansion of the U.S. nuclear arsenal. NSC-68, a high-level policy study calling for major U.S. rearmament in view of an imminent Soviet military threat to Europe and Asia, had been completed shortly before the irruption of North Korea's forces across the 38th parallel in June 1950.[10] U.S. defense spending shot across the previous ceilings imposed by the Truman administration, and the Chinese entry into the war only convinced many Americans that a Sino-Soviet bloc now threatened U.S. global interests. However, Korea was an improbable war for which American strategic planners had scarcely prepared. Expecting a global war against the Soviet Union begun in Europe, planners had given little consideration to the possibility of U.S. involvement in limited wars supported by the Soviet leadership but fought by other governments and forces.

Korea posed strategic and policymaking dilemmas in Washington. The Truman administration's decision to fight a limited war was controversial on several grounds. Field commander Douglas MacArthur chafed at political restrictions on military operations. Truman neglected to ask for a formal declaration of war against North Korea or against China after Chinese troops later entered the fighting on the Korean peninsula. The war was fought under the auspices of a

U.N. collective security operation. Since the precedent had been set for commitment of U.S. forces to limited war without a congressional declaration of war, it would be repeated to disastrous effect in Vietnam. Nor was the U.S. intervention in Korea exemplary of truly multilateral collective security operations, since it was in fact a U.S. military operation terminated according to U.S. requirements. Thus it provided no model for future uses of U.S. military power on behalf of collective security missions, a subject developed to greater depth in a later section. To the contrary, the Korean War led to the militarization of containment and to the hardening of Cold War fault lines between the Communist and capitalist worlds. The Korean War also allowed U.S. defense spending to reach a new peacetime plateau, peaking in fiscal 1953 at about 330 billion dollars (in fiscal 1990 dollars). This total was not achieved again during the Cold War, even during the Vietnam escalation or the Reagan defense expansion of the 1980s, although at its apogee Vietnam defense spending came close. Table 8.1 presents summary figures for defense outlays from slightly prior to World War II through 1991.

THE DEFENSE BUDGET

Cold War military budgets declined from Korean War levels as a result of Eisenhower's "New Look" policy emphasizing nuclear deterrence. Expenditures rose again during the Kennedy-Johnson years to a near-record 323 billion dollars in fiscal 1969. A large builddown during the Nixon-Ford years followed U.S. disengagement from Vietnam and congressional and public disillusionment with defense expenditures. Fiscal 1976 defense outlays were the lowest since before the Korean War. Budgets moved upward for defense thereafter, gradually during the Carter years and dramatically during the Reagan administration.

These oscillations in defense outlays also reflect the ambivalence of leaders and planners about the requirements for extended deterrence (of threats or attacks against U.S. allies). During the Cold War years the United States accepted unprecedented levels of peacetime commitment to European allies or to other strategic countries located in critical regions. Extended deterrence could not be supported by conventional military power alone, and in Eurasia the size of Soviet ground forces loomed large. Therefore, nuclear deterrence was relied upon not only for protection of the U.S. homeland, but also for the dissuasion of regional aggressors who might threaten U.S. European or other protectorates. Increased nuclear reliance would have important implications for U.S. strategy, force structure, and budgets throughout the Cold War years.

NUCLEAR WEAPONS AND MUTUAL DETERRENCE

The paradox of nuclear weapons was that they made the U.S. homeland vulnerable to destruction without invasion for the first time. At the same time, they gave to the United States the retaliatory power to strike back at any aggressor,

Table 8.1
U.S. Expenditures for National Defense, FY 1938–1991 (Outlays, in Fiscal 1990 Dollars)

YEAR	OUTLAYS	YEAR	OUTLAYS	YEAR	OUTLAYS
1938	13.5	1956	254.6	1974	211.2
1939	14.0	1957	258.6	1975	209.9
1940	22.2	1958	252.8	1976	203.3
1941	73.4	1959	254.0	1977	206.4
1942	248.3	1960	248.0	1978	207.3
1943	594.7	1961	248.8	1979	215.0
1944	725.7	1962	261.5	1980	221.0
1945	803.9	1963	265.3	1981	231.6
1946	415.7	1964	261.7	1982	250.7
1947	113.6	1965	236.7	1983	271.8
1948	77.8	1966	255.2	1984	284.9
1949	107.4	1967	296.5	1985	306.6
1950	105.9	1968	323.7	1986	308.6
1951	166.7	1969	314.5	1987	319.3
1952	299.6	1970	289.8	1988	314.4
1953	330.8	1971	262.7	1989	310.2
1954	314.9	1972	243.6	1990	300.0
1955	268.7	1973	221.1	1991	305.5

Source: William W. Kaufmann, *Glasnost, Perestroika and U.S. Defense Spending* (Washington, DC: Brookings Institution, 1990), Tables 1 and 3.

inflicting unacceptable damage. Therefore, a perceived sense of imminent vulnerability to possibly devastating surprise attack went hand in hand with a conviction on the part of leaders that mutual deterrence would guarantee strategic stasis. This vulnerability-invulnerability paradox left some persons confident of U.S. security based on the threat of nuclear retaliation. Other persons were equally confident that nuclear weapons would cancel themselves out, and that meaningful military competition between the United States and the Soviet Union would occur below the nuclear threshold.[11]

The arrival of the atomic bomb did not lead to an immediate restructuring of U.S. military strategy around the touchstone of nuclear deterrence. The U.S. nuclear stockpile was relatively small when Truman left office, and control of nuclear weapons in peacetime remained with the Atomic Energy Commission. Leading U.S. policy planners feared in 1950 that, absent a large American conventional and nuclear buildup, comparative U.S.-Soviet force-building trends worked against continued American security. For example, Paul H. Nitze, director of policy planning for the Department of State, contended that U.S. military weakness meant that the United States must "avoid becoming involved in general hostilities with the USSR" until a "position of strength" could be created.[12] The development of thermonuclear weapons and the eventual availability of nuclear weapons in abundance led the Eisenhower administration toward a "New Look" strategy that emphasized deterrence by threat of nuclear punishment instead of deterrence by means of conventional combat capability. Although later administration would seek a less nuclear-dependent set of military options, U.S. strategy was thereafter always under the shadow of nuclear plenty and, once the Soviet Union approached strategic nuclear parity, military gridlock.

The Korean War had seen the United States commit combat forces overseas without a congressional declaration of war. The judgment of the Truman administration had been that a formal declaration of war was neither necessary nor desirable. Nuclear weapons posed another kind of challenge to established civil-military relations.[13] The National Security Act of 1947 had established a national military establishment headed by a Secretary of Defense and responsible for the administration and combat performance of all U.S. arms of service, including the newly independent Air Force. Amendments to the National Security Act in 1949 created the Office of the Secretary of Defense and removed service secretaries from cabinet rank. Defense reorganization is considered at greater length later, but the preceding points about the initial unification of the Department of Defense (DOD) and the assumptions on which that unification was built are pertinent for the present discussion.

For reasons well understood by the framers of the U.S. Constitution and accepted by most nineteenth- and twentieth-century Presidents, the United States could not have a presidential military force. The armed forces belonged to the people and to this end were subdivided into active-duty forces, reserve forces (trained service reserves and individual ready reserve pools) and unorganized militia. The U.S. Congress had rejected universal military training (UMT) prior to the Korean War despite President Truman's strong support for it. The U.S. Constitution lodged the power to declare war in the Congress because the authors of that document distrusted executive power acting without legislative oversight. But the framers also required a congressional declaration of war for another reason: it would empower the President to conduct a war on behalf of the entire aroused nation in arms. Public opinion was thought to be the bedrock on which effective commitment of U.S. forces had to be based, and congressional assent to war was deemed improbable unless broad public support was available.[14]

Nuclear weapons called into question this carefully circumscribed relationship created by the Constitution between the executive and legislative branches of the U.S. government. They did so in two ways. First, they made necessary the avoidance of total war. Since it was easier for the public to perceive that total war was more threatening than limited war, Presidents found it harder to make the case for those kinds of wars that the nuclear constraint would permit. Second, nuclear weapons promised unprecedented destructiveness in a short time. Especially once the Soviet Union had acquired a strategic nuclear retaliatory force capable of destroying many targets in the continental United States, the United States had to devise warning and assessment systems and to create a nuclear decision-making process that by implication circumvented the constitutional luxury of a declaration of war. In case of Soviet nuclear attack against targets in the continental United States with ballistic missiles launched from land or sea, the U.S. effective warning would be measured in minutes rather than hours.

The constitutional bypass created to deal with this situation of unprecedented danger was that the President was recognized as commander-in-chief and that this status permitted him to retaliate against surprise attack without immediate congressional authorization. The Congress had other ways of reviewing and controlling the development of U.S. nuclear weapons programs and military budgets too. Therefore, the legislative branch was not frozen out of the process of force acquisition and general military-strategic planning. But the arcana of nuclear weapons target planning and the packaging of strategic and other nuclear options remained largely within the compass of the executive branch during the Cold War years.

By itself this might have been regarded as an unavoidable necessity, but the nuclear habit of presidential initiative unencumbered by legislative oversight spilled over into Cold War presidential approaches to other security and defense issues. It was no surprise that maintaining a state of permanent military preparedness raised the status of the Pentagon relative to other cabinet departments, which themselves grew in stature on the coattails of Cold War presidential power. In addition, the play of power within the national security community in response to activist Presidents, to the visibility of Cold War crises, and to the possibility of prompt nuclear surprise attack was important in its own right. As discussed in the next section, the implications of instant readiness for deterrence and for total war were far-reaching for defense reorganization. This section emphasizes the implications of the strategic paradigm shift from mobilization to deterrence for military strategy.

Nuclear weapons affected the means of defense preparedness and the expectation of surprise attack. But they did not provide usable forces in battle. Therefore, Cold War Presidents and their advisors confronted the problem of what to do if deterrence failed. This problem was partly diverted by the expectation of "extended" deterrence: nuclear weapons would deter any Soviet conventional attack against NATO Europe or other vital American interests. However, there were several problems with extended deterrence of this sort. First, not all Europeans wanted it; the French, for example, quite vociferously rejected any reliance on American nuclear protection. Second, the absolute character of nuclear weapons did not lend itself to military separatism: self-defense by threat of nuclear retaliation was intimately bound up with notions of sovereignty. Third, Presidents wanted usable options in time of crisis so that they could up the ante by using coercive measures short of war, as President Kennedy showed by his choice of blockade during the Cuban missile crisis of 1962.

Because nuclear weapons implied separate sovereignties, they complicated NATO alliance cohesion unless NATO Europeans were prepared to play only the role of U.S. military satellites. Western European economic recovery subsequent to the Marshall Plan and the creation of the European Communities led to assertive self-confidence within NATO deliberative bodies for policy consultation and for military planning. By the 1960s U.S. military strategy had to be marketed aggressively if it were to be adopted consensually by America's NATO European allies. In 1967 NATO settled on a declaratory doctrine, flexible response, that carried it to the end of the Cold War. It was a political success wrapped in a military enigma. Europeans were allowed to believe that flexible response was something other than graduated escalation, whereas American expositors contended that graduated escalation was exactly what flexible response was all about. Although NATO represented singular success in the area of peacetime military planning and coordination, under the stress of actual crisis or war the political diversity of its member states could have prevented consensual response to any Soviet challenge. Fortunately for NATO, such a challenge was not provided by Moscow.

DEFENSE REORGANIZATION

The preceding section noted that nuclear weapons and the possible outbreak of large-scale conventional war in Europe forced U.S. military planners to shift from a mobilization to a deterrence paradigm in force and policy planning. The requirement to be ready for instantaneous response and global military operations meant that both plans and budgets would have to be coordinated across service lines. This caused civilians in the Office of the Secretary of Defense (OSD) to interfere in decisions about military procurement and war planning to an extent without precedent in peacetime American history.

The battles over Planning, Programming, and Budgeting Systems (PPBS) during the McNamara years in the Pentagon do not require retelling. The political controversy during those years was not really about budgeting techniques, but about preferred strategy, doctrine, and prerogatives in determining force size. During the latter years of the Eisenhower administration, it was recognized that separate service planning for nuclear retaliation was not acceptable. The Single Integrated Operational Plan (SIOP) was established by McNamara's predecessor as a method for the coordination of Navy and Air Force strategic target planning. It followed that the same model might be extended to general-purpose forces: defining objectives and asking what mixes of forces, regardless of service ownership, would most effectively and efficiently fulfill those objectives.

McNamara and his associates knew that the battle between OSD and the services over conventional-forces programs would be more difficult than that over nuclear programs.[15] Nuclear weapons lent themselves to tight presidential control: release would be obtained only in the gravest circumstances. Conventional-forces readiness and structure were other matters, and military leaders felt with some justification that they were the experts in residence on war fighting with armies, navies, and air forces apart from nuclear deterrence. Civilians in the McNamara Pentagon doubted openly that there was any such thing as military science or military art and disparaged combat experience as a necessary constituent of fruitful policy analysis. Although the military services outlasted some of McNamara's more ambitious exertions into their domains, his lasting impact on defense decision making was to exploit the National Security Act of 1947 and the subsequent amendments of 1949, 1953, and 1958 to make the Office of the Secretary of Defense the most powerful of cabinet departments.

Nonetheless, the post-McNamara Secretaries of Defense would have their hands full. One source of trouble was the already-mentioned tradition of decentralized military decision making within each service. Another was the growth of presidential power and the derivative raising in stature of the President's advisor for national security affairs. The first person to hold formally this title was McGeorge Bundy in the Kennedy administration, and the significance of the National Security Council (NSC) advisor and his staff grew proportionately as the Cold War demands for U.S. preparedness thrust Presidents into the cockpit of military decision making. Not all of Bundy's successors necessarily enhanced the power and prerogatives of the NSC advisor, but one who surely did was Henry Kissinger. As NSC advisor to President Nixon, Kissinger became the President's *éminence grise* for all matters of security and foreign policy, eventually eclipsing Secretary of State William Rogers and finally preempting his job.[16]

Kissinger's NSC apparatus represented a threat not only to the Department of State, but also to the Pentagon. In defense of the Pentagon it must be said that Kissinger was a formidable and relentless bureaucratic opponent whose grasp of policy and power-mindedness in Washington were uncommon. Kissinger also profited during Nixon's second term from that President's preoccupation with domestic policy, especially with Watergate. But Kissinger's special talents for self-aggrandizement foraged into two areas of great military sensitivity: crisis management and arms control. In addition, the failed U.S. military strategy in Vietnam was all too apparent by the time Nixon took office, and the U.S. program of phased withdrawal for American forces from South Vietnam, termed Vietnamization, required the orchestration of military and diplomatic instruments to exploit coercive diplomacy in reverse.

Melvin Laird's and James Schlesinger's Pentagon fought off the NSC about as well as any bureaucrats could have, but the legacy left by Kissinger was an empowered NSC with the prerogative to exert control over the coordination of all matters touching upon foreign and defense policy. Once power had flowed in the direction of NSC, Presidents no longer had the choice of reinstituting a weak NSC organization and depending upon cabinet departments to take up the slack. Reagan attempted just this solution at the outset of his first term, and it failed. The NSC emerged during the Reagan administration as the locus for highly sensitive covert operations in part because the CIA wanted to avoid congressional investigations related to covert action, and in part because the expectations of experienced bureaucrats were that NSC was the place to get things done.

The tendency to empower NSC reappeared during the Bush administration. Brent Scowcroft, formerly NSC advisor in the Ford administration, accepted the same position under George Bush. NSC retained its status as a second policy-planning and crisis-management department for national security affairs. Scowcroft served as Bush's most articulate expositor of U.S. security policies, confident that defense management would be carried out according to the President's wishes by long-time Bush political colleague Dick Cheney. However, one important legacy from the Reagan administration to the Bush administration had been congressional passage of defense reform in the form of the Goldwater-Nichols legislation. This added to the power of the Chairman of the JCS, who became the principal advisor to the President and the Secretary of Defense on matters of military strategy and force structure. The Joint Staff was also reorganized and made more responsible and responsive to the Chairman. In addition, Goldwater-Nichols mandated that future officers aspiring to general or flag rank must have career-defining experiences wearing ''purple'' in specified joint assignments. Finally, the Goldwater-Nichols legislation mandated that the various commanders-in-chief of the U.S. military unified and specified commands (LANTCOM, PACOM, CENTCOM, and so forth) be given more weight in the process of developing combat and crisis management plans.[17]

Throughout the Cold War history of defense reorganization, one could with some justification divide policymakers, military professionals, and scholarly observers into two schools of thought: those who were structural optimists and believed that defense reorganization was actually related to improved policy outcomes; and bureaucratic pessimists, who rejected the possibility of any direct connection between structural reorganization and better defense policy.[18] In defense of the optimists, one could point to McNamara's introduction of PPBS and its avoidance of waste and duplication in some high-technology, expensive service programs. One could also cite the Goldwater-Nichols legislation and its apparently favorable implications for the conduct of U.S. defense planning and war-fighting strategy during the Gulf crisis and war from August 1990 through February 1991. Pessimists could argue, to the contrary, that the reach of McNamara's reforms frequently exceeded their grasp, as in the eventual demise of the tactical fighter experimental (TFX). Pessimists could also note that ''servicism'' remained even after the Goldwater-Nichols reforms an unavoidable barrier to jointness in planning and procurement: command and control systems usable by more than one service provide excellent illustrations of the pervasiveness of single-service opportunism.[19]

PERSONNEL POLICY AND MILITARY DOCTRINE

The U.S. military experience of the Cold War years was marked by unprecedented beginnings and endings with regard to personnel policy and military doctrine. The beginnings and endings in personnel policy and doctrine were related. The early Cold War years saw conscription carried over into the peacetime armed forces in the form of Selective Service. This went hand in hand with the concept of permanent preparedness for global war. The Army was of course more dependent than the Navy (including the Marines) or the Air Force on conscription. Large forces permanently stationed in Europe, Korea, and elsewhere served as trip wires to deter Soviet attack on American allies. U.S. strategy for global war during the Truman administration, given the relative scarcity of nuclear munitions and delivery vehicles compared to forces available to Truman's successors, did not envision an air-atomic offensive against the Soviet Union as capable of fulfilling U.S. wartime objectives by itself. It was assumed in late 1940s war plans that air-atomic attacks by both sides would be followed by protracted conflict between Soviet and opposed armed forces in Europe and worldwide.

The availability during the Eisenhower administration of larger numbers of nuclear weapons supported the shift to a declaratory strategy for general war of massive retaliation. While administration officials were eventually forced to retreat from this formulation in cases of less than total war, for global war against the Soviet Union Eisenhower defense planning relied mainly upon promptly delivered and massive air-atomic offensives. Special study committees such as the Gaither Committee pointed to the need for a larger menu of military responses, and Army officials chafed at the allocation of defense resources within arbitrary ceilings and under planning assumptions favoring Air Force and Navy procurement. NATO's declared objective of ninety-six active-duty and reserve divisions was far beyond any commitment its members were actually willing or able to provide. Thus reliance on nuclear weapons for extended deterrence became all the more necessary as a result of allied as well as U.S. domestic budgetary priorities.

The Army emerged from the 1950s as the fourth wheel of a defense establishment whose preferred military doctrines favored the more technical and less manpower-intensive arms of service. Under the Kennedy administration things soon changed. Kennedy preferred the strategy that became known as flexible response, calling for improved U.S. conventional forces for crisis response, forward presence, and, if necessary, actual war fighting in order to raise the nuclear threshold in Europe. This last rationale was pushed hard within NATO by McNamara, to the detriment of alliance solidarity on doctrine until the French departure from NATO's military command structure in 1966 and the promulgation of flexible response in 1967. Flexible response arguably allowed a greater role for the ground forces in U.S. military doctrine and force planning, but by the time flexible response became official NATO doctrine, the lines between Cold War "East" and "West" had solidified, and neither side seemed interested even in limited probes against the other. The outcome of the imbroglio over the Berlin crisis of 1961 and the Cuban missile crisis of 1962 had been to establish a minidetente between the superpowers on matters of high politics and security, especially on the likelihood that either side would instigate even a crisis in Europe, let alone a war.

If strategic stasis reigned in Europe, Khrushchev's insistence that wars of national liberation could be unleashed against Third World regimes supportive of U.S. policy called forth from the Kennedy administration a burst of doctrinal innovations. Special operations and low-intensity-conflict studies, as the term was later denoted, led to an emphasis on subconventional warfare, psychological operations, and nation building as constituent elements of U.S. military strategy.[20] But only a fringe of the armed forces officer corps, such as the Green Berets, committed themselves to careers along these lines. The more traditional arms of service lacked serious interest in special operations and regarded their counterinsurgency brethren with undisguised distaste. As the U.S. commitment to Vietnam escalated well beyond the engagement of special operations forces and intelligence operatives, conventional military mind-sets displaced the political side of the politico-military equation on which special operations had been predicated. U.S. conventional forces in Vietnam, on the evidence, fought well against North Vietnamese conventional forces and Vietcong units when the latter were willing to stand and fight pitched battles.

However, it became apparent by 1968 even to the Department of Defense that the United States could not win the counterinsurgency or propaganda wars at an acceptable cost: Johnson's resignation and Nixon's phased disengagement followed. Many arguments can be started in bars whether U.S. conventional or unconventional military strategy failed in Vietnam. The present discussion bypasses that temptation and emphasizes the implications of counterinsurgency displacement by conventional strategy for military personnel policy. Having decided that escalation from limited commitment to a major U.S. military campaign in South Vietnam was necessary, President Johnson nonetheless sought to balance the requirement for military escalation against his other priorities in domestic politics, especially his cherished Great Society programs recently passed by Congress. Johnson's "guns and butter" policy filled the armed forces' ranks of enlisted personnel by expanded conscription of young persons while forgoing the option to mobilize the organized reserve forces. The result of this approach was to create nationwide dissent against the war first across U.S. college campuses and then among wider audiences.

The draft more than anything else had brought the U.S. military escalation in Vietnam to a stopping point. When U.S. Commander-in-Chief William Westmoreland asked for several hundred thousand additional troops in 1968, then

Secretary of Defense Clark Clifford suggested to Johnson that he pull the plug. Johnson did so, announcing his intention not to seek another term of office and thereby conceding the failure of U.S. policy and strategy in Vietnam. However, Johnson left the nation with a major force and policy commitment to a war that would continue without complete U.S. disengagement until 1973, and with war between Vietnamese until 1975. With military disengagement from Vietnam went another look at U.S. conscription policy, and the Gates Commission recommendation to end conscription was adopted and ordered into effect beginning in 1973. In effect, the United States had come full circle to its pre–twentieth-century peacetime standard of raising armed forces by voluntary enlistment (except for the American Civil War, when both sides drafted).

The onset of the all-volunteer force coincided with post-Vietnam doctrinal revisionism. The Nixon administration changed the 1960s strategy of being able to fight two and one-half wars simultaneously to one and one-half wars, and Nixon emphasized that U.S. support for besieged allies would stop short of involving American ground forces. Voluntary enlistment dictated a strategy of selective rather than ubiquitous military engagement. Selective engagement was also facilitated by the full-blown emergence of U.S.-Soviet detente during the 1970s and Sino-American rapprochement. It was perceived by U.S. foreign and defense policy elites that diplomatic containment of Moscow's ambitions was more cost-effective than overpromising of U.S. military involvement in regional conflicts. U.S. and Soviet leaders worked to stabilize the Middle East and to create new expectations about their mutual interests in avoiding nuclear war and inadvertent military escalation. In addition, under the direction of Chief of Staff General Creighton Abrams, Army planners during the early 1970s configured the "Total Force" concept so that future Presidents could not avoid substantial reserve call-ups during any national mobilization for war.[21]

The Carter administration ended its term of office on a sour note in U.S.-Soviet relations: the invasion of Afghanistan caused Carter to ask that the U.S. Senate suspend consideration of the SALT II treaty he had negotiated. In addition, Carter called for the creation of a Rapid Deployment Force for prompt intervention in the Middle East/Persian Gulf; this force would eventually grow into the Central Command that U.S. Army General Norman Schwarzkopf would take into battle against Iraq in 1991. But Carter's belated acknowledgment of the seriousness of Soviet military potential did not lead to a full-court press with U.S. military forces against perceived Soviet vulnerabilities. Carter maintained the path of selective engagement of U.S. military power previously established under Nixon and Ford. Thus Carter was disinclined to call for a return to conscription, and Reagan was even less interested in doing so.

Although some describe the Reagan administration as a period of U.S. overcommitment to counterinsurgency or insurgency wars, Reagan's advisors were stronger on anti-Communist rhetoric than they were committed to bailing out hapless dictators or overthrowing leftist regimes. Reagan preferred to direct U.S. commitments toward counterterrorism and covert action at the low end of the conflict spectrum, and U.S. investment toward conventional high technology supportive of "air-land battle" between the Warsaw Pact and NATO at the higher end of conventional military options. The all-volunteer force, so badly underfunded that it could scarcely meet its recruitment goals during the 1970s, fared better in the 1980s after enlisted and officer compensation was raised significantly by Congress. Congress also supported the administration's emphasis on firepower-intensive as opposed to manpower-intensive military strategies. This was the case even though the DOD and the services emphasized the need to make firepower smarter through precision-guided munitions, improved capability for electronic warfare, and eventual applications of sensors and weapons based on other physical principles.

Reagan's high-tech strategic focus extended even into the heavens, where he assumed that his proposed Strategic Defense Initiative would eventually yield deployments of space-based battle stations and other accoutrements of postnuclear deterrence. This vision also seemed to require technology-intensive, not manpower-intensive, forward planning, and the vision of massive manpower wars was pushed even further from planning consciousness. A war that began in Europe might, according to Reagan planning guidance, extend into a world war, but U.S. and allied NATO strategy did not envision a repeat of any conflict as extended in time as World War II. NATO's campaign on the central front in Europe would be based on conventional deep strikes, aided by modernized sensors, battlefield computers, and precision weapons, and it would be designed to disconnect the tail of the Soviet offensive from its teeth.[22]

The modernized U.S. AirLand Battle template also remains interesting for its subsequent application to the Persian Gulf against Iraq in 1991.[23] Here U.S. military planners who contemplated how to prevail in a war between NATO and the Warsaw Pact, and who were confounded by the commingling of conventional and nuclear forces in Europe, found a more amenable theater of operations for the application of U.S. military power. A five-month period of grace for military buildup in Saudi Arabia did no harm to U.S. readiness for war in January 1991, and the U.S. AirLand Battle doctrine played successfully before a packed house. (Additional comments on the military-technical aspects of the Desert Storm air war appear in the discussions of military strategy and air power in the section "U.S. Military Choices and the Future" later in this chapter.)

The results of the Gulf War of 1991 seemed to vindicate not only U.S. conventional military strategy and technology, but also the decision in favor of the all-volunteer force taken decades earlier. Columnist Charles Krauthammer, celebrating the "unipolar moment" in which the United States had allegedly found itself by virtue of the collapse of the Soviet Union, noted:

> [I]n 1950 the U.S. engaged in a war with North Korea: it lasted three years, cost 54,000 American lives, and ended in a draw. Forty-one years later, the U.S. engaged in a war with Iraq: it lasted six weeks, cost 196 American lives, and ended in a rout. If the Roman Empire had declined at this rate, you would be reading this in Latin.[24]

However, experts recognized the ironical character of the vindication of U.S. strategy, since the AirLand Battle doctrine had been intended for a force structure that was obviously not going to be preserved intact into the post–Cold War era. The United States might not even be able to repeat Desert Storm by 1997 with forces drawn down considerably from 1990 levels even according to the Bush plan of 1991, which Congress might choose to modify. In addition, the Congress and some politico-military strategists in the executive branch were also planning to employ U.S. military capability for nontraditional or noncombat missions, including operations designed to preserve sanctuary from attack for besieged ethnic or national populations (such as Operation Provide Comfort for the Kurds in Iraq). The Bush strategy for more traditional uses of U.S. military power emphasized the performance of forward-presence and crisis-response missions intended for regional contingency operations outside of Europe, not for global warfare or for large interstate wars in Europe.

COLLECTIVE SECURITY AND U.S. MILITARY POLICY: MARSHALLING NEW THEORY AND PRAXIS

The U.S. armed forces of the Cold War years were confronted with a peacetime security environment of unprecedented complexity and perceived global responsibility. The United States used its own military power and that of allies to accomplish traditional defense and deterrence missions. Having adapted its military institutions and defense policies to the Cold War environment, the U.S. armed forces' leadership found itself in transition after 1990 to a different international system. Regional aggressors and instability were the most plausible challenges to world order.[25] American armed forces and those of allies would have to react to these challenges on the basis of collective security in addition to collective defense. Collective security might require forces specially structured and trained for peacekeeping missions. Those national forces dual hatted to U.N. command and control might be operated under two chains of command with inconsistent objectives.

Collective Security as an Approach: Traditions and Perspectives

Collective security is an approach to pacific settlement and deterrence that depends upon the willingness of most states in the international system to part with their familiar dependency on self-help for security. Collective security attempts to mobilize the forces of the law-abiding majority against one or more disturbers of the peace. In practice, collective security through peace enforcement has depended upon a select few states to act on behalf of the "law-abiding" majority. The few who take action in the name of the many are empowered to act for the "system" interest against those states designated as aggressors.[26]

U.S. military interventions of the future will favor the use of tailored forces for rapidly concluded contingency operations, as in the Bush administration's Panamanian intervention (Just Cause). Selective unilateral intervention will in all likelihood be combined with increased post–Cold War willingness to support multilateral military interventions or preventive diplomacy through the United Nations or by means of regional international organizations. One can distinguish in this regard *peacekeeping* and *peace-enforcement* operations. In the case of peacekeeping, the United Nations or another multinational body authorizes the positioning of neutral forces between combatants in order to separate their armies and to provide time for negotiations that must precede any conflict resolution. Peace enforcement means that the forces of a multilateral organization impose a solution on reluctant combatants. The United Nations Emergency Force (UNEF) deployed in Egypt from 1956 to 1967 illustrates the U.N. use of a peacekeeping force; the U.N. operation in the Congo, involving the forcible reintegration of secessionist Katanga Province, is a case study in peace enforcement.

The participation of U.S. forces in peacekeeping and peace-enforcement operations is not without difficulties. During the Cold War it was necessary for American and Soviet forces to be excluded from U.N. peacekeeping or peace-enforcement operations for obvious reasons: a regional crisis would be turned inadvertently into a superpower conflict. This difficulty no longer holds. The end of the Cold War opens the door to Security Council peacekeeping or peace-enforcement operations backed by both the United States and Russia, among other permanent members. However, the involvement of U.S. forces in multilateral operations will not be uncontroversial on the home front. The commitment of U.S. combat forces under the command of any other governments, even under the umbrella of an international organization, creates potential problems of operational integrity and political accountability. These problems did not really arise in Korea or in the Gulf War of 1991 because, although authorized by the United Nations, they were essentially U.S.-designed and directed military campaigns.

The civil war in Yugoslavia leading to the breakup of that country in 1992 and to fighting that continued into 1995 provided a case study of the difficulty in obtaining commitments by the great powers to multilateral military intervention. Reports of widespread genocide and the potential for this conflict to escalate beyond the Balkans called for some kind of concerted European or U.N. action, either to separate the combatants or to impose a cease-fire and return to the status quo ante. However, none of the European security organizations seemed able to take the lead. NATO had been designed for an entirely different mission. The Western European Union was enjoying a welcome rebirth, but it had not yet matured as a center of gravity for preventive diplomacy or for multilateral military intervention. The Conference on Security and Cooperation in Europe (CSCE) was the most inclusive body capable of taking a stand, but its very inclusiveness precluded harmonious action of a military sort. Sadly, the recognition dawned in 1992 that only a military organization with the capabilities of NATO or the former Warsaw Pact, without the aura of Cold War illegitimacy either of those organizations would carry, could intervene effectively to put a stop to the slaughter in Croatia and Bosnia.

But even if effective intervention could be obtained, the question remained on whose side intervention should be undertaken. Collective security is the political umbrella under which multilateral military intervention takes place. Collective security presupposes that one can identify an aggressor(s) and a defender(s), a good guy and a bad guy.[27] In a multinational civil war of the Yugoslav type, the problem of identifying aggressors and defenders would be one that defied consensus or political objectivity. Prominent U.S. politicians and media pundits called for military interventions of various kinds in 1992, and some made compelling cases that the chaos in the former Yugoslavia could not be ignored. However strong the imperative, the "how" remained difficult if not impossible to answer. The necessity for multilateral intervention was easier to demonstrate than the feasibility of any military operation involving multinational ground forces under U.N. or other auspices. The case of U.S. intervention in Somalia in December 1992 under U.N. auspices was a mirror image of the situation in the former Yugoslavia: feasibility was demonstrated in the initial U.S. involvement in Somalia by the deployment of a U.S. force in sufficient size to prevent Somalia warlord resistance. However, continued U.S. involvement in the later phases of the Somalia operation proved ineffective, resulting in eighteen U.S. Rangers being killed. The withdrawal of the United States from the Somalia operation occurred shortly thereafter followed by resurgence of warlord activity. On the other hand, the necessity for U.S. intervention, as opposed to that carried out by African states under U.N. sponsorship, was more controversial in the U.S. news media and in Congress.

The questions about operational feasibility of post–Cold War contingency operations, for U.S. or for multinational military forces, are the same. What is the political objective? What are the military objectives that follow from this political objective? Are these military objectives attainable with the forces that the United States or the United Nations is willing to commit? Similar questions, in case of U.S. unilateral action or U.S. commitment of troops to multistate operations, must be answered with regard to American domestic politics and its unavoidable connection with foreign policy. The Cold War experience, with a much more evident global military threat facing each administration from Truman through Reagan, was marked by great contention between Congress and the executive branch over the prerogatives held by each in security policy. In addition, the acceptability of unilateral or multilateral interventions to the U.S. public would be relevant to the Congress and, for this reason and others, to the administration.

Former Secretary of Defense Les Aspin, in his earlier role as Chairman of the House Armed Services Committee in 1992, argued for a U.S. force structure and contingency planning based on systematic threat assessment.[28] Aspin defined

Table 8.2
Potential Regional Aggressors as "Iraq Equivalents"

(FORCES)	LAND	SEA	AIR
Iraq (pre-Desert Storm)	1.0	1.0	1.0
Middle East/Southwest Asia			
Iraq (current)	.4	<.5	.5
Iran	.2	7	.4
Syria	.6	2	.8
Libya	.3	13	.7
Asia			
North Korea	.6	80	.6
China	1.4	90	2.6
Western Hemisphere			
Cuba	.2	5	.2

[a]The score assigned for Chinese land forces seems low; I assume that it estimates only military potential fighting on the offensive, not the defensive.

Source: Congressional Budget Office, using unclassified TASCFORM methodology, produced by the Analytic Sciences Corporation. TASCFORM estimates the capabilities of individual weapons systems within a force and provides summative measures for overall force combat potential. Cited in Rep. Les Aspin, Chairman, House Armed Services Committee, *An Approach to Sizing American Conventional Forces for the Post-Soviet Era: Four Illustrative Options* (Washington, DC: House Armed Services Committee, 25 February 1992), p. 11.

the major threats to U.S. post–Cold War security in rank order as countering regional aggressors; combatting the spread of nuclear and other mass-destruction weapons; fighting terrorism; restricting drug trafficking; peacekeeping missions; and humanitarian assistance. He contended that the most demanding threats would be posed by regional aggressors, for which Saddam Hussein in 1990 represented the prototype.[29] The gross size of the future U.S. force, according to Aspin, will be driven largely by the need to deter or to defeat regional aggressors; other missions require relatively smaller and more specialized forces, designed differently from forces intended to fight in large-scale regional wars. Accordingly, Aspin denoted the "Iraq equivalent" as a unit of account for future U.S. force planning: one Iraq equivalent is equal to the amount of offensive military power Iraq possessed prior to Desert Storm.[30] Aspin then provided "Iraq-equivalent" scores for potential regional aggressors who might threaten U.S. interests, based on computations by the U.S. Congressional Budget Office. These scores are shown in table 8.2.

It is instructive to recall how thin was the margin by which the U.S. Congress in January 1991 voted to authorize President Bush to use force in order to expel Iraq from Kuwait. Bush wisely avoided the trap into which President Johnson had fallen in Vietnam: marching into battle without getting Congress explicitly committed to the nation's war aims. However, in insisting on getting the explicit endorsement of Congress for Desert Storm, Bush risked a negative vote and a greater domestic obstacle course against the effective use of force. The vote in Congress was close despite the following aspects of the situation, all presumably permissive of intervention: Saddam Hussein acted the role of a textbook villain; the threat to oil supplies provided an obvious and tangible interest; the United States acted with the support not only of its former Cold War allies, but also of a majority of Middle East and Southwest Asian Arab governments; and the Soviet Union endorsed the use of force if necessary in the U.N. Security Council.

One might argue, therefore, that the U.N. support for Desert Storm represents a "best case" of international consensus behind U.S. war aims.[31] Nonetheless, public opinion polls during the U.S. Gulf military buildup and prior to the outbreak of war suggested that the American people were anxious about the feasibility of going to war and divided about the desirability of doing so. Congress reflected this ambivalence in public perceptions of the desirability and feasibility of using force: congressional and public opinion, fortified by some expert testimony on Capitol Hill, contained strong support for continued economic sanctions as an alternative to war. In the aftermath of the rapid and decisive coalition victory over Iraq, of course, public ambivalence turned into overwhelming approval. But a less successful military campaign would, on the evidence of Korea and Vietnam, have produced a more divided and contentious public policy debate.

Newer Aspects of Collective Security: Crisis Management and Conflict Termination

There exists an extensive literature on crisis management.[32] Less frequently addressed in the academic and policy literatures is the relationship between collective security and crisis management. The Bush administration's military strategy acknowledged a transition to an international order in which collective security would be combined with crisis management. Bush planning scenarios for regional conflict included war growing out of crisis in Europe and eventually requiring full mobilization; major regional crises in Korea or Southwest Asia; simultaneous major crises in Northwest and Southwest Asia; and lesser regional contingencies, including Panama. A schematic of scenario possibilities derived from the 1991 Joint Military Net Assessment appears in table 8.3.

The tactic of military interposition in support of preventive diplomacy has been used repeatedly by the United Nations to prevent the restarting of interstate or intrastate wars during the past three decades or so. Preventive diplomacy by

Table 8.3
U.S. National Military Strategy: Planning Scenarios and Missions, 1991

PEACETIME (Deterrence)	CRISIS	WAR
Strategic Nuclear	Europe	Regional
Offensive Defensive	Russia and Belarus invade Poland, Lithuania	unilateral alliance
Conventional	Simultaneous major regional crisis	Global Conventional
Presence	SWA, Korea	resurgent or emergent global threat
	Major regional Korea or SWA	
		Nonstrategic nuclear
		Strategic nuclear
	Lesser regional 2,000 nm (Panama) 6,000 nm (Philippines)	
	Counterinsurgency/counternarcotics various	

nm: nautical miles.

Source: Adapted from James John Tritten, *Our New National Security Strategy: America Promises to Come Back* (Westport, CT: Praeger, 1992), p. 23.

military interposition might be regarded as a technique of anticipatory crisis management. The presence of a U.N. force in a particular region, say Cyprus or Lebanon, gives the Security Council a rationale for meddling in the affair without seeming bumptious. During the Cold War years this technique had to be carefully used, and preferably with the active collaboration of the Americans and the Soviets. U.N. involvement in the Congo during the early 1960s showed that the commitment of U.N. forces to a situation of domestic political turmoil might involve the United Nations despite itself as the arbiter of a state's domestic political fortunes. The continuation of the operation after the Soviets and their supporters began to object strongly almost caused a financial disaster for the United Nations, and it turned Khrushchev against the United Nations at a time of rising Cold War tensions between the Americans and the Soviets.

The relationship between collective security and conflict termination may be stronger than the relationship between collective security and crisis management. Crisis management is to some extent a theory rooted in Western culture: neither the Cold War Soviets nor the post–Cold War Iraqis could be said to share the same cultural predispositions. Successful conflict termination of the Gulf War of 1991 was certainly related to the willingness of the United Nations to authorize U.S. and allied coalition actions against Iraq. Without this U.N. authorization, the United States could have acted anyway, for it effectively ran the war. However, the absence of U.N. authorization would have made it more difficult for President Bush to obtain congressional assent for the use of force (previously authorized by the United Nations). Without U.N. support, members of the coalition, including important Arab members, might have been under political pressure to defect. U.N. sponsorship also helped the government of Israel to justify its abstinence from the fighting despite Saddam's provocative Scud attacks on Israeli cities. A final point about U.N. authorization for expelling Iraq from Kuwait was that it provided legal cover for actions taken with the actual objective, at least in Washington, of reestablishing a regional balance of power.

The preceding point about a balance of power is an important one. The Bush administration determined to fight a limited war against Iraq, although with unlimited means. The objective was to weaken Iraq's power to coerce its neighbors after its expulsion from Kuwait. A regional postwar balance among Iran, Iraq, Saudi Arabia, and Israel was sought, not the permanent crippling of Iraq's political and military influence in the region. These objectives applied to an assumed postwar Iraq with Saddam having been deposed by his own armed forces. Few could foresee that Saddam might outlast George Bush in office. Therefore, by the time of President Clinton's inauguration, the expectation of Saddam's imminent departure to be replaced by President X was still a disappointed expectation. Therefore, the U.N. and U.S. short-run objective of keeping Saddam pinned in his lair conflicted with the longer-term objective of restoring Iraq to international respectability.

Collective security sanctions tend to involve both punishment and denial because of the implication that punishment is deserved by those who violate international norms. It becomes difficult within a collective security framework to employ arms in a limited fashion for specific political objectives without escalation. In fact, collective security is based upon the credible threat of "horizontal" escalation in order to deter "vertical" escalation. The great powers announce in advance that any state that violates international norms against aggressive war will be met by the combined force of all other states. Implementing this threat almost guarantees a war involving many countries and of geographically widespread character. The more states involved in a war, the more difficult it is to keep political objectives limited in view of the expanding military means.

The Gulf War of 1991 might seem to contradict the argument just made to the effect that collective security has a built-in tendency to escalation. The Gulf War fits a collective security model in the asymmetry of capability between the aggressor and the coalition that eventually liberated Kuwait. The war was terminated quickly through the successful application of overwhelming force. However, the escape from escalation was a narrow one. Involvement of Israel was a constant concern of U.S. political and military leaders: it would have split the coalition and obfuscated the political objective of further military action. The very rapid termination of the war for Kuwait, especially the short ground campaign, allowed the United States to restrain Israel and to keep together the heterogeneous coalition that might otherwise have given way to centrifugal pressures.

More typical of the escalatory tendencies inherent in collective security operations was the crisis that marked the Congo operation in 1961, when a collective security peacekeeping operation ended up requiring the suppression of rebellious Katanga Province and its forcible reintegration into the newly established post-Belgian Congo (now Zaire). Another illustration of the risk of escalation inherent in collective security was provided by the expansion of U.N. objectives in Korea at the behest of U.S. commanders. The initial purpose of U.S. involvement under U.N. authorization was to restore the status quo ante and to free South Korea of North Korean forces. The United Nations acquiesced to a U.S. change of objective from the initial aim to the liberation of all of Korea. Had the same thing occurred during the Gulf War of 1991, the United States would have followed up the ground campaign by declaring a new objective of marching on Baghdad and deposing Saddam's regime. President Bush resisted the temptation of expanded war aims; President Truman did not.

Additional escalation took place in Korea when the Chinese intervened in force in November and December 1950. In effect, it became a surrogate war between China and the United States, although nominally a war between the United Nations and North Korea. U.S. officials considered attacks against the Chinese mainland, and U.N. Commander Douglas MacArthur was sacked for publicly disputing the administration on the usefulness of military escalation. MacArthur's public advocacy for expanding military action against the Chinese mainland was an expression of the field commander's understandable desire to hit at the sources of aggression as well as at the forward ramparts of it. MacArthur's political and military superiors wanted to preclude escalation into a declared war between the United States and the People's Republic of China. Resisting the tendency toward escalation that was inherent in battlefield events, Truman and his advisors leashed MacArthur and set off a furious debate at home on U.S. war aims.

One can argue forever about might-have-beens, but the Korean War offers a clear case of potential escalation from limited to major coalition war. Few Presidents would have stood up to a military theater commander as prominent as MacArthur on the issue of what it took to win the war. Truman stood on the high ground easiest for political leaders to defend: he argued in favor of the President's right to define what ''winning'' meant, that is, what the political objectives of the United States were. Supposing, on the other hand, that Truman had been willing to endorse MacArthur's definition of U.S. military policies and political objectives, the United Nations would have found its wagon attached to a major coalition war. Soviet support for a China subject to U.S. attacks on its home territory was almost certain. This was, of course, one reason why Truman resisted MacArthur's demands.

The experience of collective security during the Cold War was limited by the circumstances of bipolarity and opposed U.S. and Soviet ideologies. Collective security was mostly removed from the arena of high politics, enforcement, and included within the more acceptable areas of low politics, peacekeeping and preventive diplomacy. The end of bipolarity and the demise of the Soviet Union create new possibilities for robustness in U.N. and great-power employment of collective security. Notwithstanding these possibilities, we must bear in mind many of the previously stated limitations and cautions. Even after the Cold War, the use of collective security is no worldwide cure-all for international instability.

U.S. MILITARY CHOICES AND THE FUTURE

The period after the Cold War presents no apparent challenge to the constitutional relationship between U.S. civil and military authority. Within this very broad constraint, opportunities exist for diverse perceptions by Presidents, planners, and congressional leaders about future roles and missions for the U.S. armed forces. Prognostication is a dangerous enterprise for scholars, but we can foresee several issues that future U.S. policymakers and planners will have to grapple with. The problem of post–Cold War strategy formulation includes both the management of domestic military policy and the development of strategy and doctrine faithful to threats posed by the international environment. What kinds of wars is the United States going to have to fight, preferably with the help of allies but perhaps alone?

Two polar views on this have been well stated by Martin van Creveld and Harry Summers. According to van Creveld, large-scale conventional war is mostly obsolete. The future of warfare lies in low-intensity conflict, terrorism, and the like.[33] The reasons are that large-scale warfare does not pay political and military dividends relative to its costs. Van Creveld argued that this trend represents the dismantling of the Clausewitzian paradigm that dominated military strategy formation from the Peace of Westphalia until the end of World War II. In Clausewitz's model of the relationship between war and policy, a trinitarian unity among people, government, and army supported the conduct of war on behalf of state interests. War was something done on behalf of the state, and only on behalf of the state. This was an important marker in Western military and political history, for it made possible, along with the political theories of Machiavelli and Hobbes, the "realist" tradition in international politics that informed generations of scholars and students.

Van Creveld argued, in essence, that the realist-statist model is no longer very realistic. The state can no longer assert its monopoly over the resort to violence.

If he is correct in this argument, the implications are profound. Once the assumption that trinitarian war is the normative model for all armed struggle is relaxed, all intellectual hell breaks loose in military studies. We return to the pre-Westphalian environment in which tribes and tribunes resorted to war with the same assumption of political legitimacy as did governments. The contemporary civil strife within the former Soviet Union, as in Georgia and as between Armenia and Azerbaijan, may be normative for the future of warfare. So, too, may the upheavals in the Balkans that have pitted ethnic and nationality groups against one another in a holy war of satanic proportions.

Harry Summers argued, in contrast to van Creveld's view, that low-intensity conflict cannot be normative for the U.S. armed forces.[34] Given U.S. political culture and military traditions, the Gulf War of 1991 is more representative of the kinds of wars that the American people and the U.S. Congress will support: high-intensity warfare in which U.S. manpower is spared, technology is exploited to the fullest, and war termination is obtained in the shortest possible time.[35] Undoubtedly the Gulf War was one of a kind, but Summers's argument holds more broadly that high-technology, conventional war is the kind of war that the United States has traditionally waged with great effectiveness. To the contrary, the U.S. track record for low-intensity warfare is dismal. One scholar noted that the United States has even failed to learn very much about low-intensity conflict from its own historical involvement in wars of this type, including nineteenth-century wars on the American continent itself.[36]

There is something to be said for both van Creveld's and Summers's positions. One does not really exclude the other. In each instance we might ask: will future Congresses and publics support the manpower, muscle, and money to fight those kinds of war? Will popular support be conditional upon combat performance, as reported through the news media and interpreted by armchair military experts having obtained their information from CNN? The questions are not frivolous. Whether the U.S. armed forces will be able to wage high-intensity warfare, low-intensity conflict, both, or neither in the future is as much dependent on the American public's understanding of the American way of war as it is on the military-technical issues such as force size and weapons modernization. Public perceptions of international threats are notoriously fickle, and Cold War policymakers deliberately exaggerated the degree of threat in order to obtain defense commitments from the U.S. Congress. One defense scholar argued that the United States was virtually free from serious threat of invasion and conquest, slow strangulation through global blockade, or nuclear attack during the Cold War years.[37] Robert J. Art compared threats to U.S. security during three eras, summarized in table 8.4.[38]

Many would argue that Art's definitions of possible dangers in the Cold War and post–Cold War eras are adequate to address worst-case scenarios. But at levels of threat or potential conflict below those worst cases, Cold War experience and events since 1990 offer less reassurance that other security objectives can be guaranteed at an acceptable cost. As John Lewis Gaddis has noted:

Table 8.4
Threats to U.S. Security in Three Eras

Type of Threat	Geopolitical Era (pre-1945)	Cold War Era (1945-1990)	Post-Cold War Era (after 1990)
Invasion and conquest	Quite difficult after 1900	Practically zero probability	Practically zero probability
Slow strangulation by global blockade	Of indeterminate feasibility	Practically zero probability	Practically zero probability
Nuclear attack from Soviet Union		Not probable	Highly improbable
Nuclear attack from states other than Soviet Union or subnational groups		Highly improbable	Not Probable

Source: Robert J. Art, ''A Defensible Defense: America's Grand Strategy after the Cold War,'' *International Security* 15, no. 4 (Spring, 1991), p. 11, table 2. I have slightly revised Art's category labels with no effect on his meaning.

[V]ictories in wars—hot or cold—tend to unfocus the mind. They encourage pride, complacency, and the abandonment of calculation; the result is likely to be disproportion in the balance that always has to exist in strategy, between what one sets out to do, and what one can feasibly expect to accomplish. It can be a dangerous thing to have achieved one's objectives, because then one has to decide what to do next.[39]

There are some cautions that we can derive from Cold War history. One caution is that forces that are optimized for high-intensity conflict against industrial-strength armies cannot simply be reduced in size and reassigned to low-intensity warfare. During the 1960s and prior to the Vietnam escalation, for example, it was assumed by planners that forces adequate for war between NATO and the Warsaw Pact would easily brush aside smaller and less heavily armed foes. It is now acknowledged that low-intensity conflict or unconventional warfare, including counterinsurgency and counterterrorism, is qualitatively different from larger-scale warfare.[40] Another caution derived from the Cold War is that low-intensity conflicts involve ambiguous political missions for which U.S. popular support cannot be assumed and must be assiduously built. A third lesson is that the U.S. armed forces' sense of military professionalism is compromised by missions outside the competency of military training and experience.[41] Assigning to military forces the mission of ''nation building'' confuses a military mission with a broader political one, to the probable detriment of both military and political objectives. Nonetheless, the post–Cold War world has already found the U.S. military involved in a number of peacekeeping, peace-enforcement, humanitarian assistance, and other nontraditional operations, which are summarized in table 8.5.

Future War

Future war is likely to be marked by a mixture of high-technology equipment and low-technology strategy. This syncretic approach to war borrows from Clausewitz the assumption that war fought without restraint tends toward the absolute in destructiveness. It borrows from Mao and other revolutionary theorists the notion that unconventional warfare can defeat conventional warfare under favorable social, political, and economic conditions.[42] Notwithstanding Summers's cautions about rewriting the U.S. military paradigm away from conventional warfare and toward unconventional warfare, the latter in some ways fulfills Clausewitz's prescription about the relationship between policy and force better than conventional war does. Few who experienced Vietnam would now argue, even if they had prior to U.S. involvement in that conflict, that counter-revolutionary wars are more military than they are political.[43] As Sam C. Sarkesian noted, in revolutionary wars

> the people of the indigenous area compose the true battleground. Clausewitzian notions and high-tech military capability are usually irrelevant in unconventional conflicts. Conventional military capability and the "largest" battalions rarely decide the outcome. The center of gravity is in the political-social milieu of the indigenous populace, rather than on the armed forces.[44]

The need to fight syncretic wars that are simultaneously conventional and unconventional in one sense drives U.S. military historians and planners back to the Revolutionary War roots of American military practice. As historian Russell Weigley has noted, General George Washington preferred to model the Continental Army along the lines of eighteenth-century European military forces.[45] Washington feared that irregular forces could not be counted on against British regular forces, and he also remained wary of the potential costs to the American social fabric of guerrilla warfare. Even his postwar efforts to shape the peacetime U.S. armed forces favored a small regular army supported by a compulsory-service and federally regulated militia.[46] On the other hand, America's revolutionary war against Britain also included successful U.S. unconventional campaigns against British regulars, such as the guerrilla attacks on Burgoyne's lines of communication and flanks contributory to his defeat at Saratoga.[47] U.S. professional military heritage from the War of 1812 was also a mixed estate. On one side stood the Battle of New Orleans, suggesting that citizen-soldiers could fight with distinction against regular British forces. On the other side stood the battles of Chippewa and Lundy's Lane, in which American

Table 8.5
U.S. Military Post–Cold War Nontraditional Operations

LOCATION	DATE	MISSION	INVOLVEMENT
USA Borders: "JTF Six"	Jun. 1990-	drug interdiction	100 military plus civilian law
Kurdistan Operation "Provide Comfort"	April-June, 1991	refugee relief	12,000 U.S. forces with 11,000 partners
Bangladesh Operation "Sea Angel"	May-June 1991	flood relief	8,000 U.S. Marines and Navy
Philippines Operation Fiery Vigil	July 1991	Mt. Inatubo volcano rescue	5,000 U.S. Navy and Marines
Western Sahara	Sept. 1991	observer force	UN military with U.S. officers
Zaire	Sept. 1991	rescue foreign nationals	French, Belgian troops with U.S. airlift
Cuba	Nov 1991- May 1992	Haitian refugee relief	U.S. Military
Russia, Operation "Provide Hope"	Dec. 1991- Feb. 1992	food relief	Western and U.S. airlift
Former Yugoslavia, "UN Protection Force"	March 1992	Peacekeeping	NATO and WEU naval deployments offshore, NATO AWACS monitor no fly zone over Bosnia
Italy, Operation "Volcano Buster"	April 1992	Mt. Etna volcano rescue	small force of U.S. U.S. Navy, Marines
California, "Joint Task Force LA"	May 1992	restore domestic order	8,000 U.S. Army, Marine Corps and 12,000 Guard

Table 8.5 Continued

LOCATION	DATE	MISSION	INVOLVEMENT
Florida, "JTF Hurricane Andrew"	August-Sept. 1992	disaster relief	21,000 U.S. Army, Air Force and Marines, and 6,000 Guard
Iraq, Operation "Southern Watch"	Aug. 1992	surveillance	U.S. Air Force, Navy
Hawaii	Sept. 1992	Hurricane Iniki disaster relief	National Guard and small U.S. Marines/Air Force
Somalia, Operation "Restore Hope"	Dec. 1992	U.S. "invasion and pacification for famine relief, restore order	all arms of service, plus allied UN forces

WEU: Western European Union.

Source: Table adapted from John Allen Williams and Charles Moskos, "Civil-Military Relations after the Cold War" (Paper prepared for delivery at American Political Science Association, Annual Meeting, 2–5 September 1993), pp. 5a and 5b.

regulars acquitted themselves well against their British counterparts in open-field battles without the use of unconventional tactics.[48]

The uniqueness of U.S. civil-military relations argued for continuing conflict between the citizen-soldier tradition and the professional-regular traditions for staffing the armed forces. The antitheses of strategy based on annihilation and those based on attrition also contended for preeminence in U.S. military schools and in the priorities of military planners.[49] The issue seemed to have been decided during World War II, in which the United States and its allies combined campaigns of annihilation into a successful war of attrition, inflicting decisive defeat on Germany and Japan. The Korean and Vietnam wars called into question again the issue of preferred military doctrine for the U.S. armed forces: wars fought for limited aims with limited means posed special constraints on strategy and force structure. Counterinsurgency was one variation of a war of attrition, and its protracted nature strained the capacity of democratic societies in France and in the United States.[50] It turned out that where local governments were sufficiently astute about maintaining popular support, U.S. support was almost superfluous; where they were not, it was useless.

The Gulf War of 1991 was either the concluding campaign of the Cold War of the first of the post–Cold War era. It was a one-sided campaign of annihilation in the model of Cannae: crushing blows against Iraqi armed forces, command systems, and military infrastructure from the air, followed by a short ground campaign based on strategic flanking movements. The need for a war of attrition of the kind that Iran had fought against Iraq during most of the 1980s had been avoided. The war demonstrated that the demise of the Soviet Union left the United States in a unique position of undisputed conventional and military superpower.[51] No state could threaten the United States with large-scale military defeat, although arms control was still necessary to winkle out of the former Soviet Union most of its residual nuclear arms. If U.S. nuclear and conventional military power made it all but invulnerable to any campaign of annihilation, its maritime supremacy as of 1991 seemed to ensure the failure of any hostile war of attrition. The odor of unipolarity was indeed in the air as the Bush administration vacated the White House.

But a large menu of problems remained for U.S. policymakers after the Cold War. Problems could be expected despite the emergence of at least temporary unipolarity, based on the absence of any power aspiring to global or European regional hegemony. Many of these problems will call for military forward presence, peacetime engagement, and other missions not previously tasked during the Cold War fixation on a one-variant war. The end of the Cold War requires that the United States disestablish a force designed for deterrence of major coalition wars. Post–Cold War U.S. forces will be smaller in size, contingency oriented instead of scenario dependent, and arguably committed to peacekeeping and other collective security missions under U.N. or other auspices.

The difficulty of using U.S. military force under any circumstances may increase, relative to Cold War precedent. For the remainder of the 1990s and in the early years of the twenty-first century, political leaders may expect to use military force in at least four kinds of situations: regional contingency operations; counterinsurgency; counterproliferation efforts; and antiterrorist raids in order to free hostages, to capture terrorist leaders, or to destroy identifiable bases of support for terrorist organizations. Of these, the involvement in regional contingencies has the greatest potential for prolonged fighting and high casualties. Historical U.S. experience and recent (1993) events in Somalia suggest that policymakers and military planners can count on little forgiveness in Congress or in the American public once U.S. casualties begin to accumulate, especially in wars for which an apparent national interest is not obvious. As shown in table 8.6, both in total numbers of deaths (battlefield and other war related) and in the percentage of national population killed, the American Civil War was the worst military disaster suffered by the United States.

Military Strategy

A U.S. military strategy based on regional contingencies may be as controversial as the containment strategy that preceded it: implemention of a contingency-oriented strategy involves complicated political, economic, and military decisions in the years ahead.[52] Declining U.S. defense budgets will create difficult trade-offs among the desired goals of preserving force size, modernizing weapons, and command, control, and communications (C^3), maintaining readiness for crisis response, and preserving sustainability for protracted conflict. On

Table 8.6
Battlefield and War-related Deaths in U.S. Wars

War	Battle Deaths	Total Deaths	Deaths as Per Cent of U.S. Population
Revolutionary War (1775-83)	6,824	25,324	.0645
War of 1812 (1812-1815)	2,260	2,260	.031
Mexican War (1846-1848)	1,723	13,283	0.057
Civil War (1861-1865)	214,938	498,332	1.585
Spanish-American (1898)	385	2,446	0.003
World War I (1917-1918)	53,513	116,708	0.110
World War II (1941-1945)	292,131	407,316	0.311
Korean War (1950-1953)	33,629	54,246	0.036
Vietnam War (1964-1973)	47,321	58,021	0.029

Source: *World Almanac and Book of Facts 1987* (New York: World Almanac, 1987), pp. 321, 337, as cited in Barry B. Hughes, *Continuity and Change in World Politics: The Clash of Perspectives* (Englewood Cliffs, NJ: Prentice-Hall, 1994), p. 114.

account of constrained U.S. resources, American forces will be dependent upon international coalitions for the conduct of major contingency operations, as they were in Desert Shield and Desert Storm. In addition, "To the extent that deterrent strategies form part of the response to today's threats and challenges, they will increasingly be implemented *multilaterally* and *economically*" (emphasis in original).[53] Beyond resource constraints, Desert Storm also suggests a qualitative dilemma for U.S. military planners. Precision-guided munitions, improved communications and command/control, and reconnaissance-strike complexes will make possible, in theory, the selective targeting of enemy military assets while minimizing collateral damage.[54] In practice, as opposed to theory, the economies and social fabrics of Third World states may be so fragile that the "precision" possible in high-technology warfare is irrelevant to those on the receiving end. In addition, coalition air attacks within and outside of the Kuwaiti

Theater of Operations (KTO) used a preponderance of other than ''smart'' munitions, as table 8.7 shows.

Air Power

Thus efforts to maintain specific political and military limitations in war, and to derive from those limitations carefully laid-down strike plans, could fail unavoidably and to the detriment of coalition management.[55] In addition, the one-sided outcome of the Gulf War of 1991 caused a hubris about the potential of U.S. air power alone to win wars or to terminate crises.[56] The Air Force–commissioned Gulf War Air Power Survey (GWAPS) noted that in some respects the coalition was unable to obtain desired damage expectancies against preferred targets, including mobile Scuds, Iraqi nuclear capabilities, and Iraqi command, control, and communications.[57] In addition, problems of interservice command and control were not absent from Desert Storm. Tensions developed between U.S. ground forces commanders and the Joint Forces Air Component Commander (JFACC), Lieutenant General Charles A. Horner, who was responsible as Commander of Central Command's Air Force component (CENTAF). General Norman Schwarzkopf Commander-in-Chief Central Command (CINC-CENT) sought to centralize control of coalition air power under one component commander, and Schwarzkopf and Horner favored target attack priorities not shared by Marine and Army corps commanders. As the Gulf War Air Power Survey noted:

> In the dispute over the best use of precision bombing in the KTO (Kuwaiti Theater of Operations) . . . Schwarzkopf made decisions which displeased his ground commanders and caused grumbling about the JFACC's [Joint Forces Air Component Commander] execution of those decisions. Not only did Schwarzkopf emphasize bombing Republican Guards rather than frontline forces, but he shared Horner's enthusiasm for ''tank plinking'' [the destruction of tanks with precision-guided bombs]—an enthusiasm that was not shared by Generals Franks (Lt. Gen. Frederick Franks, USA) and Boomer (Lt. Gen. Walter Boomer, USMC). For their part, the JFACC's air campaign planners complained that targets nominated by ground forces were often out of date and had already been disabled by previous air attacks.[58]

Communications Technology

As the use of sophisticated information-gathering, processing, and distributing systems grows, so does the dependency of commanders on those systems and the vulnerability of the entire operational plan if the high-tech command, control, communications, and intelligence (C^3I) systems are destroyed. Modern communications technology also subverts traditional, hierarchical notions of control. During the Gulf War of 1991, for example, U.S. military staffs in Colorado relayed warnings of Iraqi Scud launches directly to Tel Aviv and Riyadh; members of the Joint Chiefs of Staff and civilian policymakers had the CNN back-

Table 8.7
Munitions Employed in the Desert Storm Air War (Selected List)**

MUNITIONS	AIR FORCE	NAVY	MARINES	TOTAL
General-Purpose Bombs				
Mk-82 (500 lb)	59,884	10,941	6,828	77,653
Mk-83 (1,000 lb)		10,125	8,893	19,018
Mk-84 (2,000 lb)	10,467	971	751	12,189
Mk-117 (B-52)	43,435			43,435
CBU-52 (fragmentation bomb)	17,831			17,831
CBU-87 (combined effects munition)	10,035			10,035
CBU-89/78 (Gator)	1,105	148	61	1,314
Mk-20 (Rockeye)	5,345	6,814	15,828	27,987
Laser-Guided Bombs				
GBU-12 (laser/ Mk-82)	4,086	205	202	4,493
Air-to-Surface Missiles				
*AGM-114 Hellfire (AH-64 and AH-1W)	ARMY = 2,876	30	159	3,065
AGM-65 Maverick All Models	5,255		41	5,296

*Navy and Marine Corps also fired 283 BGM-71 TOW munitions from helicopters.

**The selected munitions displayed in this table are those that were primarily, although not exclusively, used in the Kuwaiti Theater of Operations (KTO) by coalition forces. Other types of laser-guided bombs and air-to-surface missiles were used in the war, but not primarily in KTO.

Source: GWAPS, *Abbreviated Summary*, pp. 14–33.

channel (unofficial but important information network) to supplement communications directly with the field.[59] The difficulty of bomb damage assessment during the Gulf air war shows that, notwithstanding the availability of high-tech reconnaissance systems and data-fusion centers, war remains mostly in the domain of uncertainty.[60]

CONCLUSIONS

The Cold War enlarged the size of the peacetime U.S. armed forces and imposed unprecedented requirements for the support of U.S. coercive diplomacy, crisis management, and nuclear deterrence. It also led to a reorganized military establishment through which policymakers sought to impose increasingly greater degrees of centralized control. Although more centralized control over military administration and logistics was generally regarded as contributory to improved strategy, centralized control over operations was less favorably received by professional officers. Micromanagement of operations was resisted by field commanders, and the Goldwater-Nichols reforms sought to empower the CINCs in their respective areas of responsibility.

The U.S. experience in the development of military operational art has been two-sided: one side emphasized conventional conflict between regular formations accountable to state authority, and the other aspect of U.S. doctrine tried to comprehend unconventional warfare fought by nonstate actors and with irregular methods. These two faces of U.S. military doctrine have never been fully reconciled, in strategy or in policy, despite considerable experience in both milieus from the time of the Revolution to the present. U.S. public acceptance of unconventional war as a legitimate tool of policy is always in doubt, and the American professional officer corps remains wary of partial wars backed by a divided policy elite.

Future U.S. forces will be called upon to participate in collective security operations more frequently than in the past. Collective security, even in the modified form in which great powers do the work, makes strong assumptions about the willingness of the powers to act in concert for the good of the international community. The willingness of the powers to wage coalition war against aggressor states must be supported by other means of deterrence to ensure that war waging does not become the end rather than the means of a collective security system. The United Nations has recently flexed its diplomatic and military muscle in the form of peacekeeping operations of unprecedented scope and by means of authorized military and economic sanctions against Iraq. The Iraqi case and the war in Bosnia extending from 1992 into 1995 show the difficulty of bringing about lasting war termination, even in an environment as favorable to conflict termination through collective security as now exists.

NOTES

1. See Russell F. Weigley, *The American Way of War: A History of United States Military Strategy and Policy* (New York: Macmillan, 1973).

2. On the policymaking process in U.S. national security policy, see Sam C. Sarkesian, *U.S. National Security: Policymakers, Processes, and Politics,* 2nd ed. (Boulder, CO: Lynne Rienner Publishers, 1995), pp. 53–65 and 151–162.

3. Seminal studies of U.S. civil-military relations include Samuel P. Huntington, *The Soldier and the State* (Cambridge, MA: Belknap Press of Harvard University Press, 1957); Samuel P. Huntington, *The Common Defense* (New York: Columbia University Press, 1961); Morris Janowitz, *The Professional Soldier: A Social and Political Portrait* (Glencoe, IL: Free Press, 1960); and Russell F. Weigley, *Towards an American Army: Military Thought from Washington to Marshall* (New York: Columbia University Press, 1962).

4. On U.S. security requirements and responses for the pre–Cold War or ''geopolitical'' era, see Robert J. Art, ''A Defensible Defense: America's Grand Strategy after the Cold War,'' *International Security* vol. 15, no. 4 (Spring 1991): 5–53.

5. For example, Cold War conditions posed new problems of interservice command and control. This is well treated in historical perspective by C. Kenneth Allard, *Command, Control, and the Common Defense* (New Haven: Yale University Press, 1990).

6. An expert analysis of U.S. military professionalism in the Cold War years is provided in Sam C. Sarkesian, *Beyond the Battlefield: The New Military Professionalism* (New York: Pergamon Press, 1981).

7. Gaddis Smith, *American Diplomacy during the Second World War, 1941–1945* (New York: Wiley, 1965), esp. pp. 59–80.

8. These developments can be traced in John Lewis Gaddis, *The United States and the Origins of the Cold War, 1941–1947* (New York: Columbia University Press, 1972), esp. pp. 282–352, and Adam Ulam, *The Rivals: America and Russia since World War II* (New York: Viking Press, 1971).

9. For pertinent documentation, see Walter LaFeber, *America, Russia, and the Cold War, 1945–1975,* 3rd ed. (New York: John Wiley and Sons, 1976). On the development of U.S. Cold War policy, see Gaddis, *United States and the Origins of the Cold War, 1941–1947.* For Soviet policy, see Vojtech Mastny, *Russia's Road to the Cold War: Diplomacy, Warfare, and the Politics of Communism, 1941–1945* (New York: Columbia University Press, 1979).

10. John Lewis Gaddis, *The Long Peace: Inquiries into the History of the Cold War* (New York: Oxford University Press, 1987), p. 114.

11. Robert Jervis, *The Meaning of the Nuclear Revolution* (Ithaca, NY: Cornell University Press, 1989), and Lawrence Freedman, *The Evolution of Nuclear Strategy* (New York: St. Martin's Press, 1981).

12. Paul Nitze, ''A Project for Further Analysis and Study of Certain Factors Affecting Our Foreign Policy and Our National Defense Policy,'' Project Control Papers, U.S. Air Force Historical Research Center, Maxwell AFB, Alabama, 15 September 1954, cited in Marc Trachtenberg, *History and Strategy* (Princeton, NJ: Princeton University Press, 1991), p. 112.

13. See Peter Douglas Feaver, *Guarding the Guardians: Civilian Control of Nuclear*

Weapons in the United States (Ithaca, NY: Cornell University Press, 1992), esp. pp. 3–28.

14. This case is argued in Harry G. Summers, Jr., *On Strategy: A Critical Analysis of the Vietnam War* (New York: Dell Publishing Co., 1982), chap. 1.

15. For an account from the perspective of McNamara's staff, see Alain C. Enthoven and K. Wayne Smith, *How Much Is Enough? Shaping the Defense Program, 1961–1969* (New York: Harper and Row, 1971), esp. pp. 117–164. See also William W. Kaufmann, *The McNamara Strategy* (New York: Harper and Row, 1964).

16. The evolution of the NSC is discussed in John Prados, *Keepers of the Keys: A History of the National Security Council from Truman to Bush* (New York: William Morrow and Co., 1991).

17. For assessments of the Goldwater-Nichols Act, see Robert J. Art, *Strategy and Management in the Post–Cold War Pentagon* (Carlisle Barracks, PA: U.S. Army War College, Strategic Studies Institute, 22 June 1992), and Rep. Les Aspin, Chairman, and Rep. William Dickinson, U.S. Congress, House Committee on Armed Services, *Defense for a New Era: Lessons of the Persian Gulf War* (Washington, DC: U.S. Government Printing Office, 1992).

18. For a sampling of expert assessments, see Robert J. Art, Vincent Davis, and Samuel P. Huntington, eds., *Reorganizing America's Defense: Leadership in War and Peace* (Washington, DC: Pergamon-Brassey's, 1985).

19. Art, *Strategy and Management in the Post–Cold War Pentagon,* pp. 26–27.

20. A critique of U.S. experience is provided in D. Michael Shafer, *Deadly Paradigms: The Failure of U.S. Counterinsurgency Policy* (Princeton, NJ: Princeton University Press, 1988). See also Douglas S. Blaufarb, *The Counterinsurgency Era: U.S. Doctrine and Performance, 1950 to the Present* (New York: Free Press, 1977). For evaluations of American experiences with covert action, see John Prados, *Presidents' Secret Wars: CIA and Pentagon Covert Operations since World War II* (New York: William Morrow and Co., 1986), and Roy Godson, ed., *Intelligence Requirements for the 1980s,* vol. 4, *Covert Action* (Washington, DC: National Strategy Information Center, 1983). An assessment of the impact of low-intensity conflict on American military professionalism appears in Sarkesian, *Beyond the Battlefield,* pt. 2, chaps. 4–7.

21. Harry G. Summers, Jr., *On Strategy II: A Critical Analysis of the Gulf War* (New York: Dell Publishing Co., 1992), pp. 72–73.

22. John G. Hines and Phillip A. Petersen, "NATO and the Changing Soviet Concept of Control for Theater War," in *The Soviet Challenge in the 1990s,* ed. Stephen J. Cimbala (New York: Praeger, 1989), pp. 65–122.

23. Summers, *On Strategy II: A Critical Analysis of the Gulf War,* pp. 139–150.

24. Charles Krauthammer, "The Unipolar Moment," in *Rethinking America's Security,* ed. Graham Allison and Gregory F. Treverton (New York: W. W. Norton, 1992), p. 298. U.S. battle deaths in Korea actually totaled about 34,000: total deaths raised the number above 54,000. See table 8.6.

25. James John Tritten, *Our New National Security Strategy: America Promises to Come Back* (Westport, CT: Praeger, 1992), pp. 22–23.

26. On collective security, see Inis L. Claude, Jr., *Swords into Plowshares: The Problems and Prospects of International Organization,* 3rd ed. rev. (New York: Random House, 1964), pp. 223–260. U.N. efforts in conflict termination from 1946 through 1964 are described in Sydney Bailey, *How Wars End: The United Nations and the Termination of Armed Conflict, 1946–1964,* vol. 1 (Oxford: Clarendon Press, 1982), with a companion

second volume providing more detail on the individual cases. The first volume contains an especially helpful resume of pertinent theory on conflict termination (pp. 1–15).

27. Comparison of the theoretical principle of collective security with the actual practice of it appears in Inis L. Claude, Jr., ''Collective Security after the Cold War,'' in *Collective Security in Europe and Asia,* ed. Gary L. Guertner (Carlisle Barracks, PA: U.S. Army War College, Strategic Studies Institute, March 1992), pp. 7–28. Claude noted that excessive optimism about the probable success of collective security frequently follows in the aftermath of successful coalition wars (see esp. pp. 14–15).

28. Rep. Les Aspin, Chairman, House Armed Services Committee, *An Approach to Sizing American Conventional Forces for the Post-Soviet Era: Four Illustrative Options* (Washington, DC: House Armed Services Committee, 25 February 1992).

29. Ibid., p. 8.

30. Ibid., p. 9.

31. What the Gulf War of 1991 portends for the future is explored in Aspin and Dickinson, *Defense for a New Era,* and Norman Friedman, *Desert Victory: The War for Kuwait* (Annapolis, MD: U.S. Naval Institute Press, 1991), pp. 236–260.

32. For an authoritative compendium of recent work in this field, see Alexander L. George, ed., *Avoiding War: Problems of Crisis Management* (Boulder, CO: Westview Press, 1991). For an assessment of the state of crisis management theory, see Alexander L. George, ''Findings and Recommendations,'' in George, *Avoiding War,* pp. 545–566. An excellent study of crisis-management theory is Phil Williams, *Crisis Management* (New York: John Wiley and Sons, 1976).

33. Martin van Creveld, *The Transformation of War* (New York: Free Press, 1991).

34. Summers, *On Strategy: A Critical Analysis of the Vietnam War.*

35. Summers, *On Strategy II: A Critical Analysis of the Gulf War.*

36. Sam C. Sarkesian, *America's Forgotten Wars: The Counterrevolutionary Past and Lessons for the Future* (Westport, CT: Greenwood Press, 1984), esp. pp. 155–194.

37. Art, ''Defensible Defense,'' pp. 5–53.

38. Ibid. Art offers a deliberately narrow and specific definition of security: the ability of the United States to protect its homeland from attack, conquest, invasion, or destruction (p. 7).

39. John Lewis Gaddis, *The United States and the End of the Cold War: Implications, Reconsiderations, Provocations* (New York: Oxford University Press, 1992), pp. 193–194.

40. Sam C. Sarkesian suggested that the term *unconventional conflict* is preferable to *low-intensity conflict.* Unconventional conflicts are nontraditional and not in conformity with the American way of war. These kinds of conflicts emphasize social and political variables, especially the problem of revolution and counterrevolution, instead of the military dimensions of conflict. See Sarkesian, ''U.S. Strategy and Unconventional Conflicts: The Elusive Goal,'' in *The U.S. Army in a New Security Era,* ed. Sam C. Sarkesian and John Allen Williams (Boulder, CO: Lynne Rienner Publishers, 1990), pp. 195–216.

41. Sarkesian, *Beyond the Battlefield,* chaps. 4–6.

42. For an assessment of pertinent literature, see John Shy and Thomas W. Collier, ''Revolutionary War,'' in *Makers of Modern Strategy*, ed. Peter Paret (Princeton, NJ: Princeton University Press, 1986), pp. 815–862.

43. Summers, *On Strategy: A Critical Analysis of the Vietnam War,* argued that the United States should have followed a conventional military strategy in Vietnam, leaving counterinsurgency, civic action, and the like to the South Vietnamese. In his view, U.S.

strategy failed in Vietnam because it strayed from military traditionalism into politico-military amateurism, especially graduated escalation and counterinsurgency. Sarkesian, *America's Forgotten Wars,* pp. 194–218, provided a different assessment, contending that the military aspects of the war were especially complex and involved an unusual mixture of conventional and unconventional campaigns.

44. Sarkesian, "U.S. Strategy and Unconventional Conflicts," p. 199. See also Leslie H. Gelb with Richard K. Betts, *The Irony of Vietnam: The System Worked* (Washington, DC: Brookings Institution, 1979), for an argument that bad foreign policy resulted from a U.S. domestic policymaking process that worked as it was designed to. For counterpoint to the Gelb-Betts arguments, see Shafer, *Deadly Paradigms,* pp. 240–275, esp. pp. 260–261.

45. Weigley, "American Strategy from Its Beginnings through the First World War," *Makers of Modern Strategy,* ed. Peter Paret, pp. 408–443, and Weigley, *The American Way of War.*

46. Weigley, "American Strategy from Its Beginnings through the First World War," p. 412.

47. Ibid., p. 410, and Sarkesian, *America's Forgotten Wars,* p. 107.

48. Sarkesian, *America's Forgotten Wars,* p. 110.

49. On the development of the strategy of annihilation in German military thinking, see Larry H. Addington, *The Blitzkrieg Era and the German General Staff, 1865–1941* (New Brunswick, NJ: Rutgers University Press, 1971), esp. chap. 1, pp. 3–27. On the development of the distinction between strategies of annihilation (*Niederwerfungsstrategie*) and strategies of exhaustion (*Ermattungsstrategie*) by German historian Hans Delbruck, see Gordon A. Craig, "Delbruck: The Military Historian," in Paret, *Makers of Modern Strategy,* pp. 326–353, esp. p. 341. An important Russian theorist on the difference between annihilation- and attrition-oriented strategies is Aleksandr A. Svechin, *Strategy,* ed. Kent D. Lee (Minneapolis, MN: East View Publications, 1991), pp. 240–250 (translated from the original work, A. A. Svechin, *Strategiya,* 2nd ed. (Moscow: Voennyi Vestnik, 1927).

50. Mao Tse-tung (Zedong), *Basic Tactics,* translated and with an introduction by Stuart R. Schram (New York: Frederick A. Praeger, 1967), esp. pp. 67–89.

51. For an assessment of threats to U.S. security remaining after the Cold War, see Art, "Defensible Defense," pp. 23ff. Art contended that traditional geopolitical logic exaggerated the degree of threat to U.S. interests from 1945 to 1990. Especially after 1960, the United States was faced with neither credible threats of invasion nor of slow strangulation subsequent to the conquest of Eurasia by an adversary hegemon.

52. The point is emphasized in Michael J. Mazarr, Don M. Snider, and James A. Blackwell, Jr., *Desert Storm: The Gulf War and What We Learned* (Boulder, Co: Westview Press, 1993), pp. 162–168.

53. Ibid., p. 175.

54. The term *reconnaissance-strike complexes* originated in Russian/Soviet military discourse to describe combinations of increasingly accurate conventional munitions, improved target identification and location, and enhanced control and communications systems for directing the employment of munitions against selected targets. See V. G. Reznichenko, I. N. Vorob'iev, and N. F. Miroshnichenko, *Taktika* (Tactics) (Moscow: Voenizdat, 1987), trans by Stephen Cimbala, p. 24, which noted: "In the opinion of foreign specialists, reconnaissance-strike (fire) complexes are the most effective form of high-precision weapon. High-precision reconnaissance resources and high-precision

weapons are coordinated by an automated control system, making it possible to carry out reconnaissance and destruction missions practically in real time.'' The issue continues to preoccupy the Russian military, although it will struggle to maintain the military-industrial base for future modernization. See John Erickson, ''Quo Vadis? The Changing Faces of Soviet/Russian Forces and Now Russia,'' in *The Soviet Military and the Future,* ed. Stephen J. Blank and Jacob W. Kipp (Westport, CT: Greenwood Press, 1992), pp. 33–58.

55. According to one source, ''Various offices in the Pentagon are battling for control of a dramatic new initiative for nonlethal warfare. By using blinding lasers and chemical immobilizers to stun foot soldiers and munitions with 'entanglement' warheads to stop armored vehicles on land or ships at sea, it is hoped by some that the United States could some day fight a war that did not involve death, or at least few deaths.'' Mazarr, Snider, and Blackwell, *Desert Storm,* p. 172. Life imitates art, or, at least, simulation.

56. Eliot A. Cohen, ''The Mystique of U.S. Air Power,'' *Foreign Affairs* vol. 73, no. 1 (January/February 1994), pp. 109–124.

57. Some 1,500 strikes were conducted against Iraqi ballistic missile capabilities, of which 15 percent (about 215 strikes) included attacks against mobile launchers. According to GWAPS, ''The actual destruction of any Iraqi mobile launchers by fixed-wing coalition aircraft remains impossible to confirm.'' Despite coalition attacks on leadership and C^3 targets, the Iraqi command and communications system ''turned out to be more redundant and more able to reconstitute itself than first thought.'' The redundancy, advanced status, and elusiveness of Iraq's nuclear program led the United Nations to conclude that Desert Storm had no more than ''inconvenienced'' Iraqi plans to field atomic weapons. See *Abbreviated Summary of the Gulf War Air Power Survey* (Carlisle Barracks, PA: U.S. Army War College, 1993), pp. 14–23, 14–27. The study was commissioned by the then Secretary of the U.S. Air Force, Dr. Donald Rice, in 1991 and directed by Dr. Eliot A. Cohen, Johns Hopkins University.

58. GWAPS *Abbreviated Summary,* p. 14–43.

59. Cohen, ''Mystique of U.S. Air Power,'' p. 118.

60. Ibid., p. 119.

SELECTED BIBLIOGRAPHY

Art, Robert J. *Strategy and Management in the Post-Cold War Pentagon.* Carlisle Barracks, PA: U.S. Army War College, Strategic Studies Institute, June 1992.

Art, Robert J., Vincent Davis, and Samuel P. Huntington, eds. *Reorganizing America's Defense: Leadership in War and Peace.* Washington, DC: Pergamon-Brassey's, 1985.

Aspin, Rep. Les, and Rep. William Dickinson, U.S. Congress, House Committee on Armed Services. *Defense for a New Era: Lessons of the Persian Gulf War.* Washington, DC: U.S. Government Printing Office, 1992.

Enthoven, Alain C., and K. Wayne Smith. *How Much Is Enough? Shaping the Defense Program, 1961–1969.* New York: Harper and Row, 1971.

Feaver, Peter Douglas. *Guarding the Guardians: Civilian Control of Nuclear Weapons in the United States.* Ithaca, NY: Cornell University Press, 1992.

Gaddis, John Lewis. *The Long Peace: Inquiries into the History of the Cold War.* New York: Oxford University Press, 1987.

———. *The United States and the Origins of the Cold War, 1941–1947.* New York: Columbia University Press, 1972.

Huntington, Samuel P. *The Soldier and the State.* Cambridge, MA: Belknap Press of Harvard University Press, 1957.

Janowitz, Morris. *The Professional Soldier: A Social and Political Portrait.* New York: Free Press, 1960.

Jervis, Robert. *The Meaning of the Nuclear Revolution.* Ithaca, NY: Cornell University Press, 1989.

LaFeber, Walter. *America, Russia, and the Cold War, 1945–1975.* 3rd ed. New York: John Wiley and Sons, 1976.

Prados, John. *Keepers of the Keys: A History of the National Security Council from Truman to Bush.* New York: William Morrow and Co., 1991.

Sarkesian, Sam C. *Beyond the Battlefield: The New Military Professionalism.* New York: Pergamon Press, 1981.

———. *U.S. National Security: Policymakers, Processes, and Politics.* 2nd ed. Boulder, CO: Lynne Rienner Publishers, 1995.

Summers, Harry G., Jr. *On Strategy: A Critical Analysis of the Vietnam War.* New York: Dell Publishing Co., 1982.

Trachtenberg, Marc. *History and Strategy.* Princeton, NJ: Princeton University Press, 1991.

Weigley, Russell F. *The American Way of War: A History of United States Military Strategy and Policy.* New York: Macmillan, 1973.

———. *Towards an American Army: Military Thought from Washington to Marshall.* New York: Columbia University Press, 1962.

Chapter 9

THE GULF WAR AND REGIONAL CONFLICTS

Douglas V. Johnson II

The purpose for reviewing Operation Desert Shield/Storm is to examine the most recent large-scale combined military operation. This operation will be a classic in years to come, on the order of the Battle of Königgrätz in 1866. That battle demonstrated the utility of the Prussian General Staff system just as Desert Storm demonstrated the value of the Goldwater-Nichols Reform Act and U.S. Army doctrine and training. Both battles demonstrated successful evaluation of emerging technologies and their application to tactics, operations, and strategy. Both likewise provided proof of strategic mobilization concepts and innovative strategic and operational maneuver concepts based upon decentralized execution in harmony with a uniformly understood basic plan.

The guiding concepts of the AirLand Battle doctrine and the provisions of the Goldwater-Nichols Reform Act of 1986 enabled the American military services to perform in greater harmony, with a more unified effort than ever before in American history. Unified operations prepared and executed under a single commander resulted from more than guiding operational concepts, however, as management of a unique coalition force and deployment from multiple bases at distances over 8,500 miles stretched the theater command's abilities to the limit. Here also is a clear example of the subordination of military action to political purposes as well as the proper integration of the three elements of the Clausewitzian trinity, the people, the army, and the state. In the latter half of this chapter some of these same elements are addressed within the new framework of a new national military strategy and in the context of a familiar situation with a new name, operations other than war.

SETTING THE STAGE

Historical Roots

The direct historical roots of the Gulf War lie in the eight-year Iran-Iraq War. That war, with much longer historical roots than are relevant to this case study, ended with a stunning, and very unexpected, Iraqi military victory. Iraqi military performance during the war was spotty until the stunning loss of al-Fao Peninsula to Iran in April 1986. The loss of that territory was humiliating to the Iraqis even though it actually gave little advantage to the Iranians. The humiliation was sufficient to bring about an extraordinary meeting of the Ba'ath Party in July 1986. While it is not known exactly what transpired at that meeting, everything indicates that the conduct of the war was, from that point on, placed in the hands of the professional military. The consequence of this change was the professionalization of the Iraqi military machine. December 1987 saw the last determined Iranian drive toward Basrah collapse in a welter of blood for no appreciable gain. The next year, beginning in April, the Iraqis launched their counteroffensive. With mechanical efficiency, they trained on full-scale mock-ups of their objectives, attacked with overwhelming superiority, and pounded and ground the Iranians to ruin. Launching their operations at thirty-day intervals, coinciding with the gradual advance of good campaigning weather, the Iraqis moved north along the Iranian border with their final operation, conducted largely by the forces of the People's Mujahedin of Iran (also known as the Mujahedin al Khalq), reaching almost to Kermanshah. In the process, they captured vast stores of equipment and thousands of prisoners.[1]

At the same time that Iraqi ground operations were having such unexpected success, the Iranians incautiously launched a series of confrontations against the U.S. Navy, then patrolling the Gulf and escorting Kuwaiti oil tankers. The U.S. Navy was engaged in conducting Operation Ernest Will, the escort of Kuwaiti oil tankers, reflagged to carry American colors, in order to prevent Iranian interference with the oil shipments. Iranian Revolutionary Guards naval units had been attacking neutral oil tankers sailing through the Gulf in an effort to intimidate the Gulf nations that had been supporting Iraq. In a sharp battle that lasted the better part of a day, the U.S. Navy repulsed the most determined Iranian effort, leaving roughly 25 to 30 percent of the Iranian Navy in flames. Tensions remained high, and shortly thereafter the U.S. Navy shot down an Iranian commercial jetliner, thinking it to be another Iranian attack. World opinion was muted, accepting the incident as a by-product of the hostilities. The absence of any world reaction to the deaths of more than 250 civilians, when coupled to the destruction of the Iranian Army on the ground and the continuing success of Iraqi long-range missile attacks on Iranian cities, was too much for the fanatical Iranian regime.[2] Iraq won the war in a military sense. But the war left both sides with intense bitterness remaining, and with hugh debts outstanding, particularly for Iraq.

Iraq had built its war machine from a force of about six divisions in 1980 to six corps of about fifty divisions, or almost one million men, in 1988. In the process Iraq, which had a population of only sixteen million, was obliged to import thousands of foreign laborers. Equally significant, Iraqi women were mobilized and placed in positions in business and government in gradually increasing numbers. Once the war ended, however, two major problems arose. There was no further requirement for a million-man armed force, but there was no way to demobilize it without creating internal problems. Because internal security was and is the primary consideration of the Saddam Hussein regime, it was impossible simply to demobilize major portions of the armed forces. Unemployed soldiers, the bulk of whom were the culturally and politically oppressed Shia majority, were not the people to be turned loose on an economy that was attempting to shift gears from a full wartime mode to something more normal. Immediately after the first attempt to demobilize, the American Embassy was besieged by former soldiers and officers, many with solid technical degrees, seeking visas and citing no jobs as the primary reason.[3]

The armed forces had been treated well by the government. The Air Force and the Republican Guard had been given special perks. It became impossible for discharged veterans to find jobs with wages comparable to those they had enjoyed in the service. The discharged veterans expected better than was available even if the foreign laborers departed. The Iraqi government was thus faced with a dilemma: it had to demobilize to reduce the cost of maintaining its huge army, yet its economy could not absorb the discharged veterans, and the dictates of internal security made it impossible to allow the streets to be filled with unemployed former soldiers.[4]

Worse, the Iraqi external debt had risen to approximately $40 billion. For a country with a GNP of $66 billion (1989) this was a crushing load.[5] Iraq had been managing to keep its creditors at arm's length during the war, but with the cessation of hostilities, the expectations of repayment rose rapidly. In the months following the war's end demands for payment became intense, particularly from the several nations whose defense economies had become significantly tied to arms sales to Iraq, France and the USSR in particular. Iraq began losing control of its finances when the price of oil began to drop. For a single-commodity economy, the sale of oil at a certain minimum price was vital to Iraq's recovery, but the international oil market did not take its lead from Iraqi internal needs. As the price of oil fell, the Iraqi situation worsened. Further, instead of diverting what little remaining cash it did have to internal reconstruction and economic reorientation, the Iraqi leadership perceived a renewed Israeli threat and felt compelled to take action against it. Whether the threat was valid or not is irrelevant. Whether the threat was employed as an excuse to maintain a higher-than-reasonable level of military investment is also irrelevant. What mattered was that Iraq, partly through mismanagement of its finances, found itself sliding rapidly into bankruptcy. Had there been an international Chapter 11, Iraq would have been forced into it.

As the situation worsened, it became clear that the price of oil was going to continue dropping—a consequence of OPEC overproduction especially on the part of the United Arab Emirates (UAE) and Kuwait. The UAE was notorious for poor bookkeeping; the Kuwaitis were not. If the seemingly deliberate actions of the Kuwaitis in driving the price of oil down to the point where it could be bought on the spot market at $12 a barrel were not enough, the Iraqis discovered that the oil field that they shared with the Kuwaitis had suffered a significant loss of pressure.[6] The Rumaylia oil field spans the Iraq-Kuwait border, and both nations pump from it. The Iraqis had not drawn oil from this field for most of the war and therefore expected the pressure readings to be about what they had been when production stopped on their side. A drop of pressure at the wellhead meant that the Kuwaitis had pumped a huge amount of oil from their side of the field, enough to lower the pressure throughout the field. This discovery enraged the Iraqis. The Iraqis felt that the Kuwaitis, who had admittedly loaned Iraq $10 billion during the war, had done so by selling Iraqi oil. When the Kuwaitis demanded repayment of the $10 billion plus interest, the Iraqis exploded in anger. In effect the Kuwaitis were asking the Iraqis to pay interest on assets taken from Iraq's own safety deposit box. The events that followed were poorly understood in the West mostly because of a lack of understanding of the essential background and desperate Iraqi financial situation.

Failure of Deterrence?

Negotiations over debt repayment and oil prices and quotas generated considerable hostility between Iraq and Kuwait, with harsh words being traded in the press.[7] As the Iraqis moved Republican Guard forces and other supporting units south to the Kuwait border area, diplomats from around the region sought contact with the Iraqi leadership to determine its intentions. By the time Saddam Hussein had accumulated some 100,000 troops in the southern border area, the world was thoroughly alarmed. But Saddam was calmly assuring his Arab brethren that he had no intention of actually invading; he simply wanted to put pressure on the Kuwaitis to make them behave.[8] Historians will likely condemn the American administration for failing to state clearly where it stood on these matters, for there was no serious attempt to deter Iraqi military action.

Margaret Tutwiler, spokesperson for the Department of State, stated that the United States had no formal commitments to defend Kuwait.[9] The American Ambassador to Iraq, April Glaspie, was alleged to have commented to President Hussein that the United States had no interest in border disputes. Ambassador Glaspie's actual comments were more explicitly prohibitive of military action than initially reported. Nonetheless, for many these comments were seen as a green light for Iraqi military action, just as Secretary of State John Foster Dulles's remarks excluding South Korea from the zone of vital American interests were interpreted as a "go-ahead" to North Korea. The main point is that the United States did little to deter an Iraqi invasion partly because it did not believe that it was coming. Another reason for failure to deter was American failure to understand the desperate straits in which the Iraqi regime found itself, which made deterrence a much more formidable task than it first appeared. While it is tempting and appropriate to a degree to blame the Israelis for provoking the Iraqis, it is probably incorrect to place major blame on them in creating a confrontation between Iraq and the United States. The Shamir government had overplayed its usually strong hand and alienated the American administration through its unduly harsh repression of its disenfranchised Palestinian population. The fact is that the American administration was not prepared to deter the Iraqis and, arguably, could not have done so had it chosen to.[10]

In addition, the failure of deterrence was also blamed on the often-addressed American inability to move adequate forces to the Gulf. When the Rapid Deployment Force (later the Rapid Deployment Joint Task Force [RDJTF]) was created in 1979 in response to President Carter's statement that the Gulf was a vital American national interest, that force was neither rapid, deployable, or much of a force. The American press was not shy about stating the facts, and although significant progress had been made, U.S. Central Command, which succeeded the RDJTF, was known to be short of much of its necessary strategic lift. The only training in the region had been associated with the biennial Bright Star exercises that take place in Egypt. Smaller exercises associated with this major exercise took place in other locations such as Oman and Sudan.

In order for deterrence to work, there must be a credible force, capable of moving to the scene and prepared to act. The credibility of any American deterrent in the region was minimal and was further eroded by the generally accepted proposition that the Saudis would not allow U.S. forces to operate from their soil. It was felt that the Saudis could not do this because it would profane the land of the two holy mosques of Islam in Mecca and Medina. The United States had been unable to obtain prepositioning rights in Saudi Arabia primarily for this reason even though large numbers of American contractors and American military personnel administering Foreign Military Sales and operating the Military Training Mission for the Saudi Arabian National Guard were already present. Enduring hostility between Iran and the United States over the hostage issue precluded any thought of operating from Iran. In such a circumstance, the United States had no base in the region from which it could operate should it choose to engage Iraq. Even strongly stated deterrence language would have been effectively diluted by these obvious limitations.

Invasion

The last-ditch efforts by the Saudis and others to preclude hostilities through a meeting between the antagonists in Jedda, Saudi Arabia, collapsed. Why they collapsed is uncertain, but within hours Iraqi forces launched a three-pronged attack on Kuwait. The main attack drove directly down the principal paved road, over the only terrain obstacle, which was undefended, into Kuwait City. The main attack was supported by a flanking column driving south on a parallel axis to the west. The third prong of the attack was a heliborne special operations force attack directly into Kuwait City. Ironically, the Kuwaitis had taken an impossibly strong position at the Jedda conference, refusing to give in to Iraqi demands while at the same time taking their armed forces off alert so as not to provoke the Iraqis. Consequently, Kuwaiti military resistance was minimal.[11] Within forty-eight hours after the invasion, Iraqi armored units were on the Saudi border in what appeared to be blocking positions, but with southward movement of logistic support sufficient to allow resumption of an advance.

Diplomacy

President Bush's reaction to the invasion was one of outrage. After brief consultations with the President and his national security advisor, Secretary of Defense Dick Cheney and Chairman of the Joint Chiefs of Staff General Colin Powell, a small team of experts flew to Riyadh, Saudi Arabia, to brief King Fahd on the situation as it was known to U.S. intelligence and to offer assistance.[12] The King, convinced that the threat to the kingdom was real, invited U.S. forces into Saudi Arabia to assure its defense. Within hours U.S. Air Force and Army elements began arriving as the forerunners of the most extensive deployment experienced by the U.S. military since World War II.

Initially, the Iraqis stated that the invasion was in response to a request from elements within Kuwait and that the Iraqi armed forces would withdraw as soon as a replacement government was installed. That pronouncement was quickly set aside and replaced by Iraqi statements incorporating Kuwait into Iraq as its historic nineteenth province. Among the first resolutions approved by the United Nations was one categorically rejecting Iraq's claim to Kuwait as Iraq's nineteenth province.[13]

The Iraqi Army

As noted earlier, Iraq ended the Iran-Iraq War with a million-man armed force, equipped with the most sophisticated weaponry of any Third World nation anywhere. It was also the most heavily armed nation in the region, possessing what amounted to the fourth-largest army in the world.

Iraqi Strengths

The Iraqi Army ended the Iran-Iraq War with considerable experience in countering light infantry and limited experience against mechanized or armored formations. It had established proficiency in the use of chemical weapons, including the first operational uses of the nerve gases Sarin and Tabun. The Iraqi engineers established a formidable reputation in the construction of defensive fortifications. The engineers and logisticians established a brilliantly functioning supply network—in a situation of air superiority, to be sure. For all the horrors of the regime's brutality toward its people, the Iraqi people identified with and supported the regime for the most part. How much was genuine spontaneous support is uncertain. Iraq has the most effective internal security program anywhere in the world, which may explain why neither the United States nor the vaunted Israeli intelligence agencies were able to provide any human intelligence (HUMINT) of consequence before or during the war.[14]

The Iraqis developed great ability to mask their intentions and camouflage their movements. Their ability to move units frequently and without detection by their Iranian enemies or by U.S. strategic technical means served both internal and external purposes. Internally, frequent movement served to upset coup planning; externally, it kept friend and foe uncertain of the next move. Interestingly, with the revelation of the Irangate scandal, Iraq began to rely increasingly upon its own devices for intelligence support, feeling that the United States could not be relied upon as either friend or impartial observer.[15]

Iraqi Weaknesses

Iraq never fought against major armored formations after 1981. It fought under friendly skies and with limited air support during most of the eight-year Iran-Iraq War. It demonstrated its ability to execute combined-arms maneuvers only after extensive battle drills on full-scale mock-ups. In short, set-piece battles became its principal forte, although the armored and mechanized forces demonstrated a capability to conduct counterattacks on a multidivision basis with considerable success.[16] For all the apparent loyalty of the people, the regime had to exert itself continuously to maintain internal discipline and was always bedeviled by the variations in Kurdish support. For a time there existed a large body of insurgents/deserters in the southern swamps. The Iraqis never showed the flexibility on the battlefield that the Iranians did, the latter's suicidal human-wave attacks notwithstanding. The Iraqi Air Force was essentially untested for most of the Iran-Iraq War, although it demonstrated significantly increased ability to conduct complex operations late in the war. Overcentralization of command remained the principal weakness of the military establishment throughout. The inept hand of President Saddam Hussein was everywhere evident except in rare instances and was notably withdrawn after the July 1986 Extraordinary Congress of the Ba'ath Party. Following the congress, planning and training improved sharply, and the nation mobilized as never before. Thus, when the final Iranian effort, Karbala V, was launched in December 1987, the Iraqi Army was ready and slaughtered the Iranians by the tens of thousands. Once the extent of the slaughter had sunk in, and the weather began to improve, the final Iraqi campaign was set in motion and the Iranian army was decimated. The high Iranian casualties were the product of set-piece battles with nearly unlimited resources. The Iraqis built one-to-one-scale mock-ups of the objective area, rehearsed on the mock-up for several weeks, marched directly to their lines of departure, and, following immense artillery barrages, executed their drills again against a stunned, undermanned, and demoralized enemy. About two-thirds of the entire operational stocks of the Iranian Army were destroyed or captured.[17]

The Iraqi Army, 1990

The Iraqis had attempted to demobilize their army after the Iran-Iraq War, as noted earlier, but found that they could not do so effectively. It appears that they simply allowed major proportions of the army to take leave and find whatever jobs they could. Consequently, when the call went out to mobilize for the invasion of Kuwait, only the Republican Guard Forces and, probably, those of the regular armored and mechanized forces were at combat-ready strength. As soon as the invasion was successfully completed, and following the pattern established during the Iran-Iraq War, the mechanized and armored forces were replaced on the front lines by what can be best called "fortress infantry." These units were the least well trained, the least reliable, and the most inadequately armed of all the army's units.

Furthermore, many of the units that deployed to Kuwait were at less than full strength, some estimates ranging as low as 50 percent. It had been common practice for the Iraqis to allow a high proportion of their soldiers to go on extended leave during the quiet periods of the Iran-Iraq War, knowing that when indications and warnings of an impending Iranian attack surfaced, the marvelously functioning Iraqi transportation network could deliver all the soldiers to their place of duty in plenty of time. This view seemed to prevail in 1990, even though the transportation net southward was not yet established. In any event, Western intelligence services watched as the infantry units took up positions along the Kuwaiti-Saudi border and dug in. The ever-efficient Iraqi Engineer Corps immediately undertook another huge road-building project to link the deployed infantry divisions to the sparse existing Kuwaiti network. The deployment and road building extended to the Wadi al-Batin, a dry gulch that runs roughly southwest to northeast along the border between Kuwait, Iraq, and portions of the Neutral Zone. There were few deployments beyond the Wadi and only minimal road building. From the repositioning of Iraqi mechanized and armored units, it became clear, more or less, to coalition intelligence officers what the Iraqi plan of defense was going to be—a replay of its successful practices of the last war. Armored/mechanized units were deployed as operational reserves behind the front line, some units positioned close enough to indicate tactical functions, others far enough to the rear and located along maneuver axes so as to be obvious operational reserves. The elite Republican Guard Forces Command units were positioned farthest to the rear, back in Iraq, but far enough forward to be able to act as theater reserves.

While this entire force gradually built up to about forty-two divisions, Lieutenant General John Yeosock, Commander of Army Forces, Central Command, was one of the first to notice that they were conducting no training whatsoever. From that he concluded that although they might have been positioned to counterattack, their failure to rehearse for such action was a good indicator that they would not do so, and if they were directed to, they would be used piecemeal.[18]

SELECTING THE CAST AND CONDUCTING REHEARSALS

Coalition Development

The clear articulation of U.S. national policy objectives made military planning much less difficult, and it also made coalition building easier. The four publicly stated policy objectives were the following:

1. Immediate, complete, and unconditional withdrawal of all Iraqi forces from Kuwait
2. Restoration of Kuwait's legitimate government
3. Security and stability of Saudi Arabia and the Persian Gulf
4. Safety and protection of the lives of American citizens abroad[19]

The first steps toward coalition action began almost immediately. President Bush, with the approval of the Kuwaiti Ambassador to the United States, who assumed the functions of the Kuwaiti government then fleeing for its life, froze all Kuwaiti financial assets in the United States to forestall Iraqi access. British Prime Minister Margaret Thatcher was in Aspen, Colorado, with President Bush. This served to facilitate mutually supporting declarations of the unacceptability of Iraqi actions. On that same day, in one of the most momentous acts of the decade, the Soviet Union condemned the Iraqi invasion and demanded its withdrawal.[20] Secretary of Defense Dick Cheney with a supporting team was dispatched to Saudi Arabia on 5 August to brief King Fahd on the developing situation. From that visit came an invitation for U.S. forces to help defend the kingdom against possible deeper Iraqi incursions.

United Nations Resolution 660 condemning Iraq's invasion of Kuwait passed through the U.N. Security Council (UNSC) the day of the invasion and was followed on 6 August by UNSC Resolution 661, which imposed an unprecedented financial and trade embargo. Britain and France underscored their positions that same day by dispatching warships to the region. Canada followed suit four days later, and on 12 August the Turkish National Assembly, demonstrating considerable courage and commitment, gave its national government the authority to declare war if required. The list of adherents to the anti-Iraqi coalition grew daily until some fifty nations made some kind of contribution and thirty-eight sent forces, which posed some challenging control and coordination issues.[21] The near unanimity of opinion was certainly facilitated by the blatant Iraqi acts. What remained was to fashion the uniform revulsion into tangible, coherent power against the Iraqi regime and sustain it for as long as necessary. That task fell largely to the United States.

As the coalition grew, it quickly became apparent that the forces of the Muslim nations would be uncomfortable being under the command of Western/Christian nations. Two steps were taken to overcome this problem. First, it was decided to take a risk and operate with a split chain of command. Western European/Christian forces would operate under U.S. Central Command (USCENTCOM) command, and Islamic forces would respond to the Saudis. The French briefly stayed aloof from this arrangement, but as combat operations became an increasing reality, they subordinated their forces to USCENTCOM.[22]

The second essential step in welding the coalition together was to establish a Coalition, Coordination, Communications, and Integration Center (C^3IC).[23] (Note the absence of the word *command* from the title.) General Schwarzkopf determined that he would be able to operate best with his host counterpart, General Khaled, through this somewhat unusual arrangement, which went to a considerable distance in alleviating the danger that after the war the Saudis would be accused of being stooges or lackeys of the West. At the same time this arrangement insured that American military expertise would be allowed relatively free rein. It sensitized both staffs and commanders to the other's military culture and paved the way for relatively rapid staff actions. In the words of one of the participants, "You have never seen anything as powerful as the CENTCOM staff. It is high-tech, high-energy, high-speed. It will destroy anything that comes in contact with it." The C^3IC was the reduction gear that allowed coordination between the CENTCOM and the Saudi staffs.[24]

In another act designed to allay fears of Western domination, General Schwarzkopf issued General Order Number One, announcing to all American soldiers the standards of conduct expected of them as visitors in a Muslim nation. This was an important step because one of the Saudis' reservations about allowing Americans into their country was their Vietnam-derived picture of American soldiers as drug-ridden sadists, intent upon profaning anything alien.[25]

These and many other steps taken together served to create one of the most unusual coalitions in history. How it would fight remained to be answered.

U.S. Naval Operations

As U.S. Air Force and Army elements began movement into the region, the implementation of the embargo became an immediate issue for naval forces. Maritime Intercept Operations (MIO) began before definitive guidance could be issued. The USS *Sampson* (DDG-10), an *Adams*-class destroyer, had been diverted from a routine exercise in the Mediterranean Sea to MIO duty in the Red Sea. There, on 24 August 1990, she was ordered to stop a merchant vessel en route to Aqaba, Jordan. Upon contacting the merchant vessel's master, the *Sampson* was challenged by the reply, "By what authority are you [stopping and searching] this vessel in international waters?" *Sampson* responded, "In accordance with United Nations Sanction 661, you are requested to stop your engines and prepare to receive my inspection team. Do you understand?" The master responded in the affirmative. MIO was on track.[26] This was the first of many naval actions that took on a progressively coalition flavor as the naval units of other nations arrived in theater and joined the Maritime Interception Force (MIF). This operation was unique in that no central command was established to direct it. Each national naval force received its direction through its own national command channels, but since this had been the practice for units participating in Operation Ernest Will, the protection of oil tankers in the Gulf, monthly coordination meetings proved sufficient.[27]

U.S. Army Preparations

Although the U.S. Army was already in the process of drawing down, it responded quickly to the new challenge. The deployment of XVIII Airborne Corps elements to Saudi Arabia was not entirely an ad hoc operation as portrayed in some of the media. In July 1989 USCENTCOM had conducted Exercise Internal Look. General H. Norman Schwarzkopf, Commander-in-Chief, USCENTCOM, had observed the shift in threat from the Soviet Union to Iraq and wanted to see what changes might be needed.[28] The new version of Operations Plan (OPLAN) 1002-90 that resulted from that exercise mandated earlier arrival of heavy forces to contend with Iraq's extensive, experienced armored forces. The plan was in the process of being "blessed" and the Time Phased Force Deployment List (TPFDL) was being reviewed when that plan suddenly became the basis for action.[29]

OPERATION DESERT SHIELD

As soon as King Fahd gave his approval, forces of the U.S. XVIII Corps began deploying into Saudi Arabia with advanced echelons of the U.S. Air Force. The military objectives were the following:

1. To develop a defensive capability in the Gulf region to deter Saddam Hussein from further attacks
2. To defend Saudi Arabia effectively if deterrence failed
3. To build a militarily effective coalition and integrate coalition forces into operational plans
4. To enforce the economic sanctions prescribed by UNSC Resolutions 661 and 665[30]

The primary defense objectives were the eastern Saudi oil fields and the capital, Riyadh. Of the two, the oil fields were the most vulnerable because of their proximity to the Iraqi armored forces. These oil facilities were potentially the most important since their seizure by the Iraqis would, for all practical purposes, give Iraq control of world oil. Even if the Iraqis chose to continue operating the fields in Iraq, Kuwait, and Saudi Arabia, the mere fact that they would be in a position to dictate prices and curtail the flow of the region's low-cost oil would have been enough to induce panic in the global financial community. As it was, oil prices rose almost immediately to $40 per barrel despite the fact that the market was glutted. Preservation of the free flow of low-cost oil was vital to the health of the industrialized world, and despite the fact that America was less dependent upon that oil than it had been for some years, the staggering American economy would be further affected with the prospects of oil at $40 a barrel.

After the war a captured Iraqi officer was asked about Iraqi plans to seize the Saudi oil fields. He reportedly shrugged his shoulders and replied, "You have seen our equipment, how could you contemplate such a thing?"[31] He was not a Republican Guard officer, however. For the elite Republican Guard divisions that held the Saudi-Kuwaiti border for several days, the prospects of driving another several hundred kilometers south would have been a relatively simple matter once their logistic train caught up to them.

Understanding the urgency of preventing such an act, the Commander-in-Chief Central Command (CINCCENT), adjusted his deployment schedule to place as many tank-killing units as possible at the head of the deployment order. It may be years before we know whether Saddam was deterred or simply had no plans to go further south. In any event, the change of deployment priorities meant that the logistic support structure that normally would have been woven into the deployment plan was largely excised and logistics control was lost. It never fully recovered despite herculean efforts and brave announcements that all was well. This decision is likely to be discussed and argued for years. The effect of the CINC's decision was to delay the longer-term development of offensive combat power. What was sought initially was sufficient force to dissuade and then protect. The weighting of shipping priorities in this fashion delayed development of the logistics base upon which offensive operations necessarily rested.

All afloat prepositioned stocks at Diego Garcia were shipped into Saudi Arabia and, in combination with the associated supplies of the Marine Expeditionary Brigades (MEBs) deployed to theater, were barely sufficient to sustain the initially deployed forces until the Sea Line of Communication (SLOC) closed. Some unorthodox measures were taken by commanders to insure self-sustainability as an interim measure.

Normally, the eight fast sealift ships assigned to move the 24th Infantry Division (Mechanized) would administratively load the division. The Division Commander, Major General Barry E. McCaffrey, knowing that the situation in Saudi Arabia was very tenuous, insisted upon combat loading insofar as possible and overrode shipping regulations and objections of the U.S. Navy by insisting that his equipment be loaded with fuel and live ammunition.[32] These measures compromised the ability of the assigned shipping to perform as planned, but did permit the deployment of a combat-ready force, another decision for future consideration.

During the frantic buildup period, everyone worked incredible hours attempting to make up in sweat and loss of sleep for what could not be provided in material terms. Host-nation support grew rapidly to fill some of the voids created by the inability to ship sufficient supplies. As the system gradually began to achieve a steady state, the initial exorbitant prices charged in Saudi Arabia for use of trucks were sharply reduced.[33] When it quickly became evident that the coalition was going to need every extra piece of equipment and every possible service in the kingdom, the forces of a free-market economy came into play. Trucks that had initially been rented for $1,000 per day eventually could be obtained for $50 per day.

Strategic sealift did not perform as well as hoped, although it met most initial demands. Strategic airlift and the first genuine exercise of the Civil Reserve Air Fleet (CRAF) concept worked very well. Actual airlift plans worked less well as requirements shifted dramatically. For example, because of the obvious need for antiarmor augmentation, the 82d Airborne Division required almost double the planned number of sorties.[34] Part of the problem with sealift was exemplified by the 24th Division's experience. The loading plan was significantly modified, and ships sailed at considerably less than designed carrying capacity. With the addition of vehicle fuel and live ammunition, plus extra supplies, including those for the extra-large Supercargo that included unplanned-for air defense elements, at least one ship bottomed in the mud at pierside. Also, one ship was scheduled for major repairs, the *Antares*. Since there was no suitable substitute for her, she was pressed into service and duly broke down in mid-Atlantic. The ship had to be towed into Spain and transloaded. The ship's load was critical to the 24th Division Support Command, and the delay in its arrival placed tremendous strain on that organization. By virtue of the tremendous personal effort of every soldier, sailor, and airman involved, by October a credible defensive structure was in place and growing stronger by the day.

This defensive phase has received little press, but as related by participants, it was one of the most challenging periods of their professional careers. Every day the forces available changed and the answers to the question "What actions are we to take if they attack tonight?" also changed.[35]

By mid-October 1990 the general feeling within USCENTCOM was that the defensive window of vulnerability had been closed and that there was reasonable certainty of conducting a robust defense. This came from the presence of capable coalition forces present in theater, a functioning C³I structure, a straining but operating sustainment structure, and a comfortably nonaggressive enemy. From the inside there was plenty of room for improvement, and the continuing twenty-hour work days demonstrated the continuing sense of urgency. But at the theater level there was a confidence that the Iraqis would suffer badly and probably fail should they choose to attack.

Offensive Contemplations

The USCENTCOM planners had long been considering offensive options, even in the early days when such contemplations could have been viewed as madness. The aggressive spirit of the command held firmly to the concept that the best defense was a good offense. However, as the prospects of removing the Iraqis from Kuwait without combat dimmed, the planners turned their full attention to formulation of requirements necessary to achieve that objective with force. A preliminary concept using one corps was briefed to the National Command Authority (NCA) and rejected, as was the air-only concept.[36] The four-phase plan that emerged was the product of continuous interaction among the services, the Chairman of the Joint Chiefs of Staff, the Theater CINC, the NCA, the coalition members, and the various planning staffs. The phasing of the plan was conceived in August as a conceptual device, the particulars of which were not satisfactorily put in place until 15 October when CINCCENT directed development of the wide envelopment to the west.[37] Six days later the CINC received a briefing on the new plan, accepted the basic concepts, and directed that the main effort would be focused on destruction of the Republican Guard Forces.[38] The plan developed quickly from that point, and on 15 December a combined warning order was issued to the field.[39]

In the meantime, the President had accepted the CINC's estimates of forces required to execute a successful offensive option and had alerted VII Corps in Germany for deployment to the Gulf. Because of variations in states of readiness, modernization, and training, VII Corps deployed most of its staff, the 1st Armored Division, and the 2d Armored Cavalry Regiment to Saudi Arabia. From neighboring V Corps came the 3d Armored Division. From the United States came the 1st Infantry Division (Mechanized) and the 1st Cavalry Division. There were difficult decisions involved in fielding this force since some of the organic units of these divisions were not equipped with the most up-to-date weapons systems. Modernized units of other divisions were substituted. The rapidity with which this mixture of units came together to form an effective operational team is a lasting testament to the flexibility of the officers and soldiers of the American Army. It also demonstrates how well American basic battle doctrine had been absorbed and with what relative uniformity.

Supporting the Shield

In retrospect, one of the first logistics decisions made in the 24th Infantry Division as it prepared to deploy to Southwest Asia was a prototype for logistics support to the operation. When the division was first alerted for deployment, the impression within the Division Support Command (DISCOM) was that only one brigade was going to deploy, and the supporting logistics element was immediately configured for self-sustainment.[40] Perhaps this impression was fostered by the past practice of configuring logistics support to single-brigade deployments to the National Training Center (NTC) at Fort Irwin, California. In fact, the division was in the process of recovering from one such deployment, with some of its support equipment en route to home station by rail. By the time it became clear that the entire division was going to deploy, the augmentation of the package to support the first brigade's deployment had progressed to the point of seriously disrupting the remainder of the DISCOM.[41] That the division was able to recover from this initial major problem is telling testimony to the flexibility and hard work of the entire organization. This event was a prototype in that it reflected the nondoctrinal approach to sustainment that bedeviled the logistics community from the start. For good and sufficient tactical reasons, General Schwarzkopf demanded that tank-killers be moved up in the deployment sequence to the dislocation of the planned smooth flow of support structure.[42] The armored and mechanized forces of the Iraqi Republican Guards were, after all, sitting on the Iraqi-Saudi border, approximately two days' drive from the center of gravity of the Saudi oil industry.

The fact that the Saudi economy is as well developed as it is by Western standards made it possible to compensate with commercial purchases for many of the support functions that only later flowed into theater. The benefits of prepositioning became immediately apparent when the ships from Diego Garcia arrived with their stocks, as did the Marines. While the air flow began to expand and compensate for some shortages, even the arrival of shiploads of supplies failed to alleviate shortage problems in the field because of lack of management throughout the structure. What was accomplished taxed American initiative and energy to the limit. Ad hoc arrangements abounded, but miraculously the Iraqis failed to advance. CRAF and strategic sealift went into action, and a sustainment management structure began to emerge to be progressively augmented as the situation demanded.[43] At times these demands were so severe that parts of units were detached from their parent organizations and held at one of the ports to assist with the management and processing tasks.[44] Lieutenant General William G. Pagonis's book *Moving Mountains: Lessons in Leadership and Logistics from the Gulf War* succinctly and objectively outlined the magnitude of the logistics problems caused by the changes in the deployment sequence. The book described with clarity the management approach employed to overcome these obstacles. As General Pagonis noted, there were two factors involved throughout, doctrine and sheer necessity.[45] Sheer necessity governed for the first several months and in some cases continued to govern. As an example, the decision was made not to deploy the CAPSTONE senior logistics headquarters because that would have required the establishment of a new headquarters in the midst of frantic preparations for the impending offensive. In many cases doctrine established the common ground from which the logisticians developed their innovations and variations. The principles enshrined in doctrine remained intact, but their application varied considerably.

CRAF and sealift developed momentum and, despite shortcomings, performed effectively. The real sustainment problem became that of distribution. The U.S. Army simply did not have enough trucks. In an interview following the war, Lieutenant General Gary E. Luck, Commander XVIII Corps, was asked, "If you were offered the opportunity to fix one thing in the Corps, what would it be?" His response was, "I'd get more trucks."[46] (This is reminiscent of General Dwight D. Eisenhower's problem immediately after the Torch landing in North

Africa in November 1942. Because of shipping shortages, the shipment of 5,000 two-and-one-half-ton trucks had to be delayed. This delay was significant in the Allies' failure to maintain forward movement and contributed directly to the failure to attain assigned objectives.)[47] A major complicating phenomenon was the loss of in-transit visibility and inventory control. Milvan after Milvan arrived in theater with unknown contents.[48] Some contained critical petroleum, incomplete PLL, and some mere odds and ends.[49] There were insufficient personnel and not enough time to open, inventory, and identify ownership of the hundreds of Milvans in this condition.

Gradually control was established over the logistics nightmare through the efforts of logisticians at every level. Their efforts were significantly strengthened by the unplanned deployment of a substantial number of Department of the Army (DA) civilian technicians. While their presence was vital, in some cases it also created problems for which the services were unprepared. DA civilians are not usually trained in chemical warfare defense measures, nor was their legal status clear.

As the logistic situation in support of Operation Desert Shield improved, contemplation of Operation Desert Storm was continuing. On 29 December 1990, at a Commanders Conference at General Schwarzkopf's headquarters in Riyadh, Lieutenant General Pagonis briefed the 22d Support Command (SUPCOM) plan to support the offensive operation. At the end of the briefing the CINC asked if Lieutenant General Pagonis was willing to sign something to the effect that he could execute the plan. Pagonis took his last briefing chart off the wall and signed it, "Logisticians will not let you or your soldiers down. William G. Pagonis, 29 December 1990."[50]

Having made the commitment, 22d SUPCOM turned to executing its portion of the plan. The plan required the movement of XVIII Corps and its sustaining assets approximately 500 miles west of its current location while simultaneously moving VII Corps, then west of XVIII Corps, into positions 330 miles from the arrival ports. As soon as the air war began, the logistic shift began and continued for a month. Traffic flowed at an uninterrupted rate of eighteen vehicles passing a point per minute.[51] The concept was to establish a forward logbase, Bravo, just south of King Khalid Military City (KKMC), which, when stocked with loaded trucks, served as the launching pad for the next two logbases, Charlie and Echo on the Saudi-Kuwaiti border.[52]

By 20 February 1991 Logbases Charlie and Echo had been established and stocked with mobile Class I (food), III (petroleum and oil products), and V (ammunition) supplies.[53] While this move was in progress, planning continued on further forward movement. Additional Logbases Oscar and Romeo were planned for XVIII Corps and Hotel and November for VII Corps, all according to the ninety-mile rule, the distance over which a truck could make a daily round trip. By 24 February the system had brought forward 29 days of food and water, 5.2 days of fuel, and 45 days of ammunition supplies.[54] Of course the spectacular success of the units in the combat arms put a further strain on the logistics system, but nowhere was any tactical or operational plan compromised by a failure of logistic support. The logisticians kept their promise.

Preparations before Crossing the Line of Departure

As soon as President Bush announced the decision to ship the VII Corps to Southwest Asia, it became clear that offensive action was being seriously contemplated. In fact, the CENTCOM planners had by this time convinced the NCA that sanctions were not going to produce the results required in an acceptable time frame; that it was going to be necessary to attack the Iraqi Army in Kuwait to get it out; and that a second heavy corps was required to succeed. As the VII Corps redeployed from Europe and the United States, the CINC's scheme of maneuver matured. As has so often been the case, the logistic aspects of the operation dictated the deployment of the forces. XVIII Corps would make the wide sweep to the north from the west end of the line; VII Corps, just arriving at the port of Dammam, would strike from positions astride the Wadi al-Batin. Because any major movement to the west could reveal the actual plan of maneuver, the CINC directed that no movement would commence until after the start of the air campaign. Not long after the first aircraft crossed the Iraqi border for their first strike, the massive movement of logistics facilities began. From that moment until just before H-hour, Tapline Road was one solid mass of vehicles moving westward. U.S. Army vehicles, Japanese Toyota trucks, and heavy-equipment transporters of several nations, including those of the Warsaw Pact, all carried their loads to the west, deposited one load, and returned for another.[55] Meantime, basic preassault troop-leading procedures were being carried out at all levels; deception operations were progressing on all fronts; air and missile operations were fragmenting the enemy; and the last elements of European-based VII Corps and its CONUS augmentation were rushing into line. Preassault troop-leading procedures are those actions taken at every level of command from squad upward to ensure troops are as well prepared as possible for battle. These range from personal checks of each soldier to ensure that ammunitions, rations, and special equipment are present, and that all items of personal equipment are in working order. For leaders it includes, among other things, rehearsals, review of radio codes and procedures, and if possible, reconnaissance of the objective area.

Despite the efforts of everyone involved, it was apparent that having everything in place in time was going to be a major miracle. The decisions made and not made in the opening days of the conflict had already exacted their toll. When Lieutenant General Calvin Waller, Deputy Commander-in-Chief, made a public statement that the command would not be ready to attack by 15 January as some had opined, he was simply stating the truth. This was driven by a variety of factors: decisions to front-load combat forces, not to call up the reserves until later, and to accept large numbers of volunteers from units called up later; the late date of the decision to deploy VII Corps; and the effects of national neglect of maritime health.[56]

OPERATION DESERT STORM: THE ALLIED COALITION OFFENSIVE

Air Attack

The allied air campaign began at 0130 hours (H − 90 minutes), 17 January 1991, with the first combat launch of a Tomahawk cruise missile. For the B-52s flying out of the United States, the attack began at H − 11 hrs, 25 minutes, or 16 January.[57] As the offensive planning developed, the air role was prominent in all four phases and dominated the first three. On 8 August 1990 CINCCENT had requested that the Air Staff develop a conceptual air campaign. The focus was to be on purely strategic targets in Iraq. Two days later Instant Thunder was briefed to the CINC. The resulting concept plan was effectively folded into the four-phase campaign plan that the CINC briefed to the Secretary of Defense and CJCS on 25 August:

1. Phase 1: strategic air attack against Iraq (Instant Thunder modified)
2. Phase 2: air attack of Kuwait
3. Phase 3: ground combat power attrition
4. Phase 4: ground attack

The key strategic targets identified were the following: Iraqi leadership command and control facilities; key production facilities, particularly the nuclear, biological, and chemical (NBC) facilities; infrastructure targets, particularly the lines of communications facilities; and fielded forces—initially not including the forces of the Republican Guards, which were added by the Secretary of Defense (SECDEF) as a strategic target since they comprised the support of the regime and embodied its ground striking power[58]

By H-hour, 17 January 1991, the air campaign objectives had evolved and the allocation of attack forces had been refined to integrate the air and missile attack elements of USAF, USN, USMC, U.S. Army, and the committed air elements of all coalition members. At H − 22 minutes, U.S. Army AH-64 attack helicopters struck Iraqi early warning air defense radars, opening the path for the air forces, while U.S. Navy–launched Tomahawk Land-Attack Missiles (TLAM) slammed into carefully selected targets in Baghdad, accompanied by the surprise attacks of U.S. Air Force F-117A Stealth aircraft. This simultaneous attack on Iraqi air defense and command, control, and communications nerve centers and electrical nodes was followed immediately by a flood of carefully orchestrated conventional air attacks. Within the first five minutes twenty key targets were struck; within the first hour an additional twenty-five such targets were hit.[59] The combined electronic warfare and missile/bomb attacks stunned the Iraqis and the world and effectively secured the initiative in the air for the remainder of the war.

The success of the strategic part of the air campaign was so spectacular that it gave rise to wishful thinking that air power alone might suffice. Further, the success of the centralization of control of air assets through the consolidated Air Tasking Order (ATO) was such that a feeling gradually developed that the normal allocation and apportionment decision process was being circumvented. This did not become an issue until completion of the second phase of the campaign. As the third-phase battlefield preparation commenced, ground commanders began to complain that their designated targets were not being hit as scheduled. The shift of priorities was actually accomplished, but there remains considerable acrimony over the perceived loss of control of the targeting process.[60] The thorniest issue was how to determine when the CINC's criteria for success had been achieved. General Schwarzkopf's criteria for launching the ground offensive were as follows: 50 percent degradation of the Iraqi frontline forces; 50 percent destruction of armored vehicles in the reserve formations, including the strategic reserves (Republican Guards); and 90 percent attrition of all artillery capable of hitting the proposed breach sites.[61] When these criteria were combined with the guidance noted previously, the severing of the Iraqi lines of communications (LOCs), and degradation of Iraqi command, control, communications, and intelligence, the desired effect was to produce a condition in which the coalition ground forces would be attacking a one-armed, blind, and deaf opponent.

These criteria required measuring the success of the air attack, and therein lay one of the two major problems with the air campaign. The Battle Damage Assessment (BDA) process that existed at the time was neither sophisticated nor integrated. Eventually a series of ad hoc arrangements that was sufficiently credible to satisfy the CINC was worked out by the Army Component to Central Command (ARCENT) J-2, Brigadier General John Stewart.[62] The other shortcoming was the limited ability to deal fully with the Iraqi Scud threat. There was an enormous expenditure of air effort to counter the Scuds, a true strategic threat, not because they could hit anything other than the ground, but because of the threat they appeared to pose to coalition solidarity. The Iraqis felt, and most Western members of the coalition believed, that if Scuds hit Israel and the Israelis chose to join in the attack against Iraq, the Muslim members of the coalition would withdraw. That may indeed have been a credible threat, at least until the Syrians, Israel's archenemy and the sponsor of much anti-Israeli terrorism, stated publicly that the Israelis had the right of self-defense. Nevertheless, political necessity demanded that the coalition air forces devote a tremendous effort to countering these low-tech, low-accuracy missiles.

By G-day it was evident that the devastation wrought by the air campaign was significant. How significant was not clear until after ground forces began their attack.

Ground Attack

G-day was 24 February. At 0400 hours the assault began with a combined-arms attack at three points along the Iraqi defensive system. The French 6th Light Armored Division, with the 2d Brigade of the 82d Airborne Division under its operational control (OPCON), dashed across the Saudi-Iraqi border toward Objective Rochambeau to provide protection to the western (left) flank. Three hours and 90 miles later this force attacked as-Salman airfield (Objective White) and after a brief firefight captured 2,500 Iraqi soldiers.[63] All flank objectives were secured within seven hours. Because of weather delays, the 101st Airborne Division (Air Assault) began its assault about two hours later.[64] It was the largest combat air assault operation in history, moving some 500 soldiers 93 miles deep into Iraq in just over an hour.[65] The initial objective was immediately converted into a Forward Operating Base (FOB) designated Cobra. FOB Cobra grew rapidly into a major logistics hub, setting the base for the next move, the final forward movement of the division to block Highway 8, which runs west and north between Basrah and Baghdad. As the airmobile soldiers were savoring the extent of their success, their combat service support (CSS) elements were moving north in a 700-vehicle ground convoy.[66]

Maintaining the continuity of the deception plan, the 1st Cavalry Division attacked from the center of the Coalition line along the Wadi al-Batin. Further to the east, Joint Forces Command (JFC)-North, I MEF, and JFC-East attacked north into Kuwait.

The attacks of the French and the airborne divisions were so successful that the 24th Infantry Division (Mechanized) was launched into its attack five hours earlier than planned. By midnight, G-day, the division was seventy-five miles deep in Iraq.

The main attack by VII Corps was planned for G+1, 25 February. Augmenting the success of XVIII Corps, I MEF and JFC-East drove forward at unexpected rates. Seeking to exploit this success, General Schwarzkopf ordered VII Corps' attack time moved up fifteen hours.[67] While the limited attack by the 1st Cavalry Division fixed the Iraqis' attention on the Wadi, 1st Infantry Division (Mechanized) began the process of breaking through the forward Iraqi defenses in order to allow the 1st UK Armored Division to pass through. As they were thus engaged, the 2d Armored Cavalry Regiment, followed by the 1st and 3d Armored Divisions, passed west of the Iraqi defenses toward Objective Collins, slightly south of an-Nasiryah.[68] This arm of the VII Corps was thirty miles deep in Iraq by the time the breaching operation began. Difficulties in clearing the breach required that the western arm of the Corps halt long enough for the attack through the Iraqi defenses to develop.

The supporting attacks by JFC-North and I MEF demonstrated the benefits of the long period of preparation. The multinational nature of JFC-North made acceleration of the attack hour difficult, but, employing the liaison network established earlier, the Egyptian, Syrian, Saudi, and Kuwaiti forces were all in motion by 1600 hours 24 February.

The attack by I MEF dramatically exceeded expectations. The 1st Marine Division (MARDIV) had infiltrated two task forces across the border prior to the commencement of offensive operations. Marine preparations were driven by the appreciation that they faced a sizable concentration of enemy forces and were making a frontal attack. Their preparations were so successful that by the end of G-day, I MEF had advanced twenty miles through two deep barrier systems, had shattered Iraqi forces confronting them, and had 8,000 enemy prisoners of war (EPW).[69]

JFC-East attacked at 0800 hours, 24 February, with the unique support of two American battleships, the USS *Missouri* and USS *Wisconsin.* Led by the 8th and 10th Saudi Mechanized Brigades, this multinational force pushed forward and quickly secured its objectives.

The battleships were not the only naval units engaged. As noted, naval vessels of various types launched TLAM cruise missiles while conventional operations were undertaken against remaining Iraqi naval units and feints and demonstrations were conducted to keep Iraqi eyes fixed on the amphibious possibilities represented by the afloat Marine Expeditionary Brigade (MEB). That part of the deception plan worked to perfection. After Kuwait City was liberated, a large sand-table model of the Kuwaiti coast was found indicating Iraqi concern about an amphibious attack. In addition, perhaps as many as six Iraqi divisions were fixed in coastal defense positions by the deception.[70]

G+1 (25 February 1991)

Iraqi reactions to the attack were ineffective and appeared confused. It was evident that the attacks directed against the command and control structure had been successful, particularly that of the forward-deployed Iraqi Corps. Every Iraqi unit encountered by the attacking coalition forces was crushed or badly mauled, particularly those attacked from flank or rear. At 0135 hours, 26 February, Radio Baghdad announced that Iraqi military forces had been ordered to withdraw from Kuwait, responding to the Soviet peace initiative.[71]

By midnight, G+1, the 101st Airborne Division had secured its objectives 170 miles deep in enemy territory, cutting Highway 8.[72] The forward movement of coalition forces continued through G+1 and 1 MEF making unexpectedly rapid progress to the outskirts of Kuwait City. The 1st Armored Division of VII Corps attacked north, meeting the first serious attempt by the Iraqis to counterattack. An armored brigade of the 26th Iraqi Infantry Division was destroyed in ten minutes at a range of 2,000 meters.[73] Late that evening the 2d Armored Cavalry Regiment (ACR) encountered elements of the Tawakalna Republican Guard Mechanized Division and began a fight that lasted into G+2. Meantime, the 1st Infantry Division completed breaching operations and passed 1st UK Armored Division through the gaps to attack the 12th Iraqi Armored Division, which the "Desert Rats" destroyed. JFC-East and JFC-North continued their advances in sector.

G+2

As the advance continued throughout G+2, the most significant combat action was the continuing engagement of 2d ACR with the Tawakalna Division in what is now named the Battle of 73 Easting. During the night of G+2 the regiment handed off the battle to the 3d Armored Division, which over the next day obliterated the Iraqi division. That division has been stricken from the Iraqi Order of Battle. JFC-North was to pass through the Marines and seize Kuwait City. G+2 was a memorable day for I MEF as 2d MARDIV attacked north to secure the high ground near al-Jahra, and the attached U.S. Army Tiger Brigade was sent deep to seize the high ground between Kuwait City and Iraq on the only notable terrain feature in Kuwait, al-Mutl'a Ridge. Once this ridge was secured, the Iraqi avenue of retreat for forces in and around Kuwait City was cut. Simultaneously, 1st MARDIV attacked to clear the international airport and, despite stiff resistance there and closer to Kuwait City, secured the approaches for JFC-North to move in the next day.[74]

G+3

The destruction of the Iraqi Army was proceeding beyond expectations. The offensive activities of the enemy were fragmented and clearly uncoordinated. The two Republican Guard Armored Divisions, Hammurabi and Medina, had suffered from attacks by VII Corps units. By the end of G+3 the remnants of those divisions were fleeing towards Basrah, joining the growing flood of dispirited soldiers from many Iraqi units.[75]

G+4

Offensive action ceased at 0800 hours. At that time the 24th Infantry Division stood thirty miles west of Basrah. VII Corps' divisions formed an iron sword south of the 24th Division, while I MEF secured the approaches to Kuwait City and Islamic forces of both JFC-North and JFC-East cleared the city. The combat phase of the war was over.[76]

At the time of the cease-fire, coalition military forces had accomplished their objectives as follows:

All critical lines of communications in the KTO were secure.

Organized Iraqi military forces had been ejected from Kuwait.

Kuwait City had been liberated.

The Republican Guard Forces had been badly mauled, their residual capabilities sufficient only for action against irregular forces.[77]

By CENTCOM estimate, only five of the original forty-three divisions committed to the defense of Kuwait remained capable of offensive action. About 86,000 enemy prisoners of war (EPW) were in or en route to prisoner-of-war camps. Iraqi military hardware had been reduced by two-thirds. Iraq's capacity to threaten its neighbors was reduced to negligible dimensions.[78]

Postattack Operations

Almost immediately following the cease-fire, allied forces began involvement in activities that had not been well conceived. While the restoration of civil government in Kuwait had been planned to some extent, the plans had not been fully integrated, and issues of command were not resolved. (For detailed discussion of this aspect of the operation, see Lieutenant Colonel John Fishel's excellent study, *Liberation, Occupation, and Rescue: War Termination and Desert Storm.*)[79] Further, the revolts inside Iraq's southern provinces generated an unanticipated flood of refugees. There might have been enough assets to handle the flood of refugees had efforts turned to securing Iraqi prisoners of war. At the same time, while CENTCOM was wrestling with these issues, the plight of the Kurds, who had revolted against Saddam's regime at the urging of the coalition, became critical. This was graphically shown on American television screens. American forces stationed in Turkey were directed to a new mission, "Stop the dying."[80]

While the combat actions of the coalition forces were successful, often beyond original estimates, the less satisfactory effectiveness of the postcombat phase has caused rethinking about the multitudinous issues associated with war termination. Lest impatient Americans become discouraged over these issues, they should recall that the American Revolution was not really settled until after the War of 1812, when the British finally accepted the former colonies as full members of the international system.

THEORY, PRINCIPLES, AND DOCTRINE

Theory

Clausewitz was a latecomer to the American military intellectual ranks. In fact, theory has usually been something that American military practitioners tend to neglect. Soldiers are practical men, and the applicatory method of instruction has always been the key to successfully instructing American soldiers. During World War I lectures to enlisted soldiers were not allowed to extend beyond fifteen or at the most twenty minutes. The soldiers were then immediately set to doing what they had just learned. American artillerymen arriving early in France were dumbfounded by the amount of theory their French instructors attempted to cram into their heads. Very quickly Americans became instructors and set their charges to doing practical things.

Although a practical focus may be the best in subordinate units, senior leaders must comprehend the total setting—both theoretical and practical—in which they are attempting to operate. For example, General George C. Marshall, U.S. Army Chief of Staff during World War II, learned this rather abruptly. In responding to one of President Franklin D. Roosevelt's questions about a certain matter, he began to reply, "From a strictly military point of view." The President quickly informed him that there were no strictly military points of view, clearly demonstrating that political, diplomatic, and economic matters were all intertwined at that level.

Since World War II and more particularly since Colonel Harry Summer's book on the Vietnam War, *On Strategy,* the U.S. Army has turned to the study of *On War* by Carl von Clausewitz.[81] This influential book established guiding principles that are relevant today. Many are familiar with some of his most famous comments, such as "War is a continuation of politics by other means." Other particularly noteworthy commentary includes the following:

> The first, the supreme, the most far-reaching act of judgement that the statesman and commander have to make is to establish . . . the kind of war on which they are embarking; neither mistaking it for, nor try to make it into, something that is alien to its nature.[82]

Obviously, there is a great deal more to Clausewitz than these statements. Harry Summers, following a number of Clausewitzian principles, analyzed the Vietnam War. Summers claimed, with considerable justification, that had American senior leaders been more keenly aware of the writings and philosophy of Clausewitz, the war would have developed and been fought very differently, if at all. The inculcation of Clausewitz is Summers's legacy to American military history.

The key effect of a serious study of Clausewitz is an understanding that military force is but one of the tools that nations employ to achieve policy objectives. This tool has three dimensions—the military, the government, and the people.[83] Diplomatic and economic elements are primary instruments, but when vital interests are at issue, military forces are usually employed. In order that they may play the role assigned them—first to deter—they must be prepared to undertake a variety of tasks across the spectrum. Clausewitz cautioned, however, that when it becomes necessary to employ military force, a variety of subjective forces come into play that may erode the control necessary to achieve success. But Clausewitz also cautioned that the purpose of employing forces must be the key criterion. If this is neglected or eroded, military actions take on a character and direction all their own that may well make the original object for which military operations were initiated no longer relevant. If this occurs, war will be conducted for its own sake and lose meaning and purpose. In the Gulf War the theory was put into practice and it worked; the hope is that it will continue to work, with appropriate adaptation, into the future.

Principles

The U.S. Army has possessed a set of Principles of War since 1921. They derive in part from the work of Major General J. F. C. Fuller, a British officer of remarkable imagination and energy. Though never enunciated as principles before 1921, the Principles of War are embedded in American military history.[84] The World War I experience served to point out the need for a formal statement of principles to give guidance to the American army. The lack of guidance for training officers and men during the war was the norm. With the publication of these principles and their instruction in the service schools, a common language and approach to military problem solving evolved. While cadets at the military academies learned the principles by rote, a sizable body of professional literature evolved around them, and in time they became the touchstone of professionalism.

Toward the middle of the 1970s the Principles of War as they had been understood in the past began to be questioned and some revisions and different interpretations proposed. The most prominent was the notion of "protection." This derived from the view that the next "first battle" was probably going to be in Europe, where the NATO allies felt themselves outnumbered and where preservation—protection—of the force was crucial. When the 1982 edition of *Field Manual 100-5: Operations (FM 100-5)* was published, it contained "Tenets" of the new AirLand Battle doctrine. These were not principles per se, but they tended to be elevated to that level. "Agility," "initiative," "depth," and "synchronization" became the new operative words.

The U.S. Army was in the process of recognizing some of its experience and some of the intellectual contributions of Soviet thinkers even though it would be several more years before Colonel David M. Glantz would begin to publish and lecture on the results of his studies of the Soviets' World War II performance. His work almost single-handedly set in motion a reversal of years of historical writing about that war that hitherto had relied upon German accounts of Soviet actions as interpreted by British writers. In revising this period of history, Glantz made it possible for American officers to consider new forms of operational doctrine that not only explained where the Soviets seemed to be heading, but gave impetus to changes in American doctrine and force structure.

Doctrine

In 1976 General "Bill" DePuy rewrote the Army's basic operational manual, *FM 100-5: Operations.* The Army was struggling to find itself in the aftermath of Vietnam. DePuy gave the manual and the Army a new focus called "active defense."[85] It was an uncomfortable focus since it was overtly Eurocentric and defensive. Philosophically, Americans are disinclined toward defensive doctrine, and there was considerable argument over the merits of the new doctrine. For all the philosophy, however, the doctrine represented what the Army was barely capable of doing—winning its next first battle. General DePuy's efforts were among the two or three most significant of the decade for the U.S. Army. The discussion prompted by the 1976 edition of *FM 100-5* generated a search for a more compatible doctrine and the wherewithal to execute it.

The U.S. Army designed a new doctrine in the 1982 edition of *FM 100-5* that was popularly known as AirLand Battle.[86] On the one hand, it reflected a more offensive orientation than its predecessor, one the officer corps found more acceptable. It also defined operational requirements in a way that allowed the Department of the Army to give fairly specific direction to the research and development and the acquisition communities. Earlier, there had been much talk about a concept-based requirements system, but lacking a coherent concept, what was to be done? The 1982 edition provided enough of the missing direction.

On the other hand, NATO raised an enormous hue and cry. NATO had not been consulted, nor had it been warned of the impending publication. The most disturbing aspect was in the political realm: NATO was a defensive alliance, but in the new doctrine the principal partner was adopting a clearly offensive operational doctrine. Could an offensive force structure be far behind? All the old arguments emerged—arguments about which weapons were inherently defensive and which offensive. The shift in emphasis was not lost upon the Soviets, who wasted little time in denouncing the manual and the alliance. They took the doctrinal change seriously enough that within a few years new Soviet doctrine appeared that adopted similarly overt offensive characteristics.

The greatest benefit to the U.S. Army was the impact the new field manual had on training doctrine. It provided a stepping-stone to the training revolution gradually taking shape. Many accuse armies of planning to fight the last war, and there is some measure of truth to that charge. But the Vietnam experience was so traumatic for the institution that it made a determined effort to avoid further validation of that epithet. The question "Who was responsible for the training revolution?" leads one down a fairly lengthy roster of general officers, including Paul F. Gorman and Carl E. Vuono. General Vuono will always receive much of the credit. He rose to become Chief of Staff, Army (CSA), and carried the training revolution through to conclusion. The new doctrine was vital to the development of the training revolution because it laid a coherent framework from which specific "tasks, conditions, and standards" could be derived that were relevant to combat in any location, time, or form. This training revolution existed not only at the individual soldier level, but throughout the Army's organization. For planners, the Clausewitzian concept of "center of gravity" became a key consideration (although it had existed in tactical forms for a long time) since it allowed planners to focus on objectives whose attainment contributed to a recognized, ultimately political goal. For commanders, the concept of AirLand Battle envisioned a much less centrally controlled battle; hence the "commander's intent" became central. All of this came to fruition in the Gulf War, especially the combination of the "commander's intent" and the thorough application of "tasks, conditions, and standards." There was much that worked well during the Gulf War, but the more closely one examines that conflict, the more one must be impressed by the way American soldiers of all ranks made systems work, created systems to fill voids, and accomplished monumental tasks with minimal guidance. This resulted in a spectacular military victory with minimum loss of life.

The study of theory and the application of principles continues today, resulting in the refinement of old or development of new doctrine. The essentials of soldiering will not change regardless of advances in technology. The task before the Army today is to adapt to new conditions. For example, peacemaking for the soldier is only different from combat in that the rules of engagement require considerable restraint.[87] Peacekeeping demands even more restraint, but neither differs greatly in form from any normal military operation, and the principles are much the same.

Beginning in 1984, many in the military felt the need for a new field manual. This led to the rewriting of *FM 100-5: Operations,* this time with a broader focus and with consultation with NATO allies. The basic tenets and principles remained unchanged. This effectively allowed the training and education of an entire generation of officers to be knowledgeable about essentially one doctrine. It is generally conceded that it takes about ten years for a doctrine to be assimilated. Thus, by the time of Desert Storm, every officer and noncommissioned officer in the force was conversant with the basic doctrine. Moreover, even though the Air Force was unhappy with portions of the doctrine as it applied to Europe, the senior planners knew the doctrine thoroughly and could converse doctrinally with ease with their Army counterparts. It is a rare moment in history when such a state of affairs exists—an operational concept that is well understood throughout the force and to some extent in the supporting services; an operational doctrine that has given guidance to the technical community long enough to see a good deal of its impetus translated into equipment in the hands of troops who know how to employ it.

The 1993 edition of *FM 100-5* establishes a set of principles for operations other than war (OOTW) fashioned after the form of the standard Principles of War and incorporates several adjusted for specific application.[88] Three additional principles for OOTW were written into the manual, ''Legitimacy, Perseverence, and Restraint,'' acknowledging that the application of force in these operations will be different in important ways from combat operations. Similar to the older Principles of War, these principles have their genesis in the literature of low-intensity conflict of previous decades.

NATIONAL SECURITY STRATEGY

In order to understand the process whereby regional strategy is developed, it is necessary to be familiar with the various steps, beginning with the National Security Strategy (NSS). The Bush administration produced three, the last of which was a lame-duck version, but the two that preceded were extremely useful in providing focus for the National Military Strategy (NMS) that derived from them. While the NSS varied from edition to edition in minor ways, one of the Army's primary field manuals, *FM 100-1: The Army,* has consistently attempted to reflect the long-standing NSS objectives as they have been variously articulated over the past forty-odd years. The rationale has been that although the NSS objectives do vary some on the fringes, the basic objectives do not. The basic NSS objectives stated in *FM 100-1* are the following:

1. To preserve the independence, institutions, and territorial integrity of the United States
2. To preserve U.S. and allied vital interests abroad
3. To help shape a world in which freedom and democracy can flourish in an international community in which states coexist without the use of force and in which citizens are free to choose their own governments[89]

In the Cold War era, vital national interests were linked in part to the basic national containment strategy. On the other hand, freedom of the seas has always been a vital national interest over which Americans have fought wars with Great Britain, France, and Germany. It was part of the rationale for the U.S. Navy's 600-ship strategy under Secretary of the Navy John Lehman. Free access to vital natural resources has also been key in framing America's NSS. Oil has been particularly essential and has now reached a position of such importance that it is quite possible that the United States would go to war with any nation that attempted seriously to interrupt the flow of oil to the United States or its primary allies.

It is now quite likely that the United States could consider various forms of economic behavior as impinging upon vital national interests, although this has never been stated directly. The United States also must understand in national security terms the many aspects of the information age. Information can be used as a weapon in a variety of ways. One of the most serious information threats to a vital national interest would be a situation involving manipulation or disruption of international finance. Equally serious and intimately related to all the informational aspects is the freedom of the airways and space. Interruption of the free flow of information through air and space is analogous to closing an international waterway.

These national interests external to the United States are direct interests. The multitude of indirect interests requires closer examination. In 1984 Secretary of Defense Caspar Weinberger announced his "doctrine" for the commitment of U.S. military forces. One of the major objections to it as a useful operational guide was that it was so ambiguous in interpreting vital national interests that almost anything could be included. Weinberger included the vital interests of allies within the U.S. national security perimeter. Taken literally, this could be a recipe for constant commitment of troops for a host of reasons.[90] As it is, today about 20,000 soldiers of the U.S. Army are "deployed in over 1,100 operational missions in 78 countries every day of the year.''[91] For every unit deployed somewhere on peacekeeping duty, two additional units have to be in line. One unit has to be preparing to replace the deployed unit; the other is in the process of reconstituting after its return from peacekeeping duties. The training and retraining schedules are heavy and greatly affect the quality of military life. These basic national security interests will continue, but each administration is likely to give them slightly different weight and may add considerations or even new issues, as the interdiction of drug traffic was added in the last decade.

The Clinton administration finally released a new national security strategy document entitled *A National Security Strategy of Engagement and Enlargement* in July 1994. Its thesis is simply that because the United States is the remaining superpower, it has opportunities ''to make a difference through our engagement; but . . . carefully tailored to serve our interests.'' The enlargement aspect is focused on the spread of democratic institutions, which, it is assumed, will lessen the pulse for war. In essence, this document is a statement that the United States will not revert to isolationism as it did following World War I. Russian nuclear capabilities will remain at the top of the list of potential threats, with other nuclear capable, intercontinental-range missile forces at a slightly subordinate level. Even at that level of threat the approach is from a regional perspective, for part of the Russian paranoia over nuclear weapons is directly attached to the possession of nuclear weapons by geographic neighbors. The realities of this strategy have been evident and in place long enough to allow the military services to give strategic direction to their developmental efforts.

NATIONAL MILITARY STRATEGY

As of the time of writing of this chapter, there is no formal, stated National Military Strategy (NMS). In fact, the NMS is very plain to anyone who reads what the U.S. military has published and in the budget actions on Capitol Hill. It is perfectly clear that the United States has created a force-projection NMS. It is equally important to note that this was done consciously.

When the Army withdrew from its worldwide forward-deployed positions, even as it reduced the size of its remaining forces, it began constructing a military structure that would allow the movement of flexible forces anywhere in the world in as short a time as was deemed fiscally responsible consistent with perceived threats. The Army's baseline was a strategic requirement to move five divisions anywhere in the world in seventy-five days and sustain them indefinitely. The U.S. Navy turned from the old established Mahanian theory of pure blue-water sea control to give an equal emphasis to brown-water operations.[92] Simultaneously, the Navy's land force, the U.S. Marine Corps, began lobbying for the armaments to allow it to operate more effectively against armed forces of littoral states and to operate more effectively deeper into the interior. (In fact, with the V-22 vertical takeoff aircraft, the Marines are now fond of stating that the entire United States is within the littoral region except for a small portion of northern Montana.) The U.S. Air Force almost immediately began a process of moving away from strategic bombing, its raison d'être for years, to an approach that acknowledged a need for greater balance of forces. *Global Reach, Global Power,* the Air Force's public program for change, adopted a broad strategic view including control of space. Indeed, air power does have global reach and is potentially capable of projecting global power almost anywhere in the world. The primary problem with navies and air forces, however, is that they really have the capability to do only two things, move people and things and break and destroy things. Even the enhanced Marine Corps is limited in what it can do for any period of time. It is configured, by statute, to assist the Navy with a land arm. The only force capable of enforcing a decision, restoring order, and providing a full-bodied force of intimidation, administration, or long-term assistance is the U.S. Army. T. R. Fehrenbach has been quoted too often to be novel, but the truth of his observation is timeless:

> You may fly over a land forever; you may bomb it, atomize it, and wipe it clean of life—but if you desire to defend it, protect it, and keep it for civilization, you must do this on the ground, the way the Roman Legions did, by putting your young men into the mud.[93]

Recognizing that the Army is often going to be the only service of decision, Congress and the President agreed with the Department of Defense and set about creating the structure that would make the U.S. Army a power-projection force within a Force Projection Strategy. Based principally in the United States, the Army would begin to build an infrastructure that would allow it to deploy to any place in the world quickly and with sufficient force and sustainment structure that, unpopular as the word may be, it could ''intimidate'' adversaries. As noted earlier, the objective is to be able to deploy a five-division corps with supporting force structure anywhere in the world in seventy-five days. When conceived, it was a breathtaking concept. The shipping did not exist and would take billions of dollars to build, or to lease until enough could be built. The airlift fleet had never been allowed to develop to the point where it could meet its wartime lift objectives, but again dollars found their way into the budget to begin movement toward that objective.

All this began before the Iraqis invaded Kuwait. For analytical purposes, Operation Desert Shield can be considered a huge deployment exercise with a live-fire exercise, Desert Storm, attached to it. The outcome of that massive exercise was the revelation that the domestic deployment infrastructure was in poor shape, including railroads, transshipment points (docks, heavy material, handling equipment, unloading platforms, etc.), and safety limitations, call-up procedures, and the reserve mobilization mechanisms. The periodic Emergency Deployment Readiness Exercises (EDRE) had revealed some of the shortcomings, but funds to make repairs, to change systems, and to negotiate modification of safety requirements had fallen by the wayside in the struggle to modernize the force and give life and substance to training.

Within a year after the redeployment to the United States, it became painfully apparent that the air fleet had been used up. The wear and tear on the C-5 and C-141 strategic airlift fleet far exceeded expectations.[94] As a result, Somalia was conducted on a shoestring of strategic lift. On the other hand, commercial construction of 24-knot Navy RO/RO ships received massive funding support. Further, the Army overcame service prejudice and opted to place one armored brigade aboard ships to create a floating equipment-ready reaction force. This may seem odd, since the Marines too have armored equipment afloat in their Maritime Prepositioning Ships (MPS). But an Army armored brigade is a substantially stronger force in terms of armored combat power.[95]

But what of all the other situations falling under the current title of "operations other than war"? In all probability, most regional conflicts are going to involve "operations other than war" as currently defined. War in the American political and military lexicon has a very discrete meaning. It is a legal act that can be declared only by the Congress and that sets in motion a set of other legal actions. It likewise has significant implications in international law. A declaration of war may be seen as recognition of a threat to national existence. Because it is so serious an act, the United States rarely resorts to it. In fact, the Congress has not declared war since 8 December 1941. The consequence of this is that all combat actions and all noncombat actions involving U.S. military forces since the end of World War II have taken place outside the legal realm of war. Yet it is also clear that the President has the authority to commit military forces. Since World War II U.S. forces have been committed primarily under presidential order. It is therefore most likely that all regional conflicts that will arise in the next several decades will be handled under the category of operations other than war and that each will be treated as a unique event requiring uniquely tailored support, psychological, political, legal, and material.

Regional threats will continue to emerge, although few of them will be threats to American national security. Many will be challenges to American national pride or will evoke admirable American humanitarian impulses. An entirely different set of conditions and factors will interact in these circumstances, including the public mood (itself a product of the domestic economy), confidence in the administration, and the proximity of elections. It remains unclear exactly how much confidence Americans will ever place in the United Nations or how willing they will be to support that organization's undertakings. As will be discussed later, the present administration has taken a public step away from its previous statement by declaring that American military forces will not be placed under U.N. command as preferred by the present Secretary General. Ironically, Americans seem to prefer to operate with the "blessing" of the United Nations when engaging in regional matters, and the tension will continue between those who declare that seeking U.N. approval is simply a dodge to avoid action and those who see U.N. approval as vital to collective action.

REGIONAL PLANNING

The U.S. military services are still undergoing realignment as they downsize. Regional CINCs still have extensive geographical responsibilities and are assigned minimal combat forces, especially ground combat forces. As noted earlier, the de facto NMS is one of force projection, by which a CINC receives control of certain forces with which he is supposed to handle a particular situation. He will have a library full of OPLANs, one or some of which will usually come fairly close to describing the particular situation and will contain a force list that the planners felt was appropriate for particular contingencies. This is on the assumption that the CINC staff has the time to plan and wargame its plans. Ideally, each CINC will have or obtain enough intelligence sources and assets that will identify regional "hot spots" and likely conflict scenarios.

The possibility for surprise remains strong, however. Most CINC areas of responsibility are very large, and resources are likely only available for the most important areas. Commander-in-Chief, Pacific (CINCPAC), for example, simply does not have the resources to be deeply concerned with the South Pacific archipelagoes. Principal attention must be devoted to North Korea and China as potential antagonists. Yet a watchful eye must be kept on the remnants of the Soviet Far Eastern naval forces. A hurricane disaster on Saipan in the Northern Marianas or Ulithi in the Carolines (now the Federated States of Micronesia) may call for deployment of some engineer forces from the 84th Engineer Battalion in Hawaii to restore civil works, but nothing will take priority of interest and planning when North Korea becomes restive.

The hard fact is that the United States cannot be the world's "911" service, nor do Americans necessarily want that role. As the military services shrink, there is no less need for humanitarian missions or peacemaking duties, but American military forces cannot perform them all, and the CINCs have to make the hard recommendations to the Secretary of Defense, who will then seek a final decision from the President.

The regional focus of U.S. forces now is actually little different from the past. What has changed is the relative priority in the competition for resources. Also, there are fewer assets to support decisions made to commit military forces, and most of the forces will now have to come from the United States proper. Of great significance, much of the support structure will have to come from the Reserve Components.

REGIONAL FLASH POINTS

The two most obvious regional flash points are North Korea and Iraq, although Iran also poses a potential problem. The difficulty in determining flash points is deciding what to worry about. At the very base of U.S. concerns must be Russian nuclear power, which, although diminished by the separation of the Ukraine and by various arms agreements, is still sufficient to threaten the United States. Russia is the only nation with such a capability. China has a limited capability to strike the United States with nuclear weapons, but appears focused on other concerns, primarily internal. Most recent American presidents have gone out of their way to continue reasonably amicable relations with China, even though human rights concerns continue to be aroused by China's contemporary character. Several other countries have nuclear weapons, but delivery means remain distinctly limited.

At the next level are states who hate the United States simply because it is the United States: Iran, Libya, Sudan, and of course Iraq for as long as Saddam Hussein rules. Of these, the Sudan can be discounted, and since the United States does not need Libyan oil and has responded against the Libyans once for supporting terrorism, they may also be discounted. Iran and Iraq are different. Iraq still ranks second in the world for proven oil reserves and, of perhaps greater importance, is still able to cause mischief anywhere on its borders and especially with its southern neighbors, Saudi Arabia and Kuwait. As long as the American economy runs on oil and Gulf oil is the cheapest available, the Gulf states and Saudi Arabia in particular remain very high on the list of important danger zones. Current U.S. arrangements with Kuwait demonstrate American recognition of this sensitivity. The United States maintains, at Kuwaiti expense, an armored brigade task force in that country and conducts regular training exercises, again with full Kuwaiti funding support, on an unusually frequent basis. Iraq will not likely return to its former status of the fourth-largest army with modern equipment, but it has enough material that if it should choose, it could make a suicide dash back into Kuwait and on to the Saudi Eastern Province. Rooting the Iraqi forces out could be costly, but such an invasion would likely cost Iraq its statehood, something Saddam Hussein is unlikely to risk.

Iran is a more complex problem. It retains the potential to cause trouble wherever the Moslem brethren are oppressed, and it still considers state-supported terrorism as a policy option. Its economy is in poor shape, but there is great potential in the economy, and Iran is inviting foreigners, particularly Europeans, to invest in Iran. Thus a degree of acceptable behavior is clearly in its long-term interest. Iran has and continues to develop the potential to upset the Gulf states and interfere with the shipment of oil, but for the time being it has not engaged in such activity.

There are many places where the United States could and perhaps should step in for humanitarian reasons. But lessons from Somalia showed the costs involved and the high potential for failure. The United States is now unlikely to send troops to these places or any others that do not have some other significance or in some remote way affect U.S. vital national interests. In fact, if the Russians and their neighboring republics can stabilize, their natural resources are plentiful and are likely to attract U.S. investment, shifting from any interests in the African continent.

The point to be made here is that the Somali experience provided lessons to make the United States very cautious about becoming involved even in humanitarian missions. ''Doing good'' for its own sake is attractive only when the situation at home is in order and Americans can afford to be generous. Otherwise, religious and some philanthropic organizations will have to carry the burden, and in many ways they are better suited to do so.

Drug traffic will continue to be a problem, but not one that the military is suited to address. That calls for police work, police powers, and police functions that are beyond what the active military forces of the United States are authorized to engage in.

In the final analysis, while there are wars in progress or eternally imminent in many places, none appear to threaten U.S. vital national interests. It is also the case that the use of the military should be a last resort. Diplomacy, mediation, and regional and international organizations should be the first-priority tools.

PRESIDENTIAL DECISION DIRECTIVE 25

This chapter cannot conclude without some attention to Presidential Decision Directive 25 (5 May 1994). This document will have an important impact on the conduct of operations other than war—those military undertakings short of war in the various regions of the world. The directive places limits on the employment of American military forces in peace operations. For example, when assessing American participation in a peace operation, six questions must be answered satisfactorily:

1. Will participation advance U.S. interests, and are the risks acceptable?
2. Are resources available?
3. Is U.S. participation necessary for success?
4. Do clear objectives exist, and can an endpoint be identified?
5. Do the people and Congress support the operation?
6. Are command and control arrangements acceptable?[96]

Presidential Decision Directive 25 limits all employment of American military forces and specifically limits any employment to U.S. command only. In a sense this is only a signal to the United Nations and other nations of the world that the United States will no longer respond to every ''911'' call, that the rest of the world has responsibilities to global peace and stability too. On the other hand, the directive serves to quiet domestic concern over the fears that the administration, which has appeared hostile to everything military as an article of faith, does not recognize the fact that the military are valued citizens with reasonable fears. As a long-term statement of policy it is not certain how long it will really last, nor how it will ameliorate public reaction to video footage of human tragedy. Even if public policy is unclear, the American military establishment will do its best to handle any situation for which it must assume responsibility, first by asking crucial questions, then by reacting according to tried and proven techniques that seek first to avoid bloodshed and then to limit it where it becomes necessary.

NOTES

1. Stephen C. Pelletiere, Douglas V. Johnson II, and Leif R. Rosenberger, *Iraqi Power and U.S. Security in the Middle East* (Carlisle Barracks, PA: Strategic Studies Institute, 1990), pp. 25–40; also see Anthony H. Cordesman and Abraham R. Wagner, *The Lessons of Modern War: The Iran-Iraq War,* Vol. 2 (Boulder, CO: Westview Press, 1990), p. 398, for a brief description of the Mujahedin action. A more detailed, if self-promoting, view of this action can be found in the *NLA Quarterly,* Autumn 1988, an irregularly published journal of the People's Mujahedin of Iran.

2. Cordesman and Wagner, *Lessons of Modern War: The Iran-Iraq War,* pp. 396–398.

3. Pelletiere, Johnson, and Rosenberger, *Iraqi Power and U.S. Security in the Middle East,* p. 47.

4. Lawrence Freedman and Efraim Karsh, *The Gulf Conflict, 1990–1991: Diplomacy and War in the New World Order* (Princeton, NJ: Princeton University Press, 1993), pp. 37–41.

5. *Economist Intelligence Unit: Iraq Country Report,* no. 4 (1992), p. 3.

6. R. W. Scott, "Editorial Comment—Bang," *World Oil Journal,* September 1990, p. 5.

7. On the failure of deterrence in the confrontation between Iraq and Kuwait, see Paul K. Davis and John Arquilla, *Deterring or Coercing Opponents in Crisis: Lessons from the War with Saddam Hussein* (Santa Monica, CA: Rand, 1991) (DTIC AD A255 105).

8. Michael J. Mazarr, Don M. Snider, and James A. Blackwell, Jr., *Desert Storm: The Gulf War and What We Learned* (Boulder, CO: Westview Press, 1993), pp. 21–44. This chapter contains a good discussion of deterrence theory and its application to this event. For contrast and reliance on a broader range of non-U.S. sources, see Freedman and Karsh, *The Gulf Conflict, 1990–1991,* especially chapter 3, "Iraq Confronts Kuwait." It is important to contrast these two works since both sets of authors are widely read and quoted.

9. U.S. News and World Report, *Triumph without Victory: The Unreported History of the Persian Gulf War* (New York: Random House, 1992), p. 24. There was a presumption in some quarters that because the United States was involved in Operation Ernest Will, some formal defense arrangement existed between the United States and Kuwait. In fact, prior to U.S. involvement in the tanker escort mission, Kuwait and the United States were frequently at odds.

10. Janice Gross Stein, "Deterrence and Compellence in the Gulf, 1990–91: A Failed or Impossible Task?" *International Security* 17, no. 2 (Fall 1992): 147–179.

11. Department of Defense, *The Conduct of the Persian Gulf War: Final Report to*

Congress (Washington, DC: U.S. Government Printing Office, 1992), pp. 3–4 (hereafter DOD, *Title V Report*).

12. Bob Woodward, *The Commanders* (New York: Simon and Schuster, 1991), pp. 276–277. Although this book must be used with care, those who have operated in the higher decision circles acknowledge that the tenor of the work accurately reflects the process and the personalities depicted.

13. DOD, *Title V Report,* p. 319. For the full text of all the resolutions, see U.S. News and World Report, *Triumph without Victory,* app. A, pp. 416–448.

14. Stephen C. Pelletiere and Douglas V. Johnson II, *Lessons Learned: The Iran-Iraq War* (Carlisle Barracks, PA: Strategic Studies Institute, 1991), pp. viii–xi, 61–67.

15. Pelletiere, Johnson, and Rosenberger, *Iraqi Power and U.S. Security in the Middle East,* p. 20. Irangate was the abortive American-Israeli effort to exchange arms for hostages. The hostages were American Embassy personnel seized during the riots in Tehran following the collapse of the Shah's regime in 1979. These personnel were held hostage by the student revolutionaries and adherents to the Ayatollah Khomeini. When Iran's war with Iraq found the Iranians at a severe technological disadvantage and running out of spare parts for the American equipment with which the Iranian armed forces had been equipped, various intermediaries made approaches to the American administration in an effort to secure parts and supplies. The administration engaged these intermediaries and established a flow of parts and supplies including Hawk and TOW missiles, but without any official Iranian response. The scandal ensued when administration sources lied about the administration's involvement, which was completely contrary to stated policy, in testimony before the U.S. Congress. Irangate and the perceived U.S. deception or unwillingness to accurately predict the threat to al-Fao Peninsula caused the Iraqis to turn to their own devices. It appears that the intelligence failure was largely a factor of cloud cover over Iranian assembly areas.

16. Pelletiere and Johnson, *Lessons Learned: The Iran-Iraq War,* pp. 47–63.

17. Cordesman and Wagner, *The Lessons of Modern War: The Iran-Iraq War,* pp. 395–396.

18. Lieutenant General Yeosock made this comment in an extended discussion with the officers involved in writing the U.S. Army's first "Gulf War Lessons Learned" report at Ft. Leavenworth, Center for Army Lessons Learned.

19. DOD, *Title V Report,* p. 31.

20. Freedman and Karsh, *The Gulf Conflict, 1990–1991,* p. 78. A measure of how far this decision was known is that when the aircraft carrier USS *Roosevelt* received orders to head for the Gulf, the Soviet trawler routinely following the carrier increased speed and pulled abeam the carrier, whereupon the Soviet crew assembled on deck and gave three cheers for democracy and the United States. Interview with Commander Tom Walsh, USN, pilot assigned to the USS *Roosevelt.*

21. DOD, *Title V Report,* pp. 19–25.

22. Ibid., pp. 492–494.

23. Ibid., p. 494; also see Douglas W. Craft, *An Operational Analysis of the Persian Gulf War* (Carlisle Barracks, PA: Strategic Studies Institute, 1992), p. 25; Marc Michaelis, "The Importance of Communicating in Coalition Warfare," *Military Review* 72, no. 11 (November 1992): 40–50. It should be noted that Colonel Craft worked in Central Command Deputy Chief of Staff for Plans (CCJ5) during the war and Major Michaelis worked inside the Coalition, Coordination, Communications, and Integration Center

(C^3IC). (See charts 23A, ''Desert Shield Command Relationships''; 23B, ''Desert Storm Command Relationships''; and 23C, ''Alignment of Coalition Forces on the Ground.'')

24. Interview with Major General Paul A. Schwartz, creator and director of the C^3IC.

25. Interview with a Saudi officer.

26. David M. Birdwell, ''Personal Experience Monograph,'' June 1992, U.S. Army War College (USAWC) Personal Experience Monograph Collection.

27. DOD, *Title V Report,* p. 50.

28. Interview with Colonel Gene Holloway, ARCENT G-3.

29. Craft, *Operational Analysis of the Persian Gulf War,* pp. 16–18.

30. DOD, *Title V Report,* p. 33.

31. Related to the author by a military intelligence officer involved in interrogation of Iraqi officer prisoners.

32. Interview with Major General Barry E. McCaffrey.

33. Interview with several senior U.S. Army officers involved in the process.

34. Craft, *Operational Analysis of the Persian Gulf War,* p. 19.

35. Discussions with Colonel James C. King, Commander, 24th DISCOM, and his subordinate commanders during a nine-hour videotaped ''After Action Review'' conducted at Carlisle Barracks, 1993 (hereafter 24th DISCOM Commander's interviews).

36. DOD, *Title V Report,* pp. 66–67.

37. Ibid., p. 67.

38. Ibid.

39. Ibid., p. 70. (See maps 39A, ''Ground Offensive Concept''; 39B, ''CENTCOM Command Structure (Oct '90)''; 39C, ''Ground Forces Command Structure on G-Day''; 39D, ''Task Organization''; 39E, ''Army Forces Organization for Combat''; 39F, ''IMEF Task Organization''; 39G, ''Arab Islamic Forces: JFC-North Task Organization''; and 39H, ''Arab Islamic Forces: JFC-East Task Organization.'')

40. 24th DISCOM Commander's interviews.

41. Ibid.

42. William G. Pagonis with Jeffrey L. Cruikshank, *Moving Mountains: Lessons in Leadership and Logistics from the Gulf War* (Boston: Harvard Business School Press, 1992), pp. 89–90.

43. Brooks L. Bash, *CRAF: The Persian Gulf War and Implications for the Future* (Newport, RI: Naval War College, 1992) (DTIC AD A249-892).

44. Pagonis and Cruikshank, *Moving Mountains,* p. 91.

45. Ibid., pp. 89–91.

46. Interview with Lieutenant General Gary E. Luck, Commanding General, XVIII Airborne Corps, by videoteleconference between Ft. Bragg and Carlisle Barracks.

47. Joseph H. Bykofsky and Harold Lawson, *U.S. Army in World War II, The Technical Services: The Transportation Corps—Operations Overseas* (Washington, DC: U.S. Government Printing Office, 1957), pp. 165–166.

48. A Milvan is a metal shipping/storage container that can be placed on wheels to make it into a mobile trailer.

49. PLL is the Prescribed Load List of repair parts that normally travels with a unit.

50. Pagonis and Cruikshank, *Moving Mountains,* p. 140.

51. Ibid., p. 146.

52. Ibid., pp. 141–142. (See map 52A, ''LOG Bases,'' DOD, *Title V Report.*)

53. Ibid., p. 146.

54. Ibid., p. 147.

55. Ibid.
56. Interview with Lieutenant General Calvin Waller.
57. DOD, *Title V Report,* p. 89.
58. Ibid., pp. 90–93.
59. Ibid., p. 116.
60. Interviews with several senior U.S. Army officers, including Lieutenant General Calvin Waller, Deputy Commander-in-Chief, and Major General Steven Arnold, ARCENT G-3.
61. Craft, *Operational Analysis of the Persian Gulf War,* p. 47.
62. Interviews with Brigadier General John F. Stewart, Jr., ARCENT G-2, and several other senior officers. A discussion of this issue from the perspective of the ARCENT G-2 can be found in John F. Stewart, Jr., *Operation Desert Storm, the Military Intelligence Story: A View from the G-2, 3rd U.S. Army,* (Fort MacPherson, GA: 3rd U.S. Army, locally reproduced, 1991).
63. DOD, *Title V Report,* p. 261.
64. Ibid.
65. Ibid., p. 262.
66. Ibid.
67. Ibid.
68. Ibid., p. 263.
69. Ibid., p. 265.
70. Interview with Colonel Robert Kee, U.S. Army Liaison Officer to French Forces.
71. Joseph P. Englehardt, *Desert Shield and Desert Storm: A Chronology and Troop List for the 1990–1991 Persian Gulf Crisis,* SSI Special Report (Carlisle Barracks, PA: Strategic Studies Institute, 1991), p. 70.
72. DOD, *Title V Report,* p. 270.
73. Ibid., p. 272.
74. Ibid., pp. 276–283.
75. Ibid., pp. 283–289.
76. Ibid., pp. 290–292.
77. Ibid., pp. 292–294.
78. Ibid., p. 294.
79. John T. Fishel, *Liberation, Occupation, and Rescue: War Termination and Desert Storm* (Carlisle Barracks, PA: Strategic Studies Institute, 1992).
80. Interview with Lieutenant General John Shalikashvili.
81. Harry G. Summers, Jr., *On Strategy: The Vietnam War in Context* (Carlisle Barracks, PA: Strategic Studies Institute, 1981), and Carl von Clausewitz, *On War,* ed. and trans. Michael Howard and Peter Paret (Princeton, NJ: Princeton University Press, 1976).
82. Clausewitz, *On War,* p. 88.
83. Ibid. This section describes Clausewitz's trinity in two versions. The second speaks to a trinity of "primordial violence," "chance and friction," and subordination of war to reason.
84. Headquarters, Department of the Army, *FM 100-5: Operations* (Washington, DC: U.S. Government Printing Office, 1993), pp. 2-4 and 2-5.
85. Paul H. Herbert, *Deciding What Has to Be Done: General William E. DePuy and the 1976 Edition of FM 100-5, Operations,* Leavenworth Papers Number 16 (Washington, DC: U.S. Government Printing Office, 1988).
86. John L. Romjue, *From Active Defense to AirLand Battle: The Development of*

Army Doctrine, 1973–1982, TRADOC Historical Monograph Series (Ft. Monroe, VA: U.S. Army Training and Doctrine Command, 1984).

87. See *FM 100-1: The Army* (Washington, DC: U.S. Government Printing Office, 1994) for a brief discussion of the place and purpose of rules of engagement.

88. *FM 100-5: Operations,* pp. 13-3 and 13-4.

89. *FM 100-1: The Army,* p. 15.

90. Alan Ned Sabrosky and Robert L. Sloane, *The Recourse to War: An Appraisal of the ''Weinberger Doctrine''* (Carlisle Barracks, PA: Strategic Studies Institute, 1988), particularly chapter 6, ''The Military and Operational Significance of the Weinberger Doctrine.''

91. Army Initiatives Group, *State of America's Army on Its 218th Birthday* (Washington, DC: Office of the Deputy Chief of Staff for Operations and Plans, 1993) p. 11.

92. For a summary of Admiral Mahan's theory see Russell F. Weigley, *The American Way of War: A History of United States Military Strategy and Policy* (Bloomington: Indiana University Press, 1977), pp. 174–182.

93. T. R. Fehrenbach, *This Kind of War: Korea, A Study in Unpreparedness* (New York: Pocket Books, 1964), p. 454.

94. ''C-17 Shortfall Threatens to Widen Looming US Airlift Gap,'' *Jane's Defence Weekly,* 21 May 1994, p. 18.

95. As the Soviet threat evaporated, strategic planners and intelligence experts looked about the world and drew the uncomfortable conclusion that practically anyone with an army deserving of the name had reasonably modern Soviet tanks and usually plenty of them. It is not simply the case that a tank is a tank, as the war in the Gulf demonstrated. Soviet tanks are very good. They are the equal of the Marine Corps' M-60s, of 1970 vintage, and are infinitely superior to the fast-moving, but lightly armored Marine light armored vehicles (LAVs). An Army M1A2 tank unit has no peer in the world today, and that is the way it should be. If it should be necessary to deploy American troops anywhere in the world, it is the Army leadership's intention never again to place the 82d Airborne soldiers out on a limb as potential ''speed bumps'' for some third-rate enemy with even obsolescent armored vehicles. Airborne units are great forces for rapid insertion in difficult situations, but as was painfully demonstrated during the World War II operation popularly known from Cornelius Ryan's brilliant book and the subsequent movie *A Bridge Too Far,* tanks and paratroopers do not mix well, especially in opposition. Whoever watched the Desert Shield buildup in its early stages could not help but be acutely conscious of General Schwarzkopf's dilemma in attempting to balance available airlift capacity and the competing needs for tank-killing helicopter systems against the need for logistic support systems. Tanks afloat are a singular departure for the Army, but they signal the commitment to a power-projection force within a national Force Projection Strategy.

96. Paraphrased from Presidential Decision Directive no. 25, *The Clinton Administration's Policy on Reforming Multilateral Peace Operations* (Washington, DC: The White House, May 1994).

SELECTED BIBLIOGRAPHY

Cigar, Norman. ''Iraq's Mindset and the Gulf War: Blueprint for Defeat.'' *Journal of Strategic Studies* 15, no. 1 (March 1992): pp. 1–29.

Craft, Douglas W. *An Operational Analysis of the Persian Gulf War.* Carlisle Barracks, PA: Strategic Studies Institute, 1992.

Department of Defense. *Final Report to Congress: The Conduct of the Persian Gulf War.* Washington, DC: U.S. Government Printing Office, 1992.

Fishel, John T. *Liberation, Occupation, and Rescue: War Termination and Desert Storm.* Carlisle Barracks, PA: Strategic Studies Institute, 1992.

Freedman, Lawrence, and Efraim Karsh. *The Gulf Conflict, 1990–1991: Diplomacy and War in the New World Order.* Princeton, NJ: Princeton University Press, 1993.

Godden, John, ed. *Shield and Storm: Personal Recollections of the Air War in the Gulf.* London: Brassey's, 1995.

Kindsvatter, Peter S. "VII Corps in the Gulf War: Deployment and Preparation for DESERT STORM." *Military Review* 72, no. 1 (January 1992): pp. 2–16.

———. "VII Corps in the Gulf War: Post–Cease-Fire Operations." *Military Review* 72, no. 6 (June 1992): pp. 2–19.

Pardew, James W. "The Iraqi Army's Defeat in Kuwait." *Parameters* 21, no. 4 (Winter 1991–92).

Pelletiere, Stephen C., and Douglas V. Johnson II. *Lessons Learned: The Iran-Iraq War.* Carlisle Barracks, PA: Strategic Studies Institute, 1991.

Pelletiere, Stephen C., Douglas V. Johnson, and Leif R. Rosenberger. *Iraqi Power and U.S. Security in the Middle East.* Carlisle Barracks, PA: Strategic Studies Institute, 1990.

Romjue, John L. *From Active Defense to AirLand Battle: The Development of Army Doctrine, 1973–1982.* TRADOC Historical Monograph Series. Fort Monroe, VA: U.S. Army Training and Doctrine Command, 1984.

Sabrosky, Alan Ned, and Robert L. Sloane. *The Recourse to War: An Appraisal of the "Weinberger Doctrine."* Carlisle Barracks, PA: Strategic Studies Institute, 1988.

Stewart, John F., Jr. *Operation DESERT STORM, the Military Intelligence Story: A View from the G-2, 3rd U.S. Army.* Fort MacPherson, GA: Third U.S. Army, 1991.

Interviews

Major General Steven Arnold, ARCENT G-3

Colonel Gene Holloway, ARCENT G-3

Colonel Robert Kee, U.S. Army Liaison Officer to French Forces

Colonel James C. King, Commander, 24th DISCOM

Lieutenant General Gary E. Luck, CG, XVIII Airborne Corps

Major General Barry E. McCaffrey, USAWC

Major General Paul A. Schwartz, creator and director of C^3IC

Lieutenant General John Shalikashvili, Special Assistant to the Chairman, Joint Chiefs of Staff

Brigadier General John F. Stewart, Jr., ARCENT G-2

Lieutenant General Calvin Waller, Deputy Commander-in-Chief, U.S. Central Command

Commander Tom Walsh, USN, pilot assigned to the USS *Roosevelt*

Chapter 10

PEACETIME ENGAGEMENTS

David Tucker and Christopher J. Lamb

To avoid the expense and risk of war, nations employ a variety of less belligerent means to influence, persuade, and coerce other international actors. The United States is no exception, having periodically employed demarches, shows of force, economic sanctions, and other such instruments throughout its history.[1] It has been less inclined toward and adept at such measures short of war, however, than other great powers. The tendency to see war and peace as discrete, discontinuous states partially explains the American lack of facility with measures short of war, as does the United States' geographic and often political isolation from world affairs. As one historian has noted:

> The United States usually possessed no national strategy for the employment of force or the threat of force to attain political ends, except as the nation used force in wartime. . . . The United States was not involved in international politics continuously enough or with enough consistency of purpose to permit the development of a coherent national strategy for the consistent pursuit of political goals by diplomacy in combination with armed force.[2]

World War II radically changed the U.S. view of its role in world affairs. Pearl Harbor thrust the United States into a global war from which it emerged preeminent but faced with a single, overriding, geopolitical threat to its institutions and way of life. Confronted with this challenge, the United States was forced to pay more attention to national security strategy and means short of war. It embarked upon a strategy of containing Soviet expansion through the constant engagement of countervailing American power, relying whenever possible on measures short of war.

The principal architect of U.S. containment policy, George Kennan, delivered a series of lectures on measures short of war in 1946–1947 at the new National War College in Washington, D.C. The War College was one of the many post-war national security institutions, such as the National Security Council, the Central Intelligence Agency, and the Department of Defense, that marked the passage of the United States into its role of world leadership. In the lectures Kennan argued that the United States would have to abandon an understanding of international relations as primarily a question of adjudicating or adjusting disputes and recognize that a great-power struggle fueled by competing ideologies required measures short of war not for the purpose of adjudication but for the "promulgation of power," a mutual and unceasing effort of the two great powers to exert pressure on one another for the attainment of their ends.

Kennan classified measures short of war to include economic, political, and psychological instruments as well as military and diplomatic ones. He set two conditions for their effective employment as means of avoiding the costs and risks of war. The first condition was that the United States preserve a preponderance of strength in the world. Kennan spoke not only of military strength and brilliant diplomacy, but of the moral and political fiber of U.S. society. He denigrated bluster and threats, but believed that to be effective national strength required a "readiness to use it any time if we are pushed beyond certain limits."[3]

It was not sufficient to exercise diverse, coordinated measures short of war from a position of strength, however. According to Kennan it was also necessary that these measures be employed in service of a grand strategy:

> A second condition must be met if our measures short of war are going to be effective: we must select measures and use them not hit-or-miss as the moment may seem to demand but in accordance with a pattern of grand strategy no less concrete and no less consistent than that which governs our actions in war. It is my own conviction that we must go even further than that . . . we must work out a general plan of what the United States wants in this world and pursue that plan with all the measures at our disposal, depending on what is indicated by the circumstances.[4]

During the forty-five years of the Cold War the United States employed measures short of war as a matter of course, sometimes more hit-and-miss, however, than carefully calculated to serve larger strategic goals. The United States also went to war on occasion, but it never had to fight the major conflict with the Soviet Union for which it was constantly planning and that it was prepared and engaged to deter.

POST–COLD WAR ENGAGEMENT

While historians debate how much the U.S. containment strategy was responsible for the implosion of the Soviet Union, current U.S. leadership is occupied with a massive reassessment of U.S. national security policy and strategy, and along with it a reassessment of whether and how the United States should pursue its interests in peacetime through measures short of war. Initially there was some question about whether the United States would choose to retain the mantle of world leadership at all, and by so doing, require the constant exercise of effective measures short of war. During the 1992 presidential campaign there was speculation that the United States would withdraw into a period of relative lethargy marked by flirtation with isolationism and protectionism as organizing principles for its international relations. American parochialism may still reassert itself, but for the time being the issue appears to have been resolved in favor of continued engagement. Since attaining office, the Clinton administration has forcefully announced its intention to "engage actively in the world in order to increase our prosperity, update our security arrangements and promote democracy abroad."[5]

To most observers, the objective situation requires the United States to stay actively engaged in efforts to influence the international security environment to its advantage. The end of the Cold War does not change the fact that no other great powers now protect U.S. interests as a by-product of their own security, as France and then Great Britain once did. The transcontinental reach of terrorism and the continuing spread of weapons of mass destruction and the means for their delivery further minimize the protective value of the Pacific and Atlantic oceans. For economic reasons as well the United States cannot afford a period of withdrawal from world affairs. The U.S. economy is more dependent on global economic health than ever before. In short, the traumatic lesson learned at Pearl Harbor and reinforced by forty years of the Cold War has not changed: the health and welfare of the United States cannot be divorced from events and trends elsewhere in the world. Continuing peacetime engagement in and of itself will require that the United States employ a broad range of effective measures short of war, but when, where, how, and toward what ends are questions that can only be answered in the context of a specific national security strategy.

Unfortunately, the consensus that currently prevails in favor of remaining actively engaged in world affairs does not extend to a set of organizing principles to direct U.S. policy and strategy in the post–Cold War world.[6] Thus it is not possible to articulate definitively the extent of U.S. peacetime engagement or the precise role measures short of war will play in U.S. strategy. There are, however, three sets of factors beyond the general argument in favor of engagement that suggest both the need for continued peacetime engagement in world affairs and the continuing importance of measures short of war to our national security.

Security Trends Influencing the Environment Short of War

While the end of the Cold War can only be understood as a boon to U.S. national security, it also is now clear that the end of superpower conflict has a darker side as well. While nuclear or general war on the European central front is a remote possibility now, many regional and intranational antagonisms held in check during the U.S.-Soviet superpower confrontation have erupted. For instance, Saddam Hussein might have concluded in early 1990 that in the face of declining Soviet influence in the Middle East, he had to secure his interests by force. Siad Barre's fall from power in Somalia was in good part due to the withdrawal of superpower support for his regime, a turn of events that set the stage for later U.S. and U.N. intervention in that unhappy country. Age-old animosities based on religion, culture, and ethnic rivalries also have torn apart Yugoslavia and some republics of the former Soviet Union.

A resurgence of ethnic conflict is accompanied by two trends the United States first witnessed in the opening years of the Cold War when it enjoyed unequivocal military superiority, as it does now. One trend will be an increased impetus for acquiring weapons of mass destruction by those who believe that they are necessary for great-power status, independent foreign policies, and direct attacks on established U.S. interests. The preferable means for countering the proliferation of weapons of mass destruction will be measures short of war. Where regional or subnational actors are unable to acquire weapons of mass destruction, or even where proliferation cannot be stopped and the result is an uneasy strategic stalemate, regional protagonists are more likely to resort to indirect aggression.

U.S. conventional superiority is another reason indirect aggression is likely to be a problem for the United States. When a limited deployment of U.S. conventional power in the Korean War revealed huge disparities in the efficacy of comparable Communist and allied conventional forces, the Soviet Union adopted a policy of attacking U.S. interests indirectly by instigating or manipulating Third World "wars of national liberation" and later through support for terrorists and other subversives. Similarly, in the aftermath of Desert Storm, those attacking U.S. interests will be inclined to do so through indirect aggression, using terrorism, subversion, insurgency, or insurgent tactics to pursue their agendas. In short, Mohammed Farah Aidid is a more likely model for future resistance to American interests than Saddam Hussein.

Intertwining Threats and the Environment Short of War

A second reason America must remain engaged and use measures short of war effectively is that threats are not discrete. It is true that the United States no longer views a threat in one region in terms of its linkage to a larger, more dire global geopolitical threat. This does not mean, however, that threats are isolated. In fact, most threats intertwine in complex ways. For example, a state that sponsors terrorism against the United States as part of a general struggle against alleged imperialism also gains prestige and power in its region, which can complicate American efforts to maintain a favorable balance of power there. An alternative example would be the revolution in Iran, which not only changed the balance of power in the Middle East but also led to more terrorist attacks on Americans and U.S. allies as well as to increased drug trafficking. Disputes about how best to respond to this upsurge in terrorist activity complicated our alliance relationships, while profits from drug trafficking helped to finance terrorism and other activities contrary to U.S. interests. An American response to one category of threat can also undermine other security interests. U.S. support for the insurgency in Nicaragua, for example, caused friction with certain European allies at a time when the United States confronted a strenuous Soviet effort to break the NATO alliance.

In addition, how America deals with a threat in one region has a limited transitive effect through its impact on U.S. prestige.[7] Prestige accrues from employing power with consistency, decisiveness, and resolve and is always an important asset to be developed and preserved. Any setback will diminish a state's reputation for the effective employment of power, and this fact alone guarantees that threats have some cumulative potential. Many observers believe, for example, that the military junta in Port-au-Prince was emboldened to greater resistance to U.S. pressure for democratization by the precipitous U.S. decision to withdraw from Somalia. When, on 11 October 1993, the USS *Harlan County* tried to dock at Port-au-Prince, Haiti, and disembark U.N. personnel, they were turned away by a threatening crowd shouting "We are going to turn this into another Somalia!"[8] The event demonstrated that in an era of instantaneous communications, the U.S. reaction to events on another continent was known and appreciated by those bent on thwarting U.S. policy toward their own country.

The fact that threats can reinforce and intertwine with one another explains why the United States should not respond only to the most dire perils. Moreover, cumulative effects of lower-level threats can also erode American security. The United States will be especially vulnerable to this slow but steady erosion in the uncertain and disorderly world of the years to come, in which it is not likely to face an obvious and immediate threat to its well-being. To borrow a term from the old Soviet vocabulary, the United States should try to prevent any "correlation of forces," whether coordinated or coincidental, from threatening the American people, American institutions, American economic vitality, or the American way of life. Terrorist resort to weapons of mass destruction, the spread of protectionist blocs, or militant religious fanaticism targeted at U.S. interests require different but nonetheless determined responses because they can have a cumulative adverse effect as they interact with one another and with other threats faced by our allies. While the stakes in war are high and defeat can have devastating consequences, in the long run, inadvertence in peace can be just as ruinous as incompetence in war.

Efficiency and Increasingly Scarce Resources

The third reason to remain engaged and use measures short of war effectively is that the post–Cold War challenge to U.S. leadership is magnified by the relentless decline in U.S. foreign assistance, security assistance, and defense budgets, which reduces the means available to the United States for influencing regional actors and security threats short of war. Even though the United States commands a position of world leadership, domestic needs and the diffusion of political, economic, and military power in the world require the United States to exert leadership with relatively fewer human and material resources than during the Cold War. The U.S. military's movement away from attrition warfare in conventional conflict scenarios was required by Soviet numerical superiority. A similar improvement in efficiency is now necessary when the United States pursues its interests with measures short of war.

Efficiency in the environment short of war is difficult. In peacetime, when the threats America faces are less immediate, the normal tendency toward bureaucratic specialization and simplification takes over. The United States can more easily become fixed on narrow objectives, tolerate ineffective means, or allow government agencies to work at cross-purposes. In addition, problems are more complex and public support less certain. It may be widely recognized that U.S. leadership is still more often than not the indispensable catalyst for regional conflict resolution, but it is also true that the United States must now deal with the complexity of numerous competing principles, interests, and actors, including an American public that will have difficulty understanding how ambiguous conflicts overseas require the allocation of American blood and treasure.

PEACETIME ENGAGEMENTS

Promoting and defending America's interests will continue to require a nuclear strategic deterrent and unparalleled war-fighting ability, but since the threats the United States faces are no longer nuclear annihilation or even global war, post–Cold War peacetime engagement now requires that the United States place greater emphasis on developing and applying instruments of persuasion in the environment short of war. The challenge is to infuse U.S. diplomacy and defense policies with a new creativity, so as to exercise and even expand U.S. influence while expending fewer resources.

As Kennan suggested in 1947, a "hit-or-miss" approach to measures short of war is not likely to be very economical or effective. Much preferable would be a concerted effort to guide and coordinate measures short of war in the context of an overarching national security strategy. Such an approach presumes answers to two broad sets of questions that are explored in the rest of this chapter. First, when, where, and how ought the United States to engage its limited resources, and toward what ends? We do not lay the foundation for the entirety of a national security strategy here, as would be necessary to address in detail the appropriate criteria for peacetime engagement, but we do suggest a broad set of peacetime engagement criteria that current circumstances would seem to impose upon the nation at large and the Department of Defense more specifically. Second, we explore the general requirements for success in the environment short of war by first discussing national imperatives and then more specific capabilities and programs for the Department of Defense. Before proceeding to these tasks, however, we must distinguish between the environment short of war and war.

THE ENVIRONMENT SHORT OF WAR

The Distinction between Peace and War

Compared with the volumes written about war and what victory requires, little has been done to define the environment short of war and explain how to act effectively in it. If war has its own logic and demands, the same may be true of the environment short of war. Indeed, we will see as we consider this environment that effective action in it requires strategies different from those that are appropriate for war, as well as an understanding of the relation between politics and force different from the one that prevails in war.

The first step in understanding this environment is to distinguish it from war. When states declared war and ended it with formal surrenders, this was more easily done. Since states no longer observe these conventions, we must distinguish peace and war by their inherent characteristics. One way to do this is to consider in general terms how conflicts arise and how they are resolved.

When the objectives of actors in international politics conflict, and the objectives are important enough that the actors want to pursue them even though this may cause the conflict to escalate, two courses of actions are open: the actors can try to change each other's behavior—the actions that prevent them from attaining their objectives—or they can try to destroy the capability of their adversary to act in such a way. Since trying to destroy capabilities to act in certain ways is both more costly and more dangerous than trying to change behavior through persuasion, states first attempt to resolve disputes with persuasion. They posture, negotiate, threaten, and coerce, for example, using diverse measures short of war. If, as a result of such actions, one of the states changes its position or both do to some degree, the conflict may be resolved. If neither does and even one believes that the interests at stake are important enough, it may decide to go beyond using persuasion. It may aim instead to destroy those physical capabilities that stand in the way of attaining its objectives. This decision means going to war.

What going to war entails depends on the objective at issue. If the objective is to expel an invader from some territory, the unconditional surrender or destruction of all his forces may not be necessary. It may be necessary to destroy only the ability of his forces to resist in that territory. When the objective is the destruction of a nation's way of life, as it was in World War II, then it will probably be necessary to demand unconditional surrender and destroy organized resistance to achieve it.

Persuasion and war are means to larger ends, such as the safety or aggrandizement of a society, its institutions, or its rulers. National security strategy encompasses these ends and the various means national leaders use to achieve them. It includes tools of both persuasion and war. Viewing operations short of war, war, and national security as a continuum, we see that operations short of war focus on persuasion, war on destruction, and national security strategy on both persuasion and destruction. When formulating national security strategy, statesmen use all the policy instruments at their disposal, as they do when confronting problems short of war. But when they make the decision to concentrate on destroying the physical capabilities of an opponent so that the opponent cannot attain his objectives, they make the decision to go to war and in so doing give precedence (although not free rein) to the military instrument.

Recognizing the National Security Continuum

Influencing behavior and destroying capabilities form a continuum because they are interdependent (destroying capabilities may influence behavior, and influencing behavior may affect capabilities) and because conflict is resolved by one or the other, or by a combination of the two. It is important to recognize the national security continuum as consisting of two interdependent means of pursuing objectives in order to avoid a false dichotomy: the sometimes appealing but nevertheless incorrect notion that resort to force begins where political intercourse (diplomacy) ends, and vice versa. In fact, in pursuit of their objectives, states may try over time in varying degrees to change behavior through political intercourse and to destroy capabilities to behave in unacceptable ways.

For example, an actor may try to persuade an opponent by destroying valued or symbolic targets. Similarly, when an actor has made the decision to destroy the ability of his opponent to resist, at least relative to a certain objective, the actor may still attempt through psychological warfare, strategic deception, or other means to persuade the opponent to change his behavior in a particular instance or more generally. In some cases it may be difficult to determine which is the primary means an actor is using to achieve his objectives. One or both sides in a conflict may mistakenly believe that the other side has or has not made the decision to forgo persuasion and concentrate on destruction. Vietnam is a case in point. U.S. strategy failed because it confused the political struggle in the South for a war and the conflict with the North for an effort at persuasion. Americans attacked the insurgents more aggressively than their political base and tried to persuade the North to desist from aggression rather than destroy its ability to launch aggression, either before or after it actually did so. As a result the United States failed to defeat the insurgency and also ultimately North Vietnam's army as well.

Recognizing the Threshold between War and Operations Short of War

War, then, can be distinguished easily in theory as a middle ground of sorts between applying measures short of war in "campaigns of persuasion," or what more broadly might be called operations short of war, and national security strategies writ large. In war, the primary focus is on destruction of capabilities. Operations short of war, on the other hand, focus on political relationships, while national security requires alternatives to both political relationships and war-making capabilities. The thresholds separating war fighting from grand strategy and operations short of war are, however, less clear in practice than in theory. As they approach war, operations short of war rely more on force, blurring the distinction between these operations and war itself. Above the threshold of war, national security strategy combines both war fighting and persuasion.

Recognizing the difference between war and other national security activities is important for two reasons. First, it makes clear why traditional U.S. military strategy is suitable only for war and not for the environment short of war. This strategy is designed to protect military capabilities from attack (deterrence) and to destroy an adversary's capabilities if he attacks (defense). This strategy is sufficient only for war fighting because it is only in war fighting that destroying or defending capabilities is essential. In the environment short of war destroying or defending capabilities is only a small part of the effort. What are required for peacetime uses of the military are strategies of persuasion.[9]

Second, the relationship between military requirements and political objectives in war differs from their relationship in peace. In war, those measures necessary to attain military objectives take precedence over all but those few core political objectives for which the war is being fought, and in war all political objectives are in doubt to the extent that the struggle to destroy an adversary's capabilities is in doubt.

In the environment short of war, on the other hand, those measures necessary to attain military objectives are subordinate to many political considerations because military force is employed not to destroy or defend capabilities but primarily to directly influence political relationships. The more important the focus on immediately influencing behavior through measures short of war, the more important it is that all national policy instruments, including force, be coordinated in pursuit of immediate political goals, and that political objectives guide the details of military operations. In sum, as an adversarial relationship escalates through increasingly intense stages of conflict, at some point it stops being an attempt to persuade and becomes an effort to unequivocally impose a solution by force of arms. That point is the threshold between war and peace.

Activities in the Environment Short of War

Before discussing the elements of strategies appropriate for persuasion in contrast to war, it will be helpful to look a bit more closely at the environment short of war and the activities that occur there. Persuasion is not all that actors do in this environment. In addition to limited support to law-enforcement and other domestic agencies, activities in the environment short of war fall primarily into two categories, persuasion and relief operations. Persuasion, as noted earlier, consists of all the measures short of war the United States takes to influence the behavior or choices of other actors, whether states or subnational groups, so that they do not act in ways that hinder or prevent the United States from attaining its objectives. Security operations are all those activities undertaken by the United States, such as noncombatant evacuation operations (NEOs), to ensure the security and welfare of U.S. citizens or of others.

Persuasion

In the first instance, persuasion means influence building, the general measures America takes to keep on good terms with other nations and to keep them well disposed toward American objectives. These would include state visits, aid projects, training missions, combined and joint exercises, U.S. Information Agency (USIA) visitor programs, intelligence sharing, and military-to-military contacts. Such measures also support routine diplomatic contacts and negotiations. If negotiations fail or reach an impasse, force might be used to persuade the other side to accede to U.S. goals. The force used might be nonlethal, such as economic sanctions, for example, or a show of military force. Or the force might be lethal, such as a punitive raid. All of these efforts, including the use of lethal force, are properly called persuasion because the United States undertakes them not to destroy the capability of an opponent to act in ways contrary to American interests, but to affect his intentions so that he no longer chooses to do so.

Relief Operations

Although persuasion constitutes most of what the United States does in the environment short of war it does engage in another kind of activity: relief operations. Occasionally the United States has the luxury of acting directly overseas to ensure the safety of Americans or others and their property without connection to larger interests and issues. These operations have no potential in themselves to escalate to war. Most noncombatant evacuation operations (NEOs) would be an example of this kind of operation. In undertaking NEOs, America is not necessarily concerned with affecting the behavior of a foreign power, although the operation may have this secondary result. America's primary purpose is the security of a particular group of Americans. Humanitarian missions would be another example. Again, such missions may build goodwill and American influence, but their primary purpose is not to affect the behavior of others but to assist those in distress. Referring to NEOs and humanitarian assistance as relief operations acknowledges that such operations aim only to ensure the security and welfare of a particular group of American citizens or others and not to achieve strategic objectives that ensure the security of the nation.

When discussing relief operations, we must keep an important distinction in mind. If a NEO takes place in a nonpermissive environment, if, in other words, someone tries to stop the United States from rescuing its citizens, the situation is actually defined by the conflict between U.S. goals and those of another actor.

This case is best understood, therefore, not as a relief operation but as an adversarial relationship. If the United States meets resistance, it may have to destroy the ability of the adversary to prevent America from rescuing its citizens. Making this decision, of course, requires weighing the cost of such an operation against a variety of other considerations, but because such a decision is before the United States, at least potentially, such a situation is not a security operation as defined here.

Of these two categories of peacetime activities, persuasion is the more fundamental for two reasons. First, persuasion is the primary means used to address the most comprehensive and important American national security objectives. For this reason, persuasion points toward the possibility of war in a way that a relief operation such as a permissive NEO does not. Persuasion is also the principal means used to avoid war. Even when war is unavoidable, persuasion, properly employed, can position a nation for maximum advantage in the prosecution of war. Second, persuasion makes other operations possible. It gives America access to do many NEOs, for example.

The distinction between war and peace provides a way of understanding the various complex activities that the United States undertakes in the environment short of war so that it can deal with them more effectively. Consider counterinsurgency, for example. It is a good place to begin because, since it comes closest to the threshold of war, it is the most complex and ambiguous peacetime activity. In responding to an insurgency, in fact, a government might cross the threshold of war. In general, three different ways can be distinguished in responding to an insurgency: persuasion, war, and a combination of persuasion and a small war.

Counterinsurgency as Persuasion

A traditional approach to insurgency is to separate the insurgent from popular support. The government targets the motivations, attitudes, and behavior of the disaffected population and infiltrates, harasses, and imprisons insurgents. In this approach, aggressive small-unit tactics are used against insurgents, but their purpose is not to destroy the insurgents' physical capabilities to attack the host government but to demoralize the insurgents and provide increased local security so that the work of changing attitudes and behavior through civic action and political reform can go forward. In addition, such tactics are a way of showing that the use of force will not intimidate the government. In this approach to insurgency, persuasion is the objective, which is why this way of responding to insurgency should not be considered war.

Counterinsurgency as War

Some nations have pursued counterinsurgency with an overwhelming emphasis on destroying the insurgents, regardless of the damage done to noncombatants. This approach is adopted when there seems no hope of winning support or acquiescence from the local population, or for mere expediency when ruthlessness is valued and human rights are not. In such cases the use of force is not intended to change behavior, although it may well intimidate the remnants of the group attacked or others, but to destroy the capability of that group to resist the will of the government. This intention is clear in the measures that often accompany this approach, such as destroying traditional centers of culture or learning, forcing the dispersion or permanent relocation of target populations, or simply killing them. Such an approach to insurgency should really be considered a kind of war, that of a government against its own people, even though the term *war* normally applies only to conflict between states.

Counterinsurgency might also be fought as a war if the insurgency depended on a cult of personality or a highly organized leadership cadre. In this case targeting the leader or the leadership would be intended not to persuade them to give up the insurgency but to destroy the insurgency by effectively decapitating it. Such an approach should be considered war, although again the term is not generally used in this way.

Counterinsurgency as a Combination of Persuasion and a Small War

In some cases a government may be forced to combine a national counterinsurgency strategy of persuasion with draconian measures that are applied to selected areas that seem beyond persuasion. In addition, even as a government responds to an insurgency with persuasion, the insurgents may choose, with or without the assistance of another state, to organize themselves into conventional military units and wage war in a more or less conventional fashion. Indeed, traditional Maoist strategy sought to reach this stage. In response, the government may use its own conventional forces while continuing its efforts at persuasion, supported by efforts to increase local security. In this case the response to the insurgency combines both measures short of war and war. (At different points in its long history, the U.S. involvement in Vietnam could illustrate this point.)

Similar distinctions can be made between war and peace in the amorphous category of events called contingency operations. Operations such as shows of force, punitive attacks, and raids and freedom-of-navigation exercises are peacetime operations because the purpose in using force is to persuade, not to destroy. There are, however, contingency operations that concentrate on destruction of capabilities. These must be classified as wars. Operation Just Cause is an example. After a number of measures short of war designed to put an end to Manuel Noriega's depredations, the United States decided to destroy the Panamanian Defense Force and take Noriega captive, thereby eliminating his capability to thwart U.S. objectives.

Just Cause and contingency operations like it may best be understood as a separate category of war, however. Since, from a strictly military point of view, the issue is not in doubt, success is defined as much by the political impact of using force as by the final results of combat, which are a foregone conclusion. In such cases attention should be placed on political goals and greater limitations should be accepted on the use of military force than in wars where military success, and thus the attainment of political goals, is in doubt. Of course, political considerations should not be such as to call success into question, but they may be such as to restrict lists of targets and acceptable weapons or to cause strategy and tactics to be changed. The planning and execution of such wars should be handled accordingly.

What such restrictions amount to is the dominance of policy or politics in strategic, operational, and even tactical decisions. The U.S. military considers such detailed intrusion anathema because it has focused on war fighting. In a war, as we have argued, the scope of policy and politics is restricted by the requirements of military success. In the environment short of war and even in small wars such as Just Cause, this is not the case. In such situations policy and politics do intrude into strategy, operations, and tactics. To ensure that this intrusion does not compromise success, policy and operations must be closely coordinated. This is perhaps the critical criterion for success, as is illustrated by America's recent experience with two activities that have become more important for the United States in the post–Cold War world, peacekeeping and peace enforcement.

Peacekeeping is the interposition of a neutral force between two formerly belligerent parties with their consent. It is by definition a peacetime activity. The interposing force provides the security that encourages or permits the belligerents to reach or maintain a peaceful solution. Peace enforcement, on the other hand, is the use of force to establish peace. By definition, the third party, the enforcing party, is a belligerent, because it wishes to impose its goal, peace, whether or not both parties want it. Unlike peacekeepers, who are neutral, peace enforcers take sides. Depending on the attitude of the parties involved, such a situation can easily pass from the use of force to persuade parties to accept a peaceful solution to the use of force to destroy a party's ability to resist an imposed solution. In Somalia peace enforcement was for a time tantamount to war against Mohammed Farah Aidid. During this period political considerations were subordinated to his pursuit and the destruction of his forces to a degree that was not the case when the United Nations was attempting to persuade him to become part of the process of national reconciliation. To some degree this effort failed because while the military recognized that it had crossed the threshold from persuasion to destruction, political leaders in Washington and New York did not, at least in some cases, recognize that this threshold had been crossed and that crossing it without informing and preparing the public for the possible costs of the decision might not be politically sustainable. The resulting confusion led to what was arguably a tactical success but, nevertheless, a political defeat.

CRITERIA FOR ENGAGEMENT

Having sketched the character of the environment short of war and having indicated some of the problems of operating there, we can now consider whether and how the United States should engage in this environment. This question is open now in a way it was not during the Cold War. In the past Americans correctly viewed events around the world in the context of confrontations with the Soviet Union, since it alone among other nations had the ability to project power and influence around the globe. The Soviets' willingness to support and exploit regional and unconventional threats made them the indirect or local expression of a broader strategic challenge to the United States, involving lines of communications, resources, and political influence. Soviet involvement or the involvement of Soviet proxies gave a significance to areas and problems that they would not otherwise have had. While containment had various interpretations, in general, it forced the United States to engage globally.

In the absence of the global Soviet threat, America will not have to respond to as many adverse social, political, and military developments as before. Now that there is no global power to exploit a potential naval base in a Third World country, for example, an insurgency in that country may no longer be of sufficient interest for the United States to expend any resources in helping its government. While U.S. interests require that the United States retain a widespread diplomatic and military presence, more substantial commitments of limited resources must be made more selectively if the United States is to avoid exhausting itself and thus undermining its ability over the long term to encourage a world hospitable to the American way of life.

The traditional way to calculate where, when, and how to engage resources focuses on factors of power and politics among nations, such as political goals, the goals of enemies and friends, and their past conduct, economic power, scientific and technological developments, geography, natural resources, governmental systems, and alliance structures. This traditional view considers none of these factors decisive in itself. Rather, it considers them together and in relation to each other. It recognizes that while most of them change slowly, they do change; calculations of interest and where to engage will change accordingly. At the moment, calculating with these various factors and considerations in mind suggests that in addition to the areas near American borders, Europe, Russia, Northeast Asia, China, India, and the Middle East are the regions and countries where it is most important for the United States to engage. At the same time, U.S. economic standing, counterproliferation of weapons of mass destruction, and the so-called military technical revolution are the most important security issues.

When adopted by the United States, this traditional approach is often said to emphasize its interests at the expense of its principles. Those who make this criticism are inclined to focus on such issues as building democracy, relieving human suffering, and promoting human rights, and on such subsidiary problems as environmental damage and population control. Focusing on such issues leads to a different list of priorities. If concern for human suffering and lack of democracy are most important to the United States, then Haiti, for example, might be a central issue in U.S. foreign policy. Dealing with it would require, as a Clinton administration official said, attacking the island's indigenous poverty by reshaping the economy. . . . But that's not all. We need to work on the court system and the administration of justice, on an independent legislature, on labor unions. And most importantly, we have to professionalize the Haitian Armed Forces and teach them to respect civilian authority.[10]

Merely reading this list and reflecting on the commitments of money and energy it implies suggest why devotion to building democracy and alleviating suffering is, in practice, sooner or later, leavened by due consideration of other factors. This results not only from encountering practical difficulties but from a certain logical and moral order that exists in human affairs. In order to enjoy peacefully and to share with others a life shaped according to American principles, it is necessary first to secure American interests. Practically speaking, decisions to engage mix consideration of interests with devotion to principle, all subject to the pressure of such dramatic events as a hostage taking or a natural disaster, which can take on a public profile that outweighs all other considerations.

In this ambiguous situation it is still possible to articulate some principles and guidelines that can serve to focus the United States on where to engage. These principles and guidelines should be regarded as broad standards for judgment and not as rigid rules or formulae to be applied mechanically. The diverse, complex situations the United States confronts will permit nothing more. The principles are moderation and conservation of resources, the guidelines discrimination and flexibility.

Moderation

The post–Cold War world allows the United States greater freedom than it had during the Cold War to promote democracy and free markets, since it no longer needs to support unrepresentative governments simply because they are willing to oppose the Soviets and serve as a building block in the wall of containment. Promoting democracy and liberal economics, however, can have consequences contrary to U.S. intentions. In such circumstances instability or attacks on American citizens by challenging established interests, igniting reactionary backlashes, or encouraging radical solutions can ultimately undermine liberty and lead to tyranny. Humanitarian assistance, such as distributing food, can also produce results contrary to U.S. intentions. For example, such food aid can disrupt traditional market mechanisms, making long-term recovery and self-sufficiency more difficult. Finally, intervention on behalf of struggling regimes also can run counter to long-standing U.S. commitments to the principle of self-determination. None of these problems require that we not promote democracy or offer humanitarian assistance, but they suggest that the United States should be content with modest objectives. When one is attempting to build democracy, it is necessary to promote broad principles such as representative government and free trade while accepting the inevitable limiting factors imposed by diverse cultural and political heritages. When one is confronted with such conflicts, distinctions must be made between conflict termination, which may occur unilaterally in accordance with U.S. interests, and conflict resolution, a fundamental resolution of the underlying causes of the conflict, which may not be within the power of the United States to effect.

Conservation of Resources

The deeply rooted nature of the problems America faces means that the struggle will be both protracted and costly relative to available resources and will often result in failures. In circumstances as problematic as these, the United States should conserve its resources by working through or with multilateral or regional organizations whenever feasible. In many cases a multilateral coalition, either under the auspices of the United Nations or a regional organization, will only be effective if it is led by a determined regional or global power. The United States may occasionally play that role, but most often it will want to exert influence by leveraging its greatest noncombatant strengths. Instead of combat forces, America should offer transportation, logistics, and intelligence and be more inclined to provide limited numbers of trainers, observers, liaison elements, and advisors, for example.

More specific criteria for selective engagement may be divided into two sets of guidelines: one, discrimination, concerning the criteria that should determine whether and when to engage; and the other, flexibility, concerning the criteria that should determine how to engage and with what means.

Discrimination

The United States engages overseas because it has interests at stake, for humanitarian reasons, or, intentionally or unintentionally, for a combination of these reasons. For example, it was in America's interest to destroy the Third Reich, but World War II was also a great humanitarian effort. Operation Sea Angel (disaster relief in Bangladesh in 1991) was undertaken as a purely humanitarian effort, but it also improved U.S. relations with a country and U.S. reputation around the world. In practice, motives are likely to be mixed. For the sake of clarity in our analysis, however, we should consider separately criteria for judging American self-interested and humanitarian motives for engagement.

American interests are at stake if an important regional balance of power will shift to America's disadvantage. This could occur when a regional hegemon's aggressive acts threaten important U.S. allies; when not responding would very likely encourage adversaries to undertake more threatening activities; when the threat from a regional hegemon would shake public support for and the credibility of important alliances; or when an important regional government is threatened or destabilized.

While many crises and disasters will engage U.S. humanitarian concern,

America should only commit its resources in such situations when the intervention or the manner of undertaking it (for example, unilaterally) does not sacrifice important U.S. interests. In a permissive environment, both short- and long-term disaster relief problems ought to be left to domestic and international nongovernmental relief agencies. U.S. Agency for International Development (USAID) programs should not be configured as short-term humanitarian assistance but rather as development assistance applied in such a way as to maximize regional economic growth and U.S. influence. The American government may want to make a tangible contribution to international efforts to relieve suffering in some short-term emergencies when aid agencies are not capable of rapid-enough response. If so, local circumstances and available U.S. resources should dictate the form and means for delivering such assistance.

The United States should not engage in a humanitarian intervention in a nonpermissive environment unless the need is extreme, a pending tragedy of historic proportions. This guideline will prevent America from continually allocating precious resources to inevitably recurring problems. In addition, if nonpermissive humanitarian assistance becomes routine, it may undermine the principle of sovereignty, as well as public support for engagement. Finally, the United States should not engage in such humanitarian efforts unless there is an international consensus for intervention, preferably expressed in a U.N. resolution; the intervention is part of a multilateral effort to which others contribute troops, supplies, or money; U.S. intervention is necessary to persuade others to participate in the humanitarian effort; America can limit its commitment to the resources necessary to galvanize a multilateral effort; or it can limit its commitment to the absolute minimum expenditure of resources necessary to accomplish the immediate humanitarian objective of preventing a catastrophe of historic proportions.

Finally, decisions about whether and when to engage for self-interested or humanitarian reasons should be guided by a few general considerations. The United States should intervene (assuming sufficient interests are at stake) or may intervene (for humanitarian reasons) when necessary resources are not likely to be engaged soon in more important areas (that is, the United States should give precedence to regions and the security problems of allies most important to the United States); when the problem is most susceptible to resolution with minimum U.S. resources; and when it is reasonable to expect that the United States can limit the engagement to an expenditure of resources commensurate with the U.S. interests at stake.

Any discussion of whether and when to engage should acknowledge that anytime the United States responds to a crisis, the response can change its interests. A commitment of troops or resources overseas also commits American prestige and influence. Protecting these can become an interest in itself and give the United States an unanticipated interest in a place or unexpected outcome. This is another reason care must be taken in selecting those cases where America intervenes for humanitarian reasons.

Flexibility

An appropriate decision about whether and when to engage is only the first step in effective operations in the environment short of war. Once the United States has made the decision to engage, it then becomes necessary to decide how and with what means to do so. The crucial step here is to determine the goals of the U.S. engagement and to place them in priority ranking. There will almost always be more than one goal and often several important goals. As the situation evolves, these goals may come into conflict or even end up being contradictory. Unless the United States has explicitly stated and ranked its goals, it may end up sacrificing a more important for a less important goal as a situation unfolds.

Placing the goals in some order of priority and attention to the principles of moderation and conservation of resources can help make the engagement efficient and effective. There are several guidelines that will contribute to the same result: (1) always plan for an engagement limited to an expenditure of resources commensurate with U.S. interests at stake; (2) engage the resources most appropriate to the problem at hand (that is, avoid defining the problem in terms of the most easily available resources; Marines may be offshore, but are they best suited for the mission?); and (3) compensate for the limited resources used in operations short of war by thoroughly integrating all instruments of national power, particularly diplomatic and military.

Either in the initial planning stages or at some point as the engagement unfolds, it may be necessary to consider the use of military force. Inherently a grave matter because it puts lives at risk, using force is also a critical issue because it creates the possibility of escalation beyond what American interests dictate, possibly putting more lives at risk without justification. If the military is deployed and attacked, especially if there are significant casualties or the wounded or captured are mistreated, there is an all but irresistible urge to do whatever is necessary to destroy the attacker or bring him to justice. So strong is this urge that some argue that America should not deploy the military unless it is willing to do whatever is necessary to avenge an attack. If accepted, this argument would mean either that the United States should deploy the military only where its interests justify a large-scale commitment of military force or that any place the military is deployed automatically becomes such a place. This argument risks preventing the deployment of military force in most of the situations encountered in the environment short of war or turning any such deployment into the virtual equivalent of a commitment to go to war.

This view of what military deployment requires rests upon the conviction that if the military is deployed, suffers a defeat or setback, and then withdraws or does not punish those who have attacked, America will suffer a crippling loss of prestige. This argument had more weight during the Cold War when the United States faced one predominant enemy in a virtual global struggle whose opposition was based on ideology as well as interest, and who could exploit a failure in one place by success in another. This situation no longer applies. America faces a variety of adversaries in different regional settings. Such adversaries may have prejudices, capabilities, and predilections that weigh against peaceful resolution. On the face of it, there is no reason to believe that all such adversaries will respond similarly to a setback suffered by the United States far from its borders. If disengaging from a problem in a marginal area diminishes American prestige, quick recovery can be made by a strong performance in another important area. In short, deterring the North Koreans does not require victory over Aidid in Somalia.

When considering the use of force, it is necessary to distinguish between decisive or overwhelming force and appropriate force. War calls for decisive or overwhelming force if possible because destroying enemy capabilities is the most immediate objective. Outside of war, overwhelming force is less likely to be appropriate. Some security threats in this environment cannot be removed by sheer power because adversaries have neither conventional forces to destroy nor capitals to seize. Moreover, overwhelming force may even be counterproductive to America's larger political purposes if it arouses nationalist sentiments or otherwise increases resentment of an American or allied presence, identifies the United States too closely with an outcome whose worth or durability it cannot guarantee, or creates a greater obligation for continued or deeper involvement.

An illustration of the difference between overwhelming and appropriate force comes from *The Village,* one of the best books ever written about the fighting in Vietnam.[11] In their battle with Vietcong and North Vietnamese forces, the Marines in the village learned that they were better off without the heavy firepower that artillery or helicopter gunships could provide. The damage these instruments of war caused undermined efforts to win the support of the villagers. What the Marines needed to prevail was the intelligence they could get only from the villagers. Without it, they were overrun. Because the Marines won the trust of the villagers, they were able to get the necessary intelligence, set an ambush, and defeat a much larger enemy unit, eventually securing the village.

The difference between overwhelming and appropriate force is important not just in counterinsurgency but in all engagements in the environment short of war. Consider counterterrorism. The use of overwhelming force against terrorists is problematic, since their groups do not have the solidity of states. Against whom or what does the United States use overwhelming force? America could try to kill every member of a terrorist group, but intelligence and logistical, not to mention moral, problems make this approach mostly ineffective. In some cases it might be effective to target the leaders, but others might arise to take their places or, if the group ceased to function, its expertise and personnel might simply pass on to another group.

While using overwhelming force against the state sponsors of terrorism might make more sense, it has not been called for. Contrary to some claims made in the 1980s, states have not yet used terrorism as part of a war or an unrestrained onslaught against the United States but as one foreign policy tool to be used as part of the forceful persuasion that makes up much of international relations. For these reasons, overwhelming force is not likely to be appropriate for counterterrorism. Instead, it requires the use of force as only a small part of a much larger effort to provide disincentives to terrorist groups and their sponsors, that is, force appropriate to the objectives sought and the motivations of the adversary.

To determine what appropriate use of force requires, two questions need to be addressed: First, at what point is the use of force necessary? This question implies that the critical point is whether the use of force is the most appropriate option at any given point in time. It does not imply that in every case the United States must exhaust all nonlethal means before using force, since in some cases this would abandon the initiative to the opponent in a way that might ultimately be detrimental to American interests.

Second, is the use of force under consideration commensurate with the interests the United States has at stake? This question implies that the United States has a range of interests that may justify a range of options and levels of force, such as a ship visit, covert military training, overt air support, or intervention with combat troops. It is not the case that there is a sharp line dividing two distinct categories: interests that justify the use of force and those that do not.

As noted earlier, when America uses force, it raises the stakes in any engagement. Even when force is not used, however, engagements may suffer from "mission creep," the assumption of policy goals or operational objectives that would commit resources beyond American interests. If the United States is engaged in a situation where its vital interests are at stake, "mission creep" is not a problem. The notion of vital interests implies that America would cease to exist if these were compromised. Thus it should be willing to spare no effort to see that they are not. When the United States engages for less than vital interests, there is an implicit commitment to engage only those resources commensurate with these interests. In these situations it is important to avoid making more than this commitment. To do so, the United States should strive to make sure that policy goals stay as limited as its interests and that operational objectives coincide with American policy goals at every stage of the involvement; that the United States engage in effective public and private diplomacy, making clear its operational objectives are limited by policy goals; that America has a plan for disengaging; that the United Nations or other appropriate authorities have a plan for taking over; that U.S. duties within the coalition and the coalition's command and control relationships are clearly spelled out; that the United States undertake no activities that incrementally expand U.S. objectives; and that all contacts with political leaders are handled primarily by the United Nations or the multilateral force, thus preventing the operation from becoming an American show. This last guideline applies only in those situations where America is sure that its goals and those of the United Nations or the multilateral force coincide. If there is disagreement about goals, then allowing others to take the political lead could result in the United States being committed inadvertently to goals beyond its interests.

These various guidelines, suggestions, and pointers may help national leaders to better determine whether and when to engage and how to do so most effectively. If followed, they will also help to facilitate disengagement by limiting commitments to specific interests. Making disengagement easier is important because disengagement is a vital part of any operation in the environment short of war. In these operations the United States frequently will confront adversaries who have greater interests at stake in a given situation than the United States does. Thus they will be willing to commit more resources, human and otherwise, than the United States. When adversaries increase the stakes, the only rational decision may be to withdraw. The importance of disengagement is now generally recognized, so much so that when any possible engagement is mentioned, an exit strategy is deemed necessary. While such a strategy may provide political cover and look good on paper before the engagement begins, it is unlikely to work once the United States is committed. There are several reasons for such a situation.

Engagement may often be the action of a coalition. This substantially reduces American ability to control events. The United States cannot dictate to the United Nations, other multilateral organizations, or its allies. Decisions taken in these complex settings may irreversibly commit the United States. Often the United States may not be able to remain disengaged until all its concerns are met, or it may forfeit the role of catalyst. If unilateral engagement is the case, that may generate interests that could undo a feasible exit strategy designed before the engagement. In addition, any commitment of military force raises the stakes in many incalculable ways. For these reasons and others, effective exit strategies will be easy to construct but difficult to implement. Engagements undertaken and organized according to the principles and guidelines outlined here are most likely to allow the United States a graceful exit.

A final point to consider when engaging is how to ensure that the engagement will have positive results in the long term. In addition to applying the principles and guidelines outlined here, several things can be done in planning an engagement that will improve the chances of producing positive effects in the long term. Efforts can be undertaken to ensure that policy goals articulated to all agencies include a description of the long-term U.S. goals and that these are included in operational planning. Military planning also must be done in coordination with other agencies. Planning to destroy the Panamanian Defense Force and capture Noriega, for example, was not sufficient to ensure that intervention in Panama would have positive results. Since the State Department and other agencies were not part of or privy to military planning, the coordination between the Department of Defense (DOD) and the State Department and other agencies was faulty. Securing the positive effects of intervention requires that all operational planning be interagency planning and that this cooperation take place from the beginning. The critical point is that nonmilitary agencies be aware of the likely consequences of military action and that plans be established to coordinate military and civilian efforts or, in the case of the transition from war to the environment short of war, as in Panama, to make the transition from military to civilian authority as smooth as possible. Similarly, to ensure that humanitarian interventions produce positive long-term results, private voluntary organizations (PVOs) and nongovernmental organizations (NGOs) should be involved early in planning for the transition to their assuming leadership.

DETERMINING APPROPRIATE DOD MISSIONS

The Department of Defense has long undertaken a wide variety of missions besides war fighting. With the end of the Cold War, the number of proposed peacetime missions has grown considerably to cover everything from armed humanitarian intervention to teaching in inner-city schools. To sort through these various activities and choose those that are appropriate for DOD, we need to understand the core mission of DOD. We can define this mission as the use of organized violence to attain national objectives. This is what DOD does that no other agency of the U.S. government can do. Carrying out this mission has given DOD capabilities, such as its logistical capacity, that can be applied in ways not directly related to its core mission. American national interests may require DOD to use these capabilities to perform tasks not essentially military, such as those typically included in the term *humanitarian assistance.* Or policymakers, confronted with unanticipated situations for which DOD capabilities provide a ready-to-hand response, will call on DOD to use its capabilities in missions not related to its primary function. In either case there are several reasons not to confuse these ancillary capabilities with DOD's core mission or to allow them to eclipse this core mission.

Civilian Authority

As a matter of general principle, military influence in civilian affairs must be limited, both overseas and at home. It is a fundamental principle of American democracy that the military not assume civilian authority. For this reason, laws have long recognized a difference between federal troops and those under the authority of a state governor. The National Guard has long had only a narrow and clearly defined role in state and local affairs. There is even more reason to limit the role of federal troops in these matters. Similarly, experience over the last decades indicates that in dealing with nations that do not have well-established democratic traditions, it is prudent to discourage military involvement in civilian affairs.

Military Effectiveness

While the military can bring some formidable capabilities to bear on non-military problems—martial efficiency, effective organization and training, massive and sometimes unique assets—tackling problems in the civilian sector for an extended period would require the military to become more like its civilian counterparts. Ultimately this might blunt the very characteristics that make the military efficient at waging war. If martial efficiency and military organization and training are relevant to nonmilitary problems, the preferred solution should be to transplant these characteristics to those civilian agencies normally tasked with these problems. Generally speaking, however, these characteristics cannot be transplanted because the civilian environment imposes more constraints than does the military.

Efficiency

Expanding DOD's activities would lead to redundancy within the American government. For example, USAID can hire civilian contractors to build bridges or to teach others how to do so. Ignoring strict criteria for involving DOD in peacetime activities will create the ironic situation that increased attention to roles and missions within DOD will be accompanied by a growing willingness to tolerate confusion and redundancy between DOD and other agencies of the U.S. government.

Given these considerations, it will be reasonable to task the military to handle nonmilitary problems only in a small number of cases where military involvement can be limited and the military has unique capabilities appropriate to the problem. In this connection, two general rules are suggested:

1. DOD elements overseas have reason to be involved in nonmilitary activities only if these activities provide them with training conditions unavailable elsewhere, area familiarization, tactical intelligence, or access to a foreign military or are required by local security conditions.
2. To such factors must also be added broader geostrategic considerations. Given an option between deployment in either of two locations, the choice should be made on the basis of answers to questions such as the following: Where is it more likely that American forces will be deployed in the future? What kind of political-military signal are we sending, and to whom, by undertaking the mission in location X rather than Y?

In addition to these general principles governing the use of DOD, two nonmilitary uses of DOD should be considered because of the special questions they raise. These include nation assistance and newly defined security threats.

Nation Assistance

Combat support and combat service support capabilities, such as engineering and medical care, when used to provide assistance to other nations, are frequently grouped under the term *nation assistance.* In general, proponents of these activities cite one of two reasons for undertaking them. They argue that these are part of a civic action effort directed at winning the support of local populations for U.S. or host-nation troops or are part of a general effort to spur development, with the understanding that development will decrease the causes of conflict in a society.

Nation assistance as a civic action effort is an appropriate use of DOD capabilities because it is a necessary accompaniment to military activities, whether in training or operations, directly related to the core mission of DOD. Nation assistance as an effort to assist development, on the other hand, is inappropriate for DOD for two reasons. First, assisting development in any meaningful sense is beyond the U.S. government's and, even more so, the DOD's capabilities because the resources available for such work are insignificant compared to the work to be done. More important, the attitudes and dispositions of a local population and government are more important for development than the capital infusions and technical expertise outsiders can provide. Second, even if the American government and DOD promote development, this would not necessarily diminish conflict, since development may create the conditions for conflict.[12] Nor is economic development an adequate prophylactic for conflict generated by political aspirations or deep-seated religious or ethnic animosities. Thus development assistance aimed at general socioeconomic improvement will not diminish the virulence of terrorism or an insurgency to the extent that they derive their energy from sources unrelated to access to economic opportunities and rewards.

DOD nation-assistance missions should not be undertaken primarily to improve general social and economic development. They may still be useful, however, as part of the more modest, yet still difficult effort to increase U.S. influence. Increased influence, in turn, can mean greater ability to persuade a host government to pursue sound political and economic policies, a prerequisite for stable growth.

Newly Defined Security Threats

There is a growing trend toward defining a threat as an action or event that degrades the quality of life of the inhabitants of a state or limits the options of its policymakers. This approach argues that such events as economic decline, environmental degradation, massive earthquakes in California, overpopulation, the spread of acquired immune deficiency syndrome (AIDS), a deteriorating educational system, and resource scarcities should all be considered threats to U.S. national security. This new definition of "threat" should not be accepted because doing so will blur an important distinction. Threats traditionally have been understood to be the result of an enemy's decision or intentions. Natural disasters, on the other hand, simply happen, while bad economic or educational policies are self-inflicted wounds. Responses to these events are correspondingly different. Armed aggression, for example, can be deterred; earthquakes cannot.

States can be persuaded to change their policies; AIDS cannot be persuaded to go away. Conflating all these events into a broader definition of "threat" and "security" obscures important differences between them and makes the term *security threat* no more analytically useful than the term *bad.*[13]

This issue of conceptual clarity is important because if the definitions of "threat" and "security" become uselessly broad, clarity about activities proper to DOD will become more difficult to maintain. While elements of DOD may be able to help with the aftermath of an earthquake, for example, or with irrigation projects in the Middle East, DOD must remain focused on its primary purpose: the threat and use of organized violence in pursuit of our national interests.

PEACETIME ENGAGEMENT PRINCIPLES

Having set down some general criteria for peacetime engagement and the DOD's role, we need to consider more specifically the requirements for success in the environment short of war. Success requires above all adherence to three principles, which are discussed in this section, and also some specialized capabilities, which are reviewed in the closing section of this chapter. Briefly stated, the principles for peacetime engagement are continuous and detailed coordination of policy and operations, which means ensuring that national priorities and objectives are appropriately and consistently translated into operational and even tactical objectives; unity of effort, which requires interagency coordination of diverse policy instruments; and anticipatory and sustained engagement in problem identification and resolution. This section will explain why peacetime engagement principles are necessary for success, why they are difficult to follow consistently, and how even modest modifications to the U.S. approach to peacetime engagements with these principles in mind could improve U.S. performance in operations short of war.

Why Peacetime Engagement Principles Are Necessary

Policy-Operations Coordination

Few would object to the proposition that every security strategy ought to be formulated and implemented through a process that (1) successfully establishes policy priorities; (2) translates policy objectives into realistic operational tasks, that is, ensures that operations are a direct extension of policy requirements and that policy is consistent with operational limitations; and (3) effectively communicates these objectives and tasks to those responsible for implementing the tasks.

In short, policy and operations must be carefully conducted to ensure that operations are designed to achieve policy objectives, but also to ensure that policy does not compromise the success of operations and thus become self-defeating. This process of policy-operations coordination deserves special emphasis in operations short of war because it is both more important and more difficult to effect in these operations than in war.

In war, policy-operations coordination is critical primarily at the strategic level and only with respect to a limited number of broad issues. National policy objectives during war largely hinge upon military success. Military failure or partial success severely limits what political objectives are possible. Given the stakes, national strategy directs vast resources to the war effort, commands all instruments of national policy to support military objectives, and in general gives as much leeway as possible to military considerations in planning for the conflict. Since sacrificing the primary national objectives to military expediency would render the use of force meaningless, the President and his advisors will invariably see the need to put some constraints on the way the military goes about the task of destroying the enemy's forces and seizing his territory. Otherwise, military necessity takes precedence over all other political objectives.

The opposite is true in operations short of war. Military necessity is more subordinate to political considerations at all levels because national objectives and means are more limited, policy objectives are more fluid, and other national policy instruments are more important. Since measures short of war are adopted in order to avoid the risks and costs of war, by definition national policy limits the resources available to the effort and engages other policy instruments with greater emphasis and rigor. To the extent that military force is used, it is applied primarily not to destroy or defend capabilities, but to directly influence political relationships, which requires assistance from and close coordination with economic, political, and informational policy instruments at the strategic level, but also at the operational and tactical levels as well.

Another reason policy must more directly influence the details of operational planning in operations short of war is that policy goals are more fluid in these operations. Unlike war, measures short of war are often undertaken for less than immediately vital interests and thus are inherently more susceptible to negotiation and revision. Working with limited assets and often through third parties, operators may not be able to achieve objectives at costs that are commensurate with the interests at stake. This means that national objectives may change several times, even frequently, before the problem is resolved.

In addition, operations short of war are often more ambiguous situations in that oppositional forces are not always clearly discernible. The role of one or more adversaries may evolve; some may even switch sides. Besides the adversary, other causal factors may be complicating the problem. As relevant players and factors become known with greater precision, policy will evolve, taking on greater specificity, and operational planning will have to keep pace. Thus coordinating effective U.S. political-military measures short of war is an iterative process whereby planning must be continually reviewed and adjusted as an unfolding situation requires.

For example, as in the case of the 1965 intervention in the Dominican Republic, it may be that only a broad goal such as "prevent another Cuba" will be articulated in the first round of decision making. The first set of operational tasks derived from this general goal could be to put troops ashore to increase U.S. options, foreclose those of adversaries, and generally gain leverage. Later the precise mission assigned to the military commander—whether it be to destroy rebel forces, to supervise elections and restore order, or to act as a peacekeeping force separating belligerents who must be brought to negotiations—will be determined as the specific political and military context is clarified.

Unity of Effort/Interagency Coordination

A close corollary to the principle of policy-operations coordination is that of unity of effort, or the close coordination for maximum effect of diverse policy instruments either jointly or individually exercised by different national departments and agencies. Two of the same factors that increase the importance of policy-operations coordination also increase the importance of interagency coordination. First, the shift in focus from destroying enemy forces in war to modifying policies or political relationships in operations other than war greatly increases the importance of other policy instruments. Economic, political, and informational assets are as relevant as the military for diminishing support for insurgency or terrorism, or for increasing the likelihood that a tenuous peace agreement will be respected. Second, as noted earlier, obtaining maximum leverage in circumstances inherently constrained by limited objectives, resources, and methods requires close coordination of multiple policy instruments at the strategic, operational, and even tactical levels.

Anticipatory and Sustained Engagement

Anticipatory and sustained engagement is the third principle that ought to guide how the United States organizes for operations short of war. Too often when one is dealing with a problem short of war, the tendency is to ignore it until it demands attention, manage the resultant crisis until it is no longer in the headlines, and then abandon the effort. Reactive crisis management rather than proactive threat management is generally more expensive and less effective. While not always possible, engaging a problem sooner makes solving or managing it easier at costs that are commensurate with the interests a nation has at stake.

It also is generally true that many of the problems the United States confronts in peacetime cannot be resolved with a single decisive engagement; they require sustained attention over time. Even when military force has been used in a brief, sharp engagement, such as during Operations El Dorado Canyon, Urgent Fury, and Just Cause, securing national objectives can require sustained preparation and follow-up. The counterterrorism value of bombing Libya in 1986 came not from the immediate impact on Qaddafi's attitude so much as from follow-on counterterrorism cooperation with allies. Failure to properly plan and prepare for the invasion of Grenada, particularly with respect to gathering intelligence, compromised the attainment of national objectives and made that operation more costly than necessary, as did the failure to plan for postcrisis responsibilities following the destruction of the Panamanian Defense Force.[14]

In addition to better policy-operations and interagency coordination, therefore, success in operations short of war requires the United States to better anticipate problems and prepare for sustained engagement in their resolution. The best way to secure anticipatory and sustained engagement is to institutionalize planning that divides any operation short of war into one, several, or all of four possible mission areas: diplomacy and support for diplomacy, precrisis activities, force projection and crisis response, and postcrisis initiatives. Constant reference to these four mission areas would facilitate, if not require, greater attention to policy-operations and interagency coordination, improve planning and coordination by providing a common framework for understanding and discussing peacetime engagement, provide a framework for the development of interagency doctrine, and, most important, require systematic attention to critical mission requirements often overlooked or devalued by planners.

Diplomacy and Support for Diplomacy

By far, most peacetime engagement activities fall in the "diplomacy and support for diplomacy" mission area. In peacetime, for the most part, the Department of State takes the lead as the United States pursues its interests through influence building, persuasion, and negotiation. Therefore, DOD, USAID, Treasury, Commerce, USIA, and other U.S. agencies with overseas responsibilities largely work in support of the Department of State. DOD, for example, works to build American influence through training, security and humanitarian assistance, foreign internal defense, civil-military operations, peacekeeping operations, and disaster relief, among other activities. The fact that the Department of State has the lead does not mean that other agencies are not crucial to success. Effective diplomacy presupposes the power to reward and punish, which can be accomplished by multiple means. U.S. diplomacy, therefore, presupposes the existence of, and the will to use, all elements of U.S. national power, particularly military and economic might, as circumstances require.

Precrisis Activities

One of the principal attractions of employing measures short of war is that they hold open the possibility that the United States might be able to preclude, retard, or diminish security problems before they become crises. Normal diplomatic activities and support for these activities play a large role in fulfilling this promise, but America also needs to think of defusing incipient crises as a specific mission area. Doing this will be difficult because it goes against the U.S. disinclination to address problems aggressively before they reach the stage where they pose a visible, almost direct threat. But the effort should be made nonetheless. Even if the crisis comes, precrisis activities will have better prepared the country to deal with it.

Once an incipient crisis is recognized, there are a number of actions that can be taken. For example, the United States could begin intensified bilateral and multilateral diplomacy in order to gather allied and regional support. Technical intelligence coverage would also increase, perhaps with particular attention to the motivations and objectives of the leadership cadre. DOD assets might also be activated and moved into place both to signal U.S. intentions and to prepare for force projection and crisis response, if necessary. Most important, at this point America should be preparing clear policy objectives and guidelines for the potential crisis, as well as activating all necessary mechanisms to ensure that these objectives and guidelines are included in all operational planning.

Force Projection and Crisis Response

This mission area commonly is the focus of both military and civilian agencies. Examples include a show of force, a hostage rescue, disaster relief, a security assistance surge, or a freedom-of-navigation exercise, as well as such large-scale contingency operations as Just Cause. These examples emphasize the military aspect of crisis response, but there are also crises, such as the Mexican debt crisis of the early 1980s, that require a swift, coordinated, interagency response.

Postcrisis Activities

Because of the American tendency to think that force and diplomacy are discrete, discontinuous activities, there is a tendency not to move well from one to the other. Emphasizing "postcrisis activities" as a separate peacetime engagement mission would help to rectify this problem. It should cause various government agencies to think about what needs to be done in the aftermath of a crisis or military action in order that what was gained through effective crisis response not be lost by failure to follow up or address lingering problems. Postcrisis activities might include follow-on diplomatic initiatives such as maintaining coalition involvement, negotiating treaties or security agreements, or providing reconstruction assistance, as well as peacekeeping and sharing lessons learned among allies and coalition partners.

The four mission areas need not occur sequentially. A hijacking would immediately put the United States in a crisis-response situation, for example. A natural disaster, on the other hand, could immediately involve the American government in postcrisis initiatives. In any case, structuring planning for operations other than war with these four mission areas would naturally draw attention to the importance of policy-operations and interagency coordination, and to critical mission requirements that often are undervalued by national security planners.

Why Adherence to Peacetime Engagement Principles Is Problematic

The principles for peacetime engagement discussed here—continuous and detailed coordination of policy and operations, unity of effort, and anticipatory and sustained engagement—are difficult to follow consistently for two reasons. First, there is an inverse relationship between the requirement for policy-operations and interagency coordination in operations short of war and the attention of senior decision makers to this need. During war the entire nation's attention is focused on the task of defeating an enemy. Senior decision makers and the national security bureaucracy are alert to the need for cooperation and effective execution of policy. Moreover, policy objectives are relatively simple and revolve around defeating principal and auxiliary enemy forces. Hence cooperation between agencies is easier.

In peacetime principal decision makers must contend with competing and unrelated duties; during specific operations or crises, they must face policy objectives that are complex and evolving. The result is less attention to the innumerable operational issues that must be informed by policy and less attention to interagency coordination as well. Problems caused by inattention from senior decision makers are compounded by less attention from the bureaucracy. Unlike war, peacetime engagements do not mobilize the bureaucracy to undertake a single, focused effort. Normal bureaucratic proclivities reign; less interagency cooperation is the norm. This is especially the case when decision makers assume that they control the bureaucracy and that interagency cooperation occurs as a matter of course.

Lack of consensus on the validity of need for peacetime engagement principles is the second reason they are not followed.[15] This becomes clear when discussing operations short of war with senior leadership in the Pentagon, Department of State, Central Intelligence Agency, and National Security Council. Some maintain that there are no problems with U.S. performance in the environment short of war. Others acknowledge that the U.S. record in operations short of war is far from perfect, but they attribute this to the fact that these types of problems are inherently difficult to control and believe that all things considered, the United States manages these problems as well as they can be managed. Finally, some recognize that U.S. performance in the environment short of war suggests substantial room for improvement, but believe that the factors limiting U.S. performance are inherent in its society and government, and thus remedial action is not politically possible. All three of these points of view can be partially substantiated by some important but limited truths that are worth reviewing.

Peacetime Engagements Are Situation-Dependent

Regional experts often contend that there is no possibility for systematic improvement because they believe that each regional security problem is unique. It is true that every peacetime engagement problem is unique and requires substantial regional/local expertise to be dealt with effectively. However, a specific response that does not take into account broader regional and even global policies risks running counter to other existing national objectives or addressing short-term concerns at the expense of longer-term priorities. If functional experts are not brought in to contribute to the policy process, the response developed by the regional experts may be based on false assumptions or may risk repeating mistakes made in earlier similar circumstances known to the functional experts.

Lack of Decisive Control

Many senior national security officials believe that peacetime engagements cannot be deterred or managed. They often say that the subject matter is, after all, inherently complex and the degree of control in such political-military problems is not substantial. Thus the U.S. record is probably as good as can be expected. They usually conclude that problems short of war must be handled on the fly and that the United States really does crisis management as well as or better than other states.[16]

Measures short of war are inherently problematic and often produce ambiguous results. First of all, the problem itself is often rooted in forces not easily controlled by traditional policy instruments. Second, those policy instruments that can be brought to bear often are exercised through third parties, which significantly affect the degree of control over the effectiveness of the implementation strategy and hence the likely results. It is also true that many crises short of war cannot be anticipated and must be managed, at least initially, in a reactive mode. Finally, domestic political concerns complicate planning and crisis management.

Nevertheless, these factors do not necessarily mean that the United States cannot improve its effectiveness in applying measures short of war. Both the requirement to conduct crisis management and the way it is done can be improved. Good staff work and effective interagency coordinating mechanisms should allow national security staff to alert principal decision makers far enough in advance to occasionally permit preventive action. When a preventive response is not possible, good staff work by regional and functional experts can still prepare principals for effective decision making and implementation.

American Cultural Limitations

Finally, many believe that the steps commonly suggested for improving U.S. management of operations short of war cannot be implemented because they run directly counter to deeply embedded characteristics of the American people. Americans accept only short-term, clear-cut, inexpensive but decisive solutions. Americans tend to simplify, seeing war and peace as separate states. They prefer logical to political solutions, which often seem to compromise American values. Americans prefer to engage against antagonists only when they clearly are moral inferiors. The problems often confronted, on the other hand, are complex, deep rooted, and stubborn. The "enemy" is often hard to identify. Success is hard to measure and not always permanent. In short, Americans tend not to be sympathetic to the protracted application of multiple policy instruments to problems that will be periodically redefined, which is essentially the requirement for managing problems short of war.

It is possible to overstate the extent to which American proclivities limit the ability of statesmen to manage well operations short of war. The conventional wisdom that the American public will not tolerate casualties is a good example. The point is not that Americans will not accept sacrifice, but rather that the sacrifice must seem commensurate with the cause engaged and the prospect of success. The lower the stakes and the less likely the prospect for visible progress, the fewer the casualties that will be politically sustainable. Like other American characteristics, the great respect accorded the individual and human life in general helps define the strategy and means available to American statesmen, but does not preclude successful execution of engagements short of war according to the principles advocated.

Nevertheless, American cultural proclivities are the most serious limitation on effective employment of measures short of war. U.S. strategy in this environment must always take into account the need for public support. It can be disastrous to obscure the sacrifices required for success or overstate the level of success that is likely to be achieved. Every president has employed measures short of war, but not all have done so with due regard for public sensitivities. The prudent American statesman will fully explain the peacetime engagements for which he requires public support and avoid committing U.S. combat troops except in dire circumstances or in those cases when sacrifices are likely to be low and progress toward stated objectives steady.

PEACETIME ENGAGEMENTS: A MODEST AGENDA

Reviewing such criticisms is sobering. It suggests that while it is possible to improve U.S. performance in the environment short of war, recommendations and expectations should be modest. The first priority should be to convince senior decision makers that a proactive, sustained, and coordinated interagency effort in the environment short of war is not possible without clear guidance on policy objectives and operational taskings. For example, Presidential Decision Directives that establish guidance for operations short of war should rank priorities. Principals' meetings (cabinet-member level) should have minutes that record decisions, but not the background discussions, since this might have a chilling effect on the free flow of opinion. These minutes should be distributed to lower echelons.

Operational information—particularly in DOD—must be constantly circulated, with due regard for security, to ensure an informed, effective, iterative decision-making process for operations short of war. The Joint Staff and Office of the Secretary of Defense need to review jointly methods for constant sharing of information on policy and operations. There is also a need to develop doctrine for the integration of civilian and military operations. This is already beginning. The Joint Staff is producing a Joint Doctrine Publication 3-08 on *Interagency Coordination during Joint Operations,* which is a good first step.

With respect to interagency coordination, there are educational, structural, and procedural improvements that could be made. Temporary assignment to interagency or other agency jobs should be encouraged as a prerequisite for advancement to senior management positions in national security agencies. Unfortunately, the opposite is happening. Budget cuts and staff reductions are encouraging a reduction in the detailing of personnel from one national security agency to another. In partial compensation, educational programs should be designed to acquaint senior management with the reasons other departments and agencies tend to define problems differently. Such training would better prepare individuals for interagency problem solving.[17]

Improvements can also be made in interagency structures. The U.S. government currently has in place a variety of mechanisms, centered in the National Security Council, for facilitating interagency cooperation. For example, there are regional and functional Interagency Working Groups (IWGs). At the tactical level, the Country Team, supported by the interagency process, manages both crises and the myriad day-to-day activities that make up U.S. forward presence. While no one would argue that coordination takes place without problems at either the strategic or tactical level, missing entirely are mechanisms for interagency coordination at the operational level, at the level of the region as a whole. The IWGs focus on either articulating general policy (for example, Presidential Decision Directives) or handling particular problems or crises, while the focus of the Country Team is entirely local. Coordination is needed for Department of State and DOD regional planning based on joint periodic planning sessions between CINC representatives and robust State Department regional planning cells.

Enhancing interagency coordination will require better coordination at all three levels, strategic, operational, and tactical. Improvements at the strategic and operational levels are most important, in part because they will facilitate improvements at the tactical level. Improvements at the strategic and operational levels will require the enhancement of the NSC's role in coordinating the President's policies and in ensuring unity of effort by the U.S. government, both in crisis management and in more routine policy problem solving in the environment short of war. The following are examples:

1. The NSC should manage national security issues, not be another policy voice. Active management would facilitate interagency coordination by tasking issues, clarifying differences, and recommending issues for resolution to higher authority. Lower-level meetings should be structured to produce summaries of interagency differences so that they may be highlighted for resolution by senior decision makers.

2. The National Security Council should more regularly lead interagency coordination exercises for specific emerging problems. In the past such games have

improved interagency coordination in both the planning for and the conduct of the operations.

3. For standing issues, the NSC should institute small, high-level interagency groups to meet regularly and frequently. These groups can focus on a particular regional problem, such as democratization in Haiti, or on a functional problem, such as counterproliferation. Historically the most effective interagency groups have been small (five or six members) and high-level (Assistant Secretary) and have met regularly and frequently, developing mutual trust and effective cooperation.

Modest steps such as these to improve policy-operations and interagency coordination, along with systematic attention to the full spectrum of activities required for anticipatory and sustained engagement, should produce interagency operations better tailored to accomplish top policy priorities. As individual agencies and departments articulate policy and operational details consistent with overarching guidance and are confident that such guidance has been fully understood in the field, there should be greater willingness to leave specific implementation of plans to those on the scene. In turn, those responsible for implementing policy will receive consistent guidance, be less burdened by a cacophony of suggestions and directions, and be more able to concentrate on asking for critical guidance when they need it.

Without steps to improve the management of measures short of war, it seems certain that the United States will continue to have problems in this area. Establishing static and vague goals and hoping that the National Command Authority's intent is somehow deciphered and communicated to lower echelons and effectively translated into operational objectives have not produced a track record of success. American performance in operations short of war will not improve without a system designed to achieve the latest iteration of policy objectives both in fast-moving, ambiguous situations and in longer-term problem-solving efforts that are unlikely to attract the sustained attention of senior leaders.

PEACETIME ENGAGEMENT CAPABILITY

The peacetime engagement principles articulated in the previous section constitute the "just fighting smarter" portion of the solution to improving American performance in environments short of war. The rest of the solution is to develop the right capabilities—the proper tools in the tool box, so to speak. Of the innumerable capabilities that may be applied in peacetime engagements, most are resident within our current military forces, the Central Intelligence Agency, the Department of State, and other bureaucracies that serve our national security. There are, however, some capabilities that either are uniquely required by operations short of war or are similar to those necessary for war but are so much more important in operations short of war that they deserve special emphasis.

A full explanation of the special capabilities required by operations short of war will not be presented here for two reasons. First, many of the military capabilities necessary for the environment short of war are explained in various chapters in this book. It is more important here to provide a framework for understanding the types of capabilities required and why the Department of Defense is reluctant to provide them. Second, the focus of this book is on military capabilities. We will not address the capabilities that other agencies need to be better prepared for peacetime engagement in the post–Cold War world except as these relate to the role of the DOD.

Security assistance is a good example. Most country military assistance programs such as foreign military sales and financing or international military education and training that are designed to assist friends and allies to maintain internal stability are funded by a security assistance budget controlled by the Department of State. Security assistance programs, which determine how DOD can support many peacetime engagements, will become more important in the post–Cold War world as the United States draws down its overseas basing and reduces forward deployment and presence. However, in recent years more than 95 percent of the security assistance budget has been allocated to only a few countries in the Middle East, primarily Israel and Egypt. Even a minor reduction in the amount of funds earmarked for these countries would greatly increase the flexibility of security assistance as a policy tool for the environment short of war.

DOD Peacetime Engagement Capabilities

DOD should provide the assets and planning capabilities necessary for effective performance in the four peacetime engagement missions: support for diplomacy, precrisis activities, force projection and crisis response, and postcrisis activities. DOD has long undertaken most of the activities associated with peacetime engagement missions, which are referred to in Joint Staff doctrine as ''operations other than war,'' but usually does so with whatever resources it has available for fighting major conventional force-on-force conflicts. Despite periodically ruminating in conferences, war games, and military educational institutions about what it takes to perform operations other than war well, DOD has proven extremely reluctant to provide capabilities uniquely well suited for such activities.

The primary reason DOD will not devote separate resources to peacetime engagement capabilities is that it is rightly preoccupied with the task of deterring, fighting, and winning the nation's wars. Whenever operations short of war are introduced in war games along with a war scenario, they are dismissed as secondary problems. When it is acknowledged that success in operations other than war requires some specialized capabilities, as in the Clinton administration's recent review of defense force structure requirements, they are not addressed specifically.[18] Either they are considered to be ''below-the-line'' forces, too small to deserve inclusion with major ships of the line, Army and Marine divisions, and air wings, or they are ignored because their identification would require resource allocation in a time of severe budget cutbacks.

Another reason DOD does not devote resources to operations other than war is that it does not really understand what capabilities are necessary for success. A large part of this confusion is due to the fact that the capabilities necessary for success often spill over into areas traditionally handled by other agencies. Therefore, even when the capabilities are specifically identified, the tendency in DOD is either to ''militarize'' the requirement so that it is more readily identified as a military mission or to demand that other agencies supply the capability.

A good example is special operations forces (SOFs). SOFs are generally recognized to be especially appropriate forces for a wide range of operations other than war. The regional, cultural, and linguistic skills of some SOFs make these ''warrior-diplomats'' good choices for dealing with complex military-political problems, but also blur their capabilities with those traditionally cultivated at the Department of State. Some SOFs also have refined abilities to use force with an absence of any collateral damage, which make them the forces of choice for rescuing hostages overseas, but also overlap with capabilities usually associated with the FBI or large urban police departments. The rest of the military often responds to the unique skills of SOFs by trying to make them more relevant to conventional military operations.

For these reasons DOD probably will never devote any major resources to peacetime engagement preparedness per se, but it might be encouraged to develop some inexpensive specialized capabilities, especially if they can be shown to have value in conventional war as well. Instead of more traditional military categories such as command, control, communications, intelligence, and force projection and protection, we categorize the unique or especially important military capabilities necessary for success in peacetime engagements in four groups that highlight their relationship to capabilities traditionally associated with other elements of national power. Doing so emphasizes how operations short of war are different from war because they focus not exclusively but primarily on persuasion rather than destruction of adversary capabilities, and why they are therefore looked at askance by the military establishment in general.

Internal Development Assistance

Often when DOD is called upon to participate in disaster relief, counterinsurgency, peace enforcement, or other contingency operations, it is required to provide immediate, short-term assistance to meet a wide range of human and social needs. DOD must undertake such activities not because it is supplanting the role of the U.S. Agency for International Development, private voluntary organizations, and other international aid organizations dedicated to development assistance, but because the environment is unstable, violent, or demanding enough that only DOD can deliver the assistance. Frequently the aid is delivered more for political than economic reasons. For example, providing assistance in order to build goodwill with a local populace may be necessary to secure the cooperation of the locals in missions more directly relevant to the exercise of armed force.

When DOD must provide development assistance, it finds most of the relevant resources included in its combat service and combat service support forces. These forces are dedicated to sustaining combat forces in an area of operations and include administrative services, civil affairs, finance, legal services, health services, military police, supply, maintenance, transportation, construction, topographic and geodetic engineering functions, food services, and other logistic services. Even with all this at hand, DOD could still provide some marginal improvements in its ability to support internal development activities. For example, DOD is currently being directed to develop new food rations that will be better received in different cultures and is investigating means for humanitarian demining over wide areas as opposed to the more relevant military mission of breaching mine fields. It might also consider the requirements for protective gear for military forces involved in disaster relief in a high–AIDS-threat environment.

For the most part, however, DOD has the necessary capabilities for supporting development and humanitarian activities and will improve them only as a byproduct of military requirements. For example, real-time computerized tracking of all DOD equipment and supplies may improve DOD's ability to support aid agencies handling large refugee flows, but it will be developed first and foremost to improve DOD logistics and financial accounting. What DOD must do better is plan for the employment of its combat service and combat service support forces for purposes other than combat support. Although the Marine Corps realized the importance of liaison with private voluntary organizations in Somalia, with which it had to coordinate efforts to ensure the delivery of humanitarian assistance, it underutilized Army Civil Affairs units for this purpose.

Even when the importance of these forces is recognized, it is difficult to gain access to them because so many are in the Federal Reserves. Access to some combat service and combat service support forces, such as Civil Affairs forces, through existing call-up legislation has proven to be complicated and time-consuming. A possible solution to this problem currently being worked on by the Department of Defense is to give the Secretary of Defense, when requested by a combatant Commander-in-Chief, statutory authority to call up limited numbers of Civil Affairs and other unique reserve units to participate in contingency-operation planning and execution.

Internal Security

Operations other than war also require DOD to perform a variety of missions associated with assuring internal security and law and order, missions more frequently associated with the Department of Justice. In most cases DOD works with foreign national police or paramilitary security forces when it combats terrorism, conducts counterdrug operations, assists American law-enforcement agencies, or assists allies threatened by internal subversion or insurgency. In other cases U.S. forces may be required to enforce law and order directly. In the aftermath of a disaster where public order has broken down and cannot be restored by local police, U.S. forces may impose martial law. Alternatively, following a contingency operation during which U.S. military forces have destroyed another nation's internal security forces, as happened during Operation Just Cause in Panama, or where U.S. forces intervene in an internal conflict in which local security forces are at war with one another, as happened in Somalia, the United States is required to enforce law and order with its own troops.

Any U.S. combat forces can find themselves directly engaged in internal security missions or assigned to support law-enforcement agencies, but the most obvious choices are light and special operations forces. Light units are more mobile than heavy forces and thus more appropriate for chasing down insurgents, terrorists, and narcotics traffickers or maintaining order in an urban environment. Special operations forces are even better suited to these tasks because of the cross-cultural and language skills and experience. Areas for improvement in current U.S. military capabilities to provide law and order abound. This means that the following capabilities need to be considered and developed: less lethal means of crowd control; the means to collect more detailed intelligence on individuals and subversive organizations; stealthy unmanned aerial observation vehicles for monitoring the movement of urban guerrillas; better mine countermeasures; more sophisticated psychological operations techniques and equipment; rapid and very precise countersniper and countermortar capabilities; robotic bomb disposal; rapid urban mapping and overhead electronic intelligence collection; analysis and dissemination; and unintrusive detection methods for locating weapons.

Building, Monitoring, and Destroying Political Associations

DOD is required to build, monitor, and disrupt or destroy third-party political associations. In addition to the formal defense agreements that DOD negotiates in peacetime to provide for cooperation with other nations' military forces, it conducts psychological operations to influence the attitudes of foreign audiences and maintains liaison with erstwhile friends and allies, private voluntary and international organizations, and even potential or real adversaries. DOD monitors these political relationships and tailors its operations to take advantage of, or avoid the dangers revealed by, such intelligence. While these types of activities may seem to be more the province of intelligence agencies or the Department of State, military forces find that they cannot succeed in operations short of war without conducting their own political intelligence, liaison, and psychological operations.

DOD has some forces dedicated to or especially well suited to these types of activities, such as its psychological operations forces, elements of its special operations forces, and its Foreign Area Officers. It needs to do more, however, to develop its negotiating skills and regional and country expertise. The Foreign Area Officer and similar programs need to be reinvigorated. In addition, the role of the Defense Attache and his staff needs to be reconsidered with greater emphasis placed on political-military skills and their role as liaison between the regional CINC and the Ambassador and as supervisors of military assistance.

DOD also needs to do more to tailor its intelligence capabilities to the unique requirements of operations short of war. Intelligence is always a force multiplier. It has even greater applicability in most measures short of war because they generally require a much finer grain of political and tactical intelligence. DOD needs to improve means for intelligence collection relevant for operations short of war and to provide means for the quick dissemination of intelligence in the field. It is important, particularly in peacekeeping, to be able to monitor other military and paramilitary forces over a wide area. Better barrier technology, sensors for nonintrusive verification, refined investigative techniques, and forensic and other technologies that rob protagonists of plausible deniability are other important capabilities required in this area. Instant language-translation devices and interoperability enhancements would be valuable new capabilities to have as well.

Punitive and Remedial Military Actions Short of War

Finally, there is a set of peacetime engagement activities that require the direct application of military power, but with such demanding political or military constraints that they are often not considered to be mainstream military missions. Examples are punitive raids, hostage rescues, highly mobile counterinsurgent operations, and sudden and violent seizure of a small foreign government and its limited security forces. These activities all involve the use of violent force to secure military objectives, but they are directed against unconventional adversaries and/or usually include so many political and military restrictions on rules of engagement that many military officers do not consider them mainstream military missions. Frequently they are assigned primarily to special operations forces or elite units that can be depended upon to exercise the necessary degree of discipline in exacting circumstances.

The security environment of the 1990s is likely to require greater flexibility and responsiveness from the U.S. military. Swift and convincing deployments of firepower, whether as shows of force in support of diplomacy or as contingency responses to crises, will place a premium on rapid-reaction forces, lift capabilities, and over-the-horizon fire support. The ability to locate and disarm or otherwise neutralize weapons of mass destruction will be an increasingly important military mission for elite forces.

To perform these demanding missions with few or no noncombatant casualties, American elite forces will need increasingly sophisticated enhancements, such as better night-vision equipment, ultralight body armor and rations, stealthy means of infiltration and exfiltration, and virtual reality training for extraordinary missions. A few selected light infantry units may need to be specially trained for non-war-fighting missions such as peacekeeping, humanitarian intervention, and operations to restore order. Some peacekeeping forces may need to be specially configured; for example, they may need to be bolstered with additional intelligence, psychological operations, and civil affairs capabilities, as well as liaison units for multilateral operations.

Peacetime Engagements and the Military Technical Revolution

Many strategists and military theorists believe that the world is passing through one of history's infrequent revolutions in military affairs during which new strategies, organizations, and technologies will revolutionize the way wars are fought.[19] Not infrequently the question is raised as to whether the military technical revolution is relevant to the environment short of war. Most who investigate the matter answer with a heavily qualified affirmative.[20] The qualification comes from several characteristics of operations short of war that limit but hardly eliminate the utility of sophisticated technology for improving measures short of war.

First, the principal objective of measures short of war is to influence political relationships, not take terrain and destroy forces. Adversaries employing measures short of war often do so because it is less expensive and risky than war, but also because it is a way to advance an agenda against a technologically and organizationally superior adversary in a way that negates those advantages. For example, insurgents and terrorists attack nonmilitary targets because they cannot all be defended, and they meld with the population so that they are less easily targeted themselves. The net effect of an adversary taking steps to broaden his target range while reducing his own profile is that a high-technology force may find no high-profile systems to disrupt or destroy. In such circumstances technology often has an indirect rather than direct impact on the problem; for example, language-translation aids would facilitate communication, but the experience and skills of the negotiator cannot be supplanted by technology.

Second, because operations short of war are often protracted, it is important to keep costs—material but especially human—as low as possible. Technology can help a great deal by providing improvements in mine and sniper detection or stealthy platforms for supplying third parties more directly engaged on the United States' behalf, but it will never be possible to prevent an adversary from exacting some costs from the United States. Keeping material costs low when working through third parties often means giving priority to off-the-shelf systems that are highly reliable, simple, and exportable rather than to expensive, sophisticated, gee-whiz weaponry.

Operations short of war also frequently require small-unit actions, many of which are clandestine or even covert. Here advanced technology can play a more direct role by improving the performance of the individual, including his mobility, stealth, protection, endurance, and ability to discriminate targets. Similarly, operations short of war are often highly dependent on extraordinarily detailed and accurate intelligence. It is frequently observed that much of this intelligence—such as knowledge of individual or group intentions or characteristics—must be derived from human sources. Here again, technology can assist but hardly displace human skills.

The Russian and American experiences in Afghanistan and Somalia, respectively, are illustrative. Stinger missiles had a tremendous impact on the conflict in Afghanistan, forcing the Russians to significantly alter their approach to counterinsurgency. But mules to get the missiles and other supplies to the insurgents were also critical. In Mogadishu a high-tech U.S. force could not subdue a clan leader expert in urban guerrilla operations, but when they did clash, the result was wildly disproportionate casualties in favor of the technologically superior force.

In summary, advanced technology certainly has a role to play in operations short of war, but it alone cannot guarantee success. It may be supposed that Americans, who generally speaking are so quick to take advantage of technological innovation, will find ways to apply advanced technology to operations short of war. In fact, such efforts are currently under way in the Pentagon.[21] It is much more questionable whether the United States will find and combine the necessary doctrinal and organizational innovations with advanced technology for a synergistic effect that would create a quantum leap forward in its capability to execute measures short of war effectively. The comfort level of conventional military commanders with unconventional capabilities is not great. They tend to define problems in terms of the capabilities they know best and to use familiar conventional capabilities regardless of how the problem is defined. The greatest challenge to the United States in the future will most likely not be discovering radically new technological remedies but rather changing the way Americans think about operations short of war.

NOTES

1. See, for example, U.S. Marine Corps, *Small Wars Manual* (Washington, DC: U.S. Government Printing Office, 1940); Russell Weigley, *The American Way of War* (Bloomington: Indiana University Press, 1977); Barry Blechman and Stephen Kaplan, *Force without War: U.S. Armed Forces as a Political Instrument* (Washington, DC: Brookings Institution, 1978); and John M. Collins, *America's Small Wars: Lessons for the Future* (Washington, DC: Brassey's [US], 1991).

2. Weigley, *American Way of War,* p. xix.

3. Kennan put the case eloquently:

> There is nothing that can equal or replace strength in international relations. Strength overshadows any other measure short of war that anybody can take. We can have the best intelligence, the most brilliant strategy, but if we speak from weakness, from indecision, and from the hope and prayer that the other fellow won't force the issue, we just cannot expect to be successful.

George F. Kennan, *Measures Short of War: The George F. Kennan Lectures at the National War College, 1946–47,* eds. Giles D. Harlow and George C. Maerz (Washington, DC: National Defense University Press, 1991), p. 15. See also pp. 3–5, 14–17.

4. Ibid., p. 16.

5. Anthony Lake, Assistant to the President for National Security Affairs, ''From Containment to Enlargement'' (Speech delivered at Johns Hopkins University School of Advanced International Studies, 21 September 1993).

6. Specific differences of opinion about the relative importance of ethnic conflict, proliferating weapons of mass destruction, regional hegemonies, democratization, economic growth, and environmental issues contribute to broad differences of opinion about the appropriate scope of U.S. security interests. Some argue that the United States should limit itself to engaging direct and immediate threats to vital U.S. interests, such as the spread of weapons of mass destruction to rogue states or terrorists. Others believe that U.S. security requires a broader agenda, such as the consolidation of U.S. leadership among the Organization for Economic Cooperation and Development (OECD) countries and, as a preventive means of precluding the rise of another geostrategic rival, acting as a counterbalance to aspiring regional hegemons in less important regions of the world. Still others argue for a more ambitious policy of extending the free community of market democracies wherever possible.

7. The importance of prestige as a criterion for engagement and disengagement is discussed later in this chapter.

8. Donald E. Schulz and Gabriel Marcella, *Reconciling the Irreconcilable: The Troubled Outlook for U.S. Policy toward Haiti* (Carlisle Barracks, PA: Strategic Studies Institute, 10 March 1994), p. 1.

9. For a good discussion of such strategies, see Edward N. Luttwak, *The Political Uses of Sea Power* (Baltimore, MD: Johns Hopkins University Press, 1974).

10. *Washington Post,* 5 May 1993, p. 5.

11. F. J. West, Jr., *The Village* (New York: Harper and Row, 1972).

12. For a discussion of this point, see David Tucker, ''Facing the Facts: The Failure of Nation Assistance,'' *Parameters* 23 (Summer 1993): 37–39.

13. On new security threats, see Jessica Tuchman Mathews, ''Redefining Security,'' *Foreign Affairs* 68 (Spring 1989): 162–177; Norman Myers, ''Environment and Security,'' *Foreign Policy* 74 (Spring 1989): 23–41; and Daniel Deudney, ''The Case against Linking Environmental Degradation and National Security,'' *Millennium* 19 (Winter 1990): 461–476.

14. On the failure to plan adequately for the postcrisis phase of U.S. engagement in Panama, Richard Shultz has produced an excellent study: *In the Aftermath of War: U.S. Support for Reconstruction and Nation-Building in Panama Following Just Cause* (Maxwell Air Force Base: Air University Press, August 1993).

15. There is a small number of experienced national security and foreign policy practitioners who recognize the importance of the peacetime engagement principles enumerated here. Some are retired and write eloquently on the subject, but those still active in government with experience in operations short of war usually move on to activities considered mainstream by the agencies or departments they work for, such as warfighting preparation in DOD and traditional diplomacy in the Department of State. Typically it is not career enhancing to focus on systematically improving U.S. performance in the environment short of war, and in any case, many expert practitioners consider it unnecessary or impossible to do so.

16. Some senior decision makers overestimate their ability to manage crises as they arise and underestimate the amount of detailed policy issues that must be coordinated in order to ensure unity of effort. This would seem to be a natural phenomenon, which calls

to mind the words of Tocqueville applied in another context to world leaders, that they are "too prone to imagine that everything is attributable to particular incidents, and that the wires they pull are the same as those that move the world."

17. Just such a "Senior Interagency Seminar," developed by the Office of the Assistant Secretary of Defense for Special Operations and Low-Intensity Conflict, was approved. Two pilot seminars have been conducted.

18. Les Aspin, *Report on the Bottom-Up Review* (Washington, DC: Department of Defense, October 1993).

19. Michael J. Mazarr, *The Military Technical Revolution* (Washington, DC: Center for Strategic and International Studies, March 1993).

20. Ibid., pp. 45–54.

21. "US Group to Assess Military 'Revolution,' " *Jane's Defence Weekly,* 16 April 1994.

SELECTED BIBLIOGRAPHY

Blechman, Barry, and Stephen Kaplan. *Force without War: U.S. Armed Forces as a Political Instrument.* Washington, DC: Brookings Institution, 1978.

Corr, Edwin, and Stephen Sloan, eds. *Low-Intensity Conflict: Old Threats in a New World.* Boulder, CO: Westview Press, 1992.

Handel, Michael I., *Sun Tzu and Clausewitz Compared.* Carlisle Barracks, PA: U.S. Army War College, Strategic Studies Institute, 1991.

Horne, Alistair. *A Savage War of Peace.* New York: Penguin Books/Viking Penguin, 1985.

Krepinevich, Andrew F., Jr. *The Army and Vietnam.* Baltimore, MD: Johns Hopkins University Press, 1986.

Luttwak, Edward N. *The Political Uses of Sea Power.* Baltimore, MD: Johns Hopkins University Press, 1974.

U.S. Marine Corps. *Small Wars Manual.* Washington, DC: U.S. Government Printing Office, 1940.

Weigley, Russell. *The American Way of War.* Bloomington: Indiana University Press, 1977.

West, F. J., Jr. *The Village.* New York: Harper and Row, 1972.

Chapter 11

DRUG WARS AND REVOLUTIONARY GROUPS

Cynthia Watson

One of the most complex challenges to the U.S. military is the coalition between drug cartels and revolutionary groups. Not only does such a coalition threaten the indigenous system in which it operates, it poses a long-range challenge to American domestic and national security interests. What makes such a challenge even more difficult is that effective response depends to a great deal on the indigenous governments as well as on U.S. domestic law-and-order agencies. Within the U.S. system there is much disagreement about appropriate strategies and tactical operations. Much of this focuses on the Department of Defense (DOD) and the role of the U.S. military, particularly the Army.

In 1989 then Secretary of Defense Richard Cheney stated:

> The threat of illicit drugs strikes at the heart of the Nation's values. It inflicts increased crime and violence on our society and attacks the well-being and productivity of our citizenry. One of the principal foreign policy objectives of the Administration is to reduce, and if possible to eliminate, the flow of illegal narcotic substances to the United States. Also, the Congress has by statute assigned to the Department [of Defense] the duty to serve as the single lead agency of the Federal Government for the detection and monitoring of aerial and maritime transit of illegal drugs to the US. For these reasons,

The author thanks Dr. Sharon Murphy for her incisive comments and Ms. Anna Roque for assistance on this chapter. This chapter will consider revolutionary groups only as they affect or are related to drug wars. For a more detailed treatment of the general question of revolutionary or guerrilla groups, see the chapter of Thomas Mockaitis, ''Unconventional Conflicts,'' in this volume. This chapter does not reflect the views of the National War College or any agency of the U.S. government.

the detection and countering of the production, trafficking, and use of illegal drugs is a high priority national security mission of the Department of Defense.[1]

However, in 1988 Lieutenant General Stephen Olmstead, Deputy Assistant Secretary of Defense for Drug Policy, argued:

In describing our current anti-drug abuse efforts, I often hear the world ''war.'' War, defined by Clausewitz, is a total commitment of a nation. I currently do not find that. What I find is, as one of my colleagues alluded to, ''let's make the Army the scapegoat. We don't know what the answer is to the drug problem, so let's assign it to the Army and let them try and solve it.''[2]

Few responsibilities of the U.S. armed forces have received as much recent scrutiny as those addressing narcotics wars and revolutionary groups. Political figures in the United States have used the ''war on drugs'' as a justification for military spending as well as an inducement for the military to justify specific missions that the country would support.[3] The linkage between drugs and revolutionary groups in Latin America, in particular, was the rationale for intermingling drugs and revolutionary groups into a singular challenge to the United States.

This chapter will focus primarily on the U.S. military strategy and doctrine for response to the drug/revolutionary-group challenge. Included will be attention to the American view of the proper use of military force in the context of the global problem of drugs and its ramifications regarding the political-military threat and challenges to U.S. national interests. Finally, the prospects of the use of armed force to deal with these problems in the future will be considered, including an outline of the Clinton administration's approach to the problems.

THE MILITARY MISSION

Underlying any discussion of American armed forces is the question of their basic mission. The primary mission of the U.S. military is to win the nation's wars—success in battle. ''Nontraditional'' or ''unconventional'' conflicts are not within the mainstream military strategy or doctrine. The characteristics of such missions or conflicts are usually contrary to the American way of war (see chapter 8), in terms of both the expectations of the American people and military principles.

The mainstream military is best disposed and prepared for conventional conflicts in which the political-military objectives are clearly defined and militarily doable, and that are seen as necessary for the protection of American national interests—the 1991 Gulf War is a case in point. The primary driving force for shaping the U.S. military has historically been the principles articulated by Carl von Clausewitz. These principles spell out the need for a correlation between the leaders, the military, and the people. Underpinning this notion is that the "center of gravity" of battle is on the adversary's armed forces. The defeat of the armed forces means that the victor can impose his will on the adversary.

The relative clarity of political and military objectives in World War II faded with the Korean War and more specifically in the Vietnam War. The notion of limited war became the most prominent characteristic of these post–World War II conflicts. Further, the military felt that it had been severely constrained by political directions from the national leadership that led to failure or limited success. Indeed, Vietnam and, to a lesser extent, Korea have left their negative mark on the U.S. military psyche. This is based partially on the belief that the military was not allowed to use appropriate force or operational principles for decisive victory.

Vietnam, in particular, contrasts sharply with the "successes" in Grenada, Panama, and the Gulf War.[4] Not only were these latter conflicts aimed at a different type of target, but the United States had established identifiable and relatively more clearly defined goals. In Grenada the New Jewel Movement was defeated when the U.S. October invasion rooted out any possible Soviet-inspired leaders who might be threatening U.S. citizens (specifically medical students). During the same month U.S. involvement in the Beirut expedition failed when a suicide bomber killed more than 200 Marines in a Sunday attack. These various operations and conflicts show that clear military goals combined with relevant operational directions and appropriate doctrine are essential for success. Success also depends upon the degree of support from the American people.

The military has approached the task of countering drug trafficking with some trepidation. This is not only because of the ill-defined and uncertain military objectives, but because of the difficulty at the national level of determining measures of success and effective domestic response. Every president from Richard Nixon to Bill Clinton has declared the goal of ending illegal drug consumption in the United States and stopping the flow of drugs from external sources. This multidimensional character often highlights internal domestic drug problems.

For example, President Reagan and his wife Nancy used television as a platform to implore students to "Just Say No," at least partially in reaction to the shocking, high-profile deaths of University of Maryland basketball player Len Bias and Cleveland Browns football player Don Rogers. Both men died of cocaine overdoses about ten days apart in June 1986. Cocaine had been a glamour drug of the wealthy and the young, taking on a particular cachet during the high-rolling 1980s. Later in the decade a particularly insidious form of cocaine, crack, took on a deadly role in the inner city, where its lower cost but greater potency contributed to crime and urban decay.

Characteristics of Unconventional Conflicts

Unconventional conflicts are usually characterized by protractedness and guerrilla tactics and are focused on the political infrastructure, with a subsidiary role for the insurgent military.[5] These are complicated by the coalition of drugs and revolutionary groups, making successful response by indigenous governments and the United States extremely difficult.

Further, both revolutionary groups and drug trafficking appear in areas of the world where the very legitimacy of the central governments is in question. One of the reasons that the Vietnam War was so controversial was the fact that the Saigon government was perceived by a significant portion of the Vietnamese population as lacking legitimacy. There is a similar legitimacy problem in many areas where drugs and guerrillas exist.

Various political systems confronted with drug and revolutionary-group problems often display similar characteristics. Significant gaps in income levels breed social and political inequality. Crime is a problem that leads the government to respond by using the police and the military to maintain order. The military and the police are usually corrupted by all sorts of groups, as are the governments themselves. Bribery is usually the key to the activities of the wealthy elite—an elite who exist at a far distance from the vast majority of the population. Clearly democracy, in the Western sense, does not exist in such societies.

While the view in the U.S. government is most often that elections are a sufficient condition of a regime's legitimacy, the experience in much of the rest of the world is different. Regimes around the world often hold sham elections with clearly manipulated results, with little attention to the needs of the population. More often than not, many of these regimes are seen by the indigenous population as repressive, dictatorial, and often puppets of outsiders. In such circumstances it is difficult for the United States to bring about a democratic sense to the efforts for the indigenous regimes. Indeed, what is lacking is a democratic culture. Hence the United States is often accused of playing favorites with nondemocratic regimes. Yet others argue that if such regimes were democratic, they would not need American assistance.

U.S. National Interests

For the United States, involvement in primarily Third World counterdrug missions is particularly complex and difficult. First, the United States values stability and gradual political change. Second, there is a dichotomy in the United States between those advocating stability versus groups seeking to bring about socioeconomic change. Thus countering the drug cartel within an indigenous system may well lead to socioeconomic change that flies against the grain of the ruling elite. Moreover, within the indigenous system the problem of drugs may be viewed from a different perspective.

As one military analyst wrote, ''What the United States views as an 'eradication' effort for our military may be a counter-insurgency for the nation contending with the drug trafficking.''[6] By conducting such efforts, to populations around the world the United States appears, more often than not, to use the military to preserve the status quo ante that favors U.S. interests exclusively, even when those interests conflict with avowed U.S. national goals such as democracy and human rights. Finally, by choosing between stability and socioeconomic change, the United States tends to support regimes that are likely to be ultimately challenged by groups at home—regardless of both the end of the Cold War and the end of Marxist-Leninist movements around the world.

During the Cold War counterinsurgency had a much greater priority than did counterdrug efforts. In the post–Cold War era drug trafficking has assumed a much higher priority in U.S. threat assessments. Moreover, the scope of U.S. security assistance and aid has become increasingly limited and unable to replace the relatively large resources available through drug trafficking and profiteering. Thus those involved in indigenous drug growing and trafficking find few non-drug substitutes for the high monetary value of their drug crops. Consequently, an incentive may exist for governments to increase projections of drug production and trafficking. At the same time, such governments must contend with nationalistic opposition to involvement by the United States. One result is that it is particularly difficult for the United States to determine appropriate and acceptable strategies and operations as well as trying to fix relevant critera to measure the effectiveness of the counterdrug effort.

DRUG TRAFFICKING AND REVOLUTIONARY GROUPS

Drug trafficking is not a new phenomenon. Drugs have been a part of U.S. history, whether in the form of substantial alcohol consumption in the colonial era or the cocaine base of Coca-Cola at the turn of the twentieth century. ''Drug trafficking'' as a term, however, became part of the common vocabulary in the United States and part of the public policy and political debates during the 1960s. The use of drugs had been spreading through society as a manifestation both of the experimentation of the ''hippie'' generation and of the increasing desire to escape military service in Vietnam. Richard Nixon declared a ''war on drugs'' on 17 June 1971, and in response the Coast Guard and Border Patrol developed missions accordingly.[7] The Coast Guard, however, was (and is) technically not the military but resides in the Department of Transportation. The U.S. Border Patrol is located bureaucratically within the Immigration and Naturalization Service. The Customs Service is within the Department of the Treasury.

As part of the counterdrug effort, the United States has been sending assistance—financial, training, and materiel—to various Latin American countries for at least a generation. One former senior U.S. military leader has charged, however, that the materiel was inappropriate for the needs of the governments seeking to stop the export of drugs.[8]

Drugs: The Undesired Mission

One of the most contentious debates in American society related to the military's role in curtailing drug use in the United States when a succession of presidents announced a series of "wars on drugs." The military did not want any part in the war on drugs for a variety of reasons; as discussed earlier, the most compelling reason was the nontraditional nature of the mission.

By the mid- to late 1980s, however, the strategic landscape had changed. The Cold War was cooling off and the military was finding it necessary to take on newer tasks in response to budgetary challenges. The Pentagon's Inspector General reported in 1991 that "many officers saw the drug war 'as an opportunity to subsidize some non-counternarcotics efforts struggling for funding approval.' "[9] It was difficult to justify the massive funding for the U.S. military to fight a declining threat (the Soviet Union) in the rest of the world at the same time that a different, more diffused, and more immediate challenge of crime was growing in the United States.

The issue of narcotics trafficking became particularly visible after the appearance of increasingly obvious "narcoterrorism" in the late 1980s, particularly in Colombia. Colombian Justice Minister Rodrigo Lara Bonilla was murdered in April 1984 by *secarios,* motorcyclists paid by the *narcotraficantes* to kill Colombians who agreed with the Extradition Treaty to the United States. The very public assassination of Liberal presidential candidate Luis Carlos Galan in August 1989 at a public campaign rally in Bogota attracted much attention. Even as the Colombian government was coming under assault, the Bush administration needed its cooperation in the quest to end drug exports to the United States. President Bush reiterated his predecessors' decisions to curb drugs in the United States, elevating drugs to a serious threat to the country.[10] The campaign against the traffickers was expanded. Congress provided increased funding for U.S. forces to help train and arm the Colombians, Peruvians, and Bolivians as part of what President Bush labelled the Andean Strategy.

In the main, however, in such circumstances Congress has usually been reluctant to increase funding to levels comparable to those of traditional national security concerns. There has always been congressional reluctance to fund any foreign assistance, reflecting deep societal concern that the United States is disproportionately paying for activities for other countries. Even during the period of growing concern about drug consumption in the mid-1980s this was true. The assistance to the Andean states was in the millions rather than billions of dollars, leading some commentators to question whether the United States was seriously interested in stopping drug traffickers. Colombia received $65 million in emergency assistance at the height of narcoterrorismo in 1989, while the traffickers have multibillion-dollar fortunes at their fingertips. Other critics charged that a better way to deal with drugs was either through treatment programs or complete legalization of illicit drugs. Such views were contrary to those of the U.S. government position that the military had a role in this fight.

Posse Comitatus

An even broader public debate took place in the 1980s about whether the military could be used domestically to curtail the importation of drugs. In the

1970s the military had been vocal in its opposition to any direct role in countering drug infiltration into the United States.[11] The armed forces cited the nineteenth-century arguments relating to *posse comitatus* whereby the military would not be used within U.S. borders. The 1878 Posse Comitatus Act states:

> Whoever, except in cases and under circumstances expressly authorized by the Constitution or Act of Congress, willfully uses any part of the Army or the Air Force as a posse comitatus or otherwise execute the laws shall be fined not more than $10,000 or imprisoned not more than two years, or both.[12]

The U.S. Navy is not mentioned specifically in the law but is treated as if it were and is prevented from a law-enforcement role.

The *posse comitatus* restrictions on the military were eased in 1981 as a result of the efforts of Senator Sam Nunn, who believed that the military had a useful mission in trying to curb the spread of narcotics across the United States. The 1982 Defense Appropriation Act allowed the military to take a support role by supplying intelligence and some logistical support to the civilian agencies prosecuting the drug fight.[13] The American Civil Liberties Union (ACLU), among several groups, raised serious constitutional and privacy questions about the use of the military against its own citizens. The use of the military in domestic law-and-order matters was contrary to practices in the past.[14]

Private groups such as the ACLU and privacy advocates were joined by the armed forces themselves in opposing the inclusion of counternarcotics measures as a military mission. Nevertheless, the DOD mission of drug enforcement became an increasingly important part of the department's responsibility, with its narcotics budget allocation going from $4.9 million in fiscal 1982 to almost $1 billion a decade later.[15]

During the early period of the Reagan administration, the military and its civilian leadership opposed the drug responsibility. At the time, the Reagan administration was heavily engaged in the military buildup focused on the perception of a heightened Soviet threat, not one from drugs penetrating the U.S. borders. The military believed that being charged with countering drug traffickers would interfere with its ability to confront the Soviets. Yet in the 1980s some analysts viewed the drug issue as a manifestation of Soviet attempts to bring down the United States.[16] The armed forces were also skeptical about the effectiveness of interdiction programs for which they were responsible. To many in the services, Congress was placing the military in a no-win position.

On 8 April 1986 President Ronald Reagan reacted to the increased threats posed by narcotics by elevating the issue to a national security concern, issuing National Security Decision Directive 221. This directive called for the U.S. military to become engaged in at least four important actions:

1. Considering drug control activities in foreign assistance planning
2. Taking an increased part in helping with counterdrug programs

3. Allowing the U.S. intelligence community to take a more active role in working to stop narcotics trafficking
4. Putting greater concern on drugs as a national security problem as the United States dealt with other states[17]

Internal Military Drug Issues

In the 1980s the military adopted an aggressive program against drug consumption within its own ranks. This had been a serious problem during the Vietnam era when drug use in the field escalated. One retired Marine Corps general officer argued that the drug consumption in Vietnam was influenced by the availability of heroin, a factor not present in other areas where U.S. forces operated.[18] By the early 1980s, however, fatal accidents during U.S. military deployments and training exercises led to serious self-examination about the real levels of drug consumption within the armed forces. It was learned that drugs were affecting U.S. military readiness at a time when the United States sought to greatly improve its military effectiveness. As a consequence, the armed forces took a dramatic step to institute what became known as "zero tolerance" for drugs. Troops were (and remain) subject to random drug tests. A positive result leads to immediate dismissal from the service. It struck some as ironic, then, that the military—with its heightened concern about the consumption within its own ranks—was reluctant to undertake missions to counter drug infiltration into the United States.

In the second Reagan administration the armed forces still argued against a more active role in the counterdrug efforts. One news weekly commented, "The Pentagon objects [to direct involvement in drug arrests], saying soldiers are *trained to kill adversaries,* not to advise them of Miranda rights" (italics in original).[19] Weinberger's successor as Secretary of Defense, Frank Carlucci, maintained the opposition to using the military in the counterdrug campaign. He charged, "The defense budget is not a slush fund for drug enforcement."[20] Congress, however, reacted to growing public hysteria about drugs by pushing the military to become more involved in the drug war.[21]

THE EXPANDED MILITARY ROLE

By the late 1980s and into the Bush administration, the reluctance on the part of the services diminished as the realities of the changing world environment crystallized. It became increasingly difficult to argue for high defense budgets when the American people were beginning to question the real sources of threats to national security. Critics argued that the United States had brought the Soviet Union to its knees but that the socioeconomic costs to citizens at home were leading to the growth of drug consumption in the inner cities.

The military's role in countering the drug trade took a significant shift with the 1988 congressional decision to make DOD the lead agency in this effort.

Further, DOD was to integrate command, control, communications, and technical intelligence into an effective arrangement for the effort. Congress also charged the military with overseeing the use of the National Guard in this effort.

The National Guard is not technically part of the Department of Defense, being under the control of individual state governors. In the mid-1980s states began utilizing the guard for state counternarcotics operations, such as marijuana eradication. In 1988 more than thirty states had used the guard in more than 450 missions against drug targets.[22] The 1988 Omnibus Drug Law of the Fiscal Year 1989 DOD Authorization Act apportioned to the guard $40 million of the total $300 million for drug operations.[23] As a result, the National Guard has become one of the mainstays of border patrols and various other surveillance operations to counter narcotics entering the United States.

As noted, revision of *posse comitatus* in 1981 allowed the armed forces to participate in what is often considered domestic law enforcement. Further, on 3 November 1989 DOD received a Justice Department legal opinion allowing the military to seize narcotics traffickers overseas, even without host-nation approval. The 1987 capture of Colombian kingpin Carlos Lehder Rivas had occurred because of agreement between the governments in Bogota and Washington, abiding by the existing Extradition Treaty. The new interpretation, however, did change the U.S. role.

Organization of the War on Drugs

The Chairman of the Joint Chiefs of Staff's Report *Roles, Missions, and Functions of the Armed Forces of the United States,* issued in February 1993, dedicated just over a page to ''Counter-Drug Operations.'' This report cited the 1988 decision to charge the active-duty and reserve elements of the U.S. military with this nontraditional mission. These responsibilities include stopping the flow of drugs at the source, in transit, and inside the United States. The military is also concerned with detection and monitoring. The report also cited the specific force capabilities in the various services to carry out these tasks, such as using North American Air Defense (NORAD) surveillance and specially configured maritime patrol aircraft.[24] The Commander-in-Chief for the particular area of responsibility currently most connected with this problem is the CINCSouth, headquartered in Panama, with responsibility for threats from Panama south to Tierra del Fuego.[25]

In addition, the Pacific and Atlantic commands have pivotal parts in the counterdrug action. Each command is central to the Joint Task Forces set up in early 1989 to provide surveillance information as well as to coordinate the activities between the Navy, the Coast Guard, the Customs Service, and various other players. Finally, the Army runs a Joint Task Force for southern border control.[26]

The military is only one part of the U.S. government's efforts against drugs. The U.S. military works in coordination with several other government agencies, including the Office of National Drug Control Policy (the ''Drug Czar''), the Department of the Treasury, the Drug Enforcement Administration (Department of Justice), the National Narcotics Border Interdiction System, and the Bureau of International Narcotics Matters. In an era of ''jointness'' in which interservice rivalries are being played down, the effort has gone beyond the various services and involves the government bureaucracy as a whole.[27] The attempts to stop drug trafficking are expected to continue, but more often than not, the effectiveness of this effort is plagued by bureaucratic competition.

The move to militarize the campaign against drugs accelerated with the Reagan and Bush administrations. A significant portion of the cooperation between the United States and other nations in confronting the drug traffickers is not necessarily related to the U.S. military. Instead, linkages between the law-enforcement administrations of nations often form the basis for the attempts to curb the spread of drug trafficking. The military links between countries encourage cooperation but do not guarantee success.

Operation Blast Furnace

There are also joint U.S. operations with foreign states. One of the most visible occurred between July and November 1986 when U.S. troops, in coordination with Bolivian counterparts, actually moved into Bolivia to burn out coca-processing plants. This highly publicized action, called Operation Blast Furnace, was intended to show the extent of U.S. commitment to the drug war. Blast Furnace destroyed almost two dozen cocaine-processing labs, but did not lead to arrests or major drug seizures. The aviation battalion commander for that operation questioned whether Blast Furnace, which was hailed at the time as a great success, managed to achieve anything.[28] The violation of Bolivian sovereignty by using U.S. troops did inflict a price, however, on the government in La Paz, undercutting other antidrug activities in that country.[29]

The most prominent military activity against narcotics trafficking was the December 1989 invasion of Panama to seize General Manuel Antonio Noriega. The charges that linked Noriega to drug trafficking surfaced in the spring of 1987, although critics of the Bush administration charge that the United States knew of his drug ties for years.[30]

By the end of the Bush administration, more than 200 U.S. military advisors were physically located in South America, prompting questions about escalation and quagmire.[31] This reflected domestic controversy about involvement of U.S. forces on the ground in Latin America that had been circulating earlier. But President Bush insisted that the host nations were willing to accept U.S. troops. However, the Presidents of Peru, Bolivia, and Colombia all voiced concern that U.S. forces and the continuing moves to ''militarize'' the counterdrug activities were triggering strong nationalist opposition in those states.[32]

MERGING DRUGS WITH REVOLUTIONARY GROUPS

The vast majority of the U.S. military experience with both narcotics and revolutionary conflict together relates directly to Latin America, where U.S. security interests appeared to be challenged. Revolution—in the sense of attempts at sustained and enduring social, political, and economic upheaval—began in the Western Hemisphere with the Mexican Revolution's outbreak in 1910. U.S. forces were posted along the border in an attempt to prevent the spread of revolutionary conflict into America. Mexicans sporadically retreated into U.S. territory to avoid the central government in Mexico. The Wilson administration inserted U.S. troops into the Mexican Revolution (the Punitive Expedition) to counter several of the revolutionary groups, primarily that of Pancho Villa.

For the purposes of this chapter, revolutionary groups are those that take up arms to change the political and social conditions of a state. They tend to have a disruptive influence on a society, leading to a strong response on the part of the existing government seeking to create a more peaceful atmosphere in the society.[33] With few exceptions, these revolutionary groups are a twentieth-century phenomenon.[34] Others might broaden that definition, however, to consider advocates of certain controversial policies, such as abortion or drug legalization itself, to be revolutionary because of the changes that could result. Often the term *revolution* is used simply to indicate a radical change in a particular policy or an unanticipated development.

An early U.S. experience with countering revolutionary groups was at the turn of the century in its control of the Philippines. Following the end of the Spanish-American War (1898) and the transfer of control over the Philippines to the United States, nationalist reaction against continuing foreign control led to what has been called the Philippine Revolution. The Philippine nationalist leader Emilio Aguinaldo turned his guerrilla activities against the new government. Seeking independence, not merely a transfer of colonial ownership, Aguinaldo launched armed activities against the new colonial administration, and the United States faced some of its earliest nontraditional actions. Following the end of the Filipino revolt, various Moslem guerrilla groups continued to fight U.S. colonial ownership until the 1930s, making Washington respond to the problem of smaller-scale, more random warfare than it had seen in prior periods.[35] (The very term *guerrilla* simply means little war.)

The Huk rebellion in the Philippines, between 1949 and 1953, was further work for the U.S. military—albeit on a strictly advisory basis. The Hukbong Bayan Laban sa Hapon had been an early 1940s creation from the union of Philippine Communists and Socialists, fighting initially to oust the Japanese from the islands. The Hukbong Mapagplayang Bayan (the People's Liberation Army) came from a postwar and postindependence Philippines and began a guerrilla campaign against the government in Manila.[36]

The United States viewed this social rebellion as evidence of Moscow-controlled communism threatening a key U.S. ally in the same time frame as the People's Liberation Army victory in China and the conflict on the Korean peninsula. Washington sent a number of advisors to work with the Filipinos to defeat the rebels. Washington also encouraged its favored candidates to instigate socioeconomic reforms that would undercut any popular and ideological appeal that the rebels offered. The most prominent of these individuals was Ramon Magsaysay. The Huks were eventually defeated by the Philippine military in the mid-1950s. Yet the legacy of the Huk rebellion continues today among the Islamic groups in the outer islands that are in conflict with the central government. In that rebellion U.S. ground troops were not deployed, but advisors funded by the Central Intelligence Agency trained the Filipino armed forces to end the threat.[37] Washington hoped that this "success" in a key geostrategic asset would provide solid lessons for combatting other guerrilla problems.

The Philippines was unique, however, in several ways. It was geographically isolated from any other parts of Southeast Asia, U.S. troops were not used, and there was a relatively long history of U.S.-Philippines relationship. Nevertheless, this conflict was important because it began the idea of setting up a surrogacy to combat threats that U.S. allies might face.

The earliest sustained revolutionary groups in the Western Hemisphere developed in Colombia as a result of the civil war known as La Violencia (1948–1963). Liberal self-defense groups from La Violencia evolved gradually into armed antigovernment groups in the 1960s. The most infamous of these groups, the Fuerzas Armadas Revolucionarias Colombianas (FARC), dates its formal founding to 1964. Over the course of the 1960s and 1970s, about half a dozen groups with various stated goals began launching operations against the central government in Bogota. The United States believed that Fidel Castro was behind them, although these groups often had ideological goals that actually disagreed profoundly with those of the Havana ideologues. M-19, for example, was created after an alleged theft of the presidency by the traditional powers in the 1970s who refused to allow a rightist former military dictator to assume power. The M-19 showed characteristically schizophrenic behavior, as well, as it carried out not particularly ideological but highly publicized attacks on Colombian society.

It was in the post–World War II period that the United States was confronted with a number of challenges by revolutionary groups. The most often-cited reason for the spread of revolutionary groups in the early 1960s in Latin America was Fidel Castro's active funding and ideological support for various movements. While Castro's goals were clearly to create problems for the United States, the real motivation for many groups in Latin America (and the developing world in general) was likely to have been a form of nationalism.

MERGING DRUG AND REVOLUTIONARY ADVERSARIES

The issue of drug trafficking linked to revolutionary groups is relatively new. The realization has its roots in the concept that both drugs and revolutionaries have short-term common interests, part of which is to challenge the United States. Some analysts believe that the spread of drugs into the United States was explicitly and clearly linked to the activities of the "Evil Empire"—the Communists.[38] In this view, the Communists have "use[d] drugs over many decades as weapons designed to damage and weaken—if not destroy—the stability of Free World states. The top target is and always has been, of course, the United States."[39] This argument rejects any ideas that drug traffickers are involved in their enterprises simply for economic self-aggrandizement. According to this view, the links between revolutionaries under Soviet control and drug traffickers are logical and self-evident and must be removed to preserve the national security of the United States. Specific traffickers were linked with leftist political figures around the world such as Chilean Socialist President Salvador Allende Gossens as proof that the traffickers were in cahoots with the Communists.[40] Implied in this analysis is an understanding that the citizenry of the United States would not voluntarily engage in drug consumption and that the wicked, diabolical Communists seeking to defeat the United States are the root cause.[41] In this view, responding to both traffickers and revolutionaries is crucial and completely necessary to defend the United States.

Not all analysts see the linkage so clearly, however. Indeed, several take quite the opposite position—that drug trafficking is in direct opposition to the goals of the revolutionary groups.[42] This argument points out that the traffickers almost always seek to protect their economic gains from the types of socioeconomic redistribution that the revolutionaries seek to institute as part of their ideological goals. The groups are most often in direct competition rather than traffickers seeking to further the ideological goals of revolutionary groups.

Those analysts who are skeptical of the Communist-narco links tend to put the blame for narcotics spread on socioeconomic problems and corruption in the states where the raw drugs are grown. One cannot help but notice that drugs are not grown for massive export in the industrialized states of the West but appear in societies with massive government corruption and less than optimal prospects for sustained employment.

This is not to say that guerrilla groups and narcotics traffickers do not operate in collusion at times. There have been clear instances of such linkages. The Sendero Luminoso (Shining Path) movement in Peru has benefited greatly from the profits from coca production in the Upper Huallaga Valley, allowing the brutal revolutionaries to further their war against the central government in Lima. In another part of the world, the various groups seeking to seize control of the Kabul government have profited from the poppy trade in Afghanistan. There were predictions in the 1970s about the spread of drug production to Afghanistan. One analyst argued:

> [I]t is only a matter of time before the Afghan opium merchants realize that by refining the opium gum to morphine base before it leaves Afghanistan, they have a much more readily concealed product which can bring them much higher profits in the west. It is

believed that with the increased influx of organized western criminals into Afghanistan, this trend will increase significantly.

Much more important in terms of its immediate impact on the United States and the western world is the growing traffic in hashish which has its prime origin in the Afghanistan-Pakistan area.[43]

Further, numerous allegations were made over a decade that the Nicaraguan contras were supported not only by the Reagan administration but by cocaine profits.[44] During his testimony before the Iran-Contra Committee of the U.S. Congress, Lieutenant Colonel Oliver North seemed to imply that cocaine dangers were infinitely smaller than anything that the Nicaraguan government and its links to the Salvadoran guerrillas could have thrust forward.[45]

One result of the years of widespread counterdrug and counterrevolutionary activities was the merger of the two activities. This led to U.S. forces trying to respond to a combination of drug producers and revolutionary groups in the same country. Drug production was centered in those countries where the predominant economic system was not accessible to all sectors of society. In those cases drug trafficking offered economic opportunities that either supplemented or substituted for the minimum existing benefits. The farmers and youth predominantly engaged in helping the producers were often also those who would be politically disenfranchised and most susceptible to the ideological promises of the revolutionary groups. While the direct links between any narcotics production and a particular rebel group must be considered on an individual basis, the socioeconomic basis of these societies often bred the political upheaval to which the United States responded.

The Colombian Case

Critics of U.S. policies in the 1980s, often on the political left, claimed that the United States was using the shield of narcotics for conducting widespread political violence against ideological opponents around the world. It is noticeable that the states with some of the most active revolutionary movements in the Cold War were precisely those that produced and reprocessed various drugs. Examples include Colombia, which is the major production site for cocaine from coca imported from Peru and Bolivia. Colombia has had active revolutionary movements dating from the mid-1960s.[46] Bolivia and Peru are the two sources for the raw coca leaf. Both have faced revolutionary movements over the past half century, with limited results. The two major types of groups were "indigenist" (the disenfranchised native populations who felt that their rights were excluded by the ruling population) and revolutionaries such as Sendero Luminoso.

The Colombian case shows that the merger of revolutionary groups and drug traffickers is more complicated than generally presumed. In the middle 1980s Colombian President Belisario Betancur Cuartas (1982–1986) attempted to reintegrate the guerrillas into the political system through a national dialogue. The major outcome was the creation of the Union Patriotica (UP) political party. The UP has contested the entrenched Liberal and Conservative parties in Colombia in elections at all levels. Perhaps the most startling UP characteristic has been the death rate among its candidates. Between 1985 (the year of its creation) and 1994, more than a thousand UP candidates have been killed by paramilitary groups on the political right. The UP, a leftist party, has taken positions that oppose the *narcos,* leading one to conclude that the groups are not in collusion. The drug barons have become vast landowners, and several have participated in a number of political campaigns from a rightist position.[47] The group Muerte a Secuestradores (Death to Kidnappers) was founded by the *narcotraficantes* to kill left-wing revolutionaries who had begun to kidnap the families of the *narcos* as a way to finance their struggles.[48] Muerte a Secuestradores was followed by a large number of other paramilitary groups aimed at destroying the leftists in Colombia, including the UP.[49] Instead of supporting the status quo (which would help the nouveau riche *narcos*), the UP appears bent on changing the political gridlock in Colombia, along with terminating drug trafficking because it exploits society.

Formal links between *narcotraficantes* and revolutionary groups in Colombia have long been charged by U.S. counterdrug officials, but the evidence of such ties is weak. The spectacular November 1985 seizure of the Palace of Justice in Bogota, however, did indicate that the drug forces did work with the guerrillas on occasion. In this instance three dozen M-19 revolutionaries seized the Palace of Justice and killed close to one hundred people, including the Chief Justice of the Supreme Court and various other judicial luminaries of the Republic. While the M-19 guerrillas were killed in the attack and subsequent liberation of the building, the indications are that the assault took place to prevent the Colombian judiciary from extraditing drug traffickers to the United States.[50]

The Extradition Treaty was a significant source of tension between the United States and Colombia during the 1980s and 1990s because of a divergence in goals between the two states. President Cesar Gaviria Trujillo (1990–1994) made it clear soon after his inauguration that his goal was to stop the violence related to drug trafficking in his country rather than the broader issue of narcotics trafficking itself.[51] The United States pressed the Colombians to maintain the Extradition Treaty existing between the two states. Colombian officials were far less wedded to this treaty for at least two reasons. First, the Colombian judiciary was considered to be rife with drug-funded corruption. The bribery penetration of Colombia's legal system was not surprising; too many "clean" judges were gunned down in the streets for the society to ignore the trend.[52] Corruption is not unique to Colombia or to a society with much violence and social upheaval. The levels of violence in Colombia, however, were some of the highest in the world.[53] More important, Colombians were aware of the sovereignty questions that arose from an extradition arrangement with the United States. While U.S. officials believed in making *narcos* pay the price for their illegal acts by serving in U.S. facilities, Colombians saw the issue as the United States infringing on Colombia's right to enforce its laws. This issue triggered much opposition, which was to be expected in light of the fact that many in Colombia today accept the view of earlier U.S. culpability in the loss of a national territory (Panama). Also, the United States has never been willing to distinguish between narcotrafficking and narcoterrorism; they are regarded as the same problem to be eliminated.[54]

Another obvious merging of drug suppliers and revolutionaries was the Tranquilandia facility. This site was a revolutionary-controlled coca-reprocessing laboratory in the plains area east of Bogota known as the *llanos.* The Colombian military and U.S. Drug Enforcement Administration agents found at this location not only drug reprocessing but evidence indicating ownership by the oldest Colombian revolutionary group, the Fuerzas Armadas Revolucionarias de Colombia (FARC). FARC has been an active guerrilla movement since 1964, but many of its members gave up the struggle to join the UP political party.

The Peruvian and Other Cases

In Peru the Sendero Luminoso (Shining Path) burst on the scene in 1980 as a Maoist insurgency aimed at destroying the societal fabric of Peru. Sendero Luminoso inflicted considerable brutality on the Peruvian population, particularly in rural areas, threatening anyone who cooperated with the national authorities in trying to curb the insurgents. This cadre of revolutionaries funded much of its war against the Peruvian nation through the sale of coca grown in the Upper Huallaga Valley of the interior. Sendero Luminoso collected a tax from the sales of the raw coca leaves to Colombian and other nationals who reprocessed the leaves into cocaine for export to the United States. This relationship was closer to the links that U.S. officials cite as examples of threats to the United States. However, the revolutionaries in Peru are most often not the drug producers themselves.

President Alberto Fujimori of Peru instituted a more centralized and strong-handed administration in Peru. Using tactics that, according to critics, were hardly democratic President Fujimori brought significant change including major improvement in the economy, stability to the political-economic environment, and the virtual destruction of the Sendoro Luminoso guerrillas. According to one account, "The Maoist Shining Path guerrilla movement which nearly paralyzed the country during the 1980s and early 1990s is all but defunct, and its leader, Abimael Guzman Reynoso, is in prison."[55] In April 1995, President Fujimori was elected by a landslide to a second term; an unusual feat in Latin America.

Drugs do not originate exclusively in the Western Hemisphere. The Golden Triangle, located across Burma, Thailand, and Laos, is a major source for growing opium poppies that are used to make heroin for transit through Malaysia, Singapore, China, and Hong Kong.[56] Afghanistan and Pakistan are also sources of heroin production. A potentially significant conduit for narcotics transportation in the future is some former Soviet states, particularly Uzbekistan and Tadzhikistan. Drugs are also produced in some states that do not have significant revolutionary movements, such as Turkey (with its transshipment of heroin from Asia) and Mexico. The key appears to be the existence of a sizable portion of the population that will engage in the "illegal" activity primarily because that population has no alternative source of income.[57]

Confronting the drug traffickers has not always been separate from confronting the revolutionary groups operating in these states. Human rights groups and other analysts have long questioned whether assistance targeted for antidrug campaigns was not actually directed against revolutionary groups.[58] In the Colombia case one source claimed that 85 percent of the $65 million in emergency counternarcotics aid allocated after Luis Carlos Galan's assassination went to the military, while the police have actually made 80 percent of the cocaine seizures.[59]

THE CLINTON DRUG POLICY AND ITS RELATIONSHIP WITH THE MILITARY

Bill Clinton came into office with a number of Americans questioning his character and past activities. For example, candidate Clinton admitted that he had smoked marijuana but claimed that he had not inhaled. A sizable number of personnel in the military already had serious reservations about the President's personal integrity because he had not fought in Vietnam and had indeed protested the war. The drug admission, compounded further by the new President's campaign promise to eliminate the armed services' discrimination against gays in the military, only exacerbated an already-tense relationship.

The nature of the relationship has not improved markedly because the administration has been accused of being ambivalent on a drug strategy. The criticism has come not only from groups within the United States but also from its South American partners in the drug war. In late May and early June of 1994 the Clinton administration appeared to backtrack on its goals of wiping out drugs at the source, announcing that the U.S. military would cut back on the information that U.S. radars provided to South American governments fighting the traffickers.[60] Many Latin Americans were left unsure of how to proceed and how highly Washington valued the mission.

The timing was particularly crucial because of two related stories regarding Colombia's fight against drugs. Against the wishes of 85 percent of the population, the Colombian Supreme Court in May declared that the consumption of drugs for personal use was not illegal.[61] This was a blow to the hemispheric solidarity effort against drug trafficking. Later, in June, Colombian president-elect Ernesto Samper was accused of funding his presidential campaign through drug-trafficking money. The charges came within hours of the runoff election that saw Samper win by only 190,000 votes over Conservative Andres Pastrana.

The irony was that eventually both Pastrana and Samper were at least nominally tainted by the possibility that each had received contributions from the *narcos.* These recriminations came within the same month as testimony before Senator John Kerry's committee from a former drug trafficker, Gabriel Taboada, that the Colombian political system from the presidency on down was infiltrated by drug money.[62] The already highly critical Colombian Prosecutor General (who was perhaps tainted himself) charged that the tape recordings of the alleged presidential candidate bribery by the drug barons were supplied by the United States because it sought to violate Colombian sovereignty by affecting the credibility of the election.[63]

These indicators of a breakdown in the hoped-for regional solidarity in the war on drugs came when the Clinton administration was acting upon the de facto state of affairs in the United States about drugs. The issue simply had faded dramatically from its prominence during the late 1980s and the early 1990s. The administration's policy of trying to reduce the federal deficit while trying to implement other social programs placed the drug wars in a much lower priority. The counterdrug effort was simply not seen as crucial. The military's reluctance to tackle drug trafficking was a further factor that made it hardly surprising that the Clinton administration decided to decrease the emphasis on drugs. Additionally, the military persisted in its efforts to reduce its role in nontraditional missions championed by recent administrations (counternarcotics, Somalia, Haiti, Operation Provide Comfort, and the cleanup after Hurricane Andrew, to name only a few). The military fears that such involvement hurts readiness and leads to unrest in the military.[64]

One major change that has occurred during the Clinton period is the use of the National Guard in trying to curtail drugs in Puerto Rico. While the arguments swirled about the use of the military for domestic drug issues, the use of the guard in the Commonwealth was perhaps a somewhat easier decision. Puerto Rico may be legally part of the United States, but the use of the guard there differs from its use in a particular state. The President had vetoed the use of the National Guard when requested by District of Columbia Mayor Sharon Pratt Kelly in 1993 for the purpose of fighting the drug problem.[65]

The Clinton administration also has other real if more indirect problems in trying to craft a drug policy that involves the U.S. armed forces. While the United States as a society tends to see its national security interests as clear and obvious, the nationalism of other states may play a powerful role in thwarting those interests. Indeed, the concerns of other states often center around economic goals that U.S. interests may harm. But even if direct interests are not challenged, the perception that the United States has acted unilaterally without appreciation for the rights and requirements of other societies makes U.S. actions suspect. Again, in the Colombian case, outgoing President Cesar Gaviria Trujillo was charged by his own Prosecutor General (held in low regard by U.S. authorities, who fear his drug ties) with being "subservient to the United States."[66] While Gaviria Trujillo denied the attacks, the vitriolics extended beyond drug-trafficking questions to anything that linked the U.S. military to Colombia, for example, the use early in 1994 of the U.S. forces as engineers in remote areas of the country for construction.[67] The Colombian Prosecutor General ultimately decried the drug war as a failure and received Colombian congressional support for his assertion.[68]

This apparent unraveling of the hoped-for regional solidarity in the war on drugs came when the Clinton administration sought to build regional cooperation. When the solidarity broke down on drugs, the issue of U.S. pressure on these states became a nationalist cry in other areas of the bilateral relationship. Latin American nationalism became extremely sensitive to U.S. visibility in the region. Fears of the ''Colossus from the North'' became part of the nationalistic response.

CONCLUSIONS

The role of the U.S. armed forces in countering both drug operations and revolutionary groups has expanded dramatically during the twentieth century. As budgetary constraints grow, so do the many demands on the military. Quite likely the military will draw more assignments in these fields as the complications of the post–Cold War world become apparent. Operations other than war (OOTW) have become an institutionalized concept.

The military is not entirely comfortable with these supposedly ''nontraditional'' responsibilities. Part of this is simply reaction to a series of tasks that seem different from traditional defense of the homeland. Other reactions relate to U.S. military reluctance to be dragged into anything that might lead to a prolonged, draining conflict such as that of Southeast Asia. Regardless of proclamations that the Vietnam syndrome is dead, the military retains significant apprehension about engagements that might become anything except clear, clean, decisive victories.

But herein lies the rub. Most conflicts around the world in the years since the Berlin Wall fell have been ill defined. This is the case with drug wars and revolutionary groups. Drugs, in the broadest sense, offer an enemy that is as obscure as are any guerrillas, yet as pervasive in its damage as any social upheaval. Yet some analysts (and some in the military itself) question the term ''war on drugs'' because of the nature of the threat as well as the response to it.

One would expect that revolutionary conflicts will offer a far smaller job for U.S. forces into the future. With the end of the Cold War, few sources of funding for guerrilla groups are apparent. Even Castro's Cuba declared in the early 1990s that it would no longer financially support revolutionaries in Latin America. The apparent victory of capitalism and its link to economic and political prosperity would seem to relegate revolution, in the twentieth-century meaning of the word, to the dustbin of history.

The endurance of capitalism may be solid, but there may also be related social and political upheavals that can breed armed resistance. Indeed, while the United States has always believed that revolutionary groups had to be funded directly or indirectly by a central government (such as Havana or Moscow), alternative scenarios are possible. Illegal narcotics traffickers shut out of their political systems could very well subsidize some revolutionary groups, much as has occurred in Peru under Sendero Luminoso. Alternatively, the burgeoning Russian Mafia could finance groups aiming at social upheaval. In short, the triumph of capitalism does not guarantee the end of history or of revolutionary groups.

The very frustrations and concerns that make the U.S. military most uncomfortable are those conflicts and contingencies to which it must increasingly respond. Into the foreseeable future it is unlikely that there will be significant budget allocations to create different forces to deal with international threats posed by "nontraditional" sources. While heightened public anxiety calls for various actions to address the drug threat, few Americans will actually support widespread use of the U.S. military in South America or Central Asia to burn the drug crops.

The reduced defense budgets will have an additional impact on the military. The military faces a "utility of force" problem with the public; the military is "paid for" and should therefore be used in a variety of capacities regardless of the armed forces' comfort level with a particular type of mission. This includes socially relevant contingencies.

The armed forces of the United States will continue to face adjustments in the domestic and strategic landscape, including how forces are deployed in reacting to revolution and drugs. As other chapters in this handbook indicate, the military is undergoing a number of fundamental changes as it seeks to more clearly delineate its role as the United States enters the twenty-first century. The military is particularly reluctant to engage in those conflicts, like the drug war, that seem most difficult, at best, to win. Such fears are fueled by the ill-defined political and military objectives of many operations other than war and the tendency for conflict characteristics to be contrary to the American way of war. The military's reluctance is also exacerbated by the fear that another morass will result and that the public support that the military has gained since the mid-1980s would evaporate.

One of the most challenging aspects of countering both drugs and revolutionary groups is trying to maintain the distinctions between these two challenges. According to some, merging counterdrug with counterrevolutionary efforts tends to focus the U.S. military on counterinsurgency in which U.S. forces operate.[69]

In addition, a fundamental problem exists for the United States and its armed forces. It is impossible for the United States to control most conditions in foreign states. Countering both drugs and revolutionary groups requires operations mainly outside of U.S. borders. Thus there are any number of independent variables outside the influence of the United States. For example, indigenous governments or members of such governments might, on the one hand, welcome

U.S. support. On the other hand, these governments and individuals act to thwart the effectiveness of particular U.S. initiatives.

Further, the involvement of the U.S. military in foreign states for counterdrug missions may have unexpected consequences. For example, after a decade of action the Medellin cartel in Colombia was effectively destroyed. However, the flow of cocaine continued when the Cali cartel in Colombia replaced the Medellin cartel. The Cali organization actually began exporting heroin as well as cocaine.[70] Rather than clearing out the enterprise, action against a particular group only led to the growth of another organization with the same goals in mind. Many possible reasons for this result exist, but one certainly is that the behavior in Colombia is not entirely under the control of the United States and its policymakers and implementers. Among important reasons why such developments occur is that the United States does not control the law-and-order system in Colombia—nor should it.

In an era of fundamental change, the U.S. military will in fact continue its involvement in drug wars and counterrevolutionary efforts as well as any number of contingencies under operations other than war. Additionally, national security is likely to take on new meanings in America, including a host of environmental and demographic elements. Indeed, it is likely that OOTW will be undertaken less reluctantly not only because some of these contingencies may well be serious national security issues, but also to justify defense budgets.

Nonetheless, the new strategic landscape and the contingencies in operations other than war will seriously test the U.S. military. While the military will perform effectively as it has in the past, it is important that the American people and its elected leaders understand the challenge that these contingencies and conflicts pose to the U.S. military.

NOTES

1. Richard Cheney, ''Department of Defense Guidance for Implementation of the President's National Drug Control Strategy,'' 18 September 1989.

2. David Isenberg, ''Military Options in the War on Drugs,'' *USA Today,* July 1990, p. 26.

3. Comments by a prominent Republican congressman before the National War College Class of 1993, the National War College, Washington, D.C., December 1992. This individual went further to suggest that the military might be used ''in the Andean ridge to combat drug problems.''

4. These operations were initially judged as successes by the Presidents involved (Reagan and Bush) at the time. Further reflection, however, has caused some skepticism about these claims. In the case of Panama, the regime of drug trafficker Manuel Antonio Noriega's successor, democratically elected Guillermo Endara, has been charged with being even more prolific in the trafficking of narcotics. Iraqi president Saddam Hussein's army was indeed ousted from Kuwait, but he retains power in Iraq and has killed off many of his countrymen, particularly those in the south known as the ''marsh Arabs''

whom Hussein sees as an insurgency for Iran. In sum, the question of winning and losing is often a function of how the end state or goal of the particular effort is defined.

5. Colonel Dennis W. Drew, USAF, ''Insurgency and Counterinsurgency: American Military Dilemmas and Doctrinal Proposals,'' *Cadre Paper* (Maxwell Air Force Base, AL: Air University Press, 1988), pp. 9–18. This *Cadre Paper* is useful in describing the problems that face the U.S. armed forces as they confront the broader questions of insurgency versus conventional conflict.

6. Major Mark P. Hertling, USA, ''Narcoterrorism: The New Unconventional War,'' *Military Review,* March 1990, p. 25.

7. General Lewis W. Walt, USMC (ret.), *The World Drug Traffic: A Report to the Senate Subcommittee on Internal Security* (14 September 1972), p. 4.

8. Remarks by retired Southern Command Chief General Paul Gorman in Chicago, National Strategy Forum Meeting, April 1988.

9. David Morrison, ''Police Action,'' *National Journal,* 1 February 1992, p. 268.

10. See Cheney, ''Department of Defense Guidance'' and Dale E. Brown, ''Drugs on the Border: The Role of the Military,'' *Parameters* 21, no. 4, Winter 1991/1992, p. 50.

11. Walt, *World Drug Traffic,* p. 94.

12. Brown, ''Drugs on the Border,'' p. 57.

13. Bruce Michael Bagley, ''Myths of Militarization,'' in *Drug Policy in the Americas,* ed. Peter H. Smith (Boulder, CO: Westview Press, 1992), p. 130.

14. Miriam Davidson, ''Militarizing the Mexican Border,'' *Nation,* 1 April 1991, p. 406.

15. Bagley, ''Myths of Militarization,'' p. 131, and William J. Durch, ''Protecting the Homeland,'' in *The American Military in the Twenty-First Century,* ed. Barry Blechman, William Durch, David Graham, John Henshaw, Pamela Reed, Victor Utgoff, and Steven Wolfe (New York: St. Martin's Press, 1993), p. 241.

16. See Joseph Douglass, *Red Cocaine* (Atlanta: Clarion House, 1990), for a detailed articulation of this position. Additionally, U.S. Ambassador to Colombia Lewis Tambs charged that the revolutionaries operating in Colombia were actually a further manifestation of communism threatening the United States. Peter Dale Scott and Jonathan Marshall, *Cocaine Politics* (Berkeley: University of California Press, 1991), pp. 94–96.

17. Michael Abbott, ''The Army and the Drug War: Politics or National Security?'' *Parameters* 68, no. 4 (December 1988): p. 99.

18. Walt, *World Drug Traffic,* p. 8.

19. *U.S. News and World Report,* 23 May 1988, p. 28.

20. Eliot Marshall, ''News and Comment: A War on Drugs with Real Troops?'' *Science* 241 (1 July 1988): 13–15.

21. Paul Mann, ''Congress Pressures Military to Assume Direct Antidrug Role,'' *Aviation Week and Space Technology,* 23 May 1988, pp. 25, 27.

22. Captain Jean Marie Brawders, *National Guard,* August 1989, p. 22.

23. Ibid., p. 23.

24. Chairman of the Joint Chiefs of Staff, *Report on the Roles, Missions, and Functions of the Armed Forces of the United States* (Washington, DC: Department of Defense, Office of Assistant Secretary of Defense, Public Affairs, February 1993), pp. II-9 and II-10.

25. Stephen Duncan, ''Counterdrug Assault: Much Done, Much to Do,'' *Defense,* May/June 1992, pp. 16–17.

26. Durch, "Protecting the Homeland," pp. 243–244, and Duncan, "Counterdrug Assault," pp. 17–20.

27. The Goldwater-Nichols Defense Reorganization Act of 1986 mandated that the military take a more joint approach to its job, rather than getting bogged down in service rivalries that could threaten national security. "Jointness" or "purple-suitedness" (rather than a specific service color like the Army green or Air Force blue) is the key word in the upper levels of the U.S. armed services today.

28. Abbott, "The Army and the Drug War," p. 95.

29. Bagley, "Myths of Militarization," p. 136.

30. John Dinges, in *Our Man in Panama* (New York: Random House, 1990), laid out a long-term linkage between the U.S. intelligence services and Noriega. Additionally, Dinges described some of the questions that arose in the 1987–1989 period about why the United States finally decided to move against Noriega. Many of the hypotheses developed did not relate to sudden revelations about his links to drug trafficking.

31. Morrison, "Police Action," p. 270.

32. Bagley, "Myths of Militarization," p. 140.

33. I do not say that governments are only interested in returning to peaceful conditions. In many twentieth-century cases the governments that revolutionaries aim to change are indeed what might be considered by many societies "unjust," such as the Batista government in Cuba (1950s). In similar instances the unjust and unrepresentative (in the U.S. sense) governments may actually use the revolutionary threat as an excuse to further tighten repressive measures against the dissenters in society. Former Chilean President and Army General Augusto Pinochet served as an example of this behavior.

34. For one typology of insurgency and revolutionaries, see Bard O'Neill, *Insurgency and Terrorism: Inside Modern Revolutionary Warfare* (Washington, DC: Brassey's [US], 1990).

35. Ian Beckett, "The United States Experience," in *The Roots of Counter-Insurgency,* ed. Ian Beckett (London: Blandford Press, 1988), p. 105.

36. For a recent history of the Philippines and the social conditions that bred the Huk insurrection, see Stanley Karnow, *In Our Image* (New York: Random House, 1989), pp. 336–355.

37. Ibid., pp. 351–354.

38. One of the most detailed articulations of this position is Douglass, *Red Cocaine.* Douglass argued passionately that the United States has been under siege by the two centers of Communist activity, the former Soviet Union and the People's Republic of China. He acknowledged that the "surrogates" of these states, such as Cuba and Nicaragua, have also pushed this infiltration of the United States. Douglass's assessment is quite controversial. Because the book was written before the formal end of the Soviet Union, it is not clear whether the author would transfer his charges from the Soviet Union to Russia. In other words, it is not clear whether this is an ideologically based position or one that sees the former Soviet Union and now Russia as the main threats to the United States.

39. Douglass, *Red Cocaine,* p. xvii.

40. Walt, *World Drug Traffic,* p. 61.

41. Ibid., p. 62.

42. This author has pointed out the conflict of interest between these groups. In Colombia, for example, the drug traffickers have been aligned much more with conservative interests in the socioeconomic system. The revolutionary groups seek to redistribute

power within Colombia, while the *narcotraficantes* want to enter the political system that currently exists. See Cynthia Watson, ''Guerrilla Groups in Colombia: Reconstituting the Political Process,'' *Terrorism and Political Violence* 4, no. 2 (Summer 1992): 84–102. Other authors draw the dichotomy even more sharply. See Jonathan Marshall, *Drug Wars* (Forestville, CA: Cohan and Cohen Publishers, 1991), and Scott and Marshall, *Cocaine Politics.*

43. Walt, *World Drug Traffic,* pp. 44–45.

44. See Marshall, *Drug Wars,* pp. 43–45.

45. Daniel K. Inouye and Lee H. Hamilton, *The Iran-Contra Affair* (New York: Times Books, 1988). See the sections on Oliver North. For further information, also see various works by the National Security Archive in Washington, DC, which looked at this case in excruciating detail.

46. Depending on how one wants to interpret this, it could be argued that Colombia's guerrillas actually date back to the civil war from 1947 to 1963 when various groups were created across the country to challenge the existing political system. Hence the definition of revolutionary groups becomes a somewhat relevant one for the purpose of deciding when they appeared.

47. Carlos Lehder Rivas, an original cocaine king in Colombia before his 1987 capture and extradition by the United States, was a virulent anti-Semite and pro-Nazi figure. Lehder Rivas advocated the creation of an extreme nationalist party in the Republic, in complete opposition to any leftist views. See Guy Gugliotta and Jeff Leen, *Kings of Cocaine* (New York: Simon and Schuster, 1989).

48. Ibid., chap. 9, ''MAS.''

49. For an appraisal of the problem of political violence and political participation in recent Colombia, see Watson, ''Guerrilla Groups in Colombia,'' pp. 84–102.

50. See Gugliotta and Leen, *Kings of Cocaine,* chap. 25, ''Palace of Justice.''

51. Various *Latin American Weekly Report* editions after his 7 August 1990 inauguration described his positions.

52. See Gugliotta and Leen, *Kings of Cocaine,* throughout the book.

53. Carlos Mauro Hoyos, the Attorney General, was assassinated by the drug dealers during a trip to Medellin in 1988. Numerous other officials were killed by youths on motorcycles who were assassins paid by the *narcos.*

54. The Colombians made clear their interest in changing the economic conditions at home as a precondition to ending the drug problems. Rather than seeing drugs as some sort of isolated, indigenous disease to be cured, the Colombians joined other Latin Americans in pointing out that the United States engaged in a somewhat unique view of the solutions necessary. At the same time that Washington leaned on the Colombians about narcotics trafficking and sought to get the military much more involved in the fight, the United States refused Colombia's requests for other, more indirect forms of assistance. In particular, the Bush administration in 1989 refused both to agree to the International Coffee Agreements, which would have set price supports for Colombia's main legal export, and to drop protective tariffs against Colombian flower imports. These two indications led many skeptics around the world to charge that the United States was seeking another way to fight some war while refusing Colombians the very economic support that they needed.

55. Kerry Luft, ''For Peru's Leader, Good May Outweigh Bad,'' *Chicago Tribune,* 9 April 1995, Section 1, p. 23.

56. Bertil Lintner, "New Routes for Heroin," *World Press Review,* September 1990, p. 65.

57. Rensselaer Lee, *Drugs in Post-Communist Societies* (Washington, DC: National Council for Soviet and East European Research, 1992).

58. As one example, see Jenny Pearce, *Colombia: inside the Labyrinth* (London: Latin American Bureau, 1990), pp. 265–273. See also Scott and Marshall, *Cocaine Politics.*

59. Isenberg, "Military Options in the War on Drugs," p. 26.

60. *Washington Times,* 23 June 1994.

61. *Foreign Broadcast Information Service (FBIS),* FBIS-LAT-94-091, 11 May 1994, pp. 37–38.

62. *FBIS,* FBIS-LAT-94-082, 28 April 1994, p. 57.

63. *FBIS,* FBIS-LAT-94-130, 7 July 1994, pp. 36–37.

64. A National War College Class of 1992 student essay, "The Origins of the American Military Coup of 2012" by Lieutenant Colonel Charles Dunlap, USA, raised these questions in a provocative manner. See also Bradley Graham, "Pentagon Officials Worry Aid Missions Will Sap Military Strength," *Washington Post,* 29 July 1994, p. 29. A detailed discussion of the problems that President Clinton has had with the military is in Cynthia Watson, "Peacetime Engagements: Global and Regional," Paper presented at National Strategy Forum Workshop, April 1993, Cantigny Estate, IL.

65. *Washington Post,* 30 June 1994.

66. *FBIS,* FBIS-LAT-94-079, 25 April 1994, p. 49.

67. *FBIS,* FBIS-LAT-94-080, 26 April 1994, pp. 52–53.

68. *FBIS,* FBIS-LAT-94-087, 5 May 1994, pp. 22–23.

69. There is a long list of sources on this point, ranging from human rights groups in Latin America to those in Asia. The criticism is almost always the same: nothing is as important as countering ideological enemies of the government rather than truly worrying about narcotics trafficking.

70. *Washington Post,* 16 June 1994, pp. A27–A28.

SELECTED BIBLIOGRAPHY

Abbott, Michael H. "The Army and the Drug War: Politics or National Security?" *Parameters* 68, no. 4 (December 1988): 95–112.

Bagley, Bruce Michael. "Myths of Militarization." In *Drug Policy in the Americas,* ed. Peter H. Smith (Boulder, CO: Westview Press, 1992), pp. 129–150.

Brown, Dale E. "Drugs on the Border: The Role of the Military." *Parameters,* Winter 1991/1992, pp. 50–59.

Cheney, Richard B. "DoD Role in Drug Control." *Defense Issues* 4, no. 30 (Speech, 18 September 1989).

Duncan, Stephen M. "Counterdrug Assault: Much Done, Much to Do." *Defense,* May/June 1992, pp. 12–23.

Korb, Lawrence J. "Drug War Front." *Defense,* February 1985, pp. 17–20.

Mabry, Donald. ed., *The Latin American Narcotics Trade and U.S. National Security.* Westport, CT: Greenwood Press, 1989.

Sarkesian, Sam C. *America's Forgotten Wars: The Counterrevolutionary Past and Lessons for the Future.* Westport, CT: Greenwood Press, 1984.

Chapter 12

NONCOMBAT OPERATIONS

James B. Motley

Military operations are conducted in three diverse environments: peacetime, conflict, and war. In seeking to achieve their strategic objectives in these environments, U.S. policymakers use all elements of national power—political, economic, and military—to achieve America's strategic objectives.

During peacetime U.S. policymakers attempt to influence world events through those political and economic actions that routinely occur between nations. Conflict is characterized by hostilities short of war to secure strategic objectives. The last environment, war, involves the use of U.S. armed forces in combat operations against an armed enemy.[1]

The primary mission of the U.S. armed forces is war fighting, that is, preparing for and conducting combat operations against an armed enemy when directed to do so by the President of the United States. Noncombat operations are also critical missions performed by the U.S. military.[2]

The political decision to engage U.S. armed forces in combat and noncombat operations places American lives and U.S. prestige at risk before the international community. In addition, the success or failure of these operations may have significant consequences for U.S. national security.

Noncombat operations to be discussed in this chapter include peacekeeping, humanitarian assistance, and security assistance. Peacekeeping operations are intended to prevent conflict and to resolve ongoing conflict. These operations usually involve deployment of United Nations military and/or police personnel, and frequently civilian personnel as well, in the field with the consent of all the parties concerned.[3] Humanitarian assistance includes the delivery of food and relief aid and also actions that protect civilian lives, prevent atrocities, or otherwise promote the welfare of the people of a country, while minimizing the potential for engagement in hostile actions.[4] Security assistance by the United States to another country is authorized by the Foreign Assistance Act of 1961, as amended, by the Arms Export Control Act of 1976, as amended, and by other related statutes. Under these programs the United States provides defense equipment/materiel, military training, and other defense-related services by grant, credit, or cash sales to further U.S. national policies and objectives.[5]

Noncombat operations, given a declining Department of Defense [DOD] budget, an unpredictable international landscape, and waning support by the American public for overseas involvement, have significant organizational and operational consequences for U.S. policymakers and raise important and complex questions: What are the potential long-term effects of noncombat operations on the effectiveness of the U.S. armed forces? What are the benefits and limitations of committing U.S. military forces to noncombat operations? What are the implications of increased use of U.S. armed forces in noncombat operations for U.S. military force structure, doctrine, and training? These consequences and questions are beyond the scope of this chapter, but must be addressed as the United States approaches the twenty-first century. Given the events in Somalia and the former Yugoslavia in the early 1990s, it appears that noncombat operations will become an increasingly important role for U.S. armed forces in restoring and maintaining peace throughout the world. U.S. leadership and the support of the American public are essential if such missions are to be successful.

SHAPING A NEW FUTURE

During the Cold War era U.S. national security was voiced through expressions of political resolve (the Korean and Vietnam wars), acts of diplomatic brinkmanship (the Cuban missile crisis), and numbers of nuclear weapons (the U.S.–Soviet Union military balance). The 1 September 1993 release of *The Bottom-Up Review* (a six-month effort to rethink the shape and purpose of the post–Cold War military) by the Clinton administration, however, placed new emphasis on nontraditional military missions such as peacekeeping and humanitarian assistance, as well as on curbing the spread of nuclear weapons.[6]

There is a threefold importance to this review. First, it forms the intellectual foundation for current and future DOD defense spending plans to support a smaller U.S. military force. Second, according to former Secretary of Defense Les Aspin, it ''is a product of a comprehensive broadly collaborative review based upon the real dangers that face America in the new era.''[7] Third, the review is at the heart of the U.S. efforts ''to chart the course of our national defense for the future.''[8]

In keeping with these ''real dangers,'' it is a major premise of this chapter that peacekeeping, humanitarian operations, and security assistance activities are important means by which the United States can shape the post–Cold War international security environment. A former senior U.S. government official maintained that U.S. participation in peacekeeping and humanitarian operations "helps to energize global collective security institutions through which we hope to build a more just and stable world order." Security assistance, he added, "sustains our forward presence and strengthens friends and allies with whom we share common goals."[9]

Because of the significant changes that have occurred throughout the international landscape since 1989, the U.S. national strategy has shifted from a focus on a global threat (the former Soviet Union) to one of regional challenges and opportunities. The intent of this new regional defense strategy is "to enable the U.S. to lead in shaping an uncertain future."[10] In an international environment no longer characterized by Cold War bipolarity, and within the broader framework of U.S. national security "of encouraging the spread and consolidation of democratic government and open economic systems," the new emphasis on peacekeeping operations and humanitarian and security assistance is well founded.[11]

Historically, U.S. armed forces have performed a wide range of noncombat operations. During the 1990s U.S. armed forces joined allies to carry out peacekeeping and humanitarian missions in northern Iraq and southern Turkey (Kurdish refugees), Bosnia-Herzegovina (the former Yugoslavia), Russia, other newly independent states of the former Soviet Union, and Somalia. Elements of the U.S. armed forces also supported civilian authorities in disaster relief to victims of Hurricanes Andrew and Iniki and typhoon damage in Guam and responded to the Los Angeles riots.

With this background, we now turn our attention to a discussion of noncombat operations. For a more in-depth understanding of the topics addressed, readers are encouraged to consult the sources listed in the chapter notes.

PEACEKEEPING OPERATIONS

Modern peacekeeping efforts evolved after World War II with the establishment of the United Nations.[12] Although the U.N. Charter did not make provisions for peacekeeping forces, the United Nations gradually developed a body of thought and doctrine about peacekeeping. The term *peacekeeping force* was first used in 1956 when the U.N. Emergency Force (UNEF) was established to supervise the disengagement of forces after the invasion of Egypt by Great Britain, France, and Israel in the Suez War.

In 1956 the United Nations created a Special Committee on Peacekeeping Operations to conduct its peacekeeping activities. Since its establishment in San Francisco in 1945, the United Nations has introduced international military observer groups, missions, and forces into global hot spots on numerous occasions. Once deployed, these elements have monitored cease-fires, patrolled borders, supervised troop disengagements, provided internal security, preserved essential government functions, and interposed themselves between hostile neighbors. In any discussion of peacekeeping operations, it is important to remember three key points. First, such operations occur simultaneously with and support diplomatic and political efforts to achieve long-term resolution of the conflict. Second, each conflict is different. Underlying political, social, and economic situations demand different military approaches. Third, peacekeeping operations are established in keeping with the following principles:

1. Agreement and continuing support by the U.N. Security Council
2. Agreement by the parties to the conflict and consent of the host government
3. Unrestricted access and freedom of movement by the operation within the countries of operation and within the parameters of the peacekeeping mandate
4. Noninterference by the operation and its participants in the internal affairs of the host government[13]

Military forces participating in peacekeeping operations share common characteristics, which include the following:

1. Clearly and carefully prescribed political limits (a nonmilitary objective)
2. Development and constant updating of contingency plans for evacuation and self-defense (even though the peacekeeping force is required to maintain a nonprovocative posture)

For almost half a century, whenever U.S. policymakers discussed foreign policy, they did so within the context of U.S.-Soviet rivalry (the Cold War). U.S. military planning was almost always related, directly or indirectly, to the Soviet threat. With the disintegration of the Soviet Empire and the end of the Cold War, an avenue for greater multilateral cooperation, which had long been limited by the U.S.-Soviet rivalry, became available—U.N. peacekeeping.[14]

Since 1989 there has been a dramatic increase in requests for U.N. assistance in resolving ethnic and other conflicts in places as diverse as Bosnia-Herzegovina, Cambodia, El Salvador, the Middle East, Namibia, and Somalia. In a 23 September 1993 address at the National War College, U.S. Ambassador to the United Nations Madeleine K. Albright said, "More peace-keeping operations [were conducted] in the past 5 years than in the previous 43; [with] a sevenfold increase in troops; a tenfold increase in budget; and a dramatic but immeasurable increase in danger and complexity." She added:

> At their best, UN peace-keeping operations can be very effective. Obviously, they cannot be a substitute for fighting or winning our own wars, nor should we allow the existence of a collective peace-keeping capability to lessen our military strength. But UN efforts have the potential to act as a "force multiplier" in promoting the interests in peace and stability that we share with other nations.[15]

A number of recent and current U.N. peacekeeping forces and their related missions are described here. Cost estimates are for the total U.N. effort. Personnel data are as of January 1994.[16]

Africa

U.N. Mission for the Referendum in Western Sahara (MINURSO)

MINURSO was established on 29 April 1991 and includes 348 personnel (22 U.S.) at an estimated cost (1995) of $85 million. The mission is to conduct a referendum on whether Western Sahara, a former colony from which Spain unilaterally withdrew, should become independent or be integrated into Morocco. MINURSO's mandate was expected to terminate in January 1992, but failure by the parties to agree on procedures for the conduct of the referendum led to an extension of MINURSO's deployment. The extension of the mandate requires progress toward holding the referendum by October 1995 with the mission concluding as soon as possible thereafter. Twenty-eight countries have provided civilian or military personnel to MINURSO.

U.N. Angola Verification Mission (UNAVEM II)

UNAVEM II was established 30 May 1991 with 74 personnel (0 U.S.) at an estimated cost (1995) of $290 million. The mission's original mandate was to monitor a cease-fire between government forces and UNITA (revolutionary movement in Angola) rebels, assist in preparation for elections in September 1992, and monitor the polls. Elections proceeded relatively well, but UNITA rebels disavowed the results and resumed full-scale warfare. In November 1994, the warring sides signed the Lusaka (Zambia) Accord. The mandate for the observer force was changed to monitor the cease-fire that took effect with this accord. This included plans to establish UNAVEM III to monitor the cease-fire and assist in demobilizing warring groups. Approximately twenty-four countries have participated in this mission.

U.N. Operation Mission in Somalia (UNOSOM II)

UNOSOM II was established March 1993 with 25,000 personnel (1,400 U.S., not including 4,300 ashore and 3,800 offshore with the Joint Task Force) at an estimated cost (1994) of $900 million. The mission had an original mandate to monitor a cease-fire in Mogadishu and to provide security for humanitarian assistance personnel. After the situation on the ground deteriorated, the U.N. Security Council on 3 December 1992 authorized member states to utilize "all necessary means" to establish a secure environment for humanitarian relief operations. This became the U.S.-led Unified Task Force (UNITAF). In November 1994, the U.N. Security Council ordered the withdrawal of all UNOSOM forces by 31 March 1995.

U.N. Operation in Mozambique (ONUMOZ)

ONUMOZ was established 16 December 1992 with 6,498 personnel (0 U.S.) at an estimated cost (1995) of $22 million. The mission is to assist in the implementation of the agreement between the government of Mozambique and the Mozambique National Resistance (RENAMO) to end Mozambique's civil war. The U.N. forces will monitor the cease-fire and demobilization of combatants and provide security for humanitarian relief missions. On 5 November 1993 the ONUMOZ mandate was renewed for six months, subject to a report by the United Nations on progress in disarmament and demobilization and other terms of the Rome Peace Accords. Elections were completed in October 1994. A new government was inaugurated in December and the U.N. Security Council ended the mandate in January 1995. Major troop contributors are Bangladesh, Botswana, Italy, Uruguay, and Zambia.

U.N. Observer Rwanda/Uganda Mission (UNOMUR)

UNOMUR was established 22 June 1993 with 81 personnel (0 U.S.) at an estimated cost (1993) of $6–$8 million. The mission is to deploy on the Ugandan side of the border and verify that no military assistance to Rwandan rebels is transported across the border from Uganda. UNOMUR's initial six-month mandate expired in December 1993 and was renewed for another six months, ending in June 1994.

U.N. Assistance Mission for Rwanda (UNAMIR)

UNAMIR was established 5 October 1993 with 1,260 personnel (additional forces were authorized on 6 January 1994) at an estimated cost for six months of $63 million. The mission was to deploy lightly armed U.N. peacekeepers to Rwanda to monitor observance of the 4 August peace accords leading to national elections within twenty-two months, and to assist with mine clearing, repatriation of refugees, and the coordination of humanitarian assistance activities in Rwanda. UNAMIR's initial six-month mandate expired 5 April 1994, and extended until the end of December 1995.

U.N. Military Observers in Liberia (UNOMIL)

UNOMIL was established 22 September 1993 with 650 personnel (330 military and 320 civilians) at an estimated cost for a seven-month mandate of $140 million. The mission is to augment the Economic Community of West African States' current cease-fire monitoring group. The U.N. Security Council concurred in December 1993 that the mission be continued. In June 1995 the mission continued.

Americas

U.N. Observer Mission in El Salvador (ONUSAL)

ONUSAL was established 20 May 1991 with 310 personnel (0 U.S.) at an estimated cost (1993) of $49 million and $4 million in 1995. The initial mandate was to monitor the human rights agreement between the government of El Salvador and the Farabundo Marti National Liberation Front (FMLN). This mandate was expanded 14 January 1992 to include monitoring the cease-fire, separating combatants, and observing the dismantling of the FMLN and its incorporation into Salvadoran society. The U.N. Security Council extended its mandate through the scheduled March 1994 elections. The force withdrew in April 1995.

U.N. Mission in Haiti (UNMIH)

UNMIH was established 23 September 1993 with 1,267 personnel (to include approximately 600 U.S. Seabees and military trainers) at an estimated cost of $50 million for the first six months. The mission was to oversee democratic elections and monitor human rights. On 31 August 1993 the U.N. Security Council approved an advance team of not more than thirty persons for not more than thirty days to prepare for possible deployment of the proposed peacekeeping forces. Deployment of forces was suspended 14 October after an armed gang blocked a ship carrying the U.N. forces from docking in Port-au-Prince. In July 1994, U.N. Security Council Resolution 940 established a Multinational Force (MNF) in Haiti with the United States as the main participant. This led to the commitment of 20,000 troops, mostly from the United States, which were reduced to 6,500 by March 1995. This was followed by the establishment of UNMIH under Resolution 940 with 6,000 troops, including 2,400 from the United States (550 quick reaction forces and 550 special forces).

Asia

U.N. Military Observer Group in India and Pakistan (UNMOGIP)

UNMOGIP was established 5 January 1949 with 39 personnel (0 U.S.) at an estimated cost (1995) of $8 million. The mission is to assist in the implementation of the cease-fire agreement of 1 January 1949 between India and Pakistan. UNMOGIP observes, reports, and investigates complaints from the parties on violations of the cease-fire. UNMOGIP's mandate is of indefinite duration. States providing personnel are Belgium, Chile, Denmark, Finland, Italy, Norway, Sweden, and Uruguay.

U.N. Transitional Authority for Cambodia (UNTAC)

UNTAC was established 28 February 1992 with 20 personnel (0 U.S.). The costs of this mission were not available. The mission was to restore and maintain peace, promote national reconciliation, and ensure the exercise of the right to self-determination of the Cambodian people through free and fair elections. Its mandate expired with the formation of a new government in September 1993. The withdrawal of UNTAC's personnel was completed in December 1993. More than thirty countries provided troops or observers.

Europe

U.N. Force in Cyprus (UNFICYP)

UNFICYP was established 4 March 1964 with 1,221 personnel (0 U.S.) at an estimated cost (1995) of $44 million. The mission is to halt violence between the Turkish Cypriot and Greek Cypriot communities and to help maintain order on the island. UNFICYP's six-month mandate has been renewed each May and December. Argentina, Austria, and the United Kingdom are the major troop contributors.

U.N. Protection Force (UNPROFOR)

UNPROFOR was established in the former Yugoslavia 21 February 1992 with 27,000 personnel (556 U.S.) at an estimated cost (1993) of $900 million. The mission was initially established with a twelve-month mandate as an interim arrangement to create the conditions of peace and security required for the negotiation of an overall settlement of the Yugoslav crisis. Through subsequent U.N. Security Council resolutions, functions were added to its mandate, including providing security at Sarajevo Airport, monitoring areas in Croatia, protecting humanitarian convoys, deploying observers in Macedonia, and enforcing an arms embargo on Bosnia-Herzegovina. More than thirty nations contribute personnel. In June 1995 the United Nations authorized an increase of 10,000 personnel, including French, British, and Dutch troops. These were for the purpose of establishing quick reaction forces to protect UNPROFOR. However, it was not clear what final impact the United Nations would have in the former Yugoslavia. Fighting continued, sometimes sporadically, sometimes intensely, with civilians the major casualties. Complicating the situation, Bosnian Moslem forces went on the offensive around Sarejevo in June 1995. As of this writing the situation in Bosnia-Herzogovina remains unclear and unpredictable.

U.N. Observer Mission in Georgia (UNOMIG)

UNOMIG was established 24 August 1993 with 55 personnel (0 U.S.) at an estimated cost of $16 million for six months and $22 million in 1995. The mission was to monitor compliance with the cease-fire agreement reached between the Republic of Georgia and Abkhaz separatist forces on 27 July 1993. The mission was expanded in July 1994 by the United Nations to include monitoring of the cease-fire and separation of forces agreement, which was signed in May 1994. This included the deployment of about 1,900 Russian troops to monitor the cease-fire and oversee the safe return of refugees.

Middle East

U.N. Truce Supervision Organization (UNTSO)

UNTSO was established in 1948 with 216 personnel (16 U.S.) at an estimated cost (1995) of $32 million. The mission was to supervise the truce in the Arab-

Jewish hostilities called for by the U.N. Security Council at the end of the British mandate in Palestine. UNTSO was established with a mandate of indefinite duration. Approximately twenty countries furnish observers.

U.N. Disengagement Observer Force on the Golan Heights (UNDOF)

UNDOF was established 31 May 1974 with 1,027 personnel (0 U.S.) at an estimated cost (1995) of $32 million. The mission is to monitor the buffer zone between Israeli and Syrian forces on the Golan Heights. UNDOF's six-month mandate has been renewed each November and May. Troops are provided by Austria, Canada, Finland, and Poland.

U.N. Interim Force in Lebanon (UNIFIL)

UNIFIL was established on 19 March 1978 with 5,427 personnel at an estimated cost (1995) of $135 million. The mission is to assist in restoring peace in southern Lebanon. UNIFIL's six-month mandate has been renewed each January and July. Fiji, Finland, France, Ghana, Ireland, Italy, Nepal, Norway, Poland, and Sweden furnish troops.

U.N. Iraq-Kuwait Observation Mission (UNIKOM)

UNIKOM was established on 9 April 1991 with 1,510 personnel (15 U.S.) at an estimated cost (1995) of $66 million. The mission is to monitor the demilitarized zone between Iraq and Kuwait established in the aftermath of the Gulf War. UNIKOM's mandate continues indefinitely until all five permanent Security Council members agree to terminate its operations. Thirty-three countries furnish observers.

In his 27 September 1993 address to the 48th session of the U.N. General Assembly, President Clinton said:

> UN peacekeeping holds the promise to resolve many of this era's conflicts. The reason we have supported such missions is not, as some critics in the United States have charged, to subcontract American foreign policy, but to strengthen our security, protect our interests, and to share among nations the costs and effort of pursuing peace.

He added: "Peacekeeping cannot be a substitute for our own national defense, but it can strongly supplement them."[17] The President was referring to the reinforcement of American national defense by the effective use of peacekeeping forces. Yet, in 1995 many in the United States as well as those in a number of Western countries viewed U.S. peacekeeping policy as indecisive and obscure. A case in point was the U.S. policy in Bosnia-Herzegovina. Even with the successful rescue of U.S. Air Force Captain Scott O'Grady (shot down by a surface-to-air missile while flying a U.N. air mission over Bosnia-Herzegovina in June 1995), the United States continued to appear as an indecisive and reluctant superpower.

HUMANITARIAN ASSISTANCE

Humanitarian crises arising from civil wars in Somalia and in the former Yugoslavia assumed center stage in the international arena during the early 1990s.[18] Such conflicts, with their large-scale suffering, are likely to persist and are the principal source of pressure for a more effective international response to humanitarian crises. They do not, however, present policymakers with easy decisions.

The U.S. government has established procedures for providing humanitarian assistance that go beyond the scope of this discussion.[19] The U.S. embassy, the Agency for International Development, and/or the DOD may coordinate the initial U.S. government response within the affected country.

The DOD's congressional authority to provide foreign disaster assistance is derived from a series of provisions contained in the Foreign Assistance Act of 1961 and Titles 10 and 31 of the United States Code.[20] In 1985 the DOD created the Office of Humanitarian Assistance (OHA) to coordinate DOD assistance with that from other U.S. agencies. Since then, subsequent organizational changes have occurred in OHA. In February 1994 OHA was redesignated the Office of Humanitarian Assistance and Refugee Affairs, responsible to the Assistant Secretary of Defense, Special Operations/Low-Intensity Conflict.

The U.S. armed forces have a number of capabilities that make them well suited to provide humanitarian assistance on a timely basis. Military personnel, often civil affairs officers drawn from both the active and reserve units, are well trained in a variety of disciplines and readily available to execute humanitarian assistance missions. Engineering equipment, medical teams, and water-purification and communication systems are essential resources that the U.S. military can provide in support of humanitarian assistance operations.

Is it wise for the United States to deploy its armed forces for humanitarian purposes? Public opinion surveys are ambiguous. They indicate general public support for overseas humanitarian efforts, provided that other countries share the burdens for such efforts, and public support for reduced U.S. involvement in world affairs. For example, questions remain about what the United States really accomplished in Somalia. Many predicted an upsurge in violence once U.S. military forces were no longer in the country. They argued that economic-related criminal activity and large-scale looting would be difficult to contain in a country that was without jobs and had no government to provide services to its people. The "tactical redeployment" of U.S. military combat troops from Somalia has been viewed by some as "the biggest military-political misadventure since U.S. forces went to Lebanon in 1983."[21]

The U.S. military's humanitarian assistance in the Kurdish relief effort in northern Iraq and southern Turkey at the close of the 1991 Persian Gulf War (Operation Desert Storm) represented a continuing DOD involvement in such activities. The level of aid provided by the military was unprecedented (at least since the end of World War II).[22] In the closing moments of the Gulf War, hundreds of thousands of Kurds fled into the mountains of northern Iraq and southern Turkey to avoid the wrath of Saddam Hussein. The United Nations and other relief agencies were overwhelmed by the sheer numbers of fleeing Kurds, the inaccessible terrain, and adverse weather conditions. U.S. armed forces launched and led a major relief effort (Operation Provide Comfort) on 6 April. Other members of the allied coalition also participated. Approximately 16,000 tons of supplies (tents, blankets, food, clothing, and water) were provided to the Kurds by a combination of air and ground transportation.[23]

This effort showed that the U.S. armed forces have the capabilities to deal with the challenges that are likely to be important to civilian victims of internal wars as well as with military challenges. These capabilities include health care, construction, and the means to deliver food, water, and medical supplies to remote areas. In a report to Congress, former Secretary of the Air Force Donald B. Rice said, "Part of global power is the means to extend a helping hand, and to use airpower for diplomatic and humanitarian purposes, or in support of international objectives."[24]

Although U.S. unilateral or U.S.-dominated humanitarian assistance operations are rare, they provide a number of advantages to the United States when they occur. Most notably, the United States retains control over the operation. In addition, such operations serve as a means of maintaining U.S. influence and stature abroad. The infrequency of U.S. unilateral or U.S. dominated operations is undoubtedly due in part to the reluctance of policymakers to commit U.S. armed forces in political conflict situations for purely humanitarian reasons.[25]

The lessons of Somalia (Operation Restore Hope) may have an important bearing on future decisions to undertake unilateral or U.S.-dominated humanitarian operations. The December 1992 U.S. intervention to provide security for humanitarian reasons in Somalia may set a precedent for U.S. armed forces to participate increasingly in international or regional efforts to restore order and maintain peace in civil conflicts. (The U.S.-led operation ended on 4 May 1993, at which time responsibility for security in Somalia was assumed by a U.N. force. Subsequently the U.N. force was withdrawn in early 1995.) If so, it will behoove U.S. policymakers to refresh themselves with four lessons learned during the initial U.S. troop buildup in Somalia, the first international effort to impose peace by force on a warring country and to rebuild its society. The following are principles that should guide U.S. involvement in international efforts:

1. Given the political situation in a country, a clear understanding of the objective and the resources required to accomplish that objective is essential.
2. The resources, including managerial and logistical, available to accomplish the objective must be known in advance.
3. It is essential to know how long it is going to take to accomplish the mission and the likely cost, both financial and in casualties.

4. Prior to the deployment of U.S. troops on such a mission, the U.S. President must insist on having the support of Congress and the American public.[26]

Those who support future U.S. armed humanitarian operations argue "that the United States should support the use of force in responding to humanitarian crises, largely on moral grounds but also to demonstrate continued U.S. leadership and promote regional stability."[27] President Clinton has commented that "if peacekeepers are to be effective agents for peace and stability in Somalia and elsewhere, they must be capable of using force when necessary."[28]

The U.S. and U.N. involvement in Haiti presented (and presents) a particularly difficult problem for U.S. policymakers and the military. Although the restoration of the Aristide government had been accomplished, in mid-1995 much remained to be done in developing a stable political and economic environment in Haiti. This remained even with the elections held in June 1995.

With the recent proliferation of civil conflicts resulting in a large number of civilian casualties, a wider range of possible military operations for humanitarian purposes in the future is possible. The objectives of such operations are obvious: to protect civilian lives, to prevent atrocities, to provide relief, and to promote the welfare of the people of the country concerned. Some ways in which military force might be used for humanitarian purposes during civil strife are presented in table 12.1.[29]

Civil conflicts, fueled by ancient hatreds, ethnic rivalry, and political instability, are permanent features of world politics. The United Nations is assuming an expanding role in humanitarian operations, as witnessed by operations in Cambodia and the former Yugoslavia. Expectations are that this role will continue under the leadership of U.N. Secretary General Boutros Boutros-Ghali, who supports a more active role for the United Nations.[30]

The caution that the United Nations must observe is that because of its diverse membership, deployment of military units can be delayed and restricted, thus making it difficult for the United Nations to respond to humanitarian needs. The prolonged delay in the arrival of U.N. troops in Somalia in 1992 while negotiations dragged on with warlords in the Somali capital is an example. Outbreaks of civil strife in Afghanistan, Africa, Burma, and Europe are but a few of the conflicts that are beyond the capacity of the United States to resolve or the capability of the United Nations or the international community to ameliorate.

SECURITY ASSISTANCE

Security assistance involves a range of U.S. governmental programs that "employ funding and legal authorities to provide defense assistance, economic support, peacekeeping, nonproliferation, and counter-narcotics assistance to key friends and allies."[31] It is offered primarily on a grant basis, thus enabling recipient countries to devote their financial resources to economic development.

Table 12.1
Possible Uses of Force for Humanitarian Purposes in Civil Strife

Armed Activity	Possible Objectives
Armed military forces deliver relief aid, using force only in self-defense and to protect relief supplies.	Provide relief aid with increased security for relief forces while deterring interference by armed hostile groups.
Armed military forces enforce sanctions and/ or blockade.	Pressure the offending government to modify its behavior to better protect civilians; deprive it of arms that might be used against civilians.
Armed suppression of military air traffic in the offending country.	Prevent or reduce air attacks on civilians; protect delivery of relief supplies; pressure the government to modify its behavior.
Air strikes against selected military targets.	Prevent use of weapons against civilians, punish the offending combatant, demonstrate resolve to protect civilians.
Air, ground, and/or naval action against the armed forces of one or more combatants.	Deter or reduce attacks on civilians or relief shipments; pressure the offending government or other combatants to modify behavior.
Armed forces create safe havens and defend them against local combatants.	Shelter displaced civilians until the conflict subsides.
Armed forces monitor a ceasefire or peace agreement with the consent of the combatants.	Protect civilians and encourage a resumption of a normal life through efforts to prevent a resumption of hostilities.
Armed occupation of territory to enforce terms not accepted by the government and/or other parties.	Restore peaceful conditions and allow resumption of normal life; arrange a transition to a new regime more likely to respect civilian lives.

A jointly prepared fiscal year 1994 report by the Department of State and the Defense Security Assistance Agency to Congress states:

The U.S. offers security assistance to strengthen the national security of friendly nations and to support existing or prospective democratic institutions and market economies. As we seek to shape the emerging post–Cold War international environment, security assistance provides a vital element of continuity and contributes to secure, stable relationships.[32]

An instrument of response to the challenges of the post–Cold War international security environment, security assistance involves a complexity of diplomatic, financial, political, and security issues that are beyond the scope of this chapter. The following information, however, will provide the reader with helpful insights into some of these issues.

Major Programs

Major appropriated U.S. security assistance programs include Foreign Military Financing (FMF), the Economic Support Fund (ESF), International Military Education and Training (IMET), Peacekeeping Operations (PKO), and the Nonproliferation and Disarmament Fund (NDF). A discussion of each follows.[33]

FMF is used to help countries provide for their defensive needs through the acquisition of U.S. military articles, services, and training. It also promotes U.S. national security interests by strengthening coalitions with U.S. friends and allies and improving military-to-military relationships. FMF supports U.S. regional security cooperation with allies in their defense capabilities through major modernization programs. (Egypt, Israel, and Turkey are key recipients of U.S. security assistance.) It finances equipment and services in support of peacekeeping operations and helps Latin American and Caribbean nations acquire aircraft and other items to fight the war on drugs. Almost all FMF is spent in the United States, thus strengthening the U.S. economy by financing sales of defense items. These sales lengthen production runs, which in turn results in lower unit costs for DOD purchases and creates jobs.

The ESF provides economic as well as counternarcotics assistance to U.S. allies and strategically important developing countries. The U.S. Agency for International Development (USAID) implements the ESF program under the direction of the administrator of USAID with overall foreign policy guidance from the Secretary of State.

The ESF provides balance-of-payments support to U.S. friends and allies through cash transfers or through financing of commodity imports from the United States for acquisition of critical raw materials and capital goods when foreign exchange is not readily available. If longer-term political and economic stability is the primary concern, ESF finances infrastructure or other capital projects and development projects that benefit the poor.

Recognized as one of the most cost-effective components of U.S. security assistance, the IMET program provides military education and training on a grant basis to students from allied and friendly nations. (The scope and purpose of the IMET program have been expanded in recent years by the Foreign Operations, Export Financing, and Related Programs Appropriations Act, 1991 and 1993, to provide training for foreign military and civilian officials from ministries other than Defense, such as the Foreign Ministry and equivalents of the Department of the Treasury and Office of Management and Budget.)

"Since 1950, IMET and its predecessor programs have trained more than 500,000 foreign officers and enlisted personnel in areas ranging from professional military education to basic technical and nation building skills."[34] The training received not only enables these officers and enlisted personnel to improve the capabilities of their own military forces but also exposes them to America's democratic values and institutions. One of the long-term benefits of the IMET program is the friendships established between foreign and U.S. military personnel. Significant numbers of IMET students eventually assume prominent military and civilian positions in their own countries.

As discussed earlier in this chapter, peacekeeping operations (PKO) have increased dramatically since 1989 and can be expected to increase further in the years ahead. The Foreign Assistance Act of 1961, Part II, Chapter 6, as amended, authorizes assistance to friendly countries and international organizations for PKO that further U.S. national security interests. Funding under this statute has for the most part been limited to support of the UNFICYP and the Multinational Force and Observers in the Sinai (MFO), although assistance has been provided to other peacekeeping activities. (The security assistance budget covers nonassessed, that is, voluntary contributions to bilateral or multilateral operations. A separate and much larger account covers assessed U.N. peacekeeping activities, but it is not classified as a security assistance program.)

Nonproliferation has moved to the forefront of the U.S. national security agenda. According to Thomas Graham, Jr., acting director of the Arms Control and Disarmament Agency (ACDA), it "is the number one foreign policy issue and will continue to be so for a number of years."[35] The NDF is a new element in the security assistance budget and demonstrates the increased priority given to nonproliferation and disarmament programs. The DOS, the DOD, the Department of Energy, and the ACDA are all involved in implementing these programs, major objectives of which include the following:

1. To reduce and restructure Russia's strategic nuclear force into a smaller and less destabilizing force
2. To assist in dismantling existing systems of proliferation that are a concern in the states of the former Soviet Union
3. To increase the effectiveness of existing nonproliferation and arms-control agreements and promote arms control and security in regions of tension[36]

Principal Agencies

U.S. security assistance programs require close coordination among several agencies of the executive branch, including the National Security Council (NSC), Office of Management and Budget (OMB), Department of State (DOS), and DOD. Congress enacts the laws that authorize U.S. security assistance programs and provides the authority to expend funds to implement the programs discussed earlier.[37]

Although the Clinton Administration attempted to develop a new approach in foreign aid, the Republican-controlled Congress (resulting from the November 1994 election and voter repudiation of the Democratic Party agenda) opposed the President's agenda. Congress established limits and placed some reduction in foreign aid and, in the main, is skeptical about using U.S. forces for peacekeeping operations under a U.N. mandate. This is particularly true with respect to Bosnia-Herzegovina.[38]

The following agencies are involved in the security assistance process: The President, supported by the NSC, establishes U.S. national security policy objectives. These policies define the priorities and implementation of the various security assistance programs. Members and advisors of the NSC include the President, the Secretaries of State and Defense, the Chairman of the Joint Chiefs of Staff (JCS), and the Director of the Central Intelligence Agency (CIA).

The OMB oversees the preparation of the President's budget and determines the amount of the budget to be used for security assistance. The budget is then submitted to Congress.

The U.S. Congress exercises its legislative and oversight responsibilities in the security assistance arena through four committees: Senate Foreign Relations, House Foreign Affairs, and the Senate and House Appropriations committees. These committees review the proposed security assistance legislation, budgets, and programs, which are presented to the committees by senior officials of DOS and DOD.

The overall supervision and major policy, program, and priority decisions regarding the U.S. security assistance program rest with the Secretary of State and his department. The Secretary of Defense (SECDEF) is responsible for the management, operation, and administration of the security assistance programs. Within the DOD, the JCS provides military advice to the SECDEF regarding the coordination of security assistance with U.S. military readiness, plans, and programs. The DOD organizations responsible for the implementation of security assistance programs are the Defense Security Assistance Agency (DSAA) and the military departments (Army, Navy, which coordinates the Marine Corps and Coast Guard programs, and Air Force).

The DSAA is responsible for the administration, coordination, formulation, negotiation, and execution of U.S. security assistance programs. It maintains security assistance program data, prepares (in conjunction with DOS) the annual security assistance budget for submission to Congress, and establishes policies and procedures for the implementation of the security assistance program by the military departments and other DOD agencies.

PROSPECTS FOR THE POST–COLD WAR ERA

Although the Cold War is over and no serious threat to U.S. security interests exists at present, the world remains a dangerous place, as witnessed by the ethnic, religious, and national violence in Asia, Europe, and elsewhere.[39] The realities of the new international security environment, made more dangerous by the spread of high-technology weapons, present complex and difficult challenges to U.S. policymakers for the remaining years of the twentieth century and beyond.

Although the United States no longer faces the single defining Soviet threat that dominated U.S. policy for more than forty years, the dangers are more diverse.

> Ethnic conflict is spreading and rogue states pose a serious danger to regional stability in many corners of the globe. The proliferation of weapons of mass destruction represents a major challenge to our security. Large scale environmental degradation, exacerbated by rapid population growth, threatens to undermine political stability in many countries and regions.[40]

While the United States cannot become the world's policeman and assume responsibility for solving every international security problem, U.S. assistance to peacekeeping efforts and the provision of humanitarian and security assistance can help preclude some conflicts by encouraging American values and democratic government. Of the three noncombat operations discussed in this chapter, that of peacekeeping operations has received the greatest attention in the early years of the post–Cold War era. Armed humanitarian operations are perhaps the most controversial because they are undertaken against the wishes of the government concerned and are contrary to the principle of sovereignty of states. Security assistance remains an important concept, but is remote to all but those select few who are intimately involved in this area.

Peacekeeping has become an important word in the post–Cold War vocabulary. As events in Somalia and Bosnia have demonstrated to both the Bush and Clinton administrations, peacekeeping in all of its manifestations presents a major challenge to U.S. presidents for the foreseeable future. One author wrote: "[Peacekeeping] is not an optional extra, something that we may choose to do or refrain from doing. . . . it is an integral part of doing business in the new security environment." He added: "Peacekeeping is a powerful tool for policy makers. When effective, it can also make a tremendous impact on the lives, security, and well-being of countless people around the world, encouraging the development of democracy and creating global goodwill for America."[41]

But the cost of peacekeeping operations can be high, as witnessed by the deaths of eighteen U.S. servicemen in Somalia in early October 1993. This event caused American public sentiment to swing against future U.S. involvement in U.N. peacekeeping operations in countries where the security environment is unstable and the prospects of casualties are high. In the final days of the March 1994 withdrawal of U.S. combat forces from Somalia, General John Shalikashvili, chairman of the Joint Chiefs of Staff, emphasized in repeated interviews with the media the need to inform the public and Congress better about the inherent risks of casualties in humanitarian and peacekeeping missions. (U.S.

casualties from the time U.S. troops arrived in December 1992 in Somalia until mid-March 1994 were 30 killed and 175 wounded in combat.)[42]

Congressional support for peacekeeping and humanitarian operations also has weakened. Senator John McCain, for example, wrote:

> As the events of 1993 have demonstrated, it is in neither the U.S. interests nor the international community's to subject U.S. decisionmaking on grave matters of state, and the lives of American soldiers, to the frequently vacillating, frequently contradictory, and frequently reckless collective impulses of the United Nations.[43]

The United States is drifting away from its initial post–Cold War support for U.N. peacekeeping operations. Acknowledging that the success of collective peacekeeping operations is important, one senior U.S official argued that the United Nations "has tried to do too much too soon."[44] Whether the United States elects in the future to participate solely in traditional peacekeeping observer missions as before or to move more forcefully into "assertive multilateralism" remains to be seen.

It is a political-military fact of life that without U.S. leadership key European allies will not stay involved in distant peacekeeping or humanitarian assistance operations. Responding to the withdrawal of all U.S. combat troops from Somalia on 31 March 1994, France, Germany, and Italy also withdrew their peacekeeping troops. To adapt to the withdrawal of U.S. and European forces from Somalia without giving up the U.N. effort to rebuild Somalia, Secretary General Boutros Boutros-Ghali proposed to reduce the U.N. role in Somalia and hoped that a range of African countries, India, and Pakistan would provide the necessary troops to fulfill that role.[45] All of these plans ended with the withdrawal of U.N. forces in early 1995.

One of the least publicized DOD programs that supports U.S. foreign policy objectives is humanitarian assistance. This assistance takes many forms, for example, the donation of excess food, clothing, and medical supplies, construction of schools and roads by American servicemen, and the transportation by U.S. military aircraft of privately donated humanitarian cargoes. Since 1990 the DOD has played a major role in providing assistance to the Kurdish people in northern Iraq, to states in Central and Eastern Europe, to the new states of the former Soviet Union, and to the people suffering from armed conflicts in Bosnia, Ethiopia, and Somalia. DOD assistance has also been provided in major crises in the United States.

The U.S. military is uniquely equipped by virtue of its air- and sealift capacity to deliver (on short notice) food, medical supplies, and other provisions worldwide. Historically, DOD has conducted humanitarian assistance programs in support of broader U.S. foreign policy objectives. This assistance, provided to over one hundred countries between 1985 and early 1994, enhanced military-to-military relations, improved relations with other nations, and made a major contribution to the relief of human suffering.[46]

DOD policy supports military involvement in U.S. humanitarian assistance operations. But officials favor an expanded role for the U.S. military in providing humanitarian aid only as long as American military forces support and do not lead such operations. Indications are that the following criteria must be present for DOD involvement:

1. Large numbers of people must be affected.
2. There must be a sense of urgency to the operation (people must be helped in a matter of hours or days).
3. The level of assistance required must be of the magnitude of thousands of tons of food and/or relief items.[47]

For those who advocate a wider use of the armed forces to assist civilians during internal conflicts, the operations conducted in northern Iraq and southern Turkey, Cambodia, and Somalia and under way in the former Yugoslavia may be precedents for the future. Although each operation was undertaken for a variety of reasons, humanitarian concerns were paramount. Their collective lessons may lead to more effective operations in the future.

For the foreseeable future, if U.S. policymakers consider increasing the use of American armed forces in humanitarian operations, they will be confronted with a number of questions. Will such operations be compatible with the DOD's primary mission? Is the use of American armed forces in humanitarian operations cost-effective? What will the budgetary implications be for DOD? Will DOD compete with domestic interests in humanitarian operations?[48]

Security assistance programs of the United States have underwritten American foreign policy for over forty years "and are regarded worldwide as tangible evidence of American commitment to national independence and peaceful development."[49] They can continue to assist the United States to meet the challenges of the post–Cold War international security environment. These challenges include aggressive nationalism, regional threats, and unprecedented opportunities for multinational cooperation on security matters.

The ability of the United States to utilize security assistance effectively, however, is impaired by declining resources. For example, funding for the FMF program, which finances defense purchases for more than fifty countries in support of U.S. foreign base and access rights, Middle East peace and stability, counterdrug efforts, and democratic developments, has declined steadily in recent years. Grant aid to a number of key U.S. allies—Greece, Portugal, and Turkey—has been terminated by Congress.[50]

Promoting regional stability has been a consistent, historical U.S. interest in areas where America has important strategic or economic objectives. This interest will not change. In the aftermath of over forty years of U.S.-Soviet rivalry, DOD policies and activities are adjusting to a new regional defense strategy, based not on a world of Cold War tensions, but on a world that remains unpredictable with both challenges and opportunities yet to come.

Noncombat operations—peacekeeping, humanitarian assistance, and security assistance—are indispensable elements to the regional defense strategy. They can assist in shaping the international security environment in ways that can further enhance U.S. security for the remainder of the 1990s and beyond. In commenting on the military forces required to respond to crises in the post–Cold War era, General Colin L. Powell, former chairman of the Joint Chiefs of Staff, said:

> It means a force that can participate more fully in peacekeeping and humanitarian operations. Nothing gives your warriors greater satisfaction than to use their skills not to destroy life but to relieve human sufferings, as they have done around the world over the last several years.[51]

NOTES

1. For a more detailed discussion of these diverse environments, see Headquarters, Department of the Army, *FM 100-5: Operations* (Washington, DC: U.S. Government Printing Office, June 1993), pp. 2-0 and 2-1.

2. The terms *roles, missions,* and *functions* are often used interchangeably within the military, but the distinctions between these terms are important. *Roles* are the broad and enduring purposes for which the military services were established by Congress in law. *Missions* are the tasks assigned by the President or Secretary or Defense (SECDEF) to the combatant Commanders-in-Chief (CINCs). *Functions* are specific responsibilities assigned by the President and SECDEF to enable the services to fulfill their legally established roles. "The main purpose of assigning roles, missions, and functions is to protect America." Chairman of the Joint Chiefs of Staff, *Report on the Roles, Missions, and Functions of the Armed Forces of the United States,* February 1993, Executive Summary, pp. iv, xxi.

3. Adapted from United Nations Secretary General Boutros Boutros-Ghali's report, United Nations, General Assembly and Security Council, *An Agenda for Peace: Preventive Diplomacy, Peacemaking, and Peacekeeping.* Report of the Secretary General, U.N. Document A/47/266, E/2411 (New York: The United Nations, 17 June 1992), p. 6.

4. The humanitarian crises arising from civil wars in Somalia and the former Yugoslavia have become central international problems in the post–Cold War era. Such wars are likely to persist in view of ethnic and political tensions afflicting other countries. For an excellent discussion of the humanitarian role of armed forces, see Raymond W. Copson, *The Use of Force in Civil Conflicts for Humanitarian Purposes: Prospects for the Post–Cold War Era,* Congressional Research Service Report for Congress, 2 December 1992.

5. *U.S. Department of Defense Dictionary of Military Terms* (Arco Publishing, 1988), p. 315.

6. The review identified four threats to U.S. national security: nuclear proliferation, regional conflict, internal threats to democracy in the former Soviet Union and the developing world, and a weak domestic economy. These threats are the basis for subsequent scenarios that will be used to shape the U.S. military's force structure and DOD mod-

ernization plans. For a succinct discussion of the review, see John Lancaster, ''Pentagon Issues Plan for Future,'' *Washington Post,* 2 September 1993, pp. A1, A12.

7. Ibid., p. A12.

8. News Release, Department of Defense, Office of Assistant Secretary of Defense (Public Affairs), Washington, D.C., ''Remarks Prepared for Delivery by Secretary of Defense Les Aspin at the U.S. Air Force Senior Statesman Symposium, Andrews Air Force Base, MD,'' 24 June 1993, p. 1. The focus of these remarks was on the ''broader area of major importance highlighted by'' the bottom-up review—''the need to ensure a strong peacetime presence of U.S. military forces around the world'' (p. 2).

9. Richard Cheney, Secretary of Defense, *Annual Report to the President and the Congress* (Washington, DC: U.S. Government Printing Office, January 1993), p. 14 (hereafter cited as Cheney, *ARC*).

10. Secretary of Defense Dick Cheney, *Defense Strategy for the 1990s: The Regional Defense Strategy,* January 1993, p. 1. This document provides an excellent discussion of the shift in the U.S. focus from a global threat (the former Soviet Union) to one of regional challenges and opportunities. See Chairman of the Joint Chiefs of Staff, General Colin L. Powell, ''U.S. Forces Challenges Ahead,'' *Foreign Affairs,* Winter 1992/1993, pp. 32–45, for a discussion of the variety of missions that the U.S. armed forces will be required to perform in containing future regional threats.

11. Cheney, *Defense Strategy for the 1990s,* p. 3.

12. The following sources were extremely helpful in developing this section: Lieutenant Colonel Charles M. Ayers, USA, *Peacekeeping Tactics, Techniques, and Procedures* (Langley Air Force Base, VA: Army–Air Force Center for Low Intensity Conflict, April 1989); Colonel John W. McDonald, USA (retired), *Military Operations to Restore Order and Maintain Peace,* Association of the U.S. Army Institute of Land Warfare, Landpower Essay Series No 93-1, March 1993; Marjorie Ann Browne, *United Nations Peacekeeping: Issues for Congress,* Congressional Research Service Issue Brief, 16 June 1993; and Center for Army Lessons Learned, U.S. Army Combined Arms Command, Fort Leavenworth, Kansas, Newsletter no. 93-X, Final Draft—17 November 1993, *Operations Other Than War,* vol. 9, *Peace Operations.*

13. Browne, *United Nations Peacekeeping,* p. CRS-4.

14. See, for example, Boutros Boutros-Ghali, ''Empowering the United Nations,'' *Foreign Affairs,* Winter 1992/1993, pp. 89–102.

15. Madeleine K. Albright, ''Use of Force in a Post–Cold War World,'' *U.S. Department of State Dispatch* 4, no. 39 (27 September 1993): 667.

16. Compiled by the author using public source information provided by the Department of State, Office of Peacekeeping.

17. The White House, Office of the Press Secretary (New York, New York), *Address by the President to the 48th Session of the United Nations General Assembly,* 27 September 1993.

18. The following material from the Center for Army Lessons Learned, U.S. Army Combined Arms Command, Fort Leavenworth, Kansas, provided background for the development of this section: Newsletter no. 92-6, December 1992, *Operations Other Than War,* vol. 1, *Humanitarian Assistance;* Newsletter no. 93-6, October 1993, vol. 2, *Disaster Assistance;* and Newsletter no. 93-7, November 1993, vol. 3, *Civil Disturbances.*

19. For a succinct discussion of these procedures, see Patrice K. Curtis, *Providing Humanitarian Assistance: Using the U.S. Military Overseas,* Congressional Research Report for Congress, 31 July 1992, pp. CRS-3 and CRS-4.

20. Ibid., p. CRS-8.

21. For assorted views, based on public survey opinions, see Copson, *Use of Force in Civil Conflicts for Humanitarian Purposes,* pp. CRS-11 through CRS-13. For a sobering discussion of the events that might occur in the wake of U.S. military forces' withdrawal from Somalia, see Keith B. Richburg, ''GIs Quitting Somalia Leave by Back Door,'' *Washington Post,* 7 March 1994, p. A14; Bradley Graham, ''Chairman of Joint Chiefs Bucks Up Troops Being Pulled out of Somalia,'' *Washington Post,* 14 March 1994, p. A12.

22. The Berlin Airlift was the first demonstration of modern U.S. military capability in providing large-scale humanitarian aid. The largest military emergency assistance effort to date, it began on 26 June 1948 in response to the Soviet blockade of Berlin, Germany. At the time the airlift concluded (September 1949), the U.S. military and the British Royal Air Force had airlifted 2.3 million tons of goods (coal, food, and miscellaneous supplies) into Berlin. Curtis, *Providing Humanitarian Assistance,* p. CRS-5.

23. Ibid., p. CRS-6.

24. Cheney, *Annual Report,* p. 138.

25. Humanitarian operations are viewed by some as situations where U.S. forces could become ''bogged down in complex, poorly understood foreign conflicts.'' The American experiences in Vietnam and Lebanon are often cited as examples against U.S. ''entanglement in foreign civil conflicts.'' Copson, *Use of Force in Civil Conflicts for Humanitarian Purposes,* pp. CRS-18 and CRS-19.

26. For a discussion of the broader implications of the U.S. intervention in Somalia for U.S. foreign policy, see Raymond W. Copson, *Somalia: Operation Restore Hope and UNOSOM II,* Congressional Research Service Issue Brief, 18 June 1993, pp. CRS-13 and CRS-14. Lessons learned are adapted from comments to reporters by Robert B. Oakley, chief U.S. representative in Mogadishu during the initial U.S. troop buildup. Thomas W. Lippman, ''Clinton Envoy Cites Lessons of Somalia,'' *Washington Post,* 18 December 1993, p. A8.

27. Copson, *Use of Force in Civil Conflicts for Humanitarian Purposes,* summary.

28. The quote is extracted from News Release, Office of Assistant Secretary of Defense (Public Affairs), Washington, D.C., ''Secretary of Defense Les Aspin's Remarks before the American Israel Public Affairs Executive Committee, Dinner Park Hyatt Hotel'' Washington, D.C., 14 June 1993, p. 1.

29. Adapted from Copson, *Use of Force in Civil Conflicts for Humanitarian Purposes,* pp. CRS-1 and CRS-2.

30. The Secretary General's 1992 report, *An Agenda for Peace,* has become a major focus for his discussion on strengthening the United Nations. Also see Boutros-Ghali, ''Empowering the United Nations.''

31. Department of State and the Defense Security Agency, *Congressional Presentation for Security Assistance Programs,* Fiscal Year 1994 (Washington, DC: Department of Defense, Office of the Assistant Secretary of Defense, Public Affairs, 1993), p. 3. This document is jointly prepared by the Department of State and the Defense Security Assistance Agency. Hereafter the document is referred to as CPD.

32. CPD, p. 4.

33. In discussing these programs, I have drawn heavily from CPD, pp. 19, 27–28, 38, 44, and 48. This document, in addition to narrative discussions, includes proposed security assistance regional and country program funding and tables with relevant economic and assistance data. For those interested in statistical tables dealing with security assis-

tance programs, see Department of Defense Security Assistance Agency Publication, *Foreign Military Sales, Foreign Military Construction Sales, and Military Assistance Facts, As of September 30, 1992* (by FMS Control and Reports Division Comptroller, DSAA).

34. CPD, pp. 27–28.

35. Thomas W. Lippman, ''For Nuclear Arms Control Professional Negotiating Treaty Extension Is Job 1,'' *Washington Post,* 13 February 1994, p. A14.

36. CPD, p. 48.

37. For additional information on these and other agencies, see Cheney, *Annual Report,* pp. 18–19; Association of the United States Army Institute of Land Warfare Special Report, ''Security Assistance: An Instrument of U.S. Foreign Policy,'' June 1990, pp. 8–10; and *Commitment to Freedom: Security Assistance as a U.S. Policy Instrument in the Third World,* a paper by the Regional Conflict Working Group submitted to the Commission on Integrated Long-Term Strategy (Washington, DC: U.S. Government Printing Office, May 1988).

38. During 1993, when this new approach was being considered within the Clinton administration, opposition to it developed in the Democratic Party–controlled Congress. For example, see Thomas W. Lippman, ''U.S. Foreign Aid Overhaul Urged,'' *Washington Post,* 18 September 1993, p. A1; and John M. Goshko and Thomas W. Lippman, ''Foreign Aid Shift Sought by Clinton,'' *Washington Post,* 27 November 1993, p. A1.

39. According to a Central Intelligence Agency report, as reported by the *Washington Post,* the only countries that ''currently have the capability to strike the continental United States with land-based ballistic missiles'' are China, Russia, and some republics of the former Soviet Union. Because of economic or other reasons, there is a ''low probability that any other country [Iraq, Libya, and North Korea] will acquire this capability during the next 15 years.'' Thomas W. Lippman, ''ICBM Threat to U.S. Is Called Slight,'' *Washington Post,* 24 December 1993, p. A9.

40. The White House, *A National Security Strategy of Engagement and Enlargement* (Washington, DC: U.S. Government Printing Office, February 1995), Preface, p. 1.

41. Joseph Kruzel, ''Peacekeeping and the Partnership for Peace,'' in *Peace Support Operations and the U.S. Military,* ed. Dennis J. Quinn (Washington, DC: National Defense University Press, 1994), p. 93.

42. Graham, ''Chairman of Joint Chiefs Bucks Up Troops Being Pulled out of Somalia,'' p. A12.

43. Senator John McCain, ''The Proper U.S. Role in Peacemaking,'' in Quinn, *Peace Support Operations,* p. 91.

44. Madeleine K. Albright, ''Measured Success at the United Nations,'' *Washington Post,* 6 January 1994, p. A27.

45. For an excellent discussion of the need for U.S. leadership and support in the post–Cold War era, see Jim Hoagland, ''Retreat from Intervention,'' *Washington Post,* 23 December 1993, p. A23. For details on the reduced U.N. mandate, see Julia Preston, ''UN Hopes to Reorganize, Trim Operations in Somalia,'' *Washington Post,* 7 January 1994, p. A13.

46. Cheney, *Annual Report,* p. 22.

47. Curtis, *Providing Humanitarian Assistance,* p. CRS-8.

48. These questions are examined in depth in Curtis, *Providing Humanitarian Assistance,* pp. CRS-13 through CRS-16.

49. *Commitment to Freedom: Security Assistance as a U.S. Policy Instrument in the Third World,* p. 1.

50. Cheney, *Annual Report,* p. 19.

51. ''Remarks by General Colin L. Powell, Chairman of the Joint Chiefs, at the Harvard University Commencement,'' Harvard University, Cambridge, Massachusetts, 10 June 1993, p. 5.

SELECTED BIBLIOGRAPHY

Aspin, Les, Secretary of Defense. ''Remarks at the National Defense University Graduation.'' Ft. McNair, Washington, DC. Washington, DC: News Release, Department of Defense, Office of Assistant Secretary of Defense (Public Affairs), 16 June 1993.

Boutros-Ghali, Boutros. ''Empowering the United Nations.'' *Foreign Affairs,* Winter 1992/1993, pp. 89–102.

Chairman of the Joint Chiefs of Staff. *Report on the Roles, Missions, and Functions of the Armed Forces of the United States.* Washington, DC: Department of Defense, Office of the Assistant Secretary of Defense (Public Affairs), February 1993.

Cheney, Richard, Secretary of Defense. *Defense Strategy for the 1990s: The Regional Strategy.* Washington, DC: Department of Defense, Office of Assistant Secretary of Defense (Public Affairs), January 1993.

Department of State and the Defense Security Assistance Agency. *Congressional Presentation for Security Assistance,* Fiscal Year 1994. Washington, DC: Department of Defense, Office of the Assistant Secretary of Defense Office (Public Affairs), 1993.

Quinn, Dennis J., ed. *Peacekeeping Support Operations and the U.S. Military.* Washington, DC: National Defense University Press, 1994.

White House, The. *Address by the President to the 48th Session of the United Nations General Assembly,* 27 September 1993. Washington, DC: White House, Office of the Press Secretary.

White House, The. *A National Security Strategy of Engagement and Enlargement.* Washington, DC: U.S. Government Printing Office, February 1995.

Chapter 13

UNCONVENTIONAL CONFLICTS

Thomas R. Mockaitis

No area of conflict in the twentieth century has been more pervasive and yet more problematic for the U.S. military than unconventional war. The very term bespeaks a discomfort with what is seen as atypical and abnormal. The shifting, often-confusing array of military labels for this type of warfare reveals a corresponding difficulty in coming to grips with it. ''Limited war'' gave way to ''counterinsurgency,'' which in turn yielded to ''low-intensity conflict,'' which has only recently been displaced by ''operations other than war.'' These terms share one common element: they are catchall categories for activities that the U.S. military considers other than its proper role.

Current U.S. doctrine, exemplified by the Army's latest operations manual, reveals this tendency to lump nontraditional activities under a single ''other'' category. ''Operations other than war'' include non-combatant Evacuation Operations, Arms Control, support to Domestic Civil Authorities, Humanitarian Assistance and Disaster Relief, Security Assistance, Nation Assistance, Support to Counterdrug Operations, Combatting Terrorism, Peacekeeping Operations, Peace Enforcement, Support for Insurgencies and Counterinsurgencies, and Attacks and Raids.[1] Most of these activities are ''noncombat operations'' (see chapter 12 in this volume). ''Attacks and raids'' can be conducted in support of conventional campaigns or discrete operations to achieve a limited, short-term objective. Counterterrorism is a relatively new category including hostage rescue, defense against terrorist attacks, and preemptive strikes against terrorist organizations. Like attacks and raids, such activities are short-term and highly focused. Of all the ''operations other than war,'' only insurgency and counterinsurgency are fully developed unconventional conflicts, although peace-enforcement and counterdrug operations (see chapter 11 in this volume), both of which are relatively new, may prove to have many of the characteristics of counterinsurgency. Insurgency and counterinsurgency also form the bulk of America's unconventional experience and have shaped its response to all unconventional operations.

INSURGENCY

Insurgency is a hybrid form of war in which a revolutionary group seeks to gain control of a country from within through a combination of subversion and guerrilla warfare. Starting from a position of numerical weakness and lacking the resources to engage in an open bid for power, insurgents seek to win converts to their cause while making the country ungovernable through hit-and-run attacks on its infrastructure and personnel. Revolutionary movements have developed out of legitimate grievances of oppressed people in many parts of the world. These grievances often include economic hardship or political oppression. Often motivated by an ideology such as nationalism or Marxism, insurgents win the loyalty of disaffected people with promises of a better life tomorrow in return for practical assistance today. They also use intimidation to compel cooperation. During the Cold War the United States understood insurgency as a purely Communist phenomenon whose most successful practitioner, Mao Tse-tung, sought to export his form of revolution throughout Asia and Latin America. Maoist revolution envisioned rural insurgents swimming like fish amid a sea of peasants who would provide them aid and succor. The insurgents would develop a regional base, driving out government forces through attacks on vulnerable targets, such as supply lines, small police or army units, and government offices. They would always avoid contact with numerically superior and better-armed regular units, blending in with the general population from whom they were indistinguishable. Operating out of a secure base area, the insurgents would expand to dominate the countryside as a whole, drowning the cities in a sea of proletarian revolutionaries. As the insurgency progressed, the guerrillas might develop the capability to engage the government in conventional battle, as they did during the final phase of the conflict in China.[2]

The preoccupation with insurgency as a purely Communist phenomenon has blinded Western analysts to other relevant examples. The Philippine War of 1899–1902, the Anglo-Irish War of 1919–1921, and the Zionist struggle for Palestine in 1945–1948 serve as examples of non-Marxist "people's wars." As the United States learned in Nicaragua, insurgency and counterinsurgency are ideologically neutral terms. During the 1980s the American military aided insurgents in one country while training counterinsurgency forces in another. This Cold War mentality also led the United States to support oppressive regimes merely because they opposed Communist revolutions.

Another result of equating insurgency with Maoist people's war has been misunderstanding of the nature of the insurgency environment. Asian wars of national liberation have been overwhelmingly rural. The insurgency/counterinsurgency environment, however, need not be confined to this arena. The British campaign against Greek nationalists in Cyprus (1954–1959), the Algerian Civil War (1954–1962), and the current struggle in Northern Ireland all occurred in part in built-up areas. The common salient feature of both environments is the human terrain in which the conflicts have to be fought.

Internal war, it has often been noted, is a struggle for the "hearts and minds of the people." Insurgents operate within a disaffected population, drawing on it for sustenance, using it for cover, and subverting it through propaganda. Attacks on the government aim at provoking its forces into conducting reprisals that drive more people into the insurgents' camp. For both parties to such a war, military measures must be subordinate to political considerations.

Another feature distinguishing insurgencies from conventional wars is the protracted nature of such conflicts. Indeed, the goal of revolutionaries has been to wear down their militarily superior foe. Mao took over twenty years to gain control of China; the Vietnam War lasted almost as long. The Algerian Civil War lasted eight years and the Malayan emergency twelve. The duration of insurgent wars makes them particularly difficult for the United States to fight. Neither American culture nor the American political system are conducive to protracted war.

COUNTERINSURGENCY

As the prefix "counter" suggests, counterinsurgency consists of denying revolutionaries their objective of overthrowing the government. The simplest way of achieving this goal would appear to be to destroy the insurgent guerrillas. However, as Clausewitz has reminded soldiers for generations, in war the simplest thing can be extremely difficult. The insurgents must be identified before they can be eliminated. Virtually every authority on the subject notes the primacy of intelligence gathering in internal war. "The problem of defeating the enemy," wrote retired British general and counterinsurgency expert Frank Kitson, "consists very largely of finding him."[3] Information on the insurgents can best be gathered by the police, who usually know their threatened area and its people like a patrolman on his beat. However, since the police are often no match for heavily armed guerrillas, they must pass on intelligence to the armed forces in a timely manner. Cooperation between the police and the military is thus essential.

No matter who gathers it, good, up-to-date intelligence must come from the people threatened with subversion. These people will only help the government if they are certain that its forces can protect them and if they perceive that they will gain by doing so. Since insurgencies invariably develop out of legitimate grievances, threatened governments must meet the needs of disaffected people. In most internal wars material improvements in the standard of living are more effective inducements to cooperation than ideology. The threatened governments must outbid the insurgents for the loyalty of their own people. In more developed areas, however, the emotive force of an idea can be more powerful than any economic incentives. A massive urban-renewal campaign in Northern Ireland has failed to persuade Catholic insurgents and their supporters to abandon their twenty-five–year struggle for union with the Irish Republic. In any case, an information campaign, what the U.S. military calls psychological operations, can help to counter insurgent propaganda.

Once a more cooperative population begins to provide information on insurgent whereabouts and activities, government forces can conduct operations against them. To defeat insurgents operating in small, highly mobile guerrilla bands, armies need to reject much of the conventional war wisdom about concentration of mass and firepower. Counterinsurgency campaigns have been won by breaking conventional units into smaller components under the leadership of junior officers given considerable latitude in conducting operations to beat the insurgents at their own game. Robert Thompson, one architect of the British victory in Malaya, called this the "same element approach." He likened a country threatened by insurgency to an alley disrupted by a tough tomcat. To get rid of the nuisance, most people would send in a dog to chase the cat, who merely hides to return another day. The real solution is to send in a tougher tomcat.[4] With its high-technology, massive-firepower approach to conventional war, the U.S. military has, not surprisingly, been infatuated with the dog approach to counterinsurgency.

Counterinsurgency, then, requires a comprehensive approach to combatting insurgents while removing the causes of unrest on which they feed. In such a strategy military measures must be subordinate to economic, social, and political ones. The government must create an apparatus linking the civil, police, and military organizations under unified command. Intelligence gathering is of primary importance, and the armed forces must be prepared for protracted war. Despite their superior resources, Western armies have found counterinsurgency problematic, and a string of victories by Communist revolutionaries in the 1950s and 1960s led some to deem this form of warfare practically invincible.[5]

With the Americanization of the war in Vietnam, the U.S. military became for a brief period obsessed with solving the problem of people's war. Although the American approach ultimately proved disastrous, this early infatuation with counterinsurgency and later reaction against it has profoundly shaped U.S. doctrine on unconventional war. The approach to Vietnam in turn developed from historical experience. The United States noted the examples of other Western powers beset with Communist insurgency, notably France and Britain, and more particularly drew from its own encounters in Greece, the Philippines, and Korea. However, the overwhelmingly conventional character of the U.S. military establishment and the dictates of American culture determined which examples it emphasized. As a result, analysts ignored some very relevant campaigns in the early twentieth century and drew the wrong conclusions from postwar conflicts.

UNCONVENTIONAL WAR AND CONVENTIONAL ARMIES

Despite their reluctance to engage in unconventional operations, virtually every Western military establishment has had some experience combatting insurgency. The post–World War II period in particular provided a host of such conflicts that precipitated the withdrawal of European colonial powers from their empires in Africa and Asia. The U.S. Army, whose own experience with internal conflict was much more limited, tried to glean valuable lessons from at least some of these wars in order to forge its own doctrine. Foremost among these examples was the British victory over Communist insurgents in Malaya.

Malaya

When the British returned to their colony at the end of World War II, the seeds of revolution had long been sown and would soon bear fruit. The Marxist-led Malayan Peoples Anti-Japanese Army, equipped and partially trained by the British, transformed itself into the Malayan People's Anti-British Army (later the Malayan Races Liberation Army). This force of perhaps 4,000 insurgents supported by perhaps three times as many passive supporters engaged the British and the Malayan government in a twelve-year struggle for control of Malaya.[6] They had many advantages. Malaya was a loosely organized federation of nine semiautonomous states and three crown colonies with a total population of nearly 5,000,000 people, divided into 2,428,000 Malays, 1,885,000 Chinese, and various other groups.[7] The British Army, its prestige badly damaged by the surrender at Singapore, was in a period of postwar retrenchment and had just been unceremoniously ushered out of Palestine. The minority Chinese population on which the insurgency fed was a permanent underclass, many of whom were squatters along the jungle border, where they could easily be subverted by the insurgents.

For the first two years the British foundered.[8] The army conducted large-scale sweeps described by one battalion commander as "remarkable for the grandiloquence of their titles, the largeness of their scale, and their complete lack of success."[9] The situation changed dramatically following two changes in the campaign: the forging of a comprehensive strategy and the appointment of a supreme commander to oversee it. Named for its creator, General Harold Briggs, the Briggs plan recognized that defeating the insurgency was not primarily a military problem. Unless the government could separate the insurgent "fish" from the peasant "sea," it could never defeat them. To accomplish this separation, the plan called for the forcible relocation of the Chinese "squatters" from the jungle fringe to new villages in more secure areas. This illiberal measure was accompanied by some real improvements to win the support of the people. The new villages often had running water, a school, and a hospital.

Peasants who supported the government received what they most desired: legal title to their own farms.

The hearts-and-minds campaign in general contributed to intelligence gathering, but trust took a long time to win. To produce more immediate results, Briggs instituted a generous surrender policy and reward system. Realizing that it was far more productive to convert insurgents than to kill them, the government offered attractive cash incentives to those who would leave the jungle and report on the whereabouts of their erstwhile comrades. To coordinate police efforts, especially intelligence gathering, with the development campaign and military operations, the British created an elaborate joint committee system.

Although the foundation for success had been laid, the strategy failed to function as well as it might have for want of leadership. As long as the civil government and the police answered to the British High Commissioner and the army to the Director of Operations, unified command would never be achieved. Following the assassination of High Commissioner Hugh Gurney, the Churchill government solved the problem by appointing Gerald Templer, a four-star general, both High Commissioner and Director of Operations. Templer energized the campaign, seeing that those at the operational end got the resources they needed and the freedom to use them.

With the plan and the leader in place, defeating the insurgent guerrillas would now be only a matter of time. The British won the shooting war, not with the application of massive firepower, but with small-unit operations. Assigning a battalion to a single area for a long period of time gave units the chance to learn the terrain and get to know its inhabitants. From battalion bases, individual platoons were sent into the jungle, either on routine patrols or following up on hot intelligence. Malaya was a platoon commander's war. Endless man-hours of patrolling, patient ambushes, and systematic denial of food forced the insurgents into situations in which they could be destroyed. Still, the war lasted twelve years. During that time the British employed 28,000 police and 30,000 troops to defeat the insurgents. They suffered 4,425 casualties, including some 500 dead, and killed 13,509 insurgents at a cost of $487 million, over half of which was paid for by the Malayan government.[10] Malaya received its independence in 1957 and has remained a member of the British Commonwealth ever since. It was an impressive victory by any standards.

The Malayan emergency has been the subject of extensive acrimonious debate within the academic and defense communities. During the early 1960s the U.S. military pored over every aspect of the campaign, eager to apply its apparent lessons to the worsening situation in Vietnam. American army officers attended the jungle warfare school in Johore, and Robert Thompson, who had helped to design the Briggs plan, was hired to advise the South Vietnamese and U.S. governments. Defeat in Southeast Asia led to an inevitable reappraisal of the British campaign. Malaya, it now seemed, had been an exception, a colonial campaign in which the British had enjoyed advantages entirely lacking in Vietnam. Critics pointed to authoritarian emergency regulations that the government could enact at will, the smaller scale of the insurgency, its confinement to the minority Chinese population, and the relative isolation of the Malay Peninsula.

These criticisms were of course valid, but they missed an important point. The British won in Malaya neither because they enjoyed overwhelming advantages nor because they had discovered the magic formula for counterinsurgency in that one campaign. They won because they had been combatting internal unrest for most of the twentieth century. Historical accident had given them a culture of restraint and produced a small, highly decentralized army ideally suited to counterinsurgency operations. From Ireland to India they had fought numerous small wars within an empire spanning a quarter of the globe. They were defeated in Ireland (1919–1921) and forced to withdraw from Palestine (1945–1948). But in a host of other campaigns in India proper, on the Northwest Frontier, in Burma, and in the Middle East they had succeeded and from their experience developed a highly successful approach to combatting insurgency. Based on three broad principles, minimum force, civil-military cooperation, and tactical flexibility, this approach reached its fullest development in Malaya.[11] The British would experience other victories, most notably the Dhofar War in Oman (1970–1975), and other defeats, particularly in South Arabia (1963–1967). The real lesson for the United States or any other nation wishing to reproduce the Malayan victory was that it is impossible to distill a nation's military experience from a single isolated campaign.

French Indochina

If the British provided the model for successful counterinsurgency, the French offered the best examples of how not to fight an internal war. Like the British, their colonial empire had given them ample opportunity to deal with unrest; unlike the British, they practiced a form of cultural imperialism that produced a doctrinaire, inflexible approach to counterinsurgency. "Pacification," as the French colonial strategy came to be called, did entail economic development. Indeed, one of its theorists, Marshall Joseph Gallieni, compared occupation forces to pools of oil concentrated at one point to permeate the surrounding area. However, the strategy also involved the concentration of maximum force at the outbreak of disturbances, the wielding of the proverbial sledgehammer to crack a nut, in the belief that such a firm demonstration of resolve would bring disturbances to a speedy conclusion and have a salutary effect on others contemplating rebellion. The technique worked well enough against poorly armed indigenous peoples in Algeria, Morocco, and Indochina. However, pacification was far more effective as an instrument of colonization than as a coherent strategy for combatting insurgency in an already-occupied area. Pacification also produced needlessly high casualties. The French killed 60,000 people in crushing the 1947–1948 revolt in Madagascar. In the anticolonial postwar era, however, such heavy-handed methods proved increasingly unacceptable to an international audience and within metropolitan France itself.[12]

France's counterinsurgency campaigns came on the heels of a humiliating defeat by the Germans, four years of occupation, and the creation of a Fourth Republic reflecting deep divisions within French society. Despite its weakened condition, France determined to reassert its place as a colonial power and reoccupied Indochina following the defeat of Japan. As in Malaya, the colony contained a vigorous Marxist-nationalist movement, which had provided the only indigenous resistance to the Japanese. When it became clear that France had no intention of granting independence, the nationalist leader Ho Chi Minh launched his Vietminh forces against French positions, only to be repulsed by superior firepower. Far from being defeated, the insurgents retreated to the remote northeastern area of the country to rebuild their forces and strengthen political control of the countryside. Three years of neglect by the French coupled with Mao's victory in China, which gave them a source of resupply, enabled the Vietminh to take the offensive again in 1949.

French strategy consisted of constructing a defense perimeter around the Red River Delta and fortified points throughout the country. The approach played into the hands of the insurgents, who attacked isolated outposts and ambushed convoys on the tenuous supply routes linking them together. However, their success in repelling with heavy losses Vietminh assaults on well-defended positions convinced the French that the key to victory lay in drawing the enemy into attacking such positions under circumstances in which superior French firepower could be brought to bear on them. This assessment led to the debacle of Dien Bien Phu, 170 miles west of Hanoi, far outside the French defense perimeter. Paratroopers were dropped into the valley, the advance guard of a larger force that constructed an airfield and command post surrounded by fortified bunkers. The goal of the operation was to interdict enemy supplies into Laos, provide a base for counterinsurgency operations, and perhaps draw the Vietminh into a conventional engagement. Instead, the insurgent commander, General Vo Nguyen Giap, concentrated overwhelming force on the isolated position and overran it with fierce fighting. The French lost 7,000 killed and 11,000 captured and sued for peace.[13]

The French defeat in Indochina, repeated in Algeria (1954–1962), was of singular significance to the Americans who would inherit the conflict. The United States had been supplying the French and during the siege of Dien Ben Phu even considered direct intervention. The defense establishment proposed two scenarios: a massive campaign directed at Communist China, mistakenly perceived to be the real source of the insurgency, and a Korean-conflict–style ground war requiring between seven and twelve U.S. divisions.[14] President Eisenhower vetoed both options. The administration blamed the French for perpetuating colonialism, while the defense establishment concluded that they had remained holed up in fortified positions instead of going on the offensive against the Vietminh.[15] Significantly, the American appraisal never questioned the

French approach to counterinsurgency. Although the U.S. military recognized that the French lacked the resources to win, it shared their confidence in a superior-firepower, conventional solution to the problem of people's war. This conclusion goes a long way in explaining why the United States concentrated on building a South Vietnamese army ill equipped for counterinsurgency. However, the conventional focus of the U.S. military stemmed more from its own historical experience than from imitating the French or misunderstanding the British.

THE UNITED STATES AND LIMITED WAR

Despite oft-repeated claims that unconventional war is somehow un-American, the U.S. military has had considerable experience with this type of conflict. In fact, with the brief exception of the Spanish-American War (1898) and World War I, which for the United States lasted less than eighteen months, unconventional conflict was the primary task of American armed forces between 1865 and 1941. The "pacification" of the West involved extensive campaigns against highly skilled, often well armed irregulars. Far from requiring anything like winning hearts and minds, however, these operations entailed concentration of native American peoples onto reservations and the destruction of their primary resource, the buffalo. The absence of this political and economic dimension and the lack of the emotive force of nationalism on the part of the native Americans make it difficult to classify these campaigns as counterinsurgency.

The Philippines

America's first encounter with nationalist revolution came not on the Great Plains but in the Far East. During the Spanish-American War the U.S. Army enlisted the aid of an indigenous revolutionary movement led by Emilio Aguinaldo in capturing the Philippines. Once the Spanish had been defeated, however, the McKinley administration made clear its intention of annexing the islands. The decision led to hostilities between the nationalists and the American occupation force. In a pattern to be repeated throughout the twentieth century, the insurgents were easily defeated in conventional engagements against better-armed and organized regulars. The insurgents then reverted to guerrilla warfare in the countryside. Aguinaldo divided his country into commands and subdistricts with the aim of conducting a protracted war that would wear the Americans down from "disease and exhaustion" and lead the American public to demand withdrawal.[16] In a different age such a strategy would be the formula for victory in more than one anticolonial war, but in 1899 American public opinion was too underdeveloped, the 35,000-man volunteer force too small to create a demand to "bring the boys home." Still, it was to take the Army three years to defeat the insurgents. In doing so it developed an approach to counterinsurgency that if carefully preserved and properly studied would have served it far better than later models.

Historians who view the Philippine campaign as an illustration of colonial ruthlessness and those who see it as a model campaign combining military activity with political and economic development will find ample evidence to support their conclusions. As Brian McAllister Linn has ably demonstrated, there was no monolithic counterinsurgency campaign. In a concession to the terrain, the lack of effective communications, and the breakup of Aguinaldo's forces into guerrilla bands, the American commanders, first General Elwell Otis and later General Arthur MacArthur, divided the forces into four military districts and further subdivided these into local commands. The commanders thus relinquished centralized command and control, allowing their subordinates considerable latitude in the conduct of operations. What emerged were in fact four separate campaigns, some characterized by heavy-handed measures such as martial law, reconcentration of populations, and atrocities; others marked by the skillful combination of military action and civil development, including construction of roads and schools.[17] Decentralization itself may have been the real key to success. Officers stationed in an area for a protracted period got to know its terrain and people. They could win the trust of the locals and acquire valuable intelligence on the guerrillas.

Internal Conflicts and Unlearned Lessons

The Philippine insurrection introduced the United States to a new and challenging form of conflict. It was not to be an isolated incident. Throughout the interwar period the American military, particularly the Marine Corps, was repeatedly embroiled in internal conflicts in the Caribbean. The Spanish-American War followed by construction of the Panama Canal gave the United States a strategic stake in the region, a stake underscored by economic investment. In the era of gunboat diplomacy the United States felt justified in intervening to protect these interests. The goal of such intervention was usually to insure preservation of a solvent regime, preferably democratically elected, capable of paying its debts and providing a stable business environment.[18] With these goals in mind U.S. forces intervened in Honduras six times between 1911 and 1925. They occupied Haiti for nineteen years, the Dominican Republic for eight (1916–1924), and Nicaragua for seven (1926–1933). Troops landed at Vera Cruz, Mexico, in 1914 and crossed the Rio Grande in pursuit of Pancho Villa in 1916.

These campaigns involved U.S. forces in a whole range of counterinsurgency activities. They pursued bandits in the Dominican Republic and repressed a revolt in Haiti. From 1927 to 1933 the Marines played a cat-and-mouse game with nationalist leader Augusto Sandino in Nicaragua. The campaign underscored the importance of small-unit operations based on good intelligence, which was not always forthcoming. Nicaragua also saw considerable use of tactical air power in support of counterinsurgency operations.[19] In addition to military operations, the Caribbean campaigns also entailed political reforms and material improvements in the quality of life such as roads, bridges, railroads, and sanitary reforms that improved health and reduced infant mortality.[20]

Thus on the eve of World War II the U.S. experience with insurgency was as diverse and continuous, if not as extensive, as that of the French and the British. Almost as striking as the range of this experience was its failure to produce any lasting impression on American military institutions or their doctrine. Only the Marines came close to developing such an approach. With their mission and therefore their existence in question, the Marines had perhaps most to gain from embracing what looked to be a recurring source of employment. In any event, their officers and men had by far the greatest small-war experience. Veterans of the Caribbean campaigns got nineteen hours of instruction on internal conflict mandated at field officer school in Quantico, Virginia, and later increased it to forty-five hours. They even produced a *Small Wars Manual* that numbered 428 pages in its 1940 edition and covered every aspect of counterinsurgency from hearts-and-minds to small-unit operations.[21] By the time of the Cold War, however, any trace of this experience had virtually disappeared.

The failure of this significant legacy to make any lasting impression requires considerable explanation. Part of the explanation lies in the nature of the military's small-war experience. While the list of U.S. interventions during the first half of the twentieth century is impressive, the experience was in many respects as shallow as it was extensive. With a few notable exceptions American soldiers never got to know the local people. They were often heavy handed in imposing reforms, even if these were clearly beneficial to the inhabitants, and brought American racist attitudes with them. While many officers appreciated the importance of restraint, atrocities still occurred. The Marines killed 3,250 Haitians during the 1919 Cacos rebellion while suffering only 13 combat deaths themselves.[22] Most important, the Americans never came with the intention of staying, even though some of their interventions dragged on for years. They sought to promote stability and so concentrated on creating police forces and gendarmeries that could maintain order once the Americans left; these forces became armies, the breeding ground for dictators.[23] In time American administrations would find it more expedient to work with these dictators than to try to promote democracy. The new approach was epitomized by President Franklin Roosevelt's assessment of Anastasio Somoza, the dictator who had seized power in Nicaragua and murdered Sandino: "He may be a son of a bitch, but he's our son of a bitch!" This attitude would survive down to the 1980s, when the Reagan administration supported more than one dictator as long as he was not Communist.

World War II and the Cold War

Memory of the prewar insurgencies was also crowded out by new experiences that seemed more relevant and were at least more consonant with American values. Four years of global conventional war transformed the U.S. military into the most formidable fighting force the world had ever seen. America's ability not only to fight a two-front war but to supply and bankroll its allies as well contributed to the creation of what might be called a strategy of abundance. Massive firepower augmented by the latest technology, coupled with seemingly inexhaustible reserves and apparently limitless material resources, provided the key to victory. The need to occupy both Germany and Japan at the end of the war, combined with the almost immediate onset of the Cold War, signalled by the Berlin Blockade (1948), meant that the United States never totally transferred its forces to a peacetime role. Creation of the North Atlantic Treaty Organization (1949) and the onset of the Korean War (1950) signalled American willingness to defend the free world, a defense that would require large-scale conventional forces.

While the nuclear stalemate decreased the likelihood of another world war, the U.S. military never abandoned its conventional approach to all forms of conflict. Throughout the Cold War era the primary mission of American ground forces remained (1) to deter and if necessary stop a massive Soviet armor attack through the Fulda Gap in Germany and (2) to prevent Communist forces from ever again crossing the 38th parallel into South Korea. Since U.S. forces expected to be outnumbered in both theaters, they relied heavily on superior firepower provided by high-technology weapons. In such a defense establishment there could be little room for an unconventional-war doctrine, and none was developed. From the outset of the Cold War, however, the United States had to confront insurgencies. Unfortunately, its first experiences with Communist wars of national liberation seemed to confirm the belief that the conventional approach would work, even in unconventional war.

The Greek Civil War

The Greek Civil War (1946–1949) provided the West its first direct experience of Communist insurgency. Initially it was the British who bore the brunt of defending the recently liberated country while its government regrouped and prepared for the protracted struggle. However, the announcement of Prime Minister Clement Attlee that the British would terminate aid to Greece as of March 1947 led to American assumption of that responsibility. A Joint U.S. Military Advising and Planning Group was created in December 1947. The United States sent 1,500 advisors, 800 of whom were military personnel, and $723.6 million.[24] Such massive aid of course came at a price: the Greeks would fight their war America's way.

''The American military strategy,'' wrote one analyst, ''was largely conventional: to pin down Democratic Army [insurgent] forces with massed troops and overwhelming firepower, and systematically to clear the adversary from mountain redoubts.''[25] Fortunately the insurgents played right into the Greek/American hands. Insurgent forces numbering possibly 23,000 with another 8,000 in reserve were concentrated in the northern part of the country up against the friendly Albanian and Yugoslav borders. The Greeks relocated the population of the threatened area to create a linear front and remove people from the threat of subversion. It was, however, the Communists' decision to concentrate their forces for conventional operations, perhaps out of a desire to achieve a quick victory before U.S. aid tipped the scales, that led to their defeat.[26] The Greek army, numbering 145,000 and backed by American-supplied aircraft and artillery, destroyed the insurgents in their mountain strongholds.

The Korean War

The conventional approach to unconventional war fostered in Greece was strengthened by the Korean War. While the North Koreans crossed the 38th parallel in division strength, the war did have an irregular dimension. As the South Koreans and their U.N. allies recovered and drove the invaders back north, they had to combat guerrillas who infiltrated their lines and whose numbers were augmented by stragglers from the retreating North Korean forces. The American and South Korean units deployed against these guerrillas employed conventional patrolling and a combined-arms approach, which were made more effective by the guerrillas' often-desperate need for supplies.[27] American assessments of the Korean War reinforced the already strong tendency to see all guerrillas as partisans, irregular forces operating in support of or preparatory to conventional operations, who could be defeated by conventional means.[28]

The Philippines

The one American-directed counterinsurgency campaign that could have yielded the right lessons occurred in the Philippines, the site of America's first exposure to people's war half a century before. The Hukbalahap were Marxist insurgents supported by an impoverished peasantry driven by land hunger. From 1946 to 1950 the insurgency made considerable gains against a government that eschewed land or political reform and conducted large-unit counterinsurgency operations that often entailed reprisals against innocent civilians. This conventional approach was actually encouraged by a Joint U.S. Military Advisor Group (JUSMAG). The situation improved dramatically with the appointment in 1950 of Defense Minister Ramon Magsaysay and an altered approach to the war. JUSMAG now advocated dividing the controverted area into four subareas, each dominated by a Battalion Combat Team (BTC). The BTC provided security, gathered intelligence, and conducted extensive small-unit patrolling. The effort succeeded because of the creation of the Economic Development Corps, which provided land to some peasants and the hope of land to countless more. By 1954 the back of the insurgency was broken.

Far from drawing the correct conclusions from the war, namely, the primacy of economic development with the military in a limited, ancillary role, the United States focused on the importance of Magsaysay. This view would lead to the disastrous insistence on a similar authoritarian figure in Vietnam. Analysts also overlooked the unique advantages that the United States enjoyed: considerable goodwill among the Philippine people and undeniable economic and political leverage with the government in Manila. Furthermore, the insurgency was isolated from outside support, and the source of unrest was limited to land hunger. As in Greece, the insurgency was unique.[29]

Lessons Learned?

In his incisive study of the evolution of U.S. counterinsurgency doctrine, Larry Cable demonstrated that the experiences of Greece, Korea, and the Philippines led to misunderstanding of the nature of insurgency and to a tendency to treat all guerrillas as partisans rather than insurgents, an assessment that proved disastrous in Vietnam. This analysis begs a larger question: Why did the United States so willingly fixate on the Greek and Korean examples while misunderstanding the Malayan and Philippine ones and ignoring half a century of its own small-war experience? The answer lies beyond historical examples and deep in the roots of American culture. Robert Osgood's conclusion that there might be something un-American about limited war hits at the essential problem.[30] Neither the American political system nor American values are conducive to fighting low-intensity protracted wars. The separation of powers, which requires the Congress to declare a war and the President to fight it, makes it difficult to build and sustain support for any but the most urgent of conflicts. Biennial House of Representatives elections bring national issues before the voters every two years, and First Amendment guarantees of free speech and a free press strip military operations of even a modicum of secrecy. To these structural characteristics must be added a historical isolationist tendency that makes the public unwilling to hazard American lives unless U.S. interests are overwhelmingly clear and demonstrable. Unprecedented industrial growth and scientific accomplishment have produced a strident faith in the power of technology to solve almost any problem. This faith in technology is evident in the education of officers at all of the service academies, where cadets receive an engineering degree.

The American character is impatient, setting short-term goals and seeking immediate gratification. The military services within this egalitarian democracy tend to be rigidly hierarchical, with little two-way flow of information and almost no decentralization of command and control. Such attitudes inhibit the military's ability to adopt a small-unit, area-based approach to counterinsurgency. Collectively these cultural characteristics have made it very difficult for the United States to adapt to unconventional war. Lady Bird Johnson perhaps said it best: "It is unbearably hard to fight a limited war," although she might have added a qualifier, "for Americans."[31]

Within this historical and cultural landscape, Vietnam is best understood not as a watershed but as an aberration. The conflict produced a brief flirtation with an approach to conflict alien to the American experience, demonstrated the limits of American power, and forced development of a doctrine of unconventional war more in keeping with the American tradition and character.

VIETNAM

The tortuous and confusing conduct of the Vietnam War has been matched by an equally elaborate historiographic debate over who was to blame for the defeat. As Peter Dunn has aptly demonstrated, the war was from start to finish a hybrid war entailing every aspect of the conflict spectrum from classic insurgency to partisan war to conventional operations. There were, in fact, several Vietnams—different types of conflicts fought at different times and places by different sorts of forces.[32] Still, Larry Cable's assessment remains the most penetrating: for the most part the United States got the kind of war it wished to fight; counterinsurgency was subordinated to conventional war. This salient characteristic of the Vietnam experience explains in large measure its impact on later unconventional operations and doctrine.

Following the French defeat at Dien Bien Phu and the signing of the Geneva Accords that created Laos and Cambodia and divided North and South Vietnam at the 16th parallel, the United States concentrated on building up the South as a bulwark against further Communist expansion in the region. Development consisted of military assistance and economic aid. Convinced that the North would seek to unify the country by force, especially after the South reneged on the Geneva promise to hold national elections, the Defense Department concentrated on building the Army of the Republic of Vietnam (ARVN) into a formidable conventional force. Working through the Military Advisory and Assistance Group (MAAG) and supplied with $85 million a year in equipment, the United States pared the ill-equipped, poorly trained and led French colonial force of over 200,000 down to a leaner army of 150,000 grouped into six heavy and four light divisions, many of whose officers would be trained in the United States.[33] Some analysts would later criticize MAAG for preparing for an unlikely invasion while ignoring the real threat from insurgency; others maintained that the structure of ARVN reflected the realistic threat assessment for the years 1956–1958, during which the force was created.[34] Still, the dismantling of all four light divisions within three years, concentration on divisional maneuvers, and training that involved twenty-mile marches with fifty-pound packs showed no real appreciation of the combat environment or the French experience.[35]

The other leg of America's Vietnam strategy was to create a stable political regime in the South. Based on the experiences of Greece and the Philippines, the United States had concluded that a single strong leader was essential to the creation of an anti-Communist regime.[36] The man of the hour was Ngo Dinh Diem, who assumed the premiership in the summer of 1954. Despite French warning that Diem was a megalomaniac, Washington built the new country around him; it was enough for Secretary of State John Foster Dulles that the new premier appeared "competent, anti-Communist, and vigorous."[37] With his contempt for democracy, cronyism, political repression, failure to conduct land reform, and disregard for the religious sensibilities of his Buddhist countrymen, Diem created favorable conditions for an indigenous insurgency. Ironically, the

North Vietnamese had instructed Communist cells in the South to lie low so as to avoid confrontation with the United States; only when Diem created favorable circumstances for revolution did the Vietcong campaign begin.[38] In 1958 the Communist insurgents assassinated 700; in 1960, 2,500.[39]

Growing awareness of the South Vietnamese insurgency corresponded fortuitously with the election of John F. Kennedy and the end of the Malayan emergency. The new President was committed to opposing wars of national liberation. He could not, however, fundamentally alter the institutional culture of his armed forces. The 1960s have been labelled the counterinsurgency era, but the term is misleading. While the President and some of his civilian advisors were enamored of the British victory and tried to create both counterinsurgency forces and doctrine, the defense establishment remained committed to the conventional approach to unconventional war. Kennedy elevated the status of special forces, handing out green berets at Fort Bragg, and encouraged the development of doctrine. Until 1962 the standard *Operations* manual (*FM 100-5*) did not even mention counterinsurgency. Later editions discussed such operations within a conventional-war framework. Only the Special Warfare Center at Fort Bragg produced really useful doctrine, but its impact on the army as a whole remained limited indeed.[40] Based on its experiences in Greece and particularly Korea, the Army persisted in seeing all guerrillas as partisans operating in support of conventional forces or as a prelude to invasion.[41] This dichotomy led to the creation of two conflicts: a counterinsurgency campaign conducted largely by special forces and aimed at separating the insurgents from the general population; and a conventional strategy concentrating on killing Vietcong with superior firepower.

To make matters worse, the American-trained ARVN proved inept at both the unconventional and the conventional approaches to counterinsurgency. Amply supplied with helicopters, aircraft, and artillery, South Vietnamese units relied on heavy, often-indiscriminate firepower that further alienated the peasants. While the Diem regime adopted the Strategic Hamlet Program, it ignored most of Robert Thompson's advice on how to set it up. An architect of the Malayan victory, Thompson insisted that the hamlets be well defended and therefore advocated beginning the program in areas where government influence was still strong. After securing these base areas, the program could be gradually extended into threatened provinces. Instead the Saigon government built too many hamlets too fast, set them up in areas that could not be adequately defended, and handed out weapons indiscriminately to local peasants.[42]

ARVN ineptness led both to increased North Vietnamese aid and to a corresponding Americanization of the war. In 1964 Hanoi improved the Ho Chi Minh Trail through Laos and stepped up supplies to the South. This logistic effort confirmed the established conviction that guerrillas were partisans, a belief that justified interdiction of supplies through strategic bombing, first of the trail and later of the North itself.[43]

Beginning in 1965, the United States gave up the delusion that it could remain in an advisory role and win the war. The American force, which eventually numbered 543,000, shunted the ARVN aside and adopted a strategy of attrition epitomized by Secretary of Defense Robert McNamara's emphasis on ''body count'' and by Commander Military Assistance Command Vietnam (MACV) General William Westmoreland's terse reply that the answer to insurgency was ''firepower.''[44] Besides alienating the local population, this conventional emphasis had two other unfortunate effects. First, commanders had no incentive to develop effective counterinsurgency techniques. Second, despite its size, the U.S. force had small ''tooth-to-tail'' ratio. Of the 543,000 personnel in the country, only 80,000 were combat troops—a firepower and mobility war requires extensive logistics support. Consequently, MACV had too few soldiers available for the really useful pacification programs employed with notable success but on a limited basis.[45]

Escalation of the conflict, increasing U.S. casualties, and the strategic bombing campaign, occurring amid a complex confluence of domestic circumstances, made the war increasingly unpopular in the United States. Following the 1968 Tet Offensive (''the victory from which we never recovered''), the Pentagon determined that the war could not be won at acceptable cost under prevailing political circumstances.[46] ''Vietnamization'' preceded American withdrawal, which was completed by 1973, two years before the fall of Saigon to North Vietnamese forces.

The American defeat in Southeast Asia must not obscure the fact that the war produced some notable experiments in unconventional warfare. Various programs aimed at ''pacification,'' the clearing, holding, and developing of Vietcong-threatened areas. In the early 1960s Green Berets lived among the Montagnards conducting a grass-roots hearts and minds campaign with positive results. The Strategic Hamlet Program was, of course, a failure, but largely as a result of its misapplication. Local defense forces were reorganized in 1964. Regional Forces (RFs) operated at the provisional level while Popular Forces (PFs) protected villages and hamlets. Like so many aspects of the war, however, pacification lacked a unified approach. A step in the right direction was the creation of Civil Operations and Rural Development Support (CORDS) in 1967, led by Robert Komer, who operated directly under Westmoreland. One of the most promising developments was the Combined Action Program of the U.S. Marine Corps. In 1965 Marines in the North received tactical command of some PFs. These units were then meshed with Marine squads to defend local areas and gather intelligence with promising results. The Phoenix program was a scheme aimed at attacking the Vietcong infrastructure through covert agents who would gather intelligence, make arrests, and carry out intelligence.[47]

Despite their promising results, these pacification programs never received the priority or the resources necessary to affect the outcome of the war. When MACV gained control of Special Forces, it increasingly used them for reconnaissance and out-of-area activities in support of conventional operations. The ARVN received the pick of the conscripts; those passed over went into RF and

PF units, which were often poorly supplied. Most pacification schemes and organizations operated outside of the mainstream and so had little impact on U.S. strategy overall.[48] They provide examples of how things might have been done.

UNCONVENTIONAL WAR IN THE AFTERMATH OF VIETNAM

The Vietnam War ended America's brief, uncomfortable flirtation with counterinsurgency. On the surface the military establishment appeared to learn nothing from Vietnam, except that in the future such conflicts should be avoided entirely. Nowhere is the American failure to understand the war clearer than in a 1975 exchange between a North Vietnamese and an American Colonel meeting in Hanoi. "You never defeated us on the battlefield," the American observed. "That may be so," his Vietnamese counterpart replied. "It is also irrelevant."[49] Convinced that the Washington establishment, the media, and the kids on the streets of Berkeley and Chicago had sold them out, the U.S. military could persuade itself that it had not really lost the war and that it therefore had no reason to abandon its conventional focus. Since the strategic commitments to NATO and South Korea had not changed, there seemed little incentive to reconsider this conclusion.

The United States did not, however, totally abandon its unconventional capability; however, it made clear that future involvement in internal conflict would be indirect. Even before the Vietnam War had ended, the 1969 Nixon Doctrine asserted that the host country would bear primary responsibility for counterinsurgency.[50] Both Army and joint services doctrines during the early 1970s shifted their emphasis from direct involvement by U.S. forces to logistics support and training. The 1976 version of *FM 100-5* omitted any mention of operations other than war.[51] The change aptly reflected the mood of the country, which had been unwilling to sanction intervention in Angola the previous year. The Central Intelligence Agency would continue to conduct limited covert operations as it always had. Special forces too survived the Vietnam War, although they remained as much out of the mainstream as they were when John F. Kennedy handed out the first green beret. These units predated Vietnam, as the U.S. military had always maintained a commando capability as part of its force structure. Special forces were, however, given a new, counterterrorism focus in keeping with the threat posed by terrorist organizations, particularly in the Middle East. Delta Force was created in 1977 to deal with just such a threat. The unit was based on the experiences of German and Israeli strike forces and organized on the model of the British Special Air Service.[52] Although the force performed poorly during the abortive Iran hostage rescue operation in 1980, special forces remain at the center of the U.S. approach to unconventional war to this day. This new focus on special forces conformed with the conventional-war posture of U.S. forces. In antiterrorist operations special forces function like traditional commandos conducting out-of-area operations. Given a very precise short-term mission, they deliver an intense but highly selective blow at a precise moment in time. Their presence within a force structure does not an unconventional-war capability make.

While determination to avoid direct participation in protracted internal wars has persisted to the present, the nonintervention stance of the 1970s has not. The election of Ronald Reagan in 1980 and subsequent deepening of Cold War tensions led to renewed interest in supporting friendly regimes threatened by Communist-inspired insurgencies. The United States also confronted a new phenomenon: the perceived need to support insurgents against Marxist regimes in Nicaragua and Afghanistan. In all of these endeavors the new administration, however, preferred covert to overt assistance, at least for the military side of counterinsurgency. The new Secretary of Defense, Caspar Weinberger, acknowledged this shift when he stated that the military skills for low-intensity conflict, the new term for unconventional war, were to be found primarily ''in our special operations forces.''[53]

This rhetoric was matched by the reality of a considerable special forces buildup. Active-duty special forces personnel, which had peaked at 13,000 in 1969, had been reduced to 3,000 by 1980. The Reagan and Bush administrations increased this total to 11,600 in 1981, 14,900 in 1985, and 20,900 in 1990. Of particular importance to the new emphasis were the Military Mobile Training Teams, composed largely of special forces personnel, sent to train counterinsurgency forces abroad. By 1986, 260 of these teams were assisting military establishments in 35 countries.[54] U.S. aid to threatened regimes was not, however, purely military. Many policymakers and some soldiers had learned from Vietnam that insurgencies arise from legitimate grievances, that economic and political development lies at the heart of counterinsurgency, and that destruction of insurgent guerrillas should not be the primary focus even of military operations.

Organizational changes also accompanied the special forces buildup. The hydra-headed array of units under separate service leadership was gradually pulled together under a unified command. In 1982 the Army created its first Special Operations Command (SOCOM) at Fort Bragg, and the Navy followed suit with a Special Warfare Directorate. These changes did not prevent the lack of service cooperation during the invasion of Grenada, which led to congressional pressure for a joint services command.[55] After considering a number of alternatives, including a separate service, Congress passed legislation in 1986 to create a Special Operations Unified Command, which was given considerable autonomy. Headquartered at MacDill Air Force Base in Florida, SOCOM controlled its own budget, procurement, and operations and reported directly to the newly created Assistant Secretary of Defense for Special Operations and Low-Intensity Conflict.[56] The new command would oversee three service commands and one joint command: U.S. Air Force Special Operations Command, U.S. Army Special Operations Command, U.S. Naval Special Warfare Command, and Joint

Special Operations Command. In addition to making special forces more effective and beefing up the military's counterterrorism capability, Congress clearly envisioned special operations as an alternative to direct involvement. Special forces were to be "the military mainstay of the United States for the purpose of nation building and training friendly foreign forces in order to preclude deployment or combat involving the conventional or strategic forces of the United States."[57]

Doctrine reflected the force buildup and institutional change. The new American approach to unconventional war was distilled in the 1981 version of *FM 100-20: Low-Intensity Conflict.* This doctrine recognized the social, economic, and political roots of insurgency. It provided that military assistance would come through a Military Assistance and Advisory Group, which would include a special forces Mobile Training Team.[58] Such military assistance would presumably be part of a total aid package including economic assistance aimed at helping the host government outbid the insurgents for the hearts and minds of the people. The CIA would of course conduct its own covert operations. Significantly, *FM 100-20* (1981) was translated into Spanish and used at the School of the Americas, the Army's training facility for Latin American military personnel.[59] Central America in particular was to provide the United States its main unconventional battleground throughout the 1980s.

El Salvador

The first major operation came in El Salvador. In 1979 a smoldering insurgency coalesced into a coherent Marxist revolution. The Farabundo Marti National Liberation Front (FMLN), named for labor leader and Communist organizer Farabundo Marti, launched an aggressive campaign against the Salvadoran army. In a country in which 1 percent of the population owned 70 percent of the land, "the United States found a society with a completely unjust legal system and an unyielding upper class that, with the aid of the armed forces, consistently and brutally blocked reforms."[60] Under such circumstances the FMLN had no trouble winning converts, but they were Marxist and received aid from Cuba, so the prevailing wisdom of the Reagan era dictated that they must be opposed. For the next decade the United States supported the Salvadoran government in a sordid war involving the murder of American nuns and Salvadoran priests as well as labor leaders and countless others by right-wing death squads with ties to the military. While U.S. advisors coached Salvadoran officers in small-unit tactics and the need to win local support, the Salvadoran army clung to conventional operations, reflecting perhaps that many of its soldiers had been trained by the United States before the insurgency. At the outset of the conflict it conducted reprisals against alleged supporters of the FMLN such as the infamous massacre of 700 civilians at the village of El Mozote by the American-trained elite Atlacatl battalion in 1981. Considerable evidence suggests that the United States knew of these atrocities, but reported that the human rights record of the Salvadoran army was actually improving.[61] U.S. pressure for land and legal reform met resistance from the entrenched elite who controlled both the government and the army.[62] While two U.S. administrations pressured the Salvadorans to reform, neither went so far as to make American aid contingent upon a commitment to lasting structural change. Ironically, the United States was repeating its experience of the 1920s and 1930s when American forces found it expedient to bolster pro-U.S. regimes regardless of how they treated their own people. The results of such a shortsighted approach became obvious in 1989: after almost a decade of U.S. aid devoted to suppressing it, the FMLN was still in a position to launch a major offensive. Finally, in January 1992 the United Nations succeeded in brokering a peace accord between the FMLN and the government. Although much of the agreement was on the government's terms, the FMLN had accomplished much by surviving to sign it. Given that the U.S. goal had been to eradicate the Marxist insurgency within its own backyard, El Salvador can hardly be considered a triumph for U.S.-led counterinsurgency.

The experience of El Salvador raises serious questions about the relationship between unconventional-war doctrine and operations in the U.S. military. Although *FM 100-20* (1981) outlined a sound approach to counterinsurgency, there is some doubt as to how closely U.S. advisors followed it. One special forces advisor to El Salvador was asked if U.S. low-intensity conflict principles applied there. He asked what they were and in which field manual they could be found.[63] At least one analyst, however, has astutely pointed out that the problem of counterinsurgency in El Salvador and Vietnam lay elsewhere: no doctrine and no amount of aid can save a regime determined to resist change. ''It is one thing to have the key; it is an entirely different matter to force another to use it to unlock a door through which he does not wish to go.''[64]

Nicaragua and the Contras

At the same time that U.S. advisors trained Salvadorans in counterinsurgency, the Central Intelligence Agency was aiding an insurgency against the Marxist government of Nicaragua. The successful revolution by the Sandinistas (named for Augusto Sandino) in 1979 stemmed from America's misguided policy of supporting Nicaraguan strongman Anastasio Somoza. American-supplied and trained contras conducted a campaign to overthrow the Cuban-backed Marxist revolutionary government. The contra war demonstrated emphatically that insurgency and counterinsurgency are ideologically neutral terms. However, the almost visceral tendency to equate revolution with communism perhaps encouraged the Reagan administration to keep aid for the insurgents as quiet as possible. Special forces played a limited role in what was predominantly a CIA show. Navy SEALs mined Nicaraguan harbors, and regular forces created an infrastructure in Honduras to support the contras and, if need be, launch a conventional invasion.[65]

The covert war did, however, create serious problems for the Reagan administration. During the 1984 presidential election campaign the CIA's Nicaragua manual, *Psychological Operations in Guerrilla Warfare,* came to light. Most of the manual dealt with how to conduct propaganda campaigns, but a disturbing section on "Selective Use of Violence for Propagandistic Effects" explained that "it is possible to neutralize carefully selected and planned targets, such as court judges, mesta judges, police and State Security officials, CDS chiefs, etc."[66] This open invitation to murder created a certain dissonance among Americans used to equating such behavior with America's enemies. Far more damaging was the Iran-contra scandal of 1987, which revealed that arms had been sold to Iran in exchange for the release of American hostages in Lebanon and the money diverted to the contras. The affair revealed the limited abilities of an open and democratic society to conduct covert operations.

In addition to El Salvador and Nicaragua, CIA and special forces operatives and advisors conducted a host of other operations. The United States provided aid to the Mujahadeen guerrillas opposing the Soviet-backed regime in Afghanistan. American advisors assisted the government in Peru to oppose the Marxist-led Sendero Luminoso insurgency. The CIA conducted covert operations in the Middle East. Special forces also participated in major conventional campaigns, conducting out-of-area operations in Grenada, Panama, and Iraq.

Lessons Learned?

One striking feature of all these activities was steadfast determination not to become embroiled in another Vietnam. U.S. ground forces would not be tied down in a protracted internal war in someone else's country. This determination led inexorably to the special forces buildup. Unwilling to commit its own conventional forces directly, the United States could either abandon its unconventional capability entirely or shift to the covert/special forces side of operations. Given the prevalence of unconventional war, the first choice was hardly an option. The second choice carried both advantages and liabilities. Covert operations conducted by special forces composed of volunteers would not usually produce intense media coverage or public debate. However, the pall of secrecy presented its own problems. Special forces quietly helping a host nation conduct counterinsurgency operations can easily become participant observers in atrocities, which happened in El Salvador. Such forces may also find it hard to resist the temptation to act outside the law and in defiance of congressional oversight and restraints, as happened during the Iran-contra affair. These dangers notwithstanding, the special forces/covert approach remains the only viable option for a country whose cultural traditions make it exceedingly difficult to fight what General John Galvin has called "the uncomfortable wars."[67]

CURRENT CAPABILITIES AND DOCTRINE

The U.S. military's unconventional-war capability, or at least that portion dealing with internal conflicts, resides almost entirely within a formidable array of special forces. The unified Special Operations Command directs more than 46,000 troops from all branches of the armed forces. The Army contributes 30,000 troops, grouped as Green Berets, Army Rangers, the 160th Special Operations Aviation Regiment, psychological warfare groups, civil affairs battalions, and Delta Force, the army's counterterrorism/special commando mission force. The navy contributes 5,500 Sea-Air-Land forces (SEALs), including SEAL Team 6, specializing in counterterrorism and special commando missions. The Air Force provides 9,500 air commandos, along with their special infiltration helicopters and other support aircraft. There is also a joint Army–Air Force helicopter force and intelligence unit.[68] At the end of fiscal year 1993 special forces made up less than 2 percent of the armed forces and accounted for slightly more than 1 percent of the total defense budget, a small portion of the total but up considerably from the 0.1 percent spending level of the early 1980s.[69]

Several organizations and agencies control special forces outside of SOCOM's domain. The Marine Expeditionary Units, 2,000-strong augmented battalions assigned to Navy Amphibious Ready Groups, have been designated "special operations capable."[70] The FBI has its own hostage rescue team modeled on Delta Force. The unit received unwanted publicity from its abortive assault on the Branch Davidian compound in Waco, Texas. The CIA employs a 200-strong paramilitary Special Operations Group. The organization also has the right to borrow special forces from SOCOM ("sheep-dipping").[71]

This formidable array of forces enables the United States to conduct a variety of unconventional operations worldwide. However, it must be pointed out that special forces remain outside the mainstream of a military establishment very resistant to the whole idea of unconventional war in general and to special forces in particular. Nor has the creation of SOCOM solved the problems of status and autonomy. Although SOCOM commands special forces units, the service chiefs retain administrative control of their force contributions. In addition, theater Special Operations Commands are subordinate to the theater commander. Such arrangements no doubt encourage a certain amount of turf squabbling, bureaucratic fat, and duplication of effort. Despite these shortcomings, however, current arrangements are preferable to those in the past. Special forces now have an undisputed right to exist and the resources to develop specific training programs and even weapons systems.

Current doctrine reveals the place of unconventional war in U.S. military thought. A variety of official publications present U.S. military doctrine on unconventional war. The term "operations other than war" has replaced "low-intensity conflict" (LIC) and as of this writing doctrine is being revised to address this change. The new doctrine eliminates the artificial LIC categories in favor of a range of operations types. The Army's latest version of *FM 100-5: Operations* has already incorporated the change. Chapter 13 is devoted to ''Operations Other Than War,'' most of which are noncombat contingencies. The discussion of principles germane to all such operations recognizes that the objectives may be economic or political rather than military; that the traditional desire for unity of command might occur in an atmosphere of cooperation rather than authority; and that such operations may be protracted: ''Peacetime operations may require years to achieve the desired effects. Underlying causes of confrontation and conflict rarely have a clear beginning or a decisive resolution.'' Restraint in the use of force is emphasized, and the importance of promoting the legitimacy of the threatened nation is stressed: ''Legitimacy derives from the perception that constituted authority is both genuine and effective and employs appropriate means for reasonable principles.'' Discussion of specific types of operations includes a section on ''Support for Insurgencies and Counterinsurgencies,'' which envisions the United States in a support role providing assistance to host nations ''in the context of foreign internal defense.'' Support for insurgencies is seen to be largely within the domain of special forces.[72] Army operations doctrine thus clearly reflects the difficult lessons of the past thirty years and provides a sound theoretical framework for conducting insurgency and counterinsurgency. However, more specialized publications reveal the limits to which the U.S. military is prepared to go in unconventional war.

The capstone doctrine for unconventional war, *Joint Publication 3-07: Doctrine for Joint Operations in Low Intensity Conflict* (1990), and the Army/Air Force publication, *Military Operations in Low-intensity Conflict* (*FM 100-20/AFM 2-20,* 1989), have been supplanted by updated works not yet available. However, since there has been no significant change in doctrine on ''Support for Insurgencies and Counterinsurgencies,'' both reflect current military thought in these areas. The capstone doctrine makes quite clear that military aid for counterinsurgency will be provided by ''furnishing suitable material, training, services, and advisors.'' The manual reflects the post-Vietnam reluctance to become involved in other people's wars. ''Only in exceptional cases where major US interests are at high risk will US military forces be committed to combat.''[73] Joint Army/Air Force doctrine is equally emphatic: ''The burden of carrying on the conflict must remain with the government or the insurgents. To do otherwise is to 'Americanize' the conflict, destroying the legitimacy of the entity we are attempting to assist.'' Again, the U.S. role will be advisory. ''A combat role for U.S. forces must be viewed as an exceptional event.''[74] Both publications recognized the primacy of special forces in support for insurgencies.

The new generation of joint service and Army doctrines demonstrates a refreshing flexibility absent in earlier literature. *Joint Publication 3-0: Doctrine for Joint Operations* (September 1993) eschews the earlier preoccupation with LIC categories in favor of general principles applicable to a variety of contingencies. Although the publication still prefers a ''clearly defined, decisive, and attainable objective,'' it also recognizes the primacy of political over purely military objectives and acknowledges that unity of command must be achieved in ''an atmosphere of cooperation'' with the host nation and various U.S. civilian agencies. The doctrine emphasizes the need for restraint in the use of force and warns that the rules of engagement can be subject to change for political reasons. In foreign internal defense all actions should be aimed at developing a threatened nation and promoting the legitimacy of its government. Perhaps most striking is the manual's recognition of the protracted nature of unconventional war, with emphasis shifted from a fixed end date to seeing an operation through to successful completion: ''The resolute, and persistent pursuit of national goals and objectives, for as long as necessary to achieve them, is often the requirement for success.''[75] The Army's new manual, *FM 100-7: Decisive Force: The Army in Theater Operations* (April 1994), echoes the changes of the joint service doctrine.

Encouraging as these changes in U.S. unconventional-war doctrine may be, too much should not be made of them. The American withdrawal from Somalia and public demand that the U.S. presence in Haiti be short-term confirm America's historic dislike for protracted unconventional war.

THE FUTURE

An extensive unconventional-war (now dubbed ''operations other than war'') capability will remain a significant part of U.S. military planning for the foreseeable future. So will the impressive array of special forces gathered under the wing of SOCOM and protected by a congressional mandate. In fact, special forces have so far escaped the budget-cutting axe levelled at the military during the post–Cold War retrenchment. However, despite its extensive capability in this area, U.S. military operations other than war are likely to remain confined to those areas acceptable to the American public.

The reluctance to become directly involved in protracted internal war was underscored by the recent experience of Somalia. President Clinton's assurances that the relief forces sent to Zaire to aide Rwandan refugees would not be involved in peace enforcement demonstrates how quickly the post–Cold War infatuation with policing the new world order has soured. While the United States might supply logistics, transport, and tactical air support for U.N. peacekeeping, it will avoid committing ground troops to any U.N. operations outside of its historic areas of influence. U.S. forces will sooner invade Haiti than they will enter Bosnia or Rwanda. Even Caribbean interventions will be short-term, massive-force affairs like the invasions of Grenada and Panama.

Military support for insurgency and counterinsurgency in the post–Cold War world will be confined to training and the supply of arms. The CIA will, no doubt, continue to conduct covert operations and will probably borrow forces from SOCOM to do so. The decline of international communism as the driving force behind revolution has not reduced the number of internal conflicts, potential or actual. If anything, the post–Cold War world has been characterized by greater instability and an increased number of global flash points. Future U.S. intervention will be based on self-interest rather than ideology.

The one area in which U.S. forces might well become embroiled in protracted conflict similar to insurgency is the drug war. It is not inconceivable that the United States might move into a major drug-producing area, not only to destroy a crop but to prevent its ever being replanted. Such an operation would require lengthy occupation and perhaps nation building to transform a narcotics-distorted economy.

Within its own borders the United States faces a potential insurgency of awesome proportions. The gang warfare racking the poorer neighborhoods of all major American cities has so far centered on protecting drug turf. Should the gangs cease to fight each other and combine to extend their operations into other illicit activities and their control over wider urban and even suburban areas, the federal government might find itself conducting a counterinsurgency campaign involving community development, intelligence gathering, and special operations.

Antiterrorist operations will also become an even greater concern for U.S. forces in the future. The technological revolution has made it possible for even small groups with limited funds and minimal outside support to conduct quite lethal activities, as the bombing of the World Trade Center illustrates.[76] Combatting such attacks and perhaps even preempting them will be the task of special forces. The disastrous Iran hostage rescue operation of 1980 by Delta Force and the botched assault of the Branch Davidian compound by the FBI hostage rescue unit in 1993 suggest that U.S. forces have a long way to go in developing this unconventional capability.

Current trends suggest an increasing future role for special forces. Conventional units lack the training and adaptability for the multipurpose tasks confronting the soldier on unconventional operations. Technology is making unconventional conflict as specialized as armored warfare.[77]

Despite their primacy in future wars, however, special forces remain on the periphery of respectable soldiering. It remains a truism in virtually all branches of the armed forces that an unhealthy interest in special operations significantly shortens one's career. As long as unconventional war remains so marginalized, America's capability in this vital area will be correspondingly weakened no matter what its force capabilities are.

NOTES

1. These are discussed in detail in Headquarters, Department of the Army, *Field Manual 100-5: Operations* (Washington, DC: U.S. Government Printing Office, June 1993), pp. 13-4 to 13-8.

2. Mao Tse-tung, *Guerrilla Warfare,* trans. Samuel B. Griffith (Baltimore, MD: Nautical and Aviation Publishing Company, 1992).

3. Frank Kitson, *Low Intensity Operations: Subversion, Insurgency, Peace-keeping* (London: Faber and Faber, 1991; 1st ed. 1971), p. 96.

4. Robert Thompson, *Defeating Communist Insurgency: Experiences from Malaya and Vietnam* (London: Chatto and Windus, 1966), pp. 119–120.

5. See Robert Taber, *The War of the Flea: A Study of Guerrilla Warfare Theory and Practice* (New York: Lyle Stuart, 1965); for the counterargument, see J. Bowyer Bell, *The Myth of the Guerrilla: Revolutionary Theory and Malpractice* (New York: 1971).

6. Figures are those given by Edgar O'Ballance, *Malaya: The Communist Insurgent War, 1948–1960* (Hamden, CT: Archon Books, 1966), pp. 44, 111.

7. Anthony Short, *The Communist Insurrection in Malaya, 1948–1960* (London: 1975), p. 254.

8. See John Coates, *Suppressing Insurgency: An Analysis of Malayan Emergency, 1948–1954* (Boulder, CO: Westview Press, 1992).

9. Ian Wight, cited in Thomas R. Mockaitis, *British Counterinsurgency, 1919–1960* (London: Macmillan, 1990), p. 163.

10. The figures are given by Robert Komer, *The Malayan Emergency in Retrospect: Organization of a Successful Counterinsurgency Effort* (Santa Monica, CA: Rand Corporation, 1972), pp. 22–23, 38, 47.

11. See Mockaitis, *British Counterinsurgency,* for elaboration of this argument.

12. The preceding discussion of pacification is based on John Pimlott, ''The French Army: From Indochina to Chad, 1946–1984,'' in *Armed Forces and Modern Counter-Insurgency,* ed. Ian F. W. Beckett and John Pimlott (New York: St. Martin's Press, 1985), pp. 47–49, and Francis Toase, ''The French Experience,'' in *The Roots of Counter-Insurgency,* ed. Ian F. W. Beckett (London: Blandford Press, 1988), pp. 40–59.

13. The preceding discussion of the Indochina conflict is based on Pimlott, ''French Army,'' pp. 49–54.

14. Andrew F. Krepinevich, Jr., *The Army and Vietnam* (Baltimore, MD: Johns Hopkins University Press, 1986), pp. 18–19.

15. George Herring, *America's Longest War: The United States and Vietnam, 1950–1975* (New York: Alfred A. Knopf, 1986; 1st ed., 1979), pp. 25, 42.

16. Brian McAllister Linn, *The U.S. Army and Counterinsurgency in the Philippine War, 1899–1902* (Chapel Hill: University of North Carolina Press, 1989), p. 16.

17. Ibid., pp. 163–170.

18. ''The Week in Review,'' *New York Times,* 24 July 1994, sec. 4, p. 1.

19. Ian Beckett, ''The United States Experience,'' in Beckett, *The Roots of Counter-Insurgency,* p. 122.

20. Larry Rother, ''Remembering the Past, Repeating It Anyway,'' *New York Times,* 24 July 1994, sec. 4, p. 1.

21. Beckett, ''United States Experience,'' p. 123.

22. Ibid., p. 111.

23. Rother, ''Remembering the Past,'' p. 4.

24. Michael McClintock, *Instruments of Statecraft: U.S. Guerrilla Warfare, Counter-insurgency, and Counter-Terrorism, 1940–1990* (New York: Pantheon Books, 1992), p. 12.

25. Ibid., p. 13.

26. Ibid., p. 16.

27. Larry Cable, *Conflict of Myths: The Development of American Counterinsurgency Doctrine and the Vietnam War* (New York: New York University Press, 1986), pp. 38–40.

28. Ibid., pp. 40–41.

29. The assessment of the American view of the Huk campaign is from Cable, *Conflict of Myths,* pp. 62–68.

30. Robert Osgood, *Limited War: The Challenge to American Strategy* (Chicago, IL: University of Chicago Press, 1957).

31. Cited in George Herring, " 'Cold Blood': LBJ's Conduct of Limited War in Vietnam," Harmon Memorial Lectures in Military History, no. 33, USAF Academy, Colorado, 1990, p. 24.

32. Peter M. Dunn, "The American Army: The Vietnam War, 1965–1973," in Beckett and Pimlott, *Armed Forces and Modern Counter-Insurgency,* p. 77.

33. Herring, *America's Longest War,* p. 58.

34. Ibid., p. 59.

35. Krepinevich, *Army and Vietnam,* pp. 23–24.

36. Cable, *Conflict of Myths,* p. 200.

37. Herring, *America's Longest War,* p. 63.

38. Ibid., p. 67.

39. Ibid., p. 68.

40. The discussion of U.S. Army counterinsurgency doctrine is based on Krepinevich, *Army and Vietnam,* pp. 38–42.

41. Cable, *Conflict of Myths,* p. 41.

42. See Thompson, *Defeating Communist Insurgency,* and Robert Thompson, *Make for the Hills* (London: Leo Cooper, 1989), pp. 127–131.

43. Herring, *America's Longest War,* pp. 123–131.

44. Krepinevich, *Army and Vietnam,* pp. 194–197.

45. Ibid., p. 197.

46. Herring, " 'Cold Blood,' " p. 22.

47. The details on counterinsurgency experiments are from Dunn, "American Army," pp. 94–99.

48. Krepinevich, *Army and Vietnam,* pp. 232–233.

49. Harry Summers, Jr., cited in Jennifer Morrison Taw and Robert C. Leicht, *The New World Order and Army Doctrine: The Doctrinal Renaissance of Operations Short of War?* (Santa Monica, CA: Rand Corporation, 1992), p. 12.

50. Rod Paschal, "Low-Intensity Conflict Doctrine: Who Needs it?" *Parameters* 15, no. 3 (Autumn 1985): 42.

51. Ibid., p. 21.

52. McClintock, *Instruments of Statecraft,* pp. 325–326.

53. Cited in McClintock, *Instruments of Statecraft,* pp. 350–351.

54. The details on the special forces buildup are from McClintock, *Instruments of Statecraft,* p. 351.

55. Ibid., p. 345.

56. Ibid., pp. 346–347.

57. Defense Authorization Act, 1986, cited in John M. Collins, *Special Operations Forces: An Assessment* (Washington, DC: National Defense University Press, 1994), p. 3.

58. Taw and Leicht, *New World Order and Army Doctrine,* pp. 14–15.

59. Paschal, "Low-Intensity Conflict Doctrine," p. 43.

60. Benjamin C. Schwarz, *American Counterinsurgency Doctrine and El Salvador: The Frustrations of Reform and the Illusions of Nation Building* (Santa Monica, CA: Rand Corporation, 1991), pp. 9, 44.

61. Michael Reid, "Something Happened That Should Not Have," review of Mark Danner, *The Massacre at El Mozote: A Parable of the Cold War* (New York: Vintage Books, 1993), *New York Times Book Review,* 17 July 1994, pp. 8–9.

62. For detailed discussion of these matters, see Schwarz, *American Counterinsurgency Doctrine and El Salvador.*

63. Cited in Taw and Leicht, *New World Order and Army Doctrine,* p. 19.

64. Schwarz, *American Counterinsurgency Doctrine and El Salvador,* p. 77.

65. McClintock, *Instruments of Statecraft,* p. 335.

66. *Psychological Operations in Guerrilla Warfare,* with essays by Joanne Omang and Aryeh Neier (New York: Random House, 1985), p. 57.

67. See John Galvin, "Uncomfortable Wars: Toward a New Paradigm," in *Uncomfortable Wars,* ed. Max Manwaring (Boulder, CO: Westview Press, 1991), pp. 9–18.

68. The details on SOCOM forces are taken from Douglas Waller, *The Commandos: The Making of America's Secret Soldiers from Training to Desert Storm* (New York: Simon and Schuster, 1994), p. 33.

69. Collins, *Special Operations Forces,* p. xxi.

70. Ibid., p. 68.

71. The details on non-SOCOM units are from Collins, *Special Operations Forces,* pp. 33–34.

72. *FM 100-5: Operations,* pp. 13-0 to 13-8.

73. Joint Chiefs of Staff, *Joint Pub. 3-07: Doctrine for Joint Operations in Low Intensity Conflict,* Final Draft (Washington DC: The Joint Staff, 1994), p. II-5.

74. Headquarters, Department of the Army and Air Force, *FM 100-20/AFM 2-20: Military Operations in Low Intensity Conflict* (Washington, DC: U.S. Government Printing Office, 1989), pp. 2-29 to 2-30.

75. Joint Chiefs of Staff, *Joint Pub. 3-0: Doctrine for Joint Operations* (Washington, DC: U.S. Government Printing Office, September 1993), pp. V-2 to V-4, V-10.

76. See J. Bowyer Bell, "An Irish War: The IRA's Armed Struggle, 1969–90: Strategy as History Rules OK," *Small Wars and Insurgencies* 1 no. 3 (Dec. 1990).

77. Waller, *Commandos,* pp. 355–363.

SELECTED BIBLIOGRAPHY

Barber, Noel. *The War of the Running Dogs: The Malayan Emergency, 1948–1960.* New York: Weybright and Talley, 1972.

Beckett, Ian F. W., and John Pimlott, eds. *Armed Forces and Modern Counter-Insurgency.* New York: St. Martin's Press, 1985.

Cable, Larry. *Conflict of Myths: The Development of American Counterinsurgency Doctrine and the Vietnam War.* New York: New York University Press, 1986.

Clutterbuck, Richard L. *The Long, Long War: Counterinsurgency in Malaya and Vietnam.* New York: Frederick A. Praeger, 1966.

Herring, George. *America's Longest War: The United States and Vietnam, 1950–1975.* New York: Alfred A. Knopf, 1986.

Kitson, Frank. *Low Intensity Operations: Subversion, Insurgency, Peace-keeping.* London: Faber and Faber, 1991.

Krepinevich, Andrew F., Jr. *The Army and Vietnam.* Baltimore, MD: Johns Hopkins University Press, 1986.

Linn, Brian McAllister. *The U.S. Army and Counterinsurgency in the Philippine War, 1899–1902.* Chapel Hill: University of North Carolina Press, 1989.

McClintock, Michael. *Instruments of Statecraft: U.S. Guerrilla Warfare, Counterinsurgency, and Counter-Terrorism, 1940–1990.* New York: Pantheon Books, 1992.

Mockaitis, Thomas R. *British Counterinsurgency, 1919–1960.* London: Macmillan, 1990.

Taber, George K. *The War of the Flea: A Study of Guerrilla Warfare Theory and Practice.* New York: Lyle Stuart, 1965.

Taw, Jennifer Morrison, and Robert C. Leicht. *The New World Order and Army Doctrine: The Doctrinal Renaissance of Operations Short of War?* Santa Monica, CA: Rand Corporation, 1992.

Thompson, Robert. *Defeating Communist Insurgency: Experiences from Malaya and Vietnam.* London: Chatto and Windus, 1966.

Waller, Douglas. *The Commandos: The Inside Story of America's Special Soldiers.* New York: Simon and Schuster, 1994.

Chapter 14

CONCLUSION: THE TWENTY-FIRST–CENTURY MILITARY

Sam C. Sarkesian and Robert E. Connor, Jr.

It is a popular theme that the U.S. military usually prepares for the last war. It is also commonplace to argue that military culture changes slowly. While there is some truth in both of these observations, it is the case that the U.S. military appears to be on its way to preparing for the next century, even while retaining roots in the past. The chapters in this volume show that the military is confronted with concerns not only about organizational issues and force mix, but also about the nature and characteristics of conflicts and a variety of contingencies, most in the category of operations other than war. One of the most challenging is unconventional conflicts. Yet it is also true that the military must be prepared for conventional conflicts with strategy and doctrines that have a global outlook, but a regional operational focus, while it faces a revolution in military affairs extending well into the twenty-first century. All of these matters are affected by American domestic politics and changing social and demographic dynamics. How well the military will be able to respond to these concerns and yet retain its capability in its primary purpose is problematical, given the current short-term mind-sets in many sectors of society and in some elements of the military.

The changed strategic landscape combined with the broad-based technological revolution in communications has ushered in what has been called the information age and third-wave warfare. Yet the ultimate outcome remains uncertain because it is difficult to determine with clarity where the communications revolution and its technological developments will lead military strategy and operations, or what impact they will have on the civilian sector and its relationship with the military. These developments, combined with restructuring and redeployment of the military, have created a period of uncertainty not only for the United States, but for its military.

The purpose in this final chapter is to draw broad conclusions from the chapters in this volume, with particular reference to part II, and to address these conclusions as they may project into the next century. The focus is on two major areas: the conflict environment and civil-military relations. There are a number of components to each of these areas.

THE CONFLICT ENVIRONMENT

Regardless of the changed and changing strategic landscape resulting from the end of the Cold War, military capability remains an essential component of national security. To be sure, a variety of other capabilities have become increasingly important; diplomacy, psychological strategies, and economics, among others. But the fact is that none of these can substitute for the appropriate and effective use of military power. This is especially important for the United States given its worldwide interests and the security objectives evolving from the new world order. This is not to suggest that military means should be the first or only option, but there may be times when national interests require the use of military force, although this must be considerably tempered by the nature of the conflict and the appropriate use of other instruments. In deploying the American military, the American way of war is the guiding concept. This is likely to remain the case well into the next century.

The American Way of War

The American way of war includes both American expectations of the nature and purpose of war and the military conduct of war. It has historically rested on a number of premises.

First, many Americans think that a clear distinction should be made between instruments of peace and those of war. The implements of war remain dormant until war erupts, at which time the instruments of peace fade into the background to allow those of war to do what must be done to "win." This polarization is also reflected in the way Americans tend to view contemporary conflicts. Involvement is seen as a zero-sum game: The United States is either at war or at peace, with very little attention to "no-war, no-peace" conditions.

Second, most Americans tend to view conflicts in the world through conventional lenses and mind-sets shaped by the American experience and by American values and norms. Issues of war and peace are seen in legalistic terms: Wars are declared and conducted according to established rules of law. Indeed, for many, international behavior must also abide by such rules. Seeing a new basis for American interventionism, one author has written, "The new interventionism has its roots in long-standing tendencies of American foreign policy—missionary zeal, bewilderment when the world refuses to conform to American expectations and a belief that for every problem there is a quick and easy solution.''[1] This applies equally well to conflicts.

Third, the Vietnam experience left Americans skeptical and ambivalent about the commitment of U.S. ground combat forces in overseas areas, the 1991 Gulf War notwithstanding. Even though a new generation of Americans is emerging with only vague memories of Vietnam, the Vietnam Memorial in Washington promises to keep the experience of Vietnam alive.

Fourth, U.S. involvement in war must be terminated as quickly as possible with a ''victory,'' reflecting clear decisions and final solutions. Such a mind-set assumes that every problem has a solution. As Ernest van den Haag wrote:

> And many Americans still are under the impression that a benevolent deity has made sure that there is a just solution to every problem, a remedy for every wrong, which can be discovered by negotiations, based on good will and on American moral and legal ideals, self-evident enough to persuade all parties, once they are revealed by negotiators, preferably American. Reality is otherwise. Just solutions are elusive. Many problems have no solutions, not even unjust ones; at most they can be managed, prevented from getting worse or from spreading to wider areas. . . . international problems hardly ever are solved by the sedulous pursuit of legal and moral principles.[2]

The consequences drive Americans to search for the ''doable,'' which in turn leads to oversimplification, whether the issue is strategic weaponry, defense budgets, or unconventional conflicts. With respect to unconventional conflicts, most simplistic solutions sidestep fundamental problems and reveal a lack of understanding regarding relationships between culture, modernity, political and economic change, internal conflicts, and developing systems. This American predilection is reinforced by the fact that many effective responses to conflicts, particularly unconventional conflicts, may not be within the realm of the values and norms of open systems. This does not mean that open systems such as that of the United States are not capable of effective response. What it does mean is that open systems have serious difficulties in developing acceptable policies and strategies for a variety of conflicts because of the very nature and character of open systems.

The American way of war is also part of the Weinberger Doctrine.[3] Much of this doctrine rests on the following: moral high ground, clear objectives, a clear beginning and end to any conflict, short duration, and conflict focused on clearly defined adversaries. Also, the purpose and objectives of the conflict need to be understood by the American people. Much of this doctrine is part of the prevailing military perspective, which stresses, among other things, that the military involvement needs the support of the American people, policy and strategy feasibility, and a strong argument that the use of the military is a last resort. As John Spanier said:

> Once Americans were provoked, however, and the United States had to resort to force, the employment of this force was justified in terms of universal moral principles with

> which the United States, as a democratic country, identified itself. Resort to the evil instrument of war could be justified only by presuming noble purposes and completely destroying the immoral enemy who threatened the integrity, if not the existence, of these principles. American power had to be "righteous" power; only its full exercise could ensure salvation or the absolution of sin.[4]

In sum, the ability of the United States to respond to conflicts across the spectrum is conditioned by historical experience and the American way of war. National interests and national security policy have been shaped by the premises identified here and have conditioned the way Americans see the contemporary world security environment. Yet security issues and conflicts across the spectrum may not be relevant to American perceptions, policy, and strategy. The gap between American perceptions and the realities of the security environment and the nature of conflicts poses a challenging and often-dangerous dilemma to U.S. national security policy and ultimately to the U.S. military.

The Nature of Conflicts

The changed strategic landscape and the diminishing prospect of major wars between major powers has shifted attention to a variety of lesser wars and unconventional conflicts. While concerns remain regarding the final shape of Russia and the possibility of major conflict within the former Soviet Union, increasing attention is being devoted to a variety of ethnic, religious, and nationalistic conflicts, as in the former Yugoslavia, and peacekeeping operations, as in Somalia. At the higher end of the conflict spectrum, the 1991 Gulf War represented a form of European scenario providing for some Americans guidelines for the future.[5]

> Resurgent forms of ethnic and religious violence and new forms of transnational conflict differ from traditional aggression across frontiers—but they may be equally destructive to global security. Low-intensity conflict and secret warfare—including the use of terrorism by states, private groups, and revolutionary movements—threaten the international order in new ways that transform the manner in which policymakers, diplomats, and the public must approach questions of peace and security.[6]

Complicating the conflict landscape are conflicts associated with coalitions between drug cartels and revolutionary groups, such as the Shining Path and drug-cartel linkage in Peru. Another element in the conflict environment is the threat of international criminal organizations. Criminal organizations in Russia, Colombia, and China, for example, have become transnational in scope, extending their reach into Europe and the United States. In addition, linkages between such groups and ethnic organizations not only challenge any number of systems in the less developed world, but provide an extremely lucrative channel for drug trafficking and a variety of other criminal activities. Similarly, in the United States these groups link closely with their own ethnic groups, establishing an international channel for illegal immigrants and drug movements, making it extremely difficult to uncover and to eradicate these activities.

The challenge for the United States is not only domestic, but in terms of national security. The drug trade and the linkages with ethnic groups, and the resulting corruption of government officials, make it extremely difficult for fledgling governments of less developed systems to respond effectively. In brief, criminal elements may be more effective within these indigenous systems than the government itself. The difficulty of developing effective governments, particularly in new democratic systems, poses long-range challenges to U.S. national security, based on the notion that America is intent on supporting democratic systems. The critical issue for national security policy and the U.S. military is the role, if any, for the military in U.S. response to international organized crime. The problems emerging from the perils of peacekeeping become even more pronounced in such situations.

The conflict environment makes it difficult to clearly identify adversaries and even more difficult to spell out political-military objectives. Indeed, even in the aftermath of the 1991 Gulf War, some criticized the operation because it did not finish the job of deposing Saddam Hussein of Iraq, although this was clearly not the assigned mission. In any case, likely conflict characteristics make it difficult to garner the necessary support of the American people to engage in military operations.[7] This is particularly true with respect to sustained, long-term operations. Low-visibility military operations may succeed for a time, but many see the use of military force as a blunt instrument not particularly relevant to the political-military problems likely to face the United States in the immediate future.

The military is the instrument of ''hard power,'' best employed in clear conflict situations according to clear policies aimed at protection of U.S. national interests. In the absence of an adversary that is a clear threat to the survival of the United States, and facing a changing international arena that appears to be turning into a variety of regional conflict clusters, realists can argue that none of these regional conflicts threaten the U.S. homeland and few can be translated into threats to U.S. national interests. Yet there are regional developments that may well see the rise of regional hegemons in the next century—hegemons that may challenge U.S. interests in one region or the other.

In the final analysis, conflicts in the new strategic landscape are likely to be less than major, to be less threatening to U.S. national interests (at least in the short run), and to fall into the full range of unconventional conflicts and a variety of peacekeeping missions—that is, peacekeeping, peacemaking, and peace enforcement (operations other than war). More often than not, however, the peacekeeping environment lays the groundwork for unconventional conflicts. Humanitarian missions have also become part of expected military contingencies, for example, Hurricane Andrew in Florida and the initial effort in Somalia. The U.S. intervention in Haiti, however, can be termed a mix of humanitarian assistance, peacemaking, foreign aid, and moral commitment. In mid-1995, it was not clear what eventually would emerge in Haiti, the elections in June 1995 notwithstanding. Historically, the military has effectively performed humanitarian missions and a variety of other missions under the label of "peacetime engagements."[8] But in the emerging strategic landscape and undefined world order, the notion that the U.S. military can engage in humanitarian and peacekeeping missions on a consistent basis in foreign strategic cultures raises serious questions about the impact of a U.S. military presence in various parts of the world and combat readiness. Similarly, the capability and effectiveness of the military to respond to a range of unconventional conflicts, including the drug-cartel/revolutionary coalition, remain questionable. In all of these contingencies, the support of the American people is crucial. What the U.S. military is going through during this period is best summed up by the following: "The world's greatest military seems to be on the verge of exhaustion. Incredibly, the military is not overtaxed by the demands of war, but reeling under the strain of peace."[9]

In sum, while the U.S. military must maintain its capability to deter nuclear conflict and succeed in conventional conflict (including the emerging third-wave warfare), it must be particularly concerned about operations other than war and unconventional conflicts. It is the latter conflicts and missions that are the most likely contingencies and conflicts of the future. Yet if history is any guide, the U.S. military will remain fixated on wars of a conventional nature and technological developments that affect weaponry and communications—many of which have a minimum impact on effective response to operations other than war and unconventional conflicts. This pattern appears to be well established and is likely to continue into the next century.

To develop and to maintain flexibility to respond to these potential conflicts and challenges necessitate a number of basic military capabilities. With special reference to the U.S. Army, such capability requires effective response to conventional wars and beyond, to unconventional conflicts, and to noncombat contingencies. To respond effectively, the U.S. military needs to consider a "specialization of labor" concept based on the view that the mainstream military cannot respond effectively to all conflicts across the spectrum. Moreover, in any number of noncombat missions, nonmilitary agencies may be better suited to respond. Further, the more extensive use of Federal Reserves and National Guard forces in OOTW is becoming an acceptable option. It may also be the case that privatization of some peacekeeping missions and other contingencies within OOTW may be an acceptable option.

The Conflict Spectrum

The conflict spectrum is a method of analyzing conflicts in terms of U.S. capabilities and effectiveness. It is also a method to categorize conflicts in terms of policy perspectives. In this context contemporary conflicts are placed in various categories of intensity. Figure 14.1 shows a perspective of the conflict

Figure 14.1
Conflict Spectrum

```
Operations Other Than War-------------->

*Non-     +    Unconventional Conflicts |Conventional    |Nuclear
 Combat   +                             |                |
----------+-----------------------------|--------------- |-------
          +                             |                |
          + **Special ! ***Low Intensity|  Limited/Major |
          + Operations!    Conflict     |                |
          +           ! ================|
          +           !  Revolution/    |
          +           !  Counter-       |
          +           !  revolution     |
```

Legend:

\+ Erosion of clear distinctions: any number of peacekeeping and humanitarian operations may set the stage for unconventional conflicts

* Shows of Force: military /economic aid and assistance, peacekeeping, and humanitarian contingencies

** Counterterror, hostage rescue, spearhead, surgical strikes, hit-and-run raids

***	Phase I	Combined economic and other non-military assistance and aid; weapons training teams; police training and assistance; military training cadres
	Phase 2	Special Forces "A" teams plus Phase 1
	Phase 3	Special Forces Headquarters (Teams B and C), additional A teams plus Phases 1 and 2
	Phase 4	Light infantry forces-defensive role plus Phase 1 through 3, inclusive
	Phase 5	Light infantry forces-active combat; administrative and logistical bases for expanded role plus Phase 1 through 4, inclusive. Requisite air and sea support. The Americanization of the conflict

spectrum where operations other than war and unconventional conflicts are the most likely military missions in the contemporary and future environment.

U.S. military capability varies among conflict categories. At the low end of the spectrum, the United States is capable and reasonably effective in providing military assistance ranging from military equipment and advisors to financial aid. In addition, the United States has shown effectiveness in the use of the military instrument for political purposes through shows of force and a variety of military maneuvers—now labelled operations other than war (OOTW). As seen in U.S. involvement in Somalia in 1992, it is also capable in conducting military operations as a cover for humanitarian assistance (although this ended in disaster and withdrawal of U.S. forces). All of these military contingencies are based on the presumption that there is not likely to be serious combat (or any combat) between U.S. forces and adversaries. But when such operations go beyond the peacekeeping/humanitarian contingencies, the groundwork is created for conflict, in general, and unconventional conflict, in particular.

At the opposite end of the spectrum, the United States remains well positioned in nuclear weaponry and strategic forces to deter adversaries. The end of the Cold War has led to the view that major wars and the prospects for nuclear exchange between major powers have diminished considerably. Also, treaties between the United States and Russia to reduce strategic and tactical nuclear weapons have ushered in an era of arms-control efforts extending worldwide. For example, the Presidents of the United States and Ukraine signed agreements in 1994 to eliminate strategic missiles in the Ukraine. Many such efforts were continuities from the Cold War era where agreements were concluded such as START (Strategic Arms Reduction Talks). Nonetheless, some states are developing and expanding their nuclear and chemical as well as biological capability—North Korea, Iraq, and Iran. Thus the United States must retain a credible deterrence to counter the use of such weapons and deter proliferation. Similarly, the U.S. capability in conventional conflict was well demonstrated in the Gulf War, which was primarily based on operational principles deriving from a European-oriented battle scenario.

It is the vast middle area of the spectrum where the United States is at a disadvantage, and it is OOTW and unconventional conflicts that are the most likely in the foreseeable future. Yet when Americans, most of whom place emphasis on conventional conflict categories, give any attention to this middle area, they think primarily in terms of commando-type operations or special operations shaped by counterterrorism contingencies. Further, most presume that operations other than war are primarily of a peacekeeping/humanitarian nature far removed from ground combat.

In sum, the key problem facing the military is to determine the nature and characteristics of conflicts now and in the future in order to prepare to respond effectively and maintain combat cohesion and effectiveness in the process. Part of this problem includes the need to maintain the support of society and ensure that civil-military relations evolving from the new landscape are compatible with democratic principles. To be sure, the problem does not rest solely with the military; the national leadership and the national security system share the responsibility. Nonetheless, the military does not have the luxury of waiting for others to spell out security policy and national strategy. Operational doctrine and force structure must be designed and in place, and strategic concepts must be fashioned to respond to the strategic landscape now and in the future.

Conventional Wars and Beyond

In the contemporary period the uncertain and dangerous world still requires that the United States maintain some level of effective strategic deterrence and develop defenses against nuclear as well as chemical weapons. The move by both Russia and the United States to reduce stockpiles of strategic weapons and the unlikelihood of conflict between the United States and states evolving from the former Soviet Union have reduced the need for maintaining strategic forces on the scale of the past forty years. More pressing for the U.S. military, however, is the need to maintain the ability to effectively engage in conventional war on relatively short notice. Many point to Desert Storm as a ''model'' for the future. In that conflict, according to many analysts, active forces were able to challenge and ''stand off'' the adversary until the arrival of heavy units and reconstituted forces in the form of reserve and National Guard units.

Equally important, in the Gulf War the United States was able to develop and maintain a coalition strategy that brought to bear not only U.N. political and diplomatic pressures on Iraq, but also a variety of forces from other countries, including some from the Middle East. However, using Desert Storm as a ''model'' must be viewed with some caution. While the United States can draw important lessons from the Gulf War, it is just as likely that future adversaries have also drawn a number of important lessons, the most important being not to challenge the United States overtly, visibly, or conventionally. Indeed, adversaries may have learned that the most effective way—and the least threatening to themselves—to achieve their objectives may be by covert operations and unconventional warfare using surrogates and/or third parties. Moreover, in future conflicts the United States may not have the luxury of safe ports and assembly areas to prepare for the offensive. Thus, in the long run, conventional wars such as the Gulf War may be the least likely contingencies for the United States. This does not mean that regional conflicts will necessarily diminish, but it does suggest that U.S. involvement may be the least optimum strategy, and when the United States does become involved, it may have only a minimum amount of time to respond effectively, in contrast to the 1991 Gulf War.

Operations Other Than War (OOTW)

Noncombat contingencies are under the label ''operations other than war'' (OOTW). According to U.S. Army doctrine, in operations other than war,

"Army forces and soldiers operate around the world in an environment that may not involve combat."[10] These contingencies range from arms control, support to domestic civil authorities, humanitarian assistance, and disaster relief to peacekeeping operations, peace enforcement, and support for insurgencies and counterinsurgencies.[11] There are other contingencies based on the ability to provide administrative and logistical support to political and diplomatic efforts aimed at drug control and abatement. It is usually the case that activities in operations other than war stem from civilian-initiated and implemented policies, strategies, and efforts. The key is that the role of the military, especially of ground forces, is in direct support of civilian efforts; military initiatives are minimal, if they are undertaken at all. In brief, the military role remains secondary to the political-diplomatic effort, whether initiated by the United Nations or the United States.

In the current period the U.S. military is still struggling to reconcile commitments to operations other than war with maintaining effectiveness in its primary mission. "The Army's primary focus is to fight and win the nation's wars."[12] Yet it is also clear that support for insurgencies and counterinsurgencies poses the most serious problems for the mainstream military. It is difficult for mainstream military forces to successfully engage in such operations (here termed unconventional conflicts) beyond limited administrative and logistical support without becoming engulfed in indigenous struggles and raising the specter of another Vietnam. In our view, it is also true that virtually every activity conducted in foreign lands under the rubric of operations other than war can lead to unconventional conflicts. In this respect, unconventional conflicts are critical reference points in coming to grips with most activities labelled operations other than war.

Unconventional Conflicts

Conflicts and challenges in the post–Cold war era, particularly those in the Third World, are more likely to be rooted in unconventional characteristics—revolution, counterrevolution, and terrorism. Any U.S. military involvement in such conflicts and contingencies is likely to rely heavily on ground troops. Further, such conflicts and challenges are not necessarily limited to state-to-state confrontations. They can encompass a variety of groups within states and some that are transnational in scope. But most of these conflicts and activities are not an immediate challenge to U.S. national interests or security. However, many can be in the long term, and it is this that makes it difficult to identify with any degree of confidence when and where the next conflict or threat may emerge that will require some type of response by the United States. In addition, there may be threats requiring simultaneous military contingencies.

The official literature uses labels of special operations and low-intensity conflict (SO/LIC) as well as insurgencies and counterinsurgencies to define unconventional conflict. Over the past years, however, various labels have been used to identify basically the same characteristics. These include such terms as limited wars, internal defense, guerrilla war, counterguerrilla war, insurgency, counterinsurgency, small wars, peacetime engagements, operations short of war, and now operations other than war encompassing special operations and low-intensity conflict. Moreover, efforts have been made to identify the nature of conflict by the degree of intensity: low, mid, and high. The term *unconventional conflicts* is used here because it focuses primarily on the differences between the characteristics of conflict—unconventional and conventional.

Unconventional conflict is defined as revolution, counterrevolution, and terrorism associated with each, encompassing strategies aimed at overthrowing the state using unorthodox military operations. This is primarily a political-military struggle over control of the state and involves a broad range of political, economic, psychological, social, and military means. It also includes tactics intended to achieve limited political objectives often using terrorism and covert operations. The driving strategic principles emanate from Sun Tzu rather than Clausewitz.

Characteristics of Unconventional Conflicts

Unconventional conflicts have characteristics that are unique and differ considerably from those of conventional conflicts. These are discussed in detail in a number of publications.[13] Some of the most important characteristics include the following:

Asymmetry

For the United States unconventional conflicts are limited wars, but for the indigenous adversaries these are wars of survival—total wars. The differences between the U.S. involvement and those of the indigenous adversaries shape mind-sets, resources, and commitments. As an officer in the Chilean Army noted:

> From the U.S. perspective, and based on its strategic reality, the situation in certain countries of the area requires only part of the potential US aid available which, in turn, leads to classification as low- , mid- , or high-intensity conflict. In other words the magnitude of US effort expended determines the classification of any given conflict. The countries involved have a very different viewpoint; for them it is painful bloody war, not conflict.[14]

Ambiguity

In unconventional conflicts it is difficult to determine who is winning and who is losing. In the main, conventional criteria for determining success are irrelevant. As the United States learned in Vietnam, conventional yardsticks such as body counts, prisoners, and weapons captured may be meaningless. Also, it is difficult, often impossible, to clearly distinguish the adversary's armed elements and personnel from the indigenous civilian system.

Unconventionality

Such conflicts are not only unconventional in a strategic sense but also tactically: terrorism, hit-and-run raids, ambushes, and assassinations are the common operational mode.

> Revolution is endowed with a dynamic quality and a dimension in depth that orthodox wars, whatever their scale, lack. This is particularly true of revolutionary guerrilla war, which is not susceptible to the type of superficial military treatment frequently advocated by antediluvian doctrinaires.[15]

Protraction

The long, drawn-out nature of unconventional conflicts not only challenges U.S. military doctrine but tends to erode American national will, political resolve, and staying power. Cases in point include conflicts that occurred in (or are in progress in) Angola, Malaya, Vietnam, Cambodia/Laos, Peru, and Colombia. Americans are inclined to see the proper use of strategy as seeking overwhelming use of military force to quickly end the conflict.

Differing Strategic Cultures

Unconventional conflicts are likely to take place in cultures that differ from the Western tradition. The Judeo-Christian heritage and the Anglo-Saxon legacy may not be compatible or relevant in other cultures where unconventional conflicts are most likely to occur. Among other things, the concepts of winners and losers and of the conduct of conflicts may differ in other cultures. In addition, moral and legal rules of engagement and battle conduct may differ.

Samuel Huntington's "The Clash of Civilizations" is particularly relevant in this respect. He wrote:

> Civilization identity will be increasingly important in the future, and the world will be shaped in large measure by the interactions among seven or eight major civilizations. . . . The most important conflicts of the future will occur along cultural fault lines separating these civilizations from one another.[16]

Clausewitz and Sun Tzu

The center of gravity in Clausewitzian terms is on the adversary's military. Once the military is defeated, the winning power can impose its will on the adversary. This generally means that overwhelming force at the point of decision is the key to success. According to Sun Tzu's precepts, however, the most successful general is one who wins without fighting. The center of gravity is on the political-social milieu of society. Thus secret, covert, and psychological operations are critical to success. Further, the key is to penetrate the adversary's political system and erode the will to resist. It is Sun Tzu's principles that characterize successful efforts in unconventional conflicts.[17]

It is not clear that the American public, in general, and elected officials, in particular, fully understand the range of conflicts, their characteristics, and their impact on American domestic politics. As suggested by one analyst, the propensity for the new interventionism seems to focus on wars of conscience and missionary zeal.[18] Following such perspectives, involvement in military operations can easily lead to open-ended embroilment in an unconventional conflict environment, with all that such involvement portends regarding domestic political reaction and political-military complications.

CIVIL-MILITARY RELATIONS

The relationship between the military, the national leadership, and society (civil-military relations) has a major impact on the combat effectiveness of the military. These relationships affect the military's spirit and its psychological wherewithal to engage in military contingencies. In addition, the national will, staying power, and political resolve of the American political system underpin civil-military relations. Much of this relationship is shaped by the national leadership and the strategic vision that leadership articulates.

National Leadership

The Bush Administration

In a speech at Aspen, Colorado, in August 1990, President George Bush outlined a broad strategy for ''Reshaping Our Forces'' for the new security landscape. The President stated, in part:

> The size of our forces will increasingly be shaped by the needs of regional contingencies and peacetime presence . . . A policy of peacetime engagement every bit as constant and committed to the defense of our interests and ideals in today's world as in the time of conflict and Cold War.[19]

Elaborating on the President's statement, Secretary of Defense Richard Cheney proposed four major elements of a new U.S. defense strategy[20]: (1) Strategic defense and deterrence; (2) forward presence; (3) crisis response; and (4) force reconstitution. Thus, in addition to retaining high-quality personnel and a capable industrial and technological base, the Total Force Policy has an important role in force reconstitution as well as in all other elements of strategy.

In a further elaboration of strategy as it applies to the U.S. Army, then Secretary of the Army Michael P. W. Stone stated that the Army must be prepared to fight two concurrent regional conflicts. This was based on what was labelled MRC (Major Regional Conflict) East and MRC West.[21]

Also, from the U.S. perspective, the various alliances and treaties established during the Cold War period seemed obsolete, at least in their original intent and substance. Further, a new set of relationships emerged with former adversaries, including Vietnam. Others pointed to the need for a new policy with respect to

Cuba. Equally important, the Pacific Basin area emerged as a potential for power projection and conflict as China and Japan vie for advantage in the area.[22]

During the last two years of the Bush administration plans were put into place to reduce the size of the military and reduce defense spending. These plans carried over into the Clinton administration with larger defense reductions even though there appeared to be an increase in military missions and contingencies. Yet the effectiveness of President Bush's leadership in successfully prosecuting the Gulf War reinforced and nurtured a compatible and trustworthy relationship between the President and the military. However, the high ratings for President Bush's leadership did not carry over into the 1992 election.

The Clinton Administration: The First Two Years

President Bill Clinton began his presidency with antimilitary baggage carried over from the Vietnam War. It did not help his image after becoming President that he immediately announced a policy lifting the ban on homosexuals in the military. Combined with his past activities, this created a gap between the President and the military—a gap that remains today.[23] According to Harry Summers, ''For the first time in American history we have a climate in the White House that openly scorns the military and holds those who have put their lives on the line for their country in total contempt.''[24] Contrary to the opinion of some of the President's staunchest supporters, the military has always given its complete loyalty to the Commander-in-Chief, even though some individuals in the military may question the leadership ability and character of the person occupying the Oval Office. As one consequence of the Republican sweep of congressional and gubernatorial offices in 1994, however, the climate in the White House toward the military rank and file changed.

Regardless of these issues of leadership, the fact is that the President is the official who defines issues of national security and spells out policy objectives. But only very late in the second year of his administration did President Clinton provide a national security statement. His view of U.S. national security issues was spelled out in *A National Security Strategy of Engagement and Enlargement.*[25] In concluding, President Clinton stated:

> Of all the elements contained in this strategy, none is more important than this: our Administration is committed to explaining our security interests and objectives to the nation; to seeking the broadest possible public and congressional support of our security programs and investments; and to exerting our leadership in the world in a manner that reflects our best national values and protects the security of this great and good nation.[26]

In light of the uncertain steps and a series of miscues in Bosnia and Somalia and the commitment of U.S. forces to Haiti to protect President Aristide without recourse to Congress and the American people, President Clinton's statement brought a sharp rejoinder from Harry Summers: ''There is a credibility chasm between what Clinton says and what he does.''[27] Further, one authoritative group concluded:

> One of the most striking features of the current period is the mismatch between our rhetoric and our resources. The administration's announced strategy of enlarging the community of democratic market-economy nations implies a growing demand on resources. The end of the cold war, however, has resulted in a steady and substantial decline in defense spending and other resources for intervention.[28]

In view of efforts to design a defense budget and military structure to fit budget constraints and domestic priorities, the U.S. military is faced with the prospect of doing more with less.

In response to the end of the superpower era, the Bush administration planned a reduction in the U.S. military over a five-year period. This included the trimming of the U.S. defense budget by $50 billion and the reduction of military manpower. The U.S. Army was expected to take the brunt of manpower reduction; its end strength was to be reduced by at least 25 percent to 525,000 by 1995 and below 500,000 by 1996, and by 1999, the Active Army will be reduced to ten divisions. Table 14.1 shows the approximate end strength of the U.S. military by 1999. Moreover, for the first time in decades, most of the U.S. Army will be stationed in the continental United States.

In 1993 then Secretary of Defense Les Aspin announced that the Clinton administration was planning even deeper reductions in the U.S. military.[29] For the military, not only was the additional cut in defense dollars difficult to absorb, but the reduction in total strength raised fears about military capability in responding to a variety of contingencies. The new budget revised the earlier Base Force concept and evolved from a 1992 study on ground-force structure by then Congressman Les Aspin.[30] In that study a number of options were presented using the forces employed in Desert Storm as the reference point. The option selected will reduce the active army to ten divisions.[31] Critics pointed out that the plans for reduction of forces have little to do with strategic planning, but rather deal with shifting of resources to domestic programs.

The announcement by President Clinton in November 1994 that an additional $25 billion would be provided in the defense budget over the next six years alleviated some fears regarding military preparedness. Some argued that the addition of $25 billion was too little, too late. Moreover, in the first two years of the Clinton presidency, there were not only many critics of the administration's defense policy from the Republican Party and some from within the Democratic Party, but some from observers outside government. According to one authority:

> [L]argely self-inflicted *economic* weaknesses now indirectly threaten our national security. . . . Despite the euphoria over America's success in the war in Iraq, the 1990s will be a decade of new and increasing tensions for the United States between international needs and economic constraints. As the full implications of being the world's largest

Table 14.1
U.S. Military End Strength, 1999 (Approximate)

	1990	Base Force Plan for 1995	Administration's Plan for Late 1990s
Army Divisions	28 (18 Active)	18 (12 Active)[a]	15 (10 Active)
MEFs	3	3	3
Aircraft Carriers	15 + 1 Training	12 + 1 Training	11 + 1 Reserve
Carrier Air Wings	15 (13 Active)	13 (11 Active)	10 + 1 Reserve
Battle Force Ships	546	451	346
Fighter Wings	36 (24 Active)	26 (15 Active)	20 (13 Active)
Strategic Bombers (PAA)	301	180	Up to 184
Active-Duty Manpower	2,069,000	1,644,200	1,453,000
Reserve Manpower	1,128,000	921,800	About 900,000

Notes: The Base Force Plan, the official policy of the Bush administration, would have been almost fully in place by 1995. MEF = Marine Expeditionary Force; PAA = primary authorized aircraft.

[a]Does not include two cadre divisions.

Source: Adapted from Congress of the United States, *A CBO Study: Enhancing U.S. Security through Foreign Aid* (Washington, DC: Congressional Budget Office, April 1994), p. 70.

debtor dawn on us *and* on the rest of the world, the gap between our interests and our capacities will become larger, more obvious, and more painful.[32]

Beyond 1994

As noted earlier, the 1994 midterm elections gave a majority to the Republican Party in both the Senate and the House of Representatives. For many Americans this was a repudiation of the Democratic Party agenda and of the policy and leadership of President Bill Clinton. As a consequence, a different domestic policy agenda evolved. In addition, it is likely that the Republican-controlled Congress will attempt to create a clear distinction (or firewall) between defense and nondefense spending. Also, there are likely to be changes in foreign and defense policy and limits to defense budget reductions.

In 1995 the Republican Congress passed the ''National Security Revitalization Act'' as part of the Contract with America. This Act, among other things, attempted to restrict future U.S. participation in U.N. military operations, recognized the decline in U.S. military readiness, and supported U.S. leadership in NATO. The provision to increase money for ballistic missile defense failed. While the Act did not accomplish all that was intended,

> It forced the administration to confront its readiness issues, and the Republican defense effort gave weight to Defense Secretary William Perry's request for an additional $25 billion in readiness funds. . . . There has now been a searching debate on American defense priorities. . . . Like steel passed through a fire, American defense is undoubtedly stronger for it.[33]

In another area of defense assessments serious questions were raised regarding the quality of military life and the impact this has on morale and combat readiness. These issues surfaced as the reductions in force continued and defense budgets were slashed by the Clinton administration. Quality-of-life issues became increasingly contentious and added to the fears within the military regarding careers, readiness, and the diminishing quality of the environment for military families. Additionally, this issue added fuel to efforts within the Republican Congress to increase defense spending. Yet, the balanced budget efforts in mid-1995 focused on capping, if not reducing, spending on the military.

Retired General John A. Wickham ''[A]ddressed members of the Defense Department Task Force on quality of life at the study group's first meeting . . .'' in February 1995. He said in part, ''The Army's [quality-of-life] programs are fragile and dependent on no unforeseen diversion or contingencies. . . . Put it right up front that when those things occur, your programs are broken. Don't give the impression . . . that everything is well.''[34] This will affect military force posture and likely contingencies into the next century. Much will also depend on the outcome of the 1996 presidential elections and elections to Congress.

The U.S. Military

The focus of the military in the 1990s appears to be on preparing for what has been called the revolution in military affairs.[35] At the same time, the struggle over defense dollars has triggered a new round of interservice rivalries. As the *Army Times* noted:

> The debate over which service should be doing what was prompted by the creation of the Commission on Roles and Missions of the Armed Forces. Congress ordered the independent, 11-member commission in the 1994 Defense Authorization Act.[36]

The Commission submitted its report in May 1995. This included a number of recommendations ranging from more emphasis on jointness to transferring Defense Department support services to the private sector.

> The Commission, taking its cue from the Goldwater-Nichols Act of 1986, envisions a more powerful chairman of the joint Chiefs and a strengthened Joint Requirements Oversight Council, whose job will be to decide at the very beginning of budgeting and acquisition plans what is needed and who best can do it.[37]

The Commission also recommended that 50,000 combat troops be cut from the Total Army. It also recommended shifting 60,000 troops from combat positions to support roles.[38]

Although in June 1995, Secretary of Defense William Perry had no immediate comment on the report, some criticism was expressed by outside analysts. According to some, ''[T]he emphasis on jointness, although not bad, is a cover for avoiding the big issues.''[39]

Also, the Federal Reserve and National Guard were in the process of reorganizing and reexamining their relationships with the active military. Part of this process included efforts to shift combat missions from the Federal Reserve forces to the National Guard. In addition, questions were raised about appropriate contingencies for reserve and National Guard forces both in the domestic and international arenas, particularly in peacekeeping roles. Lost in the political-military maze are the challenges posed by unconventional conflicts as well as other activities associated with operations other than war. While there is some talk of careers in operations other than war, the military still views command of mainstream units as critical to career success. Indeed, the focus on the military's primary purpose remains the driving force for all of the services. But some of this focus seems to have also spilled over into U.S. special operations forces, fashioning a conventional focus to unconventional efforts, and it is U.S. special operations forces, particularly Special Forces, that are crucial in responding to unconventional conflicts.

Complicating the problems for the U.S. military is that some find it necessary to rationalize the military's involvement in socially relevant missions and nontraditional contingencies in order to justify budgetary resources. This rests on the mistaken notion that ''shooting'' conflicts may well be a thing of the past—that all operations other than war are indeed ''peace'' missions or that no internal conflicts in foreign lands are (or can become) matters of national interest. Such arguments also presume that the U.S. military is capable of maintaining its capability across the conflict spectrum, even if it is increasingly engaged in noncombat missions. We feel that this is a dangerous misconception, as is the notion that involvement in a variety of ''peace'' missions establishes and maintains military relevancy in the eyes of the American public as well as the national leadership.

To follow such notions places the military in the unenviable position that was recognized by General Gordon Sullivan in 1993—the stress on the military, particularly the Army, is significant.[40] Adding to that stress is the notion of some that the U.S. military must replicate society, responding to a variety of domestic demographic and social issues. To presume that the military must replicate society is, we believe, another dangerous notion. While the military must represent society, it cannot replicate society without eroding the very basis of the military's purpose and cohesion.[41]

There also is a military institutional mind-set that U.S. military forces are capable across the conflict spectrum. This is based on the view that preparation for war also prepares the military for operations other than war and unconventional conflicts. But some argue that this is a mistaken notion:

> U.S. forces are well structured and prepared for high-intensity operations, but less so for peace operations and lower-intensity intervention. . . . While U.S. forces are sufficient for large-scale intervention, they are not optimized for peacekeeping and other peace operations, or for other types of low-level conflict. These operations demand specialized training and preparation.[42]

While conventional contingencies and major-power security relationships remain major concerns, the concept of operations other than war (OOTW) gained prominence in early 1990s as the United States became involved in Rwanda, Haiti, Somalia, and Bosnia-Herzegovina.[43] This concept includes peacekeeping contingencies and humanitarian missions. For some, many missions in operations other than war are driven by moral indignation, wars of conscience, and ''video'' images. If these views are taken to their logical conclusions, the U.S. military may become engaged in a variety of operations that may have little to do with national interests. In the strategic landscape of the 1990s, operations other than war seem to be becoming the rule rather than the exception. Further, the operational doctrine and the mind-set appropriate for operations other than war differ from the primary purpose of the U.S. military—success in combat. This places considerable pressure on the military to balance the skills, operational techniques, and mind-sets required for success in combat with those required for peacekeeping and humanitarian missions, including unconventional conflicts.

One of the greatest dangers for the U.S. military and its extended involvement in OOTW is the cost to readiness in performing its primary purpose. In testimony before Congress, a number of senior army officers stressed the costs to readiness. In his testimony General Carl Vuono, the former Chief of Staff of the U.S. Army, stated the following: ''Will today or tomorrow's peacetime commitments leave enough [soldiers] for properly tailoring a robust, major contingency power-projection package? As far as I'm concerned, they will not.''[44] At the same hearing ''Maxwell R. Thurman, former commander of the US Southern Command,'' testified, ''After a peacekeeping mission . . . soldiers have to go through an extensive training regime to regain the level of operational proficiency which they held at the outset of that duty.''[45] In other words, combat readiness suffers. In response to these problems, General John Shalikashvili, Chairman of the Joint Chiefs of Staff, is reported to have stated: ''The Defense Department is looking for ways to reduce operating tempos by changing historic operating routines. . . . Carrier battle groups may be making shorter deployments. And the Marines may travel less often to relatively untroubled places like the Mediterranean.''[46]

To argue that the United States as the only superpower has a worldwide moral obligation and presumes that such an obligation includes a military commitment is tantamount to accepting the notion that the United States is the world's hegemon. The reduction of U.S. military forces and the changed strategic orientation, combined with resource limits and the American domestic political-social agenda, challenge the concept of America as the only superpower with its attendant obligations. Moreover, such presumptions ignore the rise of regional associations such as the European Community and developments in the Pacific Basin as well as the China-Japan linkage. Demographics and resources in a variety of areas in the world seem to indicate the rise of major powers in the next century that may make the concept of the United States as the only superpower irrelevant.

Special Operations Command

Most of the skills and specialized training in operations other than war and unconventional conflict are in the special operations forces, particularly Special Forces. The United States Special Operations Command was created in 1986 by Congress (Public Law 99-661) and strengthened by subsequent legislation (Public Laws 100-1809 and 100-456).[47] The legislation included provisions for an Assistant Secretary of Defense for Special Operations and Low-Intensity Conflict and a unified command for special operations forces and prescribed a Board for Low-Intensity Conflict within the National Security Council (NSC). In 1987 other legislation provided for, among other items, the publication of a charter for the Assistant Secretary of Defense for Special Operations and Low-Intensity Conflict and designated the Secretary of the Army as acting Assistant Secretary of Defense for SO/LIC until the office was formally filled for the first time. In addition, provisions were made for a separate SOF budget. The Special Operations Command is the primary organization designed to respond to unconventional conflicts. The organizational structure of the United States Special Operations Command (USSOCOM) is shown in figure 14.2.

While much has been done to strengthen and improve the special operations system, much remains unresolved. Some of this has to do with the distinctions between mainstream military and special operations forces—a distinction that places career special operations forces officers almost on the periphery of military system. This is particularly true of Special Forces officers who have their own career branch. Moreover, plans and their implementation as well as rela-

Figure 14.2
Organizational Structure of the U.S. Special Operations Command

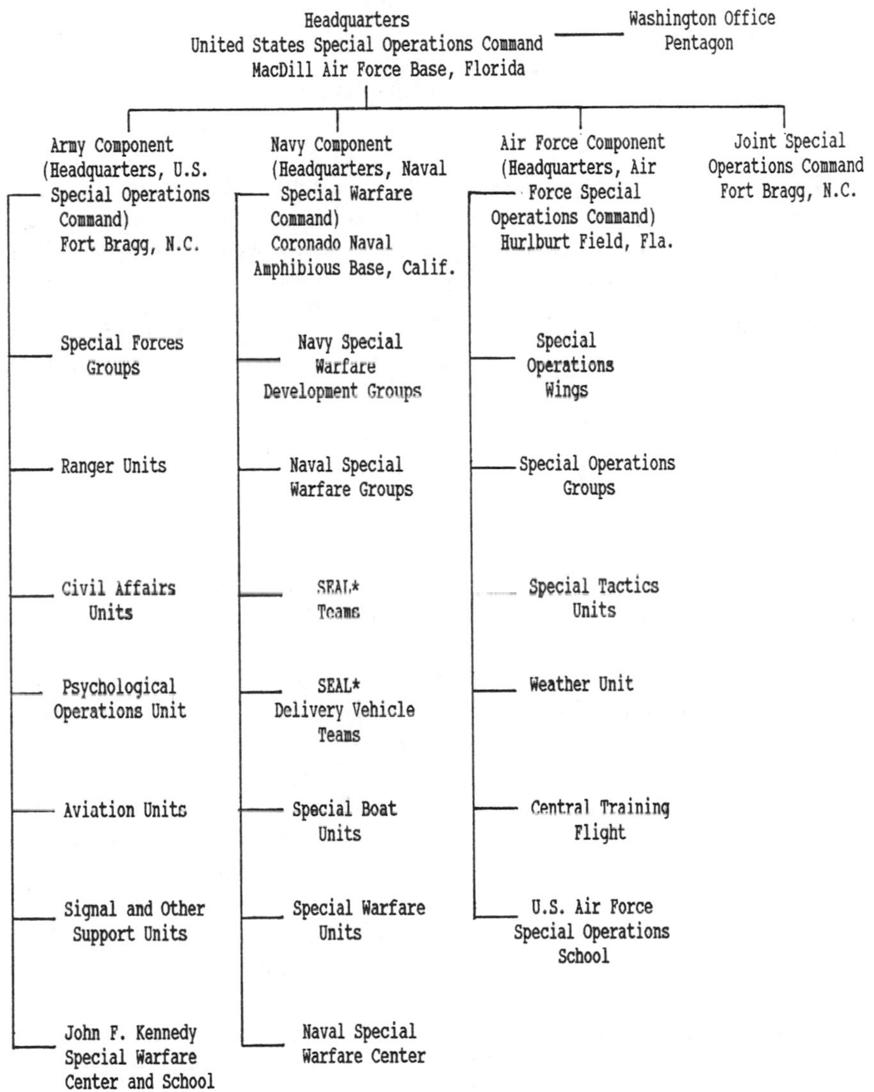

*Sea-Air-Land Units.

Source: Adapted from Dick Cheney, Secretary of Defense, *Annual Report to the President and the Congress* (Washington, DC: U.S. Government Printing Office, January 1991), p. 83.

tionships within the highest levels of government involving special operations reflect problems and misconceptions of the role of special operations. As John Collins observed, "Conflicts with the JCS Chairman, the Joint Staff, and USSOCOM over planning responsibilities remain unresolved. Successive Secretaries of Defense have declined to correct such conditions."[48]

Problems also remain regarding the employment of special operations forces and their relationship to mainstream military forces. These include the overcommitment of special operations forces and continuing problems of an institutional nature.

> [M]ilitary "cultures" are changing more slowly. Mutual distrust and misunderstandings still separate conventional forces from SOF, because not many of the former fully understand SOF capabilities and limitations. Too few special operations specialists have enough Pentagon experience to make "The System" work for them instead of against them. SOF constituencies on Capitol Hill, among U.S. military services, and in industry remain scant and tenuous; consequently, appropriate acceptance of Special Operations Forces will come only after all parties concerned complete a learning process and put doctrine into practice.[49]

It is also the case that the best use of special operations forces, particularly Special Forces, is to develop a "preventive maintenance" strategy, that is, the effort to support an indigenous system or those fighting against an indigenous system while minimizing the American presence in order to prevent the enlargement of the conflict. Indeed, the commitment of such forces with their ability to minimize U.S. presence may be the best strategy short of Americanizing the effort—an effort that may well erode American support of the military effort and engulf American forces in a Vietnam-type environment. The Americanization of the conflict should be considered only if such involvement is clearly necessary to protect American national interests.

Unfortunately, there is a tendency in the public as well as in segments of the U.S. military to misread the training, skills, and focus of Special Forces within the Special Operations Command. In the public realm many Americans too often view Special Forces as seen in *Rambo I* and *Rambo II* movies. Some in the military view the role of Special Forces through conventional lenses rather than as individuals who must meld into the political-social milieu of an indigenous system and prepare to remain over the long term. Moreover, the training and education of Special Forces remain distant from the mainstream career paths. As suggested earlier, this causes tension between Special Forces and some special operations personnel as well as for many in mainstream military units.

Society and the Military

Combined with the rise of a new generation of national leaders first signalled in 1992 and made particularly prominent in the 1994 midterm elections, the military/society relationship may be becoming more complex. On the one hand, in the military there may be a degree of replication of society and its expectations and characteristics. On the other hand, an increasing military isolation from society may occur to limit societal forces from imposing too heavily upon the military.

Issues of homosexuals in the military, women in combat, multiculturalism, demographic changes, and socially relevant contingencies are major parts of the military/society relationship. These in turn have an impact on the relationship between the national leadership and the military. The fundamental issue turns on the relative degree of closeness between the military and society. This convergence or divergence is partly a function of how the military responds to and handles political-social issues deeply felt by many Americans.

As suggested earlier, it would be a mistake to rationalize military utility on the grounds of social relevancy or budget-driven motives. To do so could be a major step in eroding the raison d'être of the military and eroding the confidence of the military profession in civilian and military leadership. Moreover, to presume that the world has seen the end of major U.S. adversaries, or that there is an unstoppable movement toward peaceful democracies, or that the world has seen the end of major conventional wars, is simply to ignore lessons of history. As George Santayana was to remind his contemporaries at the beginning of this century, "Those who cannot remember the past are condemned to repeat it."

CONCLUSIONS

In the final analysis, the U.S. military is facing the prospect of an uncertain strategic environment and an unclear national security agenda. Yet it must develop a strategic posture and force structures that are attuned to these uncertainties. While the posture and structures cannot be set in concrete, they must have a degree of relevancy with the contours of the new security environment. They must not only be focused on the contemporary period, but be flexible enough to carry over into the next century. Thus there must be a serious analysis of the philosophical and intellectual basis for strategy and force structures, an analysis that is linked to the realities as well as the uncertainties of the security landscape and American domestic imperatives. This is particularly true regarding operations other than war and unconventional conflicts. Adding to the difficulty is the fact that the concept of national security has broadened and the military has been drawn into a variety of contingencies that may have little to do with its primary purpose. All of this development must be done with less resources and manpower.

It is acknowledged that to develop a comprehensive strategy relevant now and into the next century is not an easy task. It seems clear, however, that the military profession must adjust to the new realities of a transition period in which major wars may be a thing of the past. Even with an uncertain strategic landscape and questions regarding U.S. national security goals, military strategies and force structures must be reshaped and redesigned. The U.S. military does not have the luxury of standing pat, waiting for a clarification of the security landscape and the certainty of a new world order. At the minimum, strategies and force structures must be attuned to the fluidity of the emerging landscape and must develop some congruence between military posture, new definitions of power, and the utility of military force.

The support of the American people for military involvement rests primarily on military contingencies conforming to the American way of war, virtually excluding support for involvement in various forms of operations other than war—particularly those that can lead to unconventional conflicts. This does not necessarily mean that Americans will not support noncombat military missions, but these missions need to be carefully considered and implemented only when there is a reasonable assurance of success. Further, coalition strategies and nonmilitary instruments should be given first priority in such circumstances.

The use of the U.S. military is inextricable from the attitudes and views of the American people. As General Fred Weyand stated with respect to the U.S. Army in the aftermath of the Vietnam War, "The American Army is really a people's Army in the sense that it belongs to the American people who take a jealous proprietary interest in its involvement. . . . the American Army is not so much an arm of the Executive Branch as it is an arm of the American people."[50] This is as true today as it was in the immediate aftermath of Vietnam.

While the superpower era demanded a particular global political-military capacity and strategic thinking, the strategic landscape of the new world order demands a different strategic mind-set and operational capacity. The transition from one to the other has resulted in an ad hoc mixture of strategic and operational guidelines and political-military capacity. Complicating the dilemma, there has emerged in the United States a notion of wars of conscience, policy driven by moral indignation, and the "do-something" syndrome.[51]

Another complicating development for the military is the seemingly contradictory efforts to try to reconcile interservice rivalries and the notion of "jointness." This is the concept that each service must be prepared operationally and doctrinally to operate effectively with other services in order to succeed in assigned missions. This also means that there must be a common institutional base from which effective joint operations can be implemented. On the one hand, the services seem to be struggling to defend their operational turf and even extend it to the detriment of other services. While this has been an on-again, off-again struggle over the past decades, it now seems to be driven by budgetary considerations, response to the new strategic landscape, socially relevant missions, and protection of operational turf. For example, the U.S. Air Force and Army are struggling over weaponry and doctrines in space. The U.S. Navy and the Air Force argue over strategic weapons and the control of air power. The U.S. Army and the Marines have had a constant struggle over light infantry and rapid-response missions.

On the other hand, lessons of the Gulf War showed the need for joint operations and cooperation among services that required experience in "jointness."

In Haiti, for example, U.S. Army forces and their helicopters were deployed from a U.S. Navy aircraft carrier. Moreover, the stress on "jointness" has made it extremely important that officers seeking to advance their careers into the highest ranks develop joint experience on joint staffs, among other things.

Contradictions arise when officers of one service on joint staffs become involved in the military strategy and policy process that may affect their individual services—either to the service's advantage or disadvantage. Moreover, serving on a joint staff does not break the career link between the individual officer and his own service.

In trying to respond to these apparent contradictions, joint staff officers and commanders are faced with the prospect of trying to clarify the role of the U.S. military and each service in a confusing strategic environment. Equally important, many military contingencies may be contrary to the American way of war—such as any number of contingencies in operations other than war, particularly unconventional conflicts. Yet conventional conflicts and nuclear contingencies easily fall into the realm of "jointness." But mainstream U.S. military forces are not disposed nor doctrinally oriented to effectively engage in many OOTW or unconventional conflicts. However, the strategic landscape is replete with situations that are within the scope of operations other than war and unconventional conflicts, and in the long run some of these may develop into serious threats to American national interests. There is a serious need, therefore, to clarify the meaning of U.S. national interests with respect to Third World instability, to rethink strategic orientation, and to reconsider the utilization of the U.S. military. It may be best that the United States not become involved in any number of operations other than war or unconventional conflicts, lest U.S. involvement change the dynamics of the situation to the disadvantage of American interests.

> While no one can predict the kinds of conflicts the United States may face in the coming decade, it is reasonably clear that instability and internal conflicts in the Third World are likely. . . . The most difficult challenges . . . are those posed by unconventional conflicts. . . . [These] pose complex and difficult policy questions for the United States, involving Third World cultures, different levels of growth, and different types of political systems. The United States has yet to learn how to deal with the driving forces in these non-Western cultures.[52]

When U.S. involvement becomes necessary because of U.S. national interests, those in the political and military realms need to understand the characteristics of unconventional conflicts and what operations other than war mean in terms of such conflicts. In addition, if such involvement is a matter of national necessity, then it may require the "Americanization" of the involvement, with all that this may mean in terms of the American way of war.

But there are limits to what the United States can reasonably accomplish without resorting to major war, particularly in delving into foreign strategic cultures. Indeed, even in major wars it is not clear what the future holds with respect to the character of the adversary and the limits or nonlimits placed on the lethality and character of weapons employed. In operations other than war and unconventional conflicts, the primary factor shaping the views of many Americans, both civilian and military, may well be the fear of a Vietnam-type quagmire. Accordingly, the United States should not be involved unless the issues are clear, the political and military objectives are well defined, and there is a high degree of certainty that the United States will succeed. Given the nature of the new strategic landscape and the characteristics of operations other than war and unconventional conflicts, adopting such a view may leave the field open to adversaries and adversely affect long-term U.S. interests. But involvement in operations other than war and unconventional conflicts requires a serious rethinking of U.S. interests and national objectives combined with a cautious and prudent use of Special Forces and, as a last resort, the mainstream military—if national interests dictate it. This is not an easy task. As shown in this study, the primary military intellectual and operational focus is on developing capability in third-wave warfare and in conventional conflict. Other missions seem to be secondary to the military effort, rhetoric to the contrary notwithstanding.

Finally, that the U.S. military is in a period of transition in an uncertain environment may well be an understatement. High-tech weaponry, the communications revolution, the disorderly world, the lack of a clear major adversary, and the changing domestic political-social character of the United States not only drive this transition period, but cloak it with an ill-defined strategic landscape and uncertain future.

Complicating the problems for the U.S. military are the apparent contradictions between the revolution in military affairs and the concepts of leadership, strategy, and doctrine. Information-age and third-wave warfare stress electronic sophistication and information-superhighway mind-sets. These focus on managerial competence, technicians, and information-age specialists. Lost in this maze may well be the art of leadership and competent leaders who can go beyond electronic decision making. It is also the case that regardless of electronic warfare, precision-guided weapons, and the ability to conduct "push-button" warfare, the end objective of war is to control the adversary's governing system and the political-economic infrastructure. It is difficult to see how this can be done without placing American military forces into the adversary's domain on the ground, regardless of what may be seen as the emergence of "war at a distance."

Also, the revolution in military affairs may have minimal impact on the nature of conflicts characterized by operations other than war and unconventional conflicts. The basic objective in such conflicts and contingencies evolves from Sun Tzu's notion that the center of gravity is in the political-social milieu of society, not on the adversary's military forces.

The broader problem for the U.S. military is to reconcile these apparent contradictions and retain its relationship with society without compromising its uniqueness as a military institution. The primary focus of the U.S. military on the emerging third-wave warfare and jointness, combined with the American way of war and the characteristics of the most likely conflicts and contingencies, may cause irreconcilable developments between the military and society. The most acceptable development may be in accord with the conclusions in a recent study:

> [T]hat the nurturing of a cohesive military, fine-tuned to respond to contingencies across the conflict spectrum, can be achieved, maintained, and nurtured only by ensuring that some distance remain between society and the elite and special operations forces; a degree of distance must remain between society and the mainstream ground combat arms. Combat support and combat service support elements of the military can readily absorb the political-social demands of society and create a link among these, the ground combat arms, and the elite and special operations forces.[53]

This distinction is reinforced by the force mix, weaponry, organization, and operational doctrine associated with each of the three types of forces.

Perhaps the best that can be said at this time—as commonplace as it may be—is that the U.S. military must prepare for the worst-case scenario and hope and work for the least bad scenario both in the contemporary period and into the next century. In the process civilian and military leaders need to consider a fundamental principle underpinning the precepts of Sun Tzu: If one tries to do everything well, nothing will be done well. This means that the "specialization of labor" emerging from the civilian sector needs to be applied to the military. At the same time, the highest levels of the military chain of command must retain a global perspective and strategic view not limited by microintellectual rigidity. This is no mean task.

NOTES

1. Stephen John Stedman, "The New Interventionists," *Foreign Affairs* 72, no. 1 (1993): 4.
2. Ernest van den Haag, "The Busyness of American Policy," *Foreign Affairs* 64, no. 1 (Fall 1985): 114.
3. For an examination of this doctrine, see Alan Ned Sabrosky and Robert L. Sloane, *The Recourse to War: An Appraisal of the "Weinberger Doctrine"* (Carlisle Barracks, PA: Strategic Studies Institute, 1988).
4. John Spanier, *American Foreign Policy since World War II,* 11th ed. (Washington, DC: CQ Press, 1988), p. 11.
5. See, for example, Douglas W. Craft, *An Operational Analysis of the Persian Gulf War* (Carlisle Barracks, PA: Strategic Studies Institute, 31 August 1992).
6. Samuel W. Lewis, "Point of View: The Decade of the 1990s," *United States Institute of Peace Journal* 3, no. 1 (March 1990): 2.
7. For a detailed discussion of the characteristics of unconventional conflicts, see Sam C. Sarkesian, *America's Forgotten Wars: The Counterrevolutionary Past and Lessons for the Future* (Westport, CT: Greenwood Press, 1984).
8. See President George Bush, "Reshaping Our Forces," speech delivered at the

Aspen Institute, Aspen, Colorado, 2 August 1990, *Vital Speeches of the Day,* 1990, p. 677.

9. William Matthews, "Stretched to the Limit," *Army Times,* 2 January 1995, p. 8.

10. Headquarters, Department of the Army, *FM 100-5: Operations* (Washington, DC: U.S. Government Printing Office, June 1993), p. 13-0.

11. Ibid., pp. 13-4 to 13-8.

12. Ibid., p. 13-0.

13. See, for example, Sam C. Sarkesian, *Unconventional Conflicts in a New Security Era: Lessons from Malaya and Vietnam* (Westport, CT: Greenwood Press, 1993).

14. Major Eduardo Aldunate, "Observations on the Theory of LIC and Violence in Latin America," *Military Review,* June 1991, pp. 80 and 86.

15. Mao Tse-tung, *Guerrilla Warfare,* translated and with an introduction by Samuel B. Griffith (New York: Praeger, 1961), p. 7.

16. Samuel P. Huntington, "The Clash of Civilizations," *Foreign Affairs* 72, no. 3 (Summer 1993): 25.

17. This is a brief summary of major themes on the nature of war that are in Sun Tzu, *The Art of War,* trans and with an introduction by Samuel B. Griffith (New York: Oxford University Press, 1971), pp. 77–84 and 144–149.

18. See Stedman, "New Interventionists."

19. Bush, "Reshaping Our Forces," p. 677. The concept of peacetime engagements was also detailed in the White House, *National Security Strategy of the United States* (Washington, DC: U.S. Government Printing Office, January 1993).

20. Dick Cheney, Secretary of Defense, *Defense Strategy for the 1990s: The Regional Defense Strategy* (Washington, DC: Department of Defense, January 1993), p. 11. For a detailed discussion of each of these elements see pp. 11–18.

21. Michael P. W. Stone, Secretary of the Army, in a speech delivered at the National Strategy Forum, Chicago, Illinois, 20 February 1992.

22. See James Schlesinger, "Quest for a Post–Cold War Foreign Policy," *Foreign Affairs* 72, no. 1 (1993): 28.

23. David Silverberg, "Clinton and the Military: Can the Gap Be Bridged?" *Armed Forces Journal International,* October 1993, pp. 53–54 and 57.

24. Harry Summers, "White House Climate Spurns Military Loyalty," *Army Times,* 22 March 1993.

25. The White House, *A National Security Strategy of Engagement and Enlargement* (Washington, DC: U.S. Government Printing Office, July 1994). Also see The White House, *A National Security Strategy of Engagement and Enlargement* (Washington, DC: U.S. Government Printing Office, February 1995). The 1995 version varies slightly from the 1994 statement.

26. Ibid., p. 29.

27. Harry Summers, *Army Times,* 12 September 1994, p. 63.

28. *U.S. Intervention Policy for the Post–Cold War World: New Challenges and New Responses,* Final Report of the Eighty-Fifth American Assembly (Harriman, NY: American Assembly), 7–10 April 1994, p. 5.

29. See *FY 1994 Defense Budget Begins New Era,* News Release (Washington, DC: Office of the Assistant Secretary of Defense—Public Relations, March 1994). See also Jim Tice, "Drawdown Accelerates," *Army Times,* 12 April 1993, p. 4.

30. See Les Aspin, Chairman, Committee on Armed Services, House of Representatives, Memorandum, "Sizing U.S. Conventional Forces," 22 January 1992. Also see

charts by Representative Les Aspin on "The New Security: A Bottom-Up Approach to the Post–Cold War Era," U.S. House of Representatives, Armed Services Committee, n.d.

31. Tom Donnelly, "100,000 More Troops Could Be Cut by 2000," *Army Times,* 19 April 1993, p. 26.

32. Peter G. Peterson and James K. Sebenius, "The Primacy of the Domestic Agenda," in *Retinking America's Security: Beyond Cold War to New World Order,* ed. Graham Allison and Gregory F. Treverton (New York: W. W. Norton, 1992), p. 61.

33. David Silverberg, "The National Security Status Quo Act," *Armed Forces Journal International,* March 1995, p. 13.

34. Paulette Walker, "Quality Control: A Look at the Quality of Life in the Army," *Army Times,* 13 March 1995, p. 16.

35. See, for example, Steven Metz and James Kievit, *The Revolution in Military Affairs and Conflict Short of War* (Carlisle Barracks, PA: U.S. Army War College, Strategic Studies Institute, 25 July 1994), and Paul Bracken and Raoul Henri Alcalá, *Whither the RMA: Two Perspectives on Tomorrow's Army* (Carlisle Barracks, PA: U.S. Army War College, Strategic Studies Institute, 22 July 1994).

36. Sean D. Naylor, "Defense Trends: Faces Change, Roles Debate Goes On," *Army Times,* 2 January 1995, p. 40.

37. Patrick Pexton, "Roles Unit: Jointness is the Way to Go," *Army Times,* 5 June 1995, p. 3.

38. Sean D. Naylor, "Roles Panel Seeks Cut of Total Army by 50,000," *Army Times,* 5 June 1995, p. 3.

39. Ibid., p. 3.

40. General Gordon R. Sullivan and Lieutenant Colonel James M. Dubik, *Land Warfare in the 21st Century* (Carlisle Barracks, PA: U.S. Army War College, Strategic Studies Institute, February 1993).

41. For a discussion of this issue, see Sam C. Sarkesian, John Allen Williams, and Fred B. Bryant, *Soldiers, Society, and National Security* (Boulder, CO: Lynne Rienner Publishers, 1995).

42. *U.S. Intervention Policy for the Post–Cold War World,* pp. 6–7.

43. Sullivan and Dubik, *Land Warfare in the 21st Century,* p. 11.

44. John G. Roos, "The Perils of Peacekeeping: Tallying the Costs in Blood, Coin, Prestige, and Readiness," *Armed Forces Journal International,* December 1993, p. 17.

45. Ibid.

46. William Matthews, "Force May Get a Breather in '95," *Army Times,* 2 January 1995, p. 6.

47. John M. Collins, *Special Operations Forces: An Assessment, 1986–1993, CRS Report for Congress* (Washington, DC: Congressional Research Service, 30 July 1993), includes detailed analysis of congressional legislation. Collins's report is one of the best analyses of special operations forces. Also see John M. Collins, *Special Operations Forces: An Assessment* (Washington, DC: National Defense University Press, 1994).

48. Collins, *Special Operations Forces: An Assessment,* p. 18.

49. Ibid., p. 149.

50. General Fred C. Weyand, from "Vietnam Myths and American Realities," *Cdrs Call,* July–August 1976. As quoted in Harry G. Summers, Jr., *On Strategy: The Vietnam War in Context* (Carlisle Barracks, PA: U.S. Army War College, 1981), p. 7.

51. Donald M. Snow, *Peacekeeping, Peacemaking, and Peace-Enforcement: The U.S.*

Role in the New International Order (Carlisle Barracks, PA: Strategic Studies Institute, February 1993), p. 6.

52. Sarkesian, *Unconventional Conflicts in a New Security Era,* pp. 188–189.
53. Sarkesian, Williams, and Bryant, *Soldiers, Society, and National Security,* p. 162.

SELECTED BIBLIOGRAPHY

Allison, Graham, and Gregory F. Treverton, eds. *Rethinking America's Security: Beyond Cold War to New World Order.* New York: W. W. Norton, 1992.

Builder, Carl H. *The Masks of War: American Military Styles in Strategy and Analysis.* Baltimore, MD: Johns Hopkins University Press, 1989.

Diehl, Paul F. *International Peacekeeping.* Baltimore, MD: Johns Hopkins University Press, 1994.

Godson, Roy, and Wm. J. Olson. *International Organized Crime: Emerging Threat to US Security.* Washington, DC: National Strategy Information Center, 1993.

Haass, Richard N. *Intervention: The Use of American Military Force in the Post–Cold War World.* Washington, DC: The Brookings Institution, 1994.

Handel, Michael I., ed. *Clausewitz and Modern Strategy.* London: Frank Cass, 1986.

Huntington, Samuel P. "The Clash of Civilizations." *Foreign Affairs* 72, no. 3 (Summer 1993): pp. 22–49.

———. *The Soldier and the State: The Theory and Politics of Civil-Military Relations.* New York: Vintage Books, 1964.

Janowitz, Morris. *The Professional Soldier: A Social and Political Portrait.* New York: Free Press, 1971.

Leckie, Robert. *The Wars of America.* 2 vols. New York: HarperCollins, 1992.

Odom, William E. *America's Military Revolution: Strategy and Structure after The Cold War.* Washington, DC: American University Press, 1993.

Prados, John. *The Hidden History of the Vietnam War.* Chicago, IL: Ivan R. Dee Publisher, 1995.

Sabrosky, Alan Ned, and Robert L. Sloane. *The Recourse to War: An Appraisal of the "Weinberger Doctrine."* Carlisle Barracks, PA: Strategic Studies Institute, 1988.

Sarkesian, Sam C. *America's Forgotten Wars: The Counterrevolutionary Past and Lessons for the Future.* Westport, CT: Greenwood Press, 1984.

———. *U.S. National Security: Policymakers, Processes, and Politics.* 2nd ed. Boulder, CO: Lynne Rienner Publishers, 1995.

Sarkesian, Sam C., John Allen Williams, and Fred B. Bryant. *Soldiers, Society, and National Security.* Boulder, CO: Lynne Rienner Publishers, 1995.

Shultz, Richard, Roy Godson, and Ted Greenwood, eds. *Security Studies for the 1990s.* Washington, DC: Brassey's (US), 1993.

Shultz, Richard H., Jr., and Wm. J. Olson. *Ethnic and Religious Conflict: Emerging Threat to US Security.* Washington, DC: National Strategy Information Center, 1994.

Snow, Donald M. *Peacekeeping, Peacemaking, and Peace-Enforcement: The U.S. Role in the New International Order.* Carlisle Barracks, PA: Strategic Studies Institute, February 1993.

Spanier, John. *American Foreign Policy since World War II.* 12th ed., rev. Washington, DC: CQ Press, 1992.

Sun Tzu. *The Art of War.* Translated and with an introduction by Samuel B. Griffith. New York: Oxford University Press, 1971.

White House, The. *A National Security Strategy of Engagement and Enlargement.* Washington, DC: U.S. Government Printing Office, July 1994 and February 1995.

GLOSSARY

This glossary does not include all of the acronyms appearing in this study. However, many of the most common acronyms are listed.

AAV	Amphibious Assault Vehicle
AC	Active Component
ACE	Aviation Combat Element
ADT	Active Duty for Training
AFRES	Air Force Reserve
AFSOF	Air Force Special Operations Forces
AGR	Active Guard/Reserve
AMC	Air Mobility Command
ANG	Air National Guard
ARCENT	Army Component to Central Command
ARCOM	Army Reserve Command
ARNG	Army National Guard
AT	Annual Training
ATGM	Anti-Tank Guided Missile
C^3I	Command, Control, Communications, and Intelligence

This Glossary was compiled with the assistance of Charles E. Heller, author of chapter 6.

C^3IC	Coalition, Coordination, Communications, and Integration Center
CE	Combat Element
CENTCOM	Central Command
CINC	Commander-in-Chief
CINCPAC	Commander-in-Chief Pacific
CJCS	Chairman of the Joint Chiefs of Staff
CJTF	Commander, Joint Task Force
CONUS	Continental United States
CS	Combat Support
CSS	Combat Service Support
CSSE	Combat Service Support Element
CVBG	Aircraft Carrier Battle Group
DOD	Department of Defense
FMSP	Foreign Military Sales Program
FOB	Forward Operating Base
FSSG	Force Service Support Group
GCE	Ground Combat Element
HUMINT	Human Intelligence
HUMMV	High Mobility Multipurpose Wheeled Vehicle
IDT	Inactive Duty for Training
IFV	Infantry Fighting Vehicle
IRR	Individual Ready Reserve
JCS	Joint Chiefs of Staff
JFC	Joint Force Commander
JFSOCC	Joint Forces Special Operations Component Commander
J-STARS	Joint Surveillance and Target Attack Radar System
JTF	Joint Task Force
LAV	Light Armored Vehicle
LVT	Landing Vehicle Track
MAGTF	Marine Air-Ground Task Force
MARDIV	Marine Division
MARESFOR	Marine Reserve Force
MAW	Marine Aircraft Wing
MEB	Marine Expeditionary Brigade
MEF	Marine Expeditionary Force
MLRS	Multiple-Launch Rocket System

MOS	Military Occupation Specialty
NATO	North Atlantic Treaty Organization
NCA	National Command Authority
NGB	National Guard Bureau
NSS	National Security Strategy
OCAR	Office, Chief Army Reserve
ODT	Overseas Deployment Training
OOTW	Operations Other Than War
ORC	Organized Reserve Corps
RC	Reserve Components
RDJTF	Rapid Deployment Joint Task Force
RFPB	Reserve Forces Policy Board
SEAL	Sea, Air, Land
SOC	Special Operations Forces
STARC	State Area Command
TAG	The Adjutant General
TAR	Training and Administration of Reserves
TOW	Tube-launched, Optically tracked, Wire Command-Link Guided Missile
TPU	Troop Program Unit
TSSAM	Tri-Service Standoff Missile
TTAD	Temporary Tour of Active Duty
UNSC	United Nations Security Council
USAFE	United States Air Force Europe
USAR	United States Army Reserve
USARC	United States Army Reserve Command
USCENTCOM	United States Central Command
USCGR	United States Coast Guard Reserve
USCINCCENT	Commander-in-Chief, United States Central Command
USMCR	United States Marine Corps Reserve
USNR	United States Naval Reserve
USSOCOM	United States Special Operations Command
USSOUTHCOM	United States Southern Command

INDEX

ABOUT THE EDITORS AND CONTRIBUTORS

STEPHEN J. CIMBALA is Professor of Political Science at Pennsylvania State University, Delaware County, and has contributed to the field of national security studies for many years. His recent publications include *Military Persuasion* (1993).

ROBERT E. CONNOR, JR., recently retired from the Army with over twenty years of service as an infantry officer. He has published articles on military history for the Command and General Staff College Press and has contributed articles for publication in *Historical Dictionary of the United States Army* (forthcoming).

CHARLES E. HELLER is currently Assistant Chief of Staff, U.S. Army Reserve, Combined Arms Center at Fort Leavenworth. His most recent publication is ''The Total Force Policy'' in *U.S. Domestic and National Security Agendas: Into the Twenty-First Century,* edited by Sam Sarkesian and John Flanagin (1994). He is co-editor of *America's First Battles* (1985).

DOUGLAS V. JOHNSON II is Research Professor of National Security Affairs at the Strategic Studies Institute, U.S. Army War College. He was the principal author of the last two editions of *FM 100-1: The Army.* He is writing *FM 100-3* (title forthcoming) and has published several studies and articles on a variety of subjects. His latest study is *The Impact of the Media on National Security Decision Making.*

DANIEL J. KAUFMAN, Colonel in the U.S. Army, is Professor of International Relations and Deputy Head of the Department of Social Sciences at the U.S. Military Academy at West Point. He is the author of a number of books and articles on national security issues; his latest book is *Understanding International Relations* (1994).

CHRISTOPHER J. LAMB is Director of Policy Planning, Office of the Assistant Secretary of Defense for Special Operations and Low-Intensity Conflict, and an Adjunct Professor in the National Security Studies Program at Georgetown University. He is the author of *How to Think about Arms Control, Disarmament, and Defense* (1988) and *Belief Systems and Decision Making in the Mayaguez Crisis* (1989).

ALLAN R. MILLETT is General Raymond E. Mason, Jr., Professor of Military History and Associate Director of the Mershon Center, Ohio State University. He has authored or coauthored five books, including *Semper Fidelis: The History of the United States Marine Corps* (rev. ed., 1991) and, with Peter Maslowski, *For the Common Defense: A Military History of the United States* (rev. and exp. ed., 1994). With Williamson Murray he coedited *Military Effectiveness* (3 vols., 1988) and *Calculations: Net Assessment and the Coming of World War II* (1992).

THOMAS R. MOCKAITIS is Associate Professor of History at DePaul University in Chicago. He is the author of *British Counterinsurgency, 1919–1960* (1990) and *British Counterinsurgency in the Post-Imperial Era* (1995).

JAMES B. MOTLEY is a retired U.S. Army Colonel and an internationally known writer and lecturer on low-intensity conflict.

JAMES A. MOWBRAY is currently Professor of Doctrine and Strategy at the Air War College, Air University, Air Education and Training Command, United States Air Force. He has presented papers and published articles on Air Force doctrine.

SAM C. SARKESIAN is Professor Emeritus of Political Science at Loyola University, Chicago. Some of his most recent books include *U.S. National Security: Policymakers, Processes, and Politics,* 2nd ed. (1995); *Unconventional Conflicts in a New Security Era: Lessons from Malaya and Vietnam* (1993); and *Soldiers, Society, and National Security* (with John Allen Williams and Fred B. Bryant) (1995).

DAVID TUCKER is Deputy Director for Low-Intensity Conflict, Policy Planning, Office of the Assistant Secretary of Defense for Special Operations and

Low-Intensity Conflict. He has published essays and reviews on American history, American strategy and foreign policy, and the war in Vietnam.

CYNTHIA WATSON is Professor of National Security Policy at the National War College. She has written extensively on political violence and guerrilla groups in Latin America, with articles appearing in *Third World Quarterly* and *Terrorism and Political Violence.*

JOHN ALLEN WILLIAMS is Chairman of the Department of Political Science, Loyola University, Chicago, and Vice Chairman and Executive Director of the Inter-University Seminar on Armed Forces and Society. He is coauthor (with Sam C. Sarkesian and Fred B. Bryant) of *Soldiers, Society, and National Security* and coeditor (with Sam C. Sarkesian) of *The U.S. Army in a New Security Era.*

HARDCOVER BAR CODE